MODERN PERSPECTIVES IN PSYCHIATRY
Edited by John G. Howells

13

MODERN PERSPECTIVES IN THE PSYCHIATRY OF THE AFFECTIVE DISORDERS

MODERN PERSPECTIVES IN PSYCHIATRY

Edited by John G. Howells

1. Modern Perspectives in Child Psychiatry (2nd ed. 1967)
2. Modern Perspectives in World Psychiatry (1968). Introduction by Lord Adrian, O.M., and Gene Usdin, M.D.
3. Modern Perspectives in International Child Psychiatry (1969). Introduced by Leo Kanner, M.D.
4. Modern Perspectives in Adolescent Psychiatry (1971)
5. Modern Perspectives in Psycho-Obstetrics (1972)
6. Modern Perspectives in the Psychiatry of Old Age (1975)
7. Modern Perspectives in the Psychiatric Aspects of Surgery (1976)
8. Modern Perspectives in the Psychiatry of Infancy (1979)
9. Modern Perspectives in the Psychiatry of Middle Age (1981)
10. Modern Perspectives in Clinical Psychiatry (1988)
11. Modern Perspectives in Psychosocial Pathology (1988)
12. Modern Perspectives in the Psychiatry of the Neuroses (1989)
13. Modern Perspectives in the Psychiatry of the Affective Disorders (1989)

Modern Perspectives in the Psychiatry of the Affective Disorders

Edited by

JOHN G. HOWELLS
M.D., F.R.C.Psych., D.P.M.

BRUNNER/MAZEL, *Publishers* • New York

Library of Congress Cataloging-in-Publication Data

Modern perspectives in the psychiatry of the affective disorders /
edited by John G. Howells.
p. cm. — (Modern perspectives in psychiatry ; 13)
Includes bibliographies and index.
ISBN 0-87630-531-1
1. Affective disorders. I. Howells, John G. II. Series.
[DNLM: 1. Affective Disorders—diagnosis. 2. Affective Disorders—therapy. W1 MO167P v. 13 / WM 207 M691]
RC537.M625 1989
616.85′27—dc19
DNLM/DLC
for Library of Congress 89-636
CIP

Published by
BRUNNER/MAZEL, INC.
19 Union Square
New York, New York 10003

MANUFACTURED IN THE UNITED STATES OF AMERICA

10 9 8 7 6 5 4 3 2 1

EDITOR'S PREFACE

The Modern Perspectives Series is an international encyclopedia of psychiatry. The 12 volumes already published include coverage of the psychiatry of all age periods—infancy, childhood, adolescence, adulthood, middle age, and old age—together with explorations into world psychiatry, psychoobstetrics, the psychiatric aspects of surgery, a special volume on general clinical psychiatry, and another on psychosocial pathology.

The Series continued with two volumes devoted to main nosological entities—the neuroses and the affective disorders. The former has already been published.

The present volume is *Modern Perspectives in the Psychiatry of the Affective Disorders*. Affective disorders are here understood to be a group of clinical conditions characterized by significant degrees of excess of depression and elation. The volume starts with a discussion of a number of general issues pertaining to affective disorders. It continues by describing the presentation of affective disorders in a number of symptoms and syndromes. The volume concludes with a consideration of methods of treatment for affective disorders.

The aim of each volume in the Series has remained as stated in the first volume of the Series. *Modern Perspectives in the Psychiatry of Affective Disorders* is thus planned to bring the facts from the growing points of psychiatry, and pertinent related fields, to the attention of the clinician at as early a stage as possible. A complete coverage of the field is not attempted. A single volume is not a textbook. To give an international flavor to the Series the Editor feels free to wander over the world inviting acknowledged experts to present a topic to the readership. Each contributor has the task of selecting, appraising, and explaining the available knowledge on his subject for the benefit of colleagues who may be less well acquainted with that field. Special consideration is given to the requirements of psychiatrists in training. The Editor eschews any interests or biases of his own. Thus, ranging over the possible topics, it becomes apparent that those to be covered select themselves. Together, they speak of eclecticism. Although leaning toward the clinical, applied and basic sciences, clinical and biobehavioral sciences, dynamic and biological psychiatry stand comfortably together.

The Editor gratefully acknowledges the help given by his assistant, Mrs. Janet Hodge, who tackled matters of overview and detail with equal ease. The index displays the skill and punctiliousness of my indexer, Mrs. Lesley Horrocks, for which my thanks is also due.

CONTENTS

MANAGEMENT

MODERN PERSPECTIVES IN PSYCHIATRY
Edited by John G. Howells

13

MODERN PERSPECTIVES IN THE PSYCHIATRY OF THE AFFECTIVE DISORDERS

GENERAL

1

THE EPIDEMIOLOGY OF THE AFFECTIVE DISORDERS

JOHN J. SCHWAB, M.D.

Professor and Chairman,
Department of Psychiatry and Behavioral Science,
University of Louisville School of Medicine,
Louisville, Kentucky

About 150 years ago, in writing about melancholia, Esquirol (12) emphasized that it "borrows its character, and finds again the causes which produce it, in the different periods of society" (p. 736).

INTRODUCTION

In 1970, in a short article entitled "Coming in the '70s: An Epidemic of Depression" (34), I speculated that the "age of anxiety," described by Auden and Camus (2), was passing and that it was possible that we were entering the decades of depression. My thoughts were based on reports from university health services about many depressed youths seeking treatment, the increasing number of suicides among the young, and the widespread use of mood-elevating drugs, particularly the amphetamines, possibly for self-treatment. I feared that the apparently large number of cases of depression among young people would result in many cases in the future because, when a person has responded to stressors early in life with a specific emotional disorder such as depression, he or she will tend to respond to stressors, disappointments, and adverse circumstances in later life with the same type of emotional disorder.

In the late 1960s, it seemed that many of the young were experiencing rapid social change during a period in their development when attachments, drives, and reaction patterns were being consolidated. Consequently, many of them would be exceedingly vulnerable to disappointments and to losses and thus susceptible to depression in the future. Also, I mentioned the possibility that "the too-high aspirations of young people in the late 1960s might leave them vulnerable to depression" (p. 6).

During the past 15 years, in both the Western world and the developing nations, there has been "epidemic" interest in the affective disorders, particularly depression. That interest reflects concern about the already high prevalence of depression and fears that it is becoming much more common than it was in the recent past. As early as 1971, Slater and Cowie (40) noted that first-admission rates in Great Britain for affective disorders rose sharply from 1952 to 1966—for males aged 20 to 24 from about 7 per 100,000 population in 1952 to about 44 per 100,000 in 1966, and for females aged 20 to 24 from about 15 per 100,000 in 1952 to about 80 per 100,000 in 1966.

Slater and Cowie concluded that the increased "morbidity over such a short time must be attributed to a change in both public and medical attitudes; though one cannot exclude the possibility that the rapid social changes . . . are carrying with them an increasing real burden of psychiatric illness for young people" (p. 74). They emphasized that such rapid changes in morbidity are independent "of gene frequencies, which must be regarded as remaining very constant over a few decades" (p. 75).

Another source of heightened concern about depression has been the high suicide rate in young persons. Although it declined slightly during the past few years, the suicide rate in adolescents and young adults doubled and the suicide attempt rate quadrupled from the mid-1950s to the late 1970s (3, 42). Also, recent studies of suicide rates in Canada and the United States indicate that a birth cohort effect (25, 41) might be influencing rates in those born after 1940 and could have dire portents for the future.

Egeland and her colleagues' (8) recent report of some cases of bipolar disorder being linked to DNA markers on chromosome 11 has stimulated interest in depression in scientific circles and among the general public. The popular press has been devoting considerable attention to depression. For example, in 1973, Rona and Laurence Cherry (6) had an article in the *New York Times Magazine* entitled "The Common Cold of Mental Ailments: Depression," and quite recently, *Newsweek* (13) carried an extensive article on depression which emphasized that: "It is hitting young adults harder than ever before, but researchers are gaining new understanding of the emotional disorder that afflicts millions" (p. 48). The epidemiology of the affective disorders is becoming an increasingly pertinent topic in view of the concern about a possible increase in the frequency of depression and some new findings that have societal, clinical, and public health implications.

FREQUENCY OF THE AFFECTIVE DISORDERS

Prevalence Rates

In 1984 in the United States, data on a random sample of about 9,500 adults aged 18+ from the three sites participating in the Epidemiologic Catchment Area (ECA) study indicated that, as determined by the Diagnostic Interview Schedule (DIS), the six-month prevalence rate (28) for a DSM-III diagnosis of an affective disorder ranged from 4.6 to 6.5 per 100 in the various sites—2.7 to 4.6 per 100 for men and 6.0 to 8.3 per 100 for women. The most common diagnoses were: (1) major depressive episode without bereavement—the six-month prevalence rate was 2.2 to 3.5 per 100 (1.3 to 2.2 per 100 for men, and 3.0 to 4.6 per 100 for women); and (2) dysthymia—the six-month prevalence rate was 2.1 to 3.8 per 100 (1.2 to 2.6 per 100 for men, and 2.9 to 5.4 per 100 for women).

The lifetime prevalence rate (31) of a DSM-III diagnosis of an affective disorder ranged from 6.1 to 9.5 per 100 in the various sites—2.3 to 4.4 per 100 for men, and 4.9 to 8.7 per 100 for women. For major depressive disorder, it was 3.7 to 6.7 per 100, and for dysthymia, 2.1 to 3.8 per 100. Weissman and her colleagues' (50) review of seven studies of lifetime risk of nonbipolar major depression in northern Europe and the United States indicated that there was remarkable consistency for lifetime prevalence—8% to 12% for men and 20% to 26% for women—when risk was reported either as "lifetime prevalence" or as "disease expectancy" and included both treated and untreated subjects.

For a manic episode, the ECA study reported six-month prevalence rates (28) of 0.4 to 0.8 per 100 adults in the populations sampled and lifetime prevalence rates (31) of 0.6 to 1.1 per 100. Both the six-month and the lifetime prevalence rates were about the same for men and for women. Those data are consistent with Zerbin-Rüdin's (53) 1967 summary of reports from the United Kingdom and Scandinavia which indicated that the expectancy rate for bipolar disorder was about 1%.

Incidence Rates

Concern about the high prevalence rates has raised questions about a possible increase in the incidence of the affective disorders, particularly depression. Weissman and her colleagues' (50) 1986 summary of 17 Scandinavian and British community and treatment studies of nonbipolar major depression revealed that the incidence ranged from 82 to 201 per 100,000 men per year, and from 247 to 598 per 100,000 women per year. Results of three studies of the incidence rates of bipolar disorder also varied greatly—from 9 to 15.2 per 100,000 men per year and from 7.4 to 32 per 100,000 women per year. Weissman et al. stated that these studies probably underestimated the incidence because many of the ill never receive treatment. Also, only prospective studies of a population over time can yield the data needed to ascertain whether there has been a true increase or decrease in the rate of new cases, not just an apparent increase resulting, for example, from increased population.

The most comprehensive study of the incidence of mental illness is the Lundby study (16). Almost all of the approximately 2,500 inhabitants of that small Swedish town were evaluated by psychiatrists in 1947, 1957, and 1972. In their interesting article "Are We Entering an Age of Melancholy?" Hagnell and his colleagues (17) reported that the cumulative probability of contracting depression up to the age of 80 rose in almost linear fashion for both men and women in Lundby, Sweden, from 1947 to 1972. For example, for men it increased from about 12% in the period 1947–1957 to about 26% in the period 1957–1972, and for women from about 29% in 1947–1957 to about 49% in 1957–1972.

THE SWITCH TO HYPOMANIA AND MANIA

Since unipolar and bipolar disorders were dichotomized by Leonhard et al. (23) in 1962, there has been concern about how many unipolar patients switch to hypomania or develop manic episodes, necessitating changes in diagnosis. In his review of cases at the Burghölzli Hospital, 1920–1982, Angst (1) emphasized that there have been major changes in the patient populations. In recent decades, admissions for bipolar disorder have doubled or tripled and more patients have been admitted with frequent episodes of bipolar illness. But the switch of unipolars to bipolars, which was about 2.7% in 1920–1957, has increased nonsignificantly to only 3.8% since 1958. Also, even though there have been many more admissions of both bipolars and unipolars in recent decades, the ratio between the two types of illness has not changed significantly. Angst's findings suggest that more switches are being observed simply because more patients with affective disorders are being admitted. He and others agree that we do not have the data needed to determine whether there has been an increase in the incidence of bipolar disorders in recent years.

AGE DISTRIBUTION

The relationship between age and the frequency of the affective disorders is disturbing. Many community surveys conducted in the 1950s reported an increased frequency of depressive symptomatology with advancing age. For example, in both the Stirling County (27) and the Midtown Manhattan (43) studies, depressive symptomatology was more frequent in the older than in the younger respondents. But, in 1973, we (37) reported that data on the random sample of 1,645 adults aged 16 to 92 in our Florida Health Study showed that respondents aged 16 to 19 years had high mean depression scale scores. Those aged 20 to 29 and 30 to 39 had the lowest mean scores, but the mean scores increased in almost linear fashion for those above the age of 40 and were high for those aged 70+. Also, 3.8% of respondents aged 16 to 19 admitted to thoughts of suicide "often and/or all the time," and in another report on suicidal ideation and behavior in the general population, we (38) found that almost all of the 2.7% who admitted to having made a suicide attempt at some time in their lives were under the age of 30.

Although there was considerable variation across the three ECA study sites, the six-month prevalence rates (28) reported in 1984 for the affective disorders were higher in the younger than the older respondents. In those aged 18 to 24 it was as high as 7.5% for men and 9.1% for women, and in those aged 25 to 44 it was as high as 5.4% for men and 11.4% for women. In the age group 45 to 64 it was about 3% for men and 6% to 9% for women and for those aged 65+ it was about 2% for men and 3% to 5% for women. Lifetime prevalence rates (31) for major depressive disorders were higher in the age group 25 to 44 (7.5% to 10.4%) than in either the younger age group, 18 to 24 (4.1% to 7.5%), or the two older age groups, 45 to 64 and 65+ (4.2% to 5.2% and 0.8% to 1.8%, respectively). The respondents in the age group 25 to 44 would be the counterparts of those aged 16 to 19 who, we reported, had high depression scores in the early 1970s (37).

The ECA study reported that the six-month prevalence rates (28) of manic episodes were higher in the younger than in the older respondents. In the age groups 18 to 24 and 25 to 44 for men it was 0.7% to 1.4% and for women 0.3% to 2.0%. Manic episodes were reported infrequently by both men and women over the age of 45. Likewise, the lifetime prevalence (31) of manic episodes was higher in the age groups 18 to 24 (0.1% to 2.1%) and 25 to 44 (1.5% to 1.7%) than in the age groups 45 to 64 (0.4% to 0.5%) or 65+ (0% to 0.1%).

In contrast, European studies report that hypomanic and manic episodes are not so very rare in persons in their 50s. According to Weissman and Boyd (47), some British studies of the incidence of mania show that "half of the new cases occurred in persons over the age of 50" (p. 765). In 1978, Klerman (19) reported that: "The peak admission rate for manic-depressive and involutional depressive reactions occurs in patients aged forty-five to sixty-four" (p. 269). However, all of us should be aware that a hypomanic or a manic episode in late middle-aged or elderly persons may have an *organic* cause (52).

Changes in the age distribution of the affective disorders, particularly depression, have been occurring. For many years, depression was considered to be a disorder of midlife; the age of onset was usually in the late 30s or early 40s. Just a generation ago, involutional melancholia was a common diagnosis. In 1987, Boyd and Weissman (4) compared recent U.S. data with older U.S. and European data and concluded that: "The median age at onset (now) seems to be in the mid 20s, and increasing studies are reporting high rates in younger populations" (p. 5). Also, the median age of onset of the affective disorders in the NIMH Collaborative Study on the Psychobiology of Depression was the mid- to late 20s (47). Bipolar illness tended to have an earlier age of onset, usually in the early 20s, than unipolar depression, which generally began in the later 20s.

BIRTH COHORT EFFECTS

In discussing their 1984 ECA findings, Weissman et al. (49) emphasized that the age of onset of depression was younger and that the overall rates of depression were higher in cohorts who matured after World War II than in those born earlier in the century. They stated that a possible birth cohort effect was one of their most interesting findings. Also, in 1978, Weissman and Myers (51) found some preliminary evidence of a birth cohort effect in their study of depression in another random sample of respondents in New Haven, Connecticut.

Cohort Trends, Period Effects, and Age Effects

Evaluations of birth cohort trends are complicated by period effects and age effects that may be impossible to distinguish. Cohort effects refer to differences in illness rates in groups of individuals born during defined time periods, usually either 5- or 10-year periods. Klerman and his colleagues (20) note that the effect of the "baby boom" of the 1950s on suicide rates in adolescents is an example of a cohort effect. In contrast, period effects refer specifically to changes in rates associated with certain historical events: for example, the increased suicide rate during the Great Depression. And age effects refer to changes in age-specific rates: for example, changes in the age at which coronary artery disease is occurring.

Obviously, there are interactions among cohort trends, period effects, and age effects, and it is difficult to distinguish birth cohort effects from age-period interactions. Elder and Rockwell's (11) study of cohorts of Oakland men (born 1920–1921) and Berkeley men (born 1928–1929) who went through the Great Depression either as adolescents or as young children found that the younger Berkeley men showed more adverse consequences of the Depression and less psychological well-being in their life course than the older Oakland cohorts. Those findings suggest that the economic deprivations sustained by the families had more long-term effects on young children than on adolescents.

Recently, Klerman (20), Lavori (21), and Gershon (14) and their colleagues have conducted studies of birth cohort trends and rates of depression. Klerman et al. (20) evaluated 2,289 relatives of 523 probands with affective disorders and reported that there had been an earlier age at onset of first depressive episodes and increasing rates of depression for successive birth cohorts throughout the 20th century. Even though successive cohorts showed increased hazard and the "birth cohort effect was highly significant," the investigators pointed out that they could not control for the possible " . . . effect of ambient risk on the age-specific rates of depression" (p. 691). Artifacts that might be responsible for the results included selective mortality with disproportionately large numbers of depressives dying in midlife, greater rates of institutionalization of older depressives, geographical mobility, the possibility that older persons forget depressive episodes, and changes in labeling attitudes over time. However, Klerman et al. mention that "similar trends suggestive of cohort effects have been reported for suicide [rates], homicide among black men, automobile accidents" and for such "social and economic events . . . [as] the age of entrance into the labor force, . . . and of age of termination of maternal child-rearing function [the empty nest]" (p. 692).

In a later, ingenious study, Lavori and Klerman et al. (21) evaluated 1,144 siblings, born between 1930 and 1959, of patients with major affective disorders. For sisters born after 1930, the rate of major depression more than doubled, from 6% to 13%, in the late 1960s and early 1970s, but leveled off in the 1975–1983 period. For brothers born after 1930, the rate for major depression increased from 4.5% in the 1960s to 9% in the period 1970–1978 and was followed by a small drop in the rate since 1975. Lavori et al. stated that there had been "a dramatic increase of risk in all siblings (between age 15 and 50) of affectively ill patients, beginning at about the mid-1960s and continuing at least through the 1970s" (p. 30). Sophisticated analyses suggested that a powerful period effect may have been responsible for the increased rates of major depressive disorder in young people in the 1960s and 1970s and that there may have been a "period of melancholy" for young adults in the United States. Some of them have a high lifetime risk of depression and may develop incapacitating depressions; consequently, secondary prevention efforts are needed for those who are clinically ill and primary prevention efforts could help their relatives.

In another study of this interesting topic, Gershon and his colleagues' (14) evaluations of 823 relatives of affectively ill patients showed that rates of schizoaffective, bipolar, and unipolar disorders were higher in the cohorts born after 1940 than in those born before that time. Gershon et al. assert that "the higher rates seen at younger ages in the recent cohorts predict still higher rates of illness as they age" (p. 318).

These investigators' findings are consistent with the impression that there has been an increase in the frequency of depressive disorder in recent decades and also that there is an increased family aggregation of depression. Klerman and his colleagues (20) suggest that some complex type of gene-environment interaction may be responsible. Environmental risk factors could include such biological ones as changes in nutrition or the role of viruses and such nonbiological ones as urbanization or changes in family structure.

Suicide Rates and Cohort Trends

The suicide rate in Alberta, Canada, increased between successive age cohorts during the years 1951–1977 and in the United States it increased between successive cohorts during the years 1949–1974. Both Solomon and Hellon (41) in Canada and Murphy and Wetzel (25) in the United States suggest that the increased suicide rate in the young, aged 15 to 29, might indicate that those birth cohorts would continue to have high suicide rates later in life.

In contrast, Goldney and Katsikitis's (15) Australian study showed no consistent increase in suicide rates in recent birth cohorts, although there was a general increase in the risk of suicide in the young and a peaking of the suicide rate early in life. And in England and Wales, Elaine Murphy and her colleagues (24) found no discernible trend in suicide rates in the younger cohorts during the years 1921–1980. Those reports cast doubt on the validity of predictions about a cohort's suicide rates in the future that are based on that cohort's suicidal behavior earlier in life.

Murphy and her colleagues also found a decline in the suicide rates in successively older cohorts that they attributed to the impact of period events, specifically, World War II and the detoxification of domestic gas in the 1950s. In addition to that period effect, there was some evidence for a more prolonged cohort effect—the prevalence of depression in the elderly may be dropping as a result of such economic factors as Social Security that have supplied a greater degree of financial security for the elderly than formerly. For respondents aged 65+, the three-site ECA study reported an unexpectedly low lifetime prevalence (31) for major depression, 0.8% to 1.8%.

Thus, there are contradictory data from English-speaking nations regarding cohorts' suicidal behavior (24). Investigators agree that the suicide rate is high in cohorts born after 1930 or 1940 but disagree about whether the high rates early in adult life are predictive of continuing high suicide rates for those cohorts later in life. It is possible that the suicide rates for cohorts born after 1940 peaked at a relatively early age and will level off later in life.

The recent study by Holinger and his colleagues (18) presents the possibility that just the proportion of persons aged 15 to 24 in the population in the United States was significantly related to their suicide and homicide rates, 1933–1982. During those years, suicide and homicide rates rose for those aged 15 to 24 when the relative size of that age group increased and the rates fell when the relative size of that age group decreased. But increases in proportions of those aged 35 to 44, 45 to 54, and 55 to 64 were associated with declining suicide and homicide rates. It is postulated that the young are a relatively powerless group and that an increase in their numbers leads to increased competition for academic and athletic success and, presumably, stress that may result in depression and violence to self and others.

SEX DISTRIBUTION

In Western society, almost all studies have shown that major depression and dysthymia are about twice as common in women as in men. However, Rice and his associates' (30) recent life-table calculations of depression in relatives of probands with affective disorders showed that, in recent cohorts, the male-female differences in rates of depression were minimal. Also, Egeland and Hostetter's (9) Old Order Amish (OOA) study reported that about an equal number of men and women were depressed, possibly because of the relatively large number of bipolars in the OOA population.

Also, role stability and cultural factors may affect the distribution by sex among the OOA.

Jane Murphy and her colleagues (27) recently reported that in the 1970 sample of Stirling County adults, the rates for anxiety and depression in men aged 40 to 69 were only a few percentage points less than those of women in the same age group. Compared to their 1952 Stirling County findings, rates for middle-aged men had increased whereas rates for women had decreased. These findings are especially interesting because Stirling County is a rural province in Nova Scotia in which major sociocultural changes occurred between 1952, when the first prevalence study was carried out, and 1970, when the second was completed. Between 1951 and 1971, the percentage of women entering the labor force increased from 16% to 27%, whereas the percentage of males decreased from 76% to 64%. Murphy et al. ask whether such socioeconomic changes increase or decrease the risk of anxiety and/or depression for the various age-sex groups.

Early epidemiologic studies indicated that manic-depressive illness was more common in females than males. But newer studies show that sex ratios are probably equal (47); for example, the three ECA sites reported equal sex ratios for bipolar disorder.

Many epidemiologists maintain that the sex differences in the rates of major depression and dysthymia are real although it is recognized that relatively more women than men obtain psychiatric treatment. A widely publicized and accepted explanation for the sex differences in the frequency of depression is that men are more likely to "act out" their emotional distress than women, who, generally, tend to internalize their emotional distress (48). Those ideas are substantiated, at least in part, by the ECA reports on the frequency of all mental disorders studied. The female-male ratio was almost equal—54 : 46. Although lifetime rates for major depression were almost twice as great for women as for men, the rates for alcoholism, drug dependence, and antisocial personality were much greater for men than women (31).

The narrowing of the male-female differences in the rates of depression suggested by recent cohort trends (30) and the recent Stirling County report (27) needs careful monitoring. Major changes in male-female, age group, or social class rates of illness are traditional indicators of sociocultural influences on vulnerability.

RACE

The three-site ECA study did not report the racial distribution for the six-month prevalence rates of the affective disorders, and there were no statistically significant racial differences in lifetime prevalence rates for major depressive disorder or for dysthymia (31). Lifetime prevalence rates for major depressive episode for blacks ranged from 3.7% to 5.7%, and for nonblacks, from 3.8% to 6.8%. For dysthymia, the lifetime rates for blacks ranged from 1.8% to 3.6%, and for nonblacks, from 2.3% to 3.9%.

In our study of a north Florida county (36) in the early 1970s, more blacks than whites scored high on our depression scale. But controlling for socioeconomic status erased the apparent black-white differences in the frequency of depressive symptoms (45).

Although the percentages of blacks and nonblacks reporting a manic episode at some time in life were almost the same in two ECA sites (0.5% to 1.0% for blacks, and 0.7% to 1.2% for nonblacks), in St. Louis significantly more blacks (2.5%) than nonblacks (0.7%) reported manic episodes. Even though no relationship between bipolar disorder and race has been established, for many years in the southern United States it was believed that "Negroes" were extremely susceptible to manic disorders and unusually resistant to depressive conditions. Some 19th-century (35) southern writers maintained that blacks were intellectually and culturally protected against depressive disorders.

SOCIAL CLASS

In the 1970s, we and others reported that data from community surveys revealed that there was an inverse relationship between depressive symptomatology and socioeconomic status. For example, in our Florida Health Study (36), 29.7% of those in the lowest quintile scored in the high-risk range for depression compared to only 4.9% of those in the highest quintile.

The three-site ECA report did not present six-month prevalence rates of mental disorder controlled for educational level—the social class measure used. For lifetime prevalence (31), no significant relationships were reported between either major depression or dysthymia and educational levels. The lifetime prevalence rates for major depression ranged from 4.6% to 7.1% in college graduates, and from 3.6% to 6.6% in those with less education. For dysthymia, the rates for college graduates ranged from 2.2% to 3.7%, and for those with less education, 2.1% to 3.9%.

The difference between the finding that social class was inversely related to depressive symptomatology but not to diagnosed depression is difficult to explain. For persons in the lower socioeconomic strata, depressive symptomatology may reflect anomie, not necessarily clinical depression, or a chronic, low-grade depressive syndrome that just does not meet criteria for a DSM-III diagnosis may exist, or reported results may be subject to methodological and other biases.

Generally, bipolar disorders have been considered to be more common in the middle and upper than in the lower sociocultural strata. The ECA study did not report six-month prevalence rates for a manic episode controlled for educational levels and there were no statistically significant differences in lifetime prevalence rates (31) according to educational levels. Rates for a lifetime diagnosis of a manic disorder were about the same for college graduates, 0.3% to 0.4%, as for the less well educated, 0.2% to 0.3%.

MARITAL STATUS

For decades, investigators have reported that married persons have lower rates of affective disorders than the unmarried. Recently, Weissman and her colleagues (50) emphasized that currently married or single persons have the lowest rates of depression and that the separated and divorced have the highest rates, but they pointed out that some of the relationships between depressive and marital status are complicated because they are different for men than for women.

In the late 1970s, Radloff (29), Eisenberg (10), and others suggested that higher rates of depression in females were limited to married females—that unmarried females did not have higher depression rates than unmarried males. They theorized that for many women in contemporary society, marriage entailed diminished status, restricted roles, limited opportunities for self-expression, numerous responsibilities, and few adult interactions.

In our Florida Health Study (36), we found that married respondents had the lowest mean depression scale score and the separated the highest mean score. Both single and married females had significantly higher mean scores than their male counterparts, but there were no sex differences in the depression scores of the widowed, separated, or divorced. Those findings supported, in part, the views advanced by Radloff (29) and Eisenberg (10). The ECA study has not yet reported data on marital status and depression.

Bipolar disorders are slightly more common among single and divorced persons than among the married. In the Iowa 500 study, 51% of the manics were married (7), in contrast to 58% of the general population (50). In Scandinavia, Weeke and her associates (46) found that manic-depressives were less likely than general population controls to be married. However, such findings may be complicated because bipolar disorder often leads to divorce. In a study of bipolar disorder and marital status, Targum et al. (44) reported that 53% of well spouses, compared to 5% of bipolar patients, indicated that they would not have married their spouses if they had known more about the risk of bipolar illness.

TREATMENT

Despite intensive continuing educational programs for physicians, the affective disorders continue to be underdiagnosed, and although effective therapies are available, they are not being utilized. In 1971, Lehmann (22) summarized the available data; only one in five depressed persons was receiving medical treatment, only 1 in 50 was being hospitalized, and 1 in 200 was committing suicide.

In 1984, the three-site ECA data on the utilization of health services showed that only about 31% of all adults with diagnoses of affective disorders had obtained treatment in the preceding six months; 12% to 15% received treatment from a general medical provider only, and only 16% to 19% received treatment from a mental health specialist (39).

CONCLUSION

The epidemiology of the affective disorders has become a much more interesting topic than it was just a few decades ago. In the Western world, fears about a possible epidemic of depression have been sparked by a number of findings: (1) the prevalence of depression is increasing in young persons and may be decreasing among the elderly; (2) as shown by the Lundby study (16), the incidence has been increasing; (3) the age of onset is now younger than before; and (4) there are cohort trends that Gershon and his colleagues (14) aver are "the most dramatic finding on risk differences yet reported in the epidemiology of affective illness" (p. 319).

Changes in prevalence may be a result of such artifacts as greater awareness of symptomatology on the part of the young, a lessening of stigma, and/or increased psychological-mindedness. But the findings are dramatic, and along with the possible narrowing of the male-female differences in the frequency of the affective disorders, they suggest that profound social and cultural factors are influencing the development of the affective disorders. And the possibility of a contagion effect cannot be dismissed.

In 1970, I (34) mentioned the decades of depression, and in 1978 Klerman (19) pointed out that "we may now be entering an 'age of melancholy,' precipitated in part by . . . 'doomsday' prophecies concerning nuclear warfare, overpopulation, and ecological destruction" (p. 253). Unfulfilled expectations, Klerman (cited in *Psychiatric News* [5]) has mentioned, may contribute to susceptibility on the part of the young (p. 9).

As we have seen, genetic factors cannot account for such rapid changes in the frequency and distribution of an illness. Klerman and his colleagues (20) suggest the possibility of complex gene-environment interactions. Traditionally, such epidemiological changes as are occurring with the affective disorders are indicative of multiple etiological factors. Of those, sociocultural influences are bound to be powerful. In their Lundby report, "Are We Entering an Age of Melancholy?" Hagnell and his colleagues (17) pointed out: "For men in the 20–39 year group . . . the risk of exhibiting the disorder (depression) is ten times higher during the period 1957–72 compared with the period 1947–57" (p. 284). They attributed this increased risk to such social-psychological factors as structural changes in the Swedish economy.

Concern about sociocultural factors contributing to a "new age of melancholy" (13) is not limited to the Western world. I have been told by psychiatrists in some of the developing nations that they have observed a drastic increase in depression during the past 20 years. In their World Health Organization (WHO) report on the collaborative study of the assessment of the depressive disorders, Sartorius and his colleagues (32) maintain that there are probably 100 million depressives in the world and that the number may be increasing because of deleterious sociocultural effects, demographic changes, psychological factors, the increased numbers of patients with chronic medical disorders, and the widespread use of medications that have depressive side effects. Also, data from five WHO research centers (33) indicate that there is a basic "core" of depressive symptomatology that consists of sadness, joylessness, anxiety and tension, lack of energy, loss of interests, difficulty concentrating, and feelings of worthlessness. Sartorius et al. conclude that the cross-cultural similarities of the manifestations of the depressive disorders outweigh the cross-cultural differences.

Finally, only a fraction of the patients with affective disorders are receiving adequate treatment. The failure to obtain treatment and the emergence of new populations at risk have especially ominous implications that call for vigorous therapeutic and preventive efforts. In an article entitled "Affective Disorders and Mortality," Jane Murphy and her colleagues (26) reported that depression was significantly associated with excess mortality. They pointed out that "men are more likely to die of it [depression], while women are more likley to be disabled by it" (p. 479). Overall, when mortality data were combined with data about subsequent psychiatric morbidity, 82% of those who had been depressed at baseline 16 years earlier had a poor outcome. Thus, we can see that clinical and public health measures are urgently needed to minimize the morbidity and mortality produced by the affective disorders.

REFERENCES

1. Angst, J. (1985). Switch from depression to mania—A record study over decades between 1920 and 1982. *Psychopathology, 18*(2–3), 140–154.
2. Auden, W. H., & Camus, A. Cited by: Schwab, J. J. (1970). Coming in the '70s: An epidemic of depression. *Attitude, 1*(2), 4.
3. Blum, R. (1987). Contemporary threats to adolescent health in the United States. *JAMA, 257*(24), 3390–3395.
4. Boyd, J. H., & Weissman, M. M. (1987). Epidemiology of major affective disorders, Chap. 13. In R. Michels, J. O. Cavenar, Jr., A. M. Cooper, et al. (Eds.), *Psychiatry*, Vol. 3 (pp. 1–16). Philadelphia: Lippincott.
5. C. F. B. (1987). Post WWII generation faces rising rates of depression. *Psychiatr. News, 22*(10), May 15, pp. 8–9, 11.
6. Cherry, R., & Cherry, L. (1973). The common cold of mental ailments: Depression. *New York Times Magazine*, Nov. 25, pp. 38, 117–120, 126, 134.
7. Clancy, J., Tsuang, M.-T., Norton, B., et al. (1974). The Iowa 500: A comprehensive study of mania, depression and schizophrenia. *J. Iowa Med. Soc. 64*(9), 394–396, 398.
8. Egeland, J. A., Gerhard, D. S., Pauls, D. L., et al. (1987). Bipolar affective disorders linked to DNA markers on chromosome 11. *Nature, 325*(6107), 783–787.
9. Egeland, J. A., & Hostetter, A. M. (1983). Amish study, I: Affective disorders among the Amish, 1976–1980. *Am. J. Psychiatry, 140*(1), 56–61.
10. Eisenberg, L. (1977). Psychiatry and society: A sociobiologic synthesis. *N. Engl. J. Med., 296*(16), 903–910.
11. Elder, G. H., Jr., & Rockwell, R. C. (1979). Economic depression and postwar opportunity in men's lives: A study of life patterns and health. In R. G. Simmons (Ed.), *Research in community and mental health*, Vol. 1 (pp. 249–303). Greenwich, CT: JAI Press.
12. Esquirol, J. E. D. Cited in: Hunter, R., & Macalpine, I. (Eds.) (1963). *Three hundred years of psychiatry 1535–1860* (p. 736). London: Oxford University Press.
13. Gelman, D., Hager, M., Doherty, S., et al. (1987). Depression. *Newsweek, 109*(18), 48–57.
14. Gershon, E. S., Hamovit, J. H., Guroff, J. J., et al. (1987). Birth-cohort changes in manic and depressive disorders in relatives of bipolar and schizoaffective patients. *Arch. Gen. Psychiatry, 44*(4), 314–319.
15. Goldney, R. D., & Katsikitis, M. (1983). Cohort analysis of suicide rates in Australia. *Arch. Gen. Psychiatry, 40*(1), 71–74.
16. Hagnell, O. (1986). Mental disorder in the welfare state—Sweden. A prospective longitudinal psychiatric-epidemiological study of a total population over 25 years, 1947–1972. The Lundby study. *Am. J. Soc. Psychiatry, 6*(4), 230–248.
17. Hagnell, O., Lanke, J., Rorsman, B., et al. (1982). Are we entering an age of melancholy? Depressive illnesses in a prospective epidemiological study over 25 years: The Lundby study, Sweden. *Psychol. Med., 12*, 279–289.
18. Holinger, P. C., Offer, D., Ostrov, E. (1987). Suicide and homicide in the United States: An epidemiologic study of violent death, population changes, and the potential for prediction. *Am. J. Psychiatry, 144*(2), 215–219.

19. KLERMAN, G. L. (1978). Affective disorders, Chap. 13. In A. M. Nicholi, Jr. (Ed.), *The Harvard guide to modern psychiatry* (pp. 253–281). Cambridge, MA: Belknap Press of Harvard University Press.
20. KLERMAN, G. L., LAVORI, P. W., RICE, J., et al. (1985). Birth-cohort trends in rates of major depressive disorder among relatives of patients with affective disorder. *Arch. Gen. Psychiatry, 42*(7), 689–693.
21. LAVORI, P. W., KLERMAN, G. L., KELLER, M. B., et al. (1987). Age-period-cohort analysis of secular trends in onset of major depression: Findings in siblings of patients with major affective disorder. *J. Psychiatr. Res., 21*(1), 23–35.
22. LEHMANN, H. E. (1971). Epidemiology of depressive disorders. In R. R. Fieve (Ed.), *Depression in the '70s: Modern theory and research* (Proceedings of the Symposium, New York, NY, October 1970) (pp. 21–30). Amsterdam, The Netherlands: Excerpta Medica.
23. LEONHARD, K., KORFF, L., & SCHULZ, H. (1962). Temperament in families with monopolar and bipolar phasic psychoses. *Psychiatr. Neurol. Med. Psychol., 143*, 416–434.
24. MURPHY, E., LINDESAY, J., & GRUNDY, E. (1986). 60 years of suicide in England and Wales: A cohort study. *Arch. Gen. Psychiatry, 43*(10), 969–976.
25. MURPHY, G. E., & WETZEL, R. D. (1980). Suicide risk by birth cohort in the United States, 1949 to 1974. *Arch. Gen. Psychiatry, 37*(5), 519–523.
26. MURPHY, J. M., MONSON, R. R., OLIVIER, D. C., et al. (1987). Affective disorders and mortality: A general population study. *Arch. Gen. Psychiatry, 44*(5), 473–480.
27. MURPHY, J. M., SOBOL, A. M., NEFF, R. K., et al. (1984). Stability of prevalence: Depression and anxiety disorders. *Arch. Gen. Psychiatry, 41*(10), 990–997.
28. MYERS, J. K., WEISSMAN, M. M., TISCHLER, G. L., et al. (1984). Six-month prevalence of psychiatric disorders in three communities: 1980 to 1982. *Arch. Gen. Psychiatry, 41*(10), 959–967.
29. RADLOFF, L. (1975). Sex differences in depression: The effects of occupation and marital status. *Sex Roles, 1*(3), 249–265.
30. RICE, J., REICH, T., ANDREASEN, N. C., et al. (1984). Sex-related differences in depression: Familial evidence. *J. Affective Disord., 71*, 199–210.
31. ROBINS, L. N., HELZER, J. E., WEISSMAN, M. M., et al. (1984). Lifetime prevalence of specific psychiatric disorders in three sites. *Arch. Gen. Psychiatry, 41*(10), 949–958.
32. SARTORIUS, N., DAVIDIAN, H., ERNBERG, G., et al. (1983). *Depressive disorders in different cultures: Report on the WHO collaborative study on standardized assessment of depressive disorders* (p. 1). Geneva, Switzerland: World Health Organization.
33. SARTORIUS, N., JABLENSKY, A., GULBINAT, W., et al. (1980). WHO collaborative study: Assessment of depressive disorders. *Psychol. Med., 10*, 743–749.
34. SCHWAB, J. J. (1970). Coming in the '70s: An epidemic of depression. *Attitude, 1*(2), 2–6.
35. SCHWAB, J. J. (1978). Nineteenth century studies of mental illness in southern blacks. *Interaction, 1*(4), 21–25.
36. SCHWAB, J. J., BELL, R. A., WARHEIT, G. J., et al. (1979). *Social order and mental health: The Florida Health Study* (pp. 76–78, 202–203). New York: Brunner/Mazel.
37. SCHWAB, J. J., HOLZER, C. E., III, & WARHEIT, G. J. (1973). Depressive symptomatology and age. *Psychosomatics, 14*(3), 135–141.
38. SCHWAB, J. J., WARHEIT, G. J., & HOLZER, C. E., III (1972). Suicidal ideation and behavior in a general population. *Dis. Nerv. Syst., 33*, 745–748.
39. SHAPIRO, S., SKINNER, E. A., KESSLER, L. G., et al. (1984). Utilization of health and mental health services: Three epidemiologic catchment area sites. *Arch. Gen. Psychiatry, 41*(10), 971–978.
40. SLATER, E., & COWIE, V. (1971). *The genetics of mental disorders* (pp. 74–75, 78). London: Oxford University Press.
41. SOLOMON, M. I., & HELLON, C. P. (1980). Suicide and age in Alberta, Canada, 1951 to 1977. A cohort analysis. *Arch. Gen. Psychiatry, 37*(5), 511–513.

42. Somers, A. R. (1976). Violence, television and the health of American youth. *N. Engl. J. Med.*, *294*(15), 811–817.
43. Srole, L., & Fischer, A. K. (1980). The Midtown Manhattan longitudinal study vs 'the mental paradise lost' doctrine: A controversy joined. *Arch. Gen. Psychiatry*, *37*(2), 209–221.
44. Targum, S. D., Dibble, E. D., Davenport, Y. B., et al. (1981). The family attitudes questionnaire: Patients' and spouses' views of bipolar illness. *Arch. Gen. Psychiatry*, *38*(5), 562–568.
45. Warheit, G. J., Holzer, C. E., III, & Schwab, J. J. (1973). An analysis of social class and racial differences in depressive symptomatology: A community study. *J. Health Soc. Behav.*, *14*, 291–299.
46. Weeke, A., Bille, M., Videbech, T., et al. (1975). Incidence of depressive syndromes in a Danish county: The Aarhus County investigation. *Acta Psychiatr. Scand.* *51*, 28–41.
47. Weissman, M. M., & Boyd, J. H. (1985). Affective disorders: Epidemiology, Section 18.2. In H. I. Kaplan & B. J. Sadock (Eds.), *Comprehensive textbook of psychiatry/IV*, Vol. 1 (4th ed.) (pp. 764–769). Baltimore: Williams & Wilkins.
48. Weissman, M. M., & Klerman, G. L. (1977). Sex differences and the epidemiology of depression. *Arch. Gen. Psychiatry*, *34*(1), 98–111.
49. Weissman, M. M., Leaf, P. J., Holzer, C. E., III, et al. (1984). The epidemiology of depression: An update on sex differences in rates. *J. Affect. Disord.*, *71*, 179–188.
50. Weissman, M. M., Merikangas, K. R., & Boyd, J. H. (1986). Epidemiology of affective disorders, Chap. 60. In R. Michels, J. O. Cavenar, Jr., H. K. H. Brodie, et al. (Eds.), *Psychiatry*, Vol. 1 (pp. 1–14). Philadelphia: Lippincott.
51. Weissman, M. M., & Myers, J. K. (1978). Affective disorders in a US urban community: The use of research diagnostic criteria in an epidemiological survey. *Arch. Gen. Psychiatry*, *35*(11), 1304–1311.
52. Wells, C. E. (1985). Other organic brain syndromes, Section 19.5. In H. I. Kaplan & B. J. Sadock (Eds.), *Comprehensive textbook of psychiatry/IV*, Vol. 1 (4th ed.) (pp. 875–877). Baltimore: Williams and Wilkins.
53. Zerbin-Rüdin, E. Cited by: Slater, E., & Cowie, V. (1971). *The genetics of mental disorders* (pp. 76–78). London: Oxford University Press.

2

NEUROCHEMISTRY OF DEPRESSION

DAVID HEALY, M.D., MRCPSYCH.
and
E. S. PAYKEL, M.A., M.D., FRCP., FRCPSYCH.

Department of Psychiatry, University of Cambridge, Addenbrooke's Hospital, Cambridge, United Kingdom

INTRODUCTION

There are several possible justifications for studying the neurochemistry of depression. One might be the search for a chemical abnormality, detectable in body fluids of depressed persons, which might assist diagnosis of the disorder or of particular diagnostic subgroups or which might predict response to antidepressants and electroshock therapy. While useful, this would be a limited application of neurochemistry, akin to the measurement of cardiac enzymes following myocardial infarction, beneficial diagnostically but uninstructive regarding the substrates of the disorder. A further justification for neurochemical studies in depression lies in attempts to elucidate the modes of action of antidepressant treatments. Developments in this area might permit the design of more effective therapeutic agents. However, the most compelling justification must be the search for the causes and substrates of the affective disorders. Inferences from the mode of action of drugs may be invalid as they may effect recovery by a compensatory mechanism rather than by an action on the primary disorder.

There has been an association between monoamines and mental life since Cannon demonstrated the involvement of the sympathetic nervous system in the peripheral manifestations of the emotions (44). The more immediate impetus to their investigation in mental illnesses arose on the one hand from structural similarities between norepinephrine and mescaline together with the sympathomimetic effects of amphetamine and on the other hand from the similarities between 5-HT and LSD, and the discovery that breakdown products of 5-HT such as dimethyltryptamine had potent hallucinogenic properties (14). In addition, there were early discoveries of dopaminergic deficits in Parkinson's disease and cholinergic changes in senile dementia, although these illnesses are characterized by gross motoric disturbances or profound cognitive loss rather than affective change.

THE ORIGINAL AMINE HYPOTHESES

History

Against this background the introduction of antidepressant drugs gave neurobiologists their first specific tools to probe the cerebral substrates of the affective disorders. In the late 1950s, tricyclic iminodibenzyls and monoamine oxidase inhibitors (MAOIs) were found to have antidepressant properties (125, 132). Subsequent basic research suggested that the MAOIs increased synaptic noradrenaline concentrations (204) and brain catecholamine levels (205). The tricyclics were found to inhibit amine reuptake (12, 13), to potentiate the effect of amines postsynaptically (203), and to protect against the depleting effects of reserpine (214, 215). These findings were complemented by reports that reserpine, used in the treatment of hypertension, could precipitate depression in up to 15% of those taking it (78, 95). The demonstration by Carlsson and co-workers that reserpine depleted catecholamines from brain (45) and indoleamines from platelets (46) set the scene for the first specific proposal concerning the neurochemistry of depression: that there was a consistent relationship between drug effects on catecholamines and mood, with agents causing depletion of noradrenaline leading to depression and antidepressant action being mediated through an increase of, or potentiation of, brain noradrenaline (40, 186). Comparable hypotheses concerning the role of the indoleamine serotonin (5-HT) in the affective disorders were put forward by Coppen (61) and Glassman (86). These hypotheses stimulated a considerable amount of clinical research attempting to find evidence for a simple deficit of catechol- or indoleamines or their metabolites in depressed persons. In particular, urinary and cerebrospinal fluid (CSF) MHPG and CSF 5-HIAA and postmortem brain metabolites and receptors have been studied.

MHPG

3-Methoxy-4-hydroxyphenylglycol (MHPG) has until recently been considered the major metabolite of central noradrenergic systems, leading to interest in its investigation in the urine and CSF of depressed subjects. A number of early reports suggested that urinary MHPG might be reduced in persons who were depressed (136, 137, 187). In general, however, such findings have not been consistently borne out. The difficulties of research in this area have become increasingly apparent as urinary MHPG has been found to have a wide range of normal values (104), to be affected by diet (154) and by physical activity (3, 75) and also to be influenced by weight, age, sex, urinary pH, or the consumption of alcohol or nicotine (3). In addition, it appears that little of the MHPG found in urine is derived from central sources (32). This has led to a consensus that urinary MHPG is too influenced by external factors to indicate reliably central noradrenergic function (177).

CSF MHPG potentially offers a more dependable indication of cerebral functioning, although here too there are problems, as MHPG is unstable, it may be transported into the CSF from the blood as well as in the opposite direction, and also its levels may primarily reflect aspects of behavior such as activity or anxiety at the stress of lumbar sampling (3, 250). Findings to date have been mixed (see Table 1), with studies showing increased, un-

Table 1
CSF MHPG

Depressives lower than normal controls	
Post et al. (171)	1973
Subrahmanyan (212)	1975
Depressives similar to normal controls	
Wilk et al. (239)	1972
Shaw et al. (196)	1973
Berger et al. (23)	1980
Oreland et al. (158)	1981
Depressives greater than normal controls	
Vestergaard et al. (234)	1978
Koslow et al. (123)	1983

changed, or decreased CSF MHPG in a manner suggesting a normal distribution rather than any consistent change.

Another noradrenergic metabolite recently the focus of interest has been dihydroxyphenylglycol (DHPG), which is specific to neuroendocrine tissues and hence can usefully be measured in blood, unlike MHPG, which also derives from liver and other sources (185). In addition, although there have been few attempts to study norepinephrine as it is highly unstable in plasma and difficult to measure accurately (21), a number of recent studies have examined it and DHPG. In general, there has been no convincing indication from these studies of a depletion of noradrenergic activity in depression (181, 202).

5-HIAA

There has been a similar pattern to research on CSF 5-hydroxyindoleacetic acid (5-HIAA), the metabolite of 5-HT. A number of earlier reports suggested that it was lowered in depressed persons (8–10). Additional research suggested that its accumulation in the CSF, after its egress from the CSF had been blocked by probenecid, was also reduced (90, 229). By 1979 there had been 14 studies of this metabolite but the majority of these found no abnormality in depression (3). Even were it lowered, there would be grounds for caution in the interpretation of the findings since amine metabolites may reflect metabolism but not necessarily function (91). Furthermore, 5-HIAA passes directly into the bloodstream and therefore CSF levels may reflect altered hemodynamics rather than altered cerebral function (170). The results are also affected by activity (145). In addition, it has been argued that lumbar sampling may reveal no more than the metabolism of the lumbar cord (39).

In contrast to the lack of consistent findings in depression, evidence for an association between diminished CSF 5-HIAA and aggression or autoaggression has recently been strengthening. Starting from the early studies by Asberg et al. (9), it appeared that depressed subjects with lowered CSF 5-HIAA were more likely to have attempted suicide during the course of the index illness, especially by violent means. A number of studies now support the possibility of a link between this variable and suicidal behavior, cutting across psychiatric diagnosis (see Table 2). It has been suggested that diminished serotonergic function as reflected in 5-HIAA levels may correlate with poor impulse control (232). Lowered 5-HIAA levels also appear to predict future suicide attempts (224).

Table 2
CSF 5-HIAA in Suicide

Suicidal depressions have lower 5-HIAA		
Asberg et al. (9)	1976	
Agren (2)	1980	
Oreland et al. (158)	1981	
Traskman et al. (223)	1981	
Van Praag (230)	1982	
Banki and Arrato (16)	1983	
Banki et al. (17)	1984	
Lopez-Ibor et al. (133)	1985	
Suicidal depressions do not have lower 5-HIAA		
Roy et al. (179)	1984	
Vestergaard et al. (234)	1978	
Nondepressed and suicidal have low 5-HIAA		
Traskman et al. (223)	1981	Personality disorder and anxiety
Oreland et al. (158)	1981	Personality disorder and anxiety
Banki and Arrato (16)	1983	Personality disorder and anxiety
Van Praag (231)	1983	Schizophrenia

DEVELOPMENT OF THE AMINE HYPOTHESES

Hypotheses based on a simple deficit of amines in depression are not easily sustained at present. The evidence that reserpine causes depression has been questioned (149). Among the other sympatholytic antihypertensives, only methyldopa is clearly associated with depression (165). Reserpine induces a behavioral syndrome in animals (blepharoptosis, hypothermia, and sedation) which was reversed by the prototypical antidepressants (138). It has been assumed that this is due to a depletion of monoamines. However, while reserpine does deplete amines, it mainly affects storage pools of noradrenaline and 5-HT rather than functionally active neurotransmitters (76, 124).

Furthermore, this syndrome is not reversed by all of the currently effective antidepressants (138), and failure of reversal seems to occur particularly with antidepressants that neither inhibit deamination nor block uptake. There is evidence also that many classical antidepressants, far from increasing brain amines, may do nothing to overall amine levels or may indeed decrease them through actions on amine turnover or through inhibition of amine biosynthesis (38, 47, 157). A logical consequence of the simple deficit hypotheses was that amine precursors would be effective in the treatment of depression and amine-depleting agents in the treatment of mania, but these requirements have not been met (3, 134, 149).

There is, furthermore, a notable delay in the onset of therapeutic action compared with the rapid reversal of the reserpine syndrome or the immediate onset of pharmacological effects on the monoaminergic systems. This delay along with the development of antidepressants, such as iprindole and mianserin, which had no apparent effects on monoaminergic systems led to a search for another focus of antidepressant actions. These anomalies along with evidence that receptors might undergo adaptation led Ashcroft et al. in 1972 (11) to suggest that the pathological lesion in depression might lie postsynaptically in aminergic receptors rather than simply in amine levels. This alternative emphasis has led to hypotheses of beta-adrenoceptor supersensitivity (235), $alpha_2$-autoreceptor supersensitivity (64), and 5-HT_2-receptor supersensitivity (4, 197). These hypotheses have been put forward supported by claims that antidepressants produce the requisite receptor adaptations following chronic but not acute exposure. The beta- and alpha-receptor hypotheses are logically consistent with the earlier hypotheses in that hypersensitive $alpha_2$ receptors, if presynaptic, might bring about a functional depletion of noradrenaline and beta adrenoceptors are a postsynaptic target for noradrenaline. These hypotheses offered the possibility of finding a common mechanism of antidepressant action and one that would be consistent with the time course of clinical response.

Beta-Adrenoceptor Supersensitivity

Vetulani et al. (235) reported that antidepressant agents of differing pharmacological types brought about a down-regulation of rat cortical beta-receptor density. This led to the inference that beta receptors might be supersensitive in depression, with antidepressants acting to down-regulate them (216). It has been reported that all current antidepressants bring about a reduction in beta-receptor number following chronic but not acute administration (216, 217). These results have been replicated widely except for the tetracyclic antidepressants (62, 213). However, it also appears that the effects can be brought about by chlorpromazine (31), cocaine, and amphetamine (15). The length of time taken to induce down-regulation can be as short as a few days (6, 191, 195). Particularly rapid down-regulation has been induced with combinations of imipramine or desipramine and yohimbine (110, 183) and various antidepressants combined with phenoxybenzamine (65), but none of these combinations have been reported to bring about comparably rapid clinical response (52). In addition, there have been problems in attempting to replicate the findings in species other than the rat (107) and even in all strains of rats (122). It appears that there are regional variations in antidepressant effects on beta receptors and even variations within the population of limbic beta receptors, with some down-regulating and others not (29). Given the heterogeneity of these findings, one would like to know the functional effects of altered receptor density before deciding whether the changes are clinically relevant.

Nevertheless, as beta-receptor down-regulation is one of the most consistently reported effects of antidepressants, occurring in response to antidepressants of a variety of pharmacological classes, there has been considerable interest in investigating the beta-receptor hypothesis in clinical populations. Suitable peripheral models have been difficult to find. Lymphocyte beta receptors have been used, but care must be taken in interpreting the results since lymphocyte populations are heterogenous and both subsets of lymphocytes and their receptors show pronounced circadian variation (97). Bearing this in mind, Healy et al. (97) have reported an increase in lymphocyte beta-adrenoceptor density in depression, which normalized on recovery, but Mann et al. (141) found no differences between depressed and control groups. Using a method potentially free of the above complications but also far removed from conditions that might exist in a depressive illness, Wright et al. (247) found decreased beta-adrenoceptor density on cells in lymphoblastoid cell cultures from manic-depressive patients compared to unaffected relatives and other controls. A further approach has been to examine pineal beta receptors by assessing melatonin output following challenge with the beta-receptor antagonist clenbuterol (222). Results from this study did not indicate significant beta-receptor down-regulation during the course of antidepressant treatment.

Alpha-Adrenoceptor Hypersensitivity

It has been postulated that noradrenergic neurons carry presynaptic $alpha_2$ autoreceptors, which act to reduce synaptic release of noradrenaline (211). In 1978 (64), Crews and Smith reported that $alpha_2$ receptors adapt to chronic desipramine treatment and that this adaptation takes three weeks to become established and involves effects on noradrenergic transmission that are substantially greater than those occurring acutely, in response to blockade of noradrenaline reuptake. These findings led to the proposal that the $alpha_2$ autoreceptor might be supersensitive in depression, leading to a functional depletion of noradrenaline, and that antidepressants might act to desensitize it (56). There have been difficulties in replicating this finding for antidepressants other than desipramine (190). In addition, it appears that there are regional variations in effects on alpha$_2$-receptor number after desipramine with desensitization occurring in some brain areas but not in others (111, 183).

Alpha$_2$ receptors in depression and after antidepressants can readily be measured in clinical populations by binding studies of platelet alpha$_2$ adrenoceptors, and their function can be tested by neuroendocrine challenge tests of pituitary alpha$_2$-receptor function. In 1981 (81), Garcia-Sevilla and co-workers reported that platelet alpha$_2$ receptor density was increased in depressed patients, returning to normal with effective antidepressant treatment. There has been some support for this finding from studies using either [^{3}H]clonidine or [^{3}H]dihydroergocriptine as radioligands. Both these agents are alpha$_2$ agonists. Studies using radiolabeled antagonists, such as [^{3}H]yohimbine or [^{3}H]rauwolsceine, have failed to find increased platelet alpha$_2$-receptor density (see Table 3). A recent study by Theodorou et al. (221) using the agonist ligand ^{3}UK 14,304 also failed to find increased receptor density. Variations based on the radioligand used suggest caution in the interpretation of the findings (114). It must also be kept in mind that changes in platelet receptors may be epiphenomena of the illness rather than indicative of some generalized adrenoceptor defect. There have, for example, also been reports that platelet alpha-receptor density is increased in anorexia nervosa, suggesting perhaps effects of undernourishment or hormonal changes (103, 135). Furthermore, Horton et al. (105) have reported effects of antidepressants on platelet alpha$_2$-receptor number, independent of changes in clinical state. These findings emphasize the necessity of studying only drug-free subjects or subjects who have been withdrawn from antidepressants for considerable lengths of time.

An alternative avenue for the investigation of alpha$_2$-adrenoceptor function has been through neuroendocrine challenge testing. Infusions of clonidine, an alpha$_2$ agonist, produce increases in plasma growth hormone concentration (54). In depressed patients this increase has consistently been reported to be attenuated (53, 55, 117). It has been argued that this blunting is indicative of an alpha$_2$-adrenoceptor defect in depression (53). However, these findings are not necessarily consistent with the hypothesis of Crews and Smith, which involved presynaptic autoreceptors, as the alpha$_2$ receptor involved in the release of growth hormone appears to lie postsynaptically (64).

Table 3
Platelet Alpha-Receptor Binding

B_{max} lower than controls	
Wood and Coppen (243)	1980
Carstens et al. (50)	1981
No difference	
Daiguji et al. (67)	1981
Pimoule et al. (168)	1983
Lenox et al. (127)	1983
Stahl et al. (207)	1983
Campbell et al. (43)	1985
Horton et al. (105)	1986
Theodorou et al. (221)	1986
Braddock et al. (34)	1986
Georgotas et al. (84)	1987
B_{max} greater than controls	
Kafka et al. (112)	1981
Garcia-Sevilla et al. (81, 82)	1981/7
Siever et al. (200)	1984
Healy et al. (96, 97)	1983/5
Doyle et al. (74)	1985

In addition, Siever and Uhde (199) found that responses were reduced in unipolar but not bipolar patients and that there were significantly lower responses in postmenopausal female controls than in other controls, a finding replicated by Horton et al. (105). In separate studies, Siever and coworkers found reduced responsiveness in obsessive-compulsive disorders (198) and in panic disorders (228). There also appear to be abnormalities in the basal output of growth hormone in depressed patients (151) with an increase in its output in depression, which might have a negative feedback effect, inhibiting further release on challenge testing, prohibiting inferences to an adrenoceptor defect. In addition, Katona et al. (117) reported an association between blunted response to clonidine and dexamethasone nonsuppression, which raises the possibility that findings in this system may be secondary to hypercortisolemia. It has become more apparent also that hormonal challenge responses reflect responses in complex systems rather than necessarily the functioning of single receptors (85).

5-HT Receptors in Depression

Attempts to investigate 5-HT receptor function in depression have been hampered by gaps in our basic knowledge of these receptors and technical problems in studying them. The number of 5-HT receptors identified has been growing recently, with four distinct subtypes currently characterized (77) and others suspected. There are not yet specific agonists or antagonists for each of these receptors, so that it is neither possible to measure them nor to determine their function unequivocally. Aprison et al. (4) and Sherman (197) have postulated that there is a supersensitivity of serotonergic systems in depression. Peroutka and Snyder (166) reported that chronic antidepressant treatments down-regulate 5-HT_2-receptor densities. Subsequent receptor-binding studies suggest that most, but probably not all, antidepressants bring about decreases in 5-HT_2-receptor density following chronic administration (62). In addition, electrophysiological studies indicate a change in 5-HT_2 receptor function after chronic treatment with antidepressants (70), although these findings indicate a sensitization of 5-HT_2 function, rather than the desensitization that decreased receptor density might lead one to expect.

Decreased receptor sensitivity was found for platelet 5-HT_2 receptors by Healy et al. (97) using 5-HT-stimulated platelet aggregation as a test of function. With response to treatment there was an increase in receptor sensitivity. Wood et al. (245) have replicated these effects of treatment but not the original decrease in sensitivity. Cowen et al. (63) have reported no differences between control and depressed platelet 5-HT_2-receptor density, but they also found that antidepressant treatments increase 5-HT_2-receptor density on platelets from depressed patients, a finding that contrasts with the effects of these drugs on rat cortical 5-HT_2-receptor numbers. Such findings indicate the ambiguities associated with receptor research: the precise relations between changes in functional sensitivity and receptor number are as yet unknown.

There have been a number of attempts to develop a neuroendocrine challenge test of central 5-HT-receptor sensitivity. While a number of studies have reported changes in cortisol, prolactin, and growth hormone in response to neuroendocrine challenges and inferred alterations in 5-HT-receptor function from their findings (87), such inferences are open to question. Studies to date have used a variety of challenging agents, doses, and routes of administration. The 5-HT precursors 5-HTP and L-tryptophan have been used, as well as the 5-HT agonist quipazine, the antagonist methysergide, and 5-HT uptake inhibitors such as clomipramine. None of these agents are specific either to any one 5-HT receptor or to the 5-HT system as a whole, since most also have pronounced catecholaminergic effects (233).

5-HT Transport and [^{3}H]Imipramine Binding

In contrast to studies of 5-HT receptors, the measurement of the 5-HT uptake system in platelets and synaptosomes is a sensitive and reproducible assay. Rather than investigations arising from antidepressant effects found in animals, abnormalities in the 5-HT transport systems of depressed patients have been discovered empirically. In 1976 (225), Tuomisto and Tukiainen reported that the uptake rate (V_{max}) of platelet 5-HT was reduced in persons who were depressed. This finding has since been replicated extensively (see Table 4) and appears to be specific to depression, not being found in schizophrenia (5, 206) or other disorders (102). The reduction in uptake rates appears to be restored to normal by effective treatment with antidepressants (97, 147) and appears to occur whether the patient is being treated with drugs active at the uptake sites, such as nortriptyline (147), dothiepin (97), or fluvoxamine (244), or agents having no effect at this

Table 4
Platelet 5-HT Uptake Rates (V_{max})

Depressives lower than controls	
Tuomisto and Tukiainen (225)	1976
Coppen et al. (59)	1978
Tuomisto et al. (226)	1979
Scott et al. (193)	1979
Born et al. (33)	1980
Malmgren et al. (139)	1981
Aberg-Wistedt et al. (1)	1981
Meltzer et al. (147)	1981
Stahl et al. (206)	1982
Meltzer et al. (148)	1983
Wood et al. (244)	1983
Healy et al. (96, 97)	1983
Healy et al. (98)	1986 (9 A.M.)
Butler and Leonard (41)	1986
No difference	
Kaplan and Mann (116)	1982
Healy et al. (98)	1986 (noon)
Roy et al. (181)	1987

uptake site, such as mianserin, nomifensine, or ECT (41, 60, 99). It is not yet clear how such a normalization is brought about, as it is not a natural consequence of simple exposure of these transport proteins to antidepressants (102).

Recent technical advances have revealed the existence of a high-affinity [^{3}H]imipramine binding site, found on serotonergic nerve terminals and on platelets and apparently associated with the 5-HT transport site (35, 161). There have been reports of reductions in the number of these binding sites on platelets in depression, apparently consonant with findings of reductions in 5-HT uptake in depression (147, 162). However, a number of studies recently have failed to replicate the finding of reduction in [^{3}H]imipramine binding in depression (see Table 5). In addition, unlike diminished 5-HT uptake, which appears clearly to be a state-dependent phenomenon, normalizing with recovery, decreased [^{3}H]imipramine binding has been reported long after the index depression had resolved (172). Subsequent studies have hinted at a delayed return to normal with therapeutic recovery (169), and animal studies have shown that chronic antidepressant treatment leads to an up-regulation of [^{3}H]imipramine binding sites (18).

The precise relation between high-affinity [^{3}H]imipramine binding sites and 5-HT uptake is still obscure. Binding to this site occurs at concentrations of imipramine in the nanomolar (10^{-9}M) range, whereas uptake inhibition needs considerably higher concentrations (10^{-7}M) of the drug (194, 224). At the concentrations necessary to inhibit uptake, imipramine also binds to a low-affinity site (108, 176) and it is not yet clear what effects binding to this site might have on 5-HT uptake. When first reported, high-affinity [^{3}H]imipramine binding sites were thought to be generic antidepressant binding sites, but this appears not to be the case, as other antidepressants, such as [^{3}H]desipramine, bind at high affinity to distinctly different sites (26), as do [^{3}H]mianserin (62) and [^{3}H]nortriptyline (27). It has been reported that all antidepressants investigated bind at therapeutic concentrations to low-affinity [^{3}H]imipramine binding sites, raising the possibility that it may be a generic antidepressant binding site (28). However, neither the functional effects of binding to this low-affinity site nor the densities of these sites in depressed subjects have been elucidated.

POSTMORTEM STUDIES

A number of studies have examined receptor binding in postmortem brain tissue of suicides. While concentrations of some neurotransmitters,

Table 5
Platelet [^{3}H] Imipramine Binding in Depression

Depressives lower than controls	
Asarch et al. (7)	1980
Briley et al. (36)	1980
Paul et al. (162)	1981
Raisman et al. (172)	1981
Suranyi-Cadotte et al. (218, 219)	1982/5
Wood et al. (246)	1983
Lewis and McChesney (130)	1985
Wagner et al. (236)	1985
Schneider et al. (188, 189)	1985/7
Poirier et al. (169)	1986
Nankai et al. (155)	1986
No change	
Mellerup et al. (146)	1982
Berrettini et al. (24)	1982
Gentsch et al. (83)	1982
Baron et al. (19, 20)	1983/6
Whittaker et al. (238)	1984
Tang and Morris (220)	1985
Hrdina et al. (106)	1985
Carstens et al. (51)	1986
Horton et al. (105)	1986
Braddock et al. (34)	1986
Muscettola et al. (153)	1986
Georgotas et al. (84)	1987
Kanof et al. (115)	1987
Roy et al. (181)	1987
Desmedt et al. (71)	1987

metabolites, and enzymes change after death, most neurotransmitter receptor sites appear stable for up to 96 hours postmortem (94, 178). Increase in 5-HT$_2$-receptor numbers in cortex was reported by Stanley and Mann (142, 209) but not replicated by Owen et al. (159). Increased muscarinic cholinergic receptor binding was reported by Meyerson et al. (152) but not by Stanley (210) or Kaufman et al. (118). Increase in beta-adrenergic-receptor binding was found by Zenko and Biegon (248) and Mann and Stanley (140) but not by Meyerson et al. (152). Decreased imipramine binding sites were reported in the frontal cortex by Stanley et al. (208) and by Crow et al. (66) and in the hypothalamus by Paul et al. (163), but Meyerson et al. (152) found increased binding and Owen and colleagues were unable to replicate their earlier findings (160). Recent developments such as quantitative histochemistry and autoradiography, which permit more precise measurement of variation within brain areas (30), may lead to greater consistency among future findings, as undoubtedly some of the apparent discrepancies result from sampling different brain areas. These developments may also assist in the determination of the neurophysiological significance of whatever findings emerge.

These studies do not necessarily bear on depression since suicides are a heterogenous group and most studies have also included alcoholics, schizophrenics, and personality-disordered patients. The only study in elderly depressives dying of natural causes found diminished imipramine binding (167). There are complications of studying natural deaths also, as the mode of death, e.g., anoxia because of respiratory distress, intercurrent physical illnesses, and recent drug treatment may also cloud the issue. But the above findings of alterations in serotonergic systems in suicides if confirmed would complement the findings from CSF 5-HIAA studies indicative of abnormalities in serotonergic systems in suicidal states.

OTHER NEUROTRANSMITTERS

Neurotransmitters other than noradrenaline or serotonin have also been implicated in depression. There has been a dopamine hypothesis (73, 173), and a considerable amount of evidence can be offered that antidepressants bring about changes in dopaminergic systems following chronic administration (128, 240). Dopamine, of all the catecholamines, seems most involved in motivation and in the reinforcement of ongoing behavior (80, 240). However, if dopamine depletion were responsible for depression, one might expect a high incidence of neuroleptic-induced depression, which does not occur.

Hypotheses related to acetylcholine have also been put forward (72, 109). Cholinergic mechanisms have been implicated in the disturbances of sleep, particularly REM sleep disturbances, and in the lack of drive found in depression, as well as the pathophysiology of cortisol hypersecretion (72). However, while the most marked acute clinical effects of many antidepressants are their atropinic side effects, antidepressant efficacy generally does not correspond to potency on cholinergic receptor systems (62).

There are also some grounds for implicating opioids in depression (69). Opiates have long been known to give symptomatic relief in depression

(126), and endogenous opioids appear to be mobilized in distressing circumstances and to modulate dysphoria (57, 69). Cohen et al. (57) administered high-dose naloxone infusions to volunteer subjects with no ill effects other than a mild degree of loss of concentration and a mild dysthymia. The same challenge administered to a schizophrenic population appears to have produced beneficial effects (58). However, when given to depressed persons this challenge test elicited pronounced dysphoria (57). Allied to this are the findings that patients with a major depressive disorder are less sensitive than controls or other psychiatric patients to painful stimuli (68). Antidepressants also interact with opiate and other receptors in the brain (25, 174).

More recently it has been suggested that there may be a decrease in GABAergic tone in depression (32). In support of such a hypothesis there is some evidence that the GABA agonists progabide and fengabine have antidepressant effects (129). There are also findings of lowered GABA levels in CSF of depressed subjects (131).

This plethora of proposed mechanisms of action and discovered abnormalities need not necessarily be as contradictory as may appear at first sight. Neurotransmitters may be implicated in different individual clinical features of the illness rather than have a single central role. For example, dopamine, or the balance between dopamine and Ach balance, might be involved in deficits of motivation and Ach in sleep disturbance. In this vein, Carlsson has argued that 5-HT is the principal substrate for mood, whereas noradrenaline mediates the level of motor activation or arousal, and it was this hypothesis that led to the recent formulation of antidepressants with specific 5-HT uptake inhibiting properties (48). Serotonin has also been associated with both anxiety (156) and aggression, especially autoaggression (232). There has long been a tradition that noradrenaline is particularly important to levels of arousal and vigilance (121), and the most marked effect of sympatholytic agents, such as clonidine, is sedation rather than dysphoria (165). One can also implicate the various neuropeptides in the production of the final clinical picture. For example, increased secretion of corticotropin-releasing factor (CRF), which leads to the secretion of ACTH and thereby cortisol, may be responsible for the hypercortisolemia found in depression but may also be anxiogenic (37).

Alternatively, although one neurotransmitter may be of primary importance in the production of the illness, interactions between several different neurotransmitters may be responsible for the final clinical picture as particular clinical features tend to vary from case to case. For example, while the monoamines are known to be involved in appetite control and therefore an abnormality of a single monoamine neurotransmitter might give rise to an appetite disturbance, one would expect that disturbance to be of a fixed nature. However, depression may show anorexia, hyperphagia, or feelings of satiety. Evidence is emerging that in addition to amine involvement in the control of appetite, there are also several peptide transmitters, CCK and Satietin for instance (120). It may take interactions between all these neurotransmitters to bring about the final appetite states encountered clinically.

Consistent with the possibility that derangements of differing neurotransmitters may underlie individual clinical features is a little evidence that it is possible to manipulate clinical features by actions on specific transmitter systems. Thus naloxone exacerbates the dysphoria found in depression, without causing dysphoria to other subjects (57). Administration of L-dopa may lead to increases in activity without changes in mood. But neither opiates, amine agonists, amine precursors, nor neuropeptides appear to be antidepressants. While most antidepressants have a common chronic effect to down-regulate beta adrenoceptors, they also appear to have similar effects on a number of neurotransmitter systems, bringing about down-regulation of 5-HT_2 receptors and up-regulation of $GABA_b$ binding sites (62) and 5-HT transport proteins (102), altered opiate receptor number (175), and altered responsiveness to the opiate neuromodulator substance P (110). They bind to muscarinic, histaminergic, serotonergic, opiate, and adrenergic receptors (157, 194). It is possible that antidepressant efficacy resides in having multiple actions on a number of different neurotransmitter systems.

HORMONES AND RHYTHMS

There appear to be abnormalities in the output of most hormones in depression, including cortisol (79, 182), prolactin (93, 150), TSH (119, 237), growth hormone (151), melatonin (22), and beta endorphin (143). These studies have all reported abnormalities in the 24-hour pattern of hormone secretion on serial sampling, where none had been apparent on single sampling. Common to these reports is a consistent elevation or reduction in the hormone, giving a diminished range in the levels of the hormone found over a 24-hour period. Such blunting or reduced variability appears to go hand in hand with abnormalities in neuroendocrine challenge tests. Thus there is a failure of suppression of cortisol in response to dexamethasone challenge (49) along with blunting of the TSH response to TRF (88) and a blunting of growth hormone output in response to alpha-adrenergic agonists (55, 117).

It has been suggested that this general abnormality in many hormones reflects a generalized dysregulation of neurotransmitter systems in depression (201). Most of the hormones involved are regulated by dopaminergic, noradrenergic, serotonergic, opioid, cholinergic, GABAergic, and peptide influences (227). The pattern of defects found in depression does not suggest one common neurotransmitter abnormality. Indeed, one neurotransmitter abnormality would be unlikely to give such a widespread pattern of defects, as the pituitary system has considerable inbuilt redundancy (85). While description of the findings in depression in terms of dysregulation is consistent with current knowledge, a hypothesis that dysregulation is the disturbance in depression lacks explanatory power. It does not yield precise predictions, as any abnormal finding can be termed the consequence of a dysregulation. Nor does it permit inferences about the probable origin of such a disturbance.

An alternative hypothesis is one of circadian rhythm disturbance. There has long been an association between circadian rhythm disturbance and mental illness, but until recently few specific hypotheses about the mechanism of their linkage (184). Recently a number of specific proposals have been put forward. Hallberg (92) has suggested that depression is associated with a desynchronization of rhythms; Goodwin et al. (89) found that there is a phase advance of rhythms in depressed subjects. Schulz and Lund (192) have noted a diminished amplitude in the rhythms of depressed patients. The dysregulation hypothesis of Siever and Davis (201) could be explained in terms of circadian rhythm disruption (100). Von Zerssen et al. (249) have noted the additional possibility that the disease process in depression might act as an abnormal synchronizing signal for internal rhythms or might itself be entrained to some rhythmic variable. However, it is worthy of note that antidepressants are among the few drugs known to affect circadian rhythms. They have been reported to advance the phase of rhythms and enhance their amplitude (241), and they bind to the recently discovered central circadian "clock," the suprachiasmatic nucleus (242). Also of note are diurnal rhythms in receptor number of the order of magnitude brought about by antidepressants (42, 113). Hence delayed changes in receptor number might occur as a consequence of the action of antidepressants on circadian rhythms rather than by virtue of an intrinsic action of antidepressants on the receptor systems reported to change (102). If not the therapeutic locus of action, such an action remains a possible source of delayed-onset receptor changes, whose status would then become that of side effects (101).

CONCLUSIONS

Findings on the neurochemistry of depression are currently in a state of flux and it is difficult to be certain where they will settle. The simple amine depletion theories of depression have become less easily tenable and the evidence much more complex. They originated from two lines of evidence: known pharmacological effects of antidepressant drugs and studies of amine metabolites in depressed patients. The latter findings are now clouded: there do appear to be consistent changes in urinary or CSF noradrenergic metabolites, and diminished serotonin turnover appears more closely related to suicidal and aggressive behavior than depression. Findings for drug effects are not clear-cut, but the acute effects of almost all antidepressants still do appear to involve potentiation of norepinephrine, serotonin, or both.

The investigation of receptor changes has brought new complications. A convergence of antidepressant effects in down-regulation of the beta adrenoceptor does suggest a common pattern of action. However, the significance of these changes is still obscure. Receptor studies in depression have yielded inconclusive results. A stable trait abnormality in platelet or lymphocyte markers might reflect a more widespread genetic abnormality underlying depression, but no such change has yet been conclusively shown.

The last 10 years have seen a rejuvenation of neuroendocrinology in psychiatry. Endocrine challenge tests in depression, however, measure the functional state of a system rather than simply the sensitivity of a particular receptor. As such the interpretation of consistently reported findings, such as the blunting of growth hormone output in response to clonidine, is difficult, as it may be influenced by baseline growth hormone levels and diurnal changes in receptor sensitivity. Other strategies currently being introduced include studies of intact brain functioning by noninvasive techniques such as positron emission tomography (PET) and magnetic resonance spectroscopy. These are likely to replace peripheral model systems such as the platelet or lymphocyte in the near future. Molecular biological techniques are also being introduced. They too may further contribute to our understanding of the interaction of biological and psychosocial factors that shape a depression.

Brain systems interact with the external environment. There is considerable evidence that social causes such as life events are important in depression (164). There is no contradiction between psychosocial and biological causes of depression in that psychologically perceived stress must in the long run have its substrates in brain function and neurotransmitter-mediated systems so that in the long run psychological and neurochemical causes may summate and interact.

In neurochemical studies the historical focus on monoamines may have been unwarranted. There is evidence pointing to the possible importance of other neurotransmitters and neuromodulators. Nevertheless the association between monoamines and affective disorders has been consistent, and although the association may not be exclusive, the link between monoamines and affective disorders still has more evidence in its favor than does any other neurochemical abnormality.

REFERENCES

1. Aberg-Wistedt, A., Jostell, K. G., Ross, S. B., & Westerlund, D. (1981). Effects of zimelidine and desipramine on serotonergic and noradrenergic uptake mechanisms in relation to plasma concentrations and to therapeutic effects during treatment of depression. *Psychopharmacology, 74*, 297-305.
2. Agren, H. (1980). Symptom pattern in unipolar and bipolar depressions correlating with monoamine metabolites in the cerebrospinal fluid. *Psychiatr. Res., 3*, 225-236.
3. Annitto, W., & Shopsin, B. (1979). Neuropharmacology of mania. In B. Shopsin (Ed.), *Manic illness* (pp. 105-164). New York: Academic Press.
4. Aprison, M. H., Takahashi, R., & Tachiki, K. (1978). Hypersensitive serotonin receptors involved in clinical depression—A theory. In B. Naber & M. H. Aprison (Eds.), *Neuropharmacology and behaviour* (pp. 23-53). New York: Plenum Press.
5. Arora, R. C., & Meltzer, H. Y. (1982). Serotonin uptake by blood platelets of schizophrenic patients. *Psychiatr. Res., 6*, 327-333.
6. Asakura, M., Tsukumoto, T., & Kasegawa, K. (1982). Modification of rat brain $alpha_2$ and beta adrenergic receptor sensitivity following longterm treatment with antidepressants. *Brain Res., 235*, 192-197.
7. Asarch, K. B., Shih, J., & Kulesar, A. (1980). Decreased ^{3}H.imipramine binding in depressed males and females. *Commun. Psychopharmacol., 4*, 425-432.
8. Asberg, M., Bertilsson, L., Tuck, D., Cronholm, B., & Sjoqvist, F. (1973). Indoleamine metabolism in the csf of depressed patients before and during treatment with nortriptyline. *Clin. Pharmacol. Ther., 14*, 277-283.
9. Asberg, M., Thoren, P., Traskman, L., Bertilsson, L., & Ruigleergen, N. (1976). Serotonin depression—A biochemical subgroup within the affective disorders? *Science, 191*, 478-479.
10. Ashcroft, G., Crawford, T., & Eccleston, E. (1966). 5-hydroxyindole compounds in the csf of patients with psychiatric or neurological diseases. *Lancet, 2*, 1049-1052.
11. Ashcroft, G., Eccleston, D., & Murray, I. (1972). Modified amine hypothesis for the aetiology of affective illness. *Lancet, 2*, 573-577.
12. Axelrod, J., Whitby, L., & Hertting, G. (1961). Effect of psychotropic drugs on the uptake of ^{3}H.noradrenaline by tissues. *Science, 133*, 383-384.
13. Axelrod, J., & Inscoe, J. K. (1963). The uptake and binding of circulating serotonin and the effect of drugs. *J. Pharmacol. Exp. Ther., 141*, 161-165.

14. Axelrod, J. (1972). Biogenic amines and their impact on psychiatry. *Semin. Psychiatry, 4*, 199–210.
15. Banerjee, S. P., Sharma, V. K., Kung-Cheung, L. S., Chanda, S. K., & Riggi, S. J. (1979). Cocaine and dextro-amphetamine induce changes in central beta-adrenergic sensitivity: effects of acute and chronic drug treatment. *Brain Res., 175*, 119–130.
16. Banki, C. M., & Arato, M. (1983). Amine metabolites and neuroendocrine response related to depression and suicide. *J. Affect. Disord., 5*, 223–232.
17. Banki, C. M., Vojnik, M., Papp, Z., Balla, K. Z., & Arato, M. (1985). Cerebrospinal fluid magnesium and calcium related to amine metabolites, diagnosis and suicide attempts. *Biol. Psychiatry, 20*, 163–171.
18. Barbaccia, M. L., Gandolfi, O., Chuang, D. M., & Costa, E. (1983). Modulation of neuronal serotonin uptake by a putative endogenous ligand of imipramine recognition sites. *Proc. Natl. Acad. Sci. USA, 80*, 5134–5138.
19. Baron, M., Barkai, A., Gruen, R., Kowalik, S., & Quitkin, F. (1983). ^{3}H.imipramine platelet binding sites in unipolar depression. *Biol. Psychiatry, 18*, 1403–1409.
20. Baron, M., Borkai, A., Gruen, R., Peselow, E., Fieve, R. R., & Quitkin, F. (1986). Platelet ^{3}H.imipramine binding in affective disorders: State vs trait characteristics. *Am. J. Psychiatry, 143*, 711–717.
21. Barrand, M. A., & Callingham, B. A. (1983). The catecholamines; adrenaline, noradrenaline and dopamine. In C. H. Gray & V. H. T. James (Eds.), *Hormones in blood* (3rd Ed.). New York: Academic Press.
22. Beck-Frijs, J., Lyungren, J-G., Thoren, M., von Rosen, D., Kjellman, B. F., & Wetterberg, L. (1985). Melatonin, cortisol, and ACTH in patients with manic-depressive disorder and healthy humans with special reference to the outcome of the dexamethasone suppression test. *Psychoneuroendocrinology, 10*, 173–186.
23. Berger, P. A., Faull, K. F., Kilkowski, J., et al. (1980). Cerebrospinal fluid monoamine metabolites in depression and schizophrenia. *Am. J. Psychiatry, 137*, 174–180.
24. Berrettini, W. H., Nurnberger, J. I., Post, R. M., & Gershon, E. S. (1982). Platelet ^{3}H.imipramine binding in euthyroid bipolar patients. *Psychiatr. Res.*, 7, 215–219.
25. Biegon, A., & Samuel, D. (1979). Binding of a labelled antidepressant to rat brain tissue. *Biochem. Pharmacol., 28*, 3361–3366.
26. Biegon, A., and Rainbow, T. C. (1983). Localisation and characterisation of ^{3}H.desmethylimipramine binding in the rat brain by quantitative autoradiography. *J. Neurosci., 3*, 1069–1076.
27. Biegon, A. (1984). The complex binding of tricyclic antidepressants to rat brain: The case of nortriptyline. *Brain Res., 32*, 347–351.
28. Biegon, A. Localisation and characterisation of low affinity binding sites for tricyclic antidepressants in the brain. *J. Neurochem.* (submitted).
29. Biegon, A., & Israeli, M. (1986). Localisation of the effects of electroconvulsive shock on beta adrenoceptors in the rat brain. *Eur. J. Pharmacol., 123*, 329–334.
30. Biegon, A. (1986). Effect of chronic desipramine treatment on dihydroalprenolol, imipramine and desipramine binding sites; a quantitative autoradiographic study in the rat brain. *J. Neurochem., 47*, 77–80.
31. Blumberg, J., Vetulani, J., Stawarz, R., & Sulser, F. (1976). The noradrenergic cyclic AMP generating system in the limbic forebrain: Pharmacological characterisation and possible role of limbic noradrenergic mechanisms in the mode of action of antipsychotic drugs. *Eur. J. Pharmacol., 37*, 357–366.
32. Blumberg, P., Kopin, I., Gordon, E., Markey, S., & Ebert, M. (1980). Conversion of MHPG to VMA: Implications for the importance of urinary MHPG. *Arch. Gen. Psychiatry, 37*, 1095–1098.
33. Born, G. V. R., Grignani, G., & Martin, K. (1980). Long term effects of lithium on the uptake of 5-hydroxytryptamine by human platelets. *Br. J. Clin. Pharmacol.*, 9, 321–326.

34. Braddock, L. E., Cowen, P. J., Elliot, J. M., Fraser, S., & Stump, K. (1986). Binding of yohimbine and imipramine to platelets in depressive illness. *Psychol. Med.*, *16*, 765–773.

35. Briley, M. S., Raisman, R., & Langer, S. Z. (1979). Human platelets possess high affinity binding sites for 3H.imipramine. *Eur. J. Pharmacol.*, *58*, 347–348.

36. Briley, M. S., Langer, S. Z., Raisman, R., Sechter, D., & Zarifian, E. (1980). 3H.imipramine binding sites are decreased in platelets of untreated depressed patients. *Science*, *209*, 303–305.

37. Britton, K. T., Lee, G., Dana, R., Risch, S. G., & Koob, G. P. (1986). Activating and anxiogenic effects of corticotrophin releasing factor are not inhibited by blockade of the pituitary-adrenergic system with dexamethasone. *Life Sci.*, *39*, 1281–1286.

38. Bruinvels, J. (1972). Inhibition of the biosynthesis of 5-hydroxytryptamine in rat brain by imipramine. *Eur. J. Pharmacol.*, *20*, 231–237.

39. Bulat, M. (1984). Some criteria for the study of biochemical processes in CNS by analysis of cerebrospinal fluid. *Clin. Neuropharmacol.*, *7* (suppl. 1), S153.

40. Bunney, W. E., & Davis, J. M. (1965). Norepinephrine in depressive reactions. *Arch. Gen. Psychiatry*, *13*, 483–494.

41. Butler, J., & Leonard, B. E. (1986). Postpartum depression and the effect of nomifensine treatment. *Int. Clin. Psychopharmacol.*, *1*, 244–252.

42. Campbell, I. C., Wirz-Justice, A., Krauchi, K., McKernan, R. M., & Durcan, M. J. (1985). Circadian studies of neurotransmitter receptors. In P. H. Redfern, I. C. Campbell, J. A. Davies, & K. F. Martin (Eds.), *Circadian rhythms in the central nervous system* (pp. 95–110). Basingstoke: Macmillan.

43. Campbell, I. C., McKernan, R., Checkley, S., Glass, I., Thompson, C., & Shur, E. (1985). Characterisation of platelet alpha$_2$ adrenoceptors and their measurement in control and depressed subjects. *Psychiatr. Res.*, *14*, 17–32.

44. Cannon, W. B. (1929). *Bodily changes in pain, hunger, fear and rage*. New York: Appleton-Century.

45. Carlsson, A., Rosengren, E., Bertler, A., & Nilsson, J. (1957a). Effect of reserpine on metabolism of catecholamines. In S. Garattini & V. Ghetti (Eds.), *Psychotropic drugs*. Amsterdam: Elsevier.

46. Carlsson, A., Shore, P. A., & Brodie, B. B. (1957b). Release of serotonin from blood platelets by reserpine in vitro. *J. Pharmacol. Exp. Ther.*, *120*, 334–339.

47. Carlsson, A., Corrodi, H., Fuxe, K., & Hokfelt, T. (1969). Effect of antidepressant drugs on the depletion of intraneuronal brain 5-hydroxytryptamine stores caused by 4-methyl-alpha-ethyl-meta-tyramine. *Eur. J. Pharmacol.*, *5*, 357–366.

48. Carlsson, A. (1982). Rationale and design of a selective inhibitor of 5HT reuptake. *Br. J. Clin. Pract.* (Symp. Suppl.) *19*, 19–22.

49. Carroll, B., Curtis, G., & Mendel, J. (1976). Neuroendocrine regulation in depression. (ii) Discrimination of depressed from nondepressed patients. *Arch. Gen. Psychiatry*, *33*, 1051–1057.

50. Carstens, M. E., Engelbrecht, A. H., Russell, V. A., Aalbers, C., Gagiano, C. A., Chalton, D. O., & Taljaard, J. J. F. (1986). Alpha$_2$ adrenoceptor levels on platelets of patients with major depressive disorder. *Psychiatr. Res.*, *18*, 321–331.

51. Carstens, M. E., Engelbrecht, A. H., Russell, V. A., Aalbers, C., Gagiano, C. A., Chalton, D. O., & Taljaard, J. J. F. (1986). Imipramine binding sites on platelets of patients with major depressive disorder. *Psychiatr. Res.*, *18*, 333–342.

52. Charney, D. S., Price, L. H., & Heninger, G. R. (1986). Desipramine-yohimbine combination treatment of refractory depression. *Arch. Gen. Psychiatry*, *43*, 1155–1161.

53. Charney, D. S., Heninger, G. R., Sternberg, D. E., Hafstad, M., Griddings, S., & Landis, D. H. (1982). Adrenergic receptors sensitivity in depression: Effects of clonidine in depressed patients and healthy patients. *Arch. Gen. Psychiatry*, *39*, 290–294.

54. Checkley, S. A. (1980). Neuroendocrine tests of monoamine function in man: A review of basic theory and its application to the study of depressive illness. *Psychol. Med.*, *10*, 35–53.
55. Checkley, S. A., Slade, A. P., & Shur, E. (1981). Growth hormone and other responses to clonidine in patients with endogenous depression. *Br. J. Psychiatry*, *138*, 51–55.
56. Cohen, R. M., Campbell, I. C., Cohen, M. R., Torda, T., Pickar, D., Siever, L. J., & Murphy, D. M. (1980). Presynaptive noradrenergic regulation during depression and antidepressant drug treatment. *Psychiatry Res.*, *3*, 93–105.
57. Cohen, M. R., Cohen, R. M., Pickar, D., Sunderland, T., Muelle, E., & Murphy, D. L. (1984). High dose naloxone in depression. *Biol. Psychiatry*, *19*, 825–832.
58. Cohen, M. R., Pickar, D., & Cohen, R. M. (1985). High dose naloxone administration in schizophrenia. *Biol. Psychiatry*, *20*, 573–575.
59. Coppen, A., Swade, C., & Wood, K. (1978a). Platelet 5HT accumulation in depressive illness. *Clin. Chim. Acta*, *87*, 165–168.
60. Coppen, A., Ghose, K., Swade, C., & Wood, K. (1978b). Effect of mianserin hydrochloride on peripheral uptake mechanisms for noradrenaline and 5-hydroxytryptamine in man. *Br. J. Clin. Pharmacol.*, *5*, 13S–17S.
61. Coppen, A. J. (1967). The biochemistry of affective disorders. *Br. J. Psychiatry*, *113*, 1237–1264.
62. Costa, E., Ravizza, L., & Barbaccia, M. L. (1986). Evaluation of current theories on the mode of action of antidepressant drugs. In G. Bartholini, K. G. Lloyd, & P. L. Morselli (Eds.), *LERS—Laboratoires et recherches synthelabo*, *4*, 9–21. New York: Raven Press.
63. Cowen, P. J., Charig, E. M., Fraser, S., & Elliott, J. M. (1987). Increased platelet 5-HT receptor binding during tricyclic antidepressant treatment. *J. Affect. Disord.*, *13*, 45–50.
64. Crews, F. J., & Smith, C. B. (1978). Presynaptic alpha receptor subsensitivity after longterm antidepressant treatment. *Science*, *202*, 322–324.
65. Crews, F. T., Paul, S. M., & Goodwin, F. K. (1981). Acceleration of beta receptor desensitisation in combined administration of antidepressants and phenoxybenzamine. *Nature*, *290*, 787–789.
66. Crow, T. J., Cross, A. J., Cooper, S. J., Owen, F., et al. (1984). Neurotransmitter receptors and monoamine metabolites in the brain of patients with Alzheimer-type dementia and depression and suicides. *Neuropharmacology*, *23* (12B), 1561–1569.
67. Daiguji, M., Meltzer, H. Y., & U'Prichard, D. C. (1981). Human platelet $alpha_2$ adrenergic receptors: Labelling with ^{3}H.yohimbine, a selective antagonist ligand. *Life Sci.*, *28*, 2705–2717.
68. Davis, G. C., Buchsbaum, M. S., & Bunney, W. E. (1979). Analgesia to painful stimuli in affective illness. *Am. J. Psychiatry*, *136*, 1148–1151.
69. Davis, G. C. (1983). Endorphins and pain. *Psychiatr. Clin. North Am.*, *6*, 473–487.
70. De Montigny, C., & Aghajanian, G. K. (1978). Tricyclic antidepressants—Longterm treatment increases responsivity of rat forebrain neurones to serotonin. *Science*, *202*, 1303–1306.
71. Desmedt, D. H., Egrise, D., & Mendlewicz, J. (1987). Tritiated imipramine binding sites in affective disorders and schizophrenia—Influence of circannual variation. *J. Affect. Disord.*, *12*, 193–198.
72. Dilsaver, S. C. (1986). Pathophysiology of the "cholinoceptor supersensitivity." *Biol. Psychiatry*, *21*, 813–829.
73. Downs, N. S., Britton, K. T., Gibbs, D. M., Koob, G. F., & Swerdlow, N. R. (1986). Supersensitive endocrine responses to physostigmine in dopamine-depleted rats a model of depression. *Biol. Psychiatry*, *21*, 775–786.
74. Doyle, M. C., George, A. J., Ravindran, A. V., & Philpott, R. (1985). Platelet alpha adrenoceptor binding in elderly depressed patients. *Am. J. Psychiatry*, *142*, 1489–1490.

75. Ebert, M. H., Post, R. M., & Goodwin, F. K. (1972). Effect of physical activity on urinary MHPG excretion in depressed patients. *Lancet, 2*, 766.
76. Farnebo, L. O. (1971). Effect of d-amphetamine on spontaneous and stimulation induced release of catecholamines. *Acta Physiol. Scand.* (Suppl.) *371*, 45–52.
77. Fozard, J. R. (1984). Neuronal 5HT receptors in the periphery. *Neuropharmacology, 23* (1B), 1473–1486.
78. Frize, E. D. (1954). Mental depression in hypertensive patients treated for long periods with high doses of reserpine. *N. Engl. J. Med., 251*, 1006–1008.
79. Fullerton, D., Wenzel, F., Lohrenz, F., & Fahs, H. (1968). Circadian rhythm of adrenal cortical activity in depression. *Arch. Gen. Psychiatry, 19*, 674–681.
80. Gallistel, C. R., Shizgal, P., & Yeomans, J. S. (1981). A portrait of the substrate for self-stimulation. *Psychol. Rev., 88*, 228–273.
81. Garcia-Sevilla, J. A., Zis, A. P., Hollingsworth, P. J., Greden, J. F., & Smith, C. B. (1981). Platelet alpha$_2$ adrenergic receptors in major depressive disorder. Binding of tritiated clonidine before and after tricyclic antidepressant drug treatment. *Arch. Gen. Psychiatry, 38*, 1327–1333.
82. Garcia-Sevilla, J. A., Udina, C., Furster, M. J., Alvarez, E., & Casas, M. (1987). Enhanced binding of ^{3}H.(−)adrenaline to platelets of depressed patients with melancholia: Effect of longterm clomipramine treatment. *Acta Psychiatr. Scand., 75*, 150–157.
83. Gentsch, C., Lichsteiner, M., Gastpar, M., Gastpar, G., & Feer, H. (1985). ^{3}H.imipramine binding sites in platelets of hospitalised psychiatric patients. *Psychiatr. Res., 14*, 177–187.
84. Georgotas, A., Scweitzer, J., McCue, R. E., Armour, M., & Friedhoff, A. J. (1987). Clinical and treatment effects of ^{3}H.clonidine and ^{3}H.imipramine binding in elderly depressed patients. *Life Sci., 40*, 2137–2143.
85. Gibbs, D. M. (1986). Vasopressin and oxytocin: Hypothalamic modulators of the stress response: A review. *Psychoneuroendocrinology, 11*, 131–140.
86. Glassman, A. (1969). Indoleamines and affective disorders. *Psychosom. Med., 31*, 107–144.
87. Glue, P. W., Cowen, P. J., Nutt, D. J., Kolakowka, T., & Grahame-Smith, D. G. (1986). The effect of lithium on 5HT mediated neuroendocrine responses and platelet 5HT receptors. *Psychopharmacology, 90*, 398–402.
88. Gold, M., Potash, A., Ryan, N., Sweeney, D., Davies, R., & Martin, D. (1980). TRF induced TSH response in unipolar, bipolar and secondary depressions: Possible utility in clinical assessment and difficult diagnosis. *Psychoneuroendocrinology, 5*, 147–155.
89. Goodwin, F. K., Wirz-Justice, A., & Wehr, T. (1982). Evidence that the pathophysiology of depression and the mechanism of action of antidepressant drugs involve alterations in circadian rhythms. *Adv. Biochem. Psychopharmacol., 31*, 1–11.
90. Goodwin, F. K., & Post, R. M. (1974). CSF amine metabolites in affective illness. *J. Psychiatr. Res., 10*, 320.
91. Green, A. R., & Grahame-Smith, D. G. (1975). 5-Hydroxy and other indoles in the C.N.S. In L. L. Iversen, S. D. Iversen, & S. H. Snyder (Eds.), *Handbook of psychopharmacology*, vol. 3 (169 seq.). New York: Plenum Press.
92. Hallberg, F. (1968). Physiological considerations underlying rhythmicity with special reference to emotional illness. In J. G. de Ajuriaguerra (Ed.), *Cycles biologique et psychiatrie*. Paris: Geneve & Masson.
93. Hallbreich, J., Grunhaus, L., & Ben-David, M. (1979). Twenty-four hour rhythm of prolactin in depressed patients. *Arch. Gen. Psychiatry, 36*, 1183–1186.
94. Hardy, J. A., & Dodd, P. R. (1983). Metabolic and functional studies on postmortem human brain. *Neurochem. Int., 5*, 253–266.
95. Harris, T. H. (1957). Depression induced by rauwolfia compounds. *Am. J. Psychiatry, 113*, 950.

96. Healy, D., Carney, P. A., & Leonard, B. E. (1983). Monoamine related markers of depression: changes following treatment. *J. Psychiatr. Res.*, *17*, 251–260.

97. Healy, D., O'Halloran, A., Carney, P. A., & Leonard, B. E. (1985). Peripheral adrenoceptors and serotonin receptors in depression: Changes associated with treatment with trazodone and amitriptyline. *J. Affect. Disord.*, 9, 285–296.

98. Healy, D., O'Halloran, A., Carney, P. A., & Leonard, B. E. (1986a). Variations in platelet 5HT uptake in control and depressed populations. *J. Psychiatr. Res.*, *20*, 345–354.

99. Healy, D., O'Halloran, A., & Leonard, B. E. (1986b). Increases in platelet 5-HT uptake following treatment with "uptake inhibiting" drugs. *Int. Clin. Psychopharmacol.*, *1*, 332–339.

100. Healy, D., & Williams, J. M. G. (1988, March). Dysrhythmia, dysphoria and depression; the interaction of learned helplessness and circadian dysrhythmia in the pathogenesis of learned helplessness. *Psychol. Bull.*, *103* (Part 2), 163–178.

101. Healy, D. (1987). Rhythm and blues: Neurochemical, neuropharmacological and neuropsychological implications of a hypothesis of circadian rhythm disturbance in the affective disorders. *Psychopharmacology*, *93*, 271–285.

102. Healy, D., & Leonard, B. E. (1987). Monoamine transport in depression; kinetics and dynamics. *J. Affect. Disord.*, *12*, 91–105.

103. Heufelder, A., Warnhoff, M., & Pirke, K. (1985). Platelet alpha$_2$ adrenoceptors and adenylate cyclase in patients with anorexia and bulimia. *J. Clin. Endocrinol. Metab.*, *61*, 1053–1060.

104. Hollister, L. E., Davis, K. L., Overall, J. E., & Anderson, J. E. (1978). Excretion of MHPG in normal subjects. *Arch. Gen. Psychiatry*, *35*, 1410–1415.

105. Horton, R. W., Katona, C. L. E., Theodorou, A. E., Hale, A. S., Davies, S. L., Tunnicliffe, C., Yamaguchi, Y., Paykel, E. S., & Kelly, J. S. (1986). Platelet radioligand binding and neuroendocrine challenge tests in depression. In *Antidepressants and receptor function*. Ciba Foundation Symposium, no. 123, Chichester: Wiley.

106. Hrdina, P. D., Lapierre, Y. D., Horn, E. R., & Bakish, D. (1985). Platelet ^{3}H.imipramine binding: a possible predictor of response to antidepressant treatment. *Prog. Neuropsychopharmacol. Biol. Psychiatry*, *9*, 619–623.

107. Hu, H. Y., Davis, J. M., Heinze, W. J., & Pandey, G. N. (1980). Effect of chronic treatment with antidepressants on beta adrenergic receptor binding in guinea pig brain. *Biochem. Pharmacol.*, *29*, 2895–2896.

108. Ieni, J. R., Zukin, S. R., & van Praag, H. M. (1984). Human platelets possess multiple ^{3}H.imipramine binding sites. *Eur. J. Pharmacol.*, *106*, 669–672.

109. Janowsky, D. S., El-Youssef, M. K., Davis, J. M., & Serkerke, H. J. (1972). A cholinergic-adrenergic hypothesis of mania and depression. *Lancet*, *2*, 632–635.

110. Jones, R., & Olpe, H. (1983). Cortical neuronal responsiveness to substance P is enhanced following chronic but not acute administration of antidepressants. *Eur. J. Pharmacol.*, *87*, 171–172.

111. Johnson, R. W., Reisine, T., Spotnitz, S., Weich, N. L., Ursillo, R. C., & Yamamura, H. I. (1980). Effects of desipramine and yohimbine on alpha$_2$ and beta adrenergic sensitivity. *Eur. J. Pharmacol.*, *67*, 123–127.

112. Kafka, M. S., van Kammen, D. P., Kleinman, J. E., Nurnberger, J. I., Siever, L. J., Uhde, T. W., & Polinsky, R. J. (1981). Alpha-adrenergic receptor function in schizophrenia, affective disorders and some neurological diseases. *Commun. Psychopharmacol.*, *4*, 477–486.

113. Kafka, M., Wirz-Justice, A., & Naber, D. (1981). Circadian and seasonal rhythms in alpha and beta adrenergic receptors in the rat brain. *Brain Res.*, *207*, 409–419.

114. Kafka, M. S., & Paul, S. M. (1986). Platelet alpha adrenergic receptors in depression. *Arch. Gen. Psychiatry*, *43*, 91–95.

115. Kanof, P. D., Coccaro, E. F., Johns, C. A., Siever, L. J., & Davis, K. L. (1987). Platelet ^{3}H.imipramine binding in psychiatric disorders. *Biol. Psychiatry, 22*, 278–286.
116. Kaplan, R. D., & Mann, J. J. (1982). Altered platelet serotonin uptake kinetics in schizophrenia and depression. *Life Sci., 31*, 583–588.
117. Katona, C. L. E., Theodorou, A. E., Davies, S. L., Yamaguchi, Y., Tunnicliffe, C. A., Hale, A. S., Horton, R. W., Kelly, J. S., & Paykel, E. S. (1986). Platelet binding and neuroendocrine responses in depression. In J. F. W. Deakin (Ed.), *The biology of depression* (pp. 121–136). Oxford: Arlen Press.
118. Kaufman, C. A., Gillin, J. C., O'Laughlin, T., et al. (1983). Muscarinic binding in suicides. In *New research abstracts*, Proc. 136th Annual Meeting of American Psychiatric Association. Washington, DC: American Psychiatric Association.
119. Kjellmar, B., Beck-Friis, J., Harrygren, J., & Wetterberg, L. (1984). Twenty-four hour serum levels of TSH in affective disorders. *Acta Psychiatr. Scand., 69*, 491–502.
120. Knoll, J. (1985). Satietin, a blood-borne glycoprotein in the regulation of food intake. In F. Lal, J. Labella, & F. Lane (Eds.), *Endocoids* (pp. 515–522). New York: Alan R. Liss.
121. Koella, W. P. (1982). A modern neurobiological concept of vigilance. *Experientia, 38*, 1426–1437.
122. Kopanski, C., Turek, M., & Schultz, J. E. (1983). Effects of longterm treatment of rats with antidepressants on adrenergic receptor sensitivity in cerebral cortex: structure-activity study. *Neurochem. Int., 5*, 649–659.
123. Koslow, S. H., Maas, J. W., Bowden, C. L., Davis, J. M., Hanin, I., & Javaid, J. (1983). Cerebro- spinal fluid and urine biogenic amines and metabolites in depression and mania. *Arch. Gen. Psychiatry, 40*, 999–1010.
124. Kuhn, D. M., Wolf, W., & Youdim, M. (1985). 5-Hydroxytryptamine release in vivo from a cytoplasmic pool; studies on the 5-HT behavioural syndrome in reserpinised rats. *Br. J. Pharmacol., 84*, 121–129.
125. Kuhn, R. (1958). The treatment of depressive states with G22355 (imipramine HCl). *Am. J. Psychiatry, 115*, 459–464.
126. Kuhn, R. (1970). The imipramine story. In F. J. Ayd & B. Blackwell (Eds.), *Discoveries in biological psychiatry* (pp. 205–217). Philadelphia: Lippincott.
127. Lenox, R., Ellis, J., Van-Riiper, D., Ehrlich, Y., Peyser, J., Shipley, J., & Weaver, L. (1983). Platelet alpha$_2$ adrenergic receptor activity in clinical studies of depression. In E. Usdin, M. Goldstein, A. J. Friedhoff, & A. Georgotas (Eds.), *Frontiers of neuropsychiatric research*. London: Macmillan.
128. Leonard, B. E. (1984). Pharmacology of new antidepressants. *Prog. Neuropharmacol. Biol. Psychiatry, 8*, 97–108.
129. Leonard, B. E. (1986). Neurotransmitter receptors, endocrine responses and the biological substrate of depression: A review. *Hum. Psychopharmacol., 1*, 3–22.
130. Lewis, D. A., & McChesney, C. (1985). Tritiated imipramine binding distinguishes among subtypes of depression. *Arch. Gen. Psychiatry, 42*, 485–488.
131. Lloyd, K. G., Thoret, F., & Pilc, A. (1986). GABA and the mechanism of action of antidepressant drugs. In G. Bartholini, K. G. Lloyd, & P. L. Morselli (Eds.), *LERS—Laboratoires et recherches synthelabo, 4*, 33–42. New York: Raven Press.
132. Loomer, H. P., Saunders, J. C., & Kline, N. S. (1957). A clinical and pharmacodynamic evaluation of iproniazid as a psychic energiser. In R. A. Cleghorn (Ed.), *Research in affect*. Psychiatric Research Reports, Vol. 8.
133. Lopez-Ibor, J. J., Saiz-Ruiz, J., & Perez de los Cobos, J. C. (1985). Biological correlates of suicide and aggressivity in major depressions (with melancholia). *Neuropsychobiology, 14*, 67–74.
134. Luchins, D. (1976). Biogenic amines and affective disorders. A critical analysis. *Int. Pharmacopsychiatry, 3*, 135–149.

135. LUCK, P., MIKHAILIDIS, D., DASHWOOD, M., BARRADAS, M., SEVER, P., DANDONA, P., & WAKELING, A. (1983). Platelet hyperaggregability and increased alpha adrenoceptor density in anorexia nervosa. *J. Clin. Endocrinol. Metab.*, *57*, 911–914.

136. MAAS, J. W., FAWCETT, J. A., & DEKIRMENJIAN, K. (1972). Catecholamine metabolism depressive illness and drug response. *Arch. Gen. Psychiatry*, *26*, 252–262.

137. MAAS, J. W. (1975). Biogenic amines and depression. *Arch. Gen. Psychiatry*, *32*, 1357–1361.

138. MAJ, J., PRZEGALINSKI, E., & MOGILNICKA, E. (1984). Hypotheses concerning the mode of action of antidepressant drugs. *Rev. Physiol. Biochem. Pharmacol.*, *100*, 1–74.

139. MALMGREN, R., ASBERG, M., OLSSON, P., TORNLING, G., & UNGE, G. (1981). Defective serotonin transport mechanism in platelets from endogenous depressive patients. *Life Sci.*, *29*, 2649–2658.

140. MANN, J. J., & STANLEY, M. (1984). Postmortem monoamine oxidase enzyme kinetics in the frontal cortex of suicide victims and controls. *Acta Psychiatr. Scand.*, *69*, 135–139.

141. MANN, J., BROWN, R., HALPER, J., SWEENEY, J., KOCSIS, J., STOKES, P., & BILEZIKIAN, J. (1985). Reduced sensitivity of lymphocyte beta-adrenergic receptors in patients with endogenous depression and psychomotor agitation. *N. Engl. J. Med.*, *313*, 715–720.

142. MANN, J. J., STANLEY, M., MCBRIDE, P. A., & MCEWEN, B. S. (1986). Increased serotonin$_2$ and beta adrenergic receptor binding in the frontal cortices of suicide victims. *Arch. Gen. Psychiatry*, *43*, 954–959.

143. MATTHEWS, J., AKIL, H., GREDEN, J., CHARNEY, D., WEINBERG, V., ROSENBAUM, A., & WATSON, S. (1986). Beta-endorphin/beta-lipotropin immunoreactivity in endogenous depression. *Arch. Gen. Psychiatry*, *43*, 374–381.

144. MCWILLIAM, J. R., AND MELDRUN, B. S. (1983). Noradrenergic regulation of growth hormone secretion in the baboon. *Endocrinology*, *112*, 234–239.

145. MEEK, J. L., & NEFF, N. H. (1973). Is csf the major source for the removal of 5-hydroxyindole acetic acid from the brain? *Neuropharmacology*, *12*, 497–503.

146. MELLERUP, E., PLENGE, P., & ROSENBURG, R. (1982). ^{3}H.imipramine binding sites in platelets from psychiatric patients. *Psychiatr. Res.*, *7*, 221–227.

147. MELTZER, H. Y., ARORA, R. C., BABER, R., & TRICOU, B. J. (1981). Serotonin uptake by blood platelets of psychiatric patients. *Arch. Gen. Psychiatry*, *38*, 1322–1326.

148. MELTZER, H. Y., ARORA, R. C., & GOODNICK, P. (1983). Effect of lithium carbonate on serotonin uptake in blood platelets of patients with affective disorders. *J. Affect. Disord.*, *5*, 215–221.

149. MENDELS, J., & FRAZER, A. (1974). Brain, biogenic amine depletion and mood. *Arch. Gen. Psychiatry*, *30*, 447–451.

150. MENDLEWICZ, J., VANCAUTEN, E., LINKOWSKI, P., L'HERMITE, M., & ROBYN, C. (1980). The 24 hour profile of prolactin in depression. *Life Sci.*, *27*, 2015–2024.

151. MENDLEWICZ, J., LINKOWSKI, P., KERKHOFFS, M., DESMEDT, D., GOLSTEIN, J., COPINSCHI, G., & CAUTER, E. VAN (1985). Diurnal hypersecretion of growth hormone in depression. *J. Clin. Endocrinol. Metab.*, *60*, 505–512.

152. MEYERSON, L. R., WENOGLE, I. P., ABEL, M. S., COUPET, J., LIPPA, A. S., RAU, L. E., & BEER, B. (1982). Human brain receptor alterations in suicide victims. *Pharmacol. Biochem. Behav.*, *17*, 159–163.

153. MUSCETTOLA, G., DI LAURO, A., & GIANNINI, C. P. (1986). Platelet ^{3}H.imipramine binding in bipolar patients. *Psychiatr. Res.*, *18*, 343–353.

154. MUSCETTOLA, G., WEHR, P., & GOODWIN, F. K. (1977). Effect of diet on urinary MHPG. *Am. J. Psychiatry*, *134*, 914–917.

155. NANKAI, M., YOSHIMOTO, S., NARITA, K., & TAKAHASHI, R. (1986). Platelet ^{3}H.imipramine binding in depressed patients and its circadian variation in healthy controls. *J. Affect. Disord.*, *11*, 207–212.

156. NISHIKAWA, T., & SCATTON, B. (1986). Neuroanatomical site of the inhibitory influence of anxiolytic drugs on central serotonergic transmission. *Brain Res.*, *371*, 123–132.

157. Ogren, S. O., Ross, S. B., Hall, H., Holm, A. C., & Renyi, A. L. (1982). The pharmacology of zimelidine: A selective 5HT reuptake inhibitor. *Br. J. Clin. Pract., 19* (Symp. suppl.), 27–41.

158. Oreland, L., Widberg, A., Asberg, M., Traskman, L., Sjostrand, L., Thoren, P., Bertilsson, L., & Tybring, G. (1981). Platelet monoamine oxidase activity and monoamine metabolites in cerebrospinal fluid in depressed and suicidal patients and in healthy controls. *Psychiatr. Res., 4*, 21–29.

159. Owen, F., Cross, A. J., Crow, T. J., Deakin, J. F. W., Ferrier, I. N., Lofthouse, R., & Poulter, M. (1983). Brain $5HT_2$ receptors and suicide. *Lancet, 1*, 1256.

160. Owen, F., Chambers, D. R., Cooper, S. J., Crow, T. J., Johnson, J. A., Lofthouse, R., & Poulter, M. (1986). Serotonergic mechanisms in brains of suicide victims. *Brain Res., 362*, 185–188.

161. Paul, S. M., Rehavi, M., Skolnick, P., & Goodwin, F. K. (1980). Demonstration of specific high affinity binding sites for ^{3}H.imipramine on human platelets. *Life Sci., 26*, 953–959.

162. Paul, S. M., Rehavi, M., Skolnick, P., Ballenger, J. C., & Goodwin, F. K. (1981). Depressed patients have decreased binding of tritiated imipramine to platelet serotonin transporter. *Arch. Gen. Psychiatry, 38*, 1315–1317.

163. Paul, S. M., Rehavi, M., Skolnick, P., & Goodwin, F. K. (1984). High affinity binding of antidepressants to a biogenic amine transport site in human brain and platelets: Studies in depression. In R. M. Post & J. C. Ballenger (Eds.), *Neurobiology of mood disorders* (pp. 845–853). Baltimore: Williams & Wilkins.

164. Paykel, E. S. (1982). Environmental factors (life events) and depression. *Br. J. Clin. Pract.* (Symposium suppl.) *19*, 3–6.

165. Paykel, E. S., Fleminger, R., & Watson, J. P. (1982). Psychiatric side-effects of antihypertensive drugs other than reserpine. *J. Clin. Psycho. Pharmacol., 2*, 14–39.

166. Peroutka, S. J., & Snyder, S. H. (1980). Longterm antidepressant treatment decreases spiroperidol-labelled serotonin receptor binding. *Science, 210*, 88–90.

167. Perry, E. K., Marshall, E. F., Blessed, G., Tomlinson, B. E., & Perry, R. H. (1983). Decreased imipramine binding in the brains of patients with depressive illness. *Br. J. Psychiatry, 142*, 188–192.

168. Pimoule, C., Briley, M. S., Gay, C., Loo, H., Sechter, D., Zarifian, E., Raisman, R., & Langer, S. Z. (1983). ^{3}H.rauwolsceine binding in platelets from depressed patients and healthy volunteers. *Psychopharmacology, 79*, 308–312.

169. Poirier, M. F., Benkelfat, C., Loo, H., Sechter, D., Zarifian, E., Galzin, A. M., & Langer, S. Z. (1986). Reduced Bmax of ^{3}H.imipramine binding to platelets of depressed patients free of previous medication with 5HT uptake inhibitors. *Psychopharmacology, 89*, 456–461.

170. Post, R., Kotin, J., & Goodwin, F. (1973). Psychomotor activity and csf. amine metabolites in affective illness. *Am. J. Psychiatry, 130*, 67–72.

171. Post, R. M., Gordon, E. K., & Goodwin, F. K. (1973). Central norepinephrine metabolites in affective illness: MHPG in the CSF. *Science, 179*, 1002–1003.

172. Raisman, R., Sechter, D., Briley, M. S., Zarifian, E., & Langer, S. Z. (1981). High affinity ^{3}H.imipramine binding in platelets from untreated and treated depressed patients compared to healthy volunteers. *Psychopharmacology, 75*, 368–371.

173. Randrup, A., & Braestrup, C. (1977). Uptake inhibition of biogenic amines by newer antidepressant drugs; relevance to the dopamine hypothesis of depression. *Psychopharmacology, 53*, 309–314.

174. Reichenberg, K., Gaillard-Plaza, G., & Montastrue, J. L. (1985). Influence of naloxone on the antinociceptive effects of some antidepressant drugs. *Arch. Int. Pharmacodyn., 275*, 78–85.

175. Resine, T., & Soubrie, P. (1982). Loss of rat cerebral cortical opiate receptors following chronic desmethylimipramine treatment. *Eur. J. Pharmacol.*, 77, 39–44.

176. REITH, M. E., SERSHEN, H., ALLEN, D., & LAJTHA, A. (1983). High and low affinity binding of ^{3}H.imipramine in mouse cerebral cortex. *J. Neurochem.*, *40*, 389–395.
177. RIDGES, A. P. (1980). The amine hypothesis in relation to the present understanding of depressive illness. *Br. J. Clin. Pract.* (Symp. Suppl.), 7, 12–21.
178. ROSSER, M. (1984). Biological markers in mental disorders: Post-mortem studies. *J. Psychiatr. Res.*, *18*, 457–465.
179. ROY, P., POST, R. M., RUBINOW, D. R., LINNOILA, M., SAVARD, R., & DAVIS, D. (1984). CSF 5HIAA and personal and family history of suicide in affectively ill patients: A negative study. *Psychiatr. Res.*, *10*, 263–274.
180. ROY, A., PICKAR, D., LINNOILA, M., et al. (1985). Plasma norepinephrine in affective disorders: Relationship to melancholia. *Arch. Gen. Psychiatry*, *42*, 1181–1185.
181. ROY, A., EVERETT, D., PICKAR, D., & PAUL, S. M. (1987). Platelet ^{3}H.imipramine binding and serotonin uptake in depressed patients and controls. *Arch. Gen. Psychiatry*, *44*, 320–327.
182. SACHAR, E., HELLMAN, L., ROFFWARG, H., HALPERN, F., FUKUSHIMA, D., & GALLAGHER, T. (1973). Disrupted 24 hour pattern of cortisol secretion in psychotic depression. *Arch. Gen. Psychiatry*, *28*, 19–24.
183. SALAMA, A., GARCIA, A., WANG, C. H., LIN, L., & U'PRICHARD, D. (1983). Relationship between adaptive changes in brain alpha$_2$ and beta adrenergic receptors following repeated imipramine, yohimbine and electro-convulsive shock treatment to rats. In E. Usdin, M. Goldstein, A. J. Friedhoff, & A. Georgotas (Eds.), *Frontiers of neuropsychiatric research*. London: Macmillan.
184. SAMPSON, G. A., & JENNER, F. A. (1975). Circadian rhythms and mental illness. *Psychol. Med.*, *5*, 4–8.
185. SCATTON, B., LOO, H., DENNIS, T., BENKELFAT, C., GAY, C., & POIRIER-LITTRE, M. F. (1986). Decrease in plasma levels of 3,4-dihydroxyphenylethyleneglycol in major depression. *Psychopharmacology*, *88*, 220–225.
186. SCHILDKRAUT, J. J. (1965). The catecholamine hypothesis of affective disorders: A review of supporting evidence. *Am. J. Psychiatry*, *122*, 509–522.
187. SCHILDKRAUT, J. J., ORSULAK, P., SCHATZBERG, A., GUDEMAN, J., COLE, J., ROHDE, W., & LABRIE, R. (1978). Towards a biochemical classification of depressive disorders. *Arch. Gen. Psychiatry*, *35*, 1427-1439.
188. SCHNEIDER, L. S., SEVERSON, J. A., & SLOANE, R. B. (1985). Platelet ^{3}H.imipramine binding in depressed elderly patients. *Biol. Psychiatry*, *20*, 1232–1234.
189. SCHNEIDER, L. S., FREDERICKSON, E. R., SEERSON, J. A., & SLOANE, R. B. (1987). ^{3}H.imipramine binding in depressed elderly: Relationship to family history and clinical response. *Psychiatry Res.*, *19*, 257–266.
190. SCHOFFELMEER, A., HOORNEMAN, E., SMINIA, P., & MULDER, A. (1984). Presynaptic alpha$_2$ and postsynaptic beta adrenoceptor sensitivity in slices of rat neocortex after chronic treatment with various antidepressant drugs. *Neuropharmacology*, *23*, (2A), 115–119.
191. SCHULTZ, J. E., SIGGINS, G. R., SCHOCKER, F. W., TURCK, M., & BLOOM, F. E. (1981). Effects of prolonged treatment with lithium and tricyclic antidepressants on discharge frequency, norepinephrine responses and beta-receptor binding in rat cerebellum: a physiological and biochemical comparison. *J. Pharmacol. Exp. Ther.*, *216*, 28–38.
192. SCHULZ, H., & LUND, R. (1985). On the origins of early REM episodes in the sleep of depressed patients; a comparison of 3 hypotheses. *Psychiatr. Res.*, *16*, 65–77.
193. SCOTT, M., READING, H., & LOUDON, J. (1979). Studies on human blood platelets in affective disorders. *Psychopharmacology*, *60*, 131–135.
194. SEGONZAC, A., SCHOEMAKER, H., TATEISHI, T., & LANGER, S. Z. (1985b). 5-Methoxytryptoline, a competitive endocoid acting at ^{3}H.imipramine recognition sites in human platelets. *J. Neurochem.*, *45*, 249–256.

195. SETHY, V. H., & HARRIS, D. W. (1981). Effect of norepinephrine uptake blockade on beta adrenergic receptors of the rat cerebral cortex. *Eur. J. Pharmacol.*, *75*, 53–56.
196. SHAW, D. M., O'KEEFFE, R., & MACSWEENEY, D. A. (1973). 3-Methoxy-4-hydroxyphenylglycol in depression. *Psychol. Med.*, *3*, 333–336.
197. SHERMAN, A. (1979). Time course of the effects of antidepressants on serotonin in rat neocortex. *Commun. Psychopharmacol.*, *3*, 1–5.
198. SIEVER, L. J., INSEL, T., JIMERSON, D., LAKE, C. R., UHDE, T., ALOI, J., & MURPHY, D. M. (1983). Growth hormone response to clonidine in obsessive-compulsive patients. *Br. J. Psychiatry*, *142*, 184–187.
199. SIEVER, L. J., & UHDE, T. W. (1983). New studies and perspectives on the noradrenergic receptor system in depression: Effects of the $alpha_2$ adrenergic agonist clonidine. *Biol. Psychiatry*, *19*, 131–156.
200. SIEVER, L. J., KAFKA, M. S., TARGUM, S., & LAKE, C. R. (1984). Platelet alpha adrenergic binding and biochemical responsiveness in depressed patients and controls. *Psychiatry Res.*, *11*, 287–302.
201. SIEVER, L. J., & DAVIS, K. L. (1985). Overview: Toward a dysregulation hypothesis of depression. *Am. J. Psychiatry*, *142*, 1017–1031.
202. SIEVER, L. J., UHDE, T. W., JIMERSON, D. C., LAKE, C. R., KOPIN, I. J., & MURPHY, D. L. (1986). Indices of noradrenergic output in depression. *Psychiatr. Res.*, *19*, 59–73.
203. SIGG, E., SOFFER, L., & GYERMEK, L. (1963). Influence of imipramine and related psychoactive agents on the effect of 5HT and catecholamines on the rat's nictitating membrane. *J. Pharmacol. Exp. Ther.*, *142*, 13–20.
204. SPECTOR, S., SHORE, P. A., & BRODIE, B. B. (1960). Biochemical and pharmacological effects of the maoi's, iproniazid, i-phenyl-2-hydrazinopropane (JB 516) and 1-phenyl-3-hydrazinobutane (JB 835). *J. Pharmacol. Exp. Ther.*, *128*, 15–21.
205. SPECTOR, S., HIRSCH, A. O., & BRODIE, B. B. (1963). Association of behavioural effects of pargyline, a non-hydrazide monoamine oxidase inhibitor with increase in brain norepinephrine. *Int. J. Neuropharmacol.*, *2*, 81–93.
206. STAHL, S. M., WOO, D. J., MEFFORD, I. N., BERGER, P. A., & CIARANELLO, R. D. (1983). Hyperserotonemia and platelet serotonin uptake and release in schizophrenia and affective disorders. *Am. J. Psychiatry*, *140*, 26–30.
207. STAHL, S. M., LEMOINE, P. M., CIARANELLO, R. D., & BERGER, P. A. (1983). Platelet $alpha_2$ adrenergic receptor sensitivity in major depressive disorder. *Psychiatry Res.*, *10*, 157–164.
208. STANLEY, M., VIRGILIO, J., & GERSHON, S. (1982). Tritiated imipramine binding sites are decreased in the frontal cortex of suicides. *Science*, *216*, 1337–1339.
209. STANLEY, M., & MANN, J. J. (1983). Increased $serotonin_2$ binding sites in frontal cortex of suicide victims. *Lancet*, *1*, 214–216.
210. STANLEY, M. (1984). Cholinergic binding in the frontal cortex of suicide victims. *Am. J. Psychiatry*, *141*, 11–14.
211. STARKE, K. (1977). Regulation of noradrenergic release by presynaptic receptor systems. *Rev. Physiol. Biochem. Pharmacol.*, *77*, 1–124.
212. SUBRAHMANYAM, S. (1975). Role of biogenic amines in certain pathological conditions. *Brain Res.*, *87*, 355–362.
213. SUGRUE, M. F. (1980). Changes in rat brain monoaminergic transmission following chronic antidepressant administration. *Life Sci.*, *26*, 423–429.
214. SULSER, F., & BICKEL, M. H. (1962). On the role of catecholamines in the antireserpinic action of desmethylimipramine. *Pharmacologist*, *4*, 178.
215. SULSER, F., BICKEL, M. H., & BRODIE, B. B. (1964). The action of desmethylimipramine in counteracting sedation and cholinergic effects of reserpine like drugs. *J. Pharmacol. Exp. Ther.*, *144*, 321.
216. SULSER, F. (1978). Functional aspects of the noepenephrine-coupled adenylate cyclase system in the limbic forebrain and its modification by drugs which precipitate and alleviate depression. *Pharmacopsychiatry*, *11*, 43–52.

217. Sulser, F. (1984). Regulation and function of noradrenergic receptor systems in the brain. *Neuropharmacology, 23*, 255–261.

218. Suranyi-Cadotte, B. E., Wood, P. L., Nair, N. P. V. & Schwartz, G. (1982). Normalisation of platelet ^{3}H.imipramine binding in depressed patients during recovery. *Eur. J. Pharmacol., 85*, 357–358.

219. Suranyi-Cadotte, B. E., Gauthier, S., LaFaille, F., De Flores, S., Dam, T. V., Nair, N. P. V., & Quirion, R. (1985). Platelet ^{3}H.imipramine binding distinguishes depression from Alzheimer's dementia. *Life Sci., 37*, 2305–2311.

220. Tang, S. W., & Morris, J. M. (1985). Variation in human platelet ^{3}H.imipramine binding. *Psychiatry Res., 16*, 141–146.

221. Theodorou, A. E., Hale, A. S., Davies, S. L., Katona, C. L. E., Yamaguchi, Y., Horton, R. W., Kelly, J. S., & Paykel, E. S. (1986). Platelet high affinity adrenoceptor binding sites labelled with the agonist ^{3}H.UK14304 in depressed patients and matched controls. *Eur. J. Pharmacol., 126*, 329–332.

222. Thompson, C., Mezey, G., Corn, T., Franey, C., English, J., Arendt, J., & Checkley, S. A. (1985). The effect of desipramine upon melatonin and cortisol secretion in depressed and normal subjects. *Br. J. Psychiatry, 147*, 389–393.

223. Traskman, L., Tybring, G., Asberg, M., & Sjostrand, L. (1981). Monoamine metabolites in the CSF and suicidal behaviour. *Arch. Gen. Psychiatry, 38*, 631–636.

224. Tuomisto, J. (1974). A new modification for studying 5HT uptake by blood platelets: A reevaluation of tricyclic antidepressants as uptake inhibitors. *J. Pharm. Pharmacol., 26*, 92–100.

225. Tuomisto, J., & Tukiainen, E. (1976). Decreased uptake of 5-hydroxytryptamine in blood platelets from depressed patients. *Nature, 262*, 596–598.

226. Tuomisto, J., Tukiainen, E., & Ahlfors, U. G. (1979). Decreased uptake of 5-hydroxytryptamine in blood platelets from patients with endogenous depression. *Psychopharmacology, 65*, 141–147.

227. Tuomisto, J., & Mannisto, P. (1985). Neurotransmitter regulation of anterior pituitary hormones. *Pharmacol. Rev., 37*, 249–332.

228. Uhde, T. W., Vitone, B. J., Siever, L. J., Kaye, W. H., & Post, R. M. (1986). Blunted growth hormone response to clonidine in panic disorder patients. *Biol. Psychiatry, 21*, 1081–1084.

229. Van Praag, H. M., Korf, J., & Schut, D. (1973). Cerebral monamines and depression; an investigation with the probenecid technique. *Arch. Gen. Psychiatry, 28*, 827–831.

230. Van Praag, H. M. (1982). Depression, suicide and the metabolism of serotonin in the brain. *J. Affect. Disord., 4*, 275–290.

231. Van Praag, H. M. (1983). CSF 5HIAA and suicide in non-depressed schizophrenics. *Lancet, 1*, 977–978.

232. Van Praag, H. M. (1986). Biological suicide research: Outcome and limitations. *Biol. Psychiatry, 21*, 1305–1323.

233. Van Praag, H. M., Lemus, C., & Kahn, R. (1987). Hormonal probes of the central serotonergic activity: Do they really exist? *Biol. Psychiatry, 22*, 86–98.

234. Vestergaard, P., Sorensen, T., Hoppe, E., Rafelson, O. J., Yates, C. M., & Nicolaou, N. (1978). Biogenic amine metabolites in cerebrospinal fluid of patients with affective disorders. *Acta Psychiatr. Scand., 58*, 88–96.

235. Vetulani, J., Stawarz, R. J., Dingell, J. V., & Sulser, F. (1976). A possible common mechanism of action of antidepressant drugs. *N. S. Arch. Pharmacol., 293*, 109–114.

236. Wagner, A., Aberg-Wistedt, A., Asberg, M., Ekqvist, B., Martensson, B., & Montero, D. (1985). Lower ^{3}H.imipramine binding in platelets from untreated depressed patients compared to healthy controls. *Psychiatr. Res., 16*, 131–139.

237. Weeke, A., & Weeke, J. (1980). The 24 hour pattern of serum TSH in patients with endogenous depression. *Acta Psychiatr. Scand., 62*, 69–74.

238. Whittaker, P. M., Warsh, J. J., Stancer, H. C., Persad, E. C., & Vint, C. K. (1984). Seasonal variation in platelet ^{3}H.imipramine binding: Comparative values in control and depressed populations. *Psychiatr. Res.*, *11*, 127–131.
239. Wilk, S., Shopsin, B., Gershon, S., et al. (1972). Cerebrospinal fluid levels of MHPG in affective disorders. *Nature*, *235*, 440–441.
240. Willner, P. (1983). Dopamine and depression: A review of recent evidence. *Brain Res.*, *287*, 211–246.
241. Wirz-Justice, A., & Wehr, T. A. (1983). Neuropsychopharmacology and biological rhythms. *Adv. Biol. Psychiatry*, *11*, 20–34.
242. Wirz-Justice, A., Krauchi, K., Morimasa, T., Willener, R., & Feer, H. (1983). Circadian rhythm of ^{3}H.imipramine binding in the rat suprachiasmatic nuclei. *Eur. J. Pharmacol.*, *87*, 331–333.
243. Wood, K., & Coppen, A. J. (1981). Platelet alpha-adrenoceptor sensitivity in depressive illness. *Adv. Biol. Psychiatry*, *7*, 85–89.
244. Wood, K., Swade, C., Abou-Saleh, M., Milln, P., & Coppen, A. (1983). Drug plasma levels or lithium in patients with affective disorders. *Br. J. Clin. Pharmacol.*, *15*, 365S–368S.
245. Wood, K., Swade, C., Abou-Saleh, M., & Coppen, A. J. (1985). Apparent supersensitivity of platelet 5HT receptors in lithium treated patients. *J. Affect. Disord.*, *8*, 69–72.
246. Wood, P. L., Suranyi-Cadotte, B. E., Nair, N. P. V., LaFaille, F., & Schwartz, G. (1983). Lack of association between ^{3}H.imipramine binding sites and uptake of serotonin in control, depressed and schizophrenic patients. *Neuropharmacology*, *22*, 1211–1214.
247. Wright, A. F., Crichton, D. N., Loufdon, J. B., Morten, J. E. N., & Skell, C. M. (1984). Beta-adrenergic binding defects in cell lines from families with manic-depressive disorder. *Ann. Hum. Genet.*, *48*, 201–214.
248. Zenko, M. T., & Biegon, A. (1983). Increased beta-adrenergic receptor binding in human frontal cortex of suicide victims. *Proceedings 13th Annual Meeting of Society for Neuroscience*, Boston, Abstract no. 210.5.
249. Zerssen, D. von, Barthelms, H., Dirlich, G., Doerr, P., Emrich, H. M., Lindern, L. V., Lund, R., & Pirke, K. M. (1985). Circadian rhythms in endogenous depression. *Psychiatr. Res.*, *16*, 51–63.
250. Zis, A. P., & Goodwin, F. K. (1982). The amine hypothesis. In E. S. Paykel (Ed.), *Handbook of the affective disorders* (pp. 175–190). Edinburgh: Churchill Livingstone.

3
IMMUNITY AND DEPRESSION

JOHN FARRANT, PH.D.

Scientific Staff, Medical Research Council,
Division of Immunological Medicine,
Clinical Research Centre,
Northwick Park Hospital,
Harrow, Middlesex, United Kingdom

and

MARGARITA PEREZ, M.D., M.R.C.PSYCH.

Consultant Psychiatrist, Department of Psychiatry,
Frimley Park Hospital,
Camberley, Surrey, United Kingdom

INTRODUCTION

In recent years, there has been an increased interest in understanding the nature and significance of interrelationships between the central nervous system (CNS) and the immune system (3, 9, 50, 60, 134) although the excessive fervor of enthusiasts in this field has been criticized (39, 106).

In this chapter, we illustrate the relationship between depression and the immune system, both in depressive illness and in several physical illnesses. Studies suggest that the normal CNS does have a two-way functional linkage with the immune system. Since depression is an abnormal manifestation of mental processes involving the CNS, one would therefore expect that it is associated with disturbances to the immune system. This evidence we will describe. Although the data for such an association are strong, many more controlled scientific studies on the relationship of depression to

We would like to thank Dr. M. Denman for his helpful criticism of the manuscript.

the intricate immunological networks of local hormones (lymphokines) and cells needs to be done.

In clinical practice, ideas on a linkage between the CNS and the immune system are common, but ill defined. Some physicians believe that patients presenting with a particular disease are more likely to have a characteristic personality. Also, an unhappy life event such as bereavement can trigger depressive or autoimmune illness.

The dichotomy of man into the two separate entities of mind and body has been detrimental to the understanding of man and his ailments, as well as splitting the discipline of psychiatry into those who believe in organic causes and those who consider only psychological factors, with both groups neglecting the dialogue between the two entities.

One can envisage many important developments for medicine once the connection between depression and immunity has been clarified. These will include an awareness of predisposing factors for both mental and physical illness, the possibility of psychological treatment for some aspects of those illnesses that involve the immune system, and finally an increase in the understanding of causal relationships between self, the environment, and disease.

We plan in this chapter to compare and contrast the CNS and the immune system, to give a short description of the immune system, and to describe links between the two systems both through the hypothalamic pituitary axis and via other routes. We will then relate stress to the release of neurohormones and describe their effects on the immune response. Finally, we will discuss changes in the immune response in depressive illness itself and then consider some aspects of depression in a number of other diseases.

CNS AND IMMUNE SYSTEM

Before discussing either depression or abnormal immunological responses, it is important to compare and contrast the CNS and the immune system, to distinguish the functions they have in common, and to describe what is known about connections between them.

Conventionally, the CNS with its external equipment of sensory and motor nerves handles inputs from both the external and internal worlds and, using its central abilities resident in brain and mind (whose relationships are beyond the mandate of this chapter), reacts and responds. The classical five senses are inputs to the CNS. The centralized processing involves concepts such as discrimination, learning, memory, tolerance, sensitivity, etc., which are integrated with incoming information before any "output" action is done.

The immune system involves memory, tolerance, and so forth, just like the CNS. It is also fundamentally involved in responding to the two worlds of self and nonself. For example, it needs to identify and deal with a foreign and potentially pathogenic organism. It also should be able to distinguish between a normal cell ("self") and a malignant cell (and deal with the latter if certain theories of immune surveillance of cancer are correct). Concepts of "self" and "nonself" are integral to normal functioning. Without making any definitions of what is "normal" or "abnormal," mental illness, including depressive illness, involves a defect of one or more links in this chain.

Like the CNS, the immune system can itself be damaged or malfunction. In some infectious diseases, e.g., AIDS, the immune defenses are attacked directly and subsequently fail. In other circumstances, e.g., autoimmune disease, the immune system reacts inappropriately and attacks self components.

THE IMMUNE SYSTEM

Since most psychiatrists may be more familiar with depressive illness than immunology, we thought that it might be useful to provide a short description of the immune system. An excellent recent review is that of Roitt et al. (135). The immune system can best be thought of as an organ of the body that is designed to deal with foreign substances and organisms and that is distributed throughout the whole organism rather than being localized.

Cells of the immune system are derived from pluripotential stem cells from the bone marrow and other hemopoetic areas. The nature and extent of the immune response is at several complex levels. The fundamental specificity of the response by the immune system is controlled by lymphocytes. There are only a few lymphocytes in the body with a specific receptor for each single foreign antigen. If one or more of these cells "sees" the antigen for the first time, the cells divide to make progeny with the same antigenic specificity. One effect of this "primary" response is to leave behind memory cells with the same specificity so that when the same foreign antigen is encountered in the future the response is both accelerated and amplified ("secondary" response). This is the principle of vaccination. Foreign organisms and foreign molecules usually contain more than one antigenic site (epitopes) for each of which there exists a specific set of lymphocytes.

The origin of the diversity available to the immune system in being able to relate to all potentially foreign antigens is not totally understood, but all the evidence points to the preexisting availability of cells specific for potential epitopes rather than to the more common-sense view that the system could learn from a new antigen and develop the specific cell required.

A simplified network of the cell interactions in the immune response is shown in Figure 1.

Before an antigen is seen by a lymphocyte, the antigen is processed by a monocyte or macrophage (examples of antigen-processing cells). Processing consists not only of proteolytic digestions of large-molecular-weight antigens into smaller molecules but also of unfolding of molecules leading to exposure of antigenic sites. Processed antigen is then presented to T lymphocytes by antigen-presenting cells (sometimes the same cell as the processing cell). Traditionally, the monocyte or macrophage was thought to be the presenting cell, but it is now clear that many cell types including the dendritic cell and the B lymphocyte can present antigen to T lymphocytes.

The antigen-presenting cell has to have the identical self histocompatibility locus antigen (HLA) class II as the responding lymphocyte. The T-cell receptor thus sees the antigen but only in association with a self-identification signal of the same HLA type. This response is therefore restricted and requires "dual recognition."

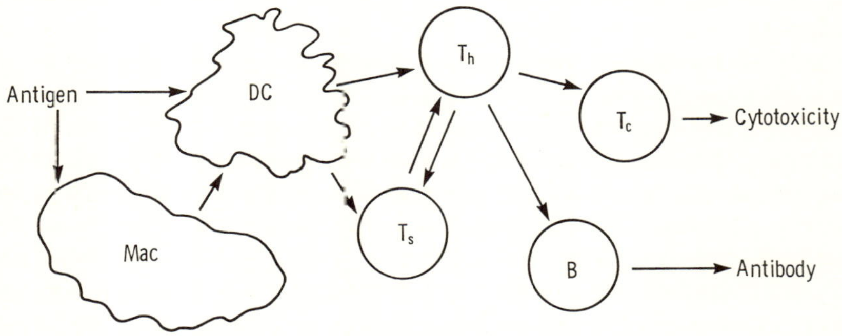

Figure 1. Simplified network of cell interactions in the immune response to an antigen. Mac=macrophage/monocyte; DC=dendritic cell; T_h=T helper lymphocyte; T_s=T suppressor lymphocyte; T_c=T cytotoxic lymphocyte; B=B lymphocyte.

The responding cell, often a T helper lymphocyte, then secretes lymphokines (local hormones) to activate (help) an effector cell, for example a B lymphocyte, which will then secrete an antibody specific for the original antigen. To be effective the antibody will neutralize the antigen by acting as a linkage molecule, attaching at one end to the specific antigen (e.g., an infectious agent), and at its other end to receptors (Fc) on phagocytic and endocytic cells. This attachment then permits inactivation of the foreign antigen.

Another important effector cell is the T cytotoxic cell (see Figure 1), which when activated by a T helper cell is able to identify and destroy the appropriate antigen-bearing target cells.

T suppressor lymphocytes are another component of the system leading to one mechanism of negative feedback control. They too need activation but can then turn off T helper cells and damp down the immune response.

All these cell interactions are mediated at several levels. First there is the geographical localization of the cells. The appropriate cell types come together when required either at a local site of inflammation or in specialized areas within organs such as lymph nodes or the spleen. Then the cells communicate by an intricate network of immunohormones called interleukins. These include gamma-interferon (gamma-IFN), interleukin 1 and 2 (IL-1 and IL-2), and helper and suppressor factors. To study these networks it is possible to set up model systems of an immune response in vitro using a particular antigen to trigger specific clones of lymphocytes.

The main reason for describing the intricacies of the cellular and humoral immune response is to show the multiple ways by which the system may be perturbed. For example, in disease, there may be cell types lacking or defective (either by underactivity or by overactivity), or there may be excessive or insufficient production of interleukins or a breakdown in the self recognition system.

As we will discuss later, the lymphocytes have receptors for many neurohormones. Because of the complexity of the immune system, with many examples of positive and negative feedback controls, there are many possible ways that the CNS could influence the immune system. As will be discussed later, it is therefore unfortunate that most of the literature on CNS-influenced changes to the immune response uses the least sensitive and most unrealistic test system of the immune response—that of the in vitro response to mitogens. The mitogens used are plant-derived compounds called lectins which bypass the antigen receptor specificity of the lymphocyte and use a nonspecific carbohydrate receptor to stimulate most of the cells. This response is nonphysiological but appears to be popular with those immunologists who have dared to do joint experiments with psychiatrists!

LINKS BETWEEN THE CNS AND THE NORMAL IMMUNE SYSTEM

We begin by demonstrating relationships between the CNS and the homeostatic functioning of the immune system in normal individuals by describing two remarkable studies. In that of Black, Humphrey, and Niven (21), five male subjects, previously shown to be susceptible to hypnosis, were studied. Four were tuberculin (Mantoux) positive and one was a negative control. The response to intracutaneous antigen (PPD) was standardized before hypnosis began. During a course of hypnosis in which it was suggested to the subjects that they would not now react to PPD, a second inoculation was carried out. The Mantoux-positive response of the four subjects before hypnosis was converted to Mantoux negative after the treatment, as judged by the levels of swelling and erythema. It was interesting that the hypnotic treatment did not prevent lymphocyte infiltration into the site of inoculation but did reduce the extent of fluid exudate and swelling.

In the second study (153), a woman subject who was experienced in meditation was able to reduce her own delayed-type hypersensitivity skin test reaction to varicella zoster virus from that observed before meditation. Later she was able to allow the response to return to control levels. The skin test data, which reflect the function of T lymphocytes in vivo, was supported by the finding that antigen-driven lymphocyte proliferation in vitro was also significantly depressed ($p < .001$) when the lymphocytes were collected from the peripheral blood during meditation. Again, the response subsequently returned to control levels.

It has also been shown that a conditioned response (e.g., camphor smell) can alter immune function (e.g., activity of natural killer cells) (53). This is discussed in more detail in the section on cancer.

THE HYPOTHALAMUS-PITUITARY-ADRENAL AXIS

The most important and obvious mechanism by which the CNS can modulate the immune response is via the hypothalamus-pituitary-adrenal axis (Figure 2).

Adaptation to environmental changes imposed by physical or psychosocial demands requires a succession of responses—behavioral, neuroendocrine, autonomic, and metabolic—in order to maintain homeostasis. It seems natural that the immune response should also be included in this list.

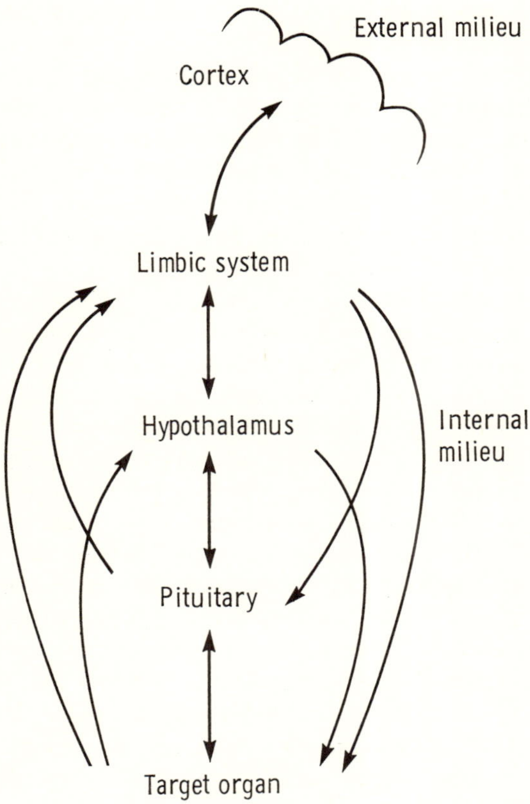

Figure 2. The hypothalamus-pituitary-adrenal axis. Interactive feedback loops occur at all levels.

Cannon was the first to suggest that such a homeostatic function was the result of an interaction between brain behavior and the endocrine function (30).

The stress theory of Selye (146) proposed that the pituitary-adrenal system was the basis for physiological adaptation and even that "mere emotional stress" such as immobilization activates the pituitary-adrenal system. He thought, however, that such a response was not specific. Later, it was recognized that psychological or social stimulae are among the most potent events in activating the pituitary-adrenal system (99, 108). Extra-hypothalamic brain structures related to emotions (122) have been recognized in the control of pituitary-adrenal function (23, 150). Other pituitary hormones such as prolactin, vasopressin, and endorphins are also activated by psychosocial stimuli (139, 165).

More recently, discoveries in neurobiology suggest that the brain is not only the controller of the endocrine system, but also the direct producer of peptides and other hormones. The action of hormones in the brain serves the organization of specific and nonspecific behavioral and other physiological responses. Mason postulated that the CNS acts as the "organizer" of these multiple hormonal responses via the autonomic system and the hypothalamus-pituitary-endocrine axis (110).

Bohus has proposed four levels of organization of endocrine response to environmental stimulae and suggested that the same levels of organization can apply to the immune system as well (24) (Figure 2).

The limbic-midbrain region in conjunction with cortical areas acts as the first level. This level is composed of the amygdaloid complex, the septal nuclei, the hippocampus, and the ascending reticular activating system (RAS). It should also include the ascending projection of the aminergic system, which originates from noradrenergic, dopaminergic, and serotonergic nuclei of the brain stem. The major function of the limbic midbrain system could be summarized as integration of sensory information (external milieu) and visceral and endocrine signals (internal milieu) and organization of adaptive processes such as learning, memory, and motivation, including the emotional background of behavior (23, 62, 81). Studies of the regulatory function of the limbic system on the pituitary adrenal system showed that amygdaloid structures have an activating role, while septal and hippocampus structures have an inhibitory one. The RAS is generally activator, but ascending serotonergic fibers carry inhibitory information (23, 150).

The second level of organization is the hypothalamus. Classically, the hypothalamus has been considered the integrative center of neuroendocrine regulation. In the case of emotional stimulae the integrative function may be questionable. The extensive anatomical connections between the limbic system, midbrain, and hypothalamus may provide the morphological connections between the first and second levels of organization. The hypothalamus may have more than one function in the organization of neuroendocrine response to stress. First it is suggested that the information provided by the limbic midbrain system in the form of neurotransmitters (neural messages) is "translated" into hormonal messages, that is, the synthesis and/or release of activating/inhibitory factors or hormones. These factors are at the same time dependent on the feedback of peripheral hormones and subject to circadian variations. The releasing/inhibitory factors reach the pituitary gland and thereby regulate the release of stress-related hormones. Some releasing hormones may have a direct effect on brain function as shown in animal experiments (161). In addition, the hypothalamus is the site of synthesis of neurotransmitter peptides that are transported to the posterior pituitary gland. The release of adrenal catecholamines is under direct control from the hypothalamus by neural connection through the spinal cord.

The fact that the hypothalamus contains cell bodies of the peptidergic neural system that terminate in the midbrain, the hindbrain, and the spinal cord represents another aspect of its neuroendocrine function. That the hypothalamus is directly involved in the regulation of the immune response following exposure to antigen is confirmed by studies with implanted electrodes. The firing rates of neurons of specific nuclei of the hypothalamus increase following immunization (16, 18). This supports the hypothesis of Solomon and Amkraut of a feedback loop between immune response and the hypothalamus (157).

We must also mention the work of Stein et al., who have reviewed the effect of hypothalamic lesions on the immune system (159). In general, immune responses, including lethal anaphylaxis, are reduced by such lesions.

The third level of organization of endocrine response corresponds to the pituitary gland. The release of stress-related hormones from the hypophysis is controlled by both hypothalamic factors and circulating peripheral hormones. That these hormones function as stress hormones has been suggested by behavioral studies. Stress-related functions of the endorphins have also been suggested (66). The release of the various stress hormones is interrelated, as suggested by a number of studies. For example, stress-induced release of prolactin can be blocked by pretreatment with dexamethasone (47, 140) and also by the opioid antagonist naloxone.

The fourth level of organization is that of the target organs, including the adrenal gland itself. The classical theories on stress consider the peripheral organ or organs in the cardiovascular, neuromuscular, and immune systems (target organs type 1) as the only sites at which stress hormones can affect bodily functions. The discovery that the brain is also a major target site for stress hormones (target organ type 2) opens a new field in the understanding and interpretation of the adaptive functions of the neuroendocrine system and closes the circuit, with the brain being a major organizer and controller of both neuroendocrine and, as we are discussing in this chapter, of immunological interactions.

There are a number of findings that we will now describe that support the concept that the immune and neuroendocrine responses are similarly organized and that the neuroendocrine response may serve as an important link in the course of host defense. Also, products of the immune system itself may regulate the activity of the pituitary–adrenal system and thus affect the release of other stress hormones. Regulation of immune activity by these hormones again demonstrates a closed circuit between the brain and the immune system involving a neuroendocrine link.

STRESS, NEUROHORMONES, AND IMMUNE RESPONSE

In order to put the relationship between depression and immunity into context, the relationship between stress and immunity should be discussed first.

Stress

Perhaps the most accepted definition of stress, taking into account subjectivity, is that of David Glass: "Stress is the perception of threat to physical or psychological well-being and the realization that the individual's response is inadequate to cope" (78, p. 430).

Stress and Neurohormones

Selye's views (146) of nonspecific biological responses to stress are no longer substantiated or supported (109) since the nature of the stress may determine the specific pattern of response. As an example, both public speaking and physical exercise produce increased plasma concentrations of both noradrenaline and adrenaline (43). Levels of noradrenaline are higher than those of adrenaline in exercise stress while the opposite is true for the stress of public speaking.

The importance of factors such as expectancy, certainty, or uncertainty and the establishment of coping strategies are relevant to the pattern of acute stress response. The status of an animal in its social hierarchy influences the levels of the resting pituitary system and its responsiveness. Environmental variables such as the possibility or impossibility of coping mechanisms also affect the temporal responsiveness of the pituitary-adrenal response to stress. For example, passive avoidance produces a gradual increase in cortisol levels in rats reaching a maximum 15 min after starting the test (24). This occurs only if the experimental animal was allowed to determine its own behavior. If it was prevented from escaping or avoiding the stress, the maximum increase in cortisol was reached more promptly after only 5 min.

Social aggressive interactions and pituitary-adrenal responsiveness can also be affected by a familiar or unfamiliar environment. Increases in the cortisol levels are higher and more prolonged in a winner than in a loser. This suggests that the response to psychological challenge of diverse parameters of the pituitary-adrenal system is regulated in a very subtle way.

A framework has been proposed to delimit three primary elements in stress, health, and disease (45). These are: activator in the environment, reaction to the activator, and the competence of the reaction. This framework permits identification of potential stressors for specific situations of individuals and consideration of conditions that make a particular stress stressful. This framework also provides an approach to modulators that may be involved in the sequence activity—reaction—consequence.

Neurohormones and the Immune Response

The relationship between neuroendocrinological hormones and the immune response has been well reviewed by Solomon and Amkraut (157).

Corticosteroids. One of the most important and best-studied hormones in the association between stress and immune response is cortisol. Lymphocytes have been shown to have receptors for corticosteroids (28). Although the finding is neglected, Ambrose showed that corticosteroid can be essential for an immune response (7) and in addition corticosteroid can enhance immunoglobulin production by B lymphocytes following in vitro stimulation by the plant lectin pokeweed mitogen (PWM) (33).

Most data show, however, that addition of cortisol will suppress the immune response (10, 49, 173). For example, in humans, corticosteroids produce profound monocytopenia, lymphocytopenia (with selective depletion of T cells), eosinopenia, and neutrophilia (49). Also, glucocorticoids can suppress interferon production (67, 68, 142). Corticosteroids may also have a role in suppressing T-cell reactions to autoantigens that might be relevant to the effect of stress in autoimmune disease (80).

Despite these overall immunosuppressive effects, the biphasic nature of complex biological responses is relevant to this system as to others. For example, Monjan and Collector showed that mice stressed over a period of 40 days gave reduced responses to the mitogens lipopolysaccharide (LPS) and concanavalin A (ConA), with a corresponding increase in the levels of cortisol (114). Later, however, when the cortisol levels had returned to normal, the proliferative response to mitogens increased to greater than control values.

Although the traditional view has been that increased glucocorticoid levels in stress augment the body's defenses, a more realistic hypothesis that explains the immunosuppressive effects is that the rise in glucocorticoid levels protects against an excessive and perhaps damaging level of the defense mechanisms themselves (115). This is in accord with the generally down-regulating actions of raised glucocorticoid levels.

Other hormones. Lymphocytes and thymocytes have receptors for a number of hormones and neurotransmitters. The list includes insulin (72, 94, 154), testosterone (2, 54, 64), beta-adrenergic agents (69, 149), estrogens (65), histamine (141), acetylcholine (131), growth hormone (52), ACTH (87, 88), the endorphins (55, 71, 87), and the neuropeptides substance P, somatostatin, and vasoactive intestinal peptide (120, 123, 126).

These receptors have been found to play a role in differentiation and control of the activity of lymphocytes. For example, thyroid function and TSH are thought to stimulate immune reaction (4, 8). Insulin can modulate lymphocyte activity (31). Catecholamines and histamine have been shown to activate the immune system. During immunization a decrease in noradrenaline in the spleen has been recorded (4, 17, 25).

These neuromodulators may affect immune function in a variety of ways, both qualitatively and quantitatively (22). For example, beta-endorphin increases T-cell proliferation to mitogens in the rat (55) and augments natural killer (NK) activity in humans (107), yet alpha-endorphin inhibits both T and B cells in humans (71). ACTH decreases antibody production in vitro (87), and decreases the production of gamma-interferon induced by mitogens (88). TSH increases production of antibody in vitro (22).

Different regimes of stress have been shown to be related to opioid or nonopioid mechanisms (100). In rats, an opioid-mediated stress will suppress NK activity and decrease resistance to tumor challenge (148).

What is not clear is what part these neurohormones play in the normal physiological functioning of the immune system in its response to the environment.

Stress and the Immune Response

In animals, early life experiences such as handling and rearing in isolation seem to affect physiological response to stress and to immunity as well (73, 156). Adrenocortical activity precedes anticipated unfamiliar experience. Mastering of the situation produces stabilization, but activation is higher when coping is required (128). Adrenocortical hormonal response to stress is varied; for instance, growth hormone (GH) response to stress may be influenced by personality characteristics such as "neuroticism" (132) and susceptibility to coronary attacks (51).

Most hormones are secreted in a pulsatile, episodic fashion. Many hormones have 24-hour rhythms, and mechanisms of immunity also show a 24-hour periodicity. In some instances a direct correlation has been observed (163). Timing of stress in relation to natural rhythms may influence immunological response. It is, however, not clear how these multiple responses are interrelated and what their ultimate effect is at the level of the tissue target.

Stress Affecting Lymphocytes

Most work in both animals and humans suggests that increased stress depresses immune function. This has been reviewed by Stein et al. (158).

Animal experiments. Reite et al. (130) studied separation experiences in primates and found decreased T-cell mitogen responses following separation for a period of two weeks. Mitogen responses returned to baseline within several weeks of reunion.

Laboratory studies have demonstrated a relationship between intensity of an acute stressor and the degree of suppression of T-lymphocyte function in rats (90). A graded series of stressors applied over 18 hours, including restraint in an apparatus, low-level electrical tail shock, and high-level shock, produced a progressively greater suppression of both the number of circulating lymphocytes and PHA-induced stimulation of peripheral blood lymphocytes. Laudenslager et al. (98) showed that the psychological state of the animal influences the suppression of lymphocyte stimulation induced by stress. They found that PHA and ConA stimulation of lymphocytes was suppressed in rats exposed to inescapable uncontrollable electric tail shock. Animals receiving the same amount of shock but able to terminate the stressor did not decrease the lymphocyte activity.

Further examples of the immunosuppression induced by stress include the following findings. Rotational stress in mice reduced the white blood cell count (133). Stressed mice have less delayed hypersensitivity reactivity (127), less NK activity (1, 145), and less skin rejection (171). Also, avoidance learning stress decreases the susceptibility of mice to passive anaphylaxis (128).

The effect of stress on the humoral immune system is complex and is related to the nature and intensity of the stimulus as well as to the biological and social characteristics of the organism. This is discussed by Joasoo and McKenzie (85), who found that rats that were kept in isolation gave reduced responses to an antigen (thyroglobulin) in comparison to those kept together. Isolation of monkeys depressed responses to mitogens (130). By contrast, mice in groups had reduced antibody responses compared to isolated mice (167), but rats handled in infancy had greater antibody response to flagellin than unhandled animals (156).

The production of specific antibody could be suppressed in a variety of species by disturbing environmental stimuli such as noise, light, movement, and housing conditions (167). Both primary and secondary antibody response could be suppressed (77, 155). Other studies supported the observations that acute exposure to stress can suppress humoral immune responses, but repeated exposure seems to result in an apparent adaptation to stress and in some cases can enhance the response (56, 85, 114).

Bereavement and other forms of stress in humans. In humans, bereavement depresses responses to the T-cell mitogens PHA and ConA (11). Linn et al. (101) also showed in a group of 60 men who had experienced family death or illness in the previous six months that the lymphocyte response to PHA was significantly reduced. The level of depression affected the response. Bartrop et al. (11) also showed that these changes to lymphocyte function were not accompanied by changes in measured serum levels of cortisol, prolactin, growth hormone, thyroxine, or triiodothyronine.

Epidemiological studies in bereavement have shown an increased risk of mortality especially during the first six months after the death of the spouse (82). Depressed immune response may be one of the factors involved. Young et al. (172) found a higher risk of mortality for the widowed in the first six months of bereavement but no rise in mortality after four to eight years. In a prospective study McNeill (105) also found widowed people under 60 years old at greater risk during the first six months after bereavement. There were sex differences; women were more predisposed to the development of malignant neoplasms. Cobb (32), in a retrospective study over a period of 10 years, concluded that widowed individuals had a higher risk of mortality compared with those who were single, divorced, or separated. Men were more at risk than women, with a peak risk of mortality between the ages of 20 and 34 years.

Other forms of stress also affect immune response in humans. For example, sport stress increases cortisol levels and depresses mitogenic and antigenic responses (46). In a later study, Dorian et al. (44) divided students taking examinations into stressed and highly stressed groups. The highly stressed group showed raised numbers of T and B lymphocytes together with a reduction in B-cell function (plaque-forming cells) and T-cell function (mitogen response to PHA and ConA). In another study, reduced T-cell numbers and mitogen responses were observed in students under the stress of examinations (57). Also, work stress in mines has been shown to reduce the serum levels of immunoglobulin over a single working shift (168). Although anxiety increases the number of circulating lymphocytes (48), in general, stress depresses immune function.

Mediators of Immune Origin Affecting the CNS

There is much less work on how the immune response itself affects the function of the CNS. However, this axis does exist and is very important in closing the circuit from the periphery to the CNS.

Besedovsky and his group have done the most work in this area (for reviews see Besedovsky and Sorkin [19]; Besedovsky et al. [15]). This group showed that an immune response that was detected by an increase in plaque-forming cells (B-cell response) was paralleled by endocrine changes including a rise in corticosterone and thyroxine levels (18, 20). Besedovsky et al. (19) also showed in rats that antigen stimulation is able to fire neurons in the hypothalamus. Later, Besedovsky et al. (16) provided evidence that the immune response evokes changes in brain noradrenergic neurons. Also, it has been shown that lymphocytes can synthesize neurohormones, including thymosins, ACTH, TSH, and endorphins (70, 151, 152).

DEPRESSIVE ILLNESS

We now consider depressive illness itself.

Mitogen Responses in Depressive Illness

Kronfol et al. (93) compared the in vitro immune response of cells from patients with major depressive disorder with cells from normal individuals. The depressed subjects had a significant reduction in the proliferative response to the primarily T-cell mitogens, PHA and ConA, and to the primarily B-cell mitogen, PWM. The severity of clinical depression of the patients on the Hamilton Depression Rating Scale correlated with the reduction in the PWM response.

Similarly, Schleifer et al. (145) compared mitogen responsiveness in cells from patients in hospital with major depressive disorder who had a mean rating of 28 on the Hamilton Depression Scale with the responsiveness of cells from outpatients with a mean depression rating of only 3. Responses to PHA, ConA, and PWM were reduced significantly in the hospital patients. The numbers of both T and B cells in the circulation were reduced in the inpatients, who also showed a raised plasma level of cortisol. Later, Schleifer et al. (144) showed that ambulatory depressed patients (mean Hamilton Depression Rating of 19) did not have different mitogen responses to controls. Since being in hospital did not change the immune responses for other groups (e.g., schizophrenic patients or surgical patients), it was argued that it was the severity of the depression that determined the immune response.

These conclusions have been challenged by Albrecht et al. (5), who found no difference in lymphocyte mitogenesis (to PHA, ConA, and PWM) between *drug-free* patients with depression and normal controls. This lack of effect was maintained even when they considered the subgroup of dexamethasone nonsuppressors. However, Albrecht and his colleagues did find a significant reduction in the response to PHA and ConA following treatment with tricyclic antidepressants or ECT. Previously, Sengar et al. (147) showed no effects on B- or T-cell responses with drug-free patients who were remitted from major depressive disorder.

Later, Kronfol et al. (91) repeated his previous work with patients who were drug free for at least two weeks before the immune function test and found again a significant reduction in mitogen blastogenesis in the patients. Unexpectedly, they also showed no correlation with either blood cortisol levels or levels of urinary free cortisol excretion. The impairment in lymphocyte function cannot therefore be explained solely on the level of cortisol.

Cortisol or Not?

Further evidence for noncortisol mechanisms has been obtained by Calabrese et al. (29). With drug-free patients they found that the reduction in the in vitro response to mitogen stimulation was associated with significant elevations in the plasma levels of prostaglandins of the E series. However, these hormones may affect cortisol levels indirectly since these prostaglandins can stimulate the hypothalamic pituitary axis.

Lowy et al. (103) have linked the dexamethasone suppression test, cortisol levels, and the reduction in immune function. They showed that mitogenesis was reduced by the dexamethasone administration itself but only in those patients (and normals) who responded to the test with suppressed cortisol levels. They conclude that the number of receptors to glucocorticoids plays an important part in these relationships. Recently this has been confirmed, for it has been shown that the patients whose cortisol levels are suppressed by dexamethasone have few receptors to glucocorticoids on their lymphocytes (61). In addition, the number of receptors was unchanged after dexamethasone, in contrast to the reduction in receptors seen in both normal subjects and patients whose cortisol levels responded to the dexamethasone suppression test. Syvalahti et al. (162) have recently challenged that there is any immunological difference between the two groups of depressed patients, that is the suppressors or nonsuppressors, in the dexamethasone suppression test.

Nemeroff et al. (118) described an elevation in the levels of corticotropin-releasing factor (CRF) in the cerebrospinal fluid of drug-free patients with major depression. This suggests that the hyperactivity of the hypothalamic-pituitary-adrenal axis seen in major depression leading to raised cortisol levels is in part due to raised levels of CRF. Also, Holsboer et al. (79) showed that patients who were nonsuppressors in the dexamethasone suppression test had raised levels of ACTH as well as cortisol. They speculated that the raised cortisol levels stem from the increase in ACTH. It has also been shown that free triiodothyronine is significantly lower in patients with unipolar major depression (121).

Neuroamines and Depression

Interesting links between neurotransmitters and hormonal response are suggested by the fact that the catecholamine systems are related to reward and positive behavior while serotonin neurons are related to avoidance and punishment. Serotonergic neurons seem to mediate the effects of noxious stimuli, including withdrawal, negative incentive, and perhaps extinction and habituation, all features present in depressive symptomatology. It has been suggested that the monoamine hypothesis of affective disorders should be reformulated: depression results from hypoactivity of the catecholamine neural system and anxiety from hyperactivity of serotinergic punishment systems, the two systems interacting with each other such that anxiety and depression represent correlated dimensions of disturbance (36).

Neuroendocrine changes during depressive illness tend to correlate with an increase in cortisol levels in response to serotonin (5-HT) in depressed patients (112, 113). Furthermore, the peak cortisol level in response to 5-HT correlates significantly with the severity of the depression, thus suggesting a link between serotonergic hyperactivity, increased cortisol response, and depressive symptomatology (34). This relationship adds further support to the hypothesis that cortisol may be one of the important factors in the relationship between depression and immune response and strengthens the role played by stress both in the development of depressive symptoms and in the decrease of the immune response. Paykel's well-established studies of life events in the six months preceding the onset of depressive illness highlight the role played by stress (124).

Since the decrease in immune response following stress mediated by raised cortisol levels has been suggested by Munck et al. (115) to be (paradoxically) a protective mechanism against an excessive defense response, one could speculate that in some cases depression may also be a protective reaction against increasing and noxious levels of anxiety caused by stress.

Tissue Type (HLA) and Depression

It is now well established that certain diseases (especially autoimmune diseases) are more common in individuals with a particular tissue type. Usually the HLA type is not the sole trigger for the disease; environmental cofactors (e.g., viruses, chemicals, etc.) are also needed. The relationship of HLA and affective disorders has also been studied. Despite some contradictory reports in the literature reviewed by Suarez and Reich (160), their final conclusion (which includes their own data) is that there is no support for the hypothesis for a linkage between HLA type and major affective disorder. There is, however, some evidence for an HLA association in schizophrenia (138), but in this study also no linkage was found with major depression.

Autoantibodies

A surprising finding was that antinuclear factor antibodies were found in 30% of patients admitted with depression (the proportion in normal individuals is about 3%) (37). Rosenblatt et al. (137) have described an association between rheumatoid factor and endogenous depression.

Gold et al. (58) suggested that "symptomless autoimmune thyroiditis" should be considered in patients complaining of depression. In fact, Nemeroff et al. (117) found that a proportion of depressed patients (20%) had elevated levels of antithyroid autoantibodies (both antimicrosomal and antithyroglobulin). It is possible, however, that drug therapy might explain their data.

Are Viruses Causally Related to Some Depressions?

A report by Allen and Tilkian (6) shows that 12 patients with depression did not develop infectious mononucleosis during an epidemic to that illness. All had evidence of a chronic viremia caused by the Epstein-Barr virus (EBV), the infectious agent in infectious mononucleosis. There was a positive correlation between the intensity of depressive symptoms and the cellular response to EBV. Although this evidence is weak, it would be interesting to see whether other evidence for viral involvement could be obtained in depressive illness. However, Roos et al. (136) have screened serum and CSF from depressed patients (and schizophrenics) and found none. Some reduction in nonspecific serum IgM levels has been noticed in depressive illness (38).

Immunopsychiatry

This term was coined by Jankovic et al. (84) to denote the involvement of immune processes in the pathogenesis of several mental disorders. For example, in depressive subjects, 94% of 34 patients gave a positive delayed-type skin hypersensitivity response to the human brain protein S-100 in comparison with only 7% of 58 control subjects (83).

DEPRESSION IN OTHER DISEASES

There are at least three classes of diseases involving the immune system:

1. Diseases involving infectious agents in which the immune response is (at least initially) functioning normally and the immune phenomena are those associated with attempts to neutralize the invading organism. In some diseases the immune defenses subsequently fail or are attacked directly (as in AIDS).
2. Diseases involving malignancy in which the postulated theory of immune surveillance is either overwhelmed or broken down.
3. Diseases in which the immune system itself is abnormal in that it reacts inappropriately (e.g., against self-components as in auto-

immune disease) or, conversely, it fails to react when required as in immunodeficiency (e.g., hypogammaglobulinemia).

We felt that it would be most convenient to list diseases in which there are indications of a relationship between depression and immunity.

AIDS

It is now clear that some patients with the acquired immunodeficiency syndrome (AIDS) present with psychiatric symptoms including depression and dementia (14). This is related to the invasion of the CNS by the virus and must be distinguished from the depression induced in AIDS victims and others by their awareness of having a fatal disease.

Allergy

Matussek et al. (111) found a positive correlation between aggression and allergic disorders in depressive patients. This relationship was not confined to depressive illness since they also showed a correlation between aggression and depression in a control group.

Asthma

Deter and his colleagues (41, 42) have shown that psychodynamic group therapy in patients with asthma reduced the number of working days lost and the dependence on therapeutic drugs in comparison with patients not in psychotherapy. It is well known that some sufferers of asthma have attacks that are precipitated by emotion. Neild and Cameron (116) demonstrated that in such individuals suggestion could induce a change in the forced expiratory volume which was blocked by an inhaled anticholinergic agent.

Autoimmune Thyroiditis

Gold et al. (59) described the association between hypothyroidism and depression. It is thought that decreased thyroid function may predispose to depression and that increase in thyroid hormones may be involved in recovery from depression (170), although others (56) have suggested that it is the treatment of depression with lithium or carbamezapine that reduces thyroid function.

Do the same detrimental life events that lead to depression, e.g., loss of partner, bereavement, etc., trigger autoimmune disease? Recently, in a careful study Gray and Hoffenberg (63) have shown that there was no significant difference in life events for control individuals and patients with Graves' thyrotoxicosis.

Cancer

The association between depression and cancer has recently been reviewed by Noyes and Kathol (119). Early studies on the role of depression in the etiology of malignancy had the shortcomings that the cancer was already present and could have caused the depression. There is little evidence to show that psychological characteristics are risk factors in cancer. Also there is no agreement that depression increases mortality in cancer or alters the rate of disease progression significantly. Two recent surveys do show that depression is higher in cancer patients than in normal individuals (27, 40). Noyes and Kathol (119) conclude that "clearly, not all depression in cancer patients is psychological in origin."

Depression appears to be associated with an impairment of cell-mediated immunity (92, 101). The theory of immune surveillance as a physiological means of dealing with malignancy would involve cell-mediated immunity (125). Ghanta et al. (53) showed that restraint stress in mice with an experimental myeloma was detrimental and led to the early death of the mice. They also showed that for this tumor the restraint stress neutralized the beneficial effects of therapy with poly I:C. They were also able to strengthen the therapeutic effect of poly I:C as measured by an increase in NK activity by conditioning the host with camphor smell. Similar findings with rotation stress or housing stress were shown by Riley (132, 133) and Kandil and Borysenko (89). Also, Shavit et al. (148) showed in rats that a footshock stress mediated by opioids decreased resistance to tumor challenge. However, with an osteosarcoma, a tumor with little evidence of regulation by T cells, Ghanta et al. (53) also showed an opposite effect, that is a prolongation in survival by stress.

A hypothesis has also been put forward that cancer presenting with depression could be an autoimmune disease involving autoantibodies to the 5-HT receptor or even that antiidiotypic antibodies are involved in the pathogenesis (26), but there is little supporting evidence for this.

Diabetes

The classical studies of stress in diabetes are those of Hinkle and his group (74–76) as well as Vanderbergh et al. (166) in which stress was associated with raised ketone levels and lower glucose levels in the blood.

Linn et al. (102) show that type I diabetics feel more stressed and score higher on anxiety than type II diabetics. They also have reduced immune function. Stress reduction has been shown to reduce the fluctuation in blood glucose levels (96). Thomas et al. (164) showed that a depressed patient with insulin-dependent diabetes who was given electroconvulsive shock therapy (ECT) three months later no longer needed insulin and had a normal glucose tolerance test.

Multiple Sclerosis

Multiple sclerosis (MS) is a demyelinating disease of the CNS. It has lymphocytic involvement and the autoimmune reaction appears to be primarily cell mediated.

Affective disorder may be a presenting or complicating feature of multiple sclerosis (104, 143). Whitlock and Siskind (169) showed that MS patients were more depressed than a set of matched patients with other chronic neurological syndromes. The MS group also had more bouts of depression before any neurological symptoms had developed, so it is difficult to argue that the depression was solely a reaction to the awareness of the disease. However, group psychotherapy decreased depression (35), as did cognitive behavior therapy (97).

One group has shown a loss of T suppressor cells in MS (129).

Rheumatoid Arthritis

Patients with rheumatoid arthritis (RA) have a number of psychological symptoms including depression, but there is no true premorbid study to ascertain whether the depression can precede the physical symptoms, and it is likely that the depression is a reaction to the pain and disability of the disease (12).

DISCUSSION

In our approach to the study of depression and immune response, we have made a parallel between the CNS, site of the emotions, personality, and ego defenses, and the immune system, site of the discrimination between self and nonself. Both systems serve functions of adaptation and defense and both intervene in the relationship between the organism and the external environment. There are therefore philosophical reasons to postulate links between the two. Both systems embody the principles of recognition, learning, memory, and the transmission of meaningful information. Furthermore, it has been suggested, and there is evidence, that the function of one system is affected by the function of the other and that the CNS, as the major translator and integrator of the stimuli arriving from the external environment, is at the same time the controller of the adaptive responses originating in the internal milieu.

We have seen that immune response can be influenced by the mind (hypnosis, conditioned response, etc.) and that psychological perturbations in animals as well as in humans show that early experiences such as stress and separation will influence the range of immune response later in life. We have also seen that in situations of particular psychological significance for the individual (social status, coping or noncoping) the scope of the immune response varies accordingly with a degree of specificity for each individual. Noxious psychological stimuli of various kinds can affect the immune response as well as the individual capacity to learn, memorize, and retain acquired patterns of behavior. This process of adaptation can be at fault if the psychological circumstances are so adverse as to disrupt the normal pattern of both psychological and immune response.

A third level of organization, also involved in the process of adaptation, is the neuroendocrine system. This acts as a link and often as a common path between the CNS and the immune system. At different levels, there is evidence of the effect that psychological situations (e.g., stress) have on neurohormones, of the effect neurohormones have on the immune response, and of the effect of stress on the immune response. Within the individual the three levels must be in constant and fluid dialogue with each other in order to achieve a harmonic homeostatic balance (Figure 3). The psychological response of the CNS and the immunological response of the immune system cannot be discussed in a simplistic manner, and any attempt to force a cause-effect relationship falls short in explaining the complexity of the interaction. Fragmented evidence for direct *causal* correlation between the CNS and the immune system has led some, erroneously in our view, to discard a possible connection.

The CNS is the main communicator with the external milieu, and whatever the occurrence in the environment, this has a repercussion in the adaptive response of the individual. The three systems have an enormous complexity of their own. In order to achieve meaningful homeostatic balance they have to be in constant internal dialogue at the different levels of biological organization. For example, what happens at the target organ is fed back at various levels of response, creating a harmonious yet interdependent relationship whose end result is the adaptive behavior of the indi-

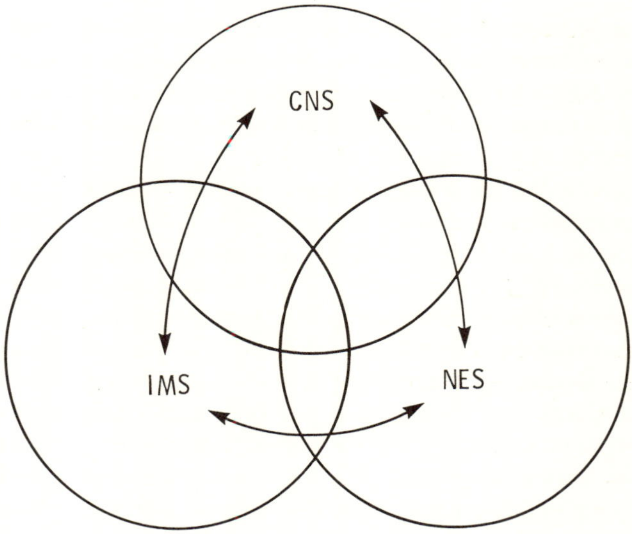

Figure 3. Homeostasis demands a dynamic dialogue between three systems: the central nervous system (CNS), the neuroendocrine system (NES), and the immune system (IMS).

vidual either externally or internally. The internal response is fed back to the environment, and the changes occurring will again have repercussions on the adaptive response of the individual.

There is therefore a continuity and overlapping of communication within the internal environment, each participating with the other and with the external environment. At all levels of organization there has to be interaction, from the molecular to the cellular and thence through the whole individual to the community. Any breakdown of communication at any one level will therefore precipitate an anomalous response resulting in maladaptive behavior, whether it be physiological (illness) or behavioral (avoidance, withdrawal, etc.) or both.

In order to understand the relationship between depression and immune response, in addition to the concept of internal dialogue, we should also consider the concept of functional subordination. Koestler has written on the seriality and integration of levels of biological organization and the relationship of the part to the whole in establishing biological identity: "The part has to maintain its individuality, otherwise the organism would lose its articulation and revert to amorphous heterogeneity: at the same time, it has to behave as a *part* in the whole, that is, in functional subordination" (see Bennette [13, p. 354]). In the model we have described, not only do the immune and neuroendocrine systems appear to be "subordinated" to the CNS as the major controller and integrator of external information, but each system has a direct influence or dialogue with the CNS. This constant dialogue between interpreter and interpreted, between interrogator and interrogated appears to happen at all levels, from the most sophisticated centers, cortex, limbic system, etc., to the target organs, adrenal glands, muscles, etc., thus affecting the totality of the psychological immune response.

In our review of depression and immune response, stress seems to be the common path for both. However, it is important to avoid the simplistic notion of stress and psychological experience as the "cause" of disease, but rather to view stress as having a complex interaction with the personality and biology of the host and hence with the expression of disease. Most studies have concentrated on the effects of acute stress but little is known of the effects of chronic stress. In clinical depression, stress during the six months preceding the onset of the illness is of importance in the genesis of the disease although there is depressive illness that occurs in the absence of life events. Cortisol level seems to be one of the relevant factors common to both depression and decrease in immune response. A decrease in immune response following stress seems paradoxical at first sight, yet we have seen that this reaction may be a protective mechanism against a loss of control in the immune reaction to stress.

It does not seem logical that an individual faced with stress should evolve with depression, a nonadaptive response. Although it is difficult to dissociate anxiety from depressive symptoms, we have proposed one explanation which is that depression may have a logical function in protecting the individual against increasing and noxious levels of anxiety.

However, the issue may not be primarily one of logic (13). Emotions are not logical. The study of evolving biographies of people, including episodes of illness, is concerned with issues that are certainly not those of logic. Laing quotes Sartre as saying, "There is no such thing as the psychological. Let us say that one can improve the biography of a person" (95; and 13, p. 354).

The overall conclusion one can make from the evidence presented in this chapter is that there are important connections by which the CNS can affect the immune system, and vice versa. Depression appears to be associated with a suppression of immune responses, and the intricate mechanisms of this relationship require much more work, for example, on the detailed immunological networks of lymphokines currently being unraveled. Most immunologists have tended to neglect the role in immunoregulation of neural and other hormones of nonimmunological origin, and from the viewpoint of the psychiatrist it seems that a clearer distinction between anxiety and depression would help in clarifying the effect of states of mind on immunity. In more physical diseases the reason for the involvement of depression clearly varies from disease to disease; again, more work will help in dissecting mechanisms.

We conclude with a plea that advances in understanding the relationships between depression and immunity can only come from well-coordinated, scientifically designed clinical studies involving both psychiatrists and immunologists.

REFERENCES

1. Aarstad, H. J., Gaudernack, G., & Seljelid, R. (1983). Stress causes reduced natural killer activity in mice. *Scand. J. Immunol.*, *18*, 461.
2. Abraham, A. D., & Buga, G. (1976). 3H-testosterone distribution and binding in rat thymus cells in vivo. *Mol. Cell. Biochem.*, *13*, 157.
3. Ader, R., & Cohen, N. (1985). High time for psychoimmunology. *Nature*, *315*, 103.
4. Ahlquist, J. (1976). Endocrine influences on lymphatic organs, immune responses, inflammation and autoimmunity. *Acta Endocrinol. (Copenhagen)*, *(Supp. 206)*, *3*, 1.
5. Albrecht, J., Helderman, J. H., Schlesser, M. A., & Rush, A. J. (1985). A controlled study of cellular immune function in affective disorders before and during somatic therapy. *Psychiatr. Res.*, *15*, 185.
6. Allen, A. D., & Tilkian, S. M. (1986). Depression correlated with cellular immunity in systemic immunodeficient Epstein Barr virus syndrome (SIDES). *J. Clin. Psychiatry*, *47*, 133.
7. Ambrose, C. T. (1970). The essential role of corticosteroids in the induction of the immune response in vitro. In G. E. W. Wolstenholme, & J. Knight (Eds.), *Hormones and immune response*. Ciba Study group no. 36. London: Churchill.
8. Aoki, N., Wakisaka, G., & Nagata, I. (1976). Effects of thyroxine on T-cell counts and tumour cell rejection in mice. *Acta Endocrinol. (Copenhagen)*, *81*, 104.
9. Ballieux, R. E. (Ed.) (1984). Psychoneuroimmunology and breakdown in adaptation: Interactions within the central nervous system, the immune and endocrine systems. In: *Breakdown in human adaptation to 'stress', towards a multidisciplinary approach*, Vol. II, Part 3. Dordrecht: Martinus Nijhoff.
10. Balow, J. E., Hurley, D. L., & Fauci, A. S. (1975). Immunosuppressive effects of glucocorticosteroids: Differential effects of acute vs chronic administration on cell-mediated immunity. *J. Immunol.*, *114*, 1072.
11. Bartrop, R. W., Lazarus, L., Luckhurst, E., Kiloh, L. G., & Penny, R. (1977). Depressed lymphocyte function after bereavement. *Lancet*, *1*, 834.
12. Baum, J. (1982). A review of the psychological aspects of rheumatic diseases. *Semin. Arth. Rheum.*, *11*, 352.
13. Bennette, G. (1969). Psychic and cellular aspects of isolation and identity impairment in cancer: A dialetic of alienation. *Ann. NY Acad. Sci.*, *164*, 352.
14. Beresford, T. P., Blow, F. C., & Hall, R. C. W. (1986). AIDS encephalitis mimicking alcohol dementia and depression. *Biol. Psychiatry*, *21*, 394.

15. BESEDOVSKY, H. O., DEL REY, A. E., & SORKIN, E. (1985). Immune-neuroendocrine interactions. *J. Immunol.*, *135*, 750s.
16. BESEDOVSKY, H. O., DEL REY, A. E., SORKIN, E., DAPRADA, M., BURRI, R., & HONEGGER, C. (1983). The immune response evokes changes in brain noradrenergic neurons. *Science*, *221*, 564.
17. BESEDOVSKY, H. O., DEL REY, A. E., SORKIN, E., DAPRADA, M., & KELLER, H. H. (1979). Immunoregulation mediated by the sympathetic nervous system. *Cell. Immunol.*, *48*, 346.
18. BESEDOVSKY, H., & SORKIN, E. (1977). Network of immune-neuroendocrine interactions. *Clin. Exp. Immunol.*, *27*, 1.
19. BESEDOVSKY, H., SORKIN, E., FELIX, D., & HAAS, H. (1977). Hypothalamic changes during the immune response. *Eur. J. Immunol.*, *7*, 323.
20. BESEDOVSKY, H., SORKIN, E., KELLER, M., & MULLER, J. (1975). Changes in blood hormone levels during the immune response. *Proc. Soc. Exp. Biol. Med.*, *150*, 466.
21. BLACK, S., HUMPHREY, J. H., & NIVEN, J. S. F. (1963). Inhibition of Mantoux reaction by direct suggestion under hypnosis. *Br. Med. J.*, *1*, 1649.
22. BLALOCK, J. E., JOHNSON, H. M., SMITH, E. M., & TORRES, B. A. (1984). Enhancement of the in vitro antibody response by thyrotropin. *Biochem. Biophys. Res. Commun.*, *125*, 30.
23. BOHUS, B. (1975). The hippocampus and the pituitary adrenal system hormones. In R. L. Isaacson & K. H. Pribram (Eds.), *The hippocampus*, Vol. 1: *Structure and development* (pp. 323–353). London: Plenum Press.
24. BOHUS, B. (1984). Neuroendocrine interactions with brain and behavior: A model for psychoneuroimmunology? In R. E. Ballieux (Ed.), *Breakdown in human adaptation to "stress,"* Vol. 2 (pp. 638–652). Dordrecht: Martinus Nijhoff.
25. BOURNE, H. R., LICHTENSTEIN, L. M., MELMON, K. L., HENNEY, C. S., WEINSTEIN, Y., & SHEARER, G. M. (1974). Modulation of inflammation and immunity by cyclic AMP: Receptors for vasoactive hormones and mediators of inflammation regulate many leukocyte functions. *Science*, *184*, 19.
26. BROWN, J. H., & PARASKEVAS, F. (1982). Cancer and depression: Cancer presenting with depressive illness: An autoimmune disease? *Br. J. Psychiatry*, *141*, 227.
27. BUKBERG, J., PENMAN, D., & HOLLAND, J. C. (1984). Depression in hospitalized cancer patients. *Psychosom. Med.*, *46*, 199.
28. CAKE, M. H., & LITWACK, G. (1975). The glucocorticoid receptor. In G. Litwack (Ed.), *Biochemical actions of hormones* (pp. 317–390). New York: Academic Press.
29. CALABRESE, J. R., SKWERER, R. G., BARNA, B., GULLEDGE, A. D., VALENZUELA, R., BUTKUS, A., SUBICHIN, S., & KRUPP, N. E. (1986). Depression, immunocompetence, and prostaglandins of the E series. *Psychiatr. Res.*, *17*, 41.
30. CANNON, W. B. (1915). *Bodily changes in pain, hunger, fear and rage*. New York: Appleton.
31. CATTANEO, R., SAIBENE, V., MARGONATO, A., & POZZA, G. (1977). In vitro effect of insulin on peripheral T-lymphocyte E-rosette function from normal and diabetic subjects. *Boll. Inst. Sieroter. Milan*, *56*, 139.
32. COBB, S. (1974). A model for life events and their consequences. In B. S. Dohrenwend & B. P. Dohrenwend (Eds.), *Stressful life events: Their nature and effects*. New York: Wiley.
33. COOPER, D. A., DUCKETT, M., PETTS, V., & PENNY, R. (1979). Corticosteroid enhancement of immunoglobulin synthesis by pokeweed mitogen-stimulated human lymphocytes. *Clin. Exp. Immunol.*, *37*, 145.
34. COWEN, P. G., & ANDERSON, I. M. (1985). 5HT neuroendocrinology: Changes during depressive illness and antidepressant drug treatment. In *Biology of depression* (pp. 71–89). Gaskell Psychiatric Series, Royal College of Psychiatrists.

35. Crawford, J. D., & McIvor, G. P. (1985). Group psychotherapy: Benefits in multiple sclerosis. *Arch. Phys. Med. Rehabil.*, *66*, 810.
36. Deakin, J. F. W., & Crow, T. J. (1986). Monamines, rewards and punishments: The anatomy and physiology of the affective disorders. In *The biology of depression* (pp. 1–25). Gaskell Psychiatric Series, Royal College of Psychiatrists.
37. Deberdt, R., Hooren, J. V., Biesbrouck, M., & Amery, W. (1976). Antinuclear factor positive mental depression: A single disease entity? *Biol. Psychiatry*, *11*, 69.
38. DeLisi, L. E., King, A. C., & Targum, S. (1984). Serum immunoglobulin concentrations in patients admitted to an acute psychiatric in-patient service. *Br. J. Psychiatry*, *145*, 661.
39. Denman, A. M. (1986). Immunity and depression. *Br. Med. J.*, *293*, 464.
40. Derogatis, L. R., Morrow, G. R., Fetting, J., Penman, D., Piasetsky, S., Schmale, A. M., Henrichs, M., & Carnicke, C. L. M. (1983). The prevalence of psychiatric disorders among cancer patients. *JAMA*, *249*, 751.
41. Deter, H. C. (1986). Cost benefit analysis of psychosomatic therapy in asthma. *J. Psychosom. Res.*, *30*, 173.
42. Deter, H. C., & Allert, G. (1983). Group therapy for asthma patients: A concept for the psychosomatic treatment of patients in a medical clinic—A controlled study. *Psychother. Psychosom.*, *40*, 95.
43. Dimsdale, J. E., & Moss, J. (1980). Plasma catecholamines in stress and exercise. *JAMA*, *243*, 340.
44. Dorian, B., Garfinkel, P., Brown, G., Shore, A., Gladman, D., & Keystone, E. (1982). Aberrations in lymphocyte subpopulations and function during psychological stress. *Clin. Exp. Immunol.*, *50*, 132.
45. Elliott, G. R., & Eisdorfer, C. (1982). *Stress and human health: Analysis and implications of research.* New York: Springer.
46. Eskola, A., Ruuskanen, O., Soppi, E., Viljanen, M. K., Jarvinen, M., Toivonen, H., & Kouvalainen, K. (1978). Effect of sport stress on lymphocyte transformation and antibody formation. *Clin. Exp. Immunol.*, *32*, 339.
47. Euker, J. E., Meites, J., & Riegle, G. D. (1975). Effects of acute stress on serum LH and prolactin in intact, castrate and dexamethasone-treated male rats. *Endocrinology*, *96*, 85.
48. Farris, E. J. (1938). Increase in lymphocytes in healthy persons under certain emotional states. *Am. J. Anat.*, *63*, 297.
49. Fauci, A. S., & Dale, D. C. (1974). The effect of in vivo hydrocortisone on subpopulations of human lymphocytes. *J. Clin. Invest.*, *53*, 240.
50. Fauman, M. A. (1982). The central nervous system and the immune system. *Biol. Psychiatry*, *17*, 1459.
51. Friedman, M., Byers, S. O., Rosenman, R. H., & Neuman, R. (1971). Coronary-prone individuals (type A behavior pattern) growth hormone responses. *JAMA*, *217*, 929.
52. Gavin, J. R. (1977). Polypeptide hormone receptors on lymphoid cells: Applications to the study of receptors alterations and radioreceptor assay of polypeptide hormones. In J. W. Hadden & R. G. Coffey (Eds.), *Immunopharmacology* (pp. 357–388). New York: Plenum Press.
53. Ghanta, V. K., Hiramoto, R. N., Solvason, H. B., & Spector, N. H. (1985). Neural and environmental influences on neoplasia and conditioning of NK activity. *J. Immunol.*, *135*, 848s.
54. Gillette, S., & Gillette, R. W. (1979). Changes in thymic estrogen receptor expression following orchidectomy. *Cell. Immunol.*, *42*, 194.
55. Gilman, S. C., Schwartz, J. M., Milner, R. J., Bloom, F. E., & Feldman, J. D. (1982). B-Endorphin enhances lymphocyte proliferative responses. *Proc. Natl. Acad. Sci. USA*, *79*, 4226.

56. Gisler, R. H. (1974). Stress and the hormonal regulation of the immune response in mice. *Psychother. Psychosom.*, *23*, 197.
57. Glaser, R., Kiecolt-Glaser, J. K., Stout, J. C., Tarr, K. L., Speicher, C. E., & Holliday, J. E. (1985). Stress-related impairments in cellular immunity. *Psychiatr. Res.*, *16*, 233.
58. Gold, M. S., Pottash, A. L. C., & Extein, I. (1982). "Symptomless" autoimmune thyroiditis in depression. *Psychiatr. Res.*, *6*, 261.
59. Gold, M. S., Pottash, A. C., & Mueller, E. A. (1981). Grades of thyroid failure in 100 depressed and anergic psychiatric inpatients. *Am. J. Psychiatry*, *138*, 253.
60. Golub, E. S. (1982). Connections between the nervous, haematopoietic and germ-cell systems. *Nature*, *299*, 483.
61. Gormley, G. J., Lowy, M. T., Reder, A. T., Hospelhorn, V. D., Antel, J. P., & Meltzer, H. Y. (1985). Glucocorticoid receptors in depression: Relationship to the dexamethasone suppression test. *Am. J. Psychiatry*, *142*, 1278.
62. Gray, J. A. (1982). *The neuropsychology of anxiety: An enquiry into the functions of the septo-hippocampal system*. Oxford: Oxford University Press.
63. Gray, J., & Hoffenberg, R. (1985). Thyrotoxicosis and stress. *Q. J. Med.*, *54*, 153.
64. Grossman, C. J., Nathan, P., & Sholiton, L. J. (1978). Specific androgen receptor in the thymus of the castrate male rat. *Biol. Reprod.*, *18 (Suppl. 1)*, 48A.
65. Grossman, C. J., Sholiton, L. J., Blaha, G. C., & Nathan, P. (1979). Rat thymic estrogen receptor. II. Physiological properties. *J. Steroid Biochem.*, *11*, 1241.
66. Guillemin, R., Vargo, T., Rossier, J., Minick, S., Ling, N., Rivier, J., Vale, W., & Bloom, F. (1977). Beta-endorphin and adrenocorticotropin are secreted concomitantly by the pituitary gland. *Science*, *197*, 1367.
67. Guyre, P. M., Bodwell, J. E., & Munck, A. (1981). Glucocorticoid actions on the immune system: Inhibition of production of an Fc receptor-augmenting factor. *J. Steroid Biochem.*, *15*, 35.
68. Guyre, P. M., Morganelli, P. M., & Miller, R. (1983). Recombinant immune interferon increases immunoglobulin G Fc receptors on cultured human mononuclear phagocytes. *J. Clin. Invest.*, *72*, 393.
69. Hadden, J. W., Hadden, E. M., & Middleton, E. (1970). Lymphocyte blast transformation. I. Demonstration of adrenergic receptors in human peripheral lymphocytes. *Cell. Immunol.*, *1*, 583.
70. Hall, N. R., McGillis, J. P., Spangelo, B. L., & Goldstein, A. L. (1985). Evidence that thymosins and other biologic response modifiers can function as neuroactive immunotransmitters. *J. Immunol.*, *135*, 806s.
71. Heijnen, C. J., Bevers, C., Kavelaars, A., & Ballieux, R. E. (1986). Effect of alpha-endorphin on the antigen-induced primary antibody response of human blood B cells in vitro. *J. Immunol.*, *136*, 213.
72. Helderman, J. H., & Strom, T. B. (1978). Specific insulin binding site on T and B lymphocytes as a marker of cell activation. *Nature*, *274*, 62.
73. Henry, J. P., Meehan, J. P., & Stephens, P. M. (1967). The use of psychosocial stimuli to induce prolonged systolic hypertension in mice. *Psychosom. Med.*, *29*, 408.
74. Hinkle, L. E., & Wolf, S. (1952a). Importance of life stress in course and management of diabetes mellitus. *JAMA*, *148*, 513.
75. Hinkle, L. E., & Wolf, S. (1952b). A summary of experimental evidence relating life stress to diabetes mellitus. *J. Mt. Sinai Hosp.*, *19*, 537.
76. Hinkle, L. E., Evans, F. M., & Wolf, S. (1951). Studies in diabetes mellitus: Life history of three persons with relatively mild, stable diabetes, and relation of significant experiences in their lives to the onset and course of the disease. *Psychosom. Med.*, *13*, 184.
77. Hirata-Hibi, M. (1967). Plasma cell reaction and thymic germinal centers after a chronic form of electric stress. *J. Reticuloendothel. Soc.*, *4*, 370.

78. HOLDEN, C. (1980). Behavioral medicine: An emergent field. *Science, 209*, 479.
79. HOLSBOER, F., DOERR, H. G., GERKEN, A., MULLER, O. A., & SIPPELL, W. G. (1984). Cortisol, 11-deoxycortisol, and ACTH concentrations after dexamethasone in depressed patients and healthy volunteers. *Psychiatr. Res., 11*, 15.
80. ILFELD, D. N., KRAKAUER, R. S., & BLAESE, R. M. (1977). Suppression of the human autologous mixed lymphocyte reaction by physiologic concentrations of hydrocortisone. *J. Immunol., 119*, 428.
81. ISAACSON, R. L. (1964). *The limbic system*. New York: Plenum Press.
82. JACOBS, S., & OSTFELD, A. (1977). An epidemiological review of the mortality of bereavement. *Psychosom. Med., 39*, 344.
83. JANKOVIC, B. D. (1985). Neural type hypersensitivity in psychiatric disorders with immunologic features. *J. Immunol., 135*, 853s.
84. JANKOVIC, B. D., JAKULIC, S., & HORVAT, J. (1980). Schizophrenia and other psychiatric diseases: Evidence for neurotissue hypersensitivity. *Clin. Exp. Immunol., 40*, 515.
85. JOASOO, A., & MCKENZIE, J. M. (1976). Stress and the immune response in rats. *Int. Arch. Allergy Appl. Immunol., 50*, 659.
86. JOFFE, R. T., ROY-BYRNE, P. P., UDHE, T. W., & POST, R. M. (1984). Thyroid function and affective illness: A reappraisal. *Biol. Psychiatry, 19*, 1685.
87. JOHNSON, H. M., SMITH, E. M., TORRES, B. E., & BLALOCK, J. E. (1982). Regulation of the in vitro antibody response by neuroendocrine hormones. *Proc. Natl. Acad. Sci. USA, 79*, 4171.
88. JOHNSON, H. M., TORRES, B. A., SMITH, E. M., DION, L. D., & BLALOCK, J. E. (1984). Regulation of lymphokine (gamma-interferon) production by corticotrophin. *J. Immunol., 132*, 246.
89. KANDIL, O., & BORYSENKO, M. (1984). Stress promotes lymphosarcoma growth in C3H/HeJ mice. Possible role of impaired NK cells. *Fed. Proc., 43*, 1753.
90. KELLER, S. E., WEISS, J. M., SCHLEIFER, S. J., MILLER, N. E., & STEIN, M. (1981). Suppression of immunity by stress: Effect of a graded series of stressors on lymphocyte stimulation in the rat. *Science, 213*, 1397.
91. KRONFOL, Z., HOUSE, J. D., SILVA, J., GREDEN, J., & CARROLL, B. (1986). Depression, urinary free cortisol excretion and lymphocyte function. *Br. J. Psychiatry, 148*, 70.
92. KRONFOL, Z., SILVA, J., GREDEN, J., DEMBINSKI, S., & CARROLL, B. J. (1982). Cell-mediated immunity in melancholia. *Psychosom. Med., 44*, 304.
93. KRONFOL, Z., SILVA, J., GREDEN, J., DEMBINSKI, S., GARDNER, R., & CARROLL, B. (1983). Impaired lymphocyte function in depressive illness. *Life Sci., 33*, 241.
94. KRUG, U., KRUG, F., & CUATRECASAS, P. (1972). Emergence of insulin receptors on human lymphocytes during in vitro transformation. *Proc. Natl. Acad. Sci. USA, 69*, 2604.
95. LAING, R. D. (1959). *The divided self*. London: Tavistock.
96. LANDIS, B., JOVANOVIC, L., LANDIS, E., PETERSON, C. M. GROSHEN, S., JOHNSON, K., & MILLER, N. E. (1985). Effect of stress reduction on daily glucose range in previously stabilized insulin-dependent diabetic patients. *Diabetes Care, 8*, 624.
97. LARCOMBE, N. A., & WILSON, P. H. (1984). An evaluation of cognitive-behavior therapy for depression in patients with multiple sclerosis. *Br. J. Psychiatry, 145*, 366.
98. LAUDENSLAGER, M. L., RYAN, S. M., DRUGAN, R. C., HYSON, R. L., & MAIER, S. F. (1983). Coping and immunosuppression: Inescapable but not escapable shock suppresses lymphocyte proliferation. *Science, 221*, 568.
99. LEVINE, S., GOLDMAN, L., & COOVER, G. D. (1972). Expectancy and the pituitary-adrenal system. In *Physiology, emotion and psychosomatic illness* (pp. 281–291). Ciba Foundation Symposium. Amsterdam: Elsevier.
100. LEWIS, J. W., CANNON, J. T., & LIEBESKIND, J. C. (1980). Opioid and non-opioid mechanisms of stress analgesia. *Science, 208*, 623.

101. Linn, B. S., Linn, M. W., & Jensen, J. (1982). Degree of depression and immune responsiveness. *Psychosom. Med.*, *44*, 128.
102. Linn, M. W., Linn, B. S., Skyler, J. S., & Jensen, J. (1983). Stress and immune function in diabetes mellitus. *Clin. Immunol. Immunopathol.*, *27*, 223.
103. Lowy, M. T., Reder, A. T., Antel, J. P., & Meltzer, H. Y. (1984). Glucocorticoid resistance in depression: The dexamethasone suppression test and lymphocyte sensitivity to dexamethasone. *Am. J. Psychiatry*, *141*, 1365.
104. McIvor, G. P., Riklan, M., & Reznikoff, M. (1984). Depression in multiple sclerosis as a function of length and severity of illness, age, remissions, and perceived social support. *J. Clin. Psychol.*, *40*, 1028.
105. McNeill, D. N. (1973). *Mortality among the widowed in Connecticut*. New Haven, CT: Yale University Press.
106. Maddox, J. (1984). Psychoimmunology before its time. *Nature*, *309*, 400.
107. Mandler, R. N., Biddison, W. E., Mandler, R., & Serrate, S. A. (1986). Beta-endorphin augments the cytolytic activity and interferon production of natural killer cells. *J. Immunol.*, *136*, 934.
108. Mason, J. W. (1968). A review of psychoendocrine research on the pituitary-adrenal cortical system. *Psychosom. Med.*, *30*, 576.
109. Mason, J. W. (1971). A re-evaluation of the concept of nonspecificity in stress theory. *J. Psychiatr. Res.*, *8*, 323.
110. Mason, J. W. (1975). In L. Levi (Ed.), *Emotions: Their parameters and measurement* (pp. 143–181). New York: Raven Press.
111. Matussek, P., Agerer, D., & Seibt, G. (1984). Aggression and allergic disorder in depressives. *J. Psychosom. Res.*, *28*, 205.
112. Meltzer, H. Y., Umberkoman-Wiita, B., Robertson, A., Tricou, B. J., Lowy, M., & Perline, R. (1984a). Effect of 5-hydroxytryptophan on serum cortisol levels in major affective disorders. I. Enhanced response in depression and mania. *Arch. Gen. Psychiatry*, *41*, 366.
113. Meltzer, H. Y., Perline, R., Tricou, B. J., Lowy, M., & Robertson, A. (1984b). Effect of 5-hydroxytryptophan on serum cortisol levels in major affective disorders. II. Relation to suicide, psychosis and depressive symptoms. *Arch. Gen. Psychiatry*, *41*, 379.
114. Monjan, A., & Collector, M. I. (1977). Stress-induced modulation of the immune response. *Science*, *196*, 307.
115. Munck, A., Guyre, P. M., & Holbrook, N. J. (1984). Physiological functions of glucocorticoids in stress and their relation to pharmacological actions. *Endocrine Rev.*, *5*, 25.
116. Neild, J. E., & Cameron, I. R. (1985). Bronchoconstriction in response to suggestion: Its prevention by an inhaled anticholinergic agent. *Br. Med. J.*, *290*, 674.
117. Nemeroff, C. B., Simon, J. F., Haggerty, J. J., & Evans, D. L. (1985). Antithyroid antibodies in depressed patients. *Am. J. Psychiatry*, *142*, 840.
118. Nemeroff, C. B., Widerlov, E., Bissette, G., Walleus, H., Karlsson, I., Eklund, K., Kilts, C. D., Loosen, P. T., & Vale, W. (1984). Elevated concentrations of CSF corticotropin releasing factor-like immunoreactivity in depressed patients. *Science*, *226*, 1342.
119. Noyes, R., & Kathol, R. G. (1986). Depression and cancer. *Psychiatr. Dev.*, *2*, 77.
120. O'Dorisio, M. S., Wood, C. L., & O'Dorisio, T. M. (1985). Vasoactive intestinal peptide and neuropeptide modulation of the immune response. *J. Immunol.*, *135*, 792s.
121. Orsulak, P. J., Crowley, G., Schlesser, M. A., Giles, D., Fairchild, C., & Rush, A. J. (1985). Free triiodothyronine (T3) and thyroxine (T4) in a group of unipolar depressed patients and normal subjects. *Biol. Psychiatry*, *20*, 1047.
122. Papez, J. W. (1937). A proposed mechanism of emotion. *Arch. Neurol. Psychiatry*, *38*, 725.

123. Payan, D. G., & Goetzl, E. J. (1985). Modulation of lymphocyte function by sensory neuropeptides. *J. Immunol.*, *135*, 783s.

124. Paykel, E. S., Myers, J. K., Dienelt, M. N., Klerman, G. L., Lindenthal, J. J., & Pepper, M. P. (1969). Life events and depression: A controlled study. *Arch. Gen. Psychiatry*, *21*, 753.

125. Penn, I. (1981). Depressed immunity and the development of cancer. *Clin. Exp. Immunol.*, *46*, 459.

126. Pert, C. B., Ruff, M. R., Weber, R. J., & Herkenham, M. (1985). Neuropeptides and their receptors: A psychosomatic network. *J. Immunol.*, *135*, 820s.

127. Pitkin, D. H. (1965). Effect of physiological stress on the delayed hypersensitivity reaction. *Proc. Soc. Exp. Biol. Med.*, *120*, 350.

128. Rasmussen, A. F., Spencer, E. S., & Marsh, J. T. (1959). Decrease in susceptibility of mice to passive anaphylaxis following avoidance-learning stress. *Proc. Soc. Exp. Biol. Med.*, *100*, 878.

129. Reinherz, E. L., Weiner, H. L., Hauser, S. L., Cohen, J. A., Distaso, J. A., & Schlossman, S. F. (1980). Loss of suppressor T cells in active multiple sclerosis: Analysis with monoclonal antibodies. *N. Engl. J. Med.*, *303*, 125.

130. Reite, M., Harbeck, R., & Hoffman, A. (1981). Altered cellular immune response following peer separation. *Life Sci.*, *29*, 1133.

131. Richman, D. P., & Arnason, B. G. W. (1979). Nicotinic acetylcholine receptor: Evidence for a functionally distinct receptor on human lymphocytes. *Proc. Natl. Acad. Sci. USA*, *76*, 4632.

132. Riley, V. (1975). Mouse mammary tumors: Alteration of incidence as apparent function of stress. *Science*, *189*, 465.

133. Riley, V. (1981). Psychoneuroendocrine influences on immunocompetence and neoplasia. *Science*, *212*, 1100.

134. Rogers, M. P., Dubey, D., & Reich, P. (1979). The influence of the psyche and the brain on immunity and disease susceptibility: A critical review. *Psychosom. Med.*, *41*, 147.

135. Roitt, I. M., Brostoff, J., & Male, D. K. (1985). *Immunology*. Edinburgh: Churchill Livingstone.

136. Roos, R. P., Davis, K., & Meltzer, H. Y. (1985). Immunoglobulin studies in patients with psychiatric diseases. *Arch. Gen. Psychiatry*, *42*, 124.

137. Rosenblatt, S., Oreskes, I., Meadow, H., et al. (1968). The relationship between antigammaglobulin activity and depression. *Am. J. Psychiatry*, *124*, 1640.

138. Rosler, M., Bellaire, W., Gressnich, N., Giannitsis, D., & Jarovici, A. (1983). HLA antigens in schizophrenia, major depressive disorder and schizoaffective disorder. *Med. Microbiol. Immunol.*, *172*, 57.

139. Rossier, J., French, E. D., Rivier, C., Ling, N., Guillemin, R., & Bloom, F. E. (1977). Footshock induced stress increases beta-endorphin levels in blood but not brain. *Nature*, *270*, 618.

140. Rossier, J., French, E., Rivier, C., Shibasaki, T., Guillemin, R., & Bloom, F. E. (1980). Stress-induced release of prolactin: Blockade by dexamethasone and naloxone may indicate beta-endorphin mediation. *Proc. Natl. Acad. Sci. USA*, *77*, 666.

141. Roszkowski, W., Plaut, M., & Lichtenstein, L. M. (1977). Selective display of histamine receptors on lymphocytes. *Science*, *165*, 683.

142. Rytel, M. W., & Kilbourne, E. D. (1966). The influence of cortisone on experimental viral infection. VIII. Suppression by cortisone of interferon formation in mice injected with Newcastle disease virus. *J. Exp. Med.*, *123*, 767.

143. Schiffer, R., & Babigian, H. (1984). Behavioral disorders in multiple sclerosis, temporal lobe epilepsy, and amyotrophic lateral sclerosis: An epidemiological study. *Arch. Neurol.*, *41*, 1067.

144. Schleifer, S. J., Keller, S. E., Siris, S. G., Davis, K. L., & Stein, M. (1985). Depres-

sion and immunity. Lymphocyte function in ambulatory depressed patients, hospitalized schizophrenic patients and patients hospitalized for herniorrhaphy. *Arch. Gen. Psychiatry*, *42*, 129.

145. Schleifer, S. J., Keller, S. E., Meyerson, A. T., Raskin, M. J., Davis, K. L., & Stein, M. (1984). Lymphocyte function in major depressive disorder. *Arch. Gen. Psychiatry*, *41*, 484.
146. Selye, H. (1950). Stress. The physiology and pathology of exposure to stress. *Acta Med., Montreal.*
147. Sengar, D. P. S., Waters, B. G. H., Dunne, J. V., & Bouer, I. M. (1982). Lymphocyte subpopulations and mitogenic responses of lymphocytes in manic-depressive disorders. *Biol. Psychiatry*, *17*, 1017.
148. Shavit, Y., Terman, G. W., Martin, F. C., Lewis, J. W., Liebeskind, J. C., & Gale, R. P. (1985). Stress, opioid peptides, the immune system, and cancer. *J. Immunol.*, *135*, 834s.
149. Singh, U., Millson, D. S., Smith, P. A., & Owen, J. J. T. (1979). Identification of beta-adrenoceptors during thymocyte ontogeny in mice. *Eur. J. Immunol.*, *9*, 31.
150. Smelik, P. G., & Vermes, I. (1980). The regulation of the pituitary adrenal system in mammals. In I. C. Jones & I. W. Henderson (Eds.), *General, comparative and clinical endocrinology of the adrenal cortex*, Vol. 3, (pp. 1–55). New York: Academic Press.
151. Smith, E. M., Phan, M., Kruger, T. E., Coppenhaver, D. H., & Blalock, J. E. (1983). Human lymphocyte production of immunoreactive thyrotropin. *Proc. Natl. Acad. Sci. USA*, *80*, 6010.
152. Smith, E. M., Harbour-McMenamin, D., & Blalock, J. E. (1985). Lymphocyte production of endorphins and endorphin-mediated immunoregulatory activity. *J. Immunol.*, *135*, 779s.
153. Smith, G. R., McKenzie, J. M., Marmer, D. J., & Steele, R. W. (1985). Psychologic modulation of the human immune response to varicella zoster. *Arch. Intern. Med.*, *145*, 2110.
154. Snow, E. C. (1985). Insulin and growth hormone function as minor growth factors that potentiate lymphocyte activation. *J. Immunol.*, *135*, 776s.
155. Solomon, G. F. (1969). Stress and antibody response in rats. *Int. Arch. Allergy Appl. Immunol.*, *35*, 97.
156. Solomon, G. F., Levine, S., & Kraft, J. K. (1968). Early experience and immunity. *Nature*, *220*, 821.
157. Solomon, G. F., & Amkraut, A. A. (1981). Psychoneuroendocrinological effects on the immune response. *Annu. Rev. Microbiol.*, *35*, 155.
158. Stein, M., Keller, S. E., & Schleifer, S. J. (1985). Stress and immunomodulation: The role of depression and neuroendocrine function. *J. Immunol.*, *135*, 827s.
159. Stein, M., Schiavi, R. C., & Camerino, M. (1976). Influence of brain and behavior on the immune system. *Science*, *191*, 435.
160. Suarez, B. K., & Reich, T. (1984). HLA and major affective disorder. *Arch. Gen. Psychiatry*, *41*, 22.
161. Sutton, R. E., Koob, G. F., Le Moal, J., Rivier, J., & Vale, W. (1982). Corticotrophin releasing factor produces behavioural activation in rats. *Nature*, *297*, 331.
162. Syvalahti, E., Eskola, J., Ruuskanen, O., & Laine, T. (1985). Nonsuppression of cortisol in depression and immune function. *Prog. Neuro-psychopharm. Biol. Psychiatry*, *9*, 413.
163. Tavadia, H. B., Fleming, K. A., Hume, P. D., & Simpson, H. W. (1975). Circadian rhythmicity of human plasma cortisol and PHA-induced lymphocyte transformation. *Clin. Exp. Immunol.*, *22*, 190.
164. Thomas, A., Goldney, R., & Phillips, P. (1983). Depression, electroconvulsive therapy and diabetes mellitus. *Aust. NZ J. Psychiatry*, *17*, 289.

165. Thompson, E. A., & De Wied, D. (1973). The relationship between the antidiuretic activity of rat eye plexus blood and passive avoidance behaviour. *Physiol. Behav.*, *11*, 377.

166. Vandenbergh, R. L., Sussman, K. E., & Titus, C. C. (1966). Effects of hypnotically induced acute emotional stress on carbohydrate and lipid metabolism in patients with diabetes mellitus. *Psychosom. Med.*, *28*, 382.

167. Vessey, S. H. (1964). Effects of grouping on levels of circulating antibodies in mice. *Proc. Soc. Exp. Biol. Med.*, *115*, 252.

168. Wagner, V., Andrlikova, J., & Palek, V. (1975). Immunoglobulins under the influence of non-specific factors. II. The influence of work-stress on levels of immunoglobulins (IgG, IgA, IgM) of miners in uranium mines. *Z. Immunol. Forsch.*, *148*, 356.

169. Whitlock, F. A., & Siskind, M. M. (1980). Depression as a major symptom of multiple sclerosis. *J. Neurol. Neurosurg. Psychiatry*, *43*, 861.

170. Whybrow, P. C., & Prange, A. J. (1981). A hypothesis of thyroid catecholamine receptor interaction. Its relevance to affective illness. *Arch. Gen. Psychiatry*, *38*, 106.

171. Wistar, R., & Hildemann, W. H. (1960). Effect of stress on skin transplantation immunity in mice. *Science*, *131*, 159.

172. Young, M., Benjamin, B., & Wallis, C. (1963). The mortality of widowers. *Lancet*, *2*, 454.

173. Yu, D. T. Y., Clements, P. J., Paulus, H. E., Peter, J. B., Levy, J., & Barnett, E. V. (1974). Human lymphocyte subpopulations. Effect of corticosteroids. *J. Clin. Invest.*, *53*, 565.

4

THYROID FUNCTION IN DEPRESSION

S. P. Calloway, M.D., M.R.C.Psych., M.R.C.P.

Consultant Psychiatrist, Fulbourn Hospital, Cambridge, United Kingdom

INTRODUCTION

The thyroid hormones, thyroxine (T_4) and triiodothyronine (T_3), are released by the thyroid gland in response to thyroid-stimulating hormone (TSH), a glycoprotein secreted by the anterior pituitary gland. TSH release from the anterior pituitary is under the stimulatory control of thyrotropin-releasing hormone (TRH), a hypothalamic tripeptide, and the inhibitory control of somatostatin, a hypothalamic polypeptide. In addition, dopamine and melatonin act at the pituitary level to influence TSH output. The hypothalamopituitary-thyroid (HPT) axis also has a negative feedback system, so that as thyroid hormone levels rise, the secretion of TSH diminishes. This feedback probably acts at the pituitary level, and T_3 appears to be more important in this respect than thyroxine.

There is evidence to suggest a circadian rhythm of TSH output. There is less secretion during the day and increased secretion just before sleep (81, 101). TSH levels then decline during sleep (80). If sleep is interrupted, the levels remain high. The circadian rhythm of thyroxine and T_3 is less obvious and may be due to variation in plasma proteins. There is a seasonal variation in thyroid hormone levels, with higher levels in the colder months (43).

MEASUREMENT

Basal levels of T_4, T_3, and TSH are generally measured by radioimmunoassay (RIA) (7, 14, 78, 100). The TRH test involves measuring the TSH response to a bolus dose of TRH (3). It has been shown that the TSH response increases in a linear fashion with increasing doses of TRH up to a dose of 400 μg, but larger doses fail to produce any greater response (40, 89). The TSH response may be diminished (blunted), augmented, or delayed. In general, a blunted response is due either to increased thyroid activity, as in hyperthyroidism, leading to negative feedback, or to failure of the pituitary gland to respond to the TRH, as in hypothyroidism due to pituitary gland dysfunction (9).

VARIATIONS IN HPT AXIS FUNCTION

Thyroid function varies throughout life; there are high thyroid levels during childhood, followed by a decline at puberty and then a gradual rise in adolescence. Thyroid function is relatively stable between the ages of 20 and 50, except during pregnancy when thyroid levels increase. In older age there are no changes in absolute thyroid hormone levels, but there appears to be a gradual decline in thyroid activity. The TSH response to TRH also decreases with age, particularly after the age of 60 (89). Gender may also influence thyroid activity, with some authors reporting greater TSH responses to TRH in women (9). Estrogens, and the contraceptive pill, on the whole appear to produce augmented TSH responses (9).

Fasting tends to produce blunted TSH responses to TRH, although in protein-calorie malnutrition there are exaggerated and sustained TSH responses, with high basal TSH levels. These are probably due to low T_3 levels (9). In liver disease and a number of other physical illnesses there are decreased levels of T_3. Many factors, including physical exertion, trauma, weight loss, fever, debilitation, and surgery, may result in increased T_4 levels (43).

Many drugs are reported to affect the TRH-TSH responses. Theophylline is a mediator of TRH-induced TSH release, and there is increased TSH response after theophylline ingestion (9). L-dopa, on the other hand, appears to cause blunting of the TSH response, probably by a direct pituitary action (19). Chlorpromazine has been shown to augment the TSH response (55). Kierkegaard et al. (56) also found that haloperidol augmented the TSH response as well as increasing basal TSH levels in 10 normal volunteers. Tricyclic antidepressants have nonspecific effects, sometimes appearing to raise thyroxine levels and at other times to diminish them (35).

Lithium has been shown to decrease T_4 levels and result in exaggerated TRH-TSH responses (90, 95). It is possible that these changes may be related in some way to the therapeutic effect of lithium.

Lazarus et al. (65) showed that lithium alters thyroid function in up to a half of treated patients, most commonly producing a shift toward subclinical hypothyroidism, with increased TSH responses to TRH. Clinical hypothyroidism develops in 5% to 17% of patients on lithium (17, 79). Calabrese et al. (10) suggested that these changes may be related to the presence of antibodies. However, Lazarus et al. (65) found that there was no relationship between the development of augmented TSH responses to TRH after lithium treatment and previous antibody status. Patients with rapid-cycling manic-depressive disorder (those with four or more affective episodes in a year) seem to be more likely to develop hypothyroidism (both clinical and subclinical) on lithium treatment (13, 17). However, hypothyroidism may be more common in rapid-cycling patients who are not on lithium (24).

There is much early work on the effects of "stress" on the HPT axis. It was shown that the recollection of unpleasant experiences, difficult interviews, examinations, watching horror films, and other forms of simulated stress led to increases in measures of thyroid functions such as plasma-bound iodine (PBI) (42, 74, 99, 105).

THE HPT AXIS IN DEPRESSION

Early studies of thyroid function in psychiatric patients relied on indirect methods of measuring thyroid activity. The findings were conflicting and inconclusive (28, 76).

With the development of a convenient method for estimating PBI (5), several studies were undertaken with psychiatric patients, including those with affective disorders. Gibbons et al. (27), in a study of 19 depressed patients, found no difference between their mean PBI level and that of controls. They did, however, demonstrate that in the depressed patients there was a slight decrease in mean PBI on clinical recovery. Board et al. (8) found that depressed patients had a higher mean PBI than controls. They also found that retarded depressed patients had higher PBI levels than nonretarded patients. They also demonstrated that PBI levels dropped on clinical recovery.

A more recent study using the PBI, that of Ferrari (26), reported that 65% of 80 female patients with depression had raised PBI levels. He reported that those with endogenous depression were particularly likely to have a raised PBI, with 73% of these patients having a high PBI. He also reported that the PBI was related to anxiety levels in the patients. In 7 of 10 cases a fall in the PBI was associated with marked clinical improvement. This study did not employ controls, but used laboratory criteria to judge elevation of PBI. The criteria for selection were not stated, nor was information given on whether patients were drug-free. Yamaguchi et al. (112) found no difference in PBI between 35 depressed patients and 15 normal patients. In this case it was stated that the patients were not drug-free, with most of them being on some form of psychotropic medication. They also reported that in 12 patients who were followed up the mean PBI fell on recovery.

THYROID HORMONE LEVELS

Whybrow et al. (109) found that 6 of 30 depressed patients had levels of thyroxine (T_4) that were in the hyperthyroid range. These fell to normal within a week of treatment. There was no correlation between T_4 levels and depression or anxiety as measured by the Hamilton Rating Scale. These authors subsequently reported that in their populations of depressed patients they find that about 5% of the female patients have thyroid function tests suggestive of marginal hypothyroidism (108). Takahashi et al. (94) found a mean free thyroxine index (FTI) higher in 36 depressed patients, who were on diazepam, than in 23 nondepressed medical patients. A retrospective study of 115 patients by Kolakowska and Swigar (62) reported on the estimated free thyroxine (EFT), a measure of thyroxine and binding capacity, finding that the EFT was higher in depression than in alcohol abuse. The EFT was related to the level of depression and also to anxiety and agitation and was highest in the psychotic depressives. Targum et al. (96) found raised T_4 levels in 54 patients who met the DSM-III criteria for major depressive disorder as compared to 19 nondepressed psychiatric patients. The results, however, were only statistically significant for the male patients.

The studies of Kierkegaard et al. (53–56) and Kierkegaard and Faber (51) have generally reported high T_4 and FTI values in patients with depression that fell on clinical recovery. They also reported that in some patients with endogenous depression the levels were in the hyperthyroid range, but that T_3 and free T_3 index were normal (53). However, some studies report low T_3 levels in depressed patients (46).

A number of studies have measured reverse T_3 in affective disorders. Kjellman et al. (60) concluded that generally the results were inconclusive, but that in the most severely depressed patients there is a tendency for high reverse T_3 levels. They suggest that this might be a nonspecific effect in that in severe chronic illnesses and with physical stress there is a preferential degradation of T_4 to reverse T_3 instead of T_3 (also accounting for the low T_3 in severe illness).

In contrast to the above studies there are a number of reports of decreased levels of thyroid hormones in patients with depression. Rybakowski and Sowinski (88) found low FTI values in four unipolar and five bipolar depressed patients. The sex of the patients was not mentioned, nor whether patients were on drugs or not. Yamaguchi et al. (112) reported a lower mean FTI in 16 depressed patients, some of whom were on drugs, than in 23 normal subjects. In a study of 20 depressed inpatients, all women, Rinieris et al. (85) found the mean FTI to be lower than in control patients. The control patients, however, were inpatients with somatic illnesses. In addition, the depressed patients were being treated with diazepam during the tests. In a subsequent study Rinieris et al. (86) reported that in drug-free depressed women the FTI was lower in psychotic depressives than neurotic depressives, and that in both groups the FTI was lower than in nondepressed psychiatric controls. Gold et al. (32, 33) report that about 10% of depressed inpatients have some degree of hypothyroidism, about half of these being clinically hypothyroid.

Despite the conflicting results with regard to the levels of PBI or thyroid hormones in depressed patients, certain general conclusions do emerge. Longitudinal studies and studies that have measured PBI, T_4, or FTI levels before and after clinical recovery indicate that thyroid hormone levels fall upon clinical recovery (6, 8, 51, 53–55, 109, 112). However, some patients, more usually female, have low levels of thyroid hormones during depression (84, 85, 108). Studies of the TRH test in depressed patients also reveal a subgroup of patients with decreased thyroid function (12, 97).

Depressed patients with raised thyroid levels have been reported as being more severely depressed, more retarded (8), and more anxious and agitated (26, 62) than those with normal levels. There is also a suggestion that there may be differences between patients with unipolar and bipolar depression. Unipolar patients with depression may be more likely to have higher levels of thyroid hormones during depression, decreasing on clinical recovery, whereas those with bipolar depression show the opposite tendency (6, 56).

TSH

There have been no consistent results from measuring basal levels of TSH in depression. Dewhurst et al. (20) reported that TSH levels were high in some patients with depression, hypomania, and paranoid schizophrenia. More recent studies have measured basal levels of TSH as part of the TRH test. Most studies have not found TSH to be elevated in depression (68). Targum et al. (96) reported no differences in levels in women, but lower levels of TSH in depressed men. Kierkegaard et al. (56), in a large study of various groups of depressed patients, found no marked differences in TSH levels although 10 patients with reactive depression had high TSH levels. However, many of the patients were on medication. Maeda et al. (73) found lower TSH levels in 13 depressed patients than in 16 normal volunteers. Some studies of TSH levels in patients during depression and on recovery have not reported any change in levels with improved clinical status (25, 51), but Kjellman et al. (61) reported that TSH levels tended to be low in depression and increased on recovery.

Weeke and Weeke (104), in a study of 19 patients with endogenous depression, found a shift in the circadian rhythm of TSH secretion. They found a diminution in nocturnal TSH secretion, bringing the nocturnal levels closer to the daytime levels. In patients with more severe depression there was least difference between nocturnal and daytime secretion. Golstein et al. (36), in a small study of six normal subjects, five patients with bipolar depression, and eight with unipolar depression, found that the patients with bipolar depression did not differ from the normal subjects, but that those with unipolar depression had lower mean 24-hr TSH secretions, mainly due to the loss of the nocturnal increase in TSH secretion. This confirmed the finding (104) that there is a lower sleep/wake ratio in some depressed patients.

The above studies used RIA to assay TSH and would thus be unable to measure lower levels of TSH and establish whether TSH levels were suppressed. The newer immunoradiometric (IRMA) methods are sensitive enough to ascertain whether suppression has taken place on a basal sample (11). Thus, in the future it will be possible to use a basal TSH result instead of the TRH test. The results correlate closely with those of the TRH test, so that a high basal TSH level corresponds to an augmented TSH test result, and a low basal TSH to a blunted TRH test result. In conjunction with high thyroid levels, a low basal TSH would indicate suppression due to negative feedback. However, in the presence of low thyroid hormone levels, a low TSH result probably reflects subclinical hypopituitarism.

TRH TEST

In the course of investigating the therapeutic efficacy of TRH in patients with depression, Prange et al. (83) and Kastin et al. (49) found that a proportion of depressed patients appeared to have a blunted TSH response to a bolus dose of TRH. Ehrensing et al. (21) reported that three of eight patients with severe depression had blunted TSH response to 1000 μg of TRH, and the three patients with blunted responses were the most deeply depressed. They reported little therapeutic effect, but suggested that the main value of TRH might be in diagnosis and the differentiation of subtypes of depression. In a large study of 36 depressed patients, who were free of psychotropic medication apart from diazepam, and 23 patients with nonendocrine medical disorders acting as controls, Takahashi et al. (94) found that the depressed patients had a smaller TSH response to 500 μg TRH. Using a 5 μU/ml cutoff point they found that 12 of the 36 depressed patients and only 1 of the 23 controls had blunted TSH responses. Subsequent studies tended to confirm that depressed patients have relatively blunted TSH responses compared to controls (15, 16, 39, 56, 69, 73). Kirstein et al. (58) established the use of a 7 μU/ml cutoff point rather than one of 5 μU/ml to define a blunted response when using the test as a diagnostic aid for depression. Extein et al. (22) found that 60 of 105 patients with unipolar primary depressive disorder had blunted responses (less than 7 μU/ml) as compared to 4 of 40 patients with minor depressive disorder and none of 20 normal volunteers. Targum et al. (96) found no blunted (less than 7 μU/ml) or augmented (over 28 μU/ml) responses in a group of nondepressed psychiatric controls, whereas 33% of a group of 54 patients with major depressive disorder, endogenous subtype, had blunted responses and a further 15% had augmented responses. Gold et al. (33) found that 31 of 41 patients with primary unipolar depression had blunted responses (less than 7 μU/ml). Winokur et al. (111) found that 23% of 26 drug-free outpatients with primary unipolar depression had blunted responses as defined on the basis of their own normal control population responses. The finding of Loosen et al. (71) that a high proportion of normal volunteers with a family history or past history of depression had blunted responses as compared to those without any such history is important in the debate as to whether the test reflects state or trait.

It has thus been established that some patients with depression have a relatively diminished TSH response to an intravenous bolus of TRH. The proportion of patients found to have blunted responses depends on both the selection criteria of patients and the cutoff point of TRH response used. A cutoff point of 7 μU/ml has been established as effective in distinguishing depressed patients from normal subjects and certain groups of nondepressed psychiatric controls. The proportion of depressed patients with blunted responses varies between 23% and 75% in the different studies.

CHANGES DURING RECOVERY

Kierkegaard et al. (52) reported that the mean maximum TSH response (Δ_{max} TSH) increased on clinical recovery in eight depressed patients. Gregoire et al. (38) also reported a marked increase in the TSH response in 16 depressed patients on clinical recovery. However, Maeda et al. (73) retested seven depressed patients on clinical recovery and found that the TSH response had increased in only two. Yamaguchi et al. (113) found that four of eight patients with abnormal TRH tests (either blunted or augmented) had normal responses and four were abnormal on retesting. Of seven depressed patients with normal TSH responses, five had normal responses and two had exaggerated responses on retesting during clinical recovery. Kierkegaard et al. (55) and Kierkegaard and Faber (51) in a number of studies found that about two-thirds of patients had no rise of TSH response on clinical recovery, whereas one-third had an increase of Δ_{max} TSH of 2 or more μU/ml. Extein et al. (25) reported that of 14 depressed patients with TSH responses of less than 7 μU/ml, nine had responses greater than 7 μU/ml on clinical recovery. Linkowski et al. (66) found that the TSH responses of patients with unipolar depression tended to remain blunted on clinical recovery, whereas those of patients with bipolar depression tended to revert to normal.

Kierkegaard et al. (53) reported that an increase in the TSH response on clinical recovery was predictive of prognosis. They reported that six of seven patients with an increased response did not relapse over a six-month follow-up, whereas three patients with no rise in Δ_{max} TSH all relapsed. In a subsequent larger study Kierkegaard et al. (55) confirmed that patients with an increase in Δ_{max} TSH of over 2 μU/ml were far less likely to relapse than those with an increase in Δ_{max} TSH of less than 2 μU/ml. Similar results were reported by Langer et al. (63). Kierkegaard and Smith (51a) found that maintaining those patients who had a recovery rise of Δ_{max} TSH of less than 2 μU/ml on tricyclic antidepressants reduced the likelihood of relapse. These findings have clinical application without necessarily using the TRH test, i.e., by observing changes in basal TSH levels (measured by IRMA—see section on TSH).

CLINICAL CORRELATES

There has been less emphasis on the use of the TRH test as a diagnostic aid for categories of depression. However, the work of Gold and his colleagues has suggested that depressed patients with bipolar illnesses may differ from those with unipolar illnesses in their responses to TRH (30, 34).

Most studies, however, have not found differences in the TSH responses between bipolar and unipolar patients (1, 56, 69, 73, 94). Different patient selection criteria might account for this discrepancy. It is also possible that some of the patients classified as unipolar in different studies would be found to run a bipolar course given sufficient time. Another possible explanation is that the timing of the test during the depressive episode is important. In this context the finding of Linkowski et al. (66) is of interest. They reported no difference between the TSH responses of 27 unipolar and 24 bipolar patients, but found that after treatment the unipolar patients tended to remain blunted, whereas the bipolars had an increased TSH response. There is some evidence that patients with "endogenous" symptom profiles are more likely to have blunted responses than those with "nonendogenous" profiles (56, 84). Our own study (12) on 68 drug-free patients with primary depression revealed an association between blunting and endogenous depressive disorder as defined by the research diagnostic criteria (91). However, the high proportion (30%) of patients with nonendogenous depressive disorder who had blunting meant that the TRH test had poor specificity as a diagnostic tool.

Although older age is associated with blunting of the TSH response (89), most studies in depressed populations have not found that age was a significant variable in determining blunted status (12, 31, 94).

There have been conflicting reports about the association between severity of depression and blunting of the TSH response. Several authors have not found severity of depression to be related to blunting (31, 68), but Agren and Wide (1) reported that severity of depression differentiated patients with blunted responses from those with normal responses. Many of the studies that have considered the clinical features of patients with blunted responses have investigated patients on medication, which would obscure possible relationships (93). So far, no consistent clinical picture of patients with blunted responses has emerged, perhaps partly due to the medication effect and partly reflecting the fact that patients with blunting do not form a homogeneous group. In our study (12) patients with blunted responses were found to be more severely depressed on global rating scales than those with normal responses and to have greater depressed mood as a symptom. Certain symptoms, including retardation, agitation, restlessness, depersonalization, weight loss, and sleep difficulties, were found to be associated with blunting. The presence of agitation and depersonalization appeared to discriminate more effectively between patients with blunted responses and those with normal responses. However, only half of the patients with blunted responses presented with these features, and the significance of the finding was hard to evaluate. The finding is of interest, however, in view of the association between agitation/restlessness and suicidal behavior, and the finding of blunted responses in suicidal patients (67).

The finding that patients with blunting have greater sleep difficulties than patients with normal responses (12, 103) is of interest as it has been shown that sleep has an inhibiting effect on TSH secretion and that TSH levels rise if sleep is disturbed (80). Sleep disturbance could account for some of the observed abnormalities, as raised TSH may produce a temporary increase in output of thyroid hormones and thus produce a blunted response by negative feedback.

A number of studies have investigated both hypothalamopituitary-adrenal axis function (including the dexamethasone test [DST]) and thyroid function in the same groups of patients (1, 4, 12, 18, 23, 50, 59, 97). The results of these combined studies indicate that blunting of the TRH test cannot be explained by increased secretion of cortisols, as originally suggested by Loosen et al. (72), although this may be a significant factor in some patients.

The combined results of the DST and TRH test do not significantly increase the chances of being able to identify any particular diagnostic group of depressed patients.

RELATIONSHIP TO PSYCHOSOCIAL FACTORS

In view of the considerable literature on "stress" and thyroid function (e.g., Mason [74]), it is clearly important to consider this aspect in groups of depressed patients. In our study (12) we used the life events and difficulties schedule of Brown and Harris (8a). It was found that patients with blunted responses were significantly more likely to have experienced major long-term difficulties (those lasting a year or more) than those with normal responses. These patients with blunted responses and difficulties were much more likely to have high FTI levels. Thus it seems that at least in some patients, the mechanism for blunting might be seen as an adaptive response to long-term stress, with high thyroid output causing blunting via the negative feedback system. This is in keeping with other evidence that prolonged, continued, or repeated stress increases thyroid output (105).

SIGNIFICANCE OF BLUNTED TRH TEST RESULTS

In a review of the TRH test, Burger and Patel (9) concluded that, in general, a blunted TSH response was due either to a negative feedback mechanism from increased thyroid hormone release or to pituitary dysfunction with restricted release of TSH by the pituitary in response to TRH stimulation. The finding in some studies that patients with blunted responses had a higher mean FTI level than those with normal responses suggests that at least in some patients, the former mechanism was operating, i.e., that blunting was due to increased output of thyroid hormones with negative feedback on the TRH-TSH response. This association between blunted responses and increased levels of thyroid hormones might be obscured in those studies in which patients were on medication.

The association may also be obscured if both mechanisms that cause blunting (i.e., blunting due to "negative feedback" and blunting due to "pituitary dysfunction") may be operating in groups of depressed patients. The relationship between blunting and FTI in a particular study would then depend on the proportion of patients with the different mechanisms within that study population, i.e., how many had the "negative feedback" mechanism operating and how many had "pituitary dysfunction." If a study population consisted mainly of patients with the "negative feedback" mechanism operating, a negative relationship between FTI levels and maximum TSH response would be found. If the population consisted of patients with the "pituitary dysfunction" mechanism, this relationship would not be found.

It is probable, therefore, that in some patients blunted TSH responses are due to increased output of thyroid hormones, resulting in negative feedback. This hypothesis is supported by the results of previous studies which have shown that there are increased FTI levels in depressed patients (53, 54, 58) and increased levels of TRH in the cerebrospinal fluid (57). In our study those patients with blunting and increased FTI levels were significantly more likely to have long-term social and personal difficulties than those with normal FTI levels. They were also more likely to have experienced a separation from parents during childhood (12). It may be, therefore, that in the patients with blunting and increased FTI levels the blunting is due to increased output of thyroid hormones as part of a stress response.

However, as already stated, not all patients with blunted responses had high FTI scores. Patients with blunting and normal FTI values may represent a separate group with an alternative mechanism to account for the blunting. As already suggested, pituitary dysfunction, with failure of the pituitary to respond to stimulation by the bolus dose of TRH, would be a possible mechanism. These two different mechanisms would not necessarily be mutually exclusive within the same patient.

AUGMENTED RESPONSES ON THE TRH TEST

There have been several reports that a subgroup of depressed patients have augmented rather than blunted responses to TRH. In one of the two original reports of TSH responses to TRH, Kastin et al. (49) found that one patient had an augmented response of 28 μU/ml. Hatotani et al. (39) found a range of TSH response of 3.8–19.5 μU/ml in 20 normal subjects given 500 μg TRH. Of a group of 51 depressed patients, 31 of whom were women, they found that seven had responses greater than this. Six of these seven were women. Targum et al. (97) reported on a group of 47 drug-free patients, all of whom were classified as having primary unipolar depressive disorder. Taking a cutoff point of 23 μU/ml, they found that eight patients had augmented responses (with six of these having responses greater than 33 μU/ml). Although 12 of the original 47 patients were male, none of the eight patients with augmented responses was male. The eight women with augmented responses had somewhat lower levels of circulating thyroxine, although this was not statistically significant. In our study (12) six patients, all women, had augmented responses (a response greater than 19.5 μU/ml). Patients with the augmented responses had significantly lower free thyroxine index levels than patients with normal responses.

THE TRH TEST IN OTHER PSYCHIATRIC DISORDERS

Blunted TRH tests occur in alcoholic patients, both in the acute stage and on withdrawal (34, 70). It has been shown that patients with alcohol abuse have decreased thyroid function (62). This may reflect pituitary damage in this group of patients. A further study by Loosen et al. (72) showed that alcoholic patients have blunted TSH responses to TRH. Moreover there was a positive relationship between basal T_4 levels and the TSH response. This indicates that in this population the blunting is not due to negative feedback, but may well reflect pituitary damage. There have been reports of blunted responses in anorexia nervosa, although most studies suggest that these patients have normal or delayed responses to TRH (34). Patients with schizophrenia, on the other hand, appear not to have blunted responses (31, 69). Blunted responses have been reported in patients with mania (34). Gold et al. (31) reported that in two patients who switched from depression to mania the TRH test results changed from an augmented to a blunted response.

THYROID ANTIBODIES

Thyroid autoantibodies, both antimicrosomal and antithyroglobulin, occur more frequently in depressed patients than in controls. Nemeroff et al. (77) reported that 20% of 45 depressed inpatients had antibodies as compared to 5% to 10% of normal controls. Lazarus et al. (64) found that 45% of 37 patients with manic-depressive disorder had one or both of these antibodies. All were treated with lithium and followed up for over a year. Two of the patients without antibodies developed antithyroglobulin antibodies. Moreover, there were marked fluctuations in antibody titers in the other patients. The authors concluded that lithium had an immunomodulatory effect, but that the high proportion of manic-depressive patients with antibodies could not be accounted for by lithium treatment.

It seems, therefore, that a high proportion of depressed patients, especially those with manic-depressive disorders, have increased titers of antithyroid antibodies. The significance of this is unclear, and as yet studies have not examined the relationship between these abnormalities and the other thyroid function abnormalities found in depression.

TREATMENT STUDIES

In 1938 Gjessing reported that some cases of "periodic catatonia" responded to treatment with thyroid extract (29). Since that time there have been many attempts to treat patients with psychiatric disorders, including those with depression, with thyroid hormones or TRH. Prange et al. (82) reported that the addition of T_3 to imipramine was successful in the treatment of depression, especially in patients with retarded depression, and more so in women than in men. The patients had normal PBIs, but slow ankle reflex times, and both these indices changed after treatment, suggesting a shift toward a more hyperthyroid state. Coppen et al. (15) also reported that T_3 potentiated the effect of imipramine and confirmed that this occurred in women, but not in men. Wheatley (107) reported that T_3 potentiated the action of amitriptyline in depressed outpatients, and that the benefit was greatest in patients with lower PBI levels.

Stancer and Persad (92) suggested that patients with rapid-cycling bipolar disorders responded to hypermetabolic doses of thyroxine. Several authors have tried to relate the efficacy of treatment with thyroid hormone to the results of the TRH test. Takahashi et al. (94) reported that dried thyroid extract was of no benefit to three patients with unipolar depression with blunted responses of TSH to TRH. However, in one patient with bipolar course there was some symptomatic improvement. This patient had a normal TSH response to TRH. Yamaguchi et al. (112) treated six patients who had PBI levels within the normal range but who had low BMRs with "desiccated thyroid" and reported that this treatment aided recovery in all cases. All six had had long-standing or persistent depressive symptoms. An important study by Targum and colleagues (98) examined the effect of adding either T_4 or T_3 to treatment regimes of 21 patients with refractory unipolar depression. They reported positive results in about a third of the patients. Five of six patients with augmented TSH responses to TRH responded to the treatment whereas only 2 of 15 patients with normal or blunted responses responded to treatment. On a cautionary note, cases of manic psychosis after treatment with thyroxine have been reported (47, 48). An issue that has yet to be resolved is whether T_4 or T_3 is the most suitable treatment in depression. Plasma T_3 levels may be more important in determining intracellular T_3 content in the periphery, whereas plasma T_4 levels may be more important in determining intracellular T_3 content in the brain and pituitary (45, 46).

In 1972 Prange et al. (83) and Kastin et al. (49) both reported that female patients with depression responded to intravenous TRH with an improvement in mood lasting some hours. Wilson et al. (110) also reported that there was improvement in mental state—with relaxation, mild euphoria, and increased energy—in normal women given TRH. Itil et al. (44) reported that TRH had little effect on depressed mood, but that certain "life instincts" such as drive for work, food, and sex were increased with treatment with TRH. Herrera et al. (41) reported that women with a bipolar depression were more likely to respond to TRH than women with other forms of depression. There have been numerous subsequent studies on TRH in the treatment of depression, but results have not been promising. In a large study of 143 subjects with depression or anorexia nervosa Amsterdam et al. (2) did not find that TRH improved mood.

CONCLUSION

Neuroendocrine function is of particular interest in depression because of the areas of the brain that are involved in the regulation of the hormone-releasing factors. These include the hypothalamus, amygdala, hippocampus, and septal nuclei—sites that are also involved in the control of drive, appetite, and mood states (87). Changes in neuroendocrine status reflect underlying neurotransmitter function that may be of importance in the pathogenesis of depression (102).

There have been two major approaches to the consideration of the changes in neurotransmitter and neuroendocrine status associated with depression. These have been the "adaptive" and the "biological."

The adaptive view has been that the changes are a response to environmental or psychological "stress." There is considerable evidence to support the view that stress affects neurotransmitters (106). The adaptive benefits of such neuroendocrine changes would be due to the physiological effects of increased HPT activity. TRH has been shown to have ergotropic activity in the brain, reversing the narcotic effects of barbiturates and reversing learned immobility in rats (75). It has a similar effect to psychostimulants on the EEG (44). Thyroid hormones enhance beta-adrenergic function, promoting noradrenergic transmission (108). This would possibly accelerate recovery in transmission if there was a defect in such transmission as is postulated in the amine hypothesis.

Pertinent to the adaptive view of these changes are the findings of Goodwin and Bunney (37) that different genetic strains of animals had different biochemical responses to stress. Moreover, Mason (74) found that there were individual variations in endocrine response to stress in humans. Thus, although the endocrine changes found in depression may be in part a stress response, many other factors would be of importance in determining the extent and severity of the response.

The biological view of the endocrine changes found in depression is that neurotransmitter changes are primary or causative. Neurotransmitter abnormalities result in changes in drive and mood, and the neuroendocrine changes could be seen as epiphenomena secondary to the neurotransmitter changes. Alternatively, it has been argued that the neuroendocrine changes themselves cause the depression—in the manner of the steroid psychoses. The main argument for the biological approach has been the reported association of the endocrine changes with the "endogenous" group of depressed patients, who, by implication, are those without precipitating stressful factors.

One explanation for the many conflicting results in this area of research is that within groups of patients, and, indeed, within individual patients, both adaptive and biological processes are likely to be important at any one time. Future research should be directed toward understanding these processes rather than trying to find biological markers for diagnostic categories that as yet have little empirical basis.

REFERENCES

1. Agren, H., & Wide, L. (1982). Patterns of depression reflected in pituitary-thyroid and pituitary-adrenal endocrine changes. *Psychoneuroendocrinology*, 7, 309–327.
2. Amsterdam, J., Winokur, A., Caroff, S., & Mendels, J. (1981). Thyrotropin-releasing hormone's mood-elevating effects in depressed patients, anorectic patients, and normal volunteers. *American Journal of Psychiatry*, *138*, 115–116.
3. Anderson, M. S., Bowers, C. Y., Kastin, A. J., Schalch, D. S., Schally, A. V., Snyder, P. J., Utiger, R. D., Wilber, J. F., & Wise, A. J. (1971). Synthetic thyrotropin releasing hormone, a potent stimulator of thyrotropin secretion in man. *New England Journal of Medicine*, *285*, 1279–1283.
4. Asnis, G. M., Sachar, E. J., Halbreich, U., Nathan, R. S., Ostrow, L., Soloman, M., & Halpern, F. S. (1981). Endocrine responses to thyrotropin-releasing hormone in major depressive disorders. *Psychiatry Research*, *5*, 205–215.
5. Barker, S. B., Humphrey, M. J., & Soley, M. M. (1951). The clinical determination of protein-bound iodine. *Journal of Clinical Investigation*, *30*, 55–62.
6. Bech, P., Kirkegaard, C., Bock, E., Johannesen, M., & Rafaelson, O. J. (1978). Hormones, electrolytes and cerebrospinal fluid proteins in manic-melancholic patients. *Neuropsychobiology*, *4*, 99–112.
7. Beckers, C., Cornette, C., & Thalasso, M. (1973). Evaluation of serum thyroxine by radioimmunossay. *Journal of Nuclear Medicine*, *14*, 317–320.
8. Board, F., Wadeson, R., & Persky, H. (1957). Depressive affect and endocrine functions. Blood levels of adrenal cortex and thyroid hormones in patients suffering from depressive reactions. *Archives of Neurological Psychiatry*, *78*, 612.

8a. Brown, G. W., & Harris, T. (1978). *Social origins of depression*. London: Tavistock.

9. Burger, H. G., & Patel, Y. C. (1977). TSH and TRH: Their physiological regulation and the clinical application of TRH. In L. Martini & G. M. Besser (Eds.), *Clinical neuroendocrinology*. New York: Academic Press.
10. Calabrese, J. R., Gulledge, A. D., Hahn, K., Skwerer, R., Kotz, M., Schumacher, O. P., Gupta, M. K., Krupp, N., & Gold, P. W. (1985). Autoimmune thyroiditis in manic-depressive patients treated with lithium. *American Journal of Psychiatry*, *142*, 1318–1321.
11. Caldwell, G. (1985). A new strategy for thyroid function testing. *Lancet*, *1*, May 18, 1117–1119.
12. Calloway, S. P., Dolan, R. J., Fonagy, P., De Souza, V. F., Wakeling, A. (1984). Endocrine changes and clinical profiles in depression: II. The thyrotropin-releasing hormone test. *Psychological Medicine*, *14*, 759–765.
13. Cho, J. T., Bone, S., Dunner, D. L., et al. (1979). The effect of lithium treatment on thyroid function in patients with primary affective disorder. *American Journal of Psychiatry*, *136*, 115–116.
14. Chopra, I. J. (1972). A radioimmunoassay for measurement of thyroxine in unextracted serum. *Journal of Clinical Endocrinology and Metabolism*, *34*, 938–947.
15. Coppen, A., Whybrow, P. C., Noguera, R., Maggs, R., & Prange, A. J., Jr. (1972). The comparative antidepressant value of L-tryptophan and imipramine with and without attempted potentiation by liothyronine. *Archives of General Psychiatry*, *26*, 234–241.
16. Coppen, A., Montgomery, S., Peet, M., Bailey, J., Marks, V., & Woods, P. (1974). Thyrotrophin-releasing hormone in the treatment of depression. *Lancet*, *2*, 433–434.
17. Cowdry, R., Wehr, T., Zis, A., et al. (1983). Thyroid abnormalities associated with rapid-cycling bipolar illness. *Archives of General Psychiatry*, *40*, 414–420.
18. Davis, K. L., Hollister, L. E., Mathé, A. A., Davis, B. M., Rothpearl, A. B., Faull,

K. F., Hsieh, J. Y., Barchas, J. D., & Berger, P. A. (1981). Neuroendocrine and neurochemical measurements in depression. *American Journal of Psychiatry, 138*, 1555–1562.

19. Demeester-Mirkine, N., & Dumont, J. E. (1980). The hypothalamo-pituitary thyroid axis. In M. De Visscher (Ed.), *The thyroid gland*. New York: Raven Press.
20. Dewhurst, K. E., Kabir, D. J. E., Harris, G. W., & Mandelbrote, B. M. (1969). Observations on the blood concentration of TSH in schizophrenia and the affective states. *British Journal of Psychiatry, 115*, 1003–1011.
21. Ehrensing, R. H., Kastin, A. J., Schalch, D. S., Friesen, H. G., Vargas, J. R., & Schally, A. V. (1974). Affective state and thyrotropin and prolactin responses after repeated injections of thyrotropin-releasing hormone in depressed patients. *American Journal of Psychiatry, 131*, 714–718.
22. Extein, I., Pottash, A. L., & Gold, M. S. (1981a). The thyrotropin-releasing hormone test in the diagnosis of unipolar depression. *Psychiatry Research, 5*, 311–316.
23. Extein, I., Pottash, A. L., & Gold, M. S. (1981b). Relationship of thyrotropin-releasing hormone test and dexamethasone suppression test abnormalities in unipolar depression. *Psychiatry Research, 4*, 49–53.
24. Extein, I., Pottash, A. L., & Gold, M. S. (1982). Does subclinical hypothyroidism predispose to tricyclic-induced rapid mood cycles? *Journal of Clinical Psychiatry, 43*, 290–291.
25. Extein, I., Pottash, A. L., Gold, M. S., & Silver, J. M. (1982). Thyroid-stimulating hormone response to thyrotropin-releasing hormone in unipolar depression before and after clinical improvement. *Psychiatry Research, 6*, 161–169.
26. Ferrari, G. (1973). On some biochemical aspects of affective disorders. *Rivista Sperimentale Di Freniatria E. Medicina Legale Delle Alienazioni mentali, 93*, 1167–1175.
27. Gibbons, J. L., Gibson, J. G., Maxwell, A. E., & Willcox, R. D. C. (1960). An Endocrine study of depressive illness. *Journal of Psychosomatic Research, 5*, 32–41.
28. Gibson, J. G. (1962). Emotions and the thyroid gland: A critical appraisal. *Journal of Psychosomatic Research, 6*, 93–116.
29. Gjessing, R. (1938). Disturbances of somatic functions in catatonia with a periodic course, and their compensations. *Journal of Mental Science, 84*, 608–621.
30. Gold, P. W., Goodwin, F. K., Wehr, T., & Rebar, R. (1977). Pituitary thyrotropin response to thyrotropin-releasing hormone in affective illness: Relationship to spinal fluid amine metabolites. *American Journal of Psychiatry, 134*, 1028–1031.
31. Gold, M. S., Pottash, A. L., Ryan, N., Sweeney, D. R., Davies, R. K., & Martin, D. M. (1980). TRH-induced TSH response in unipolar, bipolar, and secondary depressions: Possible utility in clinical assessment and differential diagnosis. *Psychoneuroendocrinology, 5*, 147–155.
32. Gold, M. S., Pottash, A. L., & Extein, I. (1981). Hypothyroidism and depression: Evidence from complete thyroid function evaluation. *Journal of American Medical Association, 245*, 1919–1922.
33. Gold, M. S., Pottash, A. L., & Mueller, E. A., III (1981). Grades of thyroid failure in 100 depressed and anergic psychiatric inpatients. *American Journal of Psychiatry, 138*, 253–255.
34. Gold, M. S., Pottash, A. L., Extein, I., Martin, D. M., Howard, E., Mueller, E. A., III, & Sweeney, D. R. (1981). The TRH test in the diagnosis of major and minor depression. *Psychoneuroendocrinology, 6*, 159–169.
35. Goldberg, I. J., Lawton, K., & Ridges, A. P. (1977). The effect of depression and its treatment on serum thyroxine. *Postgraduate Medical Journal, 53*, 211–215.
36. Golstein, J., Van Cauter, E., Linkowski, P., Vanhaelst, L., & Mendlewicz, J. (1980). Thyrotropin nyctohemeral pattern in primary depression: Differences between unipolar and bipolar women. *Life Sciences, 27*, 1695–1703.

37. GOODWIN, F. K., & BUNNEY, W. E. (1973). A psychobiological approach to affective illness. *Psychiatric Annals, 3*, 19–53.
38. GREGOIRE, F., BRAUMAN, H., DE BUCK, R., & CORVILAIN, J. (1977). Hormone release in depressed patients before and after recovery. *Psychoneuroendocrinology, 2*, 303–312.
39. HATOTANI, N., NOMURA, J., YAMAGUCHI, T., & KITAYAMA, I. (1977). Clinical and experimental studies on the pathogenesis of depression. *Psychoneuroendocrinology, 2*, 115–130.
40. HEIGLER, E. D., JR., PITTMAN, J. A., JR., HERSHMAN, J. M., & BAUGH, C. M. (1971). Direct evaluation of pituitary thyrotropin reserve utilising synthetic thyrotropin releasing hormone. *Journal of Clinical Endocrinology, 33*, 573–581.
41. HERRERA, R., GARCIA, R., GALIANA, J., & CUENCA, E. (1978). Antidepressive and endocrinometabolic effects of TRH. *Archivos de Neurobiologia, 41*, 99–108.
42. HETZEL, B. S., DE LA HABA, D. S., & HINKLE, L. E., JR. (1952). Life stress and thyroid function in human subjects [Abstract]. *Journal of Clinical Endocrinology, 12*, 941.
43. INGENBLEEK, Y. (1980). Thyroid function in nonthyroid illnesses. In M. De Visscher (Ed.), *The thyroid gland*. New York: Raven Press.
44. ITIL, T. M., PATTERSON, C. D., POLVAN, N., BIGELOW, A., & BERGEY, B. (1975). Clinical and CNS effects of oral and I.V. thyrotropin-releasing hormone in depressed patients. *Diseases of the Nervous System, 36*, 529–536.
45. JOFFE, R. T., ROY-BYRE, P. P., UDHE, T. W., & POST, R. M. (1984). Thyroid function and affective illness: A reappraisal. *Biological Psychiatry, 29*, 1685–1691.
46. JOFFE, R. T., BLANK, D. W., POST, R. M., & UDHE, W. T. (1985). Decreased triiodothyromines in depression: A preliminary report. *Biological Psychiatry, 20*, 922–925.
47. JOSEPHSON, A. M., & MACKENZIE, T. B. (1979). Appearance of manic psychosis following rapid normalization of thyroid status. *American Journal of Psychiatry, 136*, 846–847.
48. JOSEPHSON, A. M., & MACKENZIE, T. B. (1980). Thyroid-induced mania in hypothyroid patients. *British Journal of Psychiatry, 137*, 222–228.
49. KASTIN, A. J., SCHALCH, D. S., EHRENSING, R. H., & ANDERSON, M. S. (1972). Improvement in mental depression with decreased thyrotropin response after administration of thyrotropin-releasing hormone. *Lancet, 2*, 740–742.
50. KIRKEGAARD, C., & CARROLL, B. J. (1980). Dissociation of TSH adrenocortical disturbances in endogenous depression. *Psychiatry Research, 3*, 253–264.
51. KIRKEGAARD, C., & FABER, J. (1981). Altered serum levels of thyroxine, triiodothyronines and diiodothyronines in endogenous depression. *Acta Endocrinologica, 96*, 199–207.
51a. KIRKEGAARD, C., & SMITH, E. (1978). Continuation therapy in endogenous depression controlled by changes in the TRH stimulation test. *Psychological Medicine, 8*, 501–503.
52. KIRKEGAARD, C., NORLEM, N., LAURIDSEN, U. B., & BJORUM, N. (1974). Thyrotropin-releasing hormone and depression. [Letter]. *Lancet, 2*, 722.
53. KIRKEGAARD, C., NORLEM, N., LAURIDSEN, U. B., BJORUM, N., & CHRISTIANSEN, C. (1975a). Protirelin stimulation test and thyroid function during treatment of depression. *Archives of General Psychiatry, 32*, 1115–1118.
54. KIRKEGAARD, C., NORLEM, N., LAURIDSEN, U. B., & BJORUM, N. (1975b). Prognostic value of thyrotropin releasing hormone stimulation test in endogenous depression. *Acta Psychiatrica Scandinavica, 52*, 170–177.
55. KIRKEGAARD, C., BJORUM, N., COHN, N., FABER, J., LAURIDSEN, U. B., & NERUP, J. (1977). Studies on the influence of biogenic amines and psychoactive drugs on the prognostic value of the TRH stimulation test in endogenous depression. *Psychoneuroendocrinology, 2*, 131–136.
56. KIRKEGAARD, C., BJORUM, N., COHN, D., & LAURIDSEN, U. B. (1978). Thyrotrophin-

releasing hormone (TRH) stimulation test in manic-depressive illness. *Archives of General Psychiatry, 35*, 1017–1021.

57. Kirkegaard, C., Faber, J., Hummer, L., & Rogowski, P. (1979). Increased levels of TRH in cerebrospinal fluid from patients with endogenous depression. *Psychoneuroendocrinology, 4*, 227–235.
58. Kirstein, L., Gold, M. S., Pottash, A. L., & Extein, I. (1981). Thyrotropin-releasing hormone test and male unipolar depression. *Biological Psychiatry, 16*, 819–824.
59. Kirstein, L., Gold, M. S., Extein, I., Martin, D., & Pottash, A. L. (1982). Clinical correlates of the TRH infusion test in 1° depression. *Journal of Clinical Psychiatry, 43*, 191–194.
60. Kjellman, B. F., Ljunggren, J. G., Beck-Friis, J., & Wetterberg, L. (1983). Reverse T_3 levels in affective disorders. *Psychiatry Research, 10*, 1–9.
61. Kjellman, B. F., Beck-Friis, J., Ljunggren, J. G., & Wetterberg, L. (1984). Twenty-four-hour serum levels of TSH in affective disorders. *Acta Psychiatrica Scandinavica, 69*, 491–502.
62. Kolakowska, T., & Swigar, M. E. (1977). Thyroid function in depression and alcohol abuse: A retrospective study. *Archives of General Psychiatry, 34*, 984–988.
63. Langer, G., Koinig, G., Matzinger, R., Schönbeck, G., Resch, F., et al. (1986). TRH-TSH as predictor of outcome. *Archives of General Psychiatry, 43*, 861–868.
64. Lazarus, J. H., John, R., Bennie, E. M., Chalmers, R. J., & Crockett, G. (1981). Lithium therapy and thyroid function: A long-term study. *Psychological Medicine, 11*, 85–92.
65. Lazarus, J. H., McGregor, A. M., Ludgate, M., Darke, C., Creagh, F. M., & Kingswood, C. J. (1986). Effect of lithium carbonate therapy on thyroid immune status in manic depressive patients: A prospective study. *Journal of Affective Disorders, 11*, 155–160.
66. Linkowski, P., Brauman, H., & Mendlewicz, J. (1981). Thyrotrophin response to thyrotrophin-releasing hormone in unipolar and bipolar affective illness. *Journal of Affective Disorders, 3*, 9–16.
67. Linkowski, P., Van Wettere, J. P., Kerkhofs, M., Brauman, H., & Mendlewicz, J. (1983). Thyrotrophin response to thyreostimulin in affectively ill women relationship to suicidal behavior. *British Journal of Psychiatry, 143*, 401–405.
68. Loosen, P. T., & Prange, A. J. (1982). Serum thyrotrophin response to thyrotropin-releasing-hormone in psychiatric patients: A review. *American Journal of Psychiatry, 139*, 405–416.
69. Loosen, P. T., Prange, A. J., Jr., Wilson, I. C., Lara, P. P., & Pettus, C. (1977). Thyroid stimulating hormone response after thyrotropin releasing hormone in depressed, schizophrenic and normal women. *Psychoneuroendocrinology, 2*, 137–148.
70. Loosen, P. T., Prange, A. J., & Wilson, I. C. (1979). TRH (protirelin) in depressed alcoholic men: Behavioural changes and endocrine responses. *Archives of General Psychiatry, 36*, 540–547.
71. Loosen, P. T., Marciniak, R., & Thadani, K. (1987). TRH-induced TSH response in healthy volunteers: Relationship to psychiatric history. *American Journal of Psychiatry, 144*, 455–459.
72. Loosen, P. T., Wilson, I. C., Dew, R. N., & Tipermas, A. (1983). Thyrotropin-releasing hormone (TRH) in abstinent alcoholic men. *American Journal of Psychiatry, 140*, 1145–1149.
73. Maeda, K., Kato, Y., Ohgo, S., Chihara, K., Yoshimoto, Y., Yamaguchi, N., Kuromaru, S., & Imura, H. (1975). Growth hormone and prolactin release after injection of thyrotropin-releasing hormone in patients with depression. *Journal of Clinical Endocrinology and Metabolism, 40*, 501–505.
74. Mason, J. W. (1968). A review of psychoendocrine research on the pituitary-thyroid system. *Psychosomatic Medicine, 30*, 666–681.

75. Metcalf, G., & Dettmar, P. W. (1981). Is thyrotropin releasing hormone and endogenous ergotropic substance in the brain? *Lancet, 1*, 586–588.

76. Michael, R. P., & Gibbons, J. L. (1963). Interrelationships between the endocrine system and neuropsychiatry. *International Review of Neurobiology, 5*, 243–302.

77. Nemeroff, C. B., Simon, J. S., Haggerty, J. J., Jr., & Evans, D. L. (1985). Antithyroid antibodies in depressed patients. *American Journal of Psychiatry, 142*, 840–843.

78. Odell, W. D., Wilber, J. F., & Utiger, R. D. (1967). Studies of thyrotropin physiology by means of radioimmunoassay. *Recent Progress in Hormone Research, 23*, 47–85.

79. Page, C., Benaim, S., & Lappin, F. (1987). A long-term retrospective follow-up study of patients treated with prophylactic lithium carbonate. *British Journal of Psychiatry, 150*, 175–179.

80. Parker, D. C., Pekary, A. E., & Hershman, J. M. (1976). Effect of normal and reversed sleep-wake cycles upon nyctohemeral rhythmicity of plasma thyrotropin: Evidence suggestive of an inhibitory influence of sleep. *Journal of Clinical Endocrinology and Metabolism, 43*, 318–329.

81. Patel, Y. C., Alford, F. P., & Burger, H. G. (1972). The 24-hour plasma thyrotropin profile. *Clinical Science, 43*, 71–77.

82. Prange, A. J., Jr., Wilson, I. C., Rabon, A. M., & Lipton, M. A. (1969). Enhancement of imipramine antidepressant activity by thyroid hormone. *American Journal of Psychiatry, 126*, 457–469.

83. Prange, A. J., Wilson, I. C., Lara, P. P., Alltop, L. B., & Brease, G. E. (1972). Effects of thyrotropin-releasing hormone in depression. *Lancet, 2*, 999–1002.

84. Ramseier, F., Gastpar, M., & Girard, J. (1980). TSH, HGH, HPr, and cortisol responses to TRH in depressed patients. *Acta Psychiatrica Belgica, 80*, 399–409.

85. Rinieris, P. M., Christodoulou, C. N., Souvatzoglou, A. M., Koutras, D. A., & Stefanis, C. N. (1978). Thyroid function in primary depression. *Acta Psychiatrica Belgica, 78*, 248–255.

86. Rinieris, P. M., Christodoulou, G. N., Souvatzoglou, A. M., Koutras, D. A., & Stefanis, C. N. (1978). Free-thyroxine index in psychotic and neurotic depression. *Acta Psychiatrica Scandinavica, 58*, 56–60.

87. Risch, S. C., Kalin, N. H., & Murphy, D. L. (1981). Neurochemical mechanisms in the affective disorders and neuroendocrine correlates. *Journal of Clinical Psychopharmacology, 1*, 180–185.

88. Rybakowski, J., & Sowinski, J. (1973). Free-thyroxine index and absolute free-thyroxine in affective disorders. *Lancet, 1*, 889.

89. Snyder, P. J., & Utiger, R. D. (1972). Response to thyrotropin releasing hormone (TRH) in normal man. *Journal of Clinical Endocrinology, 34*, 380–385.

90. Spaulding, S. W., Burrow, G. N., Bermudez, F., & Himmelhoch, J. M. (1972). The inhibitory effect of lithium on thyroid hormone release in both euthyroid and thyrotoxic patients. *Journal of Clinical Endocrinology and Metabolism, 35*, 905–911.

91. Spitzer, R. L., Endicott, J., & Robins, E. (1978). Research diagnostic criteria. Rationale and reliability. *Archives of General Psychiatry, 35*, 773–782.

92. Stancer, H. C., & Persad, E. (1982). Treatment of rapid-cycling manic-depressive disorder with levothyroxine. *Archives of General Psychiatry, 39*, 311–312.

93. Sternbach, H. A., Gold, M. S., Pottash, A. C., & Extein, I. (1983). Thyroid failure and protirelin (thyrotropin-releasing hormone) test abnormalities in depressed outpatients. *Journal of the American Medical Association, 249*, 1618–1620.

94. Takahashi, S., Kondo, H., Yoshimura, M., & Ochi, Y. (1974). Thyrotropin responses to TRH in depressive illness: Relation to clinical subtypes and prolonged duration of depressive episode. *Folia Psychiatrica et Neurologica Japonica, 28*, 355–365.

95. Takahashi, S., Kondo, H., Yoshimura, M., & Ochi, Y. (1975). Thyroid function levels and thyrotropin responses to TRH administration in manic patients receiving lithium carbonate. *Folia Psychiatrica et Neurologica Japonica, 29*, 232–237.

96. TARGUM, S. D., SULLIVAN, A. C., & BYRNES, S. M. (1982a). Neuroendocrine interrelationships in major depressive disorder. *American Journal of Psychiatry, 139*, 282-286.
97. TARGUM, S. D., SULLIVAN, A. C., & BYRNES, S. M. (1982b). Compensatory pituitary-thyroid mechanisms in major depressive disorder. *Psychiatry Research, 6*, 85-96.
98. TARGUM, S. D., GREENBERG, R. D., HARMON, R. L., KESSLER, K., SALERIAN, A. J., & FRAM, D. H. (1984). The TRH test and thyroid hormone in refractory depression [Letter]. *American Journal of Psychiatry, 141*, 463.
99. TINGLEY, J. O., MORRIS, A. W., & HILL, S. R. (1968). Studies on the diurnal variation and response to emotional stress of the thyroid gland. *Clinical Research, 6*, 134.
100. UTIGER, R. D. (1974). Thyrotropin. In H. Behrman & B. Jaffe (Eds.), *Methods of hormone radioimmunoassay*. New York: Academic Press.
101. VAN CAUTER, E., LECLERQ, R., VANHAELST, L., & GOLSTEIN, J. (1974). Simultaneous study of cortisol and TSH daily variations in normal subjects and patients with hyperadrenal cortism. *Journal of Clinical Endocrinology and Metabolism, 39*, 645-652.
102. VAN PRAAG, H. M. (1982). Neurotransmitters and CNS disease: Depression. *Lancet, 2*, 1259-1264.
103. VOGEL, H. P., BENKERT, O., ILLIG, R., MULLER-OERLINGHAUSEN, B., & POPPENBERG, A. (1977). Psychoendocrinological and therapeutic effects of TRH in depression. *Acta Psychiatrica Scandinavica, 56*, 223-232.
104. WEEKE, A., & WEEKE, J. (1978). Disturbed circadian variation of serum thyrotropin in patients with endogenous depression. *Acta Psychiatrica Scandinavica, 57*, 281-289.
105. WEINER, H. (1977). *Psychobiology and human disease*. New York: Elsevier.
106. WEISS, J. M., GLASZIER, H. I., POMORECKY BAILEY, W. H., & SCHNEIPEL, L. H. (1979). In R. A. Depue (Ed.), *Psychobiology of the depressive disorder*. New York: Academic Press.
107. WHEATLEY, D. (1972). Potentiation of amitriptyline by thyroid hormone. *Archives of General Psychiatry, 26*, 229-233.
108. WHYBROW, P. C., & PRANGE, A. J. (1981). A hypothesis of thyroid-catecholamine-receptor interaction. *Archives of General Psychiatry, 38*, 106-113.
109. WHYBROW, P. C., COPPEN, A., PRANGE, A. J., NOGUERA, R., & BAILEY, J. E. (1972). Thyroid function and the response to liothyronine in depression. *Archives of General Psychiatry, 26*, 242-245.
110. WILSON, I. C., PRANGE, A. J., LARA, P. P., ALLTOP, L. B., STIKELEATHER, R. A., LIPTON, M. A., & HILL, C. (1973). TRH: Psychobiological responses of normal women. *Archives of General Psychiatry, 29*, 15-21.
111. WINOKUR, A., AMSTERDAM, J., CAROFF, S., SNYDER, P. J., & BRUNSWICK, D. (1982). Variability of hormonal responses to a series of neuroendocrine challenges in depressed patients. *American Journal of Psychiatry, 139*, 39-44.
112. YAMAGUCHI, T., NOMURA, J., NISHIKUBO, M., TSUJIMURA, R., & HATOTANI, N. (1975). Studies on thyroid therapy and thyroid function in depressive patients. *Folia Psychiatrica et Neurologica Japonica, 29*, 221-230.
113. YAMAGUCHI, T., HATOTANI, N., NOMURA, J., & USHIJIMA, Y. (1977). Function of hypothalamo-pituitary thyroid axis in depressed patients. *Folia Psychiatrica et Neurologica Japonica, 31*, 173-181.

5

SOCIAL PSYCHIATRY AND AFFECTIVE DISORDERS

JOHN L. CARLETON, M.D., F.A.P.A.

President, World Association for Social Psychiatry, Santa Barbara, California

INTRODUCTION

Diseases have long been recognized as products of reactions between an organism and a source of trauma. The latter could be physical injury, bacterial infection, or, in the case of mental disorders, social experiences. Genetic inheritance, developmental experiences, metabolic states, temporal events, and social support systems are generally parameters of all diseases and disorders.

The goal of this chapter is to present an overview of the contributions from social psychiatry to the understanding and treatment of the affective disorders. After some brief general comments about the affective disorders, the chapter will describe social psychiatry, briefly review living systems theory, which is essential for social psychiatry, describe some research that demonstrates the influence of environment on biological expression, and review some social psychiatric modalities and approaches. A biopsychosocial ecological approach is the most rewarding general orientation to the affective disorders.

AFFECTIVE DISORDERS

The DSM-III class of affective disorders is characterized by degrees of impairment of a person's basic physical and social processes. The word *affect* may refer to emotions or to feelings. However, persons with affective disorders manifest impairment across biopsychosocial subsystems. This raises questions as to the desirability of the class name. Metabolic processes are either inhibited or speeded up in this group of disorders. We have arbitrarily divided them into those in which the predominant symptoms are of depression and decreased activity, those of increased activity and elation, and those with combinations of these characteristics. Biological research suggests that in depression, the precursors of neurophysiological and neurochemical activity leading to mentally adaptive and mastering behaviors are either deficient or impaired, and that there is an opposite kind of genetically transmitted biological diathesis in mania. Certain specific mental processes, including learning, memory, and cognition, are impaired in depression. In mania delusions and hallucinations may occur. Generalized psychomotor retardation and "vegetative" signs and symptoms are common in major depressions. Accelerated psychomotor activity, hyperalertness, indiscriminate responsiveness to external stimuli, and an increase in metabolic activity may accompany mania.

The heading *Affective Disorders* (19) is a descriptive term that refers primarily to the relative persistency of an emotion that influences all mental (and physical) processes. *Mental disorders* are bio-psycho-social events that arise within an individual. They are manifestations of complex, unique, biological, psychological, and social interactive processes that influence (the disorder's) etiological development, clinical presentation, course, prognosis, and response to therapeutic efforts.

Our scientific efforts have yet to identify neuroanatomical, neuromolecular, or neurophysiological lesions specific for the specific affective disorders. Gene influence is not immutable. Genetic encoding apparently plays a role in the transmission of a proclivity for major affective disorders. Genes are encoded information which may directly control the structural synthesis of an entity, in which case they are structural genes. Or the gene information may regulate biological "physiological" processes. Gene function must be activated before it becomes operational and its activity may be inhibited. The biochemical bath in which a gene is situated comprises its immediate environment. The totality of factors in that environment activate or inhibit gene operations. Other variables in the biochemical and neurophysiological process chain that connects genotype with phenotype control the latter to such an extent that "being isophenic does not make people isogenic and, being isogenic does not make people isophenic" (3, p. 205). Cancro describes a number of fascinating research studies that confirm these findings (3).

Depression and mania are described subjectively (i.e., by symptoms)—how a person experiences his emotional, intellectual, and physical being—and from objective observations (signs). A person is depressed if the activity of his physical and mental processes is significantly inhibited over time. A person may be manic if the activity of his physical and mental processes is, over time, significantly increased. Depression and mania may occur in degrees of severity, for shorter or longer periods of time, and may develop gradually or precipitously. Within the range of normal, some people are more vital, more active, more assertive, more emotionally expressive, creative, adaptive, productive, and successful than others. Some are more active sexually, experience better physical health, and enjoy life to a fuller extent. Still within the range of normal, other people are more inhibited, more passive, shy, less creative, take longer to adapt, are more moody, less enthusiastic, experience fewer hours of happiness, and more periods of "normal" depression. There are many depressive and manicky expressions within and beyond the normal range. Some persist at levels of severity that justify classification as disorders.

Depression occurs when mental processes are excessively controlled or inhibited. Metabolism slows, constipation often occurs, thinking is confused or less active, delusions and hallucinations may occur, people feel rejected, unwanted, and at times unrealistically guilty. They may experience anorexia and weight loss or eat more and gain weight. The risk of suicide increases apparently concomitantly with a sense of hopelessness.

Mania includes a loss of control and excessive erratic activity of mental processes. Physical and mental processes speed up, and customary sociability is often replaced by sarcastic, demanding, and abusive conduct. Expansiveness occurs, poor judgment is evident in many social and economic areas, irritability is frequent, and angry tirades and rarely violent aggressive behavior toward others may occur. Fundamentally and generally, the excessive control in depression and the lack of control in mania are manifested in social, psychological, intellectual, behavioral, emotional, and biological parameters.

SOCIAL PSYCHIATRY

The World Association for Social Psychiatry can be seen as a social psychiatric paradigm. WASP is an organization, a concrete living system between the "group" and the "society." It is global, worldwide, and holistic. It has a physical structure and operational activities. Its orientation is biological, social, systemic, and dynamic. The Constitution and By-laws state that it seeks:

> (a) to study the nature of man and his cultures and the prevention and treatment of his vicissitudes and behavioral disorders (b) to pro-

> mote national and international collaboration among professionals and societies in fields related to social psychiatry (c) to make the knowledge and practice of social psychiatry available to other sciences and to the public and (d) to advance the physical, social and philosophic well-being of mankind (7, p. 1).

Social psychiatry, the science of anthropos, is not a subsystem of psychiatry. It seeks to define and create ameliorative interactions between children and parents, families and communities, and between all of the world's societies.

Social psychiatry believes that causative factors contributing to disorders of mentation may arise from systems precursors located at any systemic level, including the cell, organ, organism, group, organization, society, or suprasocietal and from inert systems and matter. Thus the total ecology of an individual, his biological status, his family, culture, value orientations, and societal institutions, including economic, political, religious, occupational, and entertainment, may bear meaningfully on his mental processes. Social psychiatry is scientific, phenomenological, etiological, descriptive, rehabilitative, therapeutic, preventative, altruistic, and promotes mental health and global societal concordance in its orientations toward mental disorders. It is a holistic integration of all pertinent matter, energy, and information synthesized for the benefit of all humanity.

Social psychiatry incorporates all meaningful theories concerning human behavior. This orientation includes the basic and social sciences and the fine arts. Theories may address human behavior at different systemic levels and at different degrees of abstraction. These differences are not necessarily contradictory to each other. Psychoanalytic and psychodynamic theory have addressed depression and mania for almost 100 years. In general, they contend that the human organism, once conceived, is biologically motivated to strive to continue its existence. Social involvements including warm, caring, and affectionate interpersonal contacts are essential to human existence, particularly during infancy and the developmental years. These early accepting and supporting relationships encourage biological existence, the expression of assertiveness, uninhibited emotional expression (during the earliest months), curiosity, and in general a sense of inner security and comfort about the realities of developing into a person capable of joyfully embracing creative life experiences and able to employ the self-healing behaviors of grief and mourning at times of significant change, loss, or failure. A relative absence of ambivalence about successes and failures is characteristic of persons who do not experience affective disorders. "Depression" is our metaphor for antiexistential and ambivalent reactions to frustrations, change, failure, success, loss, and living. In psychoanalytic theory mania is not a genuine freedom or elation nor are its processes akin to creativity and successful adaptation. Mania is a frenzy of generalized self-defeating mental and physical hyperactivity characterized by great ambivalence in the modes of successful adaptation to frustration, change, failure, success, or loss (14).

Social experiences occurring during infancy, the developmental years, and later may interact with a biological proclivity and contribute to the formation of predominantly collapsing modes as opposed to mastering modes of mental adaptation, thus laying the substrate for affective disorders.

In 1945 Fenichel described similarities (but not sameness) in the background of those suffering impulse neuroses and addictions (9). Forty years later Cancro cited one study of the Amish (Pennsylvania) who do not suffer significant problems of alcoholism or sociopathy. The study noted no gender difference in the rate of major depression (3).

Psychological theory offers the basis for different varieties of psychotherapy, including: supportive, insight oriented, short and long term, cognitive therapies, and other psychosocial modalities. These therapies have a significant role in the treatment of the affective disorders.

LIVING SYSTEMS THEORY

Miller's (16) plan for understanding life is called living systems theory. This theory is vital to social psychiatry. A system is a complex unity formed of many diverse parts subject to a common plan or serving a common purpose. "General living systems theory is concerned with a special subset of all systems, the living ones" (16, p. 9). The concepts of "space," "time," "matter," "energy," and "information" are basic to our understanding because living systems exist in space and are made of matter and energy organized by information. "Complex structures which carry out living processes . . . can be identified at seven hierarchal levels" (16, p. 9). These are the cell, the organ, the organism, the group, the organization, the society, and the supranational organization. Systems at all these levels are open systems composed of 19 critical subsystems that process inputs, throughputs, and outputs of matter, energy, and information. Living systems theory is a general theory through which social, biological, and physical sciences can be integrated as they apply to structure and process at any of the seven hierarchal levels of living systems.

Many sciences are almost entirely relevant to this theory. They are physiology, biochemistry, genetics, pharmacology, medicine, economics, political science, anthropology, sociology, and psychology. The physical sciences and engineering also contribute. Logic, mathematics, and statistics yield methods, models, and simulations, including some involving the relatively new approaches of cybernetics and informations theory (16, p. 4).

The Grays cogently note that our "species is a uniquely and intensely systems forming one and that our human brain is primarily a system forming organ" (11, p. 151). The precursors of systemic human behaviors can be found in "states" of human existence. The Grays found that the relative absence of "comfortability and enjoyment, answering time, thinking time, easy agreeability and (of) limitations of talking space" (12, p. 16) could become system-forming precursors for the behavioral systems of delinquency. A specific relationship between the delinquent behavior and the precursor can be identified (12). Because this general theory applies to a wide range of living systems from cell to supranational systems, conceptual terms must be as nearly as possible applicable to all levels. Specificity is not always served. There are analogous processes for each critical subsystem at every level. These fundamental aspects of the theory make it particularly applicable to the needs of social psychiatry as it is defined above. Social psychiatry then is a biopsychosocial, systems-dynamic, systems-precursor, systems-forming, and ecological science. Accurate theory encourages an orderly accumulation of new knowledge and provides a fresh orientation for existing sciences.

Living systems theory encourages holistic and integrative conceptualizations of people and their mental disorders within their contingent social and physical environments. Each individual is a living system which interdigitates with interrelating sub- and supraordinate living systems. Matter, energy, and information flow into, through, and out of all living systems and between contiguous systems. Therefore, events that are occurring at one level or within one subsystem may readily be seen to affect adjacent larger or smaller systems or their parts. Medicine is accustomed to considering the influence of microscopic organisms or hormonal changes as etiological to disease processes. Medicine acknowledges the effects of larger social realities, such as poverty, on the presence or absence of specific diseases in specific locations or groups of people. Until relatively recently, however, it has been difficult for psychiatry and the other mental health disciplines to conceptualize existing relationships between social, interpersonal, and larger systems and mental health or mental disorders.

In practice, social psychiatrists may be involved in dyadic, family, group, organizational, societal, and suprasocietal interactions. WASP, an organization, impinges on societal, suprasocietal, and lesser systems. We are aware that larger systems significantly influence the mental and physical health of families and individuals.

SOCIAL PSYCHIATRY AND THE AFFECTIVE DISORDERS

The legitimacy of social psychiatry as a contributor to the understanding and treatments of affective disorders can be established by scientifically documenting existing relationships between social experience and biological expression. This documentation may arise from research originating from a number of different fields of endeavor. A social context may have specific effects on biological expression. McGuire (15) reports that there is a highly significant difference in the brain serotonin levels of a dominant male and the other male monkeys that are members of the same group. A similar relative difference is found when serotonin levels of the officers of UCLA fraternities are compared with those of regular members of the fraternity. Furthermore, the levels change if the social status of these monkeys or fraternity members is reversed.

Psychoanalytic and dynamic psychiatric theory have consistently held that there is a relationship between social (psychosocial) loss and depressive disorders (1). The loss of a primary caretaker, the absence of sufficient physical and emotional affection, and profound interference with usual self-expression behaviors during early developmental years are associated with affective disorders during infancy, childhood, and adolescence and/or contribute to a biopsychosocial characteriological predisposition to them. These traumata may arise from intrafamily experiences or they may eventuate directly from the activity of the larger systems operations of institutions, societies, and supranational systems.

Brenner (2) performed time-series regressive analysis to investigate changes in the U.S. suicide rate, by age and sex, between 1950 and 1978. Four explanatory factors were tested for their relationship to suicide rates. They were economic, separation, illness, and alcohol consumption. He found that "economic changes dominate the explanation of variance, over time, in male suicide rate. In particular, the national unemployment rate is the outstanding source of explanation" (2, p. 171).

An indiscriminate increase in coronary heart disease occurring in middle-aged and younger males beginning early in the 20th century is the basis for some interesting research. Coronary heart disease was not a concern for medicine prior to the early 1900s, a fact that supports the basic social component of its etiology. In the 1950s and the early 1960s Rosenman and Friedman (17) described the type A and type B personality behavior patterns. They noted a "complex of characteristics, including excessive competitive drive and habitual sense of time urgency," which they designated type A behavior pattern (TAB). This type "appeared to be a rather specific action-emotional complex exhibited by most patients with coronary heart disease, and particularly those suffering coronary heart disease prior to 60 years of age" (18, p. 208).

The Committee on Public Health of the New York Academy of Medicine has been concerned about the frequency of homicide in New York City. They report that: "During the years from 1973–1984 homicide was the largest single cause of death among males 15–44 years of age in New York City" (13). Although not included in the DSM-III class of affective disorders, murder is usually committed by people suffering momentary extreme loss of control of specific inhibitory mental processes, leaving more primitive hostile impulses and reactions free to behavioral expression. Homicide is the behavioral expression of a mental disorder because, by definition, "ordered" social beings do not commit murder. The vast difference between the frequency of murder in Japan and in the United States has yet to be explained by a factor of biological difference between Japanese and "American" people.

The post-traumatic stress disorders of U.S. Vietnam veterans is characterized by a mixture of excessive and deficient control of mental processes. These control problems do not follow a cyclical pattern; rather they manifest in a multitude of mental and metabolic process disorders with psychological, biological, and social signs and symptoms. These signs and symptoms are frequently found in patients suffering from illnesses classified among the affective disorders. Recurrent and intrusive recollections, marked diminution of interest in significant activities, feelings of detachment or estrangement, constricted affect, hyperalertness, sleep disturbances, memory impairments, and trouble concentrating are among the signs and symptoms of these disorders.

The physical (biological) demands of guerrilla warfare in a foreign country with radically different climate and ecology from that of the United States are greater and more prolonged than those encountered in any other existing experience in today's world except that of torture. These experiences may lead to profound biological changes. Upon induction into the armed forces soldiers experience a disruption of their traditional social support systems, necessitating the rapid development of new ones. In war, the new support systems may be literally instantaneously destroyed. In guerrilla warfare there is no opportunity to experience normal bereavement, reparative normal regression, or verbal catharsis. Further, and perhaps more critical, the people of the United States as individuals and as a society psychologically abandoned their soldiers both in Vietnam and after they returned home, rejected them for carrying out an unpopular war, and denied the legitimacy of their post-traumatic stress disorders. The story of how the veterans have responded to this denial and rejection through the creation of self-help groups, other models of therapy, and with the presentation of two impressive monuments to the people of the United States is truly a tribute to human loyalty and ingenious reparative processes.

MODALITIES OF SOCIAL PSYCHIATRY

Evolving social conditions frequently precipitate biological reactions within individuals. The reactive neurophysiological processes, in turn, become precursors of mental health and/or mental disorders. These system precursors (12) and the systems-forming activity they motivate have been largely ignored in traditional psychiatric models and methods. Psychiatry is experiencing a stressful time as it grapples with social change that has direct relevance for the profession, for the general public, and for clinical practice. A partial list of social conditions that lead to the formation of precursors of mental disorder would include the following: urban renewal, changes in working and living conditions, changes in social and hierarchal status, stigmatization, absence of local community control over events that affect one's life, disconnectedness with nature, absence of a sense of living out a life-cycle, rapidly changing technology and the accelerating pace of institutional growth, demographic changes of age and ethnicity, mass migrations (60% of children starting school in southern California do not speak English), decreasing ability of individual societies to "control" the worldwide organization of economic activities, requirements for basic societal value changes, and the expanding evolutionary changes in the roles of women (6).

Anticipating these developments, social psychiatrists have been developing treatment systems that embrace holistically the milieus of mental health services. In the 1940s Joshua Bierer, Founder of the World Association for Social Psychiatry, pioneered the development of a community psychiatric hospital—the Social Psychotherapy Center, which was later named the Marlboro Day Hospital (10). Halfway houses, self-governed therapeutic groups (self-help groups), and other innovations reflective of his new insights and integrations followed (4).

Hudolin in Yugoslavia developed a network of Clubs of Treated Alcoholics located throughout the Yugoslavia Federation. He integrated the support of concerned individuals and organizations, including the Red Cross, service organizations, unions, industry, employers, and political organizations, into a holistic system which, in collaboration with the Zagreb Institute for the Treatment of Alcohol and Other Chemical Abuses, has effectively embraced a major public health problem. Alcoholism carries with it a significant affective disorder, and as is well known, alcoholics experience a high rate of suicide (5).

Under the direction of Louis Miller, then Chief National Psychiatrist of Israel, a National Health System was developed that literally reached to the grassroots and curbstones of the country. Further, Miller developed "community theatre" as a remedial measure for many varieties of social problems, including juvenile gangs and delinquency (5).

Bierer, Hudolin, and Miller recognized that mental disorders result from the interaction of precursors arising from different systems levels. These specific precursors lead to mental-disorder, systems-forming activity. If we seek answers from only one system or subsystem, our understanding will be flawed and our treatments will be inadequate. In effect, the creators of effective mental health treatment systems are agents of social change. They must design and create complex systems of human cooperation between many different social institutions, organizations, and individuals. Successful social psychiatric treatment systems evolve from the implementation of collaboration between religious, economic, political, legal, psychiatric, and many more disciplines.

In the future psychiatrists will adopt the biopsychosocial ecological living systems approach to the diagnosis and treatment of mental disorders. In addition to being psychotherapists, we will become psychiatric case managers and work with teams and networks of people in the social management area. Duhl predicts that planning organizations and governmental bodies will

> look closely at how mental illness is being diagnosed and treated. They will explore precisely the needs of the patient, community and families and develop a comprehensive map of the issues. The issues are, undoubtedly, biological, social, psychological, and economic. The solutions will involve decentralization, community organization, and broad participation. Once the issues are mapped out through this type of participation by many people across a state, nation and world, new programs will be developed (8, p. 141).

In the future psychiatrists will be experts about the "inside" and the "outside" of human beings. Rapidly changing societies in our rapidly changing world will require social psychiatrists capable of being systems precursor agents, forerunners who will ensure that the humanitarian commitments of our profession are fulfilled.

REFERENCES

1. Abraham, K. (1927). Notes on the psychoanalytical investigation and treatment of manic-depressive insanity and allied conditions. In *Selected papers* (Chap. 17). London: Institute of Psychoanalysis and Hogarth Press.
2. Brenner, M. D. (1985). Economic change and the suicide rate: A population model including loss, separation, illness, and alcohol consumption. In M. R. Zales (Ed.), *Stress in health and disease* (pp. 160–185). New York: Brunner/Mazel.
3. Cancro, R. (1986). Social and biologic psychiatry: Fusion or fission? *American Journal of Social Psychiatry, 6*(2), 86.
4. Carleton, J. L. (1985). Front cover story: Joshua Bierer—Pioneer in social psychiatry, his spirit lives on. *American Journal of Social Psychiatry, 5*(3), 3–4.
5. Carleton, J. L. (1977). Social psychiatry. In *International Encyclopedia of Psychiatry, Psychology, Psychoanalysis and Neurology*. New York: Aesculapius.
6. Communication Era Task Force (1974). *At the crossroads*. Spokane, WA: Communications Era Task Force.
7. *The Constitution and Bylaws of the World Association for Social Psychiatry* (1978). Zollikerberg, Switzerland: World Association for Social Psychiatry.
8. Duhl, L. J., & Hynes, J. J. (1985). Environmental stress and the crisis of psychiatry. In M. R. Zales (Ed.), *Stress in health and disease* (p. 141). New York: Brunner/Mazel.
9. Fenichel, O. (1945). *The psychoanalytic theory of neurosis* (p. 387). New York: Norton.
10. Gaind, R. (1985). An obituary for Dr. Joshua Bierer. *American Journal of Social Psychiatry, 3*, 5.
11. Gray, W., & Gray, L. (1986). Origin and development of system precursors/system forming theory. *American Journal of Social Psychiatry, 6*(3), 151.
12. Gray, W., & Gray, L. (1981). The system precursor, system forming approach and general systems theory (systems specifics). *Bulletin of the American Association for Social Psychiatry, 2*(1), 16–24.
13. Hinkle, L. E. (1985). *Prevalence of homicide in New York City*. New York: Committee on Public Health of the New York Academy of Medicine.
14. Kaplan, H. I., & Sadock, B. J. (1985). *Comprehensive textbook of psychiatry/IV* (p. 762). Baltimore: Williams & Wilkins.
15. McGuire, M. (1983). Biological expression: Where the environment and social factors fit in. Annual meeting of the American Association for Social Psychiatry, Los Angeles, CA, Sept. 9, 1984.
16. Miller, J. D. (1978). *Living systems*. New York: McGraw-Hill.
17. Rosenman, R. H., & Friedman, M. (1959, 1961). Association of specific overt behavior pattern with blood and cardiovascular findings. *Journal of the American Medical Association, 169*, 1286–1296, 1959; *24*, 1173–1184, 1961.
18. Rosenman, R. H., & Chesney, M. A. (1985). Type A behavior pattern: Its relationship to coronary heart disease and its modification by behavioral and pharmacological approaches. In M. R. Zales (Ed.), *Stress in health and disease* (p. 208). New York: Brunner/Mazel.
19. Spitzer, R. L. (1980). *Diagnostic and statistical manual of mental disorders* (pp. 205–224). Washington, DC: American Psychiatric Association.

6

NOSOLOGY OF AFFECTIVE DISORDERS

BRIAN L. COOK, D.O.,
and
GEORGE WINOKUR, M.D.

*VA Medical Center and Department of Psychiatry,
University of Iowa College of Medicine,
Iowa City, Iowa*

INTRODUCTION

The nosology of affective disorders represents an area of ongoing discussion through which various ideologies and foundational concepts regarding psychiatry have been expressed. This has led to a large number of competing classification systems, in which the areas of overlap are hard to distinguish. Classification schemes have been constructed utilizing various tools throughout their history. A few such tools have included specific symptoms, precipitating events, family history, temporal relationships, and biochemical markers. This confusion has been complicated by philosophical differences among nosologists, which in turn has resulted in idiosyncratic definitions of various classifying terms.

The sources of many of the above-noted controversies were reviewed by Kendell (27) in 1976. He noted that affective disorders (depressions) provide a convenient arena for several disputes concerning the nature and classification of mental illness as a whole: whether they are independent entities or arbitrary concepts; whether they should be represented by a typology or by dimension; and what constitutes the boundary between the affective disorders and normal mood states, anxiety disorders, personality disorders, and schizophrenia or other mental disorders.

INITIAL ISSUES IN THE CLASSIFICATION OF AFFECTIVE DISORDERS

The first step in establishing a system of classification of any disorder is to define its boundaries. This is important for two primary purposes. First, one must delimit the areas that the classification must cover. Second, all aspects within these areas must be covered in the classification schema.

The Boundaries Between Normal and Abnormal Affective States

The distinction between dysphoria, sadness, and depression presents semantic as well as definitional difficulties. The use of a term such as *depression*, which is in common usage, to describe a clinically meaningful syndrome can lead to misconceptions. Furthermore, where to draw the line between the depression that represents day-to-day sadness and adaptation to life versus a morbid depression is arguable. This problem of dealing with limits of any illness is not unique to psychiatry, however, and need not lead to pessimism regarding psychiatric nosology. Such situations are common in other areas of medicine as well. For example, the definition of such diseases as rheumatic fever or multiple sclerosis presents similar diagnostic problems. In psychiatric diagnosis, recent emphasis has been on using structured interviews and diagnostic criteria to make such distinctions more reliable and hopefully more valid.

Fortunately, the distinction between mania and euthymia is more easily agreed upon. As one extends the concept of manic states to include such items as cyclothymia or hypomania, the demarkation becomes more blurred.

The Boundary Between Affective Disorders and Schizophrenia

The distinction between affective disorder and schizophrenia has been of central importance in the classification of psychotic illness in American psychiatry. The boundary that has marked the separation of these disorders has shifted at various points in time. DSM-II (18) listed the schizoaffective disorders within the schizophrenic disorders, while the research diagnostic criteria (RDC) (37) separated them from both the schizophrenias and affective disorders. DSM-III (19) left schizoaffective disorder undefined, but developed a new category of affective disorders: major depression or mania with mood-incongruent psychotic features. The relevance of mood-congruent versus mood-incongruent features in depression has been reviewed by Coryell et al. (14) and also by Winokur et al. (45). In the former study, it was noted that older depressed patients with psychotic features present with a picture more typical of severe depression. Younger subjects were also noted to display a greater familial risk for schizophrenia than the older group, suggesting greater diagnostic heterogeneity in the younger sample. The Winokur et al. (45) study examined the diagnostic value of assessing mood congruence in delusions and hallucinations and their relationship to the affective state. In that report they noted that psychotic symptoms (defined as delusions and/or hallucinations) were common in unipolar depressives (48%) and bipolar patients (42%) and were almost always seen in schizophrenics and schizoaffectives. They further reported that the affective disorders usually showed mood-congruent symptoms and the schizophrenics mood-incongruent types. A marked dissociation of affective state and mood-congruent psychotic symptoms in schizophrenics was observed. Thus, though depressed, schizophrenics usually showed only mood-incongruent psychotic symptoms. This suggests that mood-incongruent symptoms may take precedence over the affective state in diagnosis. When these same patients were evaluated in a family study of transmission of psychotic symptoms (44), the schizophrenics and schizoaffectives were noted to breed true in the transmission of psychotic symptoms, but the affective disorders did not. From these results, it was suggested that a proportion of the schizoaffectives were actually schizophrenics who were simply following the schizophrenic familial pattern of illness transmission.

These studies point out the problems of attempting to establish a clear boundary between the schizophrenias and affective disorders. Historically as the definition of affective disorders has been expanded, increased heterogeneity has been introduced into this arena. Simultaneously, the reverse has occurred in the schizophrenias.

The Boundary Between Affective Disorders and Anxiety Disorders

The overlap and diagnostic confusion between affective disorders and anxiety disorders is considerable. Anxiety symptoms, including phobic avoidance and panic attacks, are often seen in patients with depression. Secondary depression develops in about 50% of patients with anxiety disorders (7). Both disorders respond to antidepressant therapy (31). To facilitate trying to separate these disorders, multivariate analyses (34), follow-up studies (13), and family studies (15) have been employed. From this work, a picture of more chronicity is seen in anxiety disorders versus affective disorders, and anxiety disorder shows a familial excess of anxiety but not depressive disorder in relatives of probands.

The Boundary Between Affective Disorders and Personality Disorders

Studies reported by Akiskal et al. (1, 2) and Pfohl et al. (32) demonstrate that affective disorders are frequently complicated or influenced by the presence of at least one personality disorder. The boundary between these disorders is blurred by Akiskal's inclusion of subaffective disorders within the affective disorder spectrum. This view, however, may have significant treatment implications, if the characterological symptoms are responsive to pharmacological intervention. Another factor that makes distinction between these areas difficult involves the influence major affective disorder imparts on interepisode function by social disruption during episodic exacerbation of the mood disorder.

The Boundary Between Affective Disorders and Organic Mental Disorders

An area that has recently commanded increasing attention has been the relationship between organic factors and affective disruptions. Robinson et al. (33) reported on the relationship of stroke and depression, while Cook et al. (9, 10) and Shukla et al. (36) have pursued the relationship between head trauma as well as various other organic factors in bipolar illness. These data will be summarized later in this chapter. Another area where affective disorders interface with traditionally considered organic pathology involves dementia and other cognitive changes. Differential diagnosis involving elderly depressives who present with a demented picture requires careful attention to details such as past psychiatric history and family history of psychiatric illness. The mental status examination in such situations can present with very similar findings, thus highlighting the insidious ways in which affective disorders can present.

In summary, it becomes apparent that the boundary of where affective disorder begins and what the concept should encompass is controversial. Despite this problem, efforts to classify affective disorder have been useful for a number of reasons. Clinically, the classification of these disorders may be helpful in determining the choice of treatment and in predicting outcome. From a research perspective, classification of patients into homogeneous groups may facilitate understanding in the areas of biochemical correlates, genetics, and pharmacological response.

This chapter describes many of the classification systems now in use in a clinically relevant way. Furthermore, the usefulness of various systems is discussed in terms of their predictive value regarding the course of mental illness, differential response to treatment, and the relationship to external validating techniques such as laboratory markers.

CLASSIFICATION: CATEGORICAL OR DIMENSIONAL?

The question of whether classification in affective disorders is better represented by a categorical or dimensional approach has been long-standing. Kendell (27) reviewed this problem and succinctly pointed out the major advantages and disadvantages of these different techniques. He noted that a typological or categorical system provides ease of description and a conceptualization that is aligned with the remainder of the medical model of disease classification. Despite these advantages, he noted that natural boundaries are not always easily defined, as was noted earlier in this chapter. The advantages reported for dimensional systems were increased flexibility, less tendency to ignore or misinterpret atypical symptoms, and the discouragement of naïve assumptions regarding disease entities in psychiatric diagnosis. Andreasen (3) reviewed this same controversy in 1982. She noted that disadvantages involving the dimensional approach included their reliance on difficult-to-conceptualize statistical derivations, their complexity, and the lack of a means to inherently know which factors are clinically meaningful and which are statistical artifacts.

The choice of which general type of system to use may depend on its use. In clinical practice, DSM-III or ICD-9 classification may be required to facilitate insurance processing or other third-party payment. Epidemiological study utilizing large populations may be best suited to categorical classification. Various other types of research may call for other systems that uniquely fit specific needs. Thus, the choice of system must be individualized to the situation.

CLASSIFICATION SYSTEMS

Two systems of classification widely used include the *International Classification of Diseases*, ninth edition (ICD-9) (46), and the *Diagnostic and Statistical Manual of the American Psychiatric Association*, third edition, revised (DSM-III-R) (20).

ICD-9

This system of classification was developed to be used world-wide in the classification of medical and psychiatric disorders. The system as it is written presently is outdated and is soon to undergo major revisions. Terminology in the ICD-9 is confusing. The separation of bipolar and nonbipolar affective disorder is implied, but severe depressions without a history of mania are referred to as manic-depressive psychosis, depressed type. This may lead to classification errors by psychiatrists who may interpret manic-depressive illness as being synonymous with a bipolar course. This subdivision and its importance will be reviewed later. Another area in which the ICD-9 differs from other contemporary systems is with its inclusion of the schizoaffective disorders among the schizophrenias. Table 1 summarizes the classification of affective disorders in ICD-9.

Table 1
ICD-9 Classification of Affective Disorders

Affective psychosis
Manic-depressive psychosis, manic type
Manic depressive psychosis, depressed type
Manic-depressive psychosis, circular type, currently manic
Manic-depressive psychosis, circular type, currently depressed
Manic-depressive psychosis, circular type, currently mixed
Manic-depressive psychosis, circular type, currently unspecified
Other nonorganic psychoses
Depressive type
Excitative type
Neurotic disorders
Neurotic depression
Personality disorders
Affective
Acute reaction to stress
Predominant disturbance of emotions
Adjustment reaction
Brief depressive reaction
Prolonged depressive reaction
Depressive disorder, not elsewhere classified
Schizophrenia
Schizoaffective type

DSM-III-R

The DSM-III has served the needs of clinicians and researchers with diverse backgrounds since 1980. In order to update the criteria in response to knowledge gained from its utilization and to hopefully make the system more useful, various changes have been incorporated into the DSM-III-R (revised) edition. The proposed changes became available in May 1987. One alteration involves changing the name of the affective disorders to mood disorders. Table 2 summarizes the DSM-III-R categories of mood disorders.

The other major changes in DSM-III-R include reorganization such that bipolar disorders and depressive disorders are grouped together. The diagnostic threshold for the diagnosis of mania is also increased to include the requirement of marked impairment in social or occupational functioning or hospitalization. Schizoaffective disorder also has criteria specified.

A CONCEPTUAL MODEL FOR AFFECTIVE DISORDERS

As noted at the outset of this chapter, many classification systems have been debated during the history of psychiatry. The primary goal of this chapter is to present a model for classification that makes sense and can be supported with available research data. Table 3 presents such a model of classification for the major affective disorders.

Organic Affective Syndrome

The recognition that affective as well as cognitive and personality changes can follow organic insults to the brain has been a part of psychiatric literature for a considerable period of time. Clarification of such relationships has become a focus of recent research by a number of groups. Cummings (16) reviewed a host of neurological, systemic, and pharmacological factors that have been associated with depression, and these will not be reconsidered here.

In bipolar states, it has generally been thought that mania represents a rather homogeneous illness, and little work has been done to consider potential subgroups among such patients. Krauthammer and Klerman (28) summarized the French and English literature in 1978 and described various medical and/or pharmacological antecedents related to the subsequent development of mania. Their list of such factors was updated by Stasiek and Zetin (38) in 1985. More recently, head trauma (36), as well as nonspecific factors such as perinatal trauma, developmental delay, neuropsychological deficits, and birth traumas (10), has been associated with

Table 2
DSM-III-R Classification of Mood (Affective) Disorders

Bipolar disorders
Bipolar disorder, mixed
Bipolar disorder, manic
Bipolar disorder, depressed
Severity: mild, moderate, severe without psychotic features, with psychotic features, partial remission, full remission
Cyclothymia
Bipolar disorder, not otherwise specified
Depressive disorders
Major depression, single episode
Major depression, recurrent
Severity: same as in bipolar disorders
With or without melancholia
Dysthymia
Depressive disorder, not otherwise specified
Schizoaffective disorder
Adjustment disorder with depressed mood

later development of mania. This work is supported by EEG studies which have suggested that abnormal EEG tracings in bipolar subjects predict a negative family history of affective disorder (9, 17, 26), and thus a less likely familial transmission of the disorder.

As a conceptual model regarding organic factors and affective disorders, a distinction should be drawn between those disorders which are "induced" by the organic cause and those associated with structural brain changes. Such a distinction has implications in terms of course and treatment. For example, a picture of depression frequently follows withdrawal from alcoholism. Such a depression rarely requires specific antidepressant therapy, and typically resolves in a few days (5). Such depressions rarely recur unless the offending factor is reintroduced. On the other hand, depression following structural changes, such as stroke, frequently requires antidepressant pharmacotherapy (33), and the symptoms frequently relapse. The implications of structural organic factors in bipolar illness in terms of course and treatment response are less clear, but work by Himmelhoch and Garfinkel (24) and Shukla et al. (35) suggests that such patients may be refractory to standard lithium therapy and may have rapidly cycling or mixed symp-

Table 3
A Conceptual Model for Classification of the Affective Disorders

- Affective Disorders
  - Organic affective syndrome
    - Induced
    - Structural
  - Bipolar disorders
    - Bipolar I
    - Bipolar II
  - Unipolar disorders
    - Reactive depression
      - Bereavement
      - Depression secondary to medical illness
    - Endogenous–psychotic depression
      - FPDD
      - SDD
    - Neurotic–reactive DSD Secondary to neurosis, personality disorders, and substance use disorders
  - Schizoaffective disorder

FPDD, familial pure depressive disorder. SDD, sporadic depressive disorder. DSD, depressive spectrum disorder.

tomatology. In this subgroup of bipolars, the addition of carbamazepine may be indicated.

Bipolar Disorders

The division of affective disorders into unipolar and bipolar types is probably the most widely recognized dichotomy in psychiatry. Unipolar affective disorder refers to patients with depression only. Bipolar affective disorder designates an illness with both depression and mania or mania alone. The origins of the term *mania* reach deeply into history, dating to Hippocrates. The earliest use of this term referred to a mental illness with acute onset and a mood of merriment or agitation (30). The concept of an illness characterized by excitement and depression can be traced at least to the writings of Areteus in the second century A.D. By 1686, Theophile Bonet used the term *maniaco-melancholicus* to characterize a group of patients. The next century found Falret's description of "circular insanity" (1854) and Baillarger's "double-form insanity" (1854). Leonhard (29) first proposed in 1957 that bipolar and unipolar forms of affective disorder may be different and distinct illnesses.

The separation of affective disorder between those with and without a history of mania has been intensely studied, and validation of the concept has been shown through the use of genetic studies, family studies, biological studies, and evaluation of treatment response and illness course.

Two primary areas of debate concerning this dichotomy are still ongoing. The first area of debate regards whether bipolar illness is truly a separate illness from unipolar affective disorder, or rather the former is just a more severe form of the latter.

The other issue involves what threshold is appropriate for the diagnosis of mania. Akiskal et al. (2) suggested that the affective spectrum may include presentations that overlap with symptoms of various personality disorders, most prominently the borderline personality disorder.

A potential division of bipolar affective disorder into bipolar I and bipolar II disorders has recently obtained increasing attention. Bipolar II disorder is characterized by recurrent depressions with episodes of hypomania intermixed that do not require hospitalization. Several studies (21, 22) have been able to show that such a distinction appears valid along genetic and longitudinal lines. Endicott et al. (22) reported on data concerning prior course, characteristics of the index episode, and familial aggregation of the two types of bipolar disorder and concluded that the available information was sufficient to support the separation of both bipolar I and bipolar II disorders from recurrent unipolar disorder, and from each other. This view is supported by family studies which show that increased rates of bipolar II disorder are seen in relatives of bipolar II probands when compared to bipolar I or unipolar probands (12, 21, 23). These studies were further able to reject the hypothesis that bipolar II disorder is simply a less severe form of bipolar I disorder.

Unipolar Disorders

Patients who have symptoms of depression and no history of mania are probably the most heterogeneous, and thus the most difficult to categorize in a classification of affective disorders. Table 3 proposes three primary subcategories of unipolar depression.

Reactive Depression

A situational or reactive depression is a depressive illness that develops after an event or in a situation that seems likely to have contributed to the appearance of the episode of depression at that time (25). Bereavement as a model for reactive depression has been well described by Clayton et al. (8). In their studies, it has been shown that a full range of depressive symptoms is common during the first year of bereavement. Symptoms of psychomotor retardation and delusional guilt are rarely seen, and suicidal ideation does not persist beyond one month. Psychiatric hospitalization is not increased in the first year of bereavement, although the young bereaved may seek psychiatric counseling. Most symptoms begin to improve in three to four months, and recovery is usually seen in one year. Delayed grief, presenting as an affective syndrome with onset for the first time beyond one year after the death occurs, in 5% of the population.

A second type of reactive depression may be seen in response to various serious medical illnesses. Stewart et al. (39) studied 60 severely ill medical patients and showed that 20% had a clinical depression following the onset of a major medical illness. Cassem and Hackett (6) estimate that 30% of consultations on patients with life-threatening medical illness will uncover depressions. Winokur et al. (42) compared depressions secondary to medical and psychiatric illnesses and some marked differences were uncovered. Patients with depression secondary to medical illness appeared to have an illness that could be considered reactive to a relatively acute stress, and it is seen in individuals with no family background of alcoholism. The depression secondary to medical illness was noted to be more responsive to treatment and the prognosis/course was better than in depressions secondary to the listed psychiatric diagnoses.

The above-described pattern of reactive depression does not seem to be easily extended to other stressful situations. Hirschfeld et al. (25) compared situational major depressions with nonsituational major depressions, and no differences were seen in clinical characteristics or family history of psychiatric illness. Treatment response to imipramine or ECT did not seem to be influenced by the presence of a precipitating event in a large study by Avery and Lubrano (4).

Thus, while bereavement follows a rather predictable pattern following loss, and depression following medical illnesses can be separated from depression following other psychiatric diagnoses, situational depression has otherwise not been a particularly useful concept. For these reasons, only bereavement and depression following medical illness are included under the reactive depression category in Table 3.

Endogenous-Psychotic Versus Neurotic-Reactive Depression

Patients presenting with depression only which does not follow organic central nervous system insults, medical illness, or bereavement can be further subdivided. Historically the terms endogenous-psychotic and neurotic-reactive have been used to separate out the remaining patients who suffer depressive disorders. Although the terms *neurotic* and *reactive* have at times been used synonymously, evidence exists that depressions reactive to life stresses may be entirely different from those depressions that occur in the context of an unstable personality or a stormy life-style, i.e., "neurotic depression." The evidence for the lack of importance of precipitating factors in depressions other than those outlined previously has been discussed. Winokur (40) has suggested criteria for neurotic-reactive depression which includes: specific symptom criteria for depression, the presence of a stormy life-style, presence of life events that the patient attributes as precipitating the depression, specific symptoms, and personality traits. Winokur et al. (43) expanded the concept of neurotic depression to include depression secondary to neurosis (somatization disorder, anxiety disorders), antisocial personality disorder or other personality disorders, or substance abuse disorder or primary depression with a family history of alcoholism (depression spectrum disorder). By using this methodology to define neurotic depression, and thus defining endogenous depression as a depression left over by exclusion of the neurotic depressives, robust differences could be demonstrated (43). Neurotic depressives are more likely to have marital problems and are less likely to respond to hospitalization with marked improvement. The endogenous group is more likely to have melancholic symptoms, psychotic symptoms such as delusions and hallucinations, and memory problems on mental status examination. These groups have also been noted to differ on such biological markers as dexamethasone suppression testing, glucose sensitivity to insulin, imipramine binding platelet membranes, REM latency, and diurnal advance of cortisol nadir.

Endogenous-Psychotic Depression

The category of depression that remains after one carefully screens for the neurotic subtype(s) can be referred to as the endogenous-psychotic group. Such probands with definite depression, no history of mania or relevant organic factors, and in whom exclusion of the "neurotic" factors, bereavement, and medical illness is carefully performed will leave a group that can be subdivided by familial background. The familial pure depressive disease group (FPDD) shows a family history of only depression, no mania, no alcoholism, and no antisocial personality. The sporadic depressive disease group (SDD) shows no family history of alcoholism, antisocial personality, depression, or mania. When one compares the FPDD and

SDD groups, several differences become apparent. The SDD group has a later onset of illness, generally in the late 30s or 40s, versus the early 30s in the FPDD. The sporadic-group females also have more self-reproach and are more likely first-admission presentations at index. Both male and female sporadics are less likely to have an acute onset at time of hospitalization.

When the SDD group has been separated into those with an onset before and after age 40 years, interesting findings are seen. The older SDD patients are less responsive to treatment, symptomatically show less loss of interest and more tearfulness, and show less diurnal variation. The older SDD patient is also reported to be twice as likely to be a first-episode patient at the time of index admission.

While separation of the SDD and FPDD has been successful upon a variety of clinical factors, Winokur (41) does note that because sporadic depression is diagnosed on the basis of an absence of a family history, the diagnosis may be somewhat less reliable than in the FPDD. For example, some family members of the SDD group may have died relatively early, thus not experiencing the full age of risk for depression, or the SDD proband may not be aware of various family members who have experienced depression and thus are misclassified. The findings related to the older SDD group suggest that this group may constitute a distinct entity, but the earlier-onset SDD group may be a mixture of FPDD and DSD-neurotic patients.

Schizoaffective Disorder

This category of illness presents particular problems in classification. The term *schizoaffective disorder* has historically implied a mixture of schizophrenic and affective symptoms. Where schizoaffective disorder fits in relationship to these separate categories of illness is uncertain. Does schizoaffective disorder fall within the schizophrenic realm, the affective realm, or neither? At present, clinical data are inadequate to determine the question of etiology. The presence of schizophrenic symptoms mixed with affective symptoms generally predicts a poorer prognosis, but this is not always the case. Coryell (11) proposed guidelines regarding the course of illness in such patients. He concluded that in schizoaffective patients with demographic features more characteristic of schizophrenia, a relatively poor prognosis can be anticipated. Among such features, he cited early onset (before age 30), insidious onset, family history negative for clear affective disorder or positive for clear schizophrenia, chronic course, and prodromal traits such as social isolation, peculiar behavior, or long-standing role impairment. Good prognosis was implied with the converse of those features.

SUMMARY

This chapter outlines a practical guide for classification of affective disorder. The initial division of the affective disorders is based on whether specific organic factors are noted, whether mania has ever been present, or whether a mixture of schizophrenic symptoms is seen. The unipolar group is further divided into three main subgroups, but unlike previous systems the endogenous group is defined by exclusion after reactive and neurotic groups are determined. The groups thus formed have been shown to have predictive as well as treatment implications and are hopefully clinically useful.

REFERENCES

1. Akiskal, H. S. (1981). Subaffective disorders: Dysthymic, cyclothymic, and bipolar II disorders in the borderline realm. *Psychiatr. Clin. North Am., 4*, 25.
2. Akiskal, H. S., Rosenthal, T. L., Haykal, R. F., Lemmi, H., Rosenthal, R. H., & Scott-Strauss, A. (1980). Characterological depressions: Clinical and sleep EEG findings separating "subaffective dysthymias" from "character spectrum disorders." *Arch. Gen. Psychiatry, 37*, 777.
3. Andreasen, N. C. (1982). Concepts, diagnosis and classification. In E. S. Paykel (Ed.), *Handbook of affective disorders*. New York: Guilford.
4. Avery, D., & Lubrano, A. (1979). Depression treated with imipramine and ect: The DeCarolis study reconsidered. *Am. J. Psychiatry, 136*(4B), 559.
5. Borg, V., & Weinholdt, T. (1982). Bromocriptine in the treatment of the alcohol-withdrawal syndrome. *Acta Psychiatr. Scand., 65*, 101.
6. Cassem, N., & Hackett, T. (1971). Psychiatric consultation in a coronary care unit. *Ann. Intern. Med., 75*, 9.
7. Clancy, J., Noyes, R. Jr., Hoenk, P. R., & Slymen, D. (1978). Secondary depression in anxiety neurosis. *J. Nerv. Ment. Dis., 160*, 846.
8. Clayton, P. J., Desmarais, L., & Winokur, G. (1968). A study of normal bereavement. *Am. J. Psychiatry, 125*, 168.
9. Cook, B. L., Shukla, S., & Hoff, A. L. (1986). EEG abnormalities in bipolar affective disorder. *J. Affect. Disord., 11*, 147.
10. Cook, B. L., Shukla, S., & Hoff, A. L. (1987). Mania with associated organic factors. *Acta Psychiatr. Scand., 76*(6), 674.
11. Coryell, W. (1986). Schizoaffective and schizophreniform disorders. In G. Winokur & P. J. Clayton (Eds.), *The medical basis of psychiatry*. Philadelphia: Saunders.
12. Coryell, W., Endicott, J., Reich, T., et al. (1984). A family study of bipolar II disorder. *Br. J. Psychiatry, 145*, 49.
13. Coryell, W., Noyes, R., Jr., & Clancy, J. (1983). Panic disorder and primary unipolar depression: A comparison of background and outcome. *J. Affect. Disord., 5*, 311.
14. Coryell, W., Pfohl, B., & Zimmerman, M. (1986). Heterogeneity in psychotic depression. *Comp. Psychiatry, 25*, 430.

15. Crowe, R. R., Noyes, R. Jr., Pauls, D. L., & Slymen, D. (1983). A family study of panic disorder. *Arch. Gen. Psychiatry, 40,* 1065.
16. Cummings, J. L. (1985). *Clinical neuropsychiatry.* Orlando, FL: Grune & Stratton.
17. Dalen, P. (1965). Family history, the electroencephalogram, and perinatal factors in manic conditions. *Acta Psychiatr. Scand., 41,* 527.
18. *Diagnostic and statistical manual of mental disorders* (2nd ed.). (1968). Washington, DC: American Psychiatric Association.
19. *Diagnostic and statistical manual of mental disorders* (3rd ed.). (1980). Washington, DC: American Psychiatric Association.
20. *Diagnostic and statistical manual of mental disorders* (3rd ed., revised). (1987). Washington, DC: American Psychiatric Association.
21. Dunner, D. L. (1983). Subtypes of bipolar affective disorder with particular regard to bipolar II. *Psychiatr. Dev., 1,* 75.
22. Endicott, J., Nee, J., Andreasen, N., et al. (1985). Bipolar II: Combine or keep separate? *J. Affect. Disord., 8,* 17.
23. Gershon, E. S., Hamovit, J., Gurott, J., et al. (1982). A family study of schizoaffective, bipolar I, bipolar II, unipolar, and normal control probands. *Arch. Gen. Psychiatry, 39,* 1157.
24. Himmelhoch, J. M., & Garfinkel, M. E. (1986). Sources of lithium resistance in mixed mania. *Psychopharmacol. Bull., 22,* 613.
25. Hirschfeld, R., Klerman, G., Andreasen, N., Clayton, P., & Keller, M. (1985). Situational major depressive disorder. *Arch. Gen. Psychiatry, 42,* 1109.
26. Kadrmas, A., & Winokur, G. (1979). Manic depressive illness and EEG abnormalities. *J. Clin. Psychiatry, 40,* 35.
27. Kendell, R. E. (1976). The classification of depressions: A review of contemporary confusion. *Br. J. Psychiatry, 129,* 15.
28. Krauthammer, C., & Klerman, G. (1978). Secondary mania: Manic syndrome associated with antecedent physical illness or drugs. *Arch. Gen. Psychiatry, 35,* 1333.
29. Leonhard, K. (1957). *Aufteilung der endogenen psychosen.* Berlin: Akademie.
30. Menninger, K., Mayman, M., & Pruyser, P. (1977). *The vital balance. The life process in mental health and illness.* New York: Penguin Books.
31. Noyes, R., Jr. (1983). Anxiety, phobic and obsessional disorders. In H. Hippius & G. Winokur (Eds.), *Psychopharmacology* I: Pt. 2. *Clinical psychopharmacology.* Princeton, NJ: Excerpta Medica.
32. Pfohl, B., Stangle, D., & Zimmerman, M. (1984). The implication of DSM-III personality disorders for patient with major depression. *J. Affect. Disord., 7,* 309.
33. Robinson, R. G., Kubos, K. L., Starr, L. B., Rao, K., & Price, T. R. (1984). Mood disorders in stroke patients. *Brain, 107,* 81.
34. Roth, M., & Mountjoy, C. Q. (1982). The distinction between anxiety states and depressive disorders. In E. S. Paykel (Ed.), *Handbook of affective disorders.* New York: Guilford.
35. Shukla, S., Cook, B. L., & Hoff, A. L. (1987). Treatment response in mania associated with organic factors. *New Research 134, Proceedings of 140th Annual Meeting of the American Psychiatric Association,* Chicago, IL, 91.
36. Shukla, S., Cook, B. L., & Mukherjee, S. (1987). Mania following head trauma. *Am. J. Psychiatry, 144,* 93.
37. Spitzer, R. C., Endicott, J., & Robins, E. (1978). Research diagnostic criteria: Rationale and reliability. *Arch. Gen. Psychiatry, 35,* 773.
38. Stasiek, C., & Zetin, M. (1985). Organic manic disorders. *Psychosomatics, 5,* 394.
39. Stewart, M., Drake, F., & Winokur, G. (1965). Depression among medically ill patients. *Dis. Nerv. Syst., 26,* 479.
40. Winokur, G. (1985). The validity of neurotic-reactive depression. *Arch. Gen. Psychiatry, 42,* 1116.

41. Winokur, G. (1986). Familial classification of depressive illnesses. In H. Hippius, G. L. Klerman, & N. Matussek (Eds.), *New results in depression research*. Berlin: Springer-Verlag.

42. Winokur, G., Black, D. W., & Nasrallah, A. (1988). Depression secondary to other psychiatric disorders and medical illnesses. *Am. J. Psychiatry, 145*, 233.

43. Winokur, G., Black, D. W., & Nasrallah, A. (1987). Neurotic depression: A diagnosis based on pre-existing characteristics. *Eur. Arch. Psychiatr. Neuro. Sci., 236*, 343.

44. Winokur, G., Scharfetter, C., & Angst, J. (1985). A family study of psychotic symptomatology in schizophrenia, schizoaffective disorder, unipolar depression, and bipolar disorder. *Eur. Arch. Psychiatr. Neuro. Sci., 234*, 295.

45. Winokur, G., Scharfetter, C., & Angst, J. (1985). The diagnostic value in assessing mood congruence in delusions and hallucinations and their relationship to the affective state. *Eur. Arch. Psychiatr. Neuro. Sci., 234*, 299.

46. World Health Organization (1978). *Mental disorders: Glossary and guide to their classification in accordance with the ninth revision of the International Classification of Diseases*. Geneva: WHO.

7

DIAGNOSIS OF DEPRESSION

Peter Berner, Dr. Med.

Professor of Psychiatry and Head,
Psychiatric University Clinic, Vienna, Austria

INTRODUCTION

This chapter reviews topical approaches to the diagnosis of depression.

In clinical language, the term *depression* refers to "states" and does not include those who from early life onward present depressive traits. Change from a previous condition is therefore the prerequisite for diagnosis of depression. This change may be sudden or of insidious onset; it may be a completely new occurrence or just a marked aggravation of a depressive personality structure. It must, however, be noticeable either to the patient himself or to those in his environment—or to both—as a definite alteration.

The problem that then arises is how to demarcate normal states of sadness from pathological depression. Is the latter distinguished from the former by the quality or just by the intensity of the depressive features, by their duration, by their autonomous appearance in the absence of triggering environmental events, or only by the observation over time of recurrent pathological states of the same or of another—for instance manic—type? The answers so far provided to these questions vary considerably from school to school, according to which concept of depression or one of its possible subgroups they adhere to. These divergent concepts are drawn from observations and their theoretical interpretation and, in view of our lack of knowledge, still require verification. Since the different viewpoints are reflected in the various available diagnostic rules, these will be briefly described next.

When psychiatric nosology emerged in the middle of the 19th century, the clinical relevance of depression was determined by the intensity of its symptomatology which required hospitalization. The discovery by Falret

(11) and Baillarger (4) that cases primarily presenting a depressive symptomatology of clinical relevance may take a circular course in the sense of a "folie à double forme" led to the assumption that depression is the manifestation of a disease. The observation, however, that depressive states may occur in connection with distressing experiences led to the distinction of two etiologically different groups of these disorders—one biologically, the other psychologically determined.

The first group was further subdivided into "endogenous" depressions, thought to be of a constitutional-hereditary origin, and "somatic" depressions, related to demonstrable somatic illnesses. The second group was further split up into "reactive" depressive states, appearing in immediate connection with traumatizing events, and "neurotic" depressions, which were supposedly the consequence of long-term psychologically distorting influences similar to those considered to cause classical psychoneuroses. Whereas the identification of somatogenic depression is generally regarded as a problem of more practical than theoretical importance, which can be reduced to the reminder to check carefully and repeatedly the possibility of a somatic cause, the justification and feasibility of distinguishing the other three groups from each other and from normality are still controversial.

Classical psychiatry has envisaged this problem in the perspective of an endogenous-reactive/neurotic dichotomy, with the common denominator of both groups being a depressed, sad, pessimistic outlook of longer duration than normal with mood swings, accompanied by a decrease in the habitual level of energy and psychomotor retardation or agitation. Beyond these features endogenous depressions have been thought to differ from the reactive/neurotic group in regard to details of symptomatology, circumstance of onset, and course. Since endogenous depression was considered a disease, its phenomenology was searched for in features which, according to Jaspers (23), postulate that diseases—contrary to abnormal reactions and developments—produce symptoms escaping psychological understanding and are qualitatively different from normal feelings or behavior. Schneider (40) thought such a phenomenon is evident in the "vital" tinge of the mood changes in which the patient perceives his sadness as a numb sensation of fatigue or of being down on the ground. In Schneider's opinion, this specific symptom serves not only to separate endogenous depression from psychologically determined depressions, but also facilitates identification of even the mildest forms of the former by establishing a purely phenomenological distinction between endogenous depression and normal mood swings, thus making it unnecessary to estimate the severity of the symptomatology.

Pursuing Schneider's approach, numerous authors compiled lists of symptoms considered specific for endogenous depression, among which signs pointing to a basically biological disorder—such as characteristic sleep disturbances and diurnal fluctuations—are frequently held to be of primary importance.

In addition to these symptomatological characteristics, endogenous depressions were supposed to be characterized by their autochthonous manifestation, independent of external events, by a normal premorbid personality structure, and by the recurrence of depressive and possibly also manic states. However, experience has convinced many authors that, at least for individual cases, the absence of these conditions may not have great diagnostic value. Endogenous depression may be triggered by stressful experiences or occur in neurotic personalities and recurrence may not be noticed in the case of single episodes or because the time of observation is not sufficiently long (24).

Whereas the classical distinction between endogenous and reactive/neurotic depressions is categorical, the subdivision of the latter group is frequently considered to be dimensional (8, 27). Viewed from this perspective, persons occasionally manifesting reactive depression diverge from those with neurotic depression only in regard to the degree of their psychologically acquired vulnerability. The former show a reduced capacity to cope with distressing life events and subsequently react to them with a depressive response of greater intensity and/or duration than normal individuals. As far as the latter group is concerned, their level of tolerance is still lower so that even minor stress situations, scarcely identifiable as such by external observers, lead to a depressive state. Thus, there is a flowing transition from neurotic overreactive depressions to normal responsiveness, a viewpoint adopted by traditional psychiatry which holds that the reactive/neurotic depressive phenomenology is characterized by the absence of specific endogenous symptoms and only quantitatively different from normality. Under the supposition, however, that neurotic depressions have their roots in early childhood, whereas the reactive ones are triggered by traumatizations of later life, or that different learning processes are involved, other authors envisage them as separate pathogenetic categories, with the former being characterized by long-term adjustment problems and perhaps typical neurotic symptoms, and the latter being linked to stressful events and occurring in previously well-functioning persons. Reactive depressions may furthermore be of brief duration, thus frequently differing from normal grief only by intensity. Neurotic depressions, on the other hand, are thought to be long-lasting because of the patient's incapacity to resolve his psychological problems. This failure to accomplish the "work of mourning"—from a psychoanalytical perspective originally considered the cause of melancholia (16)—also explains the observation that neurotic depressions endure even longer than endogenous ones, the duration of which seems to be limited by the ordinarily episodic course of an underlying biological disturbance.

The traditional dichotomy between endogenous and reactive/neurotic depressions considered as separate etiological categories has been challenged on the grounds that most statistical analyses have not demonstrated a bimodal distribution of depressive states (30). The possibility that methodological artifacts may either produce a spurious bimodality or obscure an existing one (10, 26, 33) still enlivens the controversy—especially between the Maudsley and the Newcastle schools—as to whether a "continuum model of depressive illness" (24a) should be adopted or the traditional dichotomy be maintained (7). The first viewpoint suggests that the reactive/neurotic and the endogenous types of depression represent merely different degrees of severity to be placed on a continuum that passes without interruption into normality (19). The second school of thought defends the categorical approach and stresses, especially in reference to treatment response, that severity does not account for the separation of the two groups (8, 13). This viewpoint receives support from the fact that statistical analyses, although frequently failing to identify a distinct reactive/neurotic factor, reveal quite consistently the existence of an "endogenous depressive item profile," thus suggesting that "the widely propagated scepticism toward the diagnosis of endogenous depression is not valid" (32). Others, however, believe that symptomatology is not suitable for categorical distinctions and that these can only be maintained with reference to illness course. They stipulate, in other words, that only bipolar manic-depressive disorders and unipolar recurrent depressions characterized by complete well-being during the interval might be considered a special group to be separated from the other depressive states (19, 33).

The question, however, as to whether the distinction between a unipolar and a bipolar form of mood disorder (3, 31, 35, 47) justifies the assumption of two definite disease entities is still controversial and has led to classification of different subtypes of unipolar and bipolar illness (15, 29). Akiskal's (1) review of this issue suggests a spectrum of genetic risk, proceeding from infrequent episode unipolar (unipolar I) to recurrent unipolar (unipolar II) to bipolar II (depression and spontaneous hypomania) to bipolar I (depressive and full-blown manic episodes). He assumes that only the unipolar I type may be heterogeneous, including "nonfamilial phenocopies" as well as true endogenous depression, with the latter thought to belong, together with all the other types, to the manic-depressive spectrum. Viewed from this perspective, family history and the occurrence of manic or hypomanic states (which, according to Akiskal, appear in the unipolar II only after psychopharmacological challenge) acquire a special diagnostic meaning.

Attempts to identify subgroups of depressive disorders with regard to either neurophysiological and neurohormonal parameters or responsiveness to specific treatment have had contradictory results (19). Thus, the demarcation of depressive states from normality and their eventual subdivision remain based on pragmatic rules and hypothetical assumptions which may vary from one diagnostic system to the other.

Another important issue concerns the diagnostic value to be attributed to depressive states occurring in simultaneous or successive combination with other psychiatric disorders. The real nature of the relationship between depressive mood and such other psychopathological manifestations is generally unknown and still subject to hypothetical assumptions. Therefore, guidelines for the classification of such conditions are either based on these theoretical concepts or propose purely pragmatic rules. Among the latter, the most unbiased procedure is to accept dual or even multiple diagnoses for the same patient—chronologically as well as simultaneously—and to leave the clarification of the relation between the depressive and the other noted syndromes to further investigations. The distinction between "primary" and "secondary" depressions of the St. Louis school (37) may be placed in the same pragmatic perspective. Primary depressions are there defined as occurring in subjects with no prior history of any other mental disorder, except previous depressive or manic syndromes, whereas depressive states chronologically superimposed on a preexisting nonaffective disorder are called "secondary." This classification has been criticized because it implies that the preexisting psychiatric conditions, such as anxiety neurosis, phobia, alcoholism, and so forth, are "primary" in an etiological sense (38, 45). Although the terminology may be misleading, the "primary"-"secondary" dichotomy aims only at selection of "pure" depressions for research purposes and does not imply that secondary depressions necessarily result from the disorder that preceded or accompanied them.

The most widely applied theoretical guideline for handling the problem of coexistence of different psychiatric syndromes is Jaspers' (23) hierarchical principle, which assumes that neurotic symptoms or personality disorders are relatively "superficial," whereas affective, schizophrenic, and organic symptoms lie on deeper "levels" of the organization of brain functions. When several symptoms that belong to various "levels" occur simultaneously or consecutively, diagnosis is determined by the deepest "level" reached. As organicity is generally established with reference to objective somatic findings and neurotic symptoms or personality disorders have no excluding function, the consequences of the application of this principle vary essentially with the adopted definitions of depression and schizophrenia. Many authors, for instance, will not apply Jaspers' principle for any kind of depressive state occurring in connection with a personality disorder or "typical" neurotic symptomatology, such as hysterical, phobic, or obsessional-compulsive, but they would rule out the diagnosis of neurosis if these features are combined with an endogenous depressive item profile. The endogenous items they refer to are not necessarily symptomatological. Some would apply Jaspers' principle also in cases in which unspecific depressive features occur in connection with personality disturbances or neurotic symptoms, in a premorbid well-adjusted personality, without any relationship to a triggering event. Similarly, the application of Jaspers' principle to the demarcation between depression and schizophrenia leads to different results, independent of the definition attributed to the latter. The boundaries of depression, for instance, are narrow when schizophrenia is diagnosed with reference to Schneider's (41) first-rank symptoms, whereas they remain broad when the diagnosis of schizophrenia is restricted to the presence of formal thought disorders.

On the grounds of theoretical or empirical considerations, some diagnostic systems reversed Jaspers' principle with regard to the hierarchical relationship between schizophrenic and affective symptomatology, giving diagnostic supremacy to the latter. This means that the presence of a depressive or manic syndrome excludes the diagnosis of schizophrenia, the definition of which varies from one system to the other. In these systems (for which the DSM-III definition [9] in its present form is the most popular example) the realm of depression consequently becomes a much broader one than in the systems that adhere to Jaspers' rules in their original version. The rejection of Jaspers' principle for the demarcation between schizophrenic and affective disorders, on the other hand, makes it possible to assign both diagnoses to the same patient, and when the symptoms of both categories are present simultaneously or consecutively, the patient will be diagnosed as schizoaffective. This again restricts the boundaries of depression, making it dependent on how broadly schizophrenia is defined.

Many diagnostic systems introduce nuances into the application of hierarchical rules with regard to the time relation between the different types of symptomatology. Thus, supremacy may, for instance, be attributed to a depressive syndrome only if it occurs simultaneously with a schizophrenic symptomatology, or if it precedes it.

A final concern is demarcation of depression with delusions and possibly also hallucinations from other nonschizophrenic delusional disorders. The traditional approach to this problem is to admit the occurrence of "mood-congruent" delusions and hallucinations as compatible with the diagnosis of depression, whereas "mood-incongruent" features of this kind should be assigned either to schizophrenia or to other categories—the decision of assignation being determined by the rules adopted to distinguish schizophrenia and other delusional or delusional-hallucinatory categories.

Recent follow-up, treatment response, and transcultural studies, however, have convinced many schools to admit that even mood-incongruent delusions and hallucinations may appear in depressions. If such mood-incongruent features are not attributable in a given system to schizophrenia (because they are not, for instance, first-rank symptoms), the decision as to whether the disorder should be assigned to depression or to another (nonschizophrenic) delusional disorder is made according to guidelines similar to those applied to the demarcation between schizophrenia and depression. The diagnostic attribution is determined by the definition of depression (for instance the requirement of an endogenous item profile), the kind of combination between mood-incongruent and depressive symptoms required (some schools, for instance, rule out the diagnosis of depression when the former precede the latter), and the possible establishment of symptom hierarchy (primacy may be given either to the mood-incongruent or to the depressive features, or to none of them; the last option calls for a dual diagnosis or the stipulation of a separate entity).

TOPICAL APPROACHES TO THE DIAGNOSIS OF DEPRESSION

The preceding is merely a rough draft of the unresolved questions in regard to the definition and delineation of depression. In this context we have also referred to the debate over whether a dichotomous separation of two types of depressive disorders, supposedly qualitatively different, is justified or whether depressive subtypes merely represent different degrees of severity to be placed on a continuum. As this controversy has not been definitively resolved, both concepts should be taken into consideration in studying the nature of depression. At present, the categorical approach seems to have greater value for clinical research and practice. The dimensional strategy, on the other hand, can be useful for conceptualization, but may prove methodically sterile unless it is coupled with its typological counterpart (2).

In view of this state of affairs, even adherents of the unitarian model must use subdivisions for practical purposes, but whereas they may use simple criteria to define thresholds for different degrees of severity (25, 36), adherents of the binarian hypothesis must base the distinction between their categories on qualitative differences, identification of which is a much more subtle problem. As each of these two approaches may have its justifications, many diagnostic systems, especially those hoping for universal acceptance, attempt to couple both. Thus, the DSM-III, for instance, though admitting on principle a classification based on severity, establishes a special subgroup corresponding to the traditional concept of "endogenous depression"; others, such as the 1986 draft of ICD-10, try to resolve the problem by taking symptoms traditionally considered as "endogenous" as criteria to define "severe depression" in the frame of a basically unitarian model.

Whatever the underlying hypothesis, a paradigmatic or an operational approach to diagnosis may be chosen. The former compares the features noticeable in a specific patient with those described for "typical cases"; the latter uses algorithms based on defined, logical rules for inclusion or exclusion. As the operational criteria, which made their appearance only during the last two decades, have been mainly derived from classical descriptions still largely applied, and in view of the importance attributed by many schools to the dichotomy hypothesis, we shall take the clinical description of endogenous depression as a point of departure for discussion of the most frequently used diagnostic approaches to depressive states.

Paradigmatic Diagnosis and Differential Diagnosis

The binarian approach. Although depressions traditionally labeled as "endogenous" are presumed to have a biological basis, some authors propose to replace this term by other designations, such as melancholic, autonomous, cryptogenic, or endogenomorphic, which, they feel, better reflect our ignorance of their real nature. As none of these terminologies have yet found general acceptance, we shall still use the word *endogenous*. Up to now, no pathognomic symptoms or objective external criteria are known to establish unequivocally the diagnosis of endogenous depression. Therefore, attribution to this category must be made in several steps, each of which aims at a higher degree of diagnostic certainty. The first step is assessment of characteristic symptoms and corroboration of the diagnosis with nonsymptomatological data, such as course and outcome, factors related to onset, treatment response, or a family history of affective illness. Some of these data are not available at a first manifestation of a depressive disorder (and the symptomatology may be vague at the beginning). Thus, a long follow-up observation is sometimes needed to establish the diagnosis. Since exclusion of organic or toxic causes through appropriate tests is a prerequisite for attribution to the endogenous category, it should be taken for granted in the following discussion.

Depression in general may manifest itself by a wide range of psychological, psychomotor, functional, and behavioral symptoms whose intensity, prevalence, and combination vary considerably from patient to patient. Symptoms include depressed mood, impairment of emotional resonance, anxiety, irritability, reduction of energy, decrease of activity, fatigue, difficulty in thinking and concentration, motor retardation or agitation, loss of appetite, diminution of sexual drive, sleep disturbances or hypersomnia, functional somatic (especially vegetative) symptoms, social withdrawal, suicidal behavior, and so forth. The depressed mood need not be the most dominant feature; some of the other symptoms may be more prominent. The depressive mood-tone itself may be expressed in many different ways, such as sadness, fearfulness, dejectedness, hopelessness, feelings of worthlessness or guilt, anhedonia, incapacity of anticipation, suicidal thoughts, or painful ruminations of various content.

Clinical experience and research indicate that within this symptomatological spectrum, the following features point more specifically to the diagnosis of a mainly biologically determined *endogenous disease*: a distinct quality of depressed mood (of great intensity or otherwise different from the feelings the person has experienced previously, following a distressing event), feelings of guilt or self-reproach, a general lack of responsiveness, refractory anhedonia, lack of energy, marked diurnal variations of the symptomatology, early wakening, middle insomnia, and loss of weight.

The examples of operational definitions of endogenous depression given below demonstrate that there are only minor differences between the various diagnostic systems with regard to this list of "core symptoms." Some enumerations are slightly more comprehensive, others more restrictive (for instance, by excluding guilt feelings on the grounds of transcultural research, indicating that they are a culture-bound epiphenomenon). Many systems give the same weight to each of the symptoms and suggest that their accumulation increases the certainty of the diagnosis. Others allot the highest degree of specificity to biorhythmical changes and consider the diagnosis of endogenous depression as fairly well established only if depressive mood and impaired emotional resonance are combined with characteristic sleep disturbances and diurnal variations in the sense of an endogenous depressive core syndrome.

Genetic loading, a history of episodic or periodic affective disorders of the uni- or bipolar type (even without the manifestation of core symptoms), and the response to somatic treatments (such as ECT or antidepressants) augment beyond doubt the probability that a given depressive state is endogenous. In view of the arguments discussed previously, triggering events and abnormal personality traits support the diagnosis of an endogenous depression only if absent, whereas their presence does not exclude it. As the concept of endogenous depression is based on the categorical model, even mild mood disorders corresponding to the description given may be attributed to this diagnosis provided they fulfill the criteria of a state.

The subdivision of depressive disorders in accordance with prevailing symptomatology into agitated, retarded, anxious, and hostile types (17, 34) represented a temptation to extend the term *endogenous depression* to cases in which the anxious or hostile mood has no depressive features, on condition that it appears autonomously in a previously well-balanced personality and is accompanied by biorhythmical changes. These disorders may be qualified as endogenous anxiety states (42) or as endogenous states of irritability (43), but the term endogenous depression should, for the sake of clarity, be reserved for conditions in which the anxious or hostile moodtone is superimposed on an undoubted depressive background. The assessment of an endogenous depressive state is not yet tantamount to a nosological diagnosis, as it does not preclude the possibility that unipolar and bipolar disorders (although manifesting the same depressive symptomatology) are separate disease entities.

The paradigmatic approach to the diagnosis of *nonendogenous depression* relies above all on exclusion of features considered to be typical for endogenous depressions. This differential diagnosis procedure, which can be especially tricky if anxiety dominates the picture, may be refined through the introduction of psychopathological factors. Klein (28), for instance, stresses that "nonendogenomorphic" depressions are characterized by an impairment of anticipatory but not consummatory reward, and Zimmerman et al. (48) note that nonendogenous depressed patients blame others for their depression. Other criteria, proposed to describe positively nonendogenous depressions, such as relation to triggering events, duration, long-standing maladaptive personality patterns, and presence of distinct neurotic symptoms, hold true only for some of their subgroups and increase, at best (as pointed out in the previous discussion), the probability that a given disorder is nonendogenous but do not, on the other hand, definitely exclude an endogenous depression.

The subdivision of depressive states lacking endogenous features is essentially a matter of convention. If they appear in a previously well-balanced personality as the consequence of an acute distressing event, they are generally labeled as "reactive," whereas their emergence in the frame of long-lasting psychosocial strain will lead to the diagnosis of a "situational" depression. Nonendogenous depressions occurring in patients with maladaptive personality patterns already noticeable in early life are (based on the theoretical concepts adopted) considered either "characterological" or "'neurotic." Some authors, however, reserve the latter term for depressions characterized by the presence of specific neurotic features such as phobic, obsessive-compulsive, or hysterical symptoms. Delusions and hallucinations are generally considered incompatible with the diagnosis of nonendogenous depression.

The diagnosis of conditions in which an *endogenous depressive symptomatology* is combined with *psychopathological phenomena suggesting the possibility of schizophrenia or a nonschizophrenic delusional disorder* is made as described previously. Most of the paradigmatic diagnostic rules adhere either to Jaspers' hierarchical principle and assign such states to schizophrenia if "first-rank" or Bleulerian "fundamental" symptoms are present and to other delusional disorders if the "psychotic" symptomatology is restricted to "second-rank" or Bleulerian "accessory" symptoms. In the latter case, however, an exception is frequently made for mood-congruent delusions or hallucinations whose content concerns "personal inadequacy, guilt, disease, death, nihilism, or deserved punishment" (DSM-III).

The unitarian approach. Paradigmatic attempts to establish thresholds in the frame of the unitarian model are only alluded to in psychiatric literature, as the representatives of this viewpoint prefer to base their diagnoses on operational definitions. These descriptive demarcations are generally restricted to the statement that the loss of interest or pleasure is not pervasive but may be alleviated by affection, on one hand, and to the claim that hallucinations or delusions must be absent in cases of "mild depression," on the other. Symptoms belonging to the endogenous item profile determine the assessment of a "major depressive disorder," as exemplified by the draft formulation of ICD-10, which stipulates that a "severe depressive episode" is, in addition to the general criteria of depression, "accompanied by the so-called 'biological' or 'endogenomorphic' symptoms such as motor retardation, weight loss . . . marked diurnal variation, early morning wakening and loss of libido."

With respect to the differentiation between "major depressions" and other mental disorders, the comments made in connection with the binarian approach also hold true for the unitarian.

Operational Diagnosis and Differential Diagnosis

Operational approaches to diagnosis are conceived either as scales assigning defined weightings to each of its items, or as logic rules determining the combination of symptoms and the conditions required for attribution of a given diagnosis. The latter are called "operational diagnostic criteria" in the narrow sense of the word. Diagnostic scales require discriminant function analysis or related techniques and are used to assist differential diagnosis (39). They thus differ from scales designed to measure severity (such as, for instance, the Hamilton Depression Scale [20]) or to predict course or outcome, which are established by other mathematical derivations. Diagnostic scales are especially applied to discriminate between endogenous and nonendogenous depressions in the perspective of the dichotomy hypothesis by establishing a cutoff score. Operational criteria in the narrow sense, on the other hand, are derived from conventional clinical diagnostic habits. They are composed of different elements containing in each case a list of items out of which a given number must be present. The choice of elements and of the items they include is based on the theoretical, empirical, or pragmatic considerations described in the previous chapter. Thus, the various diagnostic criteria not only define populations of different size, but overlap only partially, depending on which elements and items are employed and in which combination they are put together. This will be illustrated by some examples.

Operational devices based on the dichotomy hypothesis

Scales. The first instrument of this kind is the *Newcastle Scale I* for differential diagnosis between neurotic and endogenous depression (7). It consists of 10 items (adequate personality, nonadequate psychogenesis, distinct quality, weight loss, previous episode, depressive psychomotor activity, anxiety, nihilistic delusions, blaming others, guilt), which are rated by scores from −1 to +2; a sum score of 5 or less leads to assignment to the neurotic group, of 6 or more to the endogenous group.

The *Newcastle Scale II* (18), designed to differentiate between endogenous and nonendogenous depression, replaces most of the items contained in Scale I, basing the aimed distinction mainly on biorhythmical changes, sudden onset, reactivity, duration, retardation, and psychological stress, whereas the reference to personality is omitted. Introducing also weightings of severity of two items, this scale requires a score of −20 or less for the diagnosis of endogenous depression.

Using the same approach, Feinberg and Carroll (13, 14) developed the *Michigan Discrimination Index* to differentiate unipolar and bipolar endogenous depressions from nonendogenous ones, defining two cutoff points in order to distinguish endogenous and nonendogenous depression from a nonclassifiable group.

All three of these scales are designed as research instruments.

Operational criteria. Based on the dichotomy hypothesis, these criteria concentrate on the diagnosis of endogenous depression. For instance, the *Vienna Research Criteria* (5) contain as obligatory elements diurnal variations, sleep disturbances (interrupted or prolonged sleep, early awakening), and at least one of the following symptoms: depressive mood, emotional response either lacking or limited to depressive responses, reduced drive, or agitation. As no hierarchical principle is applied, the diagnosis of a schizoaffective disorder—depressive type—is possible. The schizophrenic symptomatology is restricted to the presence of defined formal thought disorders.

Operational delineations in the unitarian perspective

This approach is best illustrated by the *CATEGO System* (46), which isolates only two classes of depression. Depressive psychoses are defined by depressed mood or depressive delusions or hallucinations. Both symptoms must be present, but schizophrenic symptoms (defined in the Schneiderian perspective) or a mixture with manic features excludes the diagnosis. The chief symptoms of retarded depression are: depressed mood, retardation, guilt, self-deprecation, and agitation. The first of these symptoms must be present, together with one of the others, in the absence of depressive delusions or other psychotic symptoms. If neither of these two classes applies, and if a depressed mood is combined with anxiety, the case is diagnosed as "neurotic depression" or "anxiety or phobic neurosis," according to the severity and combination of symptoms present.

Combined systems

This type of operational criteria attempts to enable the user to establish diagnoses based on severity as well as subclassifications compatible with the dichotomy hypothesis, or with other demarcations serving special purposes. The most elaborate system of this kind is the *Research Diagnostic Criteria* (RDC) (44), which includes the diagnosis of a "major depressive disorder," further subdivided into nonmutually exclusive subtypes, to permit testing of several hypotheses relevant to depression. The subtype labeled "endogenous" encompasses 10 items, all belonging to the endogenous depressive item profile (such as distinct mood quality, lack of reactivity, worse in the morning, pervasive loss of interest or pleasure, self-reproach, excessive or inappropriate guilt feelings, early-morning awakening, middle insomnia, etc.), of which at least four must be present. Other subdivisions make allowances for the distinction between "primary" and "secondary" depression (as conceived in the St. Louis Criteria) (12) and between "agitated" and "retarded" depressions. In addition, the diagnosis of "recurrent unipolar," "psychotic," "incapacitating," "situational," or "simple major depressive disorder" can be established. Bipolar I and bipolar II depressions (both also including cases in which the depression is only of "minor" severity) as well as schizoaffective disorders are not included in the major depressive disorder but are considered to be separate diagnoses.

The DSM-III, in many respects resembling the RDC, differs from the latter mainly in two points. First, the division of "major depressive episodes" (which are opposed to mild depressive states and contain a group labeled "with melancholia" corresponding to the endogenous depressive item profile) is less detailed. Second, the DSM-III subordinates the schizophrenic symptomatology to the depressive one and accordingly refers to depressions with mood-incongruent psychotic features. The RDC, on the other hand, apply no hierarchical rule and attribute to a psychotic major depressive disorder only those cases which do not meet the criteria for "schizoaffective" disorder. The latter is therefore a frequent diagnosis when using the RDC, whereas the DSM-III confines it to a few cases in which a differential diagnosis between schizophrenia and affective disorder cannot be made (however, this viewpoint has been changed in the revision of DSM-III). Regarding the assessment of schizophrenic symptomatology, both systems offer Bleulerian and Schneiderian criteria.

The choice of the system to be used

The decision as to which operational approach should be chosen depends on the purpose of the diagnostic assignment. Clinicians will prefer to rely on systems containing broad diagnostic groups, such as major depressive states, implying a high sensitivity which avoids false negative attributions. For researchers, on the other hand, the specificity of the instrument aiming at exclusion of false positive cases is of primary importance. They will therefore choose instruments that establish narrow, well-defined diagnoses, either solely or as subtypes of broader categories. In each case they have to check carefully whether the algorithm applied guarantees a patient sampling corresponding to the hypothesis to be tested. Furthermore, research studies must be validated and therefore must use instruments not containing elements pertaining to information intended to serve for validation, such as genetic data, course, outcome, etc., and which should be seconded by "separate" axes not used for the diagnostic assignment. For many research designs the application of a polydiagnostic approach (6) allowing simultaneous use of several diagnostic formulations may be advantageous, as it permits the testing of several theories in the same patient population.

REFERENCES

1. Akiskal, H. S. (1983a). The bipolar spectrum: New concepts in classification and diagnosis. In L. Grinspoon (Ed.), *Psychiatry update*. The American Psychiatric Association Review, Vol. II (pp. 271–292). Washington, DC: American Psychiatric Press.
2. Akiskal, H. S. (1983b). Diagnosis and classification of affective disorders: New insights from clinical and laboratory approaches. *Psychiatr. Dev.*, *2*, 123–160.
3. Angst, J. (1966). *Zur Aetiologie und noslogie endogener depressiver psychosen*. Berlin: Springer-Verlag.
4. Baillarger, J. (1854). De la folie à double forme. *Ann. Méd.-Psychol. 6*, 369–384.
5. Berner, P., Gabriel, E., & Katschnig, H. (1983). *Diagnostic criteria for schizophrenic and affective psychoses*. Washington, DC: World Psychiatric Association, American Psychiatric Press.
6. Berner, P., & Katschnig, H. (1983). Principles of "multiaxial" classification in psychiatry as a basis of modern methodology. In T. Helgason (Ed.), *Methods in evaluation of psychiatric treatment*. Cambridge: Cambridge University Press.
7. Carney, M. W. P., Roth, M., & Garside, R. F. (1965). The diagnosis of depressive syndromes and the prediction of E.C.T. response. *Br. J. Psychiatry, 111*, 659–674.
8. Carney, M. N. P., & Sheffield, B. F. (1972). Depression and the Newcastle Scales—Their relation to Hamilton's Scales. *Br. J. Psychiatry, 121*, 35–40.
9. *Diagnostic and statistical manual of mental disorders* (DSM-III). (1980). Washington, DC: American Psychiatric Association.
10. Everitt, B. S. (1981). Bimodality and the nature of depression. *Br. J. Psychiatry, 138*, 336–339.

11. Falret, J. P. (1854). De la folie circulaire. *Bull. Acad. Méd., 19*, 382.
12. Feighner, J. P., Robins, E., & Guze, S. B. (1972). Diagnostic criteria for use in psychiatric research. *Arch. Gen. Psychiatry, 26*, 57–63.
13. Feinberg, M., & Carroll, B. J. (1982). Separation of subtypes of depression using discriminate analysis, 1: Separation of unipolar endogenous depression from non-endogenous depression. *Br. J. Psychiatry, 140*, 384–391.
14. Feinberg, M., & Carroll, B. J. (1983). Separation of bipolar endogenous depression from nonendogenous (neurotic) depression. *J. Affect. Disord., 5*, 129–139.
15. Fieve, R. R., & Dunner, D. L. (1985). Unipolar and bipolar affective states. In F. Flach (Ed.), *The nature and treatment of depression*. New York: Wiley.
16. Freud, S. (1969). *Trauer und melancholie, gesammelte werke*, Vol. 10, *Werke aus den jahren 1913-1917* (5th ed.) (pp. 427–446). Frankfurt: S. Fischer Verlag.
17. Grinker, R. R., Miller, J., Sabshin, M., et al. (1961). *The phenomena of depression*. New York: Hoeber.
18. Gurney, C. (1983). Diagnostic scales for affective disorders. In *Proceedings of the V World Congress of Psychiatry*. Mexico City. (Quoted by Roth et al. [39].)
19. Haefner, H. (1987). Determinanten psychischer gesundheit und krankheit. *Fundamenta Psychiatr., 1*, 4–14.
20. Hamilton, M. (1960). A rating scale for depression. *J. Neurol. Neurosurg. Psychiatry, 23*, 56–62.
21. *Mental disorders. Glossary and guide to their classification in accordance with the 9th revision of the International Classification of Diseases* (1978). Geneva: WHO.
22. *ICD-10* (1968 Draft of Chapter V Categories F00–F99) (1987). Geneva: WHO.
23. Jaspers, K. (1913). *Allgemeine psychopathologie*. Berlin, Heidelberg: Springer.
24. Katschnig, H., & Simhandl, C. (1986). *New developments in the classification and diagnosis of functional mental disorders*. Psychopathology 19 (pp. 219–235). Basel: Karger.
24a. Kendell, R. E. (1969). The continuum model of depressive illness. *Proc. R. Soc. Med., 72*, 335–339.
25. Kendell, R. E. (1976). The classification of depressions: A review of contemporary confusion. *Br. J. Psychiatry, 129*, 15–28.
26. Kendell, R. E. (1981). L'échec des méthodes statistiques multivariées à resondre nos difficultés de classification. In P. Pichot, & C. B. Pull (Eds.), *La symptomatologie dépressive* (pp. 131–137). Paris: Geigy.
27. Kiloh, L. G., Andrews, G., Neilson, M., & Bianchi, G. N. (1972). The relationship of the syndromes called endogenous and neurotic depression. *Br. J. Psychiatry, 121*, 183–196.
28. Klein, D. F. (1974). Endogenomorphic depression: A conceptual and terminological revision. *Arch. Gen. Psychiatry, 31*, 447–454.
29. Kupfer, D. J., Pickar, D., & Hillelhoch, J. M. (1975). Are there two types of unipolar depression? *Arch. Gen. Psychiatry, 32*, 866–871.
30. Lehman, H. E. (1985). Affective disorders: Clinical features. In H. J. Kaplan & B. Sadock (Eds.), *Comprehensive textbook of psychiatry*/IV, Vol. 1 (pp. 786–811). Baltimore: Williams & Wilkins.
31. Leonhard, K. (1957). *Aufteilung der endogenen psychosen*. Berlin: Akademie Verl.
32. Matussek, P., Söldner, M., & Nagel, D. (1981). Identification of endogenous depressive syndrome based on the symptoms and characteristics of the course. *Br. J. Psychiatry, 138*, 361–372.
33. Mullaney, J. A. (1985). The validity of two Newcastle Diagnostic Scales in the affective disorders: Bimodality and other correlates. *J. Affect. Dis., 9*, 239–247.
34. Paykel, E. S. (1971). Classification of depressed patients—A cluster analysis derived grouping. *Br. J. Psychiatry, 118*, 275–288.

35. Perris, C. (1966). A study of bipolar (manic depressive) and unipolar recurrent depressive psychoses. *Acta Psychiatr. Scand.* (suppl. 194).
36. Pichot, P. (1986). Classification of depressive states. *Psychopathology, 19*, (suppl. 2), 12–16.
37. Robins, E., & Guze, S. B. (1972). Classification of affective disorders: The primary, secondary, the endogenous-reactive, and the neurotic-psychotic concepts. In T. A. Williams et al. (Eds.), *Recent advances in the psychobiology of the depressive illnesses* (pp. 283–292). Washington DC: US Government Printing Office.
38. Roth, M. (1981). Problems in the classification of affective disorder. *Acta Psychiatr. Scand., 63*, (suppl. 290), 42–51.
39. Roth, M., Gurney, C., & Mountjoy, O. Q. (1983). The Newcastle Rating Scales. *Acta Psychiatr. Scand.*, (suppl. 310), 42–54.
40. Schneider, K. (1925). Der begriff der reaktion in der psychiatrie. *Z. ges. Neurol. Psychiatr., 9*, 500–505.
41. Schneider, K. (1959). *Klinische psychopathologie* (5th ed.). Stuttgart: Thieme.
42. Sheehan, D., Ballenger, J., & Jacobsen, G. (1980). Treatment of endogenous and phobic, hysterical and hypochondriacal symptoms. *Arch. Gen. Psychiatry, 3J*, 51–59.
43. Snaith, R. P., & Taylor, C. M. (1985). Irritability: Definition assessment and associated factors. *Br. J. Psychiatry, 147*, 127–136.
44. Spitzer, R. L., Endicott, J., & Robins, E. (1978). Research Diagnostic Criteria (RDC) for selected groups of functional disorders (3rd ed.). New York: New York State Psychiatric Institute.
45. Van Praag, W. M. (1982). A trans-Atlantic view of the diagnosis of depression, according to DSM-III: I. Controversies and misunderstandings in depressive diagnosis. *Compr. Psychiatry, 23*, 315–320.
46. Wing, J. K., Cooper, J. E., & Sartorius, N. (1974). *Description and classification of psychiatric symptoms*. London: Cambridge University Press.
47. Winokur, G., & Clayton, P. (1967). Family history studies: I. Two types of affective disorders separated according to genetic and clinical factors. In J. Wortis (Ed.), *Recent advances in biological psychiatry*. New York: Plenum Press.
48. Zimmerman, M., Coryell, W., Stangl, D., & Pfohl, B. (1987). Validity of an operational definition for neurotic, unipolar, major depression. *J. Affect. Disord., 12*, 29–40.

8

DSM-III AND DEPRESSION

WILLIAM N. GOLDSTEIN, M.D.

Teaching Analyst, Baltimore-Washington Institute for Psychoanalysis

and

ROBERT N. ANTHONY, M.D.

Private Practice of Psychiatry and Psychoanalysis, Bethesda, Maryland

INTRODUCTION

The classification of depression in DSM-III is radically changed from that of DSM-I and DSM-II. With this in mind, this chapter examines DSM-III and also DSM-III-R, especially from the viewpoint of understanding the changes from past nomenclatures. In order to aid in this task, a brief history of diagnostic systems regarding depression is first presented. In contrast to DSM-III and DSM-III-R, many of the older systems classified depressions as subgroups of neuroses, psychoses, and personality disorders. Noting that, a closer look at depression as it relates to these larger categories is undertaken. Included is a look at the different usages of the term *neurotic*. Finally, DSM-III and DSM-III-R themselves are closely scrutinized. Changes from the past nomenclatures are highlighted and critiqued.

BRIEF HISTORY OF DIAGNOSTIC CLASSIFICATIONS OF DEPRESSION

Although depression has been studied by physicians since Hippocrates, a review of the history of the classification of this disorder may begin with the work of Kraepelin. Kraepelin's observations of the depressed and his attempt to classify different subtypes and variants of the illness sharpened and expanded over eight editions of his *Lehrbuch der Psychiatrie*. One of his major contributions was the division of mental illness into two broad classes: disorders of thought and disorders of mood. All that we call depression today he subsumed under the broad class manic-depressive insanity, as a mood disorder. His view was that this illness was endogenous, but one for which an anatomical substrate had yet to be found. By the eighth edition (30), however, he did note the existence of "psychogenic depression" as a separate entity and further determined that this disorder did not fit the organic frame of reference (22). He also mentioned a "cyclothymic temperament."

Kraepelin thus had suggested a division into organic and psychogenic depression. This dual way of looking at this disorder was sharpened by the burgeoning psychoanalytic movement, particularly inspired by Freud's "Mourning and Melancholia" (13). Here, unconscious conflict was seen to be at the bedrock of depression. Psychiatrists following Freud began to look further and further for nonorganic causes regarding the onset and course of depression. By the end of the 1920s the psychiatric community was split into nature and nurture schools of approaching the classification of depression. The former was concerned with heredity, anatomy, and pathogens; the latter was interested in the impact of early life experiences, current stressors, loss, and unconscious processes.

Lewis (33) attempted to heal this division with an exhaustive clinical review and study. He proposed looking at the illness as unified and through the range of acute to chronic or mild to severe. He seemed to have a slant toward the nurture school, because he felt that the closer one looked at depression, the more one saw of environmental influences. However, he did not belittle heredity, anatomy, or physiology. His stress was on depression as one illness with different manifestations. His view is now reflected in DSM-III and DSM-III-R.

DSM-I and Response

DSM-I, published in 1952 (1), was based largely on the *Statistical Manual for the Use of Hospitals for Mental Disease* (42). In this latter manual, manic-depressive illness appeared under the class of disorders that may or may not be of psychogenic origin. It was classed as a psychosis, as was involutional melancholia. There was no mention of anything akin to a psychotic depression or a major depressive episode in this manual. Reactive depression was classed under the neurotic disorders. There was no cyclothymia or inclusion of depression under the personality disorders. Rather than one illness, depression was seen as forms of other groupings, such as psychoses or neuroses.

In DSM-I (1), the psychotic/neurotic division continued. Affective reactions appeared for the first time as a subgroup of the psychotic disorders and included manic depressive reactions and psychotic depressive reactions. Psychotic depression was distinguished from manic depression by the presence of an environmental stressor. Involutional psychotic reactions also appeared under the psychotic disorders. Depressive neurosis replaced reactive depression as the name of the class of depressions under neurotic disorders. Under the personality disorders appeared the subheading cyclothymic personality.

DSM-I's basic nosology of depression was frequently examined and challenged. Leonhard (32) was the first to propose the distinction between unipolar and bipolar depressive illness. This distinction was supported by much research differentiating depressions in accordance with response to medication (28, 31, 35–37). In general, the bipolar depressions responded to lithium, while the unipolar responded to the tricyclics. Considerable evidence was accumulating from genetic, biochemical, familial, physiological, and pharmacological sources to support the bipolar-unipolar dichotomy (29). From another perspective, Woodruff et al. (45) developed the concept of primary versus secondary depression, a concept elaborated on by Robins and Guze (38). These researchers proposed a division of depression into cases where there was no other psychiatric illness (primary) and cases where there was evidence of a preexisting psychiatric illness (secondary). In addition, studies were emerging that utilized factor analysis to classify depressions. One of the first studies here was that of Grinker et al. (21). This study identified five different personality types suffering from depression.

DSM-II and Response

DSM-II (2) was published in 1968, but was little changed from DSM-I in regard to depression. The newer research approaches and findings were not taken into account, and the psychotic/neurotic division remained. Manic-depressive illness and involutional melancholia were classified as major affective disorders, while psychotic depression was classified under the category of other psychoses. Depressive neurosis and cyclothymic personality were classified similarly to DSM-I.

There was much criticism of DSM-II, particularly by researchers. Zung (47), for example, criticized the DSM-II classification of depression as confusing and contradictory. He thought the appearance of depression under so many categories made no sense. He proposed a new rating scale for depression from which to derive data and suggested depression be seen as one illness. Andreasen and Winokur (5), in their report from the NIMH pilot study, advocated vigorous research using the newer approaches: primary versus secondary depression, depressive versus depressive spectrum disease, research with the somatic therapies, and DST and TSH test response data. The dichotomy of depressive disease versus depressive spectrum disease relates to the work of Winokur et al. (44). This group based their classification on family history differences among two groups depending on the response to antidepressant medication. One group had families with only depression in relatives, whereas the second had families with other disorders (in addition to depression), such as alcoholism, hysteria, and sociopathy, in relatives.

The Feighner Criteria and the RDC

The two most influential works on depression regarding the composition of DSM-III were clearly those of Feighner et al. (9) and Spitzer et al. (41). Feighner et al. (9) were dissatisfied with a diagnostic system (DSM-II) based on the "best clinical judgment and experience of a committee and its consultants" and proposed instead a system they felt was validated by follow-up and family studies. Regarding depression, "primary" depression was diagnosed by three criteria. The first was the presence of a dysphoric mood characterized by symptoms such as the following: depressed, sad, blue, despondent, etc. The second demanded at least five of the following for definite diagnosis; four for probable diagnosis:

1. Poor appetite or weight loss
2. Sleep disturbance
3. Loss of energy
4. Agitation or retardation
5. Loss of interest in usual activities, or decrease in sexual drive
6. Feeling of self-reproach or guilt
7. Complaints of or actually diminished ability to think or concentrate
8. Recurrent thoughts of death or suicide including thoughts of wishing to be dead

The third required a psychiatric illness lasting at least one month, with no preexisting psychiatric condition, also in the absence of life-threatening or incapacitating medical illness. Secondary depression was diagnosed by the same criteria, in the presence of a preexisting nonaffective disorder or a life-threatening or incapacitating medical illness.

The Research Diagnostic Criteria (41) is basically an expansion and an elaboration of the Feighner classification. In the RDC, criteria were chosen based both on clinical experience and on research evidence, with emphasis placed on predicting outcome, response to treatment, and familial association. The diagnostic criteria for major depressive disorder were very similar to those of Feighner et al. The duration of symptoms required for the diagnosis was changed from one month to one to two weeks, and the exclusion criteria (especially for schizophrenia) were greatly elaborated. Whereas Feighner et al. required a dysphoric mood, the RDC allowed the presence of a pervasive loss of interest or pleasure as an alternative to that. In addition, subtypes of major depressive disorder were described. These included primary depressive disorder; secondary depressive disorder; simple major depressive disorder; recurrent unipolar depressive disorder; psychotic, incapacitating, and endogenous major depressive disorder; situational major depressive disorder; and agitated and retarded major depressive disorder. The diagnoses of minor depressive disorder, intermittent depressive disorder, and cyclothymic personality were used to describe milder depressions. The category of intermittent depressive disorder was thought to correspond to the concept of depressive personality.

DEPRESSIONS AS SUBGROUPS OF THE NEUROSES, PERSONALITY DISORDERS, AND THE PSYCHOSES

DSM-III was published in 1980 and heralded a major change in classification. The contrast between DSM-I and DSM-II, on the one hand, and DSM-III, on the other, is striking. In DSM-III depressions are no longer subdivided under psychoses, neuroses, and personality disorders, but now appear under one separate grouping, the affective disorders. This, in itself, is a major change. Before detailing DSM-III, some discussion of the former classification of depressions into neuroses, psychoses, and personality disorders is in order.

The Different Meanings of the Term Neurosis

The term *neurosis*, when referring to neurotic depression, can be used in several ways. Two distinctions need to be made. The first is between the psychoneuroses, also called symptom neuroses, and the character neuroses, also called character disorders or personality disorders. The second is between the psychoneuroses and character neuroses (personality disorders), on the one hand, and the larger category, the neurotic structural configuration, on the other hand. When DSM-I and DSM-II use the term *neurosis*, they mean psychoneurosis. However, with DSM-III, this does not appear to be the case. As will be detailed later, the DSM-III dysthymic disorder (depressive neurosis) actually appears to be a hybrid between a neurosis and a personality disorder. Technically only the term *neurotic structural configuration* clearly applies to the dysthymic disorder. In general, the term *neurotic*, in contrasting neurotic depressions with endogenous depressions, does not refer specifically to the psychoneuroses, nor does it necessarily refer to the personality disorders. Rather, it usually means a mild depression of psychogenic origin, clearly fitting into the neurotic structural configuration. For completion and hopefully not to make matters more confusing, Freud (11, 12) originally differentiated what he called the actual neuroses from the psychoneuroses. The concept of the actual neuroses is basically no longer in use and need not be elaborated here. We will now turn to a closer examination of the psychoneuroses, the character neuroses (personality disorders), the neurotic structural organization, and then the psychoses.

Psychoneuroses

The popularity and prevalence of the term *psychoneurosis* are attributed to Freud (14, 15). Psychoanalysts think of the psychoneuroses as clearly distinct entities consisting of ego-dystonic symptoms, formed by a very specific process. A simplified current version of psychoanalytic theory regarding the formation of psychoneurotic symptoms is as follows (6, 8, 15, 17, 20). In the formation of a neurotic symptom, the starting point is a present-day precipitating event. This event is usually external but can in certain circumstances be considered primarily internal. The precipitating event contains elements related to earlier childhood conflicts and stimulates an upsurge of drive. This upsurge involves either the aggressive or libidinal drive, or both, and can be thought of as absolute or relative (related to decreased ego functioning). There are unconscious fantasies (relating to childhood) connected with the increased drive. The unconscious fantasies involve predominantly the Oedipal period, but are also influenced and colored by pre-Oedipal factors.

The ego perceives the upsurge of drive (with corresponding fantasies), recognizes a danger in connection with this, and signals anxiety or depressive affect. The danger situation is conceptualized by the ego along a developmental hierarchy of dangers. These include loss of object, loss of love, the danger of castration, and superego fear. In neuroses, the primary danger is that of castration, but the other dangers, especially superego fear, also play a role. Thus, the ego recognizes the danger of castration and signals anxiety or depressive affect. All this is done on an unconscious level.

With the signal of anxiety or depressive affect, the ego uses unconscious defenses to deal with the increased drive. The libidinal and/or aggressive drives come into conflict with the ego. The superego is instrumental in making the ego take note of and oppose the increased drive, but the actual conflict is between the ego and the id. Symptoms result as compromise formations from the battle between the drives and the ego. The exact nature of the symptoms will depend on the outcome of this battle, and include such factors as the strength of the ego versus the drives, and the defenses utilized. Regression and repression are invariably among the defenses utilized. The different neuroses are characterized by typical specific defensive patterns, in addition to these two. In depression, there is a tendency to turn aggression against the self.

To understand why a particular symptom is chosen in a particular individual, we must turn to psychogenetics. This includes both constitutional and experiential factors. Experiential factors really include all aspects of early upbringing, with particular emphasis on the individual's processing of the upbringing. Thus, early traumas (real or fantasized), seductions (real or fantasized), degree of frustration versus gratification, and early fixations must all be considered. This early upbringing plus constitutional factors will help determine the specifics of drive neutralization and ego (and superego) formation. In depression, the superego is often characterized by an especially rigid and punitive conscience and a very lofty and relatively unattainable ego ideal. In all neurotics, we expect adequate early upbringing, with good neutralization of the drives, leading to the formation of a relatively strong ego. We likewise expect the individual to have obtained libidinal object constancy, in Mahler's (34) terms, by age three or so.

Although many equate neurotic depression with psychogenic depression, technically speaking, constitutional factors as well as experiential ones are noted in the above formation of neurotic symptoms. Despite this, it is fair to say that experiential factors are predominant in what most think of as neurotic depression. As already noted, the DSM-I and DSM-II definition of depressive neurosis fits the description of psychoneuroses just elaborated, whereas the DSM-III definition does not. Regarding the psychoneuroses, there does appear to be a group of depressed individuals characterized in this way, without a good place to classify them in DSM-III.

Personality Disorders

Regarding the distinction between the psychoneuroses and the character neuroses or personality disorders, the latter are expressed as ego-syntonic traits or characteristics that are chronic and ingrained in the personality. This is in contrast to the ego-dystonic symptoms of the psychoneuroses. The character neuroses (or personality disorders), like the psychoneuroses, originated in childhood conflict. However, the outcome of the conflict is a modification of the ego rather than a symptom. The result takes the form of lifelong patterns of behavior, clearly recognizable by adolescence or earlier. These patterns of behavior represent a solution to specific developmental conflicts. Regarding personality disorders, DSM-I and DSM-II list a cyclothymic personality, which can be subdivided into a depressive type. DSM-III does not list any personality disorder expressly related to depression.

In clinical practice there is a fairly common group of patients for whom the term *depressive personality* applies. A patient in this group often organizes his identity in accordance with a "bad self." He views himself as inadequate, inept, of little worth and value, sometimes even harmful. To feel decent about himself, he usually has to both live up to certain difficult internalized aspirations, ideals, and achievements and, in addition, receive repetitive external positive feedback from others. In accordance with this, he often seeks out and forms relationships where he can obtain this needed positive feedback. At times these need-fulfilling relationships can become clinging, demanding, and controlling. Even when he is feeling adequate about himself on the surface, the identity of the "bad self" is operational at a preconscious or unconscious level, motivating behavior. Various activities and acting-out behaviors might be used to ward off painful affects associated with this identity. These include the use of alcohol and drugs, sexual and antisocial behavior, and many kinds of compulsive behaviors, not all of which are necessarily destructive. In relation to the activation of the "bad self," impulsive behavior can be self-directed and self-destructive. Sometimes an unconscious desire for punishment can result in a variety of masochistic, dangerous, and self-defeating behaviors. Related to a vulnerability associated with the identity of the "bad self," there is almost always a sensitivity to negative feedback, slights, and rejections, with a particular difficulty in frustration tolerance and impulse control in this area.

The degree of acting out associated with the depressive personality varies. Many depressive personalities do little of the kinds of acting out just described. However, there is a group of patients who fit the above description and are constantly acting out in various destructive ways. This impulse-ridden group of patients might be considered to be a subgroup of the borderline personality disorder (19). In addition, many depressive personalities do not become chronically depressed and do not fit anywhere in DSM-III. Others become depressed frequently enough to meet one of the diagnostic categories in DSM-III, usually the dysthymic disorder. Regarding the former group, there appears to be a rather large group of individuals, as described above, who are vulnerable to depressions, yet do not frequently become clinically depressed. These individuals certainly display obvious psychopathology, often come for treatment, and need to be recognized in the diagnostic nomenclature.

The Different Structural Configurations

A useful diagnostic system, psychodynamically oriented and providing underlying conceptual understanding, involves classifying individuals into large groupings based on underlying structural configurations. This system, described elsewhere (18, 20), in accordance with Kernberg (24, 25), first classifies individuals into one of three large groupings: the neurotic, the borderline, and the psychotic. Each of these large groupings is characterized by a distinct underlying structural configuration, consisting of a specific pattern of ego and superego functioning, along with a specific pattern of instinctual drive organization. The pattern of ego functioning, described in the form of a profile or inventory of ego functions, by itself is sufficient to establish the differential diagnosis between these three large groupings. It is possible to conceptualize a fourth large grouping, the narcissistic (16, 18), but this will not be elaborated in the present chapter.

All individuals basically fall into one of these large groupings. In evaluation interviews it is extremely helpful to first classify individuals in accordance with these groupings. A "structural" diagnosis thus made is invaluable for conceptual understanding, therapeutic assessment, and prognostic considerations, providing the underlying framework for further discussion and evaluation. This "structural" diagnosis can serve as a superordinate or first-level diagnosis. Later, a more specific and secondary diagnosis can be added, providing further descriptive information. If one desires, DSM-III diagnoses can be used as the secondary diagnoses.

As noted, this "structural" diagnosis can be established via the profile or inventory of ego functions by itself. In fact, it is to this ego profile that one looks for this purpose. These ego functions include reality testing, thought processes, interpersonal relations, adaptation to reality, impulse control and frustration tolerance, and defenses. In addition, sense of identity and stability of affects are scrutinized.

The Borderline Structural Configuration

An examination of the borderline level of structural configuration will first be undertaken. The description of this borderline level, elaborated elsewhere (18, 20), will basically be in accordance with the work of Kernberg (23, 26, 27), with some variations. The borderline individual can be conceptualized as having an ego profile characterized by four relative ego strengths and four underlying ego weaknesses, as follows. The strengths are:

1. The relative intactness of reality testing (intact in everyday interactions but vulnerable to reality distortions and brief psychotic episodes under stress).
2. The relative intactness of thought processes (secondary process in everyday interactions but vulnerable to regressions to primary-process thinking under stress and in nonstructured situations).
3. The relative intactness of interpersonal relations (intact superficially but lacking in empathy and depth, and basically need fulfilling when viewed under close scrutiny).
4. The relative intactness of the adaptation to reality (intact superficially but revealing numerous difficulties in adaptation when viewed under close scrutiny).

The weaknesses are:

1. The combination of poor impulse control and poor frustration tolerance.
2. The proclivity to use primitive ego defenses (especially projection, denial, primitive idealization, omnipotence, devaluation, splitting, and acting out).
3. The syndrome of identity diffusion (characterized by an unstable sense of self and objects, with multiple contradictory self- and object images).

4. Affective instability (characterized by intense affect, usually depressive or hostile, and by the propensity for rapid affective shifts).

The Neurotic and the Psychotic Structural Configurations

The relative ego strengths differentiate the borderline from someone more psychotic. The underlying weaknesses, correspondingly, differentiate the borderline from someone more neurotic. Thus, the basically psychotic individual is characterized by more global defects in reality testing and thought processes, along with more obvious disturbances in interpersonal relations and adaptation to reality. Like the borderline, there is poor impulse control and poor frustration tolerance, identity diffusion, and affective instability. There is a proclivity to use primitive ego defenses, both those described as borderline and those more pathological, such as fusion, dedifferentiation, delusions, and hallucinations. The basically neurotic individual is characterized by good reality testing, secondary-process thinking, good interpersonal relations, good adaptation to reality, good impulse control and frustration tolerance, defenses typically characterized as "neurotic" or "higher level" (such as repression, isolation, reaction formation, intellectualization, and sublimation), a stable identity, and affective stability. In addition, the neurotic, in contrast to both the borderline and psychotic groupings, has attained libidinal object constancy, in Mahler's terms (34).

When one uses the term *neurotic* and contrasts neurotic and endogenous forms of depression, one is usually referring to neurotic in the larger sense of the neurotic structural configuration. In DSM-III, the dysthymic disorder clearly fits into the neurotic structural configuration, whereas the major depressions vary as to structural configuration.

DSM-III Dysthymic Disorder

DSM-III includes dysthymic disorder (or depressive neurosis) under the heading of "Affective Disorders." Although the term *depressive neurosis* appears in parentheses, the DSM-III dysthymic disorder does not really describe the traditional depressive neurosis. In order to qualify for a dysthymic disorder, an individual must have depressive symptoms most of the time for two continuous years. In addition, these symptoms, although persistent, must not be severe enough to qualify for a major depressive episode.

The dysthymic disorder, as noted, actually appears to be a hybrid between a psychoneurosis and a personality disorder. The depressive neurosis, as conceptualized along the model of symptom formation earlier described, could possibly fit into the category of dysthymic disorder, were it not for the criterion of two continuous years. Unfortunately, there is no DSM-III category more accommodating to the depressive neuroses than the dysthymic disorder. The dysthymic disorder, clearly fitting into the neurotic structural configuration, provides a way of classifying depression milder than the other depressions listed in DSM-III. Even for this diagnosis, however, one must display rather significant psychopathology.

Psychoses

Neuroses are often contrasted with psychoses, as neurotic depressions are often contrasted with psychotic depressions. Regarding the formation of psychotic symptoms, there are those (7) who employ the model of symptom formation described under the psychoneuroses to additionally explain the formation of psychotic symptoms, while others (10) explain the psychoses in a very different way. Almost everyone, however, agrees that the psychoses are distinguished from the neuroses by more severe defects in ego functioning, especially reality testing, by a regression to the pre-Oedipal period, and by a greater prominence of manifestations of the aggressive drive. Many are content with focusing on the defect in reality testing as being pathognomonic of the psychoses.

In both DSM-I and DSM-II, manic-depressive illness (including the major depressions) is listed as a psychotic disorder. The term *psychotic depression* is used to differentiate those severe depressions clearly distinguished by an environmental stressor from the manic-depressive disorders, where external precipitants are thought to play little role. In DSM-I and DSM-II, involutional psychotic reactions also appear under the psychoses. As noted, DSM-III eliminates the categories of psychotic depression and involutional psychoses. In DSM-III, all depressions are listed under affective disorders, with psychotic features designated by a fifth digit code.

Actually, both the old and new classifications have merit here. Under the old system, depressions are differentiated as to whether they are reactive (to stress) or endogenous. Basically using the definition of psychosis outlined above, the reactive depressions are then characterized as neurotic or psychotic. The manic depressions and involutional depressions are always classified as psychotic. The problem is that not all manic depressions and involutional depressions are psychotic. This difficulty is solved by DSM-III by no longer labeling these as exclusive psychotic disorders. However, eliminating the reactive versus endogenous classification seems questionable, as this classification can be particularly helpful with psychodynamic and psychotherapeutic thinking.

DSM-III ITSELF

This brings us to DSM-III (3). This third edition of the *Diagnostic and Statistical Manual of Mental Disorders* offers an atheoretical orientation, without efforts at psychodynamic understanding. It is an approach most subscribed to by a group of professionals, often researchers, who are most interested in establishing descriptions that are easily defined, reliable, and valid. Primary focus is on symptoms and traits, particularly those that can differentiate one diagnostic group from another. Literature reviews, research designs, and statistical methods are employed, where possible, to try to identify these traits and symptoms.

Regarding depression, as already noted, the contrast between DSM-I and DSM-II, on the one hand, and DSM-III, on the other, is striking. DSM-III classifies all depressions within one category, the affective disorders, regardless of etiology, precipitating events, or psychotic features. Within that one grouping, the bipolar versus unipolar distinction gains clear prominence. Affective disorders are divided into three groups: major affective disorders, other specific affective disorders, and atypical affective disorders, with each of the three groups being subdivided into bipolar and unipolar categories. Thus the major affective disorders are divided into bipolar disorder and major depression, the other specific affective disorders are divided into cyclothymic disorder and dysthymic disorder (or depressive neurosis), and the atypical affective disorders are divided into atypical bipolar disorder and atypical depression.

In the listing of the diagnostic criteria for each of the disorders, the work of Feighner et al. (9) and Spitzer et al. (41) is clearly obvious. To make the DSM-III diagnosis of a major affective disorder, five different diagnostic criteria must be met. Regarding the depressed periods, there must be a clear period of obvious dysphoric mood or severe loss of interest in activities. At least four of eight symptoms (reminiscent of the Feighner criteria and the RDC) must be present for at least two weeks. The clinical picture cannot be dominated by mood-incongruent delusions, hallucinations, or bizarre behavior when the affective syndrome is absent. Finally, the clinical picture cannot be superimposed on schizophrenia, schizophreniform disorder, or paranoid disorder or be due to any organic mental disorder or uncomplicated bereavement.

To make the DSM-III diagnosis of a dysthymic disorder, the individual must be bothered most of the time for the last two years by depressive symptoms. However, these symptoms must not be of such severity that the individual meets the diagnostic criteria of a major depressive episode. During the two years, there can be normal superimposed periods, but no longer than a few months at a time. The depressed periods must have a prominent depressed mood or marked loss of interest or pleasure in activities and be characterized by two symptoms from a list of 13. In addition, there must be an absence of psychotic features. Finally, the depression, if superimposed on a preexisting disorder, must be clearly distinguished from the individual's usual mood. Thus, the dysthymic disorder is simply a milder version of a major depression. The DSM-III classification of atypical depression is a residual category for individuals who cannot meet the other depressed diagnoses. There is also one DSM-III category involving depression outside of the affective disorders, adjustment disorder with depressed mood. This category is for depressions that do not meet the criteria for a major depression, and where there is an obvious psychosocial stressor.

The concept of primary and secondary depression is included in DSM-III by allowing for the coding of other psychiatric disorders "with depressed mood." Involutional melancholia is dropped as a diagnostic entity, but the term *melancholia* is included to emphasize those severe depressions particularly sensitive to the tricyclics, via a fifth-digit coding. Depressions with psychotic features are also designated by a fifth-digit code. Although the term *depressive neurosis* appears in parentheses after dysthymic disorder, the concept of the psychoneuroses, as noted, is actually gone. Likewise there are no DSM-III categories in the personality disorders related to depression.

DSM-III-R

DSM-III-R (4) was published in 1987. Here there are some changes in name and organization, but no changes in substance. The name *affective disorder* is dropped in favor of mood disorders. The term *depressive disorder* not otherwise specified replaces atypical depression. The categories are basically the same as in DSM-III but reorganized into two large groups: bipolar disorders and depressive disorders. Bipolar disorders are divided into bipolar disorder, cyclothymia, and bipolar disorder not otherwise specified; whereas depressive disorders are divided into major depression, dysthymia (or depressive neurosis), and depressive disorder not otherwise specified. In response to research (40) indicating that there is a cyclical form of depression beginning in early winter and ending in spring, the concept of a seasonal pattern to depression is added. The descriptions of the various DSM-III-R categories, although not identical, are very similar to those of DSM-III.

Conclusions Regarding DSM-III and DSM-III-R

It is very unclear, at the present time, whether, regarding depression, DSM-III and DSM-III-R are more advantageous than the very different DSM-I and DSM-II. There certainly is not yet any current international agreement on DSM-III. The current international classification, ICD-9 (46), for example, does not follow the DSM-III format; in fact, it is more similar to DSM-I and DSM-II. DSM-III, more than previous systems, clearly takes into account recent research. It certainly provides more precisely defined and reliable entities. The leaning is toward a unitary view of depression. The emphasis of bipolar versus unipolar is correlated with considerable evidence (genetic, familial, biochemical, physiological, and pharmacological) pointing to differences in these two types of depression. The elimination of the distinction between psychogenic (or reactive) and endogenous depressions is questionable and certainly does not aid psychodynamic and psychotherapeutic thinking. To its credit, DSM-III does allow the classification of melancholia with a fifth-digit code, to signify a type of depression particularly responsive to antidepressant medication. Because many people with bipolar (or manic depressive) illness are not technically psychotic, classifying these people only as psychotic was a previous limitation corrected by DSM-III. The removal of involutional melancholia, although in association with some recent research (39, 43) indicating no increase of depression in the involutional period, does not address the existence of this group of patients.

The elimination of the concept of psychoneuroses and thus of depressive neurosis is in accordance with the atheoretical orientation of DSM-III, but not with clinical reality. Changes regarding the neuroses were probably the most hotly debated in the making of DSM-III. The elimination of neurosis as a diagnostic class and the distribution of the subtypes of neurosis under other rubrics eventually prevailed in the 1980 *Manual*, but the utilization of parentheses and the word *or* for designating the synonymity of the traditional neurosis categories was added. Regarding depression, because of the dissimilarity of the DSM-III dysthymic disorder with the DSM-III neurotic depression, this only causes confusion. In regard to the personality disorders, no DSM-III category corresponding to the depressive personality seems limiting. In fact, removal of the milder depressions in general appears undesirable. The dysthymic disorder, the mildest of the DSM-III affective disorders, actually represents a rather marked depressive disorder itself.

DSM-III and DSM-III-R actually offer both advantages and disadvantages in comparison to DSM-I and DSM-II. Depression is far from figured out. Research is proceeding along many different lines, and one can anticipate many future changes in the nomenclature corresponding to the many endeavors here. With this in mind, DSM-III and DSM-III-R, regarding the depressions, can only be thought of as temporary classifications, clearly to be altered with time.

REFERENCES

1. American Psychiatric Association (1952). *Diagnostic and statistical manual of mental disorders*. Washington, DC: APA.
2. American Psychiatric Association (1968). *Diagnostic and statistical manual of mental disorders* (2nd ed.). Washington, DC: APA.
3. American Psychiatric Association (1980). *Diagnostic and statistical manual of mental disorders* (3rd ed.). Washington, DC: APA.
4. American Psychiatric Association (1987). *Diagnostic and statistical manual of mental disorders* (3rd ed., revised). Washington, DC: APA.
5. Andreasen, N. C., & Winokur, G. (1979). Newer experimental methods for classifying depressions. A report from the NIMH collaborative pilot study. *Arch. Gen. Psychiatry*, *36*(4), 447.
6. Arlow, J. (1963). Conflict, regression, and symptom formation. *Int. J. Psychoanal.*, *44*, 12.
7. Arlow, J. A., & Brenner, C. (1969). The psychopathology of the psychoses: A proposed revision. *Int. J. Psychoanal.*, *50*, 5.
8. Brenner, C. (1982). *The mind in conflict*. New York: International Universities Press.
9. Feighner, J. P., Robins, E., Guze, S. B., Woodruff, R. A., Winokur, G., & Munoz, R. (1972). Diagnostic criteria for use in psychiatric research. *Arch. Gen. Psychiatry*, *26*, 57.
10. Freeman, T. (1970). The psychopathology of the psychoses: A reply to Arlow and Brenner. *Int. J. Psychoanal.*, *51*, 407.
11. Freud, S. (1896). Further remarks on the neuro-psychoses of defense. In *Standard Edition*, Vol. 3 (p. 159). London: Hogarth Press. Published 1973.
12. Freud, S. (1898). Sexuality in the etiology of the neuroses. In *Standard Edition*, Vol. 3 (p. 261). London, Hogarth Press. Published 1973.
13. Freud, S. (1917). Mourning and melancholy. In *Standard Edition*, Vol. 14 (p. 243). London: Hogarth Press. Published 1973.
14. Freud, S. (1923). The ego and the id. In *Standard Edition*, Vol. 19 (p. 3). London: Hogarth Press. Published 1973.
15. Freud, S. (1926). Inhibitions, symptoms and anxiety. In *Standard Edition*, Vol. 20 (p. 67). London: Hogarth Press. Published 1973.
16. Goldstein, W. (1985). DSM-III and the narcissistic personality. *Am. J. Psychother.*, *39*, 4.

17. Goldstein, W. (1985). Obsessive-compulsive behavior, DSM-III, and a psychodynamic classification of psychopathology. *Am. J. Psychother.*, *39*, 346.
18. Goldstein, W. (1985). *An introduction to the borderline conditions*. Northvale, NJ: Jason Aronson.
19. Goldstein, W. (In press). The depressive impulse ridden character and the core borderline personality. *Am. J. Psychother*.
20. Goldstein, W., & Burris, B. (In press). DSM-III and the neuroses. In J. Howells (Ed.), *Modern perspectives for the psychiatry of neurosis*.
21. Grinker, R. R., Miller, J., Sabshin, M., Nunn, R., & Nunnally, J. (1961). *The phenomena of depressions*. New York: Harper & Row.
22. Kendell, R. E. (1968). *The classification of depressive illness*. Institute of Psychiatry Maudsley Monographs Number 18. London: Oxford University Press.
23. Kernberg, O. (1975). *Borderline conditions and pathological narcissism*. New York: Jason Aronson.
24. Kernberg, O. (1977). Structural diagnosis of borderline personality organization. In P. Hartocollis (Ed.), *Borderline personality disorders: The concept, the syndrome, the patient*. New York: International Universities Press.
25. Kernberg, O. (1980). Neurosis, psychosis, and borderline states. In A. Freedman, H. Kaplan, & B. Sadock (Eds.), *Comprehensive textbook of psychiatry*, Vol. III (3rd ed.). Baltimore: Williams & Wilkins.
26. Kernberg, O. (1980). *Internal world and external reality*. New York: Jason Aronson.
27. Kernberg, O. (1984). *Severe personality disorders: Psychotherapeutic strategies*. New Haven, CT: Yale University Press.
28. Kiloh, L. G., & Garside, R. F. (1963). The independence of neurotic depression and endogenous depression. *Br. J. Psychiatry*, *109*, 451–463.
29. Klerman, G. (1983). The nosology and diagnosis of depressive disorders. In L. Grinspoon (Ed.), *Psychiatry update*, Vol. II. Washington, DC: American Psychiatric Press.
30. Kraepelin, E. (1921). *Manic-depressive insanity and paranoia*. Translation of *Lehrbuch der psychiatrie* (8th ed.). Edinburgh: Barclay.
31. Kupfer, D. J., Picker, D., Himmelhoch, J. M., & Detre, T. P. (1975). Are there two types of unipolar depression? *Arch. Gen Psychiatry*, *32*(7), 866.
32. Leonhard, K. (1957). *Aufteilung der endogenen psychosen* (2nd ed.). Berlin: Akademie-Verlag.
33. Lewis, A. J. (1938). States of depression: Their clinical and aetiological differentiation. *Br. Med. J.*, *2*, 875.
34. Mahler, M., Pine, F., & Bergman, A. (1975). *The psychological birth of the human infant*. New York: Basic Books.
35. Overall, J. E., Hollister, L. E., Johnson, M., & Pennington, V. (1966). Nosology of depression and differential response to drugs. *JAMA*, *195*, 946.
36. Pare, C. M. B., Rees, L., & Sainsburg, M. J. (1962). Differentiation of two genetically specific types of depression by the response to anti-depressants. *Lancet*, *2*, 1340.
37. Perris, C. (1966). A study of bipolar (manic-depressive) and unipolar recurrent depressive psychoses. *Acta Psychiatr. Scand.*, *42* (Suppl.), 9.
38. Robins, E., & Guze, S. (1972). Classification of affective disorders: The primary-secondary, the endogenous, and the neurotic-psychotic concepts. In T. Williams, M. N. Katz, & J. Shield (Eds.), *Recent advances in the psychobiology of depressive illness*. Washington, DC: Department of Health, Education and Welfare.
39. Rosenthal, S. (1968). The involutional depressive syndrome. *Am. J. Psychiatry*, *124*(Supp.), 21.
40. Rosenthal, N. E., Sack, D. A., Gillin, J. C., Lewy, A. J., Goodwin, F. K., Davenport, Y., Mueller, P. S., Newson, D. A., & Wehr, A. (1984). Seasonal affective disorder: A description of the syndrome and the preliminary findings with light therapy. *Arch. Gen. Psychiatry*, *41*, 72.

41. SPITZER, R., ENDICOTT, J., & ROBINS, E. (1978). Research diagnostic criteria: Rationale and reliability. *Arch. Gen. Psychiatry, 35*, 773.
42. *Statistical manual for the use of hospitals for mental disease* (10th ed.) (1945). New York: National Committee for Mental Hygiene.
43. WEISSMAN, M., & KLERMAN, G. (1977). Sex differences in the epidemiology of depression. *Arch. Gen. Psychiatry, 34*, 98.
44. WINOKUR, G., CADOLET, R., DORZAB, J., BAKER, M. (1971). Depressive disease: A genetic study. *Arch. Gen. Psychiatry, 24*, 135.
45. WOODRUFF, R. W., et al. (1967). The natural history of affective disorders: I. Symptoms of 72 patients at the time of index hospital admission. *J. Psychiatr. Res.*, 5, 255.
46. WORLD HEALTH ORGANIZATION (1977). *Manual of the international statistical classification of diseases, injuries, and causes of death* (9th rev.). Geneva: WHO.
47. ZUNG, W. W. K. (1973). From art to science: The diagnosis and treatment of depression. *Arch. Gen. Psychiatry, 29*(13), 328.

CLINICAL SYNDROMES

9

SUICIDAL EPISODES AND RISK FACTORS IN CHILDREN

CYNTHIA R. PFEFFER, M.D.

Associate Professor of Clinical Psychiatry, Cornell University Medical College and Chief, Child Psychiatric Inpatient Unit, New York Hospital, New York

INTRODUCTION

The recognition that youth suicide occurs at an alarmingly high rate has stimulated interest in understanding the many facets involved in the etiology and prevention of this frightening problem. It has become quite apparent that suicidal behavior affects the young as well as middle-aged and elderly populations. Although there is an awareness that suicidal acts occur among teenagers, there is still great surprise in learning about a suicide attempt or a suicide of a child younger than 12 years. Yet, suicide and suicide attempts occur among preadolescents who are 6 to 12 years old, and for that matter, it has been described for children as young as three to five years. Thus, suicidal behavior occurs throughout the human lifecycle.

This chapter presents an overview of suicidal behavior among preadolescents, an age group in which clinicians have relatively little experience with regard to recognition of and intervention for suicidal tendencies. The main purpose of this chapter, therefore, is to educate psychiatrists and other clinicians about suicide and nonfatal suicidal acts among children so that preventive efforts can be more effective.

The goal of educating clinicians is especially relevant because, in the last several years, new information derived from the expansion of research efforts on this problem among children has been accumulating. Furthermore, although adolescent suicide, in contrast to childhood suicide, has rapidly increased over the last several decades, the focus of this chapter is on young children because it will provide a developmental perspective to the features of suicidal behavior among adolescents as well. Thus, the chapter will include relevant findings from empirical research with adolescents in order to highlight continuities and discontinuities of factors associated with suicidal behavior in children and adolescents.

INCIDENCE OF CHILDHOOD SUICIDE

In recent years, approximately 200 children, aged 5 to 14 years, committed suicide in the United States annually (15). In 1984, this number accounted for a rate of 0.7 per 100,000 population annually for 5- to 14-year-olds and it represents the lowest suicide rate for all age groups. It is also in sharp contrast to the 5,026 adolescents and young adults, aged 15 to 24 years, who commit suicide annually; the suicide rate for this age group is 12.5 per 100,000 population. The suicide rates for children under age 14 years have remained relatively constant in the last several decades, but the suicide rates for adolescents have dramatically increased.

Although suicide rates in different countries vary with regard to youth, the increase in adolescent suicide in the United States parallels increased incidence of other phenomena: depression, alcohol and drug abuse, homicide, and accidents (11). The reason for the increase in these phenomena in the last several decades is not entirely clear. Nevertheless, research indicates that this may be a temporal period effect that reflects some unique but unknown phenomenon affecting youth in the last two or three decades (11). Suggested evidence for such a temporal effect for adolescent suicide comes from the work of Holinger and Offer (9). In their study, comparisons were made between the number of adolescents, aged 15 to 19 years old, in the U.S. population at a given time from 1933 to 1975 and the U.S. suicide rates for adolescents. The results indicated that there was a positive association between these factors. Thus, if there are more adolescents in the population at a given time, there is an increase in suicide rate also at that time. This finding seemed specific to adolescents, and verification of this was suggested by another facet of the same study. The trends for the elderly in the United States do not show a significant association between the number of old individuals in the United States and suicidal acts. Holinger and Offer suggested that at least two psychodynamic explanations can be proposed for this: competition and/or failure and isolation from meaningful social relations. Holinger and Offer also proposed that these findings can be useful as a model for predicting trends of U.S. suicide rates in the future. Whether this trend is specific to U.S. youth suicide rates is unknown, especially since there are no similar studies in other national populations.

Suicide is the sixth leading cause of death among 5-to-14-year-olds in the United States. The most common causes of death for children of this age group are accidents, neoplasms, and congenital anomalies. Suicide is often difficult to determine among children. A percentage of deaths in youngsters may be classified as accidents when in actuality the cause of death may be suicide. Studies are needed to clarify this hypothesis.

Classification of suicide as the cause of death in the preadolescent age is done cautiously and conservatively mainly because adults think that children are unable to appreciate the concept of the finality of death. In fact, this adult belief is probably unjustified as a rationale for classifying children's suicidal wishes (16). What is more plausible is that children, as young as three years, have developed some concepts of death and, as a result, children are able to act on their wishes to die. For example, a five-year-old who may believe that death means that one can live in a more pleasant situation, even temporarily, may take large quantities of pills in order to achieve the state of death. Such a child may want to be relieved of stress and, as a result, may wish to die. In fact, children are capable of using many self-destructive methods, such as hanging, jumping from heights, ingesting toxic substances, self-stabbing, and drowning. The wish to die is the motivator, the goal is whatever the child fantasizes death to be, and the vehicle to achieve this goal is the physical method used for self-harm.

A CLINICAL EXAMPLE

In order to effectively prevent childhood suicidal behavior, it is necessary for mental health clinicians, parents, pediatricians, teachers, and others who are in regular contact with children to be able to recognize feelings and behaviors that may provide clues to imminent suicidal tendencies. The following example of a suicidal child will highlight characteristic factors that are evident among children who wish to take their own lives. This child is presented as an example to aid clinicians in appraising clinical features that they may encounter when evaluating children who have suicidal tendencies. Of course, a large variety of factors are associated with childhood suicidal behavior so that this example cannot capture all the characteristics of suicidal children.

Steven, aged 11 years, had a long history of behavior problems in school and at home, including a history of school truancy and previous psychiatric treatment. The child's outpatient psychiatrist referred him for psychiatric hospitalization after Steven attempted to stab himself in the chest. This occurred immediately after Steven had an argument with his mother about whether or not he could go outside after school. Steven had not gone to school that day, and as a punishment, his mother refused to let him go outside to play. In an intense argument between Steven and his mother, Steven felt that he was not understood and was angry about being told what to do. After the argument subsided, Steven went to the kitchen, where he found a knife. He was about to stab himself in the chest when his mother raced in and took the knife away from him.

Steven's parents had divorced three years before. They had an intensely embittered marriage. Steven's father rarely visited Steven. Since the divorce, Steven refused to go to school, had periodic episodes of violence toward his mother, and felt chronically depressed. Often he thought about suicide, especially when he felt alone and thought about his father. Steven longed for his father and also felt angry about being abandoned by him. Steven felt despondent about not having a steady relationship with his father, and Steven blamed his mother for his father's departure.

SUICIDAL RISK FACTORS

Recent research indicates that childhood suicidal behavior is a complex symptom in which many variables are simultaneously operative to increase risk (16). Factors can be clustered into those associated with psychological, environmental, and biological variables. Most consistently, signs of depression have been associated with childhood suicidal acts. Pfeffer and associates (19) reported that depressed mood and other indicators of depressive disorder such as sleep and eating disturbances, psychomotor changes, withdrawal, feelings of worthlessness and hopelessness, and death preoccupations are associated with severity of suicidal behavior in samples of 106 preadolescent psychiatric inpatients and 101 outpatients. Other studies also support the finding that severity of depression is associated with intensity of suicidal ideation. For example, Carlson and Cantwell (3) evaluated 102 child and adolescent psychiatric inpatients and outpatients by interview and self-report measurements of suicidal tendencies and depression. These researchers found that severe suicidal ideation was associated with the severity of depression. Depressed mood is a common factor regardless of the child's psychiatric disorder. In studies carried out by Pfeffer and associates (19) suicidal children were found to have many types of psychiatric disorders, and regardless of the type of disorder, depressed mood was associated with suicidal ideas and/or acts. Furthermore, Brent and colleagues (2), in a study of 231 children referred to psychiatric treatment, and Myers, Burke and McCauley (14), in a study of 348 child psychiatric inpatients, found comparable results: depression was highly correlated with severity of suicidal tendencies.

Major depression is the most significantly associated psychiatric disorder for childhood suicidal behavior (16). Signs of depressed mood and changes in sleeping, eating, social, and activity patterns, as well as death preoccupations, are characteristic of the severely depressed youngster and potentially suicidal child. Evidence regarding childhood affective disorders has three features: an increased prevalence of affective disorders in the young (11), chronicity of serious childhood affective disorders (12, 13), and an association between parental and childhood affective disorders (1). Each of these three features can contribute to the increased incidence of suicidal tendencies in the young.

Poor self-esteem and lack of hope in the future are also poignant activators of suicidal fantasies and acts. The most systematic study of the role of hopelessness in relation to suicidal risk in children was reported by Kazdin and associates (10). In their study of 66 child psychiatric inpatients, aged 8 to 13 years, measures of hopelessness, depression, and suicidal intent were evaluated. The children who were most hopeless showed more severe depression and had lower self-esteem than children who were hopeful. Children with suicidal ideas and/or acts scored higher for hopelessness than did the nonsuicidal children. Suicidal intent was more consistently correlated with hopelessness than with depression. These findings are similar to trends found for adult suicidal individuals (25).

Other behaviors, too, are significant factors for suicidal risk. Violent behavior, running away, truancy, lying, and stealing are prominent features of many suicidal youngsters. This was especially highlighted by the study of young suicides, aged 12 to 14 years, evaluated in England and Wales between 1962 and 1968 by Shaffer (22). An extensive record review of the coroner, social service, school, and medical reports of all 30 young suicides revealed that 17% had symptoms of antisocial tendencies, 57% had symptoms of both antisocial and affective symptoms, 13% had symptoms of affective problems, and 13% had neither type of symptomatology.

When the psychological characteristics of suicidal preadolescents are compared with those of adolescents, a number of similarities are found. Suicidal preadolescents and adolescents often are depressed, preoccupied with death, and exhibit antisocial behaviors (4, 17, 20). A major difference is in the association of alcohol and drug abuse among adolescents who exhibit fatal and nonfatal suicidal acts (7, 17, 23).

Often, suicidal acts are precipitated by a current crisis in the child's interpersonal involvements. A parental disciplinary act or problems with peers are major factors. It has been suggested that suicidal children, in contrast to nonsuicidal children, experience more current and past life stresses, such as family losses through parental separation and divorce. Such trends were highlighted by Cohen-Sandler, Berman, and King (5) in their study of 76 child psychiatric inpatients. The suicidal children experienced increasing and greater amounts of life stress than the nonsuicidal inpatients. Important life events associated with suicidal behavior were losses and separations. Important family constellations are the links between parental psychopathology, such as affective disorders, and propensity for violence and child abuse and a relation to childhood suicidal behavior. Weissman and associates (26) reported that children who had parents with a major affective disorder have a threefold risk for psychopathology that involves major depression, attention deficit disorder, and separation anxiety. Suicidal behavior was reported among the children of the depressed parents but not among children of nondepressed parents. Evidence for the association between child abuse and suicidal behavior was reported in populations of children and adolescents (6, 8). For example, Deykin, Alpert, and McNamarra (6) found that among 159 adolescent suicide attemptors, there was a three- to sixfold greater likelihood of being abused than among the nonsuicidal adolescents.

ASSESSMENT OF A SUICIDAL CHILD

Assessment of a suicidal child requires sufficient time to speak extensively with the child. A clinician embarking on the assessment of an acutely suicidal child should structure the initial evaluation to leave sufficient time to develop a relationship with the child. A clinician needs to evaluate the degree of openness, trust, and cooperation the child can have with the clinician. Furthermore, an assessment must be made about the extent of the commitment that the child can make in delaying any self-destructive actions and in telling the therapist about them. These factors, the ability to talk honestly and openly, to cooperate, and to delay acting out on suicidal impulses, are necessary ingredients in ensuring that the child may be safe without additional close observation and intervention.

A number of other factors must be evaluated in determining the safety of the child and in planning a treatment program. These include details about the suicidal episode (16). The specific suicidal fantasies must be evaluated. Among these are the severity of suicidal tendencies that include whether the child ever thought about hurting himself/herself, ever threatened to do harm, or whether there was a suicidal act. Concepts of what would happen if the suicidal act were carried out must be determined. The immediate circumstances of the time of the child's suicidal behavior require description. Since past suicidal tendencies often predict future suicidal tendencies, an appraisal of the child's past suicidal ideas and/or acts must become known. Finally, the child's conscious and/or unconscious motivations for suicidal behavior must be delineated. For example, did the child ever wish to reunite with a lost benevolent individual or did the child's suicidal impulse represent an act of revenge against an unempathic person?

Important risk factors should be evaluated also. Among these are the child's concepts and experiences with death, criteria for depression, and environmental stresses (16). Specific questions should focus on the child's mood, the presence of vegetative signs of sleep and appetite disturbance, the degree of involvement with others and with activities, the capacity to concentrate, and the degree of anger and/or irritability. These features are indications of depression. Since suicidal children are often intensely preoccupied with death, questions need to be asked about the child's worries, fantasies, and experiences with death. Finally, extensive discussion of environmental stresses must take place with the child. Among the issues that should be addressed are problems in the family, at school, and with peers. It is crucial to evaluate the child's perceptions of and adaptive capacities regarding these experiences.

There is no doubt that suicidal children can speak directly about their suicidal preoccupations (16). One 11-year-old said the following: "My mother yells at me a lot. She is critical of me and tells me that I should be like my friends and go to school and do my homework. I don't like school. I feel like killing myself. I think that I would be better off dead. Mom will be sorry then. She will not be able to yell at me then." Such children give clear descriptions of the despairing feelings, suicidal preoccupations, and stressful life circumstances. These life situations require detailed evaluations, too.

An initial evaluation of the suicidal child requires that the parents be involved also. A number of specific issues are of great relevance to understanding childhood suicidal behavior. The clinician must appraise the basic issue of whether there is a sincere wish "that the child be alive." Often, family turmoil due to parental strife or parental psychopathology precludes a sharp focus on the child's needs. This is often the case when the parent's psychopathology is chronic, and as a result, the child often develops a sense of responsibility of taking care of the parent. In such cases, the child may feel guilty about the family or parental problems and hopeless about remedying them. Children, in this situation, often wish to be out of the family situation and hope to be with an actual or fantasized person who is considered omnipotent and supportive. Another issue to be appraised is whether the parents do not appreciate the seriousness of the child's condition or are resistant to following through with the treatment recommendation. In such a circumstance, the child's condition may be quite unpredictable. Taylor and Stansfeld (24) reported that parental attitudes about the treatment of a suicidal youngster are significant determinants of whether effective care will be obtained. Thus, if parents are resistant or neglectful in supporting and cooperating with needed treatment for the child, added assistance through social service agencies may be required to ensure that the child obtains treatment.

TREATMENT PLANNING

There are few reports of research on the treatment of the suicidal child. Nevertheless, there are sufficient data about childhood suicidal behavior that suggest directions for effective treatment (16).

Treatment plans must be organized around the important goal of protecting the suicidal child from harm (16). Intense outpatient treatment is feasible if the child has been able to make a commitment to work in treatment, if the child is truthful about revealing feelings and suicidal impulses, and if there is sufficient environmental support from the family to collaborate with the treatment. Psychiatric hospitalization is another common setting for treatment, especially if the child demonstrates continued intense suicidal preoccupations, has poor impulse control, is unable to work consistently in treatment and/or there is insufficient parental support, or if the environmental circumstances are too tumultuous.

Pfeffer, Plutchik, and Mizruchi (18) studied the clinical characteristics that were important predictors of child psychiatric hospitalization. The study included 106 child psychiatric inpatients and 101 child psychiatric outpatients. The severity of suicidal tendencies was the best predictor for psychiatric hospitalization. Other predictor factors of psychiatric hospitalization and associated with suicidal behavior were: poor reality testing, recent depression, recent aggression, and the ego defenses of projection and regression. This study suggested that when this combination of factors is present in a given child, it accounts for 43% of the predictive influence.

The main tasks of psychiatric hospitalization of a suicidal child are to protect the child from self-destructive acts, to remove the child from stressful circumstances, to offer multimodality diagnostic assessments, and to provide ego supports on an intensive, 24-hour basis (16). The hospital staff offers constant therapeutic input while the child is in an acute suicidal state. Thus, if the child has an acute suicidal episode, the staff is immediately available to speak with the child and to physically interrupt a self-destructive act.

Whether the child is treated on an inpatient or an outpatient basis, treatment should aim to decrease suicidal impulses and the associated risk factors. Reduction of suicidal impulses can be accomplished directly by helping the child gain hope that alternative approaches to what is perceived as an unsolvable problem seems possible. The therapist must determine what the child wishes to be different and what needs are being painfully frustrated. Reduction of suicidal impulses occurs when a child feels that personal needs are sufficiently gratified.

Suicidal impulses are also decreased by lowering the degree or number of risk factors. With regard to risk factors such as depression, a psychotherapeutic orientation with or without use of medication is indicated. The most important psychotherapeutic issues to be addressed are the intensity of depression arising from loss of actual or fantasized factors. For example, discussion of the child's responses to parental divorce may help clarify the child's fears of being abandoned, the child's guilt over causing the marital disruption, and the child's anger at not preventing the situation from occurring. Loss of self-esteem may arise from feelings of being deficient physically and/or emotionally and from stressful interactions with family and peers. Clarification of these issues is required and promises to be quite therapeutic, especially if the therapist helps the child by maintaining an empathic inquisitive attitude about the child's feelings and fantasies. In this way, the child is offered the opportunity of talking about feelings and behaviors in a nonpunitive, nonjudgmental, and supportive atmosphere. Such an atmosphere is especially devoid of the stresses that have been overwhelming the suicidal child.

While biological risk factors have not been specified for childhood suicidal behavior, biological treatments must be considered. Specifically, medication aimed to relieve the child's symptoms of psychiatric disorders should be used. By decreasing associated general psychopathology, suicidal risk will diminish. For the seriously depressed child, judicious use of antidepressants is indicated. However, the most appropriate medicine for the suicidal child is determined by the symptoms targeted for resolution. With this in mind, a variety of classes of medication can be used; the most efficacious one will be dependent on the nature of the child's general level of psychopathology.

Environmental supports within the family must be amplified. The clinician, having appraised the family interactive style and whether there exists parental psychopathology, must determine target areas for family intervention. The main goal is to stabilize the family milieu so that it provides consistent support and appropriate limit setting for the suicidal child. A variety of treatment modalities may be utilized and they may include individual parent psychotherapy, psychopharmacological interventions for a parent, parental marital treatment, and/or a series of sessions with the entire nuclear family. The family treatment plan aims to decrease family strife and turmoil that ensues from parental psychopathology and marital discord.

Other important areas for intervention are to enhance other environmental supports. This is best carried out by collaborating with school professionals and other people who are routinely involved with the suicidal child. It is essential that the therapist take on a role of coordinator of communication between the child, the parent, and other important people in the environment. In this way, a treatment network is established and it can have the potential capacity of offering close observation of warning signs of impending suicidal behavior as well as immediate support for the suicidal child in distress. Such a treatment network can be more effective than the treatment offered only by the clinician working alone with the child. This type of therapeutic network also has the advantage of being able to monitor the progress of the child over an extended period of time even after the specific treatment with the therapist has been completed. The benefit of this is to make it feasible to observe an early sign that an acute suicidal episode may recur.

PREVENTION OF CHILDHOOD SUICIDAL BEHAVIOR

Prevention of childhood suicidal behavior must be multidetermined and specific to different suicidal risk factors. Most effective are approaches that enhance early recognition of the suicidal child and subsequent treatment. It is unfortunately common that children and/or their parents may be resistant to treatment. In such cases, approaches to enlist a treatment alliance are called for by means of extensive discussion and assistance from nonfamilial sources, such as social agencies. On a more practical level, removing easy access to a suicide method is helpful. In fact, firearms are the leading suicidal method among teenagers, although less commonly among children. Maintaining these weapons in secure places and removing them from the home are indicated. From a clinical perspective, prescribing practices for medication should include consistent appraisal of how much medication is given, who administers it, where it is kept, and whether other potentially toxic substances are in the home. Overdoses are a common suicidal method among children. For a school-age suicidal child, environmental supports can be elicited from school professionals, pediatricians, and others involved with children. Close collaboration with these professionals will ensure that a therapeutic network exists in which early warnings of risk can be communicated to the treating child psychiatrist who can reassess the mode of intervention. Finally, since childhood suicidal tendencies often arise within a context of family problems, these must be recognized and treated early. An important form of primary prevention is to recognize the child who is living in a high-risk family situation. Screening of children who are experiencing family breakup, the vicissitudes of parental emotional problems, or the traumas of harsh discipline is helpful from the prevention vantage point. After a screening procedure, a recommendation for more extensive evaluation and/or treatment can be formulated.

Finally, it must be realized that when prevention has been effective, a clinician may never know that it has occurred. When a child's life is saved, there will be no statistical way of measuring this. Our clinical work, therefore, must be based on satisfactions obtained by perceiving that a child has been better able to adapt, has more self-confidence, and is hopeful about future prospects. Such therapeutic work, while anxiety provoking and intense, is remarkably rewarding!

SUMMARY

This chapter focuses on suicidal behavior particularly in the preadolescent age group. Although the incidence of suicide in children under 14 years old is the lowest of all age groups, preadolescents frequently exhibit suicidal ideas, threats, and attempts (16). In addition, some reports indicate that preschool children, aged 2-$^1/_2$ to 5 years, have been observed to express suicidal acts (21).

This chapter points out that children can speak about suicidal fantasies and that a comprehensive assessment of suicidal episodes of preadolescent children is an important first step to treatment and prevention of suicidal acts. Childhood suicidal behavior is a complex phenomenon that involves psychological, environmental, and biological risk factors. Among children of this age period, depression is one of the most important risk factors. Parental psychopathology that is manifest as affective disorders, child abuse, and the occurrence of family disruption and intense stress are significant environmental risk factors. Biological correlates of childhood suicidal behavior are yet to be elucidated. Nevertheless, psychopharmacological interventions have an important place in the treatment plan. The main treatment goals are to protect a youngster from harm and to diminish risk factors as rapidly as possible. Individual child psychotherapy, family intervention, and developing an environmental support network are important treatment modalities.

Prevention of childhood suicidal behavior must be multifaceted and aimed at decreasing access to lethal suicidal methods, early recognition and effective intervention of risk factors, and screening of children in high-risk situations. Long-term follow-up of a suicidal child provides an opportunity to intervene as early as possible if a repeat suicidal episode occurs. Finally, since effective prevention can never be quantified, a clinician working with potentially suicidal children should appraise the therapeutic effects by means of outcome variables such as enhancement of self-esteem or degree of adaptive skills rather than by the outcome of whether or not suicidal acts have occurred.

REFERENCES

1. Beardslee, W. R., Bemporad, J., Keller, M. D., & Klerman, G. L. (1983): Children of parents with major affective disorder: A review. *American Journal of Psychiatry, 140*, 825–832.
2. Brent, D. A., Kalas, R., Edelbrock, C., Costello, A. J., Dulcan, M. K., & Conover, N. (1986): Psychopathology and its relationship to suicidal ideation in childhood and adolescence. *Journal of the American Academy of Child Psychiatry, 25*, 666–673.
3. Carlson, G. A., & Cantwell, D. P. (1982): Suicidal behavior and depression in children and adolescents. *Journal of the American Academy of Child Psychiatry, 21*, 361–368.
4. Chiles, J. A., Miller, M. L., & Cox, G. B. (1980): Depression in an adolescent delinquent population. *Archives of General Psychiatry, 37*, 1179–1184.
5. Cohen-Sandler, R., Berman, A. L., & King. R. A. (1982): Life stress and symptomatology: Determinants of suicidal behavior in children. *Journal of the American Academy of Child Psychiatry, 21*, 178–186.
6. Deykin, E. Y., Alpert, J. J., & McNamarra, J. J. (1985): A pilot study of the effect of exposure to child abuse or neglect in adolescent suicidal behavior. *American Journal of Psychiatry, 142*, 1299–1303.

7. Fowler, R. C., Rich, C. L., & Young, D. (1986): San Diego Suicide Study. II. Substance abuse in young cases. *Archives of General Psychiatry, 43*, 962–965.
8. Green, A. H. (1978): Self-destructive behavior in battered children. *American Journal of Psychiatry, 135*, 579–582.
9. Holinger, P. C., & Offer, D. (1982): Prediction of adolescent suicide: A population model. *American Journal of Psychiatry, 139*, 302–307.
10. Kazdin, A. E., French, N. H., Unis, A. S., Esveldt-Dawson, K., & Sherick, R. B. (1983): Hopelessness, depression, and suicidal intent among psychiatrically disturbed inpatient children. *Journal of Consulting and Child Psychology, 51*, 504–510.
11. Klerman, G. L., Lavori, P. W., Rice, J., Reich, T., Endicott, J., Andreasen, N. C., Keller, M. B., & Hirschfeld, R. M. A. (1985): Birth-cohort trends in rates of major depressive disorder among relatives of patients with affective disorder. *Archives of General Psychiatry, 42*, 689–693.
12. Kovacs, M., Feinberg, T. L., Crouse-Novak, M. A., Paulauskas, S. L., & Finkelstein, R. (1984): Depressive disorders in childhood. I. A longitudinal prospective study of characteristics and recovery. *Archives of General Psychiatry, 41*, 229–237.
13. Kovacs, M., Feinberg, T. L., Crouse-Novak, M., Paulauskas, S. L., Pollock, M., & Finkelstein, R. (1984): Depressive disorders in childhood. II. A longitudinal study of the risk for a subsequent major depression. *Archives of General Psychiatry, 41*, 643–649.
14. Myers, K. M., Burke, P., & McCauley, E. (1985): Suicidal behavior by hospitalized preadolescent children on a psychiatric unit. *Journal of the American Academy of Child Psychiatry, 24*, 474–480.
15. National Center for Health Statistics (1986): Advance Report of Final Mortality Statistics, 1984. *Monthly Vital Statistics Report, 35*, 25–31.
16. Pfeffer, C. R. (1986): *The suicidal child.* New York: Guilford Press.
17. Pfeffer, C. R., Newcorn, J., Kaplan, G., Mizruchi, M. S., & Plutchik, R. (1985). Suicidal behavior in adolescent psychiatric inpatients. Presented at the Annual Meeting of the American Psychiatric Association, Dallas, Texas.
18. Pfeffer, C. R., Plutchik, R., & Mizruchi, M. S. (1986): A comparison of psychopathology in child psychiatric inpatients, outpatients, and nonpatients: Implications for treatment planning. *Journal of Nervous and Mental Disease, 174*, 529–535.
19. Pfeffer, C. R., Plutchik, R., Mizruchi, M. S., & Lipkins, R. (1986): Suicidal behavior in child psychiatric inpatients and outpatients and in nonpatients. *American Journal of Psychiatry, 143*, 733–738.
20. Robbins, D. R., & Alessi, N. E. (1985): Depressive symptoms and suicidal behavior in adolescents. *American Journal of Psychiatry, 142*, 588–592.
21. Rosenthal, P. A., & Rosenthal, S. (1984): Suicidal behavior by preschool children. *American Journal of Psychiatry, 141*, 520–525.
22. Shaffer, D. (1974): Suicide in childhood and early adolescence. *Journal of Child Psychology and Psychiatry, 15*, 275–291.
23. Shafii, M., Carrigan, S., Whittinghall, J. R., & Derrick, A. (1985): Psychological autopsy of completed suicide in children and adolescents. *American Journal of Psychiatry, 142*, 1061–1064.
24. Taylor, E. A., & Stansfeld, S. A. (1984): Children who poison themselves. II. Prediction of attendance for treatment. *British Journal of Psychiatry, 145*, 132–135.
25. Wetzel, R. D. (1976): Hopelessness, depression, and suicide intent. *Archives of General Psychiatry, 33*, 1069–1073.
26. Weissman, M. M., Prusoff, B. A., Gammon, G. D., Merikangas, K. R., Leckman, J. F., & Kidd, K. K. (1984): Psychopathology in the children (ages 6–18) of depressed and normal parents. *Journal of the American Academy of Child Psychiatry, 23*, 78–84.

10
SUICIDE IN ADULTS

Ari Kiev, M.D., J.D.

Clinical Associate Professor of Psychiatry, Cornell University Medical College, and Director, Social Psychiatry Research Institute, New York, New York

INTRODUCTION

Despite the availability of potent antidepressant medications, a humanitarian approach to psychiatric disorder, and an increased number of people in the psychiatric health care professions, the suicide rate has not changed significantly in the past 25 years and there is no reason to assume that the rate of suicide attempts has declined.

The number of completed suicides in the United States is estimated to be approximately 25,000 to 50,000 annually. It has been the twelfth most common cause of death since 1950. Except for the fluctuations during the Depression and the world wars, the suicide rate has remained rather stable in this country. Since 1900, this rate has ranged from 18.4 per 100,000 in 1932 to a low of 9.8 per 100,000 in 1957.

Suicide risk is considerable in the elderly, the alcoholic, those with suicidal histories, and those with severe psychiatric disorders. It is the second most common cause of death in the college-age population and the most common cause of death among young black women and American Indian youths, and it is gradually becoming more and more prominent as a major cause of death among teenagers and young adults.

THE EARLY RECOGNITION AND TREATMENT OF POTENTIALLY SUICIDAL PERSONS

It is often difficult for people to recognize that they are in fact suffering from an abnormality of mood, thought, or behavior. The subjective experiences of normal life events may be so similar to the subjective experiences of emotional disorder that it is difficult for an individual to perceive any difference between the two. Some of the patients who visit therapists have been suffering from various symptoms for considerable periods of time, but the symptoms are so common in everyday life experience that they were not recognized as clinically treatable problems. People look for help only when they begin to find it difficult to function.

Even today, thousands of people associate psychiatric illness with the notion of someone going stark raving mad or having a nervous breakdown and being placed in a hospital (usually conceived of as a snakepit) in order to protect society from potential violence. This is a grossly unrealistic picture of psychiatric illness. Most psychiatric illnesses are temporary and self-limiting and do not become apparent even to the close, untrained onlooker except when he sees the person's social abilities and work performance decline.

The early symptoms of mental illness include very common experiences—difficulty in falling asleep, restless sleep, early-morning awakening, loss of appetite or compulsive overeating (with resultant weight gain), or feeling blue or down in the dumps. The person, or his family, may blame noisy streets, a heavy dinner, fatigue, or work worries for such sleep difficulties and brush them off as temporary and unimportant. Loss of appetite, sudden distaste for food, and loss of weight may go unnoticed or be rationalized as the result of a change in diet, a desire to lose weight, or gastric indigestion. The person's energy may drop, so that simple, routine tasks become burdensome or even impossible; he may find it slowly and progressively more difficult to concentrate, lose interest in work and hobbies, find that his sexual drive has dropped off, and he may become preoccupied with morbid thoughts, excessive worry, anxiety, fears, and pessimism coupled with guilt over being unable to perform or feel joy and other emotions. Sometimes the ill person will perceive the environment inaccurately and decide that co-workers or family and friends are either unsympathetic or actively hostile to him. He may find reasons to blame outside forces for the distress he feels. One of the difficulties in recognizing such a condition as a psychiatric illness is that the rationalizations sound quite plausible; he might indeed be under genuine stresses that would disturb anyone to some degree. As a matter of fact, it is precisely the degree that determines the line between normal reaction to stress and the onset of a psychiatric condition.

Other individuals may find their thinking markedly disturbed, so that they cannot adequately express ideas or they misunderstand the ideas of others. They may then react by withdrawing from ordinary life experiences rather than suffer the strain caused by attempting to function.

To the extent that many of these symptoms can be temporary exaggerations of normal experiences, they often go unrecognized as the early signs of mental illness.

Efforts to Get Relief

The person suffering from symptoms may try in many ways to get some relief. He may use tranquilizers, either prescribed or purchased over the counter, to reduce his anxiety and tension. He may get barbiturates or nonprescription sleeping pills to combat insomnia and energy tonics for temporary and partial relief, but these stopgap remedies can in the end be harmful if the underlying psychiatric illness is not recognized and treated. Some persons will search for new meanings to life or security through religion or philosophical movements; again, what for one person would be a rich, enlarging experience can, to the unrecognized psychiatric patient, be a potentially harmful experience, because the search has been motivated by an illness that will not be cured by these otherwise normal activities. When the search does not bring the longed-for relief, despair may deepen. Still others turn to excessive alcohol or experiment with LSD or other potent, dangerous, and sometimes addicting drugs which not only bring no relief, but can lead to secondary complications more serious than the original illness.

The depressed suicidal patient, not unlike many other types of psychiatric patients, is overwhelmed by feelings of despair, fear, and uncertainty. His usual methods of coping have failed; he is plagued by thoughts of guilt and overwhelming anxiety sometimes masked by lethargy. His judgment and reality testing may be poor, and he may be trying to meet his responsibilities with decreasing efficiency and success. Suicide, if considered at all, is usually viewed as a way out or as an end to suffering rather than as a clear decision to die.

The Role of Social Factors in the Causation of Psychiatric Disorders

The stresses of life associated with changes in the life-cycle such as adolescence, menopause, and increasing age; the adjustment to new life situations such as marriage; death of a loved one; graduation from school, retirement, or the onset of a new career may complicate psychiatric illnesses because of the extra demands they place on people. However, to the extent that such experiences are used to rationalize the presence of symptoms, they may lead to the failure to recognize a treatable illness. For this reason, it is important to distinguish between natural life stresses and symptoms of emotional illness. Even if one ought to feel depressed because of a dreadful experience, adequate treatment can strengthen the individual's capacity to cope.

The Onset of Psychiatric Illness

Most persons, particularly in this society, tend to blame themselves or circumstances for these symptoms; consequently they do not or cannot recognize them as early signs of psychiatric illness. Family, friends, colleagues, or the ill person himself are much more likely to feel that the symptoms are due to lack of will power, laziness, inadequacy, or personal failure. Less puritanical onlookers may blame the pressure of work, school, or family stresses. Loneliness, isolation, or recent stressful experiences are even more acceptable explanations for symptoms; at least less moral blame seems to be attached to them. But numerous studies have begun to suggest that symptoms first develop as a result of as-yet-unspecified physiological or biochemical changes in the nervous system. According to this view, interpersonal and psychological difficulties then follow the development of the symptoms.

Furthermore, old problems tend to be magnified and handled less effectively when someone is already emotionally ill. If the symptoms are successfully treated and relieved, however, the problems that seemed so overwhelming are reduced in magnitude, and the patient regains the ability to cope as well as he was able to before the onset of the illness.

Sick Role

While the assessment of psychiatric symptoms constitutes an accepted phase in the evaluation of suicidal potential, the social and psychological responses to symptoms and the juxtaposition of symptoms in relationship to other variables must also be assessed in determining what specific treatment is indicated, the likelihood of treatment being accepted, and the possibility of support or sabotage by the relevant people in the patient's social world.

The patient's acceptance of treatment obviously has crucial significance for prognosis. Prognosis is guarded to the extent that a negative attitude toward treatment, a tendency to attribute psychological problems and distress to external circumstances which cannot be controlled or to specific events which have passed, reduces the likelihood that a patient will accept treatment. This is particularly true in patients who have attempted suicide but express unwillingness to accept the notion that they have a problem and require treatment.

Some patients who refuse to assume the sick role improve simply because of the passage of time. But others, not accepting the fact of their illness or problem and incorrectly attributing depressive symptoms to lack of will power, may put themselves under tremendous pressure to continue working, and to the extent that they are symptomatic, they may continue to experience excessive guilt over failure to perform up to par and, at times, additional pressure from significant others who also do not recognize the need for treatment. All this increases suicide risk.

Some Factors Leading People to Attempt Suicide

People attempt suicide for a variety of reasons. A person experiencing the inner distress of emotional illness without recognizing that it is an illness that requires treatment is likely to find it almost impossible to explain what is happening to him or to explain his inability to perform. If he attempts to control the symptoms or makes a greater effort and still fails, his sense of guilt and despair will increase.

Added to his own feeling of self-blame may be the judgments of others who, not recognizing his real distress or the fact that his disturbances in sleep, appetite, energy, and drive are out of his control, may either criticize him or minimize his distress. They may insist that there is no real cause for his feelings and urge him to force himself to work and enjoy things. This kind of advice, well meant as it may be, will only deepen the ill person's sense of helplessness and guilt. He may develop a pressing need to escape from both his own feelings and the additional guilt of being a burden to others. It is true that most people want to live, but not in a state of crippling distress. The tension that precedes the actual suicide attempt turns minutes into hours and days into unending nights; it so alters the person's capacity for rational judgment that he cannot even imagine that this tension state is really brief and self-limited.

SUICIDAL BEHAVIOR

The gravity of a suicidal attempt, the dangerousness of the attempt, the efforts made by the patient to prevent assistance from appearing on the scene, the presence of precipitating stresses, the use of alcohol, and other factors must be weighed in evaluating risk of a subsequent attempt. The seriousness of a previous attempt is an indicator of the patient's disturbance, as well as the patient's capacity to act impulsively and self-destructively.

Impulsivity

The degree of impulsivity underscores the patient's capacity to act impulsively in a self-destructive way should the various events and circumstances such as stresses and illness be present at a later date. In our own experiences, patients with the highest scores on impulsivity have the poorest outcome. Seriousness of method employed in a previous attempt has some prognostic significance, with those choosing irreversible methods having the poorest prognosis.

Method of Attempt

Individuals who attempt suicide in the presence of others, do not take sufficient quantity to produce coma, or call for help after the attempt have a better prognosis than those who isolate themselves from the world, take precautions not to be discovered, or are accidentally discovered. Alcohol contributes to suicidal risk because of its synergistic interaction with drugs and its disinhibitory effects.

Repeated Attempts

Repeated subintentioned overdoses resulting in hospitalizations are the most common pattern of repeated attempts. Unsuccessful resolution of turbulent life situations, denial of suicidal intent, and treatment refusal are common background factors in such attempts. These patients frequently demonstrate a tendency to explosive emotional outbursts lasting several minutes to hours associated with impairments of reality-testing ability. These states, often provoked by interpersonal conflict, generate intense urges to escape the situation, eliminate the tension of uncomfortable emotional state, or strike out at others by harming themselves.

A physical illness often serves as the precipitant for the elderly who lack supportive social groups. Those who are integrated into social groups often experience excessive guilt over failure to live up to the group's expectations.

The majority of repeated attempts occur shortly after entry into treatment in patients who remain symptomatically distressed or involved in the same life circumstances that led to their initial attempt. The predisposition to repeated attempts often increases as a result of the negative attitudes of others toward the patient's behavior. Delusional thought often induces fear and revulsion in others, while withdrawal induces anger and guilt, and manipulativeness induces resentment.

EVALUATING SIGNIFICANT OTHERS

Interpersonal conflict, social isolation, and major life changes also contribute to suicidal risk. The social world of the patient, specifically his relationships, plays a far more critical role in the subsequent clinical course than does diagnosis or the severity of the patient's psychiatric condition. For both depressed and attempted suicide patients the attitudes of significant others as to the presence or absence of a treatable illness and the recognition of the fact that the patient is isolated and not functioning are important aspects of the outcome.

The best prognosis is associated with concerned relatives who are calm and not panicked in the face of increased symptoms and suicidal thoughts and who recognize the need for professional care. Prognosis is unfavorable where there are few symptoms, conflicts, use of the denial of the sick role, and panic and confusion.

It is important to consult with significant others at the time of admission or first contact with suicidal or potentially suicidal individuals, and to assess the long-term relationship and attitudes toward the patient, not just the nature of the immediate responses, which are often highly conditioned by the anxiety of the moment following the suicide attempt. There is a strong case for crisis intervention efforts at the time of the attempt and engaging significant others in the therapeutic process, so as to assist them in developing constructive attitudes and approaches to the patient.

IDENTIFYING LIFE STRESSES

A variety of changes in the patient's illness, life situation, and attitude to treatment occur prior to and following an attempt. Some patients face custody fights, divorce proceedings, and unemployment. Others encounter prejudice and feel stigmatized. Explaining new relationships to children and friends proves stressful for many.

Some patients discover the secondary gains of being treated as sick and continue to remain dependent. Some friends and relatives of patients compete with the therapist or therapeutic team, challenging the value of the medicine or criticizing the patient's efforts to improve. This creates confusion and obstructs the development of feasible objectives and goals.

Patients who cannot limit the demands of others often feel guilty about suicidal thoughts or behavior. Resentment and hostility develop from this, creating more guilt and the generation of new crises. Significant others sometimes respond to independence strivings with oppressiveness.

Some patients create crises by threatening suicide and involving others in their experience. Knowing only part of the story, such friends often act at cross-purposes, adding more turbulence to the situation. The anxiety and undisciplined response of others in turn reinforce the patient's passive dependency and manipulativeness and give some patients who fail to realize their own role in the crisis a feeling of being victimized.

Persisting social and environmental problems also create significant stress. Inadequate or noxious social relationships contribute to the patient's demoralization, sense of worthlessness, and conviction of suicide as a valid release from distress.

Increased isolation and the disruption of interpersonal relationships commonly occur in the lives of patients, making the assumption of personal responsibility more of a burden than a challenge. When a suicide attempt results from loss of a significant relationship, as after the death of a loved one, the postattempt period is often very stressful, although some patients are challenged by new circumstances to become independent and self-reliant.

Highly dependent individuals tolerate bereavement much worse than independent and resourceful individuals. The elderly often need the assistance of social services, particularly when they have built their life around a spouse.

Serious physical illness and fewer social roles in the older age groups reduce flexibility and adaptability and are likely to persist after an attempt, thus contributing to the continued suicidal risk of elderly patients.

The patient's behavior subsequent to an attempt intensifies social stress and keeps the patient at high risk. In this sense, chronic persistent stresses create more serious management problems than do discrete episodes of objective stress which do not persist. A persisting noxious relationship is perhaps the most troublesome type of stress that sometimes necessitates hospitalization to protect the patient.

Maladaptive patient patterns include excessive confessions to others, efforts to amend for past wrongdoings, a failure to pursue self-interested objectives, and involvement in complicated relationships. An increase in risk-taking behavior, alcohol abuse, or drug abuse often reflects a deflection of self-destructive trends into less obvious forms.

Reality factors such as job pressures and housing shortages add extra burdens to the recovering individual. Important parameters of employment status include length of employment, frequency and regularity of unemployment, and discrepancies between educational level and job status. Unemployment contributes to insecurity, as do highly responsible jobs or ones that restrict autonomous activity. Unemployment frequently coincides with downward social and residential mobility, advancing age, and changing attitudes of young people toward work, all of which may indirectly contribute to suicidal risk.

Those outside the usual network of friendships and relationships, such as the isolated, the alcoholic, the elderly, and the chronically ill, experience considerable stress. Social and environmental factors influence whether patients enter into treatment and/or encounter acute conflicts. Depressed patients usually experience more objective stress in their lives but enjoy better relationships than patients diagnosed as having psychotic or character disorders, the latter experiencing more interpersonal conflict than the other diagnostic groups. Interpersonal conflict creates more stress for younger patients than older ones, whose relationships often seem more stabilized. The stresses predominating in the older age groups include the death of loved ones, physical illness, physical handicaps, and employment problems.

Difficult interpersonal relationships with significant others also prove stressful for many, and must be assessed. Sympathetic at first, relatives often become unsympathetic, rejecting, and negativistic when their efforts fail to obtain favorable responses from the patient.

The parameters of relationships that can be clinically assessed include number, duration, activities, sentiments, values, and rules or characteristic patterns of the relationships. These parameters reflect stability, dependency, and intensity of involvement in the relationship.

Changes in personality and in the role assumed subsequent to an attempt occasionally lead to shifts in the environment and new pressures that often precipitate new crises. Significant others, willing to allow others to take responsibility for the patient's welfare, sometimes reduce their own efforts, which the patient interprets as rejection. Some patients improve to a better level of functioning than prior to their illness; others regress, fearful of being stigmatized or of losing control of themselves. Still others marry, divorce, leave home, or make other major changes in their lives. Difficulties persist when such decisions are viewed as solutions to unresolved problems. The requirements of new living situations tax the patient's adaptive resources, especially if others deny the validity of the patient's illness and emphasize the need for more assertions of will power.

Scapegoating and threats of rehospitalization by significant others occur most often in relation to the patient's independence strivings. Excessive protectiveness may be manifested in efforts to check up on the patient or discourage healthy activity. Such protectiveness blends into partial infantilism, as in efforts to screen a patient's mail (this generates explosive rifts and often leads to hospitalization) or, as in one case, the creation of an institutional setting at home by the inclusion of round-the-clock "babysitters." Increased reliance on social agencies also creates feelings of inadequacy, excessive dependency, and resentment in patients.

Some pathological relationships appear innocent enough on the surface. Patients may become overinvolved with parents who believe themselves to be dutiful and respectful. Such parents continually seek reassurance and demand regular telephone calls, visits, and favors from the patient, with little regard for the patient's neglect of his or her life. Such parents expect to be consulted on all decisions and rationalize their instructions as a willingness to help which could not be rejected. They find a host of reasons for almost continual interaction, continually pressuring the patient to confide all personal matters.

Changes in the patient's behavior often lead to manipulative responses in significant others, who often mistakenly interpret these changes as evidence of disturbance. The patient's rights and the significant other's obligations have to be clarified continually so that the family can learn to interact in a healthy way. Relatives, anxious for the patient's difficulties to pass, often press patients to improve, function better at their job, or return to school prematurely, failing to realize the undue burden of such expectations on the patient. Some angry spouses doubt the desirability of treatment and make efforts to undermine the patient's self-confidence. Some parents unwittingly encourage others to adopt infantile attitudes toward the patient by focusing on his helplessness, not on his performance. Such patients soon learn not to take the initiative. Checking out plans with others fosters dependency and an uncertainty about capabilities.

CLUSTER PROFILES

On the basis of cluster analytical statistical techniques, suicidal patients can be allocated to seven identifiable profile types that correlate with outcome. These profiles include data on the social setting and the seriousness of the attempt and judgments about overall functioning and interpersonal conflict as well as the input of the patient's significant others. These profiles have prognostic significance as well as implications for the treatment of suicide attempters and the education of emotionally involved significant others.

Type I: Suicidal Gesture

Type I, the largest clustering, consists of patients with characterological problems who experience few symptoms of anxiety, guilt, or depression; minimal dysfunctioning and minimal interpersonal conflict; and alcohol and/or drug abuse. Denying the presence of psychiatric difficulties or attributing the problems to situational factors, patients who fit this profile type make the least severe attempts of all seven groups. They report no plans for the attempt, minimal suicidal thoughts, and minimal discomfort before a suicide attempt. They attempt suicide with pills or by slashing their wrists in the presence of others or with others nearby. Despite repeated low-risk attempts, these patients tend to have good general outcomes; they show little increase in conflict or in symptoms at follow-up.

Type II: Acute Depressive Reaction

Type II, the second largest clustering, consists of acutely depressed patients who believe themselves to be incapable of coping with objective life stresses and attempt suicide with irreversible means in a setting that has minimal possibilities of rescue.

These patients report the highest scores on the somatic symptoms of depression, including appetite, sleep, and sex disturbances, as well as high scores on anxiety, tension, fear, and remorse. They report minimal interpersonal conflict with significant others.

The social setting of the suicide attempts of this group of patients—at a distance from others and with minimal possibility of rescue—despite the supportive attitudes of significant others, earmark this high-risk group. In the year following the attempt, these patients show high scores on increased conflict, subsequent hospitalization, increased symptoms, and subsequent attempts.

Hospitalization should be seriously considered for this group of patients. They require prompt reduction of depressive symptoms with ECT or psychopharmaceuticals. Special precautions should be taken when a patient who fits this type appears to improve but has not yet come out of his depression.

Type III: Passive-Aggressive and Passive-Dependent Personality Disorder

Type III patients report a minimum of symptoms and interpersonal conflict. Judged by significant others to be quite dysfunctional, these patients are hospitalized more often than any of the other groups. They attempt suicide in a remote and private way, using irreversible means, and make no effort to obtain help. In the year following the attempt, they make the fewest major changes in their lives and are judged generally to have the worst clinical outcomes, despite the absence of repeated attempts. They score zero or minimal on ratings of suicidal preoccupation and obsessive thoughts or acts. They show little evidence of emotional or physical blunting of affect and receive the lowest scores on unusual thoughts and behavior of any of the groups. They also have mild and minimal ratings on grandiosity, hallucinatory behavior, and bizarre thought content. They are rated as minimal to mild on anxiety, guilt, tension, and depressive symptoms.

A history of a serious suicide attempt in an isolated social setting without seeking help and a discrepancy between these patients' views of their problems (they minimize them) and the views of significant others (who may have been indifferent, rejecting, punitive, or overcontrolling in their concern for the patient's welfare) make this a high-risk group.

Treatment goals for patients who fit this type must be designed to reduce their high rate of dropping out of treatment. Brief hospitalization should be considered to reduce the pressures brought by significant others and to arrange less noxious living arrangements for these patients. Long-range supportive programs may prove to be the most satisfactory way of keeping contact with them. At the same time, significant others should be helped to reduce their excessive guilt and sense of responsibility.

Type IV: Anxiety Reaction with Interpersonal Conflict

Of the seven groups, type IV patients have the highest scores on anxiety and guilt and the second highest scores on tension, suicidal threats, and interpersonal conflict, despite reports of significant others that they were supportive of the patients and nonthreatened. While patients who fit type IV attempt suicide in close proximity to others with reversible methods—e.g., lacerations and pills—they are judged to be above average in suicide potential.

Type IV patients receive average scores for unusual thoughts and emotional and physical blunting and the lowest scores on depressive symptoms and overall dysfunctioning.

The most prominent feature of this group appears to be the marked discrepancy between the patients' high scores for interpersonal conflict and the significant others' accounts of being supportive, which no doubt contribute to the persistence of high levels of interpersonal conflict, the highest incidence of repeated attempts, and the second highest scores on symptoms at follow-up. These patients report considerable interpersonal conflict with significant others, who view themselves as supportive and minimize the patients' distress. The discrepancy between the patients' subjective sense of rejection and the reports of the significant others' indifference often leads to repeated attempts, persistence of symptoms, and continued interpersonal conflict.

Treatment for this group of suicide attempters must ultimately focus on the resolution of interpersonal conflict and reduction of related anxiety and tension. Outpatient treatment and family therapy may be most relevant because hospitalization is unlikely to resolve the problem.

Type V: Socially Isolated

Type V patients are characterized by very high scores on interpersonal conflict, suicide potential, and unusual thought and behavior; attempt suicide at a distance from others; and make no effort to be rescued. Despite this, significant others judge their functioning to be unremarkable, a finding with substantial prognostic implications. Of interest and possibly related to their social isolation, type V patients (like type VII patients, described below) are difficult to follow up.

The inclination of this group of patients to drop out of treatment should be recognized. Efforts should be made to establish a long-range supportive and contact program for these patients, with simultaneous efforts directed toward the education of significant others, who must be helped to understand the seriousness of the problem of these patients.

Type VI: Suicidal Preoccupation

Type VI patients constitute a group who are diagnostically similar to type I patients except for highest scores of any group on suicide potential. These patients report more obsessive thought and interpersonal conflict than type I patients, although their scores are close to the mean. They experience little anxiety, guilt, or depressive symptoms and only minimal dysfunctioning. They are close to the mean on emotional withdrawal and physical blunting, and they attempt suicide in close proximity to others.

At one year, type VI patients make the most major changes and make no subsequent attempts.

In essence, type VI patients present more serious characterological problems than type I patients as well as the highest scores on the factor measuring suicide potential. They make relatively nonserious attempts in close proximity to others in the face of situational problems but appear to have good one-year outcomes, probably related to the major changes they are able to make in their lives.

Type VII: Chronic Dysfunctional

Type VII patients resemble type III patients in that they have low scores on anxiety and guilt and attempt suicide at a distance from help, using irreversible means. They also have high scores on interpersonal conflict, suicide potential, and significant others' ratings of overall dysfunctioning and rejection.

They differ from type III patients in that they have higher scores on obsessive thoughts, suicidal preoccupation, and overall dysfunctioning; the highest scores on emotional and physical blunting; and some evidence of depressive symptoms.

Threatened or attempted suicide cannot be lightly dismissed as attention-seeking behavior. Pepple who attempt suicide often come close to death. Those who threaten suicide or who make less serious attempts may kill themselves in subsequent attempts.

The results of cluster analysis underscore the importance of evaluating the effects of discrete variables that may act simultaneously and perhaps synergistically to increase suicidal risk. Particular emphasis must be given to the views of significant others regarding the patient's symptoms and need for treatment, the presence of interpersonal conflict, and the discrepancy between the attitudes of the patient and of significant others.

The groups at highest risk of suicide appear to be patients suffering from psychoneurotic illnesses with depressive or anxiety symptoms who are involved in interpersonal conflict and patients with long-standing characterological problems associated with nonfunctioning and considerable interpersonal conflict. Socially isolated patients, who tend to disappear from follow-up, represent an additional high-risk group.

The attitudes of significant others toward the patient, his illness, and his suicide attempt have major significance in assessing prognosis. Patients with the highest scores on depressive symptoms and serious suicide attempts report considerable conflict with significant others at the end of one year after their suicide attempt, suggesting that increased interpersonal conflict subsequent to an attempt may be reflected in rehospitalization, increased symptoms, and subsequent attempts.

In contrast to depressed patients, those with substantial anxiety reactions report considerable interpersonal conflict, which contrasts markedly with the accounts of significant others, who consider themselves to be supportive and nonthreatened by the attempt. The discrepancy between the views of the patients and those of significant others may be reflected in the high incidence of repeated attempts and the increase in symptoms in this group of patients.

The significant others in the passive-dependent, passive-aggressive group convey indifferent and rejecting attitudes, which are at considerable variance with the average scores on interpersonal conflict reported by the patients, whose isolated attempts are above average in intention and lethality.

The significant others of the socially isolated patients also report indifferent and rejecting attitudes, but this corresponds to the perceptions of the patients, who have the highest scores on interpersonal conflict and who attempted suicide in isolation.

Psychiatric illness may too often be mistakenly rationalized as attributable to factors other than mental disease. Failure to recognize the patient's need for treatment may lead to an escalation of conflict and stigmatization of the patient unless appropriate efforts are made to educate both patients and their significant others as to the nature of the problem.

The attitudes of significant others appear to relate to the outcome of suicidal patients—whether in terms of their ignoring the presence of a treatable illness or in terms of their creating a nonsupportive, punitive, or noxious environment for the patient. These factors have relevance for assessing the immediate risk following a suicide attempt and for the continuing management of the patient. If symptoms improve but negative attitudes persist, prognosis must necessarily be guarded.

TREATMENT OF DEPRESSION

Unrecognized and untreated psychiatric illness, particularly major depressive illness, all too often leads to suicide, or at least attempted suicide. Anxiety, agitation, apprehension, and a pervasive feeling of worthlessness are the components of a depressive illness that may drive the patient to attempt to take his or her own life. Recent efforts to cope with this major public health problem have led to the development of various suicide prevention programs, relying heavily on emergency telephone hot lines, brief psychotherapeutic techniques, patient-led groups, as well as the development of comprehensive crisis intervention clinics.

As much as such programs may have ameliorative effects on the life crisis that may have precipitated the suicide attempt, by themselves they rarely have significant effects in reducing the distressing symptomatology that characterizes depressive reactions, regardless of whether they result from tangible environmental factors or develop as psychobiological responses to nonspecific life stresses. For symptomatic relief and rapid reduction of suicide potential, more specific measures, such as effective psychopharmaceuticals, are indicated.

The antidepressant drugs available today, principally the tricyclics, have proven useful in controlling the specific target symptoms of depressive illness in a rapid, economical, and relatively simple fashion. Antidepressant medication is especially useful for relieving insomnia, loss of appetite, lack of energy, depressed mood, hypochondriasis, reduced sexual drive, and feelings of emotional emptiness when these are part of the depressive state.

The risk of suicide is greatest when a period of improvement occurs before the end of a discrete period of depression. This is so because depression is a cyclical entity. For this reason, the antidepressant medication employed should provide not only prompt but sustained symptomatic relief until the patient has returned to his or her premorbid status.

The magnitude and intensity of social and psychological problems and conflicts generally decrease as the patient's symptoms are relieved and he is restored to his normal emotional state. It is much easier to assess his problem at this stage. Difficulties on the job, at home, or in interpersonal relationships produce much guilt and may seem insoluble and overwhelming to the patient; nevertheless, as the patient improves they may disappear, become completely manageable, or be reduced to just one problem area.

Still, efforts are made to alter any environmental circumstances that are clearly contributing to the person's illness. The frequency of visits to the therapist is based on the extent of the person's distress and need for support during crisis periods. Sometimes it is desirable to see the patient every day if only for brief periods. At other times, it is enough to maintain telephone contact with the patient during crisis periods. For most patients a weekly visit over a period of one or two months will carry them through until distress is sufficiently relieved so that they are coping adequately again.

Personality changes do not come about in the therapy session, but occur in real-life situations, particularly when patients are able to experiment with new ways of being and behaving. This is particularly true for individuals with chronic difficulties in adjustment and getting along. For this reason, treatment moves most rapidly when patients can focus on concrete problems in work, at home, or in interpersonal relationships, for these areas offer the greatest opportunity for trying out new ways of dealing with others, which can in turn lead to new attitudes and greater opportunities for self-realization.

The therapists act as guides in solving problems and try to assist the patient to help himself overcome those early learned habits and inhibitions that block him from pursuing his goals. While the professionals certainly do not have answers to all problems, there is good evidence that the effects of an individual's success in solving a previously insoluble problem are generalized to other areas of his life.

The majority of depressive illnesses last about three to four months. Generally, it takes two to three weeks for medication to begin to work. The course of improvement may zigzag, with good periods being followed sometimes by a temporary return of symptoms. However, the odds are that once the patient has begun to improve, overall progress will be uphill.

It takes considerably longer for attitudes and relationships to change. Once the patient discovers that each day is a new one affording him countless ordinary situations where he can try to realize himself and his potential by behaving in new ways, he can continue to progress on his own, periodically consulting with his therapist when and if new problems arise.

Lithium carbonate is a prophylactic agent potentially useful in a range of conditions often unresponsive to conventional antidepressants and tranquilizers. Lithium has been claimed to be of value in the treatment of a number of conditions, including excitement states, manic states, premenstrual tension, phobias, and obsessive-compulsive behavior. It has also been demonstrated to be an effective prophylactic agent against recurrent depressions.

SUMMARY

The social impact of attempted suicide can be broadly measured in terms of psychiatric morbidity, divorce, separation, unemployment, and other manifestations of conflict and shifts in interpersonal or family relationships.

The most striking characteristic of the social environment of most patients is the degree of life difficulties, stressful relationships, and frequent crises. Suicide attempts are generally indicative of overall maladjustments in functioning, not isolated episodic or chance occurrences. Viewed as responses to a relationship, symptoms of depression often become the focus of sadomasochistic relationships, making it difficult at times to differentiate treatable symptoms from the effects of unsatisfactory relationships.

The onset of symptoms often creates such friction in relationships, leading in turn to rejection, separations, and repeated suicidal attempts as a result of inability to handle tense interpersonal conflict while in a guilt-ridden, self-derogating depressed state.

Good treatment consists of appropriate medication and a meaningful patient-therapist relationship. The therapist's theoretical orientation counts for less than his warmth, sympathy, understanding, and orientation to reality. Treatment efforts seek to increase self-reliance, strengthen the capacity to tolerate rejection, and help to develop alternative ways of tension reduction. Patients require help in accepting reality and discovering strengths in themselves that can be maximally utilized. Crisis intervention therapy avoids intensive examination of sensitive areas which reduces the patient's sense of self-confidence. Where self-destructive behavior has become habitual, prognosis remains guarded and resocialization is required.

Crisis intervention helps patients to cope with increased stress by learning to anticipate and plan for difficult situations; reduces the duration of the recovery phase in instances of repeated attempts, the incidence of complications, and the speed of adjustment to difficult stresses; and reduces the incidence of overreaction and interpersonal conflict that often follow an initial attempt. To the extent that others believe problems are being handled, treatment reduces the concerns of others to the significance of the attempts and to the underlying distress of the individual.

The techniques and the results of successful treatment vary with different psychiatric disorders. Personality factors influence the response to both psychotherapy and chemotherapy. Some hysterical and immature patients exaggerate their distress over minimal depressive symptoms and the side effects of medication. Obsessive perfectionist patients often show little tolerance for symptoms and never believe they have improved. They judge themselves perfectionistically and rarely compare their progress to their initial depressed or disturbed state. Schizoid patients often become increasingly withdrawn.

In general, when the patient accepts help and maintains contact over time with a psychiatrist or therapeutic team, the outcome is more favorable than when the patient attends sporadically or evokes rejecting attitudes in others which reinforce the misperceptions that others don't care.

To the extent that successful treatment depends on the establishment of a working relationship between patient and therapist, positive outcome relates to maturity. The healthiest patients obtain the best results and benefit most from the therapeutic relationship. The families of patients whose illness resulted from stress change more readily. Relationships stabilize around the patient's psychopathology and efforts to change them in the families of schizophrenics and character disorders who have developed a long-standing life-style to fit the patient's special needs. Impulsive patients rapidly respond to support. Patients suffering endogenous depression require support but respond less to suggestions or encouragement. Both groups tolerate intensive psychotherapy poorly.

REFERENCES

1. KIEV, A. (1970). New directions for suicide prevention centers. *Am. J. Psychiatry, 127*, 87.
2. KIEV, A. (1971). The chemotherapy of depressive illness. *Drug Ther., 1*, 9.
3. KIEV, A. (1973). *A strategy for daily living*. New York: Free Press.
4. KIEV, A. (1974). The role of chemotherapy in managing potentially suicidal patients. *Dis. Nerv. Syst., 35*, 108.
5. KIEV, A. (1974). Lithium—drug in search of an illness. *Drug Ther., 4*, 63.
6. KIEV, A. (1974). Prognostic factors in attempted suicide. *Am. J. Psychiatry, 131*, 9.
7. KIEV, A. (Ed.). (1974). *Somatic manifestations of depressive disorders*. Princeton, NJ: Excerpta Medica.
8. KIEV, A. (1979). *The courage to live*. New York: Crowell.
9. KIEV, A. (1982). *Recovery from depression*. New York: Dutton.
10. KIEV, A. (1975). Symptom patterns and the acceptance of the "sick role" in attempted suicide. *Cur. Med. Res. Opinion, 2* (Suppl. 34), 34.
11. KIEV, A. (1975). Psychotherapeutic strategies in the management of depressed and suicidal patients. *Am. J. Psychother., 29*, 345.
12. KIEV, A. (1976). Cluster analysis profiles of suicide attempters. *Am. J. Psychiatry, 133*, 2.

11

SCHIZOAFFECTIVE STATES

PAUL V. WILLIAMS, M.D.

Staff Psychiatrist,
Chestnut Lodge Research Institute
Rockville, Maryland

and

THOMAS H. MCGLASHAN, M.D.

Director of Research,
Chestnut Lodge Research Institute
Rockville, Maryland

INTRODUCTION

The concept of schizoaffective (SA) illness developed from a need to account for the many patients not easily classified by the Kraepelinian (13) dichotomy of the psychoses into schizophrenia and manic-depressive illness. As historically determined, it comprises a broad field of heterogeneous disorders and includes any patient demonstrating an admixture of schizophrenic and affective disorder symptoms.

In this chapter we trace the history of the SA concept, outline its scope, and discuss current diagnostic and prognostic guidelines. We also propose a stepwise approach to treatment that helps to specify differential diagnosis and to minimize iatrogenic risk. Illustrative clinical cases are presented.

HISTORICAL DEVELOPMENT OF THE SCHIZOAFFECTIVE CONCEPT

The existence of psychoses with admixtures of schizophrenic and affective symptoms has long been recognized. Over the last century, however, the understanding and categorization of these descriptively "schizoaffective" psychoses has varied markedly. In the mid-19th century, the classification of mental illness was determined by a tradition that considered symptom clusters like catatonia, melancholia, mania, and dementia to be true and distinct diseases and by a widely held belief that all psychoses began with a melancholic state (3). Modern clinical psychiatry at the turn of the century was initiated by Kraepelin's (13) description of the major psychoses. He proposed that certain symptom groups, e.g., catatonia, hebephrenia, and paranoia, were part of a group of psychoses termed *dementia praecox* which ended in chronicity and deterioration. Other psychoses lacking these symptom groups and not ending in deterioration were classified as manic-depressive psychoses.

Bleuler (3) continued Kraepelin's (13) tradition of careful clinical description. He felt that schizophrenia could be "clearly distinguished" from all the other psychoses which "neither show the same symptomatology nor the same outcome" (p. 4). For Bleuler, the process of differential diagnosis began by considering schizophrenia to be the primary and more inclusive diagnosis. He felt that "all manic-depressive symptoms can also occur in schizophrenia . . . " (p. 269). Hence, if certain pathognomonic symptoms occurred, the diagnosis of schizophrenia was established regardless of the presence of manic or depressive symptoms. According to him, "Manic and melancholic symptoms are so common in our patients that we must assume that they are usually released by the disease process itself, and thus are part of the schizophrenia" (p. 268). Manic-depressive psychosis, on the other hand, was for Bleuler (3) limited to patients with a narrow group of symptoms, the essential character being an elated or depressed "tonus" of affect, association, and mobility. This included "pathological euphoria, flight of ideas, pressure of activity on the one hand; depression, blocking of thought, general motor inhibition on the other" (p. 12). He limited the scope of manic-depressive psychosis by excluding "accessory" symptoms such as delusions. He wrote, "Most of the manic and melancholic delusions of earlier writers belong here [with schizophrenia] since manic-depressive delusions are rare" (p. 215).

Bleuler (3) was not oblivious to the arbitrariness of rigidly dichotomizing schizophrenia and manic-depressive psychosis, and he made reference to confusing combinations of symptomatology. He explicitly considered the possibility that schizophrenia could occur in conjunction with other psychoses. While concluding that "combinations of schizophrenia with melancholia and mania or with manic-depressive psychosis have not yet been demonstrated with any certainty" (p. 268), he did note that "those cases [of schizophrenia], which follow the pattern of cyclic psychoses . . . are probably for the most part mixed forms of manic-depressive psychosis and schizophrenia" (p. 269).

Following Kraepelin (13) and Bleuler (3), clinicians described psychotic states that did not fit into a dichotomized scheme. Greenacre (7) reported a group of 40 cases of affective disorders with schizophrenic manifestations. He grouped the schizophrenic symptoms into five classes by content: delusions of reference, delusions of influence, hallucinations, gross distortions of body sense, and incongruous behavior. Bowman and Raymond (4) demonstrated the presence of delusions in nearly 60% of the 1,009 manic-depressive patients they studied compared to their presence in 90% of the 1,408 schizophrenic patients studied. Lewis and Hubbard (14) retrospectively studied a group of 77 patients who had been diagnosed either as manic-depressive or who had presented with an admixture of affective and schizophrenic symptoms. Contrasting the clinical picture and course of illness of these patients, they concluded that "definite schizophrenic elaborations appearing during the course of an affect disorder are unfavorable signs" (p. 604). Subclassifying these patients by polarity of mood at first admission, they found that an elated reaction was encountered twice as frequently as a depressive reaction. Regardless of initial mood, "there was an increasingly greater tendency for the content [of the psychosis] to become schizophrenic in subsequent attacks" (p. 601).

Kasanin (12) is credited with originating the specific term *schizoaffective*. He presented case studies of nine patients with "acute schizoaffective psychoses" who were premorbidly well adjusted and had the onset of an acute psychosis in reaction to clear precipitants. They showed a mixture of schizophrenic and affective symptoms, and all went on to recovery within a few months. Kasanin (12) felt that the Kraepelinian (13) classification was too rigid and that such dichotomized groups would contain "a large number of heterogeneous cases with different clinical pictures . . . " (p. 98). He asserted that progress in psychiatry depended on delineating homogeneous subgroups, and he presented his case studies as an example of such.

Hunt and Appel (10) were interested in cases that did not fit into clear-cut diagnostic groups. They stated, "We are not so much interested in trying to set up a new nosological group as in trying to find out something more about this group [i.e., schizoaffective] which undoubtedly exists, no matter how we classify it" (p. 314). They studied 30 cases presenting with an almost equal mixture of schizophrenic and manic-depressive symptoms. Their cases were followed for at least four years following admission. They reported a 37% rate of recovery for these SA patients, which was between the recovery rates they reported for schizophrenia, 21%, and manic-depressive illness, 81%. They also subdivided their patients by affective subtypes, primarily manic, depressed, or mixed. They found a greater percentage of the depressed subtype in the unfavorable outcome groups.

Kant (11) reported on a group of 39 patients, all of whom conformed to a "conventional diagnosis" of schizophrenia, but who recovered to the point of having a "complete restoration of their pre-psychotic personality, as well as an objective attitude toward the previous illness and abnormal experiences" (p. 263). He subclassified these patients on the basis of atypical features, and the majority showed predominantly affective features despite the diagnosis of schizophrenia.

Despite these reports, the SA states had no firm "official" standing in diagnostic nomenclatures. The *Diagnostic and Statistical Manual* (1) of the American Psychiatric Association in 1952 did list a schizoaffective subtype of schizophrenia "for those cases showing significant admixtures of schizophrenic and affective reactions" (p. 27). It noted, however, that "on prolonged observation, such cases usually prove to be basically schizophrenic in nature" (p. 27).

In a review of what he termed the "remitting schizophrenias," Vaillant (23) identified 15 independent reports between the years 1849 and 1960 which described schizophrenialike psychoses with admixtures of affective symptoms. He tabulated the common features of each, which included good premorbid adjustment, precipitating stress, psychologically understandable symptoms, symptoms of psychotic depression, concern with dying, and acute onset with confusion. Vaillant hypothesized that such patients had schizophrenia, but in an acute form from which they recovered. He did not support the concept of SA states per se and felt that efforts to subdivide the group of schizophrenias were premature. Thus he supported a conservative position favoring an inclusive diagnosis of schizophrenia.

Procci (17) titled his survey of the literature a decade later "Schizoaffective Psychosis: Fact or Fiction?" in recognition of the continuing doubts about the validity of this concept. He compared 11 independent descriptions of SA states reported between the years 1913 and 1975. He felt that the authors examined were describing a similar entity, characterized by good premorbid adjustment, acute onset with confusion, precipitating stress, affective symptoms, and family history of affective illness. Unlike Vaillant (23), Procci (17) felt that these SA states had little resemblance to schizophrenia beyond the presence of symptomatic features. Moreover, he concluded that SA psychosis is itself a heterogeneous entity, and he endorsed Tsuang's (19) proposal that subclassification into schizophrenic, affective, and mixed subtypes would advance research efforts. For example, he felt that the subgroup of SA states reviewed by him (cases with good outcome) would most likely fit into the affective subtype.

During the last decade, investigations of the SA states have benefited from expanding interest in systematic nosology, and especially from the development of specific operational diagnostic criteria (6, 18). Three comprehensive reviews of the current state of SA disorders prepared by Brockington and Meltzer (5), Tsuang and Simpson (21), and Harrow and Grossman (9) have appeared recently.

Brockington and Meltzer (5) reviewed pattern of inheritance, treatment response, course, outcome, and platelet 5-hydroxytryptophan uptake in SA psychosis. They rejected the hypotheses that SA disorders are variants of schizophrenia or that they represent the coincidental occurrence of two unconnected diseases. They could not reject the hypothesis that the manic subgroup is a variant of affective disorder. They concluded that SA disorders are heterogeneous and that SA symptomatology cloaks two or three distinct diseases, including schizophrenia, affective disorder, and possibly a third, small, and etiologically distinct subgroup which breeds true.

Tsuang and Simpson (21) organized their review according to whether a study supported SA disorder to be a form of schizophrenia, a form of affective disorder, or a distinct/heterogeneous illness. They concluded that the repeated differences arrived at by separate researchers constitute evidence for the heterogeneity of SA disorder and felt that an appropriate research strategy was to search for homogeneous subgroups.

Harrow and Grossman (9) reviewed retrospective and prospective outcome studies of SA disorders. They concluded that the varying profiles of clinical course and outcome left open the issue of whether SA disorders should be classified as belonging with affective disorders, with schizophrenia, or as a separate disorder.

The long-term outcome of SA psychosis, schizophrenia, and affective disorder, defined using operational research criteria, have been compared by Tsuang and Dempsey (20) and Williams and McGlashan (25). Both studies found SA patients to have an outcome between that of patients with schizophrenia and affective disorder. A prospective study of Grossman et al. (8), at the initial one-year evaluation, likewise reported that SA patients had outcomes falling between patients with schizophrenia and affective disorder. Taken together, these three studies fail to support trends subsuming SA psychosis under either schizophrenia or affective disorder.

SCOPE AND CLASSIFICATION OF THE SCHIZOAFFECTIVE DISORDERS

Schizoaffective states comprise a heterogeneous group, the understanding of which may be facilitated by the proposed heuristic model shown in Figure 1. The intersecting or overlapping parts of this Venn diagram correspond to admixtures of schizophrenic and affective symptomatology as observed clinically, including the subclassification of SA disorders by predominant psychopathology and by affective subtype. SAS represents the schizophrenic subtype, in contrast to the affective subtypes, which can be

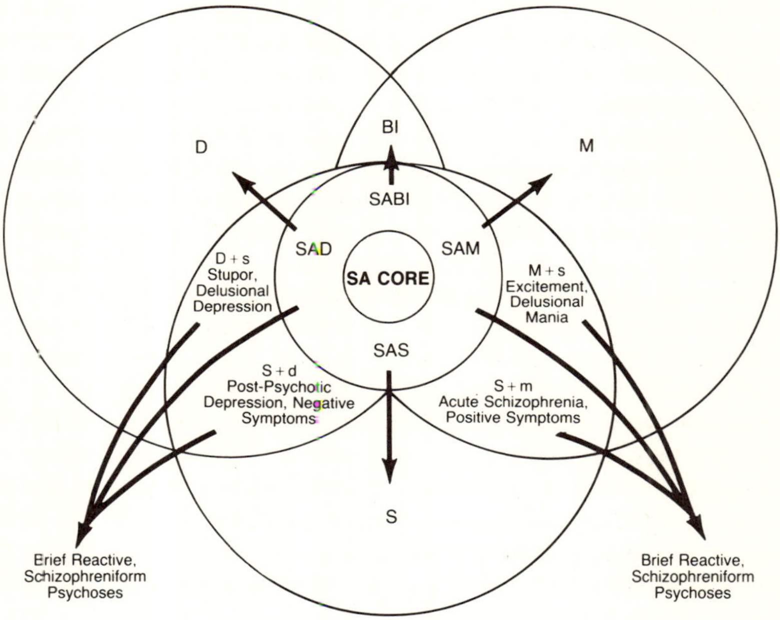

S = Schizophrenia; D = Unipolar Depression; BI = Biopolar; M = Mania
SA = Schizoaffective; SAS = Schizophrenic Subtype
SAD = Depressed Subtype; SABI = Bipolar Subtype;
SAM = Manic Subtype

Arrows indicate possible directions of diagnostic change over time. Possibly related sybtypes: S+d = primary S with D features (Post-Psychotic Depression, Negative symptoms); D+s = primary D with S features (Catatonic Stupor, Delusional Depression); M+s = primary M with S features (Catatonic Excitement, Delusional Mania); S+m = primary S with M features (Acute Schizophrenia, Positive Symptoms)

Figure 1. Schematic diagram of the heterogeneous scope and evolution of schizoaffective states.

further subclassified by polarity of mood into SA depressed (SAD), SA manic (SAM), and SA bipolar (SABI).

The diagram also depicts the possible vicissitudes of SA psychopathology over time, especially its evolution into other Axis I diagnostic categories. For example, arrows indicate possible transformation to schizophrenia (S), depression (D), mania (M), or bipolar affective disorder (BI). Some SA states may evolve rapidly into a clinical picture of brief reactive psychosis or schizophreniform disorder. A core group of SA patients may remain, at least descriptively, even at long-term follow-up. Williams and McGlashan (26) recently studied the long-term diagnostic stability of 68 SA patients and found that only 16% of them retained a clinical diagnosis of SA disorder an average of 15 years after index assessment. The majority had evolved into schizophrenia and the rest into affective disorder, primarily unipolar depression.

Finally, Figure 1 denotes several subtypes of schizophrenia and affective disorder which may or may not relate to SA psychosis. They are primary D with S features (catatonic stupor, delusional depression), primary S with D features (post-psychotic depression, negative/defect symptoms), primary S with M features (acute S, continuous positive symptoms), and primary M with S features (catatonic excitement, delusional mania).

Diagnostic Criteria

SA disorder is considered a residual diagnostic category by the DSM-III (2). Syndromes with admixtures of schizophrenic and affective symptoms are classified into other categories, especially schizophreniform disorder, affective disorder with mood-incongruent psychotic features, or schizophrenia with superimposed atypical affective disorder. DSM-III remains uncertain about whether there is a need for the SA diagnosis but retains the category without diagnostic criteria.

DSM-III (2) separates some disorders with acute onset, brief duration, and remitting course from the subacute or chronic, nonremitting states, but generally avoids the issue of admixtures of symptomatology. For example, brief reactive psychosis does not include any criteria that speak to the presence of affective symptoms. DSM-III would, as another example, probably put the acute SA psychoses observed by Kasanin (12) into the schizophreniform disorder category. DSM-III schizophreniform disorder meets all of the criteria for schizophrenia except for duration of six months. It excludes a full depressive or manic syndrome unless secondary to schizophrenic symptoms and excludes prodromal and residual symptoms due to a disturbance in mood. This diagnosis does not do justice to Kasanin's and others' attempts to distinguish the acute SA states as distinct from schizophrenia.

Many schizophrenic and affective symptom admixtures are categorized by DSM-III (2) as affective disorders with mood-incongruent psychotic features. This assumes they are variants of affective disorder, which has not been demonstrated. In so doing, DSM-III may be repeating in reverse the former mistake of holding most SA states to be variants of schizophrenia. It may also tend to blur the poor prognosis of psychoses with mood-incongruent features, as recently suggested by Harrow and Grossman (9).

Because explicit diagnostic criteria are important for investigative and prognostic purposes, other systems have provided these for SA psychosis, including RDC (18) and *modified versions* of the DSM-III (2) and Feighner et al. (6) criteria. Since the latter two systems do not have specific criteria for SA disorder, researchers (22, 25) have used them to construct a hybrid system that requires the SA patient to fulfill the diagnosis for both schizophrenia and affective disorder, minus mutual exclusion criteria.

DSM-III-R (24) provides specific diagnostic criteria for SA disorder. It defines a disturbance in which the individual experiences either a major depressive or a manic syndrome concurrent with symptoms from the A criterion for schizophrenia; however, for at least two weeks the patient must manifest delusions or hallucinations in the absence of prominent affective symptoms. This definition emphasizes a period of nonconcurrence of affective and schizophrenic symptoms, which has not been a distinguishing feature of either clinical reports or research studies. Whether such a definition selects a homogeneous subgroup of SA patients remains to be seen, but such restricted criteria certainly overlook the majority of clinically visible SA disorders.

Subclassification by Predominant Psychopathology

Two systems provide for further subclassification on the basis of predominant psychopathology, i.e., schizophrenic, affective, or other/undifferentiated. Under the RDC criteria (18), an SA patient is first subtyped by affective polarity (manic or depressed) and then further subclassified as: (1) affective subtype if affective symptoms began prior to the onset of schizophrenic symptoms and the patient had good premorbid social and occupational adjustment, or (2) schizophrenic subtype if features typical of schizophrenia were exhibited prior to the onset of the affective features or if core schizophrenic symptoms were present for at least one week in the absence of affective features. Under the Tsuang and Loyd (22) criteria an SA patient is subtyped as schizophrenic if five of the following seven criteria are met: onset before age 25, presence of auditory hallucinations, presence of motor symptoms (hebephrenic-catatonic), absence of self-reproach or euphoria, poor premorbid adjustment, poor recovery from previous episode(s), and family history positive for chronic psychotic condition. The affective subtype requires the same number of criteria from this list, modified by onset after age 30, a family history positive for remitting affective episode(s), and the opposite direction vis-à-vis the other five criteria. Affective subtype is then further subdivided into manic and depressive.

Subclassification by Affective Polarity

The affective mood polarity of an SA disorder can, following usual criteria for affective disorders, be subtyped into SA depressed (SAD), SA manic (SAM), and SA bipolar (SABI). Grossman et al. (8) conducted a prospective follow-up of 39 SA patients diagnosed by RDC (18). They found no significant differences in overall outcome at one year between SAD and SAM patients. They also found no significant differences in overall outcome between affective versus schizophrenic subtypes. McGlashan and Williams (16) studied the long-term outcome of a group of 68 SA patients diagnosed by hybrid DSM-III (2) criteria. They found that SAD showed a suggestive but nonsignificant trend toward better outcome compared to both SAM and SABI.

Classification for the Clinician

The nosological status of SA psychosis remains, as usual, in a state of speculation and controversy. This provides little direction for the clinician whose patients cannot wait for the development of valid diagnostic systems and syndromes. Because the criteria for SA psychoses are in such a state of flux at the present time, we suggest that the practicing psychiatrist follow the historical clinical tradition. That is, we suggest a SA diagnosis be considered whenever the patient presents with both schizophrenic and affective (bipolar, unipolar) symptoms, either simultaneously or in sequence. We advocate the use of these broad and inclusive criteria as the best approach at the onset of treatment to encourage full investigation of differential diagnostic possibilities, and to avoid premature closure on optimal treatment.

TREATMENT

Treatment of the schizoaffective disorders demands that the clinician have familiarity with the full range of clinical services and a knowledge of treatment techniques that have proven useful in both affective disorders and schizophrenia. For the acutely ill SA patient, this begins with inpatient hospitalization, case management, and pharmacotherapy. Once the patient stabilizes and appears out of danger, discharge is feasible, especially if referral can be effected to an aftercare setup that provides continuity of care. Long-term treatment in this context focuses on assuring an adequate living situation (in or out of the family), organizing sufficient vocational and recreational activities to structure the patient's day, and evaluating the strategy for maintenance pharmacotherapy. Specific pathogenic stresses and adaptive deficiencies are addressed by psychosocial interventions such as individual psychotherapy, group psychotherapy, social skills training, vocational rehabilitation, and family therapy. In general, the psychosocial therapies that have evolved for the treatment of schizophrenia also apply to the SA disorders. These have recently been reviewed by McGlashan (15).

The treatment of SA patients, then, can be straightforward and similar to the approaches generally developed for the psychoses. Even skilled clinicians, however, occasionally find themselves perplexed by patients with SA states. Uncertainties about treatment decisions are often a reflection of uncertainty about the diagnosis itself. In fact, clinicians frequently pursue a differential diagnosis of SA states at the same time that they are attempting to make treatment decisions. Commonly, one is pursuing a presumptive diagnosis made on the basis of a patient's response to treatment trials in progress.

The key to judicious treatment lies in remaining open to differential diagnostic possibilities and avoiding closure on diagnosis which prematurely forecloses on useful therapeutic alternatives. Forcing a "true" SA patient into a narrower diagnosis may result in partial treatment. On the other hand, failure to consider that a presenting SA picture may actually be an atypical affective disorder exposes the patient to the hazards of neuroleptics, especially tardive dyskinesia. A staged or stepwise approach to the differential diagnosis and treatment of SA states is offered here as a reasonable protocol for the majority of SA patients encountered in a clinical practice. A four-stage approach is shown schematically in Figure 2.

When evaluating a new or acute, first-episode patient, it is important to use a broadly defined diagnostic system. Then, through the process of

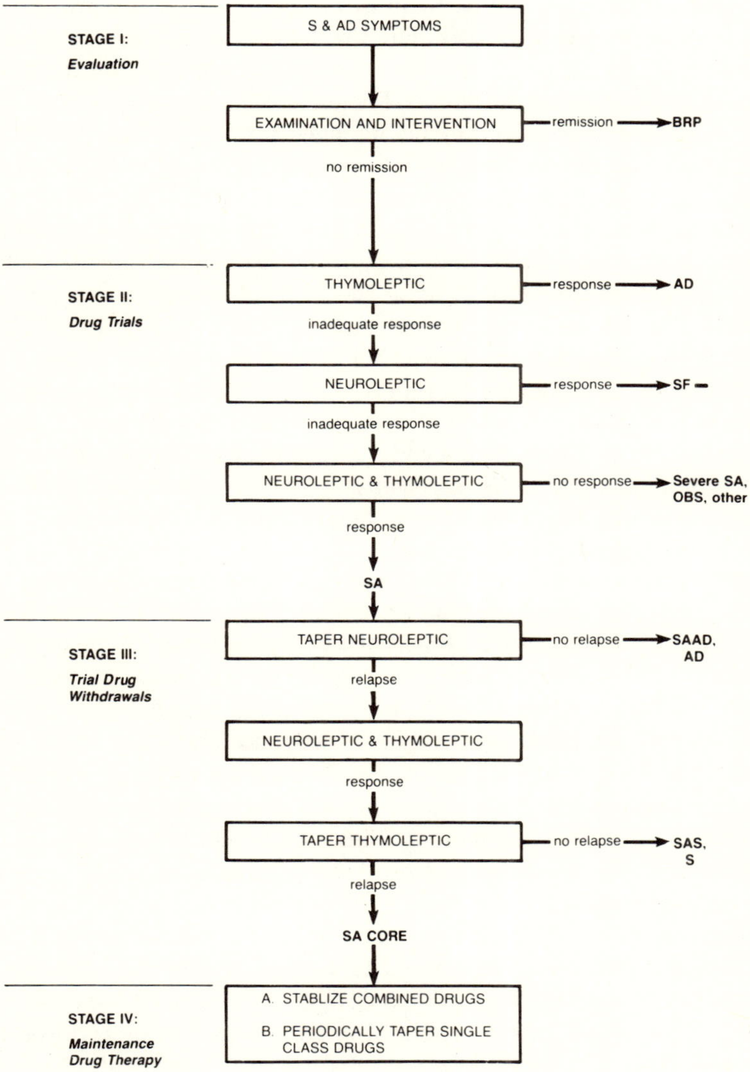

S=	Schizophrenia	OBS=	Organic Brain Syndrome
AD=	Affective Disorder	SA=	Schizoaffective Psychosis
BRP=	Brief Reactive Psychosis	SAAD=	SA, Affective Subtype
SF=	Schizophreniform Psychosis	SAS=	SA, Schizophrenic Subtype

Figure 2. Treatment and presumptive diagnosis of schizoaffective states.

treatment, differential diagnostic possibilities are tested and primary diagnosis is progressively specified. For the first-time, acutely psychotic SA patient, it is vital to consider brief reactive psychosis among the primary differential diagnostic possibilities. If such a patient is not a clinical danger to self or others, he or she may be managed for two or three weeks in the hospital without medication, or with sparing amounts, in hopes of aiding or inducing a spontaneous remission (see stage I of Fig. 2).

If the patient remains symptomatic after this period of evaluation and milieu management, single-class drug trials are begun (stage II). Thymoleptics should be used first in case the patient's condition represents an affective disorder with atypical presentation. The risk of tardive dyskinesia demands that neuroleptics be withheld unless the patient is dangerously agitated or the thymoleptic trial proves ineffective. A positive clinical response at this point to thymoleptics suggests affective disorder. A negative response to thymoleptics followed by remission with neuroleptics suggests schizophreniform psychosis, especially if the remission proves stable after subsequent neuroleptic withdrawal. Relapse following withdrawal, on the other hand, suggests schizophrenia.

If the clinician is satisfied that single-class medication has proven inadequate, combined-class drug trials are begun. The patient is placed simultaneously on the therapeutic regimens of a neuroleptic and thymoleptic. Our definition of thymoleptic includes tricyclic antidepressants, monoamine oxidase inhibitors, lithium, and, at times, ECT. Stabilization of the patient's clinical condition on combined medication provides treatment response validation of the SA diagnosis. A negative response to combined therapy at this point demands reconsideration of the differential diagnostic possibilities, as shown in Figure 2. This could include treatment-resistant SA psychosis, an organically determined psychotic state, or some other atypically presenting, functionally psychotic process.

When evaluating a subacute or chronic patient with a previous history of illness and treatment, it is important to assess the thoroughness with which prior evaluation and drug trials (stages I and II) have been conducted. Were all diagnostic possibilities considered? Were syndrome-specific treatments rendered? Was compliance with treatment satisfactory? What alternative strategies were applied, and with what results?

Once a clinical response is achieved, the treating psychiatrist is at stage III. Before a patient is locked into combined *maintenance* medication, however, discontinuation trials of one class of drugs at a time may further specify differential diagnosis. After the patient is stabilized on a combination of drugs, for example, first it may be judicious to attempt to taper and eventually discontinue the neuroleptics. This may uncover patients who have affective disorder with incongruent mood and who can be maintained on thymoleptics alone. These patients may have been misdiagnosed because of the bizarreness of their symptoms and the difficulty of their management in the past. Some atypical patients may have a prolonged latency of response to usual thymoleptic drugs. Some patients are nonresponders to the usual thymoleptic drugs and deserve a trial on MAO inhibitors or alternative drugs with thymoleptic action, for example, carbamazepine, clonazepam, or propranolol.

A second, equally essential strategy of stage III is an attempt to taper and/or discontinue the thymoleptic. A number of SA patients have an initial response to thymoleptics but then appear to lose the benefits they have acquired. These patients, probably the schizophrenic subtype of SA, may not relapse when the thymoleptic is discontinued. They can be observed for future exacerbations of affective symptomatology and again tried on a thymoleptic in combination with a maintenance neuroleptic.

Periodic drug discontinuations serve not only to articulate diagnosis, but also to provide information about what medicines and doses are necessary for effective long-term prophylaxis. For the core SA patient, combined-class drug maintenance may be optimal, although the necessity for this should always be tested from time to time (stage IV). The goals, as always, are to prevent relapse and maximize clinical gain while minimizing the risks of side effects, especially irreversible tardive dyskinesia.

BRIEF CASE STUDIES

Cases illustrating the differential diagnosis and treatment of schizoaffective (SA) disorders are presented.

Case 1: Acute SA State Evolving to Brief Reactive Psychosis

The patient was a 34-year-old, unmarried accountant brought to the hospital involuntarily by the police. He had been apprehended in an acute state of panic, agitation, and bizarre activity at the headquarters of his corporation. He had gone there with a briefcase full of documents to show his chief executive officer. He felt that these documents proved that his immediate supervisor had plotted to discredit and fire him. His agitated behavior alarmed the secretarial staff. When they tried to delay him, his panic increased and he rushed into an adjoining office screaming that he was being followed by a killer hired by his supervisor.

At the hospital, he was hyperactive and unable to sleep. At times, his consciousness seemed clouded and he was unable to respond to questions. At other times he paced the floor and became threatening to nursing staff, who had to restrain and seclude him. He refused to eat. He showed pressure of speech and had grandiose assumptions about being promoted and taking over his supervisor's position. He thought the attending psychiatrist had been threatened by his supervisor and was now forced into the deceitful position of trying to establish that the patient was crazy in order to protect himself.

At one point he thought his assassin was on the unit disguised as a patient. He burst into the nursing office screaming in terror and in confusion became assaultive. He required seclusion again and on this occasion was given a neuroleptic intramuscularly. After that, he agreed to take the medication by mouth. Within several days he reestablished a normal sleep pattern and was clear of symptoms except for residual doubts about the intentions of his supervisor. He was, however, able to reconstruct most of what had happened and felt embarrassed for having acted "foolishly."

A few days later, the patient signed out of the hospital against medical advice and refused to take medication. He did agree to come for follow-up psychotherapy interviews. Over the next several months he remained clear of symptoms. He reconstructed that for three weeks prior to the acute episode he had felt strained and quietly resentful of the criticisms of his new supervisor. He had had difficulty concentrating at work and became increasingly suspicious of his supervisor. He was very unhappy at work, contemplated quitting, but felt dependent and feared giving it up. During his follow-up convalescent period, he consciously realized these discontents and turned in his resignation, after which his lingering suspicions about the supervisor gradually resolved.

A thorough history revealed that the patient had had a prior dysfunctional period which interrupted his first year away from home at college. He was obsessed with the fear of a brain tumor and spent several months visiting medical consultants. He finally accepted referral to a psychiatrist for brief supportive therapy, which helped him return to college.

Comment. In this case, it was impossible to maintain and observe the patient free of medication because of his assaultiveness. His failure to relapse off of medication, however, identified his response as a remission. This, plus good premorbid adjustment, the presence of acute precipitants, and SA symptoms, justified the diagnosis of brief reactive psychosis. This case bears some resemblance to Kasanin's (12) original series, including the observation that in his cases there was usually a vague history of previous breakdown followed by complete recovery.

Case 2: Chronic SA State Evolving to Bipolar Affective Disorder with Mood-Incongruent Features

The patient was a married, childless, 42-year-old woman with onset at age 28 of chronic, undifferentiated schizophrenia. She had abrupt relapses with florid symptoms, usually stabilizing after a two-to-three-month admission, following which she returned home to live with her husband. Between admissions, she functioned well as a housewife. Careful questioning of both husband and patient failed to reveal noncompliance with her maintenance neuroleptics, but it remained the outpatient staff's impression that she had been periodically noncompliant.

On the ward, despite adequate doses of neuroleptics, the patient's psychosis flourished. She was sleepless. She reported bizarre delusions that she had been kidnapped overnight and sent across country in a train at the mercy of a gang of men who repeatedly raped her before they furtively brought her back to the hospital in the early morning. At times she was wildly hyperactive and displayed classic flight of ideas. Because of similar manic symptoms in the past, she had twice been given trials of lithium carbonate along with a neuroleptic, but neither trial had lasted longer than one month.

The treatment decision was made to embark on an extended trial of combined lithium and neuroleptic. Within two months a significant improvement occurred, and by three months the patient was planning for discharge. Brief marital counseling uncovered a pattern of extreme periodic stress precipitated by the husband's intermittent bouts of alcoholic intoxication. At these times of acute marital discord, she experienced breakthroughs of manic symptoms. For the five years prior to this admission, she had never experienced a period of remission lasting longer than 12 months, despite apparent compliance with neuroleptics.

Once stabilized on the combination of drugs, she was gradually tapered off the neuroleptic. Symptoms did not recur, and three-year follow-up found the patient continuously remitted on maintenance lithium.

Comment. This case demonstrates that combined drug treatment is at times necessary for treatment of affective disorders with mood-incongruent features during the acute phase, whereas lithium or thymoleptics alone may be sufficient for maintenance. Because of their refractoriness, these illnesses can easily be misdiagnosed as schizophrenic or schizoaffective.

Case 3: SA Disorder Misdiagnosed Following Partial Treatment and Requiring Combined Drugs

The patient was a 22-year-old, single man with a diagnosis of chronic paranoid schizophrenia and a three and a half year history of 10 psychiatric hospitalizations. He had adequate trials of several neuroleptics at high dosages, including injections of fluphenazine decanoate up to 100 mg i.m. every week. These diminished the intensity of some symptoms, but he had continued to experience hallucinations, delusions, and suicidal impulses regularly. His referring physician had considered the diagnosis of SA disorder and had conducted a trial of lithium carbonate for "about" six weeks without documented blood levels. The patient had been given adequate trials on tricyclic antidepressants and MAO inhibitors and a four-month trial on carbamazepine at therapeutic blood levels. When none of these produced a clinically significant benefit, the differential diagnosis of SA disorder was eliminated in favor of paranoid schizophrenia.

His course was chronic from the beginning. His many hospitalizations were accompanied by bizarre delusions and command hallucinations. He had somatic delusions that his kidneys were moving around in his body. He was convinced that he had fecal material in his throat and that something was up his rectum. Voices called him "freak" and "homosexual." He believed that people were following him and could read his mind or hear his broadcast thoughts.

During prior relapses, the patient had punched holes in walls and broken furniture, but never hurt anyone. He constantly complained of depression and made numerous suicide attempts, twice jumping out of a moving car, twice slashing his wrists, and thrice overdosing. He was constantly preoccupied with suicidal ideation and felt destined to commit suicide before his 23rd birthday.

Two weeks before index hospitalization, he stopped his neuroleptic "to join the Navy." He quickly decompensated, becoming abusive to his parents and damaging their house. As usual, his acute agitation was subdued with high doses of neuroleptics. However, his hallucinations, delusions, suicidal preoccupations, and severe mood swings continued, prompting a diagnosis of SA disorder.

Family therapy with the patient and his parents was conducted once weekly following admission. The treatment plan incorporated a full program of rehabilitation and recreational activities, but the patient was totally noncompliant. He presented with denial of illness and refused to discuss a repeat trial on lithium carbonate. His intense dislike of lithium and his fixed ideas that this drug could not help him, plus a history of "cheeking" psychoactive medications, encouraged the speculation that he had not been compliant with the previous trial of lithium.

After four months of hospitalization, his alliance with the treatment staff allowed him to accept a clinical trial on adequate levels of lithium carbonate. After eight weeks, he showed a moderate stabilization of his mood and less periods of agitation, hostility, and depressive preoccupation. The gradual improvement that he had shown during the initial four months accelerated once the trial of lithium carbonate was underway. Over the next two months, he became interested in getting out of the hospital and returning to work. He participated briefly in a sheltered workshop program and then secured a part-time job in the community.

Soon thereafter, he was discharged back to the care of his referring physician. Trial reductions of the neuroleptics under this doctor's care were generally unsuccessful because the patient reexperienced first-rank symptoms and auditory hallucinations. Accordingly, he was maintained on the combination.

Comment. This case illustrates the importance of treating both dimensions of an SA illness. Diligence in pursuing a reasonable drug protocol despite past treatment failures is essential. It is especially important to maintain skepticism about the adequacy of previous clinical trials.

Case 4: SA Disorder Illustrating Sequential Trials of Neuroleptic and Thymoleptic

The patient was a 23-year-old, single man who had several previous hospitalizations and a diagnosis of chronic paranoid schizophrenia. He had an insidious onset of illness. At age 13, he became more isolated, perfectionistic, and grandiose. Over the next few years he withdrew from his family and would eat alone in his room. He became paranoid, belligerent, and impulsive. He attempted to choke his mother and followed this by slashing his wrists. He was fanatically religious while intermittently abusing drugs. He required hospitalization at age 19 after voicing the delusion that his father had turned into the Devil, hallucinating that he was standing at the Gates of Hell, and asserting his intention to poke out his eyes and drink his urine to prove that he loved his family. Over the next several years, his condition evolved into a chronic psychosis with marginal functioning outside of hospitals.

During index hospitalization, the patient initially refused psychotropic medication. He appeared to be engrossed in psychotic hallucinations and made bizarre facial grimaces, apparently to ward off evil spirits. He was preoccupied with delusions about Hitler, religion, and the Devil. He reasoned that since Hitler had sent the mentally ill but not the criminals to concentration camps, he should murder a mental health worker to become a criminal and avoid annihilation. His affect was intense and ranged between boyish good humor and rage at delusional, persecutory objects. Thought processes and speech were pressured, tangential, and circumstantial. Diagnostic impression was SA disorder.

After attempting to burn himself, he was certified and given injections of neuroleptics against his will. On this, he became more cognitively organized and less confused, but his agitation and intense affective pressure continued. His paranoid delusions became more crystallized and he discussed them openly. After a month, he was begun on lithium, which lessened hostility and paranoid delusions. Surprisingly he looked more playfully hypomanic. He was stabilized on moderate doses of neuroleptic and lithium for two months.

A treatment plan was then formulated to reduce the neuroleptic to help make the differential diagnosis between atypical manic-depressive illness and SA disorder. Over the next two months the neuroleptic was discontinued. The patient showed intense dysphoria and malicious secretive paranoia. The latter increased to the point where he was discovered making plans to buy a shotgun in preparation for a family visit. The neuroleptic was reintroduced with good result. He was stable for some months and a trial reduction of lithium was undertaken to see whether his adjustment could be maintained on neuroleptic alone. However, he became affectively pressured, agitated, and threatened suicidal behavior, so lithium was resumed. The combination of moderate doses of both drug classes produced maximum clinical benefit, and the plan was made to maintain him on both drugs over the long term.

Comment. The patient showed a combination of a malignant, paranoid illness and a disorganizing hypomania. This SA illness responded optimally to neuroleptics and lithium. Neither drug class alone significantly affected both sets of symptoms. During long-term follow-up, further attempts to discontinue either class again failed, demonstrating the necessity for combined drug maintenance.

SUMMARY

Patients with symptoms of both schizophrenia and affective disorder have frequently aroused the interest of clinicians, occupying as they do a crucial interface in descriptive psychiatry and differential diagnosis. The clinical tradition that resists dichotomizing these patients into either schizophrenia or affective disorder appears to be warranted. Studies of the broad scope of schizoaffective disorders have led to the identification of homogeneous subgroups with specific treatment implications. Many uncertainties remain in the differential diagnosis and subclassification of schizoaffective states, and continuing investigation is indicated.

Treatment and differential diagnosis of the schizoaffective disorders can be approached through a stepwise protocol suggested herein. Understanding the usefulness and limitations of treatment with combined drug classes (neuroleptic and thymoleptic) is essential to optimal outcome. Several representative issues in the management of these disorders are illustrated through case examples.

REFERENCES

1. American Psychiatric Association (1952). *Mental disorders: Diagnostic and statistical manual.* Washington, DC: American Psychiatric Association.
2. American Psychiatric Association (1980). *DSM-III: Diagnostic and statistical manual of mental disorders* (3rd ed.). Washington, DC: American Psychiatric Association.
3. Bleuler, E. (1950). *Dementia praecox or the group of schizophrenias.* New York: International Universities Press.
4. Bowman, K. M., & Raymond, A. F. (1931). A statistical study of delusions in the manic-depressive psychoses. *Assoc. Res. Nerv. Ment. Dis., 11*, 313.
5. Brockington, I. F., & Meltzer, H. Y. (1983). The nosology of schizoaffective psychosis. *Psychiatr. Dev., 4*, 317.
6. Feighner, J. P., Robins, E., Guze, S. B., Woodruff, R. A., Winokur, G., & Munoz, R. (1972). Diagnostic criteria for use in psychiatric research. *Arch. Gen. Psychiatry, 26*, 57.
7. Greenacre, P. (1918). The content of schizophrenic characteristics occurring in affective disorders. *Am. J. Insanity, 75*, 197.
8. Grossman, L. S., Harrow, M., Fudala, J. L., & Meltzer, H. Y. (1984). The longitudinal course of schizoaffective disorders: A prospective follow-up study. *J. Nerv. Ment. Dis., 172*, 140.
9. Harrow, M., & Grossman, L. S. (1984). Outcome in schizoaffective disorders: A critical review and reevaluation of the literature. *Schizophr. Bull., 10*, 87.
10. Hunt, R. C., & Appel, K. E. (1936). Prognosis in the psychoses lying midway between schizophrenia and manic-depressive psychoses. *Am. J. Psychiatry, 93*, 313.
11. Kant, O. (1941). Study of a group of recovered schizophrenic patients. *Psychiatr. Q., 15*, 263.
12. Kasanin, J. (1933). The acute schizoaffective psychoses. *Am. J. Psychiatry, 13*, 97.
13. Kraepelin, E. (1919). *Dementia praecox and paraphrenia* (translated by R. M. Barclay). Edinburgh: E. & S. Livingstone.

14. Lewis, N. D. C., & Hubbard, L. D. (1931). The mechanisms and prognostic aspects of the manic-depressive-schizophrenic combinations. *Assoc. Res. Nerv. Ment. Dis., 11*, 539.
15. McGlashan, T. H. (1986). Schizophrenia: Psychosocial treatments and the role of psychosocial factors in its etiology and pathogenesis. In A. Frances & R. Hales (Eds.), *Annual review*, Vol. 5. Washington, DC: American Psychiatric Press.
16. McGlashan, T. H., & Williams, P. V. (1987). Schizoaffective psychosis: II. Manic, bipolar and depressive subtypes. *Arch. Gen. Psychiatry, 44*, 138.
17. Procci, W. R. (1976). Schizo-affective psychosis: Fact or fiction? *Arch. Gen. Psychiatry, 33*, 1167.
18. Spitzer, R. L., Endicott, J., & Robins, E. (1978). *Research diagnostic criteria (RDC) for a selected group of functional disorders* (3rd ed.) (updated 3/17/81). New York: New York State Psychiatric Institute.
19. Tsuang, M. T. (1974). What is schizo-affective disorder? Read before the New Research Program of the 127th annual meeting of the American Psychiatric Association, Detroit.
20. Tsuang, M. T., & Dempsey, G. M. (1979). Long-term outcome of major psychoses: II. Schizoaffective disorder compared with schizophrenia, affective disorders, and a surgical control group. *Arch. Gen. Psychiatry, 36*, 1302.
21. Tsuang, M. T., & Simpson, J. C. (1984). Schizoaffective disorder: Concept and reality. *Schizophr. Bull., 10*, 14.
22. Tsuang, M. T., & Loyd, D. W. (1986). Other psychotic disorders. In J. O. Cavenar (Ed.), *Psychiatry*. New York: Basic Books.
23. Vaillant, G. E. (1964). An historical review of the remitting schizophrenias. *J. Nerv. Ment. Dis., 138*, 48.
24. American Psychiatric Association (1987). *DSM-III-R: Diagnostic and statistical manual of mental disorders* (3rd ed., revised). Washington, DC: American Psychiatric Association.
25. Williams, P. V., & McGlashan, T. H. (1987). Schizoaffective psychosis: I. Comparative long-term outcome. *Arch. Gen. Psychiatry, 44*, 130.
26. Williams, P. V., & McGlashan, T. H. (submitted). Predicting diagnostic stability in Axis I schizoaffective and affective disorders.

12
THE VAGARIES OF THE CONCEPT OF ATYPICAL DEPRESSION

JONATHAN M. HIMMELHOCH, M.D.

*Professor of Psychiatry,
University of Pittsburgh School of Medicine,
Western Psychiatric Institute and Clinic,
Pittsburgh, Pennsylvania*

and

MICHAEL E. THASE, M.D.

*Associate Professor of Psychiatry,
University of Pittsburgh School of Medicine,
Western Psychiatric Institute and Clinic,
Pittsburgh, Pennsylvania*

> For who would lose,
> Though full of pain, this intellectual being
> Those thoughts that wander through eternity,
> To perish rather, swallowed up and lost
> In the wide womb of unrelated night,
> Devoid of sense and motion.
>
> —John Milton, *Paradise Lost*

In his seminal paper on the nosology of affective disorders, "Endogenomorphic Depression," Donald Klein (1) carefully differentiates dimensional from categorical diagnostic systems. Dimensional approaches contend that a given diagnosis, say depression, represents a single entity that expresses itself in different ways along a particular dimension, such as severity. Hence, although reactive and endogenous depression belong to the same diagnostic entity, endogenous depression looks different because it is more severe and hence able to spontaneously occur, whereas reactive depression is less severe and thereby requires a particular environmental stress, or series of stresses, to touch it off. Psychiatry has been traditionally fond of dimensional approaches to diagnosis because such an approach automatically deals with the difficult, if not insoluble, problem clichéd as "nature versus nurture." Hence, there is the process versus reactive dimension of schizophrenia that parallels the reactive versus endogenous division of the affective disorders.

Categorical nosologies are those which assert that different clinical entities arise from different etiologies; e.g., the anemias, where the syndrome of low red-blood-cell mass, weakness, and fatigue represents over 250 separate illnesses, many with obvious clinical differences from the others, but equally as many separable only through laboratory investigation. Categorical systems have generally been avoided by psychiatry despite their regular use in the other disciplines of medicine and surgery, lost like Milton's thoughts that wander through eternity. *Diagnostic and Statistical Manual II* (2) actually stated its dimensional bias by its open apposition of endogenous to reactive depression as a legitimate diagnostic maneuver. By contrast, *Diagnostic and Statistical Manual III* (DSM-III) (3) and DSM-III-Revised (DSM-III-R) (4) look much more categorical on the surface. The affective disorder entities, differentiated by multiple operational criteria, look for all the world as categorical as can be. Nevertheless, DSM-III and its modifications continue to be used by psychiatric diagnosticians in a dimensional way. Many papers have been written on the ascertainment of endogenous illness (i.e., melancholia) within the DSM-III major depressive disorder category (see, for example, Ref. 5). Moreover, operational criteria (the key mechanism of DSM-III-R and other modern psychiatric diagnostic systems) are purely descriptive and atheoretical. Categorical diagnosis, on the other hand, must always be based on a hypothesis. In one sense, the difference between categorical and dimensional approaches represents the historical ideological conflict between Kant and the logical positivism of Auguste Comte, which in most arenas has long been settled in favor of Kant. In psychiatry, however, Comte still prevails, as does his belief that "*il faut que la pensée nouvelle soit positive, c'est a dire qu'elle* *n'affirme aucune proposition qui ne se ramène en dernier ressort d'un fait d'experience. . . .*"*

Kraepelin's (7) original diagnostic approach to the affective disorders was categorical. In the early editions of his textbook he felt each carefully described affective state arose from a different etiology—some from constitutional or genetic differences, some from varying physiological influences ranging from syphilis to head injury to alcoholism. However, as he aged, he observed enough cases from one category change into another that he ended up including all the presumed constitutional affective disorders under the rubric "manic-depressive insanity" (8, 9). All that was left of his once-rich categorical conceptualization was the difference between constitutional states and those acquired secondary to medical and neurological illnesses. In 1929, Gillespie (10) completed the conversion of Kraepelin's nosology from categorical to dimensional when he split off manic-depressive insanity from milder affective states, which were called endogenous and reactive, respectively.

Over the past decades the concept of atypical depression has been evolving, and at its core lies the very problem of dimensional versus categorical diagnoses. The history of this syndrome is reviewed fully later in this chapter. For now it is sufficient to say that atypical depressive states have been split off from the more traditional affective diagnoses because:

1. They appear as distinct core clinical presentations fairly easily, descriptively differentiated from typical affective disorders.
2. They have markedly different pharmacological responses from typical (melancholic) states—most often requiring monoamine oxidase inhibitors (MAOI).
3. Recent nosological and family history research suggests that bipolar affective disorder forms a prominent etiological base for a large number of atypical depressive syndromes (11). In addition, many of the more rapid cycling bipolar states seem related to temporal-lobe syndromes, ranging from seizure-free interictal symptom profiles with or without positive electroencephalographic findings all the way to frank temporal-lobe epilepsy (TLE). The remaining cases present as panic syndromes with heavy affective loading (12) or as those chronic character disor-

*The new way of thinking must be positive, which is to say that it affirms no proposition which does not lead back, at last resort, to a *fact* of experience.

> ders that are interlaced with depressive symptomatology (13). On occasion, particularly in younger patients, symptoms of minimal brain disorders, learning abnormalities, and attention deficit disorders also make a contribution.

It is clear that our conceptualization of atypical depression, its differences from typical states, and its treatments are based on a categorical foundation. The above differences are created by varying disease states, not by a dimension, such as age or severity. Our conceptualization is shown graphically in Table 1. The affective syndromes surrounding atypical depression move from anxious-phobic atypical states, which manifest environmental reactivity and characterological coloration, toward atypical syndromes characterized by anergia and reversed vegetative profiles (i.e., hypersomnia and weight gain). The latter syndromes are closely related to both typical bipolar illness and bipolar II disorders. Temporal-lobe syndromes complete the circle, linking bipolarity back to the more anxious type of atypical depressions. Treatment approaches follow the circle as it moves from anxious to anergic back to anxious, as will be discussed in detail later.

Table 1
Features of Hysteroid Dysphoria*

1. Extreme rejection sensitivity
   a. Crashlike depressions in reaction to rejection
   b. Reaction includes either overeating (craving for sweets), oversleeping (more time in bed), or anergia (extreme fatigue, leaden paralysis)
2. At least four periods of depressed mood related to rejection during the past 2 years
3. Self-esteem is dependent on external approval
4. Depressions are nonautonomous
5. Normal personality characterized by histrionic, flamboyant, intrusive, seductive, self-centered, and demanding qualities
6. At least 3 of the following: abuses alcohol, marijuana, or sedatives when depressed; abuses stimulants on occasion; normal mood is expansive and active; chronic dieting is necessary to maintain normal weight; poor social judgment; applause is stimulating and rewarding; withdraws when depressed; makes suicidal gestures or threats; physically self-mutilating when depressed

*Adapted from Liebowitz and Klein (26).

Finally, there are miscellaneous states of atypical depression which can appear as the early syndromal manifestations of medical and surgical illness (e.g., carcinoma of the tail of the pancreas) and postinfectious and postoperative depressions. Each of these syndromes generally takes on reversed neurovegetative symptomatology. On occasion, a mixture of panic and depression follows resolution of chronic illness, such as after mitral or aortic valve replacement.

In the following sections, we first discuss the history of the concept of atypical depression, followed by a summary of current classifications and a broad discussion of our current approach to treatment of the various categories of atypical depression proposed in Figure 1. We include data from published investigations with preliminary results from our own ongoing studies, as well as impressions drawn from clinical practice.

HISTORY OF THE CONCEPT OF ATYPICAL DEPRESSION

Any discussion of atypical depression is, of course, influenced by the prevailing notion of what constitutes a "typical" episode of depression. Such understanding is dependent on the type of treatment setting and the availability of effective treatment. For example, to our knowledge the first use of the term *atypical depression* in the psychiatric literature occurred in a 1948 article by Huston and Locker (14). The context that Huston and Locker were working within was inpatient psychiatric practice, with electroconvulsive therapy (ECT) as the only reliable and effective treatment available for severe mood disorders. The label typical depression therefore related to that subgroup of inpatients who manifested the clinical features which are now well known to predict response to ECT, such as motor retardation, terminal insomnia, anhedonia, loss of mood reactivity, and, when present, mood-congruent delusions. The "atypical" depressed patients identified by Huston and Locker represented a second group of patients with a syndrome responsive to ECT, consisting of patients with increased levels of agitation, confusion, and paranoid delusions. Jarvie (15) subsequently published a report independently verifying the existence of a subgroup of "atypical" depressive patients with agitation and mood-incongruent hallucinations and/or delusions. Jarvie reported that this subgroup accounted for 12% of a large series of depressed inpatients. Further, he found that these patients were younger and exhibited a greater degree of characterological disturbance and poorer premorbid social adjustment than "typical" depression. It is interesting that, nearly 40 years later, such

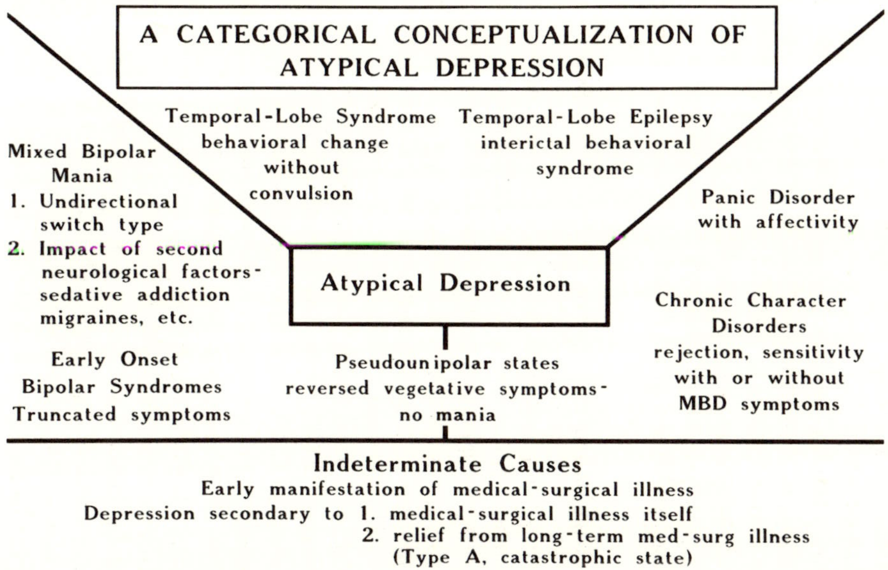

Figure 1. Schematic representation of atypical depressions.

patients are still seen in inpatient settings, but now are viewed as suffering from schizoaffective, schizophreniform, or psychotic depressive disorders. From a current perspective, these patients still do not have "typical" depressions, but no longer are classified within the framework of atypical depression.

The introduction of two distinctly different antidepressant medications, imipramine and iproniazid, some 10 years later led to the next formulation of the concept of atypical depression. Thus, the availability of alternate effective treatments for depressed patients, in concert with increased utilization of outpatient services in psychiatry, affected redefinition of atypical depression. The first and most influential report reflecting this shift was published by West and Dally in 1959 (16). West and Dally described a series of patients who responded to treatment with iproniazid (an agent that was developed initially as an antitubercular medication but subsequently was found to be an antidepressant). The stimulus for this report was the growing impression that imipramine, a tricyclic compound (TCA), and iproniazid, an MAOI, appeared to help different patients, with the tricyclic more effective in patients with clinical features similar, albeit perhaps milder, to the ECT-responsive depressive disorders. By contrast, West and Dally reported that iproniazid responders were more likely to be patients with anxiety complaints (panic, specific phobias, obsessions, and/or agoraphobia) and/or reversed vegetative symptoms, such as overeating, oversleeping, and/or increased libido. West and Dally further noted that such patients tended to have a more chronic course and associated character pathology, particularly dependent, labile, or histrionic features. Unlike the atypical depressed patients described by Huston and Locker (14) and Jarvie (15), these patients were noted to have a poor or even adverse response to ECT.

Following the seminal publication of West and Dally (16), a series of reports by other British investigators (17–20) supported and extended these initial observations about the clinical profile of patients who respond to MAOIs, including the recently introduced drugs phenelzine and tranylcypromine. Such growing evidence that a peculiar group of patients responded best to MAOI antidepressants stood in counterpoint to the publication of results from two large, multicentered clinical trials which suggested that phenelzine was relatively ineffective in more severely depressed patients (21, 22). Indeed, demonstration that MAOIs were effective in at least one subgroup of depressed patients was a critical factor in preserving interest in this class of antidepressants, since there also was a growing concern about the toxicity of MAOIs, particularly with respect to evidence of hepatocellular damage and hypertensive crises. Of course, subsequent identification of the mechanism of the so-called "cheese effect" and prescription of appropriate dietary precautions greatly lessened the risk of untoward hypertensive reactions, and the gradual replacement of the more hepatotoxic MAOIs (such as iproniazid) with safer agents, such as phenelzine and tranylcypromine, greatly improved the safety of these agents.

Throughout the 1970s, there was a resurgence of interest in the MAOIs, particularly in the United States where prescription of these agents at one point had nearly ceased (23). Moreover, there was continued interest in identifying the depressive syndromes that might respond best to these agents. In an early report from this decade, Robinson, Nies, and associates (24) operationalized the clinical criteria suggested by the earlier British studies by developing a rating scale for discrimination of atypical and typical (melancholic) depressive syndromes. Robinson et al. also demonstrated that phenelzine was a clinically effective antidepressant (relative to placebo) in patients with mixed anxiety-depressive syndromes. Paykel et al. (25) similarly reported preferential response to phenelzine in less severely depressed outpatients who manifested high atypicality scores on Nies and Robinson's rating scale. Finally, in a comprehensive review, Quitkin et al. (23) suggested that earlier descriptions of atypical depression may have mixed at least two distinct forms: depressions associated with intense rejection sensitivity and histrionic personality traits (hysteroid dysphoria) and depressions associated with phobic or panic anxiety states.

The concept of hysteroid dysphoria has been further elaborated over the past decade by the Columbia group (26–28). Liebowitz and Klein's (26) detailed criteria for a diagnosis of hysteroid dysphoria are summarized in Table 1. The key categorical component of the diagnosis of hysteroid dysphoria is the requirement of rejection sensitivity and fragility of self-esteem, the hallmarks of a long-standing maladaptive personality style (emotionally labile or histrionic), intertwined with the atypical affective syndrome. Needless to say, there is considerable overlap between hysteroid dysphoria and what is now known as borderline personality disorder (27). Prominent associated features are reactive mood, sweet cravings, substance abuse, and reversed vegetative symptoms during periods of depression, with a virtual exclusion of panic anxiety or phobic features in the diagnostic formulation. Nevertheless, a significant minority of these patients do report experiencing panic attacks (28).

Although many clinicians have found hysteroid dysphoria to be a useful clinical diagnosis (29, 30), the term has not yet found its way into the DSM-III classification system (3, 4). Indeed, Spitzer and Williams (31) found only a slight overrepresentation of patients with the constellation of signs and symptoms of hysteroid dysphoria in a large sample of depressed outpatients. Nevertheless, the cooccurrence of sweet cravings, histrionic traits, and atypical depressive features has been replicated recently (32), and from a narrower perspective, Liebowitz et al. (28) found that fully 25% of their patients with atypical depressions met criteria for hysteroid dysphoria. Preliminary evidence from several investigations suggests that hysteroid dysphoria responds more favorably to phenelzine than to TCAs or placebo (33, 34).

Returning to the earlier notion of multiple forms of atypical depression, Davidson et al. (12, 35) suggested a division into two, partially overlapping syndromes, characterized by predominantly anxious (A-type) or predominantly reversed vegetative (V-type) clinical features. As will be discussed later in more detail, Davidson et al. linked the V type of atypical depression to the bipolar spectrum, as did Kupfer et al. (36) in an earlier report of apparently unipolar (or pseudounipolar) patients who responded poorly to TCAs but favorably to lithium salts. Although not specifically discussed by Davidson et al., the V-type syndrome also would encompass many categorically distinct depressive states associated with organic etiologies, such as postviral syndromes or stimulant withdrawal syndromes.

Relating the V type of atypical depression to the bipolar spectrum recalls several earlier reports concerning the value of the MAOIs in patients with withdrawn, motorically retarded, and hypersomnic depressive states (37–40). Interestingly, we recently have collected data further supporting the value of the V-type formulation in two ongoing studies of tranylcypromine. In the first, Himmelhoch et al. (41) found that tranylcypromine was significantly more effective than imipramine in a sample of bipolar depressives prospectively identified by the V-type criteria and treated under double-blind conditions. The second study, conducted on an open-label basis with unipolar patients who had not responded to imipramine, found a clear association ($p < .01$) between response to tranylcypromine and the presence of anergia, hypersomnia, and/or weight gain (see Ref. 42).

Davidson and Pelton (35) pooled data from several different pharmacological trials to address specifically the relative efficacy of TCA and MAOIs in A- and V-type atypical depressions. Their sample consisted of 84 patients who received either phenelzine or isocarboxazid and 77 patients who received either IMI or amitriptyline. With respect to the A-type syndrome (as defined by the presence of panic attacks), MAOI treatment was superior to TCA in female, but *not* male patients. However, TCA and MAOI treatments were found to be equally effective in patients with V-type symptomatology, irrespective of patient sex. These puzzling findings certainly warrant prospective replication, particularly concerning the apparent equivalence of TCA and MAOI antidepressants (other than tranylcypromine) in the V-type patients. As noted earlier, Liebowitz et al. (28) found phenelzine to be significantly more effective than placebo or IMI in atypical depressions with reversed vegetative features when coupled with hysteroid dysphoria and/or the presence of panic attacks.

In summary, clinical and empirical studies over the past three decades have led to delineation of several clinical forms of atypical depression, perhaps best described by blending the categories of Davidson et al. (12, 35) and Klein and associates (1, 26, 27). Thus, the descriptive clinical spectrum of the forms of atypical depression reviewed so far runs from phobic/panic-anxiety states, at one extreme, to profoundly anergic, hypersomnolent depressions at the other.

CURRENT DIAGNOSTIC APPROACHES

Despite the long and rich clinical history concerning atypical depressive states, neither DSM-III (3) nor its recent revision (4) specifically include these conditions. For example, in DSM-III the classifications Atypical Depression (296.82) and Atypical Bipolar Disorder (296.70) are utilized as residual categories, i.e., for use when patients do not meet the criteria for Major Depression, Dysthymia, or Bipolar Affective Disorder. Thus, atypical here refers to not fitting into the DSM framework, rather than to a particular syndromal presentation. The DSM-III-R avoids such terminological confusion by adopting the term *Not Otherwise Specified* (NOS) to describe these residual categories.

Liebowitz et al. (28) have formalized a set of operational research criteria for atypical depression (see Table 2). These criteria, when applied uniformly, should facilitate scientific study of atypical depression across research centers. Nevertheless, even these criteria are atheoretical and, hence, are not illustrative of the multiple categories of atypical depressive states.

Both DSM-III and DSM-III-R include hypersomnia and hyperphagia/weight gain (but not increased libido) as alternate diagnostic criteria for a depressive episode. Thus nonbipolar depressions characterized by V-type symptoms usually would be classified as either Major Depression or Dysthymia unless the course of the depression is intermittent. As reversed vegetative symptoms are a common feature of bipolar depressions, particularly in younger patients (11), it is perhaps incorrect to even consider use of the term *atypical* to describe these patients. More current controversy,

Table 2
Research Criteria for Atypical Depressions*

1. Meets Research Diagnostic Criteria for major, minor, or intermittent depressive disorder
2. Maintains mood reactivity while depressed (nonautonomous depressive syndrome)
3. At least two of the following
   a. Increased appetite or weight gain
   b. Oversleeping or spending more time in bed
   c. Severe fatigue, leaden paralysis, heavy sensations in limbs
   d. Rejection sensitivity as a trait throughout adulthood

*Adapted from Liebowitz et al. (28).

however, surrounds the issue of combining or separately classifying bipolar conditions punctuated by full-blown manic episodes (bipolar I) from those characterized only by hypomanic periods (bipolar II) (43–47). In our experience, the V-type presentation occurs in both forms, although others have suggested that reversed vegetative symptoms may be more common among the "softer" cases of the bipolar spectrum, including bipolar II patients (11). Interestingly, Rosenthal et al. (48) have described a seasonal form of cyclical mood disorder, in which the fall and winter depressions are predominantly V type and are associated with hypomanic episodes in the spring. Criteria for such a seasonal pattern are specifically included in DSM-III-R for use as a subcode for each of the affective disorders diagnoses.

The A-type presentation of atypical depression also is not specifically addressed in the current editions of the DSM. The potential occurrence of phobias, obsessions, and/or panic attacks during a depressive episode is discussed in DSM-III as part of the differential diagnosis of the primary psychopathological syndrome (i.e., anxiety disorder versus affective disorder). However, it is left to the diagnostician to take the history, apply the criteria, and utilize clinical judgment to pick which of the relevant categories should be selected. As discussed later, the practical clinical importance of diagnostic precision for differentiation of primary anxiety disorders from A-type atypical depressions has been lessened by the considerable recent evidence supporting the efficacy of treatment of anxiety states with TCAs and MAOIs.

TREATMENT CONSIDERATIONS

Returning to Figure 1 and moving clockwise from panic disorder through pseudounipolar states to the interictal behavioral syndromes of TLE, a series of linked syndromes of varying etiology is described. Optimal treatment of these syndromes is dependent on careful clinical evaluation. No computer diagnostic system, nor scantily trained research technician, using any of the various research diagnostic instruments, will be able to ascertain the *categories* of atypical depressive disorder. Each syndrome is separate from the others in terms of the intensity and manifestation of anxiety, and in terms of treatment selection and response. Family history and associated neuropsychiatric "second factors" also play a role in defining which type of atypical depressive syndrome is which. In a majority of instances, each syndrome has subtle differences from the others that can be detected clinically—but only by an experienced clinician well schooled in obtaining the fine points of developmental and family history. Moreover, in the minority of cases, where the well-trained clinician cannot clinically differentiate one syndrome from the other, he will occasionally have to rely on laboratory assessments (electroencephalogram [EEG], evoked EEGs, and varying types of brain scans, including computed tomography and magnetic resonance imaging) or, more frequently, on a series of treatment trials. This empirical approach is analogous to the model that was formerly used to diagnose the etiology of macrocytic anemias, where a patient is given a clinical trial of folate to test whether he suffers from folic acid or vitamin B_{12} deficiency. The varying types of atypical depression have very little dimensional quality except for the self-evident inevitability that one patient will be older than another or will have a more severe illness than another, factors that may temper and modify treatment, but never diagnosis. The DSM-III-R categories of Major Depression, Dysthymic Disorder, or Depression NOS thus become neoplatonic procrustean beds (Figure 2) into which the dimensional diagnostician must force-fit his patient's condition and then scratch his head and wonder, "How in the world is this patient to be treated?" Categorical diagnoses, however, point strongly toward their own best treatment and suggest the only factors that go into treatment design.

Panic Disorder and Related Characterological Correlations

Although panic disorder is formally classified as an anxiety disorder in the DSM (3, 4) systems, much recent literature has shown considerable overlap with the family histories of patients with affective illness symptom-

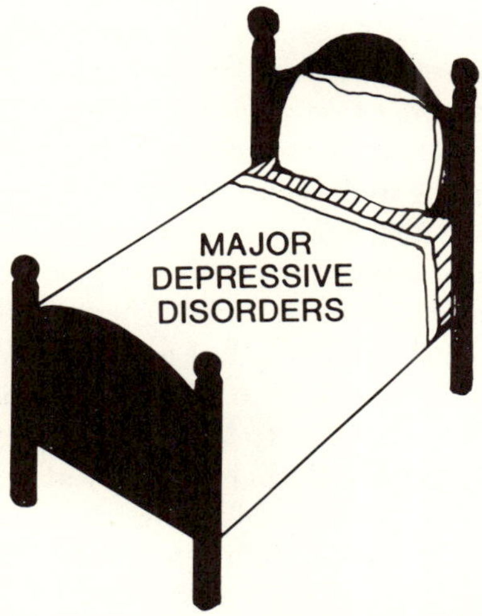

Figure 2. Conceptual restraint is imposed by atheoretical classification of categorical illness.

atology (49, 50). Detre and Himmelhoch (51) have reported patients whose affective disorder began as a panic syndrome, but, as they aged, became progressively less panicky, more somatic, and more clearly depressed. Included in this group were a number of patients who experienced panic disorder in their midtwenties and classic melancholia in their midforties. Moreover, thymoleptic medications, particularly imipramine and the MAOI phenelzine, are generally effective treatments for these syndromes. Triazolobenzodiazepines (e.g., alprazolam) are used by our group primarily as a backup treatment for patients who cannot tolerate or do not respond to tricyclics and/or MAOIs. Although these agents are often effective and even preferred by patients, well-documented problems of tolerance and withdrawal, made more intense by a short half-life, are the pharmacological factors that make triazolobenzodiazepines a less desirable treatment of anxious depression in our opinion, as well as the opinion of others (52).

Indeed, as panic is either colored or replaced by generalized social anxiety and characterological disturbance (including rejection sensitivity) as the core of the patient's maladaptation, both the triazolobenzodiazepines and the TCAs are found to be less useful—the former because of the notorious propensity for individuals with anxious character disorders to develop tolerance and sedative dependence by abusing minor tranquilizers, the latter because TCAs are not only less effective, but actually can cause paradoxical worsening of anxiety and agitation (53). Therefore, in socially anxious and/or rejection-sensitive patients, the MAOI phenelzine plus practical psychotherapy is our preferred treatment approach. In our experience, phenelzine is preferable to TRP in these cases since it seems superior as an anxiolytic. Titration of the dosage upward, as tolerated, to a usual effective dosage range of 45–90 mg per day, is crucial, since phenelzine (and probably isocarboxazid) is most effective when >80% inhibition of platelet monoamine oxidase activity is achieved. Even higher dosages are occasionally necessary to achieve therapeutic benefit. When the drug is effective, maintenance treatment with phenelzine often is necessary for an indefinite period, perhaps even several years. As demonstrated by Harrison et al. (54), relapse following drug discontinuation is common. Adherence to treatment with phenelzine and other MAOIs is complicated by the necessary dietary restrictions, as well as common side effects such as orthostasis, weight gain, and anorgasmia. Nevertheless, most patients will tolerate these nuisances in return for mood stability, particularly if successful MAOI treatment follows previous unsuccessful courses of TCAs or psychotherapy. In fact, psychotherapy may be more beneficial than ever before in concert with effective pharmacotherapy.

Since anxious, characterologically colored atypical depressives sometimes have a childhood history of hyperkinesis, learning disorders, or attention deficit disorders, TRP may be substituted for phenelzine because it is molecularly and pharmacologically more similar to *d*-amphetamine. In severe, chronic disorders, MAOIs and psychomotor stimulants can be used together, but such potentially dangerous treatment should be closely monitored by specialists in this area of psychopharmacology.

Atypical Depression and Its Relationship to the Bipolar Syndromes

The previously described treatment of atypical depressive syndromes clearly corresponds to the A-type picture so thoroughly reviewed earlier in this chapter. Figure 1 moves clockwise from type A, through hysteroid dysphoria, on to type-V atypical depressions. Here anergia, volitional inhibition, and motor retardation (rather than panic or rejection sensitivity) form the core of the syndrome and, very frequently, reversed vegetative signs, especially hypersomnia and weight gain, are prominent. Tricyclics are again often ineffective with such patients, on occasion worsening retardation (pure motor retardation as opposed to that vague concept *psycho-*

motor retardation, which occurs in every type of depressive typical or atypical, bipolar or unipolar), hypersomnia, and weight gain. Himmelhoch and associates (40–42) have shown the MAOI tranylcypromine is markedly effective in patients with anergia, hypersomnia, and weight gain.

In clinical practice, TRP is no more difficult to prescribe or to take than phenelzine. The dosage is initiated at 10 mg b.i.d. and titrated upward to the 30–60 mg per day range. While drug-induced insomnia is on occasion a problem, this is dealt with by utilizing divided daytime dosages. Further, we preferentially prescribe TRP to *hypersomnic* patients. Curiously, we recently failed to find an association between response to TRP and level of platelet MAO inhibition (unpublished data). While this might suggest that TRP works via some mechanism other than MAO inhibition, it is plausible that TRP preferentially acts on type-A MAO (in the brain) rather than type B, which is measured in the platelet.

To digress for a moment, we previously discussed the apparent relationship between V-type depression and bipolar depression. Such patients may be referred to as pseudounipolar (36) because their depression is very similar to the depressive syndrome often seen in bipolar states. As a result, it is no surprise that such an episode of atypical depression can be the first clinically significant mood swing in a bipolar patient. Indeed, young bipolar patients often present a truncated bipolar syndrome where, in milder cases, the manic phase looks like "rebellion" and, in severe cases, a paranoid episode. The depressive phase in these young subjects is almost invariably identical to Davidson et al.'s V-type atypical syndrome. Akiskal (11), Klerman (45), Dunner et al. (47), and others have noted and emphasized this phenomenological finding. They have postulated that bipolar illness is a heterogeneous affective disorder and is epidemiologically far more common than was previously thought. They have coined a number of new syndromes, such as bipolar II disorder, atypical bipolar illness, and bipolar spectrum disease, to express such heterogeneity. The increased epidemiological incidence is strongly suggested in Egeland and Hostetter's (55) "Amish Study," although such a conclusion might be avoided by insisting that the Amish are so different from other Caucasian populations that the high relative incidence of atypical and typical bipolar syndromes in their population (when compared to nonbipolar syndromes) is an aberration. If Akiskal (11) and Klerman's (45) suggestions of bipolarity are to be believed, however, the epidemiological findings in the Amish will look less and less aberrant for the general populations in the future. Our group shares Akiskal's experience above all and have reported our suspicions that bipolar illness is epidemiologically nearly as common as primary unipolar affective disorder in a mood-disorders clinic population drawn freely from a community catchment area (56).

If, as is probably the case, many type-V atypical syndromes are bipolar at their roots, then successful treatment with any antidepressant, whether an MAOI such as TRP or a more commonly used agent, will demand the addition of a mood stabilizer first to prevent the onset of hypomania or mania and second to block the induction of mood cycling. For the majority of bipolar patients this agent will be one of the lithium salts. However, it is now well known that severe and/or complicated manic illness often requires additional intervention with the temporal-lobe stabilizing agent carbamazepine (57, 58). Often such patients will present with mixed manic episodes. Himmelhoch and Garfinkel (59) have shown that mixed episodes occur first in the more severe bipolar I syndromes that fit Court's "continuum hypothesis" of manic-depressive illness (60, 61). This unidirectional, switch conceptualization hypothesizes that in bipolar I patients, depression is a mild form of illness and hypomania/mania is the severe form of illness. As depression intensifies in severity, there comes a switch phase with simultaneous features of mania and depression. Repeated surveys of lithium clinics show that approximately 30% of bipolar patients present in this switch phase (see, for example, Ref. 62). Only 50% to 60% are typical bipolar I–type illness; the rest seem to develop mixed mania from the impact of a second neuropsychiatric illness or factor on the manic episode (59). For example, in our experience, the most common "second factor" is sedative/alcohol addiction and withdrawal, but migraine, head injury, epilepsy of any type, and mild dementia can produce such mixed features and make the affected patient harder to treat (59, 62). Once again, carbamazepine and other anticonvulsants (especially phenytoin sodium or clonazepam) can be effective. Neuroleptics, calcium channel blockers, and/or alpha-adrenergic agonists, such as clonidine, are used much less frequently in the most refractory patients.

Bipolar Syndromes Related to Epileptic Change and to Epilepsy

In an earlier paper on secondary affective illness (64), we noted:

> Two and a half millennia have distilled the hypothesis [the close relationship of affective illness to epilepsy] to the straight-forward idea that limbic neuronal dysregulation produces a distinct affective coloration to behavior whether it occurs in a patient with: 1) obvious

> temporal lobe epilepsy; 2) subictal limbic foci, who either experiences no ictus whatsoever or ictal activity so subtle as to meld with his/her personality and be clinically unrecognizable; or, 3) a limbic syndrome that is not epileptic as suggested by Ballenger, Post, et al. (58). Even in patients with the [typical] interictal behavioral syndromes, affective dysregulation follows, by necessity, since the combination of heightened emotionality, a cognitive disorder and global hyposexuality (the interictal syndromes of temporal lobe epilepsy) *can look identical to an atypical affective syndrome.* (p. 276)

Blumer, Heilbronn, and Himmelhoch have recently called those syndromes occurring without manifest partial convulsions "temporal lobe syndrome" (64). Naturally, both atypical depressive episodes and rapid-cycling bipolar syndromes can occur interictally in patients with manifest or subclinical epilepsy. These syndromes, shown at the top of Figure 1, require carbamazepine or other anticonvulsants, not as a stabilizing adjunct, but as their basic pharmacological regulator. Thymoleptic medications (particularly lithium salts), the MAOIs (particularly phenelzine), or—in clinical presentations with marked somatic features, such as chronic pain—heterocyclics are used adjunctively. At this point we have closed the circle. Not only can temporal-lobe syndromes produce classic panic attacks, but many patients with temporal-lobe syndromes show compulsive hyperphagia and chocolate craving. Moreover, the heterocyclics have reappeared as effective treatment. The shift from V-type (retarded) back to A-type (anxious) atypical depression has also been completed. Anxiety in various forms crops up more and more as the table progresses from typical bipolar illness to more severe, more mixed, and more atypical forms. The temporal-lobe syndromes complete the categories of atypical depression.

CONCLUSION

In this chapter, we have reviewed a variety of conditions that present as atypical depressions. Familiarity with these categories and their treatment will greatly enhance the clinical care of such individuals.

REFERENCES

1. Klein, D. F. (1974). Endogenomorphic depression: A conceptual and terminological revision. *Arch. Gen. Psychiatry, 31*, 447.
2. American Psychiatric Association (1970). *Diagnostic and statistical manual of mental disorders* (2nd ed.). Washington, DC: APA.

3. American Psychiatric Association (1980). *Diagnostic and statistical manual of mental disorders* (3rd ed.). Washington, DC: APA.
4. American Psychiatric Association (1987). *Diagnostic and statistical manual of mental disorders* (3rd ed., revised). Washington, DC: APA.
5. Zimmerman, M., Coryell, W., Pfohl, B., & Stangl, D. (1986). The validity of four definitions of endogenous depression. *Arch. Gen. Psychiatry, 43*, 234.
6. Comte, A. (1949). Introduction by Charles le Verrier. *Cours de Philosophie Positive, Vol. I* (p. xxiii). Paris: Librairie, Gariver Neses.
7. Kraepelin, E. (1968). *Lectures on clinical psychiatry* (a facsimile of the 1904 edition). New York: Hafner.
8. Kraepelin, E. (1899). *Ein lehrbuch fur studierende und aertze*. Leipzig, Germany: J. A. Barth.
9. Kraepelin, E. (1895). *Ein lehrbuch fur studierende und aertze*. Leipzig, Germany: J. A. Barth.
10. Gillespie, R. (1929). The clinical differentiation of types of depression. *Guys Hosp. Rep., 79*, 306.
11. Akiskal, H. S. (1983). The bipolar spectrum: New concepts in classification and diagnosis. In L. Grinspoon (Ed.), *Psychiatry update, vol. 2*. Washington, DC: American Psychiatric Association.
12. Davidson, J. R. T., Miller, R. D., Turnbull, C. D., & Sullivan, J. L. (1982). Atypical depression. *Arch. Gen. Psychiatry, 39*, 527.
13. Akiskal, H. S., Rosenthal, T. L., Haykal, R. F., Lemmi, H., Rosenthal, R. H., & Scott-Strauss, A. (1980). Characterological depressions: Clinical and sleep EEG findings separating subaffective dysthymias from character spectrum disorders. *Arch. Gen. Psychiatry, 37*, 777.
14. Huston, P. E., & Locker, L. M. (1948). Manic-depressive psychosis. *Arch. Neurol. Psychiatry, 60*, 37.
15. Jarvie, H. F. (1950). On atypicality and the depressive state. *J. Ment. Sci., 96*, 208.
16. West, E., & Dally, P. J. (1959). Effect of iproniazid in depressive syndromes. *Br. Med. J., 1*, 1491.
17. Sargant, W. (1960). Drugs in the treatment of depression. *Br. Med. J., 1*, 225.
18. Pollitt, J. D. (1965). Suggestions for a physiological classification of depression. *Br. J. Psychiatry, 111*, 489.
19. Pare, C. M. B. (1979). Monoamine oxidase inhibitors in resistant depression. *Int. Pharmacopsychiatry, 14*, 101.
20. Paykel, E. S., Rowan, P. R., Rao, B. M., & Bhat, A. (1983). Atypical depression: Nosology and response to antidepressants. In P. J. Clayton & J. E. Barrett (Eds.), *Treatment of depression: Old controversies and new approaches*. New York: Raven Press.
21. Greenblatt, M., Grosser, G. H., & Wechsler, H. (1964). Differential response of hospitalized patients to somatic therapy. *Am. J. Psychiatry, 120*, 935.
22. British Medical Research Council (1965). Clinical trial of the treatment of depressive illness. *Br. Med. J., 1*, 881.
23. Quitkin, F. M., Rifkin, A., & Klein, D. F. (1979). Monoamine oxidase inhibitors: A review of antidepressant effectiveness. *Arch. Gen. Psychiatry, 36*, 749.
24. Robinson, D. S., Nies, A., Ravaris, L., & Lamborn, K. R. (1973). The monoamine oxidase inhibitor, phenelzine, in the treatment of depressive-anxiety-states. *Arch. Gen. Psychiatry, 29*, 407.
25. Paykel, E. S., Rowan, P. R., Parker, R. R., & Bhat, A. V. (1982). Response to phenelzine and amitriptyline in subtypes of out-patient depression. *Arch. Gen. Psychiatry, 39*, 1041.
26. Liebowitz, M. R., & Klein, D. F. (1979). Hysteroid dysphoria. *Psychiatr. Clin. North Am., 2*, 555.

27. Liebowitz, M. R., & Klein, D. F. (1981). Interrelationship of hysteroid dysphoria and borderline personality disorder. *Psychiatr. Clin. North Am.*, *4*, 67.
28. Liebowitz, M. R., Quitkin, F. M., Steward, J. W., McGrath, P. J., Harrison, W., Rabbin, J., Tricamo, E., Markowitz, J. S., & Klein, D. F. (1984). Phenelzine v. imipramine in atypical depression: A preliminary report. *Arch Gen. Psychiatry*, *44*, 669.
29. Sovner, R. D. (1981). The clinical characteristics and treatment of atypical depression. *J. Clin. Psychiatry*, *42*, 285.
30. Pare, C. M. B. (1987). Monoamine oxidase inhibitors in the treatment of affective disorders. *Psychiatr. Ann.*, *17*, 309.
31. Spitzer, R. L., & Williams, J. B. W. (1982). Hysteroid dysphoria: An unsuccessful attempt to demonstrate its syndromal validity. *Am. J. Psychiatry*, *139*, 1286.
32. Schuman, M., Gitlin, M., & Fairbanks, L. (1987). Sweets, chocolate, and atypical depressive traits. *J. Nerv. Ment. Dis.*, *8*, 491.
33. Liebowitz, M. R., Quitkin, F. M., Stewart, J. W., McGrath, P. J., Harrison, W., Rabkin, J. G., Tricamo, E., Markowitz, J. S., & Klein, D. F. (1984). Psychopharmacological validation of atypical depression. *J. Clin. Psychiatry*, *45*(7, sec.2), 22.
34. Kayser, A., Robinson, D. S., Nies, A., & Howard, D. (1985). Response to phenelzine among depressed patients with fears of hysteroid dysphoria. *Am. J. Psychiatry*, *142*, 486–488.
35. Davidson, J., & Pelton, S. (1986). Forms of atypical depression and their response to antidepressant drugs. *Psychiatry Res.*, *17*, 87.
36. Kupfer, D. J., Pickar, D., Himmelhoch, J. M., & Detre, T. P. (1975). Are there two types of unipolar depression? *Arch. Gen. Psychiatry*, *32*, 866.
37. Alexander, L., & Berkeley, A. W. (1959). The inert psychasthenic reaction (anhedonia) as differentiated from classic depression and its response to iproniazid. *Ann. N.Y. Acad. Sci.*, *80*, 669.
38. Feldman, P. (1959). Treatment of anergic schizophrenia with nialamide. *Dis. Nerv. Syst.*, *20*(Suppl.), 41.
39. Himmelhoch, J., Detre, T., Kupfer, J., Swartzburg, M., & Byck, R. (1972). Treatment of previously intractable depressions with tranylcypromine and lithium. *J. Nerv. Dis.*, *155*(3), 216.
40. Himmelhoch, J. M., Fuchs, C. Z., & Symons, B. J. (1982). A double-blind study of tranylcypromine treatment of major anergic depression. *J. Nerv. Ment. Dis.*, *170*, 628.
41. Himmelhoch, J. M., Thase, M. E., Mallinger, A. G., & Fuchs, C. Z. (1986). Tranylcypromine versus imipramine in manic depression. *Proc. Am. Psychiatr. Assoc. – New Res.*, *139*, 69.
42. Thase, M. E. (1985). Atypical depressions. *Directions in Psychiatry*, *5*(29), 1.
43. Coryell, W. (1982). Hypomania. *J. Affect. Disord.*, *4*, 167.
44. Endicott, J., Nee, J., Andreasen, N., Clayton, P., Keller, M., & Coryell, W. (1985). Bipolar II: Combine or keep separate? *J. Affect. Disord.*, *8*, 17.
45. Klerman, G. L. (1987). The classification of bipolar disorders. *Psychiatr. Ann.*, *17*, 1.
46. Keeler, L., & Othmer, E. (1987). Atypical bipolar disorder: Is it a distinct entity? *Psychiatr. Ann.*, *17*, 1.
47. Dunner, D. L., Dwyer, T., & Fieve, R. R. (1976). Depressive symptoms in patients with unipolar and bipolar affective disorder. *Comp. Psychiatry*, *17*, 447.
48. Rosenthal, N. E., Sack, D. A., Grillin, J. C., Lewy, A. J., Goodwin, F. K., Davenport, Y., Mueller, P. S., Newsome, D. A., & Wehr, T. A. (1984). Seasonal affective disorder. *Arch. Gen. Psychiatry*, *41*, 72.
49. Weissman, M. M., Gershon, E. S., Kidd, K. K., Prusoff, B. A., Leckman, J. F., Dibble, E., Hemovit, J., Thompson, W. D., Pauls, D. L., & Gruoff, J. J. (1984). Psychiatric disorders in relatives of probands with affective disorders. *Arch. Gen. Psychiatry*, *41*, 13.

50. Weissman, M. M., Leckm, J. F., Merikangas, K. G., Gammon, G. D., & Prosoff, B. A. (1984). Depression and anxiety disorders in parents and children. *Arch. Gen. Psychiatry, 41*, 845.
51. Detre, T., & Himmelhoch, J. (1973). Diagnosing anxiety. *Consultant, 13*, 87.
52. Alprazolam (Xanax) withdrawal: A follow-up (1987). *Massachusetts Gen. Hosp. Newsletter, Biol. Ther. Psychiatry, 10*(6).
53. Thase, M. E., & Shipley, J. H. (1987). Tricyclic and related antidepressant drugs. In C. G. Last & M. Hersen (Eds.), *Handbook of anxiety disorders*. New York: Pergamon Press.
54. Harrison, W., Rabkin, J., Steward, J. W., McGrath, P. J., Tricamo, E., & Quitkin, F. (1986). Phenelzine for chronic depression: A study of continuation treatment. *J. Clin. Psychiatry, 47*, 346.
55. Egeland, J., & Hostetter, A. (1983). Amish study. I: Affective disorders among the Amish. *Am. J. Psychiatry, 140*(9), 1263.
56. Thase, M., & Himmelhoch, J. (1983). On the Amish study. *Am. J. Psychiatry, 140*(9), 1263.
57. Okuma, T., & Kishimoto, A. (1977). Anti-manic and prophylactic effects of Tegretol. In *Abstracts of the Sixth World Congress of Psychiatry*, Honolulu, Hawaii (p. 134). Summit, NJ: Ciba-Geigy.
58. Ballenger, J. C., & Post, R. M. (1978). Therapeutic effects of carbamazepine in affective illness: A preliminary report. *Commun. Psychopharmacol, 2*, 159.
59. Himmelhoch, J. M., & Garfinkel, M. E. (1986). Sources of lithium resistance in mixed mania. *Psychopharmacol. Bull., 22*(3), 613.
60. Court, J. (1968). Manic-depressive psychosis: An alternative conceptual mode. *Br. J. Psychiatry, 114*, 1523.
61. Court, J. (1972). The continuum model as a resolution of paradoxes in manic-depressive illness. I. A systematic study of sequential behavior change. *Arch. Gen. Psychiatry, 27*, 295.
62. Himmelhoch, J., Mulla, D., Neil, J., Detre, T., & Kupfer, D. (1976). Incidence and significance of mixed affective states in a bipolar population. *Arch. Gen. Psychiatry, 33*, 1062.
63. Himmelhoch, J. (1987). Cerebral dysrhythmia, substance abuse and the nature of secondary affective illness. *Psychiatr. Ann., 17*(11).
64. Blumer, D., Heilbronn, J., & Himmelhoch, J. (In press). Indications for carbamazepine in mental illness: Atypical psychiatric disorder or temporal lobe syndrome? *Compr. Psychiatry*.

13
INVOLUTIONAL MELANCHOLIA

ROBERT N. GOLDEN, M.D.

Assistant Professor of Psychiatry,
University of North Carolina School of Medicine
Chapel Hill, North Carolina

DWIGHT L. EVANS, M.D.

Associate Professor of Psychiatry and Medicine,
University of North Carolina School of Medicine
Chapel Hill, North Carolina

and

DAVID S. JANOWSKY, M.D.

Professor and Chairman, Department of Psychiatry,
University of North Carolina School of Medicine
Chapel Hill, North Carolina

INTRODUCTION

Involutional melancholia no longer exists, at least in the United States. It has not been eradicated through primary prevention, vaccination, improved public health policies, or any of the other usual mechanisms for eliminating disease; rather, it has been "killed off" as a disease entity through changes in nosology. In the late 1970s, the American Psychiatric Association's Task Force on Nomenclature and Statistics reviewed the available data regarding the epidemiology, clinical course, and treatment response characteristics of involutional melancholia and concluded that "there is no compelling evidence that depression occurring in the involutional period is distinct from depression occurring at other ages of life" (2, p. 375). Thus American psychiatrists can no longer officially apply the diagnoses of "involutional melancholia." On the other hand, while internists are unlikely to diagnose "involutional pneumonia," they nonetheless recognize the importance of particular aspects of diagnosing and treating pneumonia in the elderly population. In this chapter, after briefly reviewing the history of the concept of "involutional melancholia," we will present the special considerations that we find helpful in evaluating and treating depressive episodes in the geriatric population.

HISTORICAL OVERVIEW

The term *melancholia* has its roots in ancient Greek culture. Hippocrates is credited with advancing the label to describe severe depressive states. He suggested that the etiology of melancholia involved the accumulation of "black bile," which influenced brain functioning, "darkening the spirit and making it melancholy . . . " (31). Centuries later, Kraepelin first delineated involutional melancholia from other affective diseases. In the early part of this century, he described an entity beginning in the late middle age in men and after menopause in women that was neither a phase of some other form of insanity nor was it preceded by other mental disorders. This condition began with the insidious onset of anxious depression and apprehension and led to more fully developed delusions. Kraepelin hypothesized that this involutional melancholia resulted from external stress, while manic-depressive insanity was constitutional in origin (29).

Dreyfus, a student of Kraepelin, disagreed with his teacher and argued that "involutional melancholia" was a form of manic-depressive illness and should not be classified as a separate disease. The German school of psychiatry agreed with Dreyfus, and even Kraepelin modified his original position. The majority of English and American psychiatrists disagreed, however, and clung to Kraepelin's original formulation that the first episode of any mental illness occurring in the involutional period and characterized by depression, agitation, feelings of unreality, somatic and nihilistic delusions, and exaggerated feelings of guilt constitutes a distinct entity, involutional melancholia (21).

The second *Diagnostic and Statistical Manual of the American Psychiatric Association* (DSM-II), published in 1968, included involutional melancholia under "major affective disorders" and described it as "a disorder occurring in the involutional period and characterized by worry, anxiety, agitation, and severe insomnia. Feelings of guilt and somatic preoccupations are frequently present and may be of delusional proportions." The continuing debate regarding the validity of the diagnosis was acknowledged: "Opinion is divided as to whether this psychosis can be distinguished from other affective disorder. It is, therefore, recommended that involutional patients not be given this diagnosis unless all other affective disorders have been ruled out" (1, p. 36).

In the 1970s the descriptive/phenomenological tradition of European psychiatry began to assume increasing prominence in the United States with a reawakening of interest in nosology. Careful, objective review of epidemiological and clinical data by prominent researchers such as Weissman at Yale University again called into question the validity of the diagnosis of "involutional melancholia" (44). Ford, the author of the chapter on involutional melancholia in the second edition of *Comprehensive Textbook of Psychiatry* (21), speculated that the subject "(would) not warrant a separate chapter in textbooks in the future." Apparently he was correct; in the third edition of the same textbook, "involutional melancholia" was relegated to a few lines in the glossary, which noted that the term has been replaced by the diagnosis "major depression, single episode, with melancholia or with mood-congruent psychotic features" (28).

The clinical presentation of "involutional melancholia" (DSM-II) or "major depression, single episode, with psychotic features, melancholic type" (DSM-III-R) is described below. The DSM-III-R diagnostic criteria were tested for reliability and validity prior to their incorporation into DSM-III-R (3). In addition to these standard criteria, a number of clinical features seemed to be especially striking to many clinicians who diagnosed and treated "involutional melancholia" in the pre–DSM-III era. Psychomotor agitation can be pronounced, with hand wringing, pacing, and episodes of frenzied movement occurring throughout the waking hours. Feelings of guilt are often intense. Patients frequently blame themselves for unpardonable sins which they believe they have committed in the past. Predictions of horrible but (to the patient) justified punishments can be accompanied by extreme fearfulness. Harsh self-accusation and self-condemnation may lead to preoccupation with death and suicidal ideation. In addition to delusions of guilt, somatic and nihilistic delusions are frequently present.

As mentioned above, the preponderance of epidemiological data suggests that involutional melancholia, i.e., psychotic, melancholic depression in the elderly, is not a distinct diagnostic entity. However, there is considerable ongoing debate as to whether "psychotic depression" in general is a specific, distinct subtype of depressive illness, or simply a more severe presentation of major depression. This question has not been answered conclusively; however, a variety of studies, including descriptive, treatment outcome, and biological marker research, suggest that psychotic or "delusional" depression may be a distinct entity. Nelson and his colleagues at Yale have studied this issue for more than a decade. They have identified distinguishing clinical characteristics for delusional (psychotic) depressives. These patients were found to have a high incidence of psychomotor disturbance, as well as impairment in concentration, short-term memory, visual-spatial ability, and visual-sequential ability. They had, on average, a larger number of prior episodes of illness compared to nondelusional depressives and were more likely to experience guilty feelings and ruminations (10, 36). Further, the form and content of prior depressive episodes were remarkably similar to the index episode for both groups; i.e., delusional depressives usually were delusional whenever they became depressed. However, there was no significant difference between the delusional and nondelusional depressives regarding age of onset of their illness.

Treatment response studies have also identified differences between psychotic and nonpsychotic depression. Nelson's group found that only 22% of their delusional depressives responded to tricyclic therapy, while 80% of their nonpsychotic patients responded (10). The delusional depressives responded well to treatment with combined tricyclic-neuroleptic (68% response rate) or with ECT (82% response rate). Earlier work by Glassman's group (22) had also uncovered a poor response to tricyclic treatment and excellent response to ECT among patients with delusional depression. Recently, Spiker et al. (42) have confirmed a low rate of treatment response to tricyclic alone (41%) and a higher response rate with combined tricyclic-neuroleptic treatment (78%) in patients with delusional depression.

Several studies of biochemical and neuroendocrine aspects of affective illness suggest that psychotic depression may be a biologically distinct subtype. Mendels et al. (34) reported that cerebrospinal fluid concentrations of the serotonin metabolite 5-HIAA were lower in psychotic depressed patients compared to nonpsychotic depressives. Meltzer's group (35) reported that serum dopamine-beta-hydroxylase activity was similar in nonpsychotic depressives compared to normal controls and schizophrenic patients but was significantly lower in psychotic depressed patients. In work conducted by Evans and colleagues here at the University of North Carolina, the dexamethasone suppression test has identified neuroendocrine correlates of psychotic depression. Specifically, psychotic depressives as a group have a higher incidence of abnormal "nonsuppressor" responses to a standard dexamethasone challenge (see below) compared to nonpsychotic depressed patients. Further, the average cortisol response is greater in the psychotic group (13, 18, 19). Thus clinical studies, including outcome and biological marker research, suggest that psychotic or delusional depression may be a distinct clinical subtype. However, the data do not support the hypothesis that psychotic depression in the elderly is clinically or biologically different from psychotic depression in the young or middle-aged.

DIAGNOSIS OF DEPRESSION IN THE ELDERLY

Although involutional melancholia is no longer recognized as a distinct diagnostic entity, physicians are becoming increasingly interested in the special health needs of our growing elderly population. Because of the concomitant illness and medication that are often present in depressed elderly patients, the diagnosis and treatment of major depression in this group of patients can be challenging (25).

A major depressive episode presents as a constellation of symptoms that includes disturbances in mood, cognition, and neurovegetative function. The DSM-III-R diagnostic criteria are listed in Table 1. Table 2 lists the specific features seen in the DSM-III-R subtype of depression "with melancholia"; this label is similar to the terms *endogenous*, *endogenomorphic*, and *vital* depression used in other classificatory schemes. Psychotic features, both mood-congruent and mood-incongruent, may also be present (Table 3). As mentioned above, major depressive episode with melancholia and/or with mood-congruent psychotic features best describes the clinical picture which in the past, when present for the first time in an older patient, would have been diagnosed as involutional melancholia.

Distinguishing Depressive Pseudodementia from True Dementia

In the elderly, depression may present with striking features that are suggestive of dementia, such as disorientation, memory impairment, and distractibility. Loss of interest and pleasure in usual activities may appear as apathy and withdrawal. Difficulty in concentration may present as inattentiveness. Thus the differential diagnosis of "pseudodementia," i.e., depression with dementialike features, from true dementia can be difficult to make (25). Certain clinical features can be helpful in making this important clinical distinction. While patients with both pseudodementia and dementia may demonstrate clinical features relating to memory, cognitive, and intellectual dysfunction, patients with pseudodementia will often "highlight" their deficits, while patients with dementia will attempt to minimize or "cover up" their symptoms. Thus depressive pseudodementia patients will often respond to questions with "I don't know" or "I can't remember" responses; demented patients may confabulate and attempt to

Table 1
Diagnostic Criteria for Major Depressive Episode

A. At least five of the following symptoms have been present during the same two-week period and represent a change from previous functioning; at least one of the symptoms is either (1) depressed mood, or (2) loss of interest or pleasure. . . .

(1) depressed mood . . . most of the day, nearly every day, as indicated either by subjective account or observation by others
(2) markedly diminished interest or pleasure in all, or almost all, activities most of the day, nearly every day . . .
(3) significant weight loss or weight gain when not dieting . . . or decrease or increase in appetite nearly every day . . .
(4) insomnia or hypersomnia nearly every day
(5) psychomotor agitation or retardation nearly every day (observable by others, not merely subjective feelings of restlessness or being slowed down)
(6) fatigue or loss of energy nearly every day
(7) feelings of worthlessness or excessive or inappropriate guilt (which may be delusional) nearly every day (not merely self-reproach or guilt about being sick)
(8) diminished ability to think or concentrate, or indecisiveness, nearly every day (either by subjective account or as observed by others)
(9) recurrent thoughts of death (not just fear of dying), recurrent suicidal ideation without a specific plan, or a suicide attempt or a specific plan for committing suicide

B. (1) It cannot be established that an organic factor initiated and maintained the disturbance
(2) The disturbance is not a normal reaction to death of a loved one . . .

NOTE: Morbid preoccupation with worthlessness, suicidal ideation, marked functional impairment or psychomotor retardation, or prolonged duration suggest bereavement complicated by Major Depression.

C. At no time during the disturbance have there been delusions or hallucinations for as long as two weeks in the absence of prominent mood symptoms (i.e., before the mood symptoms developed or after they have remitted).

D. Not superimposed on Schizophrenia, Schizophreniform Disorder, Delusional Disorder, or Psychotic Disorder Not Otherwise Specified.

Table 2
Diagnostic Criteria for Major Depressive Episode, Melancholic Type

The presence of at least five of the following:

(1) loss of interest or pleasure in all, or almost all, activities
(2) lack of reactivity to usually pleasurable stimuli (does not feel much better, even temporarily, when something good happens)
(3) depression regularly worse in the morning
(4) early morning awakening (at least two hours before usual time of awakening)
(5) psychomotor retardation or agitation (not merely subjective complaints)
(6) significant anorexia or weight loss (e.g., more than 5% of body weight in a month)
(7) no significant personality disturbance before first Major Depressive Episode
(8) one or more previous Major Depressive Episodes followed by complete, or nearly complete, recovery
(9) previous good response to specific and adequate somatic antidepressant therapy, e.g., tricyclics, ECT, MAOI, lithium

Table 3
Major Depressive Episode with Psychotic Features

Delusions or hallucinations are present. If possible, specify whether the psychotic features are *mood-congruent* or *mood-incongruent*.

Mood-congruent psychotic features: Delusions or hallucinations whose content does not involve typical depressive themes of personal inadequacy, guilt, disease, death, nihilism, or deserved punishment.

Mood-incongruent psychotic features: Delusions or hallucinations whose content does *not* involve typical depressive themes of personal inadequacy, guilt, disease, death, nihilism, or deserved punishment. Included here are such symptoms as persecutory delusions (not directly related to depressive themes), thought insertion, thought broadcasting, and delusions of control.

disguise their cognitive impairments. Additional features that distinguish the cognitive aspects of depressive pseudodementia from those of dementia include the preservation of attention and concentration, memory gaps for specific periods of events, equal loss of recent and remote memory, and marked variability in task performance in pseudodementia (see Table 4). In addition, a careful delineation of history and clinical course may help in diagnosis. The onset of illness can often be dated with some precision in patients with pseudodementia, and the patient's family are always aware of dysfunction; the families of demented patients, in contrast, often report an insidious onset of dysfunction and at times are unaware of the scope and severity of impairment. A history of previous psychiatric dysfunction, especially a history of affective disorder, should raise the index of suspicion for pseudodementia, as should a rapid progression of symptoms (45). Table 4 summarizes these and other clinical features that can be used in differentiating pseudodementia from dementia.

Table 4
Clinical Features of Dementia and Pseudodementia

Dementia	Pseudodementia
Insidious onset	Relatively rapid onset
Symptoms often present for long period of time before medical help is sought	Symptoms often of short duration before help is sought
History of previous psychiatric illness is rare	History of previous psychiatric illness is common
Family history of dementia	Family history of affective illness
Cognitive disabilities often concealed by patient	Cognitive disabilities often highlighted by patient
Behavior is often compatible with degree of cognitive impairment	Behavior often incongruent with degree of cognitive impairment
Attention and concentration often impaired	Attention and concentration often intact
Consistently poor performance on tasks of similar difficulty	Inconsistency in task performance
Recent memory often more severely impaired than remote memory	Recent and remote memory often equally impaired
Memory "gaps" for specific periods are rare	Memory "gaps" are common

Evaluating Neurovegetative Complaints in the Elderly

As described elsewhere in this volume, disturbances in neurovegetative functioning are among the cardinal features of depression and can usually be assessed with more objectivity than emotional or cognitive complaints. In the involutional population, however, "abnormal" neurovegetative function has to be evaluated with special care, since changes in some of these functions can, to a degree, be seen as part of the "normal" aging process. For example, surveys of the elderly have revealed that it is rather common for them to experience a decrease in "sleep efficiency." Most older people develop an increase in nocturnal awakenings, a decrease in total sleep time, an increase in daytime drowsiness, and, not surprisingly, a dissatisfaction with the quality of their sleep as they age in the involutional period. Thus in assessing an elderly patient's complaint of sleep disturbance, it is important to clarify the relative severity, compared to the age-expected norm, as well as the timing of the onset of the complaint (i.e., does it coincide temporally with the onset of other affective disorder complaints?).

Just as changes in sleep might reflect normal age-related patterns rather than depressive symptomatology, so might some other neurovegetative changes. Many older people experience a decrease in energy level and libido, either as a consequence of growing older, as a result of medical conditions for which they are at greater risk, or as side effects of medications that the elderly may frequently be taking. Again, carefully teasing out the chronology of these complaints relative to the onset of changes in prescriptions or signs of medical illness versus other depression-related symptoms is important. Further, some of the diagnostic criteria for melancholia are not often associated with "normal" aging or medical/iatrogenic conditions. Thus the presence of diurnal variation of symptoms or inappropriate guilt should increase the index of suspicion for affective disorder. We have found that severe anhedonia is an especially useful symptom for identifying depressive illness in this population; this point was made more than 60 years ago by Mapother, who described depression as a state of "marked dissatisfaction" without pointing to sadness or affective distress as primary (32). Finally, it is extremely useful in most cases to obtain additional history from family members, who may have a more objective and realistic perspective regarding the timing of onset and severity of symptoms.

The Dexamethasone Suppression Test

Several early reports suggested that the Dexamethasone Suppression Test (DST) might be a useful laboratory test to distinguish involutional melancholia from dementia. Originally devised as a test for uncovering Cushing's disease, the Dexamethasone Suppression Test was later used by psychiatric researchers (6, 8, 43) and has received considerable attention as a possible biological marker for affective illness (see Ref. 15 for a review). Its application is relatively simple and inexpensive; as standardized by Carroll and associates (7), the test consists of administration of a 1-mg oral dose of the synthetic glucocorticoid dexamethasone at 11 P.M., followed by serum cortisol determination at 4 P.M. and 11 P.M. the following day. An abnormal test result is generally defined as a serum cortisol concentration of greater than 5 μg/ml at either 4 P.M. or 11 P.M. Rudorfer and Clayton (38, 39) found that this test was useful in distinguishing depression from dementia; others reported similar findings (33). However, the utility of the Dexamethasone Suppression Test in this population has been variable in more recent studies. Two groups of investigators have found fairly high rates of false positive DST results in nondepressed, demented patients, calling into question the specificity of the test (37, 41); other studies have found high specificity similar to that seen in the initial reports (5, 9, 19). In the reports that found low specificity, the patients were profoundly demented, leading some researchers to speculate that the severity of dementia may be more closely related to dexamethasone responsivity than is the simple presence of dementia (24). Further research is needed to clarify these and related issues before determining the ultimate value of the dexamethasone suppression test as a clinical diagnostic tool for distinguishing involutional depression from dementia.

Medical Causes of Depressive Symptoms in the Elderly

There are a number of medical illnesses which the elderly are vulnerable to and that are frequently associated with depressive symptoms (see Table 5). Parkinson's disease, normal-pressure hydrocephalus, carcinoma (16) (especially of the head of the pancreas) (27), thyroid disease, pernicious anemia (14), stroke, or Alzheimer's disease may contribute to depression in the involutional period. Less frequently, Cushing's and Addison's diseases, hyperparathyroidism, systemic lupus erythematosus, and a variety of viral infections can be seen in association with depression. An important potential "masquerader" of depression in this population is sleep apnea. The prevalence of this condition increases with age, and it can present with

Table 5
Medical Conditions Associated with Depressive Symptoms

Endocrine/metabolic	Infectious
Thyroid disease	Influenza
Cushing's disease	Hepatitis
Addison's disease	Pneumonia
B_{12} or folate deficiencies	Chronic Epstein-Barr virus infection
Diabetes	Miscellaneous
Hypoglycemia	Malignancy, especially cancer of the pancreas
Hyperparathyroidism	Rheumatoid arthritis
	Heavy-metal poisoning
Neurological	Systemic lupus erythematosus
Parkinson's disease	Congestive heart failure and other causes of cardiovascular dysfunction
Alzheimer's disease	
Stroke	Sleep apnea
Normal-pressure hydrocephalus	

complaints of lack of energy, difficulty with concentration and memory, impotence, and change in mood—signs and symptoms that are not dissimilar from the clinical picture of major depression. A careful history, review of systems, physical exam, and, when indicated, sleep polysomnography studies should be employed to rule out this condition, especially since the diagnosis of apnea confers a relative contraindication for the use of sedative-hypnotic medication.

Table 6 lists some of the medications that are often prescribed to geriatric patients which can cause the emergence of melancholic depressive symptoms. Many of the commonly prescribed centrally acting antihypertensives, such as reserpine, propranolol, and alpha-methyldopa, appear to be associated with the emergence of depressive syndromes, although it is not clear whether this association is primarily with "at risk" individuals (i.e., those with personal and/or family histories of affective disorders). In patients who develop depressive symptoms but still require antihypertensive therapy, it might be prudent to switch to a drug that has few, if any, central nervous system effects (e.g., a thiazide diuretic) or to a drug that has relatively poor penetrance of the blood-brain barrier (e.g., atenolol). Other drugs that may cause depression in the elderly include sedative-hypnotics, alcohol, cimetidine, L-dopa, as well as certain nonprescription drugs including lecithin, choline, and bromide derivatives.

Table 6
Medications Associated with Depressive Symptoms

Antihypertensives	Cardiovascular agents
Reserpine	Digitalis
Propranolol	Procainamide
Alpha-methyldopa	
Clonidine	Antiparkinsonian drugs
Guanethidine	L-Dopa
Hydralazine	Amantadine
Hormones	Antimicrobials
Estrogen	Cycloserine
Progesterone	Sulfonamides
Corticosteroids	
	Miscellaneous
Anxiolytics	Alcohol
Benzodiapines	Choline
Barbiturates	Lecithin
Meprobamate	Cimetidine
	Metaclopramide
Analgesics/antiarthritics	Disulfiram
Indomethacin	Physostigmine
Phenylbutazone	L-Asparaginase
Phenacetin	

TREATMENT CONSIDERATIONS

In general, patients suffering from affective illness respond best to a thoughtful treatment plan which incorporates biological, psychological, and social approaches. In the elderly population, each of these aspects of treatment needs to be carefully tailored to the biopsychosocial needs and changes associated with aging.

Biological Factors

As people age, biological changes lead to changes in the pharmacokinetic and pharmacodynamic aspects of their pharmacotherapy, which in turn affect their vulnerability to side effects and the likelihood of favorable clinical response. Thus the clinician needs to carefully consider these types of age-related changes in prescribing medications to the melancholic elderly patient.

While there are no clear data to substantiate the common assumption that the absorption of drugs is decreased in the elderly, there is evidence to suggest that other aspects of pharmacokinetics are affected by aging. Body composition changes with age; lean body mass and body water decrease, while total body fat increases, thereby affecting the volume of distribution of drugs. Lithium, the antidepressant of choice for bipolar patients, is distributed in the total body water, so the decreased water content of elderly people may increase the expected plasma concentration of lithium for a given dose. Lipid-soluble drugs, such as the tricyclic antidepressants, would have a relatively greater reservoir of fatty tissue into which they could be diluted, so that their plasma concentrations might be decreased at any given total body amount. Plasma albumin, the major source of protein binding of drugs in the blood, is often decreased in the elderly. For the tricyclic antidepressants and other highly bound drugs, this may greatly increase the proportion of unbound drug that is free to cross the blood-brain barrier and exert biological effects. Drug metabolism can be affected by aging. For most drugs, the elimination half-life is increased in the elderly, and this phenomenon has been demonstrated for the tricyclic desipramine. Finally, renal function normally declines by 40% to 50% with aging, and this accounts for changes in drug excretion in the elderly. For the majority of antidepressant medications, metabolism by the liver accounts for most of the elimination; for lithium, however, virtually all of its elimination occurs via renal excretion, so that an age-related decline in renal function may have significant impact on blood levels (26).

Aging is also associated with changes in pharmacodynamics, e.g., changes in some of the specific receptors where antidepressant drugs can exert therapeutic effects and/or side effects. For example, elderly patients are especially sensitive to central cholinergic blockade and are vulnerable to the confusional effects of the antidepressants which have strong anticholinergic activity. Autopsy studies of the elderly have found decreased concentrations of choline acetylase, and a consequent deficiency of acetylcholine might explain the clinical vulnerability of the elderly to anticholinergic toxicity. Monoamine oxidase activity, on the other hand, is increased in the brain of older patients, suggesting that monoamine neurotransmitters, including dopamine, might be decreased. This in turn could relate to the clinical observation that elderly patients are quite vulnerable to the Parkinsonian side effects of antipsychotic agents. Baroreceptor sensitivity may decline with aging, and this can lead to fairly severe orthostatic hypotension related to antidepressant therapy (26). In the elderly, drug-related orthostatic dizziness can lead to hip fractures and other devastating sequelae.

Common medical problems of the elderly can also affect the biological treatment of depression. Cardiac conduction defects, glaucoma, and benign prostatic hypertrophy can be aggravated by the anticholinergic effects of many tricyclics. Central anticholinergic activity may also induce an atropinelike psychosis and either cause delirium in the depressed patient or aggravate the underlying dementia of the depressed-demented patient. Several of the "second-generation" antidepressants, such as trazodone, amoxapine, and maprotiline, have relatively mild anticholinergic effects; trazodone, in fact, is virtually devoid of anticholinergic activity (40). These agents can be especially useful in treating selected elderly patients for whom anticholinergic effects would be particularly problematic. Of the conventional tricyclic antidepressants, desipramine is the least anticholinergic and is often well tolerated in the elderly. In addition to anticholinergic effects, orthostatic hypotension, which is probably related to alpha-adrenergic-receptor blockade, is a frequent side effect of antidepressant medications. In the elderly, preexisting arteriosclerotic compromise of cerebral circulation can make orthostatic blood pressure changes especially dangerous and can lead to hip fractures and stroke. Unfortunately, trazodone, the safest drug with regard to anticholinergic toxicity, is a fairly potent alpha-adrenergic antagonist and has been associated with a high incidence of orthostatic hypotension. The tricyclic nortriptyline may be better tolerated than most antidepressants with regard to orthostatic blood pressure changes, and since it has a fairly well-defined range for therapeutic plasma concentrations, the dose can be carefully titrated to achieve the lowest amount necessary for clinical efficacy.

How can the clinician integrate all the above factors into a careful approach to treating depression in the elderly? First, one should perform a thorough physical exam, review of systems, and appropriate laboratory studies to rule out complicating medical conditions before treatment is begun. All medications, including nonprescription agents, should be reviewed and only those which are essential should be continued. In choosing which antidepressant to prescribe, consider the side effect profile that would be least troublesome for elderly patients in general and for your patient in particular. Start treatment at a relatively low dose, perhaps one-third to one-half the usual amount, and increase it gradually while monitoring the patient very carefully for the emergence of side effects.

Electroconvulsive therapy (ECT) is a highly effective treatment for depression, and for many elderly patients with coexisting medical illness, it is probably safer than aggressive pharmacotherapy. When administering ECT to these patients, two techniques may be useful in decreasing the risk of treatment-related confusion and memory loss: 1) application of unilateral treatment to the nondominant hemisphere, and 2) if preanesthetic anticholinergic medication is required, glycopyrrolate should be used rather than atropine, since the former has relatively poor penetrance of the blood-brain barrier and is therefore less likely to contribute to central side effects.

Psychological Factors

Psychological factors need to be considered in designing a treatment plan for the depressed elderly patient. These factors include the age-related developmental issues that are common for people in that stage of the life-cycle, as well as the neuropsychological and cognitive changes that are frequently seen.

Erickson (20) emphasized that the process of emotional growth and development is not limited to the early formative years, but rather is an ongoing process that covers the entire span of life, including the involutional years. At that stage, the principal challenge involves the development of ego integrity, the sense of satisfaction one feels when reflecting on a productive and meaningful life. Poor resolution of this developmental task leads to despair—the feeling that one's life has been wasted, and a sense of bitterness toward others or self-hatred. Levinson (30) has identified as a major challenge for this period in life the need to find new activities that provide a new basis for self-worth, since many of the former sources of self-esteem, e.g., work roles, are no longer available. Thus for people in the involutional phase of life, there are challenging tasks and stresses to be mastered, and the presence of an affective disorder can greatly impair their ability to do so. Some of the specific signs and symptoms of melancholia, including anhedonia, withdrawal, sense of guilt, and low self-esteem, can be especially poignant for patients in this phase of life in light of these age-related developmental issues.

Many people experience a decline in their cognitive capacities as they age. This may be especially apparent with regard to short-term memory functions. Such a change in neuropsychological status can affect biological and other aspects of treatment in that elderly depressed patients may find it extremely difficult to remember the instructions for taking medication, scheduling appointments, etc. This problem may be compounded by an age-related decrease in hearing acuity and a depression-related loss of self-esteem which makes it difficult to ask the physician to repeat instructions when they aren't heard or remembered. It is helpful to write down instructions for these patients and, when possible, to share them with involved family members.

Some psychotherapists have claimed that advanced age decreases the suitability of a patient for individual psychotherapy because of the unproven assumption that the capacity for growth and change decreases with age. However, we agree with the school of thought which holds that individual therapy can be extremely helpful for many elderly patients (4, 17, 23). There is a growing body of data to suggest that the combination of pharmacotherapy with individual psychotherapy provides additive benefits in the treatment of depression (12).

Social Factors

The social changes and pressures associated with aging should be taken into account in treating depressive illness in this population. The elderly often experience a decline in their support systems due to the loss of friends and peers from sickness and death. Many aged patients lose their mobility because of physical impairments and/or the loss of access to transportation. With retirement comes a decline in financial resources for many older patients.

With all these factors in mind, it becomes imperative that the physician strive to help his/her elderly patients increase their available support systems as much as possible. Referral to geriatric day treatment and activity programs can be very helpful. Home nursing services may be necessary for house-bound depressed elderly patients. Efforts to preserve financial resources can be enhanced by referral to social services and benefits counselors and by the judicious use, when appropriate, of less expensive generic drug preparations.

CONCLUSIONS

Major depression in the elderly, formerly referred to as involutional melancholia, can be a devastating illness; yet if physicians are aware of the age-related aspects of the diagnosis and treatment of affective disorders in the aged, the prognosis can be excellent. Comfort (11) has articulated very elegantly the importance of recognizing the unique qualities of the geriatric population:

> Older patients today account for about 25 percent of prescriptions, and a higher proportion of office case load, and their numbers are growing. Their symptoms, diagnostics, and reaction to therapies differ as sharply as those of babies from the adult norm as taught. . . . they are extremely susceptible to overmedication and mismedication with substances and doses fully appropriate to younger persons.

> Their problems with the irrational attitudes of society, which treats them as suddenly nonpeople or different people, are apt to be diagnosed as a Valium deficiency. (p. 624)

We hope that the guidelines and clinical points raised here will help eradicate "involutional melancholia," not simply through nosological changes, but by improvements in the diagnosis and treatment of depression in the geriatric population.

REFERENCES

1. American Psychiatric Association (1968). *Diagnostic and statistical manual of mental disorders* (2nd ed.). Washington, DC: American Psychiatric Association.
2. American Psychiatric Association (1980). *Diagnostic and statistical manual of mental disorders* (3rd ed.). Washington, DC: American Psychiatric Association.
3. American Psychiatric Association (1987). *Diagnostic and statistical manual of mental disorders* (3rd ed. rev.). Washington, DC: American Psychiatric Association.
4. Berezin, M. A. (1978). The elderly person. In A. M. Nicholi, Jr. (Ed.), *The Harvard guide to modern psychiatry*. Cambridge, MA: Harvard University Press.
5. Carnes, M., Smith, J. C., Kalin, N. H., & Bauwens, S. F. (1983). The dexamethasone suppression test in demented outpatients with and without depression. *Psychiatry Res.*, *9*, 337.
6. Carroll, B. J., & Davies, B. M. (1970). Clinical associations of 11-hydroxy-corticosteroid suppression and non-suppression in severe depressive illness. *Br. Med. J.*, *1*, 789.
7. Carroll, B. J., Feinberg, M., Greden, J. F., Tarika, J., Alabala, A. A., Haskett, R. F., James, N. M., Kronfol, Z., Lohr, N., Steiner. M., DeVigne, J. P., & Young, E. (1981). A specific laboratory test for the diagnosis of melancholia. *Arch. Gen. Psychiatry*, *38*, 15.
8. Carroll, B. J., Martin, F. I. R., & Davies, B. M. (1968). Resistance to suppression by dexamethasone of plasma 11-OHCS levels in severe depressive illness. *Br. Med. J.*, *3*, 285.
9. Castro, P., Lemaire, M., Toscano-Auilar, M., & Herchuelz, A. (1983). Depression, dementia, and the dexamethasone suppression test. *Am. J. Psychiatry*, *140*, 386.
10. Charney, D. S., & Nelson, J. C. (1981). Delusional and non-delusional unipolar depression: Further evidence for distinct subtypes. *Am. J. Psychiatry*, *138*, 328.
11. Comfort, A. (1977). Geriatrics: A British view. *N. Engl. J. Med.*, *297*, 624.
12. Conte, H. R., Plutchik, R., Wild, K. V., & Karasu, T. B. (1986). Combined psychotherapy and pharmacotherapy for depression: A systematic analysis of the evidence. *Arch. Gen. Psychiatry*, *43*, 471.
13. Evans, D. L., Burnett, G. B., & Nemeroff, C. B. (1983). The dexamethasone suppression test in the clinical setting. *Am. J. Psychiatry*, *140*(5), 586–588.
14. Evans, D. L., Edelsohn, G., & Golden, R. N. (1983). Organic psychosis without anemia or spinal cord symptoms in vitamin B12 deficient patients. *Am. J. Psychiatry*, *140*, 218.
15. Evans, D. L., & Golden, R. N. (1987). The dexamethasone suppression test: A review. In C. B. Nemeroff & P. T. Loosen (Eds.), *Handbook of clinical psychoneuroendocrinology* (pp. 313–335). New York: Guilford Press.

16. Evans, D. L., McCartney, C., Nemeroff, C. B., Raft, D., Quade, D., Golden, R. N., Haggerty, J., Jr., Holmes, V., Simon, J., Droba, M., Mason, G., & Fowler, W. (1986). Depression in women treated for gynecologic cancer: Clinical and neuroendocrine assessment. *Am. J. Psychiatry, 143*, 447.
17. Evans, D. L., Millicovsky, L., & Tennison, C. R. (1984). Aging, reminiscence, and mourning. *Psychiatr. Forum, 12*, 19.
18. Evans, D. L., & Nemeroff, C. B. (1983). Use of the dexamethasone suppression test using DSM-III criteria on an in-patient psychiatric unit. *Biol. Psychiatry, 18*(4), 505–511.
19. Evans, D. L., & Nemeroff, C. B. (1987). The clinical use of the dexamethasone suppression test in DSM-III affective disorders: Correlation with the severe depressive subtypes of melancholia and psychosis. *J. Psychiatr. Res., 21*, 185–194.
20. Erickson, E. H. (1968). The life cycle. In *International encyclopedia of the social sciences*. New York: Macmillan.
21. Ford, H. (1975). Involutional melancholia. In A. M. Freedman, H. I. Kaplan, & B. J. Sadock (Eds.), *Comprehensive textbook of psychiatry* (2nd ed.). Baltimore: Williams & Wilkins.
22. Glassman, A., Kantor, S., & Shostak, M. (1975). Depression, delusions, and drug response. *Am. J. Psychiatry, 132*, 716.
23. Goldfarb, A. I. (1962). The psychotherapy of elderly patients. In H. T. Blumenthal (Ed.), *Medical and clinical aspects of aging*. New York: Columbia University Press.
24. Grunhaus, L., Dilsaver, S., Greden, J. F., & Carroll, B. J. (1983). Depressive pseudodementia: A suggested diagnostic profile. *Biol. Psychiatry, 18*, 215.
25. Haggerty, J. J., Jr., Golden, R. N., Evans, D. L., & Janowsky, D. S. (In press). The differential diagnosis of dementia and pseudodementia. *Geriatrics*.
26. Hollister, L. E. (1981). General principles of psychotherapeutic drug use in the aged. In T. Crook & G. D. Cohen (Eds.), *Physician's handbook on psychotherapeutic drug use in the aged*. New Canaan, CT: Mark Powley Associates.
27. Joffe, R. T., Rubinow, D. R., Denicoff, K. D., Maher, M., & Sindelar, W. F. (1986). Depression and cancer of the pancreas. *Gen. Hosp. Psychiatry, 8*, 241.
28. Kaplan, H. I., & Sadock, B. J. (1980). *Comprehensive textbook of psychiatry* (3rd ed.). Baltimore: Williams & Wilkins.
29. Kraepelin, E. (1904). *Lectures on clinical psychiatry*. New York: Wood.
30. Levinson, D. (1978). *The seasons of a man's life*. New York: Knopf.
31. Lewis, A. (1967). Melancholia: Historical review. In A. Lewis (Ed.), *The state of psychiatry: Essays and addresses*. New York: Science House.
32. Mapother, E. (1926). Discussion on manic depressive psychosis. *Br. Med. J., 2*, 872–876.
33. McAllister, T. W., Ferrell, R. B., Price, T. R. P., & Neville, M. B. (1982). The dexamethasone suppression test in two patients with severe depressive pseudodementia. *Am. J. Psychiatry, 139*, 479.
34. Mendels, J., Frazer, A., Fitzgerald, R. G., Ramsey, T. A., & Stokes, J. W. (1972). Biogenic amine metabolites in cerebrospinal fluid of depressed and manic patients. *Science, 175*, 1380.
35. Meltzer, H., Cho, H., Carroll, B., & Russo, P. (1976). Serum dopamine b-hydroxylase activity in the affective psychoses and schizophrenia. *Arch. Gen. Psychiatry, 33*, 585.
36. Nelson, J. C., & Bowers, M. (1978). Delusional depression: description and drug response. *Arch. Gen. Psychiatry, 35*, 1321.
37. Raskind, M., Peskind, E., Rivard, M. F., Veith, R., & Barnes, R. (1982). Dexamethasone suppression test and cortisol circadian rhythm in primary degenerative dementia. *Am. J. Psychiatry, 139*, 1468.
38. Rudorfer, M. V., & Clayton, P. V. (1981). Depression, dementia, and dexamethasone suppression. *Am. J. Psychiatry, 138*, 701.

39. Rudorfer, M. V., & Clayton, P. V. (1982). Pseudodementia: Use of the DST in diagnosis and treatment monitoring. *Psychosomatics, 23*, 429.
40. Rudorfer, M. V., Golden, R. N., & Potter, W. Z. (1984). Second generation antidepressants. *Psychiatr. Clin. North Am.*, 7, 519.
41. Spar, J. E., & Gerner, R. (1982). Does the dexamethasone suppression test distinguish dementia from depression? *Am. J. Psychiatry, 139*, 238.
42. Spiker et al. (1985). The pharmacological treatment of delusional depression. *Am. J. Psychiatry, 142*, 430–436.
43. Stokes, P. E. (1972). Studies on the control of adrenocortical function in depression. In T. A. Williams, M. M. Katz, & J. A. Shield (Eds.), *Recent advances in the psychobiology of depressive illnesses*. Washington, DC: US Government Printing Office.
44. Weissman, M. M. (1979). The myth of involutional melancholia. *JAMA, 242*, 742–744.
45. Wells, C. (1979). Pseudodementia. *Am. J. Psychiatry, 136*, 895–900.

14

BIPOLAR AFFECTIVE DISORDER: REVIEW AND UPDATE

SETH COHEN, M.D.

Acting Assistant Professor,
Department of Psychiatry and Behavioral Sciences,
University of Washington,
Harborview Medical Center,
Seattle, Washington

and

DAVID DUNNER, M.D.

Professor,
Department of Psychiatry and Behavioral Sciences,
University of Washington,
Harborview Medical Center,
Seattle, Washington

INTRODUCTION

The illness referred to today as bipolar affective disorder has been recognized since antiquity. In the second century, a physician named Aretaens (1) described melancholia and mania and noted a relationship between the two states. He described the episodic course of the illness and contrasted the guilt-ridden, self-sacrificing style of the melancholic state with the gay, overactive behavior of the manic state. His teachings were ignored for many years, again being recognized by Baillarger in 1853 and labeled *folie circulaire* by Falret in 1854 (41). Falret characterized its circular and intermittent nature.

Kraepelin's work (21) was even more incisive in making the nosological distinction between dementia praecox and manic-depressive insanity. He stressed the importance of the course of illness in differentiating between these two disease states. Kraepelin noted that manic-depressive insanity had a uniform prognosis and that the end result of an episode of illness was the complete disappearance of all symptoms, whereas schizophrenia had a chronic deteriorating course. Kraepelin concluded that almost any illness with good prognosis and without deterioration could reasonably be thought of as manic-depressive insanity. Under that rubric he included periodic and circular insanity manifested by depressions and manias, simple mania, melancholia, exhaustion stupor, and periodic and good-prognosis paranoias. In addition, Kraepelin thought some patients described as psychopaths, neurasthenics, or hysterics and who also suffered from cyclical mood fluctuations should be regarded as having manic-depressive insanity. In being so inclusive, he certainly sowed the seeds for the ongoing controversy regarding the nosology of affective disorders.

Inconsistency in the diagnostic distinction between manic-depressive illness and schizophrenia was pointed out by Kramer (22) in 1961, who noted that manic-depressive illness was diagnosed nine times as often in England and Wales as in the United States. More detailed U.S.-U.K. comparative studies were then conducted which demonstrated a significant predilection for American psychiatrists to diagnose manic-depressive illness rarely and schizophrenia commonly, in contradistinction to their British counterparts (9). Greater interest in establishing diagnostic clarity eventuated in the acceptance of diagnostic criteria for bipolar affective disorder as defined in the 3rd edition of the *Diagnostic and Statistical Manual* (DSM-III). The importance of refined diagnostic ability is also partly due to the establishment of lithium as an effective treatment for the acute and maintenance phases of the illness.

In this chapter we discuss the current description of the signs and symptoms of bipolar affective disorder and briefly review its differential diagnosis, epidemiology, genetics, course, and outcome (28, 40). We then focus on treatment and special factors today's clinicians face in treating bipolar affective disorder.

CLINICAL DESCRIPTIONS

The essential feature of bipolar disorder is the occurrence of a distinct manic episode. In light of the fact that the majority of persons who experience such an episode eventually develop depressive episodes, most investigators regard unipolar manic episodes within the category of bipolar disorder.

The critical clinical feature for a manic episode is a mood that is elevated, elated, expansive, or irritable. By DSM-III criteria the episode must be at least of one-week duration or require hospitalization and be accompanied by at least three of the following symptoms (four if the mood is irritable): increased activity, pressure of speech, flight of ideas, inflated self-esteem, reduced sleep, distractibility, high risk taking, and poor judgment. There can be no mood-incongruent delusions or hallucinations and no bizarre behavior if the affective syndrome is not present. Additionally, for the diagnosis of a manic episode to be made, the symptoms cannot be associated with schizophrenia, schizophreniform disorder, or paranoid disorder and cannot be due to an organic or toxic mental disorder.

The above-noted clinical description would not account for all patients with the diagnosis of bipolar affective disorder. Evidence has accumulated to distinguish bipolar I disorder (as described above) from bipolar II patients (DSM-III atypical bipolar disorder) who suffer from either hypomania or mild mania, in addition to depressive episodes, and have not required hospitalization for the elated phase of their illness (14). Furthermore, the bipolar III patient has been defined as an individual who has had episodes of depression only, but a family history of mania (10). Another clinically useful subclassification is the rapid-cycling group. These are patients who have four or more affective events (or two or more cycles) in a one-year period (15). Special diagnostic and treatment issues related to this subgroup are described later in this chapter.

DIFFERENTIAL DIAGNOSIS

Mania has been reported in a variety of organic illnesses, and this is referred to as *secondary mania* (23). Included are the categories of prescription drugs, metabolic disturbances, infections, neoplasms, and epilepsy. Since the time of its description by Krauthammer and Klerman, secondary mania is now also described due to drugs of abuse and head trauma.

Within the realm of functional illness the most common and difficult differential is between mania and schizophrenia. Clinically useful points to consider include age of onset, course of illness, and family history. Many patients, however, have both affective and psychotic symptoms, and distinguishing between the two disorders can be extremely difficult. DSM-III reflects this difficulty in the establishment of a separate disorder, schizoaffective. The term was first used by Kasanin (20), and other labels for this entity have been established, such as schizophreniform psychosis, good-prognosis schizophrenia, atypical mania, oneirophrenia, and cycloid psychosis. Active debate continues as to whether the diagnosis of schizoaffective disorder merits independent existence.

Also to be considered in the differential is cyclothymic disorder where the affective symptoms tend to be muted. In this disorder there are elated and sad periods but the full manic and depressive syndromes are not present.

EPIDEMIOLOGY

A comprehensive review of the literature found the lifetime risk of bipolar affective disorder to range from 0.6% to 0.9% in industrialized nations (3). Depending on whether inpatients or outpatients were being considered, the annual incidence ranged from 0.009% to 0.015% for men and 0.007% to 0.030% for women. Subsequent to that review the U.S. Epidemiologic Catchment Area (ECA) study has been published (32). This study found the six-month period prevalence for a manic episode to range from 0.4% to 0.8% for men and 0.4% to 0.9% for women. Lifetime risk for the disorder was 0.9% to 1.1% for men and 0.6% to 1.3% for women.

Previous studies reported a ratio of women to men for bipolar disorder in the range of 1.3:1 to 2:1. Those studies used a diagnostic classification which included depression in the manic-depressive group. As depression is more common among women, the numbers were skewed in the direction of a higher incidence in women. Using the more specified criteria of the DSM-III, however, reveals the sex ratio for bipolar disorder to be approximately equal between men and women or slightly increased among women.

Disagreement exists regarding the age of onset of bipolar disorder. Earlier studies found a rising incidence until age 35 and then a decline. More recent studies suggest age of onset in late adolescence or the early twenties, with the incidence increasing with age. It has also been found that half of the new cases occur in those over age 50. Other retrospective studies found the age of onset to range from 24 to 31.5 years, with a modal age of onset of 30 years. As the presentation for bipolar disorder may be mixed with polydrug abuse and antisocial personality disorder, adolescents with the disorder may be misdiagnosed as having conduct disorder.

Bipolar disorder has been reported to occur more frequently in upper socioeconomic classes, yet that finding is inconstant. Furthermore, it is unclear whether being upper class is cause or consequence of the disorder. There is no apparent relationship between race and bipolar disorder. Most studies suggest that bipolar disorder is more common among divorced and single than married people. However, divorce may be a consequence of the disorder, not a precipitant.

GENETICS

Twin studies in bipolar disorder reveal the concordance rates in dizygotes to vary from 15% to 20% and in monozygotes to vary between 67% to 79%. Thus there is a fourfold increase in concordance in monozygotes, which is highly suggestive of a genetic-transmission hypothesis. Adoption studies have also been done, revealing that 31% of the biological parents of adoptees with bipolar disorder have affective illness, compared with 2% of controls. Recent studies have localized a dominant gene conferring a strong predisposition to bipolar disorder at the tip of the short arm of chromosome 11 (17).

COURSE AND OUTCOME

Prior to the 1950s when antidepressants were introduced, half of those diagnosed manic-depressive spent more than four months hospitalized with each episode. Ten percent of the patients would be hospitalized for more than four years. The death rate for females was twice normal and for males three times the normal rate. Before lithium gained widespread use in the 1960s, manic-depressives had episodes of illness on average every two to three years, each lasting about four months. With modern treatment the duration of a manic episode through complete resolution of symptoms is about three months. Most patients, however, show substantial improvement and may be functioning within three to four weeks of the start of adequate treatment. With increasing age, the interval between episodes shortens and the length of each episode increases. Thus a patient with bipolar disorder has an increasing risk of having an affective episode as he or she grows older. Some patients are often free of relapse for 10 to 20 years between the first and second episode. Following complete resolution of an attack, the next three to six months are considered to be the most vulnerable for relapse.

Excess mortality among bipolar patients is significant. Unlike the excess seen in unipolar illness, factors other than unnatural death are involved, though the increased lifetime risk of suicide is highly significant.

TREATMENT

Most of the studies that showed lithium effective for the treatment of acute mania involved acutely manic hospitalized patients who were randomly assigned to treatment with lithium versus placebo or lithium versus antipsychotic, usually chlorpromazine (13). These studies clearly support the efficacy of lithium as compared with alternate treatments in a two-to-three-week trial. Such patients generally had *typical mania*, were without a history of polydrug abuse or alcoholism, and, although sufficiently ill to require hospitalization, were voluntarily compliant with research treatment. Patients who participated in these trials may have been delusional, but if so, the delusions were generally mood congruent. Although delusions of reference and/or paranoid delusions could have been present, such delusions did not dominate the clinical picture. Thus, the research reports demonstrating efficacy of lithium were performed on relatively compliant patients who had prototypical symptoms.

One study which also included patients with overt psychosis was the VA NIMH inpatient project reported by Prien et al. (30, 31). They subdivided patients into manics and schizoaffectives, the latter group possibly meeting criteria for mania using today's standards, and they further subdivided treatment groups into those who were quite agitated and those who were mildly to moderately agitated.

The VA NIMH collaborative study showed that lithium was more effective in such patients, whether they were typically manic or acute schizoaffectives, than chlorpromazine treatment if the patient had a mild to moderate mania. If the patient was more psychotic and agitated, the antipsychotic drug was probably better since, among other reasons, the antipsychotic drug (chlorpromazine) produced sedation earlier than lithium treatment (30, 31).

In clinical practice, most acutely manic patients are treated with a combination of lithium and antipsychotic drugs. As the more potent varieties of antipsychotic medications were marketed, clinicians opted to use these drugs in preference to the less potent antipsychotic drugs, presumably because of the decrease in cardiovascular and blood pressure side effects with the more potent compounds. Furthermore, clinicians are faced with treating acutely manic patients who are less compliant, more assaultive, more psychotic, and have more intercurrent medical problems than those patients who participated in research studies. As lithium is only available as an oral preparation and many acutely manic patients will not cooperate with oral consumption of medication, the clinician is often then left with having to use intramuscular antipsychotics. Thus, although the research studies reported lithium efficacy in about 80% of acutely manic patients in a two-week trial, most clinicians experience greater difficulty in treating acutely manic patients today.

Part of the difficulty in achieving rapid response to lithium may be related to diagnostic issues, including overdiagnosis of mania, secondary mania, and manic patients who have psychotic symptoms. Evidence also suggests that the mixed manic patient is less responsive to pharmacotherapy. Many clinicians diagnose mania in a patient who has a recurrent psychotic illness but who may not have the inclusion symptoms of bipolar illness. Thus, in clinical use, the diagnosis of mania has been considerably broadened over the past 10 years to include patients who might be better diagnosed as atypical psychosis. Other patients may have *secondary mania* described in a differential diagnosis section of this chapter. Some patients who exhibit bipolar mood swings have prior histories of extensive polydrug abuse or head trauma. In our experience, such patients do not demonstrate rapid responses to lithium treatment for their manic symptoms.

An additional reason for poor response relates to today's pressure to discharge patients rapidly. The research studies demonstrating the efficacy of lithium were conducted over two-to-three-week periods. One study showed that some manics who did not respond by three weeks were responders after five weeks of treatment (38). Some clinicians are concerned if their manic patient is not responding within two weeks, but the concern relates to insurance-payment problems rather than to the patient's psychopharmacology. Manic patients treated in the "research era" may have had psychosis. However, the hospitalized manic patient in the modern era is likely to be psychotic and at times with mood-incongruent delusions.

In summary, diagnostic issues as well as differences in clinical presentation result in lowered response rates for today's manic patients as compared with those patients who were studied in research trials of lithium for acute mania. Furthermore, many patients who had prototypical mania are being maintained out of the hospital with maintenance therapy with lithium carbonate.

The bipolar patients who come into the hospital these days then tend to be treatment failures. Among the considerations for this group may be a history of alcohol or polydrug abuse, as noted above. The lithium/erythrocyte plasma ratio may be useful in adjusting the lithium level in some of these patients, since some patients have low red-blood-cell plasma ratios reflecting too low an entry level of lithium in their cells (34). Although their plasma levels seem fine, they are not being adequately treated. Thus, for some patients we would recommend a simple increase in lithium to a higher dose. In other patients, alternate treatments for acute mania may be necessary.

Most clinicians treat acutely manic patients with a combination of lithium carbonate and a high-potency neuroleptic. However, two problems are emerging associated with the use of neuroleptics in mania: neuroleptic malignant syndrome and tardive dyskinesia. Neuroleptic malignant syndrome (25) is an acute syndrome with an approximately 20% fatality rate and is characterized by confusion, fever, muscle rigidity, and elevated levels of creatine phosphokinase. This disorder has been reported to occur in the presence of neuroleptic treatment. We recently had a patient who seemed to fit these criteria but did not have any recent neuroleptic treatment, suggesting that the older syndromes, such as lethal catatonia, exhaustion syndrome, cyanotic syndrome, or other sudden-death syndromes such as Bell's mania, may be relevant to the acute, sudden-death cases seen in hospitals during acute psychosis and attributed to neuroleptic treatment (6). Although further research in this area is warranted, the clinical trend has been to try to use less neuroleptic dosage for acute mania.

The second problem relating to the use of neuroleptics is tardive dyskinesia. When one is treating patients who relapse frequently for mania, and using lithium and antipsychotic drugs, the usual tendency is to use the more potent drugs and increase the doses rather rapidly for the treatment of acute mania, and then decrease the doses when the patient goes into the postmanic depressive phase. The repeated increase and decrease of neuroleptic doses would seem to sensitize some patients for the development of tardive dyskinesia, and some research studies cite that tardive dyskinesia may be more frequent among bipolar patients treated in the above manner than among chronic schizophrenic patients (27).

Both these concerns relating to the use of neuroleptics, as well as some medical problems associated with lithium, such as chronic renal disease, make the development of newer agents for the treatment of acute mania quite useful. Such newer agents have recently been reviewed by Lerer (24) and by Dunner and Clayton (12) and include a variety of anticonvulsant and benzodiazepine-type drugs along with other cardiovascular-acting agents. Of particular note is the use of carbamazepine. This drug was developed for mania by Japanese investigators (19) and studied in this country by Ballenger and Post (2). The latter studied carbamazepine in acute manic patients and rapid cyclers and found the drug to be effective in both conditions. Although studies on large numbers of patients are lacking, carbamazepine is the single best-studied drug other than lithium for the treatment of acute manic illness. Carbamazepine has been shown to be an effective agent. One question that arises with carbamazepine is whether blood levels should be obtained, and also whether the medical tests advised in the *Physicians' Desk Reference* should be pursued as conscientiously as mentioned. The cost of obtaining frequent blood tests is usually greater than the cost of pharmacotherapy, whereas the incidence of clinically significant hematological and hepatological abnormalities due to carbamazepine is exceedingly low.

Other pharmacotherapeutic strategies for the treatment of acute mania involve benzodiazepines. When used alone benzodiazepines are devoid of complications such as neuroleptic malignant syndrome and tardive dyskinesia. Their use in combination with neuroleptics was reported by Salzman et al. to have a neuroleptic sparing effect, thus limiting neuroleptic toxicity (33). Their report involved the treatment of patients with severe disruptive behavior whose diagnosis included affective illness, schizophrenia, organic brain syndrome, and borderline personality disorder. Reports of benzodiazepine administration confined to the treatment of manic-depressive illness, manic type, are limited yet favorable (5, 26).

We have reported on the efficacy of benzodiazepines with or without neuroleptics in the first seven days of treatment of 12 acutely manic patients using two standard rating scales as objective indicators of improvement (7). We found that those patients who received benzodiazepines alone were among the better responders and that when the benzodiazepines were used in combination with neuroleptics, the dose of each drug was quite small. Side effects were minimal and included sedation, ataxia, and orthostatic blood pressure change.

An additional treatment for acute mania which is often overlooked is electroconvulsive therapy. Small has recently reported that bilateral ECT was quite effective in the treatment of lithium-refractory patients who had acute mania (36). It is important to note that lithium treatment should be stopped approximately one week prior to administering ECT so that neurotoxicity does not result (37).

The major uses for lithium are in maintenance therapy. Issues of concern to the clinician relating to maintenance therapy include determining the least effective dose of lithium that can be used. This is important since higher doses of lithium and higher plasma levels may be associated with an increased risk of medical complications such as renal disease. Although this question is not well settled, it appears that minimal doses of around .5 to .6 meq/liter are necessary to effect maintenance therapy.

A second issue is determining whether all patients who have mania should be put on lithium maintenance therapy. As discussed earlier, mania tends to be a relapsing disorder, but many patients will not relapse for several years after their initial episode. Thus, it seems prudent to follow the patient through the acute mania and the postmanic depressive episode and continue lithium for six months. If this is the first affective cycle for the patient, lithium could be stopped and the patient followed over the next year. The reason for continuing treatment for six months relates to this interval showing the highest rate of relapse in longitudinal studies (18). The reason for following the patient over the next year without lithium is that there may be a tendency to relapse at about the same time of year the patient had the initial episode. If the patient remains asymptomatic, he should be advised of manic or premanic depressive symptoms and advised to return for treatment should they recur. Patients who have infrequent relapsing mania, such as two episodes in 10 years, may opt not to have lithium maintenance. One could perform a cost-effective analysis and determine that lithium maintenance seems to be indicated if patients have two episodes within about a seven-year interval.

Lithium is also quite useful for treatment of recurrent depression, both recurrent depression with hypomania (bipolar II) and in patients with recurrent depression only (13, 16). Indeed, patients with multiple episodes of depression which require treatment should be treated with lithium maintenance therapy if they have histories of mania or hypomania and with tricyclic antidepressant and/or lithium maintenance therapy if they have histories of depression only (8). This is one of the newer findings of psychopharmacology and suggests that such treatment would be preventive for future depressive episodes.

A subgroup requiring additional note are the rapid cyclers, who are patients with four or more affective events (or two or more cycles) in a one-year period (15). Such patients have been shown to be more refractory to treatment with lithium than non–rapid-cycling bipolar patients, although they clearly benefit from lithium therapy. Our approach to treatment of the rapid-cycling bipolar patient has been aimed at preventing manic or hypomanic episodes. It appears that the manic-depressive cycle will be reduced if mania is prevented and increased if mania or hypomania is augmented. Thus, cycling patients have a higher cycle frequency if treated with tricyclic antidepressants than if treated with lithium alone (39).

Our treatment regimen for rapid cyclers has consisted of using lithium carbonate, having the patient keep a daily mood calendar, assessing for antithyroid antibodies and other evidence of thyroid dysfunction, avoiding the use of antidepressants, adjunctively using low-potency neuroleptics in low doses in addition to cognitive therapy, and physical exercise (11). The addition or use of carbamazepine may be beneficial if there is evidence of neurological dysfunction or if the patient is not responding after six months of treatment (29).

Lithium should be given so that adequate blood levels are obtained. If the patient's daily mood calendar suggests a regular pattern to the cycle, it may be helpful to increase the lithium dose (and possibly the neuroleptic dose) a few days prior to the anticipated switch from depression to hypomania. Although the patient may complain of the depressive phase of the cycle, these depressions frequently last a shorter duration than the time required for antidepressants to work. Thus, antidepressants can usually be avoided and the depressive phase treated with exercise, cognitive therapy, and by adjusting the neuroleptic.

A percentage of rapid-cycling patients have elevated titers of antithyroid antibodies (antithyroglobulin or antimicrosomal), and such patients may benefit from treatment with thyroid hormone even if they are clinically euthyroid. Also, such patients may be more prone than others to have lithium-induced hypothyroidism (4).

Carbamazepine can be a useful adjunct to lithium therapy for rapid-cycling patients (29). Neurotoxicity has been reported from the combined use of lithium and carbamazepine, and the clinician should be aware of these case reports (35). We prefer to use lithium in combination with carbamazepine, although carbamazepine alone has been reported to show anticycling activity.

In summary, lithium carbonate seems to work well for the majority of patients with bipolar affective disorder, both for treatment of acute mania and for maintenance therapy for recurrent mania or recurrent depression. Its efficacy has resulted in the patients we are seeing in hospitals being more refractory to treatment since they are the ones relapsing in spite of good maintenance therapy. Some suggestions regarding the above patients have been reviewed in this chapter.

REFERENCES

1. ARIETI, S. (1974). Affective disorders. In S. Arieti (Ed.), *American handbook of psychiatry*. New York: Basic Books.
2. BALLENGER, J. C., & POST, R. M. (1980). Carbamazepine in manic-depressive illness: A new treatment. *American Journal of Psychiatry, 137*, 782.
3. BOYD, J. H., & WEISSMAN, M. M. (1981). Epidemiology of affective disorders: A reexamination and future directions. *Archives of General Psychiatry, 38*, 1039.
4. CHO, J. T., BONE, S., DUNNER, D. L., et al. (1979). The effect of lithium treatment on thyroid function in patients with primary affective disorder. *American Journal of Psychiatry, 136*, 115.

5. Chouinard, G., Young, S. M., & Annable, L. (1983). Antimanic effect of clonazepam. *Biological Psychiatry, 18*, 451.
6. Cohen, S., Fligner, C. L., Raisys, V. A., et al. (1987). A case of nonneuroleptic malignant syndrome. *Journal of Clinical Psychiatry, 48*, 287.
7. Cohen, S., Khan A., & Johnson, S. (1987). Pharmacological management of manic psychosis in an unlocked setting. *Journal of Clinical Psychopharmacology, 7*, 261.
8. Consensus Development Panel (1985). Mood disorders: Pharmacologic prevention of recurrences. *American Journal of Psychiatry, 142*, 469.
9. Cooper, J. E., Kendell, R. E., Gurland, B. J., et al. (1972). *Psychiatric diagnoses in New York and London*, Institute of Psychiatry, Maudsley Monograph Series, No. 20. London: Oxford University Press.
10. Depue, R. A., & Monroe, S. N. (1978). The unipolar-bipolar distinction in the depressive disorders. *Psychological Bulletin, 85*, 1001.
11. Dunner, D. L. (1979). Rapid cycling bipolar manic depressive illness. *Psychiatric Clinics of North America, 2*, 461.
12. Dunner, D. L., & Clayton, P. J. (1987). Drug treatment of bipolar disorder. In H. L. Meltzer (Ed.), *Psychopharmacology: A second generation of progress*. New York: Raven Press.
13. Dunner, D. L., & Fieve, R. R. (1978). The effect of lithium in depressive subtypes. In P. Deniker, C. Radoucho-Thomas, & A. Villeneuve (Eds.), *Neuropsychopharmacology* (p. 1109). New York: Pergamon Press.
14. Dunner, D. L., Gershon, E. S., & Goodwin, F. K. (1976). Hereditable factors in the severity of affective illness. *Biological Psychiatry, 11*, 31.
15. Dunner, D. L., Patrick, V., & Fieve, R. R. (1977). Rapid cycling manic depressive patients. *Comprehensive Psychiatry, 18*, 561.
16. Dunner, D. L., Stallone, F., & Fieve, R. R. (1976). Lithium carbonate and affective disorders: V. A double-blind study of prophylaxis of depression in bipolar illness. *Archives of General Psychiatry, 33*, 117.
17. Egeland, J. A., Gerhard, D. S., Pauls, D. L., et al. (1987). Bipolar affective disorders linked to DNA markers on chromosome 11. *Nature, 326*, 783.
18. Fleiss, J. L., Prien, R. F., Dunner, D. L., et al. (1978). Actuarial studies of the course of manic depressive illness. *Comprehensive Psychiatry, 19*, 355.
19. Inoue, K., Arima, S., Tanaka, K., et al. (1981). A lithium and carbamazepine combination in the treatment of bipolar disorder—A preliminary report. *Folia Psychiatry and Neurology Japan, 35*, 465.
20. Kasanin, J. (1933). The acute schizoaffective psychoses. *American Journal of Psychiatry, 13*, 97.
21. Kraepelin, E. (1921). Manic depressive insanity and paranoia. Edinburgh: E. and S. Livingstone.
22. Kramer, M. (1961). Some problems for international research suggested by observations on differences on first admission rates to the mental hospitals of England and Wales and of the United States. In *Proceedings of the Third World Congress of Psychiatry*, Vol. 3 (p. 153). Montreal: University of Toronto Press; McGill University Press.
23. Krauthammer, C., & Klerman, G. L. (1978). Secondary mania. *Archives of General Psychiatry, 35*, 1333.
24. Lerer, B. (1985). Alternate therapies for bipolar disorder. *Journal of Clinical Psychiatry, 46*, 309.
25. Levenson, J. L. (1985). Neuroleptic malignant syndrome. *American Journal of Psychiatry, 142*, 1137.
26. Modell, J. G., Lenox, R. H., & Weiner, S. (1985). Inpatient clinical trial of lorazepam for the management of manic agitation. *Journal of Clinical Psychopharmacology, 5*, 109.

27. Mukherjee, S., Rosen, A. M., Caracci, G., et al. (1986). Persistent tardive dyskinesia in bipolar patients. *Archives of General Psychiatry, 43*, 342.
28. Paykel, E. S. (Ed.) (1982). *Handbook of affective disorder*. New York: Guilford Press.
29. Post, R. M., Ballenger, J. C., Uhde, R. W., et al. (1984). Efficacy of carbamazepine in manic depressive illness: Implications for underlying mechanisms. In R. M. Post & J. C. Ballenger (Eds.), *Neurobiology of mood disorder* (p. 777). Baltimore: Williams & Wilkins.
30. Prien, R. F., Caffey, D. M., & Klett, C. J. (1972). A comparison of lithium carbonate and chlorpromazine in the treatment of excited schizoaffectives. *Archives of General Psychiatry, 27*, 182.
31. Prien, R. F., Klett, C. J., & Caffey, E. M. (1972). A comparison of lithium carbonate and chlorpromazine in the treatment of mania. *Archives of General Psychiatry, 26*, 146.
32. Regier, D. A., Myers, J. K., Kramer, M., et al. (1984). The NIMH Edpidemiologic Catchment Area (ECA) program: Historical context, major objectives, and study population characteristics. *Archives of General Psychiatry, 41*, 934.
33. Salzman, C., Green, A., Rodriguez-Villa, F., et al. (1986). Benzodiazepines combined with neuroleptics for management of severe disruptive behavior. *Psychosomatics, 27* (Suppl.), 17.
34. Schreiner, H. C., Dunner, D. L., Meltzer, H. L., et al. (1979). The relationship of the lithium erythrocyte: Plasma ratio to plasma lithium level. *Biological Psychiatry, 14*, 207.
35. Shukla, S., Goodwin, C. D., Long, L. E. B., et al. (1984). Lithium-carbamazepine neurotoxicity and risk factors. *American Journal of Psychiatry, 141*, 1604.
36. Small, J. G. (1985). Efficacy of electroconvulsive therapy in schizophrenia, mania and other disorders. II: Mania and other disorders. *Convulsive Therapy, 1*, 271.
37. Small, J. G., Kellams, J. J., Milstein, V., et al. (1980). Complications of electroconvulsive treatment combined with lithium. *Biological Psychiatry, 15*, 103.
38. Takahashi, R., Sakuma, A., Itoh, K., et al. (1975). Comparison of efficacy of lithium carbonate and chlorpromazine in mania. *Archives of General Psychiatry, 32*, 1310.
39. Wehr, T. A., & Goodwin, F. U. (1979). Rapid cycling in manic depressives induced by tricyclic antidepressants. *Archives of General Psychiatry, 36*, 555.
40. Winokur, G., Clayton, P. J., & Reich, T. (1969). *Manic depressive illness*. St. Louis: Mosby.
41. Zilboorg, G. (1941). *A history of medical psychology*. New York: Norton.

15

PSYCHIATRIC ILLNESS AFTER CHILDBEARING

JAMES ALEXANDER HAMILTON, M.D., PH.D.

Associate Clinical Professor of Psychiatry, Stanford University School of Medicine, Emeritus

INTRODUCTION

Psychiatric illness that follows childbearing differs in many ways from other varieties of psychiatric illness. One major difference is that the symptoms which present themselves at one time may be quite different from those which present themselves at other times. Part of this is the result of an evolution of psychiatric symptoms which follows physical changes from the pregnant state. Part is a tendency for rapid and unpredictable changes to occur. A patient may exhibit the signs and symptoms of a simple depression and then suddenly become animated and express bizarre ideation, which might suggest the appropriateness of a schizophrenic diagnosis. This may give way to a period of lucidity which can be taken mistakenly for recovery. During such lucid periods there may be apparent amnesia for the bizarre ideation. Confusion is a common element of many expressions of postpartum illness, but the degree of confusion may fluctuate. The remarkable changeability of many patients, their impetuousness, and their explosive qualities create treatment problems and hazards of considerable magnitude. The adjective *mercurial* is particularly appropriate to psychiatric symptoms that follow childbearing.

Because of the mercurial quality of postpartum psychiatric illness, a presentation of a single syndrome, such as depression, would be misleading. The physician, and all those who treat or come in contact with postpartum patients, including families of patients, should be made aware of the likely mercurial qualities of symptoms and the varieties of thinking and behavior that may be expected. This chapter is divided into a historical review, an outline of syndromes, a section on etiology, and concluding remarks on treatment.

HISTORICAL REVIEW

During the 19th century, many brilliant physicians observed the symptoms and course of postpartum psychiatric illness. In 1838, J. E. D. Esquirol described 92 cases and speculated on the possible causes of the high incidence of delirium (10). The first comprehensive book on psychiatric illness associated with childbearing was that of Louis Victor Marcé, in 1858 (19). Marcé was stationed at the mental hospital at Ivry-sur-Seine, near Paris, where Esquirol had worked with postpartum patients. Marcé made a sharp distinction between patients recently delivered and patients whose illness developed after six weeks. Among the first group, he observed that many were at first delirious or manic, and that later they moved into "toutes les nouances" of other syndromes. Among the early-onset patients whose mood was depressed, he noted a high incidence of a peculiar sad delirium, "délére triste," with fleeting ideas of persecution, death, dishonor, and self-destruction.

Marcé's cases which developed after six weeks were observed to be mainly melancholic, with a high incidence of weakness, loss of weight, constipation, and menstrual disorders. Psychological symptoms and signs were confusion, vagueness, poor memory, lack of ideational clarity, and occasional odd ideas.

In speculating about the causes of postpartum illness, Marcé noted that the evolution of psychiatric symptoms seemed to follow physical changes related to the return to the nonpregnant state. He noted that some patients seemed to recover and then suffered exacerbations premenstrually. He proposed that a "connexion" must exist between the organs of generation and the mind. He gave the "connexion" a name, "sympathie morbide." Marcé's work was done a half-century before the endocrine system was outlined. Had he lived a half-century later, he would surely have identified morbid sympathy as a hormonal connection between the body and the mind.

In England, J. Webster initiated an interest and excellence at Bethlem Hospital which has continued with the work of R. Kumar today. In 1848, Webster objected to the then-current practices of bleeding and restraint and advocated sedation with opium and hemp (35). From 1875 to 1896, G. H. Savage reported continuing Bethlem studies, stressing case description and treatment and coining the term *miserable sleeplessness* to describe a common characteristic of many cases. In discussing classification and nomenclature, he said, "We have not yet got beyond what Dr. Hughlings Jackson calls the market-gardner's classification; we have not been able to form natural orders like the botanists, or at least we have not many natural orders yet. . . . We cannot classify them with any degree of precision into mania, melancholia and dementia. We shall note typical cases of each of these varieties, but I must premise by saying it is common for one to pass through all of these forms" (27, pp. 84, 89).

In the 20th century, attention to the behavior and care of patients gave way to concerns regarding the prestige of psychiatry as a "science." E. A. Strecker and F. G. Ebaugh led a troop of Americans who were determined to develop a nomenclature for all psychiatric illnesses that was free of internal inconsistencies (33). They found this difficult, but feasible if they could work out a system based on constellations of symptoms. Psychiatric illness after childbearing was an anathema, since it freely jumped from organic symptoms (confusion, delirium), to thinking disorders (delusions, dementia praecox, schizophreniform disorders), to disorders of mood (depression, mania, manic-depressive psychosis, bipolar affective disorder). The solution proposed, and enthusiastically accepted, was that the term *postpartum*, with its synonyms *puerperal* and *postnatal*, be expunged from the nomenclature of psychiatry. The success of the Strecker offensive was epitomized in the 1952 (first) edition of the *Diagnostic and Statistical Manual of Mental Disorders* published by the American Psychiatric Association (1). Psychiatric illness after childbearing, directed this official tome, must be named in such a way that the relationship to childbearing must not be indicated in the name of the illness. This position held through the DSM-III-R in 1987. With few exceptions, research and rational treatment of these cases died.

British initiative spurred a return of interest, beginning with Merton Sandler's *Mental Illness in Pregnancy and the Puerperium*, in 1978 (26). Ian Brockington, then at Manchester, called a conference on postpartum psychiatric problems in 1980. Enormous enthusiasm emerged, particularly from England, the Continent, Japan, and Australia. An international scientific organization was created, the *Marcé Society*, and research was carried out in many parts of the world. The new views were summarized in *Motherhood and Mental Illness*, an Academic Press book of 1982 by I. F. Brockington and R. Kumar (4).

Now it is possible to look at descriptions of the syndromes of postpartum illness with the benefit of information that is available regarding the physical and hormonal changes of the puerperium. Treatment, which lapsed during the dark ages of the first four-fifths of the 20th century, has begun to become rational. Leads are developing for prevention which should be particularly useful for high-risk cases. "High risk" is easily defined, since the chance of a severe psychiatric illness, 1 per 1,000 births, moves up to one per three or four births if one has had such an illness.

OUTLINE OF SYNDROMES

In the absence of an official terminology, and indeed with a near-interdiction of such adjectives as puerperal or postpartum, an unofficial jargon has grown up to designate the principal psychiatric syndromes that occur after childbearing. The syndromes are not sharply demarcated, since many cases overlap syndromes or change from one to another. Minor differences of usage occur, but those who work with these cases have, for the most part, a clear understanding of the terms used by their colleagues.

A general term for all psychiatric illness after childbearing, including a mild depressive syndrome and major psychoses, is *postpartum depression*. Carol Dix, in her excellent popular book *The New Mother Syndrome*, has shortened this to "PPD" (9). After the dark ages of most of the 20th century, when there was almost-universal ignorance of these matters, a general term like *postpartum depression* is welcome. It should not be taken to be synonymous with other uses of the word *depression*.

There are three syndromes of severe postpartum illness. The incidence of all three is equivalent to one case per 1,000 deliveries. The first is *puerperal psychosis* (5), which is characterized by agitation, confusion, insomnia, hallucinations, delusions, and violent behavior. Symptoms may change quite rapidly. They are *mercurial*. The mood may be elation or depression.

The term *puerperal* is derived from the obstetrical term *puerperium*, meaning the period during which the generative organs revert to the non-pregnant state, a time often set arbitrarily at six weeks. The term *postpartum* may have an advantage in that it has a higher recognition value, but this is not a major issue. The word *psychosis* is essential to stress the thinking disability and the associated lack of responsibility that are characteristic of this syndrome.

The second syndrome is *major postpartum depression*. This syndrome begins after the 20th day, increases slowly, and may be quite deep at the 5th or 6th week. It is more constant and less mercurial than puerperal psychosis. It is often accompanied by physical signs and symptoms: excessive fatigability, insomnia, water retention, dry skin, cold extremities, and excessive loss of hair. The mood is depressed (11).

The third severe syndrome is a combination of the first two. This is *postpartum psychotic depression*. It may begin with an earlier puerperal psychosis, or the early symptoms may be minimal or absent. However, a few weeks after delivery, the patient settles into a state of moderate to severe depression, usually with considerable confusion and with occasional gross distortions of thinking and sometimes violence. While the day-to-day behavior of these patients tends to be quite different from that of their prepregnant state, they may give the appearance of some degree of stability at a low level of adjustment. Then an episode of violent behavior, such as a suicidal attempt or violence to others, belies the apparent stability. There may be amnesia for the violent episode, or the recollection may be colored by the memory of hallucinatory material. It is important that this syndrome be called "psychotic" as well as "depressive," since the outbursts of gross psychotic behavior may not receive a proper medical or legal response if they are simply called "depressive."

The changeable, mercurial qualities of these patients, months after delivery, are less likely to be observed and reported at the present time than they were in the 19th century. In patients who are hospitalized or under medical care, the effects of neuroleptic medications tend to level off and render obscure the gross psychotic symptoms and the potentiality for violence. In patients who are not hospitalized, and with little or no medication, conscious efforts to conceal disturbed thinking may be effective and may be conducive to a diminished family alertness. Then, an episode of violence may come as a surprise.

Bernhard Pauliekhoff, at Münster, has devoted many years to the day-to-day study of the evolution of postpartum cases as they move in their symptoms with *time*, and with the involution of puerperal anatomy and physiology (22). He tries to handle his patients with a minimum of medication, using intensive nursing supervision to minimize agitation and destructive tendencies. Without much medication, he observes a phenomenon called "Amentia" in Germany. This is a state of varying degrees of confusion punctuated by occasional auditory hallucinations and transitory delusions. The delusions are dreamlike and quickly forgotten. The content of the delusions is often bizarre, and the moods vary, usually being depressive, sometimes terrorized, occasionally euphoric. There are misrepresentations of the environment, failure to identify familiar people, restlessness, wandering, episodes of violent activity, sometimes suicidal. There is usually amnesia for the delusions and the episodes of violent behavior. Recovery is gradual and requires an average of three months, sometimes much longer. After recovery, patients have little recollection of the period of Amentia.

The exact position of Amentia in relation to other syndromes is not finally determined, yet Pauliekhoff found it in 50 of 350 cases studied at Münster. Some cases of suicide or infanticide, not hospitalized and on little or no medication, appear retrospectively to have had episodes of gross psychotic behavior which, from time to time, interrupted a continuum of confusion, mild to moderate depression, and diminished cognitive capability. This would place Amentia with the broader group of postpartum psychotic depression.

Two lesser syndromes may be mentioned. The *baby blues* is a syndrome of insomnia, exhaustion, tearfulness, and sometimes transitory confusion. The time of onset is from the third to the sixth day. It occurs in one-third to one-half of all new mothers, which leads to its common consideration as a normal aspect of recovery from childbearing. It is important because puerperal psychosis is easily misdiagnosed as baby blues, at its onset (31).

The second of the lesser syndromes is *postnatal depression*. Note the slight change in language: not *postpartum*, but *postnatal*. This usage serves well to distinguish between severe illnesses and illnesses of lesser severity (18).

Postnatal depression exhibits itself as mild to moderate depression of mood, irritability, subtle changes of personality, often some physical complaints, and usually diminished sexual responsiveness. Its incidence depends on its diagnostic criteria, but a great many excellent investigators estimate its incidence in the range from 1 in 10 to 1 in 15 births. Thus, from an incidence of some rarity (the severe psychiatric illnesses that follow childbearing, the total incidence being 1 in 1,000 births), we move to a condition that can be distressing to vast numbers of women each year.

ETIOLOGY

Discussion of the cause or causes of psychiatric illness after childbearing should be preceded by this caveat: The etiology is not known with certainty. However, large numbers of studies provide a great deal of information which, as Ralph H. Paffenbarger noted, is "arranged in a tantalizing fashion, much like the pieces of a picture puzzle, partly fitted together" (21, p. 161).

Since Paffenbarger's remark, new data have appeared which suggest that the picture is coming together gradually. The etiology of postpartum illness is divided into two separate but related panels, organic and psychological factors. We begin with the organic.

From the days of Marcé, many careful observers have been impressed with the many indications of a close connection between psychological symptoms and physiological events of the puerperium. The signs of confusion and delirium, of frequent occurrence in postpartum cases, are generally associated with toxic, inflammatory, or metabolic effects on neuronal function. They are "organic" signs. Until the 20th century, however, there was little indication of the nature of the physiological mechanisms that might influence mental processes. Then, in 1910, K. Stössner reported that on Christmas day, 1906, he was called to a farm on the northern tip of the Rhineland to see a child with the measles (32).

The mother was severely depressed, dating her depression to a short time after the birth of the child. Stössner noted physical signs of thyroid deficiency, administered desiccated thyroid, and in a few weeks the woman was well. She discontinued thyroid and the symptoms returned. Resumption of the thyroid was again successful in relieving the depression. Others noted similar cases over the years. I was associated with a medical study group many years ago, and we had seen a number of cases wherein a postpartum depression had been associated with peripheral edema, diminished energy, loss of hair, and sensitivity to low temperatures. We had found "low-normal" serum thyroxine, administered thyroid, and watched the symptoms of depression disappear along with the physical evidence of a hypothyroid state (11).

There was, however, no *experimental* proof that all the signs and symptoms, physical and mental, were part of the same process. When triiodothyronine became available, this provided an opportunity to create a temporary thyroxine effect which could be programmed as a blind study, with placebos, plus self-rating of the level of depression. The ratings could be transformed into statistics which could *quantify* the study and make it an experiment. Patients with moderate depressions, not hospitalized, were used. After a few days of "experimentation" with a few patients, we received an emergency telephone call. One of the subjects was severely disturbed. She was seen immediately, the placebo code was broken, and it was learned that she had felt very encouraged after several days on triiodothyronine. Two days of the placebo had left her with a severe depression of mood. Another similar case appeared two days later. Our cavalier attempt to document the effect of thyroid in a placebo-controlled experiment, without hospital controls, was terminated hastily. To do a well-controlled study of the relationship of thyroid depletion to postpartum depression, with hospitalization of all experimental and control subjects, would have required one million dollars at that time, several million dollars now. Funds in this amount were not available then and are not available now. If funds were available, this would still be an experiment with serious human-rights questions.

Without the absolute *proof* derived from an experimental study, I have administered thyroid to over 300 postpartum depressive patients, with generally excellent results. A. A. Baker describes similar favorable results with thyroid in selected postpartum cases (2).

The rationale for the use of thyroid in postpartum cases relates to the work of Danowski, who studied serum thyroxine levels during pregnancy and for one year after childbearing. Thyroxine rises 50% above the nonpregnant level at term, drops back to the prepregnancy level at 20 days, and then coasts down to a level 18% below the prepregnancy level, where it remains for the better part of a year. These are averages, but individual records show the same trends (8).

Other endocrine parameters have been implicated. The Swiss psychiatrist V. S. Bürgi studied patients chronically ill in a public mental hospital, the onset of whose illness had been subsequent to childbearing (3). He found a high incidence of changes in hair distribution, changes in appetite reflected in marked overweight or underweight, headache, constipation, and skin and circulatory disturbances which he found similar to the physical abnormalities found in known diseases of the diencephalon. N. Hatotani and J. Nomura studied similar cases of postpartum illness which had become chronic and found a variety of deficient hormonal parameters (15).

Like the thyroid gland, the adrenal cortex was long ago suspected of involvement in psychiatric reactions subsequent to childbearing. Apart from childbearing, the hormones most clearly associated with psychosis, both in excess and in deprivation, are the adrenal corticoids and their analogs.

Ione Railton was a resident in medicine at the University of California at San Francisco in the early 1950s. This was a time of extensive use of cortisone for a wide variety of diseases. Many patients developed gross edema and other signs of toxicity, and the cortisone was discontinued. Within a very few days, many of these patients developed florid psychoses. Most of them were treated in medical wards with resumption and then gradual reduction of cortisone.

While maintaining her primary interest in medicine, Railton took a one-year fellowship on the psychiatric service in San Francisco. There, she saw several cases of postpartum psychosis, the early severe syndrome. She noted a remarkable resemblance to the cortisone-withdrawal patients she had seen on the medical wards. She consulted her endocrinology professor, Peter Forsham, and they devised an experimental program to administer prednisolone, a synthetic analog of cortisol, to the postpartum patients. Their hypothesis was that a temporary cortisol deficit might be responsible for the postpartum illness. Railton's results were excellent, and in 1961 she published the results of her observations of 16 patients treated with small doses of prednisolone, compared with 16 controls. Patients' illnesses were of moderate severity and treatment was outpatient. Experimental patients received 5 to 50 mg of prednisolone daily for three to four weeks. Control groups had equal or greater home care. The average time necessary for subsidence of moderately severe psychological symptoms in the control group was eight months. The average time for patients given prednisolone was two months (23).

This favorable report was published in the *Journal of the American Women's Medical Association* in June 1961. There was no response at all from the psychiatric profession. Railton returned to the Department of Medicine, where she continued to treat occasional postpartum patients.

The Marcé Society is a scientific organization founded after the 1980 Manchester meeting to further the study of postpartum matters. The biennial meeting of the Society was scheduled for San Francisco in the fall of 1984. Early that year I learned about Railton's paper, called her, and invited her to present her results to the Society. She did so, adding her experience with 10 more successful cases. To the best of her knowledge, no psychiatrist has ever pursued the treatment she discovered.

This has been a dreary tale, of discoveries made, of treatments described but unused by others, and of knowledge mislaid, often for many decades. One reason for this regrettable situation is that for the last half-century, few physicians believed that a real psychiatric entity could exist if its name had been amputated. Another reason is that it is difficult to see how all the stray symptoms and mechanisms hold together. It is difficult until one adds a few pieces of information from the library of obstetrical endocrinology. These bits of information may serve as mortar to bind the other information together in what may be called the hypothesis of postpartum illness and the sluggish pituitary. As this is presented remember that this is an hypothesis, not truth engraved on stone. It needs to be checked (13).

During late pregnancy, the pituitary gland is very active and produces a large amount of the hormones that stimulate the thyroid and the adrenal cortex to accelerate their hormone production. The stimulus to *pituitary* activity is the large amount of estrogen and progesterone produced mainly by the placenta. At delivery, with the loss of the placenta, estrogen and progesterone in the blood experience an enormous fall, to near zero in 24 hours. There is no overt psychological reaction to this fall. The pituitary reacts dramatically with diminished blood circulation and diminished hormone production. The thyroid and the adrenal cortex, under the control of pituitary hormones, produce less of their respective hormones, but blood levels move down slowly. This is partly because a large reservoir was built up during late pregnancy, and in the case of cortisol, because most of it is bound to a large protein molecule, transcortin (34).

The thyroxine level in the blood falls back to the prepregnancy level, passes it at about day 20, and almost always overshoots the mark. It is hypothesized that depressive symptoms after three to four weeks depend to a significant extent on this drop in serum thyroxine, which is a reflection of the sluggish postpartum pituitary.

Total cortisol is high toward the end of pregnancy and drops off a little more rapidly than thyroxine. However, an average of 90% is bound to transcortin. Only about 10% is free and active cortisol. The life-maintaining qualities of cortisol depend on this 10%, which, in turn, probably reflects mainly newly secreted cortisol from the adrenal cortex. The stimulus for new cortisol production is ACTH from the pituitary, and the pituitary is *sluggish*.

The 10% of free cortisol in the serum is only an average. This percent decreases as it is metabolized, used, or excreted and then increases in response to stimulation by ACTH. A very powerful sensor for cortisol is located in a small area in the hypothalamus, a part of the diencephalon just over the pituitary. When cortisol becomes low, the sensor in the hypothalamus stimulates the pituitary to produce ACTH. But in the postpartum state, the sluggish pituitary may respond weakly or not at all. The hypothesis is that repeated unsuccessful firing of the hypothalamic center leads to increased intensity of firing, and that this activates nearby areas which control the autonomic nervous system. This generates the bodily responses and sensations of anxiety and terror which are characteristic of early puerperal psychosis. The *mercurial* quality of early puerperal psychosis, the later postpartum psychotic depression, and the syndrome of Amentia are attributable to spurts or lags in ACTH production which are reflected in adequate and then deficient supplies of free cortisol. The confusion and the hallucinations may be the result of cortisol deficit acting directly on brain cells.

The hypothesis of the sluggish pituitary, therefore, is that many postpartum psychiatric symptoms are attributable to deficits in pituitary trophic hormones, mainly ACTH and thyrotropic hormone. The early, strange somatic sensations which are characteristic of puerperal psychosis, and which are interpreted as "unreasonable" anxiety or terror, may be caused by overstimulation of the sensor for cortisol deficit located in the hypothalamus. Since proper neuronal action depends on cortisol, the confusion and hallucinations may be a direct action of cortisol deficit. Depressive syndromes that appear later may reflect a relative thyroid deficit.

A remarkable parallel in symptomatology has been observed in postpartum hypopituitarism, or Sheehan's Syndrome, and severe postpartum psychiatric illness. Sheehan's Syndrome is a disorder in which pituitary failure after childbearing, with destruction of large numbers of pituitary secretory cells, causes permanent loss of ACTH and thyrotropic hormone, plus many physical *and* psychiatric disturbances. Studied by Professor H. L. Sheehan and many Liverpool associates, the psychiatric symptoms have many resemblances to those seen in postpartum psychiatric illness, but in Sheehan's Syndrome, the symptoms continue indefinitely. However, lifelong treatment with cortisone and thyroxine relieves the psychiatric symptoms and also much of the physical disability of Sheehan's Syndrome. Most of the symptoms seen in postpartum psychiatric cases are relieved or improve markedly after a few weeks or months (28, 29).

The foregoing hypothesis relates to the physiological components of postpartum psychiatric reactions. Equally important, and just as unique, are the psychological stresses that impinge on the new mother who has these symptoms. This is the typical story: During pregnancy, a woman puts up with a certain amount of discomfort. At delivery there may be much fear and much pain. A few hours later she may be fairly comfortable. The following day (day 1), she feels fine. She feels fine on day 2 and is anxious to be up and about, to take care of her child. She receives the admiration of her family and friends, she sees that the child is well. Some time later, days 3 to 14, probably because her free cortisol runs low and the sensor in the hypothalamus fires vigorously, her autonomic nervous system reacts and she feels intense panic. Why? She is confused. Fearfully, she searches for reasons. The doctor comes by, says the temperature is normal, no infection, not to worry. She is confused. People do not look normal. Her husband may be a stranger. The baby is abnormal, not hers. She cannot sleep. Hour after hour, day after day, attacks of meaningless terror occur, again and again. The stress is intolerable. And there is no reason for this.

Then suddenly she has an idea. She is not a good mother. This was all a mistake. She should never have had the child. Now it is too late. Depression. The dilemma is solved, but she has a terrible solution.

Or another idea, compounded of exhaustion, confusion, delirium, hallucinations. The baby is evil. The baby is a devil. The baby must be destroyed, destroyed to save us all.

Severe postpartum depressions, unless they are initiated by a puerperal psychosis, develop slowly, after the first three weeks. Exhaustion and insomnia are often the first symptoms, followed by depression of mood. Because there are no obvious physical symptoms, the patient develops self-derogatory explanatory hypotheses, as with the earlier syndrome, but she develops them more slowly.

The ailing new mother often pursues a vigorous search of her past history to look for explanations for her present predicament. Mistakes she made, peccadilloes, sins, fears—all are reviewed for their possible relevance to her present predicament. Often, a sexual transgression or irregularity, real or imagined, is seized upon as an explanation.

The careful observers of the 19th century also searched for such explanations and came up empty-handed. One early statement on the relevance of past traumatic events is that of E. P. Christian, in 1889 (6). "In my own cases, no moral cause was alleged or suggested by the recovered patients, or by friends. . . . Any emotional experience . . . might easily be believed to have been the cause, by one seeking it. When a cause is eagerly sought for, on the *post hoc, ergo propter hoc* reasoning, any emotional experience is resurrected from the forgotten past to serve the purpose" (p. 456).

My own clinical experience is in agreement with that of Christian. Ralph Paffenbarger's analysis of 126 hospital cases, the most statistically refined study in the literature, failed to identify any indications of important prepregnancy psychological predisposition (21). We believe that severe postpartum illness strikes indiscriminately, with the only important psychological predisposing factor the occurrence of a previous postpartum episode.

Contrary opinions have emerged from studies based on serial samples of patients from obstetrical services. Typical is the study of Bonnie Saks *et al.*, whose subjects were 20 unselected obstetrical patients (25). Questionnaire and some interview data were obtained during pregnancy and postpartum. On the basis of test scores, the group of 20 was split in half, the high-scoring half then being called "depressed." Comparison of test scores of the two groups revealed that the "depressed" group had higher pregnancy scores on "loneliness," "inward-directed anger," "shyness," and similar test variables.

An initial comment on this is that the population of a random sample of 20 women from an obstetrical service is hardly one from which to derive information regarding an illness that occurs once in 1,000 births. The chance of even one severe reaction among the 20 cases studied is 1 in 50.

The assumption that the studied population can derive information regarding clinical cases of depression has not been established.

A more grave possibility is that of a statistical fallacy. The group is separated on the basis of a test, wherein the measurement involves the inclination to say "Yes" to a question regarding a presumed depressive indicator. Then the subgroups are compared with regard to what they answered earlier, to answers to the same or similar questions. The question arises as to whether the criterion of separation was contaminated with the same items, or the same kind of items, as those from which conclusions about "depression" are made. In other words, could this study have simply proved that normal women who have or admit to neurotic traits during pregnancy tend to have or admit to having the same traits after they have a child?

TREATMENT AND PREVENTION

The first meeting between a physician and a patient who may have a serious postpartum reaction imposes some special requirements on the physician. The first of these is that there may be a need for an immediate decision regarding hospitalization. To help in making this decision and implementing an affirmative decision, a conference with one or more family members prior to seeing the patient may be helpful.

The initial meeting with the patient has important implications for psychological management of the case. If the physician concentrates on details of the present illness and avoids or plays down sensitive areas in the past history, the patient is encouraged to avoid rumination about disturbing past events. From my first experiences with these cases, it was my belief that they were organically determined, and my blunt statement of this, toward the end of the first interview, seemed to have a favorable psychological effect. In this interview, the painfulness of the symptoms should not be minimized, but a favorable outcome can and should be predicted. The physician who appears to be knowledgeable and decisive has an initial advantage (14).

Support groups, consisting of former patients who have personal acquaintance with postpartum illness, perform a service of enormous value. The support group member is often the first knowledgeable person contacted, usually on the Warm Line telephone. "Oh, yes, you probably have PPD. I have had it and it is awful. Can you come over and see me right now?" These may be the most important words the patient has ever heard, or will hear (16).*

Treatment with pharmacological agents is not a matter of general agreement, except for the fact that a low to moderate dose of a phenothiazine (75 mg chlorpromazine in divided doses) is a good base. Although tricyclic antidepressants are widely used, some of the most able therapists believe that they may be counterproductive. There is less objection to MAO inhibitors. My own practice was to place considerable reliance on sedatives with short half-lives, such as the barbiturates, for use as needed, thereby encouraging lucid and clear periods to facilitate communication, both with the physician and with members of a specially trained hospital staff. It is important to know the trend of thinking or the nature of hallucinations in these cases. We demonstrated real interest in sleep, and the term "bad dreams" elicited this kind of material without trauma. In a hospital with other postpartum patients, the presence of those who go home is very therapeutic. The British initiative of Mother and Baby Units has a very positive psychological effect on patients (20).

Electroshock therapy (electropexy) has an important role in the treatment of some patients. I used it for those patients whose cognitive processes were still disturbed six to eight weeks after delivery, less than 5% of hospitalized patients. It was very effective. We did not use it earlier than six weeks after delivery because of an unwarranted fear that blood clots could be dislodged. Sneddon and Kerry report that it is effective in delirium and severe puerperal psychosis much earlier in the puerperium; they use it in 15% of all cases (30).

The use of specific medication depends on the physician's experience and theoretical orientation. I became alerted early on to suspect a relative thyroid deficit in depressed cases after three to four weeks. Low-normal serum thyroxine plus symptoms sufficed for a trial, beginning with a half-grain of thyroid, which was monitored. This was done with several hundred patients with what appeared to be good results and no instances of known thyroid toxicity.

My knowledge of Railton's work came after I discontinued taking primary responsibility for patients, so I never used prednisolone. Her reported

*For information regarding support organizations, or the International Postpartum Support Network, contact Ms. Claire Delpech, Inst. of Obs. and Gynaec., Queen Charlotte's Hosp., London; Ms. Jane Honikman, Santa Barbara Birth Resource Center, 2255 Modoc Rd., Santa Barbara, CA 93101; or Ms. Nancy Berchtold, Depression after Delivery, PO Box 1282, Morrisville, PA 19067.

results correspond to what I would anticipate on theoretical grounds. However, the use of an analog of cortisol is fraught with some hazards, especially in hands unfamiliar with the possibility of iatrogenic adrenal suppression. Nevertheless, Railton's work could be a major lead to the elimination of postpartum psychiatric illness, and it must not be disregarded. Currently, we are working with the U.S. Food and Drug Administration to set up a protocol for verification of her findings safely.

Prevention of postpartum psychiatric illness is mainly a matter of reducing hazards in high-risk women, i.e., those with a history of a former episode. Most of this has centered on efforts to cushion the drop in estrogen and progesterone which seems to initiate adverse changes. I saw experimental work on lactation suppression wherein estrogen in oil was administered at delivery. I was told that an incidental observation was marked reduction in the incidence of baby blues. In desperate need of a preventive, I gave estrogen in oil at delivery followed by a few days of oral estrogen (12). Forty high-risk patients have been treated without a single recurrence. Dalton administered parenteral progesterone at delivery and for a month thereafter to patients who had had prior reactions and reported favorable results (7). Ryan, clearly working at another level of the chemistry of the illness, reported effective prevention with 50 mg of pyridoxine beginning at delivery and continuing for two months (24).

The foregoing reports of specific treatment and prevention all appear encouraging, but at the present time, nothing about specific treatment or prevention has been *proven*. Despite a resurgence of interest since 1980, the pace of research is agonizingly slow. These questions remain: what levels of proof must be demanded, what levels can we get, when can we get them, and what policy serves the best interests and wishes of those who suffer from psychiatric illness after childbearing?

REFERENCES

1. American Psychiatric Association (1952, 1980, 1987). *Diagnostic and statistical manual* (1952); DSM-III (1980); DSM-III-R (1987). Washington, DC: American Psychiatric Press.
2. Baker, A. A. (1967). *Psychiatric disorders in obstetrics*. Oxford: Blackwell.
3. Bürgi, V. S. (1954). Puerperalpsychose oder Diencephalosis puerperalis? *Schweiz. med. Wchnschr.*, *84*, 1222.
4. Brockington, I. F., & Kumar, R. (1982). *Motherhood and mental illness*. London: Academic Press.
5. Brockington, I. F., Winokur, G., & Dean, C. (1982). Puerperal psychoses. In Brockington & Kumar (4).
6. Christian, E. P. (1889). What is puerperal mania, and what constitutes puerperal insanity? *Ann. Gynaecol.*, *2*, 449–457.

7. DALTON, K. (1984). *The premenstrual syndrome and progesterone therapy* (2nd ed.). London: Heinemann. Also Report to Marcé Society, San Francisco, 1984.
8. DANOWSKI, T. S., HUFF, S. J., & MRVOS, D., et al. (1953). Is pregnancy followed by relative hypothyroidism? *Am. J. Obstet. Gynecol., 65*, 77–80.
9. DIX, CAROL (1985). *The new mother syndrome*. Garden City, NY: Doubleday.
10. ESQUIROL, J. E. D. (1838). Des Maladies mentales considérées sous les rapports medical, hygiénique et médico-legal. Paris: Baillière.
11. HAMILTON, J. A. (1962). *Postpartum psychiatric problems*. St. Louis: Mosby.
12. HAMILTON, J. A. (1977). Puerperal psychoses. In *Gynecology and Obstetrics* (Chap. 24). New York: Harper & Row.
13. HAMILTON, J. A. (1982). Model utility in postpartum psychosis. *Psychopharmacol. Bull., 18*, 184.
14. HAMILTON, J. A. (1985). Guidelines for therapeutic management of postpartum disorders. In D. G. Inwood (Ed.), *Postpartum psychiatric disorders* (Chap. 5). Washington, DC: American Psychiatric Press.
15. HATOTANI, N., & NOMURA, J. (1983). Clinoendocrine studies of postpartum psychoses. In *Neurobiology of periodic psychoses* (Chap. 6). Tokyo: Igaku-Shoin.
16. HONIKMAN, J. (1987). How to start a parents' organization. In Z. Boukydis (Ed.), *Support for parents and infants*. New York: Methuen.
17. INWOOD, D. (1985). *Postpartum psychiatric disorders*. Washington, DC: American Psychiatric Press.
18. KUMAR, R. (1982). Neurotic disorders in childbearing women. In Brockington & Kumar (4, Chap. 4).
19. MARCÉ, L. V. (1858). *Traité de la folie des femmes enceintes, des nouvelles accouchées et des nourrices*. Paris: Baillière.
20. MARGISON, F., & BROCKINGTON, I. F. (1982). Psychiatric Mother and Baby Units. In Brockington & Kumar (4, Chap. 8).
21. PAFFENBARGER, R. (1961). The picture puzzle of the postpartum psychoses. *J. Chronic. Dis., 13*, 161–173.
22. PAULIEKHOFF, B. (1964, 1984). Seelische Störungen in der Schwangerschaft und nach der Geburt. Stuttgart: Enke Verlag. Also, Address of the distinguished scholar (1984). San Francisco: Marcé Society.
23. RAILTON, I. (1961, 1984). The use of corticoids in postpartum depression. *J. Am. Med. Women's Assoc., 16*, 450. Also, The use of prednisolone for postpartum psychiatric symptoms (1984). San Francisco: Marcé Society.
24. RYAN, D. (1984). Premenstrual syndrome, postpartum depressive symptoms, and pyridoxine hydrochloride prophylaxis. San Francisco: Marcé Society.
25. SAKS, B. R., FRANK, J. B., & LOWE, T. L., et al. (1985). Depressed mood during pregnancy and the puerperium: Clinical recognition and implications for clinical practice. *Am. J. Psychiatry, 142*, 728.
26. SANDLER, M. (1978). *Mental illness in pregnancy and the puerperium*. London: Oxford Press.
27. SAVAGE, G. H. (1875). Observations on the insanity of pregnancy and childbirth. *Guy's Hosp. Rep., 20*, 83–117.
28. SHEEHAN, H. L., & SUMMERS, U. K. (1960). The syndrome of hypopituitarism. *Q. J. Med., 18*, 319.
29. SHEEHAN, H. L., & DAVIS, J. C. (1982). *Post-partum hypopituitarism*. Springfield, IL: Charles C Thomas.
30. SNEDDON, J., & KERRY, R. J. (1985). The psychiatric Mother and Baby Unit: A five-year study. In Inwood (17, Chap. 6).
31. STEIN, G. (1982). The maternity blues. In Brockington & Kumar (4, Chap. 5).
32. STÖSSNER, K. (1910). Ein Fall von Myxödem im Anschluss an Gravidität. *München. med. Wchnschr., 57*, 2531.

33. Strecker, E. A., & Ebaugh, F. G. (1926). Psychoses occurring during the puerperium. *Arch. Neurol. Psychiatry*, *15*, 239.
34. Tulchinsky, D. (1980). The postpartum period. In Tulchinsky, D., & Ryan, K. J.: *Maternal-fetal endocrinology* (Chap. 9). Philadelphia: Saunders.
35. Webster, J. (1848). Remarks on the statistics, pathology and treatment of puerperal insanity. *Lancet*, 2, 611.

16

MANIA: CLINICAL MANIFESTATIONS AND ASSESSMENT

EDWARD G. ALTMAN, PSY.D.,
PHILIP G. JANICAK, M.D.,
and
JOHN M. DAVIS, M.D.
Illinois State Psychiatric Institute
Chicago, Illinois

INTRODUCTION: THE SYNDROME OF MANIA

Mania is not synonymous with euphoria and elation, but rather refers to a syndrome with a characteristic constellation of signs and symptoms. The syndrome of mania can occur in a wide variety of disorders, and its core features involve aberrations in three primary areas: mood, behavior, and thought. Tyrer and Shopsin (16) have described and listed all possible symptoms, and Table 1 summarizes these key clinical phenomena.

The essential feature of mania is a distinct period of an elevated, expansive, or irritable mood accompanied by several other symptoms. These may include hyperactivity, pressure of speech, flight of ideas, inflated self-esteem, decreased need for sleep, distractibility, and excessive involvement in activities that have a high potential for painful consequences. An elevated mood may be described initially as unusually good, happy, or cheerful, and later as euphoric or elated. Manic patients are often in a playful or festive mood, and their gaiety may be infectious. Although the patient is unaware of his or her changing mood, it is often recognized as excessive by those who know the patient well. The elevated mood has an expansive

Table 1
Core Symptoms of a Manic Syndrome

1. Affect	Humorous, euphoric Irritability and anger Poor impulse control Disinhibited Heightened sensory impressions
2. Behavior	Increased energy Decreased sleep Pressure of speech Increased social contact Sexual overactivity Excessive financial spending
3. Cognition	Poor judgment; unrealistic planning Distractibility Litigious Flight of ideas Grandiose ideas and delusions

quality characterized by a tendency to become indiscriminately involved with people and aspects of the environment. Mood may become so expansive that some develop delusional notions about their own power and self-importance. Although an elevated mood is the prototypical symptom, the predominant disturbance may be irritability, which is most evident when the individual is thwarted in goal-directed behavior. Indeed the clinical picture can suddenly change, with the euphoric mood quickly replaced by anger and irritability. Since manic patients can be acutely sensitive to criticism, they may become contentious and easily angered, even by seemingly harmless remarks. Verbal abuse is frequent, with physical violence occurring less commonly.

An accelerated pace of psychomotor activity often accompanies mood changes. Almost invariably there is increased sociability, typically including efforts to renew old acquaintances and quick changes from one activity to another. Often sexual interest is inappropriately increased. Because of inflated self-esteem, unwarranted optimism, and poor judgment, the patient may engage in buying sprees, reckless driving, or foolish business investments. This hyperactivity may have a disorganized, flamboyant, and even bizarre quality (e.g., wearing brightly colored or strange garments or excessive or distasteful makeup). On the other hand, many patients demonstrate a marked tendency to neglect themselves (e.g., careless or insufficient dress, poor grooming, seeming indifference to physical health, and lack of concern with personal appearance).

Another cardinal feature is disturbance in speech, which can be loud, rapid, and often difficult to interrupt. The manic frequently jokes, puns, and engages in word play and droll irrelevancies. If mood is euphoric, speech often takes on a theatrical or dramatic flair. As the activity level of the manic patient increases, associations may loosen, and speech can become totally incoherent and indistinguishable from an acute schizophrenic exacerbation. If mood is more irritable than expansive, speech will more likely include complaints, hostile comments, and angry tirades.

Another common characteristic is flight of ideas. This is an almost continuous flow of accelerated speech with abrupt changes from topic to topic, at times so pronounced that it becomes disorganized and incomprehensible. These ideas are usually based on understandable associations, distracting stimuli, or plays on words.

Distractibility is common and manifested by rapid changes in speech or activity. This is a result of the patient's tendency to respond to various irrelevant external stimuli, such as background noises or objects.

Inflated self-esteem may range from uncritical self-confidence to marked grandiosity, often of delusional proportions. Patients may give advice on matters for which they are untrained and about which they have no special knowledge. Despite average talents, they may boast of extraordinary abilities, often leading to unrealistic beliefs (e.g., that they can compose music, write poetry, publish books, or design new inventions). Grandiose delusions usually involve belief in a special relationship to God or some well-known figure from the political, religious, or entertainment world.

Invariably there is a decreased need for sleep, with early awakening by several hours or a significant decrease in total sleep time. When the disturbance is severe, the patient may go for days without sleep and not feel fatigued.

ASSOCIATED SYMPTOMS OF THE MANIC SYNDROME

Lability of affect is a commonly associated clinical feature, characterized by rapid shifts from euphoria to anger or depression. Depressive symptoms (i.e., tearfulness, suicidal threats, insomnia, etc.) may last moments, hours, or, more rarely, days. Occasionally, depressive and manic symptoms intermingle or may alternate rapidly within a few days. Classic psychotic symptoms, such as delusions and hallucinations, may be present in more severe episodes and are primarily mood-congruent. However, studies on the phenomenology of mania suggest that mood-congruency may not always be necessary. Pope and Lipinski's (12) report found that "schizophrenic" symptoms were present in 20 to 50% of manic patients and that many of the delusions were mood-incongruent (i.e., delusions of persecution, catatonic symptoms, formal thought disorder, and auditory hallucinations not consistent with the mood state). In addition, Schneiderian first-rank symptoms, originally thought to be pathognomonic of schizophrenia, have been reported in 8 to 23% of manic cases (7, 14). While the DSM-III-R distinguishes between psychotic features that are either mood-congruent or mood-incongruent, the usefulness of this distinction remains controversial.

The delusions seen in mania often have a religious, sexual, or persecutory theme. Persecutory delusions (15) may be based on the idea that the individual is singled out because of some special relationship or attribute. Hallucinations may be vivid, visual (i.e., seeing God, brightly-colored flowers), and consistent with the patient's mood (6).

In addition to manifesting specific clinical symptoms during an active phase of their illness, patients may also display certain interpersonal styles that fluctuate with the course of their illness. Janowsky et al. (9) demonstrated that manic patients have a characteristic interactional style which clearly distinguishes them from schizoaffective and schizophrenic patients. They developed the Manic Interpersonal Interaction Scale to assess changes in personality style and found these patients more likely to evoke anger from staff, project responsibility onto others, attempt to divide staff through manipulative behavior, test limits, and exploit or attack others' vulnerabilities. The authors concluded that such behaviors are not attributable to one's premorbid personality, but, rather, are as characteristic of mania as are the classic short-term symptom changes (i.e., euphoria, flight of ideas, overtalkativeness, and grandiosity). They suggested that what is unique in acute mania is a change in the pattern of interpersonal interactions that fluctuates dramatically with the phases of the illness. They also reported that when manic patients were treated with lithium, this style of behavior disappeared.

DIAGNOSIS OF MANIA

When diagnosing a bipolar disorder, manic phase, it is important to consider precipitating causes in a patient with no prior history of a mania. For example, maniclike syndromes have been reported in a variety of organic mental disorders, precipitated by such diverse problems as metabolic derangements, endocrine disturbances, and drugs such as amphetamines, cocaine, and phencyclidine (2). Clearly, the diagnosis of mania should not be made if the syndrome can be explained by a known organic cause.

In the United States, the RDC (13) and the DSM-III-R (1) both provide clear inclusion and exclusion criteria for a current episode (see Table 2). Evaluation of past episodes can be made using the Schedule for Affective Disorders and Schizophrenia—Lifetime Version (SADS-L) (8). In other countries, the Present State Exam (PSE) (17) can reliably distinguish mania from other disorders. While these instruments are primarily concerned with determining the presence or absence of symptoms, they are not usually appropriate for assessing the severity of a manic episode. This requires more refined measures to assess the degree of mania once a proper diagnosis has been established.

RATING SCALES FOR MANIA

In the last two decades, a number of manic rating scales have been developed to assess the presence and severity of symptoms in various clinical settings. Prior to this, studies had employed only global ratings which were simply not sensitive enough to detect differences in response to more effective drugs. The first valid and reliable instrument was the Manic State Rating Scale (MS) designed by Beigel et al. (4), which consists of 26 items intended for use by nursing staff. Each item on the scale is rated for frequency (0 to 5) and intensity (1 to 5), and the item score is the product of these two ratings. This scale has since been refined and modified by others (5, 10). One of its major advantages is that patients can be rated over a period of time even when not directly observed. This is important since mildly manic patients can control their behavior in a structured interview, whereas ward activity may be much more representative of their true mental and behavioral state. Some disadvantages include a lengthy period to administer the scale, item redundancy, and the absence of a core feature of mania (i.e., sleep disturbance).

Murphy et al. (10) subsequently demonstrated that a subscale of 11 items from the original 26-item MS correlated significantly with two global ratings of mania; the first was the total MS scale score ($r = .84$, $p < .001$), and the second a 15-point global rating done separately by two psychiatrists ($r = .73$, $p < .01$). These items were considered by the authors not only to best characterize the elements common to mania, but also to represent the most valid indicators of severity in a given patient (see Table 3).

The Manic State Rating Scale (MS) has also been modified by Blackburn et al. (5). Their scale includes five additional items and some of the origi-

Table 2
A Comparison of DSM-III-R and RDC Criteria for Mania

DSM-III-R (1987)	RDC (1985 Update)
A. Distinct period of elevated/irritable mood	A. Distinct period of elevated/irritable mood
B. At least 3 of the following for elevated mood, 4 for irritable mood: (1) Increased self-esteem/grandiosity (2) Decreased need for sleep (3) More talkative or pressure of speech (4) Flight of ideas or racing thoughts (5) Distractibility (6) Increased goal-directed activity/agitation (7) Excessive involvement in activities	B. At least 3 of the following for elevated mood, 4 for irritable mood: (1) More active or physically restless (2) More talkative or pressure of speech (3) Flight of ideas or racing thoughts (4) Inflated self-esteem/grandiosity (5) Decreased need for sleep (6) Distractibility (7) Excessive involvement in activities
C. Marked impairment in social/occupational functioning or hospitalization	C. At least one of the following: (1) Meaningful conversation not possible (2) Serious impairment at home, work, or socially (3) Hospitalization
D. Delusions and/or hallucinations have not been present for as long as two weeks in the absence of prominent mood symptoms	D. Duration of manic features at least one week
E. Not superimposed on schizophrenia, schizophreniform disorder, delusional disorder, or psychotic disorder F. Not attributable to a known organic factor (Note: DSM-III-R also distinguishes between psychotic features which are mood-congruent or mood-incongruent.)	E. None of the following is present: (1) Delusions of control, insertion, withdrawal, thought broadcasting (2) Nonaffective hallucinations throughout the day or intermittently for one week (3) Auditory hallucinations commenting on person's thoughts/actions or two or more voices converse with each other (4) Had delusions/hallucinations for one week in absence of manic/depressive symptoms (5) Had marked thought disorder with either blunted/inappropriate affect, delusions/hallucinations, or grossly disorganized behavior for at least one week in absence of manic symptoms

Table 3
Comparison of Manic Rating Scalcs by Core Clinical Manifestations

Clinical Manifestations	Rating Scales				
	MS scale (4)	Petterson et al. (11)	MMS Scale (5)	[Y]MRS (18)	MRS (3)
Affective	Looks depressed Is irritable* Verbalizes depression Is angry* Verbalizes well-being	Elevated mood	Is depressed Is irritable Is labile Is angry Verbalizes well-being	Elevated mood Irritability	Mood
Behavioral	Is talking* Increased motor activity* Makes threats Inappropriate dress Looks happy/cheerful Seeks out others Combative/destructive Is active* Is argumentative* Talks about sex Careless dress Decreased impulse control* Demands contact* Sexually preoccupied	Pressure of speech Increased motor activity Noisiness Aggressiveness Global rating Global change	Is talking Restlessness Makes threats Looks happy/cheerful Seeks out others Is active Has disturbed sleep Careless dress Decreased impulse control Is disinhibited Demands contact Sexually preoccupied	Increased activity/energy Disruptive/aggressive Sleep disturbance Increased sexual interest Appearance Increase speech	Activity (motor) Activity (verbal) Voice/noise level Hostility/destructiveness Contact Sleep Activity (sexual) Activity (work and interests)

Cognitive	Poor judgment* Is distractible* Has grandiose ideas Is delusional Is suspicious Unrealistic plans Jumps from topic to topic*	Orientation Flight of ideas	Poor judgment Is distractible Has grandiose ideas Has grandiose delusions Is hallucinating Has persecutory delusions Flight of ideas Is religious Is suspicious Unrealistic plans Jumps from topic to topic	Insight Thought content Language/thought disorder	Flight of thoughts Self-esteem

*These items comprise a subscale from the MS Scale and are the most valid indicators of severity (10).

nal ones have been condensed. The items are scored on a 0-to-5-point scale based on severity. Although the resulting Modified Manic State Rating Scale (MMS) is carefully defined, its reliability and validity are not as high as the MS, perhaps owing to the increased number of items. While it is the most comprehensive of all the scales, several items appear redundant (e.g., grandiosity, poor impulse control, delusions) and may inflate the overall score.

Petterson and her colleagues (11) designed a rating scale that can be administered during a clinical interview. This scale is shorter and more explicit than the MS and correlates well with global manic ratings. The nine items are scored on a scale of 1 to 5 based on degree of severity. There are several shortcomings with this scale, including: (1) too few items; (2) the absence of relevant features (e.g., sleep, grandiosity); and (3) inclusion of a less relevant feature (i.e., orientation).

The Mania Rating Scale (MRS) described by Young et al. (18) consists of 11 items, most of which are rated on a scale of 0 (absent) to 4 (severe) during a 30-minute clinical interview. Each item was defined in a glossary and reliability was quite acceptable ($r=.93$) even when administered by an untrained group of psychiatric residents. The 11 items in this scale are fairly distinct and allow for a wide range of symptoms to be rated.

Finally, Bech et al. (3) developed a different, yet similarly named, Mania Rating Scale (MRS), which contains 11 items rated on a five-point scale of 0 (normal) to 4 (extreme). Since the authors were interested in rating both poles of the affective spectrum (mania and depression), they report correlations of the MRS with the seven-item Hamilton Rating Scale (0.80 to 0.95). They did not, however, report any attempts to correlate the MRS with other existing mania rating scales. While their scale does include ratings for symptoms common to mania, four of the 11 items (36%) are devoted to activity level alone (i.e., motor, verbal, sexual, work, and interests), and there are no items rating other important symptoms such as psychotic symptoms (hallucinations and delusions) and distractibility. Most of the 11 items are behavioral manifestations and only one item rates affective manifestations.

The choice of rating scale depends on the circumstances as well as the available raters. If skilled nursing raters are available, either the MS or MMS should suffice; however, with less experienced staff and in outpatient settings, the modified MS or the MRS would be preferable since they are more easily learned and administered.

CONCLUSION

In summary, it is first important to emphasize the universality of the syndrome of mania whose symptoms can overlap other illnesses, including organic affective, schizoaffective, and schizophreniform disorders. Second, the diagnosis of a bipolar disorder, manic phase, includes clearly defined inclusion and exclusion criteria which help differentiate among these overlapping disorders. Third, the recent development of clinician-administered rating scales helps to assess not only the presence or absence of symptoms and specific diagnostic criteria, but also severity of an episode. Fourth, unlike reliable self-rating scales for depression (e.g., those of Zung, Beck, Carroll), there are no such presently acceptable scales for mania.

As our concept of what constitutes mania as a diagnosis evolves, elaboration and refinement of both rater and self-administered scales should help improve diagnosis, as well as assessment of response to standard and novel treatments for mania.

REFERENCES

1. American Psychiatric Association (1987). *Diagnostic and statistical manual of mental disorders* (3rd ed., Revised) Washington, DC: Author.
2. Angrist, B., & Sudilovsky, A. (1978). CNS stimulants: Historical and clinical aspects. In I. Iverson, S. Iverson, & S. Snyder (Eds.), *Handbook of psychopharmacology*, Vol. 11 (pp. 99–165). New York: Plenum.
3. Bech, P., Rafaelsen, O. J., Kramp, P., & Bolwig, T. G. (1978). The mania rating scale: Scale construction and inter-observer agreement. *Neuropharmacology, 17*, 430.
4. Beigel, A., Murphy, D. L., & Bunney, N. E. (1971). The manic state rating scale. *Archives of General Psychiatry, 25*, 256.
5. Blackburn, I. M., Loudon, J. B., & Ashworth, C. M. (1977). A new scale for measuring mania. *Psychological Medicine, 6*, 453.
6. Carlson, G. A., & Goodwin, F. K. (1973). The stages of mania: A longitudinal analysis of the manic episode. *Archives of General Psychiatry, 28*, 221.
7. Carpenter, W. T., Strauss, J. S., & Muleh, S. (1973). Are there pathognomonic symptoms in schizophrenia? An empiric investigation of schneider's first-rank symptoms. *Archives of General Psychiatry, 28*, 847.
8. Endicott, J., & Spitzer, R. L. (1978). A diagnostic interview: The schedule for affective disorders and schizophrenia. *Archives of General Psychiatry, 35*, 837.
9. Janowsky, D. S., El Yousef, A., & Davis, J. M. (1974). Interpersonal maneuvers of manic patients. *American Journal of Psychiatry, 131*, 250.
10. Murphy, D. L., Beigel, A., Weingartner, H., & Bunney, W. E. (1974). The quantitation of manic behavior. In P. Pichot (Ed.), *Psychological measurements in psychopharmacology*. Mod. Probl. Pharmacopsychiat, Vol. 7 (pp. 203–220). Paris: Karger-Basel.
11. Petterson, U., Fyro, B., & Sedvall, G. (1973). A new scale for the longitudinal rating of manic states. *Acta Psychiatrica Scandinavica, 49*, 248.

12. Pope, H., & Lipinski, J. (1978). Differential diagnosis of schizophrenia and manic depressive illness: A reassessment of the specificity of 'schizophrenia' symptoms in the light of current research. *Archives of General Psychiatry, 35*, 811.
13. Spitzer, R. L., Endicott, J., & Robins, E. (1978). Research diagnostic criteria: Rational and reliability. *Archives of General Psychiatry, 35*, 773.
14. Taylor, M. A., & Abrams, R. (1973). The phenomenology of mania. A new look at some old patients. *Archives of General Psychiatry, 29*, 520.
15. Taylor, M. A., & Abrams, R. (1975). Acute mania: Clinical and genetic study of responders and nonresponders to treatments. *Archives of General Psychiatry, 32*, 863.
16. Tyrer, S., & Shopsin, B. (1982). Symptoms and assessment of mania. In E. S. Paykel (Ed.), *Handbook of affective disorders* (pp. 2–23). New York: Guilford Press.
17. Wing, J. K., Cooper, J. E., & Sartorius, N. (1974). *Description and classification of psychiatric symptoms*. Cambridge: Cambridge University Press.
18. Young, R. C., Biggs, J. T., Ziegler, V., & Meyer, D. A. (1978). A rating scale for mania: Reliability, validity, and sensitivity. *British Journal of Psychiatry, 133*, 429.

17
PREVENTION OF AFFECTIVE DISORDERS

L. J. Schmidt, M.D.

Associate Professor of Psychiatry,
Director of Adult Services
Western Institute of Neuropsychiatry
University of Utah School of Medicine
Salt Lake City, Utah

and

Michael R. Lowry, M.D.

Associate Clinical Professor of Psychiatry,
Medical Director, Mood Disorders Clinic, Wasatch Canyons Hospital,
University of Utah School of Medicine
Salt Lake City, Utah

INTRODUCTION

Any discussion of prevention must clearly detail *what it is we hope to prevent*. We shall review the prevention of affective disorders. The revised third edition of the *Diagnostic and Statistical Manual of Mental Disorders* published by the American Psychiatric Association (DSM-III-R) renames these disorders as mood disorders. "Mood" is considered a more descriptive and technically correct term. The terms will be used interchangeably throughout this discussion. The criterion-based DSM-III system has con-

The authors gratefully acknowledge Samuel G. Schmidt for his research assistance, and Fran Hunter and Glenda Collett for their help in preparing the manuscript.

tributed substantially to reducing the diagnostic imprecision for these disorders.

TYPES OF PREVENTION

The most common view of prevention involves stopping a problem before it gets started. This is called *primary prevention*. Technically, primary prevention is a reduction of the incidence (or occurrence) of new cases of a disorder in the population. The most effective examples of primary prevention in psychiatry lie in the field of infectious diseases (e.g., tertiary syphilis) and the correction of psychotic states resulting from nutritional disturbances (e.g., pellagra).

When there is a reduction of the duration of the disorder, this is called *secondary prevention*. In this instance, the prevalence (i.e., the number of persons in a population suffering from the disorder at any point in time) is diminished. Accurate diagnostic and treatment methods are the basis for this type of prevention.

Some disorders cause permanent impairments; others contribute to secondary effects which require adaptation. *Tertiary prevention* reduces the limitations of these impairments and may often involve strategies of rehabilitation.

PRIMARY PREVENTION OF AFFECTIVE DISORDERS

Our current knowledge of the etiology of affective disorder remains incomplete and our ability to identify individuals at high risk is at best limited. *There are no published studies in the scientific literature that demonstrate the prevention of bipolar disorder or major depression*. Indeed, recent studies (16, 22) suggest an alarming progressive increase in the rates of depression in successive birth cohorts through the 20th century. An earlier age of onset of depression has been reported for each birth cohort.

Despite this, our knowledge concerning the issues that seem to increase the risk of depression has grown significantly in the last few decades. A chorus of interested investigators (3, 28, 39, 42) has suggested that it is now time to evaluate the possible strategies that might be employed.

Affective disorders appear to be the product of *multiple causation* (2). Factors of biological vulnerability are coupled with developmental experience, critical life events, personal resources, and social status to influence the onset, course, and outcome of the disorder. Any strategy of preventive intervention, therefore, must influence one or more of these factors in reproducible ways to affect the incidence of the disorder.

Risk Factors for Mood Disorders

Although a multitude of factors have been found to relate to mood disorders, none provides a necessary or sufficient explanation for their development. This suggests that successful interventions will depend on an aggregate impact on these factors. Epidemiological study has been important in discerning these issues; a brief, selective review follows.

Biogenetic vulnerabilities. Studies of identical twins and outcomes for adopted-away offspring of mood-disordered patients strongly suggest that heredity plays a contributing role. Perhaps as much as 50% of the variance in the pathogenesis of *recurrent* affective disorders may be attributed to this factor (3). Moreover, there is considerable evidence from studies of family aggregation (4, 20, 35, 38) that mood disorders run in families. For example, when one parent is affected by mood disorder, the subsequent risk for a child is tripled, whereas when both parents have the disorder there is a 10-fold increase in risk (15). The more the phenomenon is spread across previous succeeding generations, the higher the possibility that offspring will be affected.

Identical twins show a 72% concordance for bipolar disorder and 40% for major depression (27). If heredity was the only factor at issue, we would expect 100% concordance. Obviously, issues other than genetics play a role in the expression of these disorders.

Early development. In addition to genetic contributions, children reared in the home of a parent with an affective illness experience the additional impact that an affected person brings to that environment. This may include modeling of the attitudes and behaviors typically found in the symptomatic disorder. In addition to the complex interactional difficulties that the child may experience, parental separation, divorce, or suicide may have additional emotional impact. The relevance of biogenetics and early development for prevention lies in the fact that potentially vulnerable individuals may be identified in clinical settings where preventive efforts might be initiated.

Childhood bereavement. Over the last three decades considerable research has been conducted to determine the relationship between childhood bereavement and later adult affective disorder. Lloyd (25) found the majority of these studies showed an increased rate of childhood bereavement among adult depressives. She observed that childhood loss of a parent by death generally increases adult depressive risk by a factor of two or three. Despite this association, most depressives have not experienced an early loss event, and clearly other causal factors are operative.

In a separate review, Tennant et al. (45) drew contrary conclusions. They found that methodological limitations in most studies of childhood bereavement have produced findings that are quite inconsistent. Inadequate control of potentially confounding variables and problems of match between experimental and control samples contributed to the lack of association between childhood parental bereavement and depression in later life. Later Roy (40) showed that early parental death was not significantly associated with depression. By contrast, both Roy and Tennant et al. (46) found that the early loss of a parent due to marital discord or parental illness appeared more commonly in the histories of adults with depression.

Life events and other psychosocial risks. It is clear that everyday events have an emotional impact on our lives. What is less clear is how these events have an impact on psychiatric disorders. Experiences of deprivation and loss contribute to sadness. Since sadness is a central feature of depression, it is commonly believed that extraordinary emotional events cause depression. Yet there is a difference between depression the symptom and depression the syndrome.

Hirschfeld and Cross (17) critically examined psychosocial risk factors in mood disorders. They concluded that the risk factors associated with the *symptoms* and the *syndrome* of depression are similar; the risk factors for bipolar disorder differ, somewhat.

Women have more depression than men by a 2:1 ratio. The lower the social class, the higher the rate of depression. (There are no independent racial differences.) Married persons, and those with intimates, have less depression than those who are single (9). The prevalence of depression is higher in younger age groups, though the age of onset lags behind bipolar disorder by 10 years. There are a greater number of life events, particularly in the month prior to onset (26). Undesirable and exit events and those beyond the person's control are most often associated. Personal resources (family ties, supportive relationships) offer a protective role in studies of depressive symptoms but not in major depression. Personality factors, so important in some theories of depression, have not been satisfactorily studied. Features of dependency, low self-esteem, and obsessionality have been found to be associated with depression (18).

By contrast, bipolars have an earlier age of onset, and being female and single confers no greater risk. The disorder is more prevalent in high socioeconomic, occupational, and educational levels. The role of life events and personal resources is apparently similar to that in major depression. Bipolars are more obsessive than normals but have less associated personality disorder than major depressives (1).

Problems with life events research render the value of the results suspect. First, most studies are retrospective. The life event may contribute to affective disorder or it may be a resultant of the disorder in early phase. Second, for the sake of reproducible conclusions, the events selected may be rather simplistically conceptualized and defined. Third, the methods used to collect data are open to several interpretations. For example, depressive symptoms and depressive syndromes are probably different, though overlapping, phenomena. Fourth, most studies have focused on patients drawn from clinical settings. This sampling may not be representative of depression in the population at large. Finally, the relationship between life events and depression may be reciprocal, and perhaps circular. Aneshensel and Stone (5) found that recent stress led to an increase in current depression, but depression was also found to precede the experience of stressful life events. Hirschfeld and Cross (17) discerned that correlations for events and the onset of depression are weak—in the .09 to .30 range, suggesting that life events may explain only 1 to 9% of the variance in these disorders.

POTENTIAL STRATEGIES FOR PRIMARY PREVENTION

There are only a limited number of possibilities for preventive intervention in affective disorders. These include biogenetic intervention, alterations of social status, modifications of life stresses, and bolstering personal resources.

Biogenetic Intervention

To borrow a quip from clinical rounds, the prevention of affective disorders depends on the patient selecting a different family of origin. While that is patently impossible, genetic counseling offers another potential approach to reducing the incidence and prevalence of mood disorders. Where there is a heavily laden family history in previous successive generations, particularly in the case of bipolar illness, some may choose the option of remaining childless. Without such a history, a bipolar patient would have an 80% chance of producing an unaffected offspring. For major depression, the outlook is even more favorable. Since treatment is most frequently successful, it seems unlikely that most couples would forego having their own children as a result of genetic counseling. This remains, then, a theoretical, not a practical preventive solution.

Alterations of Social Status

For those born female, the risk of depression is doubled, though it is no greater for bipolar disorder. But gender and the inevitable progression of age are not matters of choice. This leaves two status attributes that offer greater opportunity, if dubious practical relevance—marital status and social class. Statistically, marriage and intimate relationships reduce the risk of depression, yet there is no evidence that remaining in a destructive primary relationship promotes continued health. Whereas elevating one's social class is a universally accepted aim in Western culture, striving to achieve it is commonly associated with increased life stress (another risk factor). Furthermore, while improving social and political conditions for those who are disadvantaged is laudatory, it remains little more than conjecture that the incidence of major mental disorders is favorably altered thereby.

Modification of Life Stress

Some of life's cruelties are undoubtedly avoidable by the use of good judgment; others, including the loss of loved ones to death, rarely are. Parental illness, separation, divorce, and death during childhood appear to play a role in increasing the subsequent risk of developing an affective disorder as an adult.

Yet the usefulness of such information for successful prevention remains obscure. Strategies to overcome the influence of loss, to contribute to later positive mental health, and, specifically, to reduce the occurrence of subsequent affective illness have not been demonstrated. As Lowry has concluded, "it seems that scientific investigation has added little to common-sense prescriptions to work and to love (and, perhaps, to bear children in moderation)" (27, p. 79).

More proximate losses seem to affect greater impact. There is a 6.5-fold increased adult risk of developing a clinical depression within six months of a significant loss (31). Clayton (11) found that 42% of the recently bereaved meet diagnostic criteria for major depression at one month. Sixteen percent are still clinically depressed at one year. Accordingly, there has been abundant preventive research interest in this readily identifiable high-risk group. Polak et al. (32), in a carefully controlled study, found that preventive crisis intervention failed to decrease psychiatric illness, disturbed family functioning, or increased social cost for acutely bereaved families.

By contrast, Raphael (36) showed a beneficial effect from an intervention consisting of supportive mourning with recently bereaved widows. But the results have not been replicated. Also, it remains unclear whether the control group was comparable with respect to family history of depression. (If the controls had a more heavily laden family history of depression, that could explain the favorable results of the experimental group.) Thus, it remains unclear what advantages these strategies hold for preventive intervention.

Personal Resources

It is in the area of personal resources that our best hopes for preventive interventions exist. These include our coping strategies, personality characteristics, and social supports.

Few would disagree with the value of teaching children *an effective array of coping strategies* to counter subsequent problems in their lives when the primary institutions of family and community life falter. For example, Rehm (37) has suggested the application of self-management techniques with children to interdict the development of later depression. Some data support the use of a self-management program to *treat* moderate depression in children. But it remains an untested hypothesis whether this sort of intervention might have preventive value months, much less years, later.

The role of *personality characteristics* is yet another murky area. Since most studies of personality in affective disorders are drawn retrospectively, they fail to discriminate whether the distinguishing characteristics are related to the *state* of the disorder or the *traits* of the personality. Hirschfeld et al. (18) found that social introversion, interpersonal dependency, and diminished social adroitness were personality features of two groups of recovered depressed females. A suggestion, not confirmed, was that these characteristics represented preexisting traits accentuated by the clinical depression. This would imply that therapeutic efforts should focus on enhancing the social techniques of depressed patients.

Similarly, evidence suggests that *lack of intimacy* may increase the risk for developing an affective disorder. It is unclear whether the lack of intimacy is a result of an absent capacity (social introversion), a residual effect of the disorder, or a random social misfortune that is otherwise not a characteristic of the patient.

Nevertheless, *social support may serve as a protective emotional buffer* which neutralizes the effect of stressful events. For example, in one bereavement study (10), depression more often followed loss of a spouse when there were no available supportive adult children.

Psychotherapy (49) and psychoeducational procedures (7) designed to *reduce social skills deficits* associated with depression have been compared favorably with antidepressant medications. The acquisition of these skills yields symptom improvement and enhanced social functioning, and the chance of relapse may also be diminished. It seems reasonable that strategies that build and maintain effective social capacities might, when coupled with other interventions, yield a positive preventive effect.

Beck's (6) thesis that the meaning we impart to ourselves, our world, and our futures contributes powerfully to depression may also have preventive relevance. Studies demonstrating the efficacy of *cognitive behavioral therapies designed to correct these faulty attributions* have been impressive. This approach may provide fertile ground for preventive intervention testing.

San Francisco Depression Prevention Research Project

Work is at present underway on the first large-scale primary prevention effort with depression (29). The goal of the study is to evaluate a cognitive-behavioral group intervention patterned after the Coping-with-Depression program of Lewinsohn (23).

The intervention focuses in a practical fashion on many of the issues mentioned above. Topics include: how thoughts influence feelings, the effect activities have on mood, the value of interpersonal contacts, and the way these factors may be used to prevent depression. The program gives special attention to low-income minorities with appropriate representation of cultural subgroups.

Unfortunately, no results are yet available. A sample of substantial size is needed to demonstrate a preventive effect. This study deserves emphasis whether it proves to be successful or not. This appears to be our best hope of discerning what we need to know in order to develop cost-effective preventive intervention programs.

SECONDARY AND TERTIARY PREVENTION OF AFFECTIVE DISORDERS

The earlier a diagnosis is made and the more rapidly a treatment is effective, the greater the reduction in prevalence. This is the aim of *secondary prevention*. Disorders, typically chronic ones, may cause impairments (as mood disorders may impair social functioning). Intervention to minimize such complications is considered *tertiary prevention*. We will merge our discussion of secondary and tertiary prevention in the remainder of this chapter.

Importance of Public and Professional Education

As with other major public health risks such as cancer and heart disease, familiarizing both health care providers and the general public with signs of mood disorders and information about the efficacy of early intervention may lead people to seek treatment earlier. Less than 20% of those with affective disorders seek treatment from mental health specialists (43). While as many as 75% of these symptomatic patients are in the care of nonpsychiatric physicians, there is disturbing evidence that these depressions are overlooked or inappropriately treated (19, 21).

In the United States, there have been major efforts during the last several years to remedy this set of circumstances. Both the print and broadcast media have focused public attention on affective disorders. Each of the major weekly news periodicals has carried feature articles. Similar emphasis can regularly be found in women's magazines. For professionals, both the American Psychiatric Association and the National Institute of Mental Health have recently inaugurated major educational campaigns. It is too soon to tell what the impact of these efforts will be.

When people do seek treatment, a variety of effective acute treatment approaches are available (and competently reviewed elsewhere). But affective disorders are often relapsing or recurrent, leading to a chronic outcome for some.

Definitions

Relapse refers to an exacerbation of an ongoing episode of a disorder after an initial suppression of symptoms. *Continuation therapy* is directed toward preventing relapse. *Recurrence* involves the onset of a new episode of the disorder following complete recovery that has lasted at least several months. *Preventive therapy* is a longer-term effort directed toward preventing completely, or reducing the intensity or frequency of, recurrences.

PHARMACOLOGICAL PREVENTION OF RELAPSE AND RECURRENCE

A recent series of collaborative studies conducted under the auspices of the NIMH provides useful information concerning pharmacological prevention of recurrence in both major depression and bipolar disorder (33). A subsequent consensus panel also sponsored by NIMH provides an updated view of the state of the preventive art from this perspective (30).

Continuation of Medication to Prevent Relapse

When antidepressant medications are used in the treatment of major depression, patients are anxious to learn how long they may have to continue the treatment. It has long been known that premature withdrawal leads to relapse. Prien and Kupfer (34) noted that patients with residual symptoms at the time of drug withdrawal relapsed at a higher rate than those patients who showed no residual symptoms. Results suggest that a patient should be free of significant symptoms for at least 16 to 20 weeks before medication withdrawal is begun. The first 8 weeks following discontinuation of active medication is the period of greatest risk for relapse. Careful scrutiny during this time should produce the greatest preventive yield.

Who Should Be Considered for Preventive Maintenance Medication?

Manic episodes are very disruptive and carry a high risk of recurrence, potential for psychosis, and suicide. Even patients with hypomania and depression are at greater risk for recurrence and the development of psychosis when depressed. Additional indications of the need for preventive therapy for bipolars include: family history of bipolar disorder, past suicide attempts, past psychotic episodes, functional incapacity in past episodes, and compromised social functioning and affective symptoms between episodes.

A number of risk factors for recurrence of major depression have also been identified. These include: the presence of another psychiatric disorder, a chronic medical disorder, an underlying chronic affective disorder, older age of onset of the first episode, psychotic features of the current or a past episode, serious suicide attempts, and functional incapacity with a prior episode. When between episodes there have been sustained affective symptoms or a decreased level of social functioning, the severity of subsequent episodes is worse. By contrast, a rapid response to treatment and long intervals between past episodes argue against preventive therapy.

Efficacy of Medication in Modifying the Course

Lithium maintenance of bipolar disorder has been demonstrated to reduce the number of recurrent episodes by 50%, and the recurrences that do occur are less severe. Rapid-cycling bipolars (i.e., those with three or more episodes per year) do less well. Since the full efficacy of lithium's preventive effects may not stabilize for the first few months of a course of therapy, an early relapse should not lead to abandonment of this approach.

A significant number of well-controlled studies have demonstrated that lithium and tricyclic antidepressants decrease the frequency and intensity of recurrent episodes of major depression. Maintenance treatment has a 60% continuous success over two years. Assessing the severity of the disorder may be important in selecting which agent to choose, however. One study (33) has shown tricyclics to be substantially more effective than lithium when the initial episode of depression produces significant functional impairment.

Long-Term Preventive Treatment Strategies

To date, preventive doses for these medications have not been systematically determined. Doses somewhat lower than used in the acute treatment phase are usually effective. The duration of preventive treatment must be individually determined. A useful guideline suggests continuing preventive treatment for a period of time equivalent to several previous cycle lengths. The stronger the indications for preventive treatment, the longer the duration should be. Following discontinuation of medication, it may be wise to seek the involvement of family to watch for recurrence in order to alert the patient and the physician.

Compliance with Preventive Treatment

The acceptance of a long-term pharmacological strategy by patients is hampered by a number of factors. These drugs produce an array of unpleasant side effects (33) — 25% for tricyclics and 14% for lithium in the moderately severe range. In addition, patients and their families may have negative attitudes about medication for psychological symptoms. Vigorous efforts on the part of the prescribing physician to counter these forces can be effective. These include educating the patient regarding the implications of the diagnosis, risks of chronicity, and strategies for avoiding side effects. Careful and solicitous follow-up make a difference, as well.

PSYCHOTHERAPY IN THE PREVENTION OF RECURRENCE

The role of psychotherapy in the prevention of recurrent mood disorders is less securely established. Nevertheless, there have been significant advances in the study of psychotherapy for depression within the last 10 years (48). Two forms of psychotherapy merit particular interest, cognitive therapy (CT) and interpersonal psychotherapy (IPT). Each has been developed specifically with depressed patients, standardized in a fashion so that other therapists can be trained to deliver it reliably, and shown to be effective.

CT was developed within the past 20 years by Aaron T. Beck (6) and his colleagues. Observing negative cognitions in the depressed patient's view of himself, his world, and his future, Beck formulated a set of interventions using both behavioral and verbal techniques to correct the patient's faulty beliefs.

IPT was developed in the context of treating depressed outpatients in the New Haven–Boston Collaborative Depression Project. Utilizing an interpersonal framework and therapeutic techniques that are psychodynamically derived, treatment is directed to the patient's current life problems and interpersonal relationships.

Interpersonal Therapy

A number of studies (47, 49) have determined the relative benefits of IPT and antidepressant medication. The two treatments appeared to impact different symptoms and, hence, their effects were additive (13). Medication affected vegetative (somatic) elements of the disorder, while IPT had greater influence on mood, work, and interests. Social functioning was enhanced to a greater extent by IPT, as well.

Cognitive Therapy

At least three studies have claimed a superiority for CT over medication. Rush et al. (41) showed significantly greater improvement for CT on all measures of depression. Marked improvement was achieved for 78.9% of patients treated with CT, while only 22.7% of the patients treated with medication showed similar gains. Moreover, the dropout rate was substantially higher (8 : 1) for the medication group. Blackburn et al. (8) demonstrated, in a general-practice setting reported in the same study, that CT alone and in combination with drugs proved to be superior to drugs alone. A third study, by Simons et al. (44), compared CT, medication, and a combination of the two. Follow-up a year after termination of active treatment showed that patients who received CT (either with or without medication) were less likely to relapse or have a recurrence.

Since a minimum of 16 to 20 weeks of continued drug therapy following an initial response is necessary to prevent relapse (34), it is important to note that the length of treatment in these studies fell short of that minimum.

Evaluation of Combined Treatment

In an effort to determine whether combined psychotherapy and medication is superior to either alternative alone, Conte et al. (12) reviewed all appropriate controlled studies between 1974 and 1984. The combined therapies were appreciably more effective than placebo conditions, but only slightly superior to either alternative alone.

NIMH Treatment of Depression Collaborative Research Program

A large, controlled trial of psychotherapy compared with imipramine in the treatment of depression was inaugurated by the NIMH in the early 1980s (14). The study of 250 patients compared responses to CT, IPT, imipramine, and a control condition using placebo plus supportive therapy, for 16 weeks of treatment. Initial findings were reported at the annual meeting of the American Psychiatric Association in 1986. Between 50 and 60% of patients in the three active therapies had a favorable response, compared with 29% of the controls. Treatment with imipramine proved more rapid than the psychotherapies, but by the 16th week, the psychotherapies had matched the level of improvement produced by imipramine.

Psychoeducational Strategies

Several investigators have studied group psychoeducational and skill-building approaches to relieving depression. Bellack et al. (7) compared social skills training with psychotherapy and amitriptyline. While each treatment produced favorable changes, significantly more patients were substantially improved by social skills training. The dropout rate among patients taking amitriptyline was an alarming 55%.

Lewinsohn (23, 24) has developed a 12-session two-hour group intervention called the Coping-with-Depression Course. Favorable outcomes over six months have been replicated in four separate studies, with only 20% of patients remaining clinically depressed (by Research Diagnostic Criteria) one month after treatment. This outcome compares favorably with the use of medication though there was no medication control group in these studies.

Secondary Prevention Summarized

Once a diagnosis has been established, the prevention of further progression of the disorder is, appropriately, the clinician's responsibility. The patient needs education concerning the potential of a recurrent or chronic course in order to make informed choices about his care. While the individual practitioner may have little to contribute to primary prevention, careful treatment and follow-up of patients with mood disorders has a substantial impact on the prevalence of these disorders and the lives of those who suffer them.

REFERENCES

1. Akiskal, H. S., Hirschfeld, R. M. A., & Yerevanian, B. I. (1983). The relationship of personality to affective disorders: A critical review. *Arch. Gen. Psychiatry, 40*, 801.
2. Akiskal, H. S., & Webb, W., Jr. (1983). Affective disorders. I. Recent advances in clinical conceptualization. *Hosp. Community Psychiatry, 34*, 695.
3. Akiskal, H. S. (1987). Overview of biobehavioral factors in the prevention of mood disorders. In R. F. Munoz (Ed.), *Depression prevention: Research directions*. Washington, DC: Hemisphere.
4. Andreasen, N.C., Rice, J., Endicott, J., Coryell, W., Grove, W., & Reich, T. (1987). Familial rates of affective disorder. *Arch. Gen. Psychiatry, 44*, 461.
5. Aneshensel, C. S., & Stone, J. D. (1982). Stress and depression: A test of the buffering model of social support. *Arch. Gen. Psychiatry, 39*, 1392.
6. Beck, A. T., Rush, A. J., Shaw, B. F., & Emery, G. (1979). *Cognitive therapy of depression*. New York: Guilford Press.
7. Bellack, A. S., Hersen, M., & Himmelhoch, J. (1981). Social skills training compared with pharmacotherapy and psychotherapy in the treatment of unipolar depression. *Am. J. Psychiatry, 138*, 1562.
8. Blackburn, I. M., Bishop, S., Glen, A. I. M., Whalley, L. J., & Christie, J. E. (1981). The efficacy of cognitive therapy in depression: A treatment trial using cognitive therapy and pharmacotherapy, each alone and in combination. *Br. J. Psychiatry, 139*, 181.
9. Brown, G. W., & Harris, T. (1978). *Social origins of depression – A study of psychiatric disorder in women*. New York: Free Press.
10. Clayton, P. J., Halikis, J., & Maurice, W. (1972). The depression of widowhood. *Br. J. Psychiatry, 120*, 71.
11. Clayton, P. J. (1979). The sequelae and nonsequelae of conjugal bereavement. *Am. J. Psychiatry, 136*, 1530.
12. Conte, H. R., Plutchik, R., Wild, K., & Karasu, T. B. (1986). Combined psychotherapy and pharmacotherapy for depression. *Arch. Gen. Psychiatry, 43*, 471.
13. DiMascio, A., Weissman, M. M., Prusoff, B. A., Neu, C., Zwilling, M., & Klerman, G. L. (1979). Differential symptom reduction by drugs and psychotherapy in acute depression. *Arch. Gen. Psychiatry, 36*, 1450.
14. Elkin, I., Parloff, M. B., Hadley, S. W., & Autry, J. H. (1985). NIMH treatment of depression collaborative research program. *Arch. Gen. Psychiatry, 42*, 305.
15. Gershon, E. S., Hamovit, J. H., Guroff, J. J., Dibble, E., Leckman, J. F., Sceery, W., Targum, S. D., Nurnberger, J. I., Goldin, L. R., & Bunney, W. (1982). A family study of schizoaffective, bipolar I, bipolar II, unipolar and normal control probands. *Arch. Gen. Psychiatry, 39*, 1157.
16. Gershon, E. S., Hamovit, J. H., Guroff, J. J., & Nurnberger, J. I. (1987). Birth-cohort changes in manic and depressive disorders in relatives of bipolar and schizoaffective patients. *Arch. Gen. Psychiatry, 44*, 314.
17. Hirschfeld, R. M. A., & Cross, C. K. (1982). Epidemiology of affective disorders. *Arch. Gen. Psychiatry, 39*, 35.

18. Hirschfeld, R. M. A., Klerman, G. L., Clayton, P. J., & Keller, M. B. (1983). Personality and depression: Empirical findings. *Arch. Gen. Psychiatry, 40*, 993.
19. Jencks, S. F. (1985). Recognition of mental distress and diagnosis of mental disorder in primary care. *JAMA, 253*, 1903.
20. Keller, M. B., Beardslee, W. R., Dorer, D. J., Lavori, P. W., Samuelson, M. A., & Klerman, G. R. (1986). Impact of severity and chronicity of parental affective illness on adaptive functioning and psychopathology in children. *Arch. Gen. Psychiatry, 43*, 930.
21. Kessler, L. G., Cleary, P. D., & Burke, J. D., Jr. (1985). Psychiatric disorder in primary care. *Arch. Gen. Psychiatry, 42*, 583.
22. Klerman, G. L., Lavori, P. W., Rice, J., Reich, T., Endicott, J., Andreasen, N. C., Keller, M. B., & Hirschfeld, R. M. A. (1985). Birth-cohort trends in rates of major depressive disorder among relatives of patients with affective disorder. *Arch. Gen. Psychiatry, 42*, 689.
23. Lewinsohn, P. M. (1987). The coping-with-depression course. In R. F. Munoz (Ed.), *Depression prevention: Research directions*. Washington, DC: Hemisphere.
24. Lewinsohn, P. M., Breckenridge, J. S., Attonuccio, D. O., & Teri, L. (1985). A behavioral group therapy approach to the treatment of depression. In D. Upper & S. M. Ross (Eds.), *Handbook of behavioral group therapy*. New York: Plenum Press.
25. Lloyd, C. (1980). Life events and depressive disorder reviewed. I. Events as predisposing factors. *Arch. Gen. Psychiatry, 37*, 529.
26. Lloyd, C. (1980). Life events and depressive disorder reviewed. II. Events as precipitating factors. *Arch. Gen. Psychiatry, 37*, 541.
27. Lowry, M. R. (1984). *Major depression: Prevention and treatment*. St. Louis: Warren H. Green.
28. Munoz, R. F., Chan, F., & Armas, R. (1986). Cross-cultural perspectives on primary prevention. In J. T. Barter & S. W. Talbott (Eds.), *Primary prevention in psychiatry: State of the art*. Washington, DC: American Psychiatric Press.
29. Munoz, R. F. (1987). The San Francisco depression prevention research project: A randomized trial with medical outpatients. In R. F. Munoz (Ed.), *Depression prevention: Research directions*. Washington, DC: Hemisphere.
30. NIMH/NIS Consensus Development Panel (1985). Mood disorders: Pharmacologic prevention of recurrences. *Am. J. Psychiatry, 142*, 469.
31. Paykel, E. S. (1982). *Handbook of affective disorders*. New York: Guilford Press.
32. Polak, P. R., Egan, D., Vandenbergh, R., & Williams, W. V. (1975). Prevention in mental health: A controlled study. *Am. J. Psychiatry, 132*, 146.
33. Prien, R. F., Kupfer, D. J., Mansky, P. A., Small, J. G., Tuason, V. B., Voss, C. B., & Johnson, W. E. (1984). Drug therapy in the prevention of recurrences in unipolar and bipolar affective disorders. *Arch. Gen. Psychiatry, 41*, 1096.
34. Prien, R. F., & Kupfer, D. J. (1986). Continuation drug therapy for major depressive episodes: How long should it be maintained? *Am. J. Psychiatry, 143*, 18.
35. Puig-Antich, J. (1986). Possible prevention strategies for depression in children and adolescents. In J. T. Barter & S. W. Talbott (Eds.), *Primary prevention in psychiatry: State of the art*. Washington, DC: American Psychiatric Press.
36. Raphael, B. (1977). Preventive intervention with the recently bereaved. *Arch. Gen. Psychiatry, 34*, 1450.
37. Rehm, L. R. (1987). Approaches to the prevention of depression: A self-management perspective. In R. F. Munoz (Ed.), *Depression prevention: Research directions*. Washington, DC: Hemisphere.
38. Rice, J., Reich, T., Andreasen, N. C., Endicott, J., Van Eerdewegh, M., Fishman, R., Hirschfeld, R. M. A., & Klerman, G. (1987). The familial transmission of bipolar illness. *Arch. Gen. Psychiatry, 44*, 441.
39. Roberts, R. E. (1987). Epidemiological issues in measuring preventive effects. In R. F.

Munoz (Ed.), *Depression prevention: Research directions.* Washington, DC: Hemisphere.

40. Roy, A. (1985). Early parental separation and adult depression. *Arch. Gen. Psychiatry, 42*, 1987.
41. Rush, A. J., Beck, A. T., Kovacs, M., & Hollon, S. (1977). Comparative efficacy of cognitive therapy and pharmacotherapy in the treatment of depressed outpatients. *Cognitive Ther. Res., 1*, 17.
42. Rutter, M. (1982). Prevention of children's psychosocial disorders: Myth and substance. *Pediatrics, 70*, 883.
43. Shapiro, S., Skinner, E. A., Kessler, L. G., Von Korff, M., German, P. S., Tischler, G. L., Leaf, P. J., Benham, L., Cottler, L., & Regier, D. A. (1984). Utilization of health and mental health services: Three epidemiological catchment area sites. *Arch. Gen. Psychiatry, 41*, 971.
44. Simons, A. D., Murphy, G. E., Levine, J. L., & Wetzel, R. D. (1986). Cognitive therapy and pharmacotherapy for depression. *Arch. Gen. Psychiatry, 43*, 43.
45. Tennant, C., Bebbington, P., & Hurry, J. (1980). Parental death in childhood and risk of adult depressive disorders: A review. *Psychol. Med., 10*, 289.
46. Tennant, C., Hurry, J., & Bebbington, P. (1982). The relation of childhood separation experiences to adult depressive and anxiety states. *Br. J. Psychiatry, 141*, 475.
47. Weissman, M. M., Prusoff, B. A., Dimascio, A., Neu, C., Goklaney, M., & Klerman, G. L. (1979). The efficacy of drugs and psychotherapy in the treatment of acute depressive episodes. *Am. J. Psychiatry, 136*, 555.
48. Weissman, M. M. (1979). The psychological treatment of depression: evidence for the efficacy of psychotherapy alone, in comparison with, and in combination with pharmacotherapy. *Arch. Gen. Psychiatry, 36*, 121.
49. Weissman, M. M., Klerman, G. L., Prusoff, B. A., Sholomskas, O., & Padian, N. (1981). Depressed outpatients; results one year after treatment with drugs and/or interpersonal psychotherapy. *Arch. Gen. Psychiatry, 38*, 51.

MANAGEMENT

18

PSYCHOTHERAPY OF DEPRESSION

JEAN-YVES GOSSELIN, M.D.

Professor, University of Ottawa;
Director, Inpatient Psychiatric Services
Ottawa General Hospital
Ottawa, Ontario, Canada

INTRODUCTION

Anxiety and depression are common expressions of conflict and distress. Because of its broad range of manifestations, depression is perhaps present in any psychiatric condition. It is estimated that between 6 and 10% of the adult population in Europe and North America is depressed during any period of time. Depression is twice more frequent among females than males. Though psychiatrists are usually involved with the more severe of those conditions, the whole medical profession is confronted regularly by patients with symptoms of emotional decompensation diagnosed as such or expressed through organic conditions.

The mental representation of any particular illness is very specific to each individual, as it is rooted in the ontogenic and philogenetic influences. Depression, even more than any other medical condition, has a special meaning for each patient. A medical diagnosis tainted with depressive elements or the memory of a catastrophic event, including significant loss or threat of loss, could have very special negative meanings for the patients and determinant implications on the treatment and its outcome.

A depressive condition may not be recognized or diagnosed when either denied by the patient or underestimated by the physicians because of what it represents. In fact, it confronts both the patient and the physician with his limitations, deficiencies, and failure, and even more so with the problems related to one's own death. This becomes more obvious when, as physicians, we have to provide care to a colleague or a V.I.P. We may tend to deny or underestimate the severity of the patient's condition because of our identification with him, which then triggers a direct confrontation with our own depression and our own death. As expressed by Melanie Klein (9): "The major task of a human being is to reach and get over one's own depressive position" (p. 187).

CLASSIFICATION OF DEPRESSIVE DISORDERS

The DSM-III-R delineates three classes of depression, namely: major depression, dysthymia, adjustment disorder with depressed mood, and depressive disorder not otherwise specified. May I propose to add to this list, in the interest of quality care, the "somatic equivalents of depression," often identified by the treating physician or during a psychiatric consultation.

A sound clinical diagnosis will clarify the presence or absence of genetic vulnerability and of organic factors that may affect the patient's symptomatology. It is an essential step before proceeding to the dynamic formulation, and the potential benefit of psychotherapy should not serve as a deterrent to the exploration of those basic areas.

A more objective perception of the interinfluence of the organic and dynamic factors involved will be achieved. The dynamic diagnosis will define why and how the illness has developed, how it is experienced by the patient, and even how it is perceived by the therapist. It will help to delineate what pertains to a developmental deficit from what is linked to conflicts. In that respect, needless to say how important the first interview is and how, with some empathy, it could also become therapeutic.

Psychodynamic therapists do not focus on symptoms, but rather on the intrapsychic conflicts and the interpersonal contexts in which they develop. In that perspective, the symptoms are a response to an early defect reactivated by a current loss or threat of loss. A skilled therapist will visualize, during the first assessment, not only the present resources and limitations of the patient, but also the eventual problems of transference and countertransference, which should not be denied or ignored even if, at times, those unconscious reactions are difficult to recognize even for the therapist.

Until a decade ago, many psychotic depressions were considered "endogenous"; no precipitant factors were then identified and those conditions tended to be recurrent. In the meantime, more attention was paid, not only to actual or recent precipitating events, but also to remote traumatic situations expressed in what is termed *anniversary reactions*. A detailed history often reveals that besides the chronological incidence of those events, the actual complaints or symptoms expressed by the patient are like a reverberation of those either experienced in the past on the occasion of that particularly traumatic event or manifested by the other significant figure(s) linked to that situation. It is well accepted now that even if we cannot identify a cause of a depressive condition, we should not conclude that it is necessarily endogenous.

In our experience, most of the patients seen in psychotherapy after their acute depressive episode have been able to identify a precipitating factor and benefited from the treatment. A minority of them became noncompliant with the therapy, early in the process. They were either unable to establish any connection with a past significant event or not interested in that exploration. Some of them decided to get involved again after a recurrent episode of depression and were able to identify some causes, at times recent, at times remote in their history, factors either previously denied or whose importance was underestimated. It may be that the defenses mobilized in the illness interfere with the patient's capacity to even perceive the possibility of those significant connections.

It is therefore important to properly identify the defense mechanisms used by the patient, in order to provide some flexibility in the therapeutic process. Without it, the patient's resistance will soon develop, and countertransference may emerge to protect the narcissistic needs of the frustrated therapist, which may sign the end of the treatment, to the detriment of the patient.

When the level of regression is such that insight-oriented therapy is not indicated, a step treatment could instead be proposed, either with a different therapist or by the same therapist but with a different type of therapy, or a combination of therapies such as supportive psychotherapy and pharmacotherapy. This will provide continuity to the care needed and assist the reintegration of the defenses at the premorbid level. From there, the patient may be recommended or may decide to resume the exploratory process.

TYPES OF PSYCHOTHERAPY

During the past two decades, a growing number of clinical researchers, on the basis of Beck's (3) theory of depression, a cognitive triad consisting of negative perception of one's self, the external world, and one's own future, concluded that the outcome of cognitive-behavior therapy in depression is superior to results with other types of psychotherapy and even antidepressant medication. The approach is based on learned and existential elements, and the treatment goals are: to identify the negative cognition, to develop more flexible alternatives, and to repeat the exercises in order to develop new cognitive and behavioral responses. The rationale is that if we correct the behavior, we alleviate the symptoms.

This method has its main indication in the treatment of depression but it has its limitations, like any other theory and technique. Altshuler and Rush (1), comparing the theory and tactics of psychoanalytic and cognitive therapies, concluded: "Despite the major differences in language and in theory between cognitive and psychoanalytic therapies, we believe they are in practice more complementary and overlapping than mutually exclusive. . . . Finding a therapy to be effective is not validation of the theory from which it derives" (p. 14).

I will concentrate here on psychoanalytically oriented therapy or insight psychotherapy, because it contains, in my opinion, the main ingredients of many other forms of psychotherapy. It also gives the therapist more flexibility and possibilities to develop a range rather than a single type of therapy. It can be applied not only to individual psychotherapy but also to group, marital, and family therapy, which could be used as well concomitantly and contribute to a more stable outcome of the treatment.

The brief insight-oriented psychotherapy, which consists of up to 30 weekly sessions, is still widely used, alone or in combination with either psychoactive medications or another format of psychotherapy. Recent data (5, 6) indicate that the combination of medication and psychotherapy for depression seems to give better clinical results. Methodological and statistical problems make such evaluations rather difficult and their conclusions are often challenged.

Insight-oriented therapies are counterindicated during the acute phase of psychotic depression. Crisis intervention or supportive psychotherapy along with psychoactive medication is then often implemented. It is common practice in our service when a patient is hospitalized, even for a severe depression, to keep him under observation for a few days before giving regular medication unless an agitated condition or a need for control or protection develops. We frequently observe a significant improvement in his condition within the first few days of hospitalization.

The patients, hostages of their own dilemma, unable to see any acceptable solution, have no coping alternative but an "inhibition of action." An office consultation and, more so, hospitalization may contribute to development of at least some elements of solution.

The separation from a stressful milieu, the protection and care provided, and the message of confidence invested in the patient's capacity to control his aggressive impulses seem to have a sedative impact on the previous state of distress and the tendency to overgeneralize inadequacies and failures. We frequently continue this treatment during hospitalization, relying uniquely on individual, group, occupational, and milieu therapy with good results. It is considered that 30% to 40% of the patients benefit from that approach. In most instances, the patients develop a much better understanding of their emotional conflicts and a good motivation to continue psychotherapy once they leave the hospital.

Group therapy can be very helpful, according to our experience with the hospitalized patients. It gives them a way to identify and share experiences with other depressed patients. Furthermore, it provides them with an opportunity to benefit from the experience and understanding of those already able to recognize and correct openly the previously distorted perception of their inner and outside reality. It offers another opportunity to develop insight and continuity with the individual psychotherapy sessions.

Individual therapy combined with either group, marital, or family therapy has to be conducted with the same psychodynamic orientation in order for the patient to recognize the continuity of the approach. Conflicting credos and competitive partisan approaches can only create more confusion in the mind of the patient, a prime deterrent to pursue any therapy. Moreover, the highly motivated patients who have already received different approaches usually identify very promptly the type of therapy that can best help their condition and reach the roots of their problems.

It is not unusual to observe particularly rapid symptomatic improvement of patients receiving antidepressants and psychotherapy. That can hardly be explained by the effects of those medications, but rather by the other therapeutic factors mentioned previously.

The quality of the individuation-separation process is central to the quality of adjustment to adult life. It will influence the marital choice, the quality of intimacy in the couple, and the reactions to the many losses faced during a lifetime.

Even if depression in adult life may reflect a developmental deficit, it is usually triggered by factors central to the actual *raison d'être* of the patient. The spouse may be the precipitating factor, perhaps because of his inadequacies or his exaggerated expectations from or demands on the partner, or because of the patient's own inadequacies or handicap. It is not infrequent to see a depressed person who has taken over an "impossible task," whose original purpose was to compensate for his inability to fulfill a similar ambition or task during childhood or adolescence. It is therefore important to consider the addition of marital therapy, which can only succeed if both partners have the emotional resources and motivation for insight and the determination to execute the necessary changes in their attitude and behavior.

The patient may very well be the scapegoat for the spouse whom he wants to protect from an ever more severe decompensation. Such a patient usually has rather poor ego boundaries, a tendency to fuse with others in order to fulfill a strong need for security and gratification, and a concomitant feeling of responsibility for any error or problems that may develop around him.

The depressed patient may also be the emissary of a severe disorganization in the family. Family therapy may then play a major role and even take precedence over individual therapy if the members of the family have the resources and motivation to contribute to improve the previous situation. It will be discontinued if no one agrees to share the responsibility with the patient for the disintegration of the family. Specific goals have to be delineated before continuing the individual therapy sessions.

THE TREATMENT CHOICES

Many factors influence the choice of a particular type of psychotherapy, namely: the stage of the illness, the patient's accessibility, including spouse and family, and the therapist's accessibility and skills.

It is usually counterindicated to proceed with insight-oriented psychotherapy during the psychotic phase of a depression. Suffice to list some of the defense mechanisms used then by the patient to cope with the loss, namely: negation, regression, introjection, projection, splitting, identification, and idealization, to understand the degree of disorganization and to grasp the risk of provoking a more severe decompensation when imposing further demands. It could foster more helplessness in the patient, who might then decide to fuse with the lost object and die. Arieti (2) insists, though, that "the intensity of the depression should not deter the therapist from making psychotherapeutic attempts. . . . The person who is depressed to a psychotic degree does not reject the world, and acts to a certain extent, like a mother who does not reject a bad child" (p. 864). Dr. Arieti explains his psychodynamic view and therapeutic procedures of psychotic depression to support his very good results.

> The patients were nine women and three men; ten of them had suicidal ideations. The patients were treated for at least 18 months

> with a minimum of 2 sessions a week. After at least three years from termination of treatment, I can now report that full recovery with no relapse was obtained in 7 patients, marked improvement in 4, and failure in 1. (p. 864)

The therapist should be flexible in his approach. Any attempt to uncover unconscious material during the psychotic phase may increase the suicidal risk. The physician should project the image of a reliable and powerful figure, providing support and protection during that phase and agreeing to serve temporarily as a substitute for the lost object. I consider the first encounter with a patient to be a major medical or therapeutic step which should be carefully and empathically conducted. The messages are perceived by the patient through a filter sensitive to negative perceptions and interpretations of what the therapist tries to convey in his words and attitude. A simple reference to a particular problem may well generate a severe or generalized threat in the mind of the patient.

A step approach will be more conducive to the development of a good rapport with the patient and will provide more incentive to enter the therapeutic process. This initial phase is generally used to assess the conflicts, the underlying personality, and the resources available for the therapy.

Sedative or antidepressant medications are often needed to alleviate the symptoms, to obviate the emotional deterioration, and to improve the accessibility of the patient to psychotherapy.

Contrary to the opinion prevailing until recently, the medication does not necessarily interfere with the efficiency of psychotherapy. It could even be an important, if not a necessary, adjunct at least to initiate the treatment with some severely depressed patients. Psychoactive medication may be counterindicated if a patient is dependent on medication, if it interferes with a treatment (for example, the patient becomes too heavily sedated to be involved in a learning process of behavior therapy), or if the medication plays a negative role on the motivation of the patient to become more autonomous. The message received or perceived by the patient concerning the role and effects of medication plays a particularly determinant influence. Therefore, an eclectic attitude from the therapist will help the patient to better define his objectives, his role, and his responsibilities in the therapeutic process. The nonbiased attitude of the clinician is essential for an objective orientation of the therapeutic process.

The assessment of patient accessibility to psychotherapy should embrace both the intellectual and emotional resources. It is important to establish whether the depressive episode reflects a reaction to a loss or an expectation of compensation for an emotional deficit.

The most reliable indicators rest in the patient's capacity to function within his family, at work, and socially once the acute phase of depression is over. Insight-oriented psychotherapy is indicated only if such resources exist.

Frequently, such patients will identify the cause of their depression but remain unaware of the scope and depth of their significance. This is a common finding in the treatment of pathological grief reaction. Though the problem for the patient appears to be linked to the loss, as stated by Vaillant (11), the real issue is not to deal with the loss but with the remembrance.

The therapist accessibility depends on many factors, among others: the setting, the clinical orientation, and the type of therapy he is most familiar with. The clinical skills used for assessment of the patients should take into consideration the medicopsychosocial factors in the formulation of the diagnosis. The therapeutic skills developed through education and training will focus on specific areas through well-structured processes. In general, each of us is proficient at only a few types of therapies we are most familiar with and prefer using. The most effective type of therapy should be offered to the patient. A colleague's opinion could be asked, if needed, to clarify what orientation and format of treatment are best indicated.

THE PSYCHOTHERAPEUTIC PROCESS

Very little attention has been paid so far to the personality of the therapist (7, 8, 10) as an important variable in the treatment process and the outcome. Strupp (10) made a strong point to that effect: "There can be no doubt that the patient's relationship to the therapist . . . embodies one of the most powerful forces in the therapeutic entreprises" (p. 396). We all know how important mental representations are in our daily lives and how much they influence not only the intrapsychic process but also the interpersonal relationship.

The term *transference* used in the analytic therapies should not be confused with the term *therapeutic alliance* to which it is in fact antithetical in its purpose and process (7).

Many hypotheses have been developed to explain how psychotherapy works. I consider the following stages essential to the treatment efficiency, namely:

1. The stage of awareness.
2. The stage of conceptualization.
3. The stage of action or implementation.

There is a need for the patient to be receptive to internal confrontations with his own conflicts, which is the essence of any exploratory work and an essential condition for conceptualization, insight, or cognition. It is here that the help of the therapist, through interpretations or other techniques, takes on special significance. The phase of action or implementation is the key to a stable improvement. It is considered the most difficult task in psychotherapy and a frequent cause for its failure; it is called the resistance to change.

TARGET ELEMENTS

Disappointment and sadness are the back-scene on which further decompensation develops. Though these feelings appear to be directed at oneself, they are as well turned at the outside world: "I let myself down, no you let me down, no I . . . ," etc. If disappointments multiply and persist, they tend to generalize, and then a fear of losing control and facing a total disaster develops. The experience of distress that ensues creates a hopeless and helpless condition, the intensity of which triggers internally and externally oriented anger, usually at the most significant figure or its substitute.

In that respect, the development of a persistent stage of irritability and anger in a child and an adolescent is still too rarely perceived and/or identified by the parents as signal of profound insecurity. It negatively influences the process of separation-individuation, leads to interpersonal conflicts and punishments, and increases the subjective feeling of inadequacy. The signs of underachievement will often echo what the parents are themselves experiencing.

As the anger is directed against the powerful idealized parents, perceived as "refusing" to understand the deep feeling of desolation and rejection, a need to punish them emerges. Their presence may even be considered nondesirable. Wishes that they disappear are recognized at first through short-lived fantasies becoming more persistent if the distress itself persists. They are controlled only by the fear of retaliation. A fear of eventual total annihilation, or of total loss of love, will create more and more distress and anger. In the meantime, the "internal monster" appears and develops, along with a tremendous sense of guilt and a need for punishment.

Efforts are made and responses usually develop to correct those internal inadequacies. Development of alliances with other significant figures will take place, be it in school with peers or professors, in sports, at work, in a loving relationship, etc. If it succeeds, it will temporarily alleviate the pain and assist survival, but at the same time, a constant need for approval by others will emerge and set a limitation on the capacity to receive or be gratified. Such behavior is reinforced by their demands and approval. The need to give becomes a constant preoccupation along with flight into action which frequently precedes flight into illness. This becomes the price to pay and the only way to receive care as a substitute for love and the last fortress against an ongoing feeling of imminent rejection. In fact, corrections of inadequacies never take place.

The worst will come when the flight into action is interrupted by life events or circumstances, unless in the meantime some therapy provides the elements for insight and correction, [then] the split perception of the object representation becomes more integrated.

Any disappointment, problem, or failure that happens tends to be overgeneralized and perceived as punishment. Moreover, punishment, if not emanating from external agents, may be self-inflicted. It functions as a censor to forbidden satisfaction and happiness. A good clinical history should reveal the existence of such a "hostagelike" condition perpetuating the presence of the bad object and its influence on the subject. Any signal of satisfaction which could threaten that presence and evoke the death of that figure will soon be replaced by self-imposed frustrations. Hence, a lifelong feeling of hopelessness and helplessness will eventually decompensate into either a severe depression or its somatic equivalent.

TREATMENT DURATION

The duration of a treatment depends on many factors, namely: the goals established in the treatment, the availability of the patient and the therapist, the progress made by the patient, etc. In general, brief insight-oriented psychotherapy will be initiated. Sessions may last for 20 to 90 minutes in certain situations but they are usually limited to about 50 minutes. It is considered that personality conflicts greatly benefit from this type of therapy, which does not exclude the need for long-term psychoanalytically oriented psychotherapy or psychoanalysis when indicated and affordable.

The termination of therapy is usually planned early enough in the process, once the patient has reached a good level of functioning, which should ideally be superior to the one existing during the premorbid condition. In certain cases, the number of sessions as well as the specific objectives will be decided at the beginning of the therapy. The termination of psychotherapy is usually a very creative period for insight and change in attitude and adjustment, not only to outside reality but primarily to inner conflicts.

It may be indicated for some patients to continue on maintenance therapy for a longer period of time, e.g., one session a month or even one or two sessions a year. Here again, some flexibility is indicated. Over the years, we have realized that many patients benefit from the type of assistance that helped them avoid relapses, as well as from psychoactive medication used intermittently, and maintained the quality of their improvement achieved during the intensive part of the treatment.

The "no therapy" decision is often a difficult step to take because of the risks involved and should usually be made after consultation with a colleague. A crisis intervention is more appropriate to deal with acute depressive episodes of patients with ongoing negative and destructive attitudes toward their therapist and who are not showing any intention or motivation to change. Severe personality disorders, at times diagnosed also as anorexia nervosa or severe bulimia, that do not improve after years of treatment may fall in this category. A no-treatment decision may also apply for those malingering and antisocial personality disorders who use psychiatric benefits as secondary gains and for those overdependent on psychotherapy. Continuing the treatment will only perpetuate the illness behavior. A severe emotional deficit, rather than reaction to a loss, is a common finding among those individuals.

I would like to briefly address the question of the treatment-resistant patient and his hidden agenda, be it metabolic defects, lack of motivation, secondary gains, angry resistance, or a combination of factors. The patient may well use an interminable resistance to treatment as an achievement and a way of life.

CONCLUSION

Depression, like any other illness, may be influenced by a genetic vulnerability and a multiplicity of organic, emotional, and social factors. More than in other conditions, it is tainted with a sense of humiliation and punishment. It is important to help the patient to understand the meaning of his symptoms, a task of responsibility and prime importance for the therapist and of crucial implications for the patient. As expressed by Hilde Bruch (4): "The process of learning psychotherapy is lifelong; and an interminable task of creative reappraisal, of studying both failures and successes with the same objectivity and readiness to learn" (p. vii).

REFERENCES

1. Altshuler, K. Z., & Rush, A. J. (1984). Psychoanalytic and cognitive therapies: A comparison of theory and tactics. *Am. J. Psychother.*, *38*(1), 4.
2. Arieti, S. (1977). Psychotherapy of severe depression. *Am. J. Psychiatry, 134*(8), 864.
3. Beck, A. T. (1963). Thinking and depression: Idiosyncratic context and cognitive distortion. *Arch. Gen. Psychiatry,* 9, 324.
4. Bruch, H. (1974). *Learning psychotherapy: Rationale and ground rules* (p. vii). Cambridge, MA: Harvard University Press.
5. Coute, R., Plutchik, R., Wild, K. V., & Karasu, T. B. (1986). Combined psychotherapy and pharmacotherapy for depression: A systematic analysis of the evidence. *Arch. Gen. Psychiatry, 43*, 471.
6. Karasu, T. B. (1982). Psychotherapy and pharmacotherapy: Toward an integrative model. *Am. J. Psychiatry, 139*(9), 1102.
7. Karasu, T. B. (1977). Psychotherapies: An overview. *Am. J. Psychiatry, 134*(8), 851.
8. Katz, P. (1986). The role of the psychotherapies in the practice of psychiatry (the position of the Canadian Psychiatric Association). *Can. J. Psychiatry, 31*(5), 458.
9. Klein, M. (1966). Developpement de la psychanalyse. *Presses Universitaires de France*, p. 187.
10. Strupp, H. (1970). Specific vs. nonspecific factors in psychotherapy and the problem of control. *Arch. Gen. Psychiatry, 23*, 393.
11. Vaillant, G. E. (1985). Loss as a metaphor for attachment. *Am. J. Psychoanal.*, *45*(1), 59.

19

DRUG THERAPY OF DEPRESSION

BERNARD I. GROSSER, M.D.

Professor and Chairman,
Department of Psychiatry,
University of Utah School of Medicine
Salt Lake City, Utah

and

DAVID A. TOMB, M.D.

Vice Chairman,
Department of Psychiatry,
University of Utah School of Medicine
Salt Lake City, Utah

INTRODUCTION

Modern psychopharmacological treatment of depression began in the 1950s with the discovery that the antitubercular drug isoniazid (INH) and its analog iproniazid (Marsilid), a potent inhibitor of monoamine oxidase (MAO), had antidepressant qualities (45). This led to the identification of several clinically effective MAOI antidepressants. At about the same time, the first tricyclic antidepressant, imipramine, was made available (42). Although the tricyclics and MAOIs have remained drugs of choice in the treatment of depression, new agents and combinations of agents have been introduced over the past decade which make a successful drug-patient match increasingly likely. This chapter reviews both the principles of using medication to treat depression as well as the drugs that are currently available.

IDENTIFYING POTENTIAL RESPONDERS

Medication is the recommended initial treatment for most patients with major depression: correctly used, it is effective in 70 to 80% of seriously depressed patients. Unfortunately, because depression is heterogeneous, we are unable to predict with certainty who will improve with drugs; we must use a variety of clinical indicators to identify those most likely to respond. Nevertheless, it is often more important to decide with whom and how to use an antidepressant drug than it is to decide which drug to use.

Patients with major depression (depressed mood and/or a loss of interest or pleasure coupled with some mixture of additional symptoms, such as fatigue, agitation, insomnia, anorexia, and difficulty concentrating), particularly if they have melancholic features (e.g., profound loss of interest, weight loss, psychomotor retardation, sleep disruption), are most likely to improve with antidepressants. This is true whether they have a unipolar or bipolar pattern. Individuals with less severe symptoms of depression, particularly if their illness is recent or if they have atypical characteristics (e.g., irritability, emotional lability, hypersomnolence, hyperphagia, marked anxiety, reversed diurnal mood variation), features of a personality disorder (e.g., unstable relationships, impulsiveness, constant need for reassurance, antisocial behavior), or a concurrent psychiatric illness (anxiety disorder, phobia, organicity), also may respond, but more erratically and unpredictably. Antidepressants are also recommended for patients with a psychotic depression (usually combined with antipsychotics or electroshock therapy [ECT]), a depression due to a medical condition (particularly if the depression remains after the underlying medical condition remits), and for prophylaxis of a recurrent depressive illness. These medications, however, are *not* recommended for regular use in patients with normal bereavement or in those with chronic, minor depressions—cognitive (6) or interpersonal (41) psychotherapy is often a more appropriate treatment choice in minor depressions. In general, the more acute, severe, and "pure" the depression, the more likely it is to respond to medication. ECT, on the other hand, may be a better choice if the patient is imminently suicidal, medically deteriorated, frail and old, or has a profound or psychotic depression.

Other indications of potential favorable response include a family history of major mood disorder or a past personal and family history of improvement with an antidepressant. Laboratory measures predicting treatment response are currently of little practical value. Results have been intriguing but inconsistent: the present and even future value of laboratory tests has been questioned (87). Measures of pretreatment urinary MHPG

(100) and pretreatment CSF 5-HIAA (48), the DST (96), and stimulant challenge tests (26) all have presented contradictory findings and do not reliably predict a positive response to antidepressants. Moreover, recent studies that suggest that a blunted pretreatment TSH response to TRH challenge may predict a good response to treatment while a blunted post-treatment response may be prognostic of an early relapse (43) as yet lack reliability. More research is needed on all these measures.

GENERAL PRINCIPLES OF ANTIDEPRESSANT USE

More than a dozen antidepressant drugs are currently available (Table 1). Because of familiarity and proven effectiveness, the classical tricyclics (imipramine, amitriptyline) are often the first medications chosen to treat depression. Other tricyclics (TCAs), the MAOIs, and the newer antidepressants then serve as alternative drugs, should the standard TCAs fail to produce adequate improvement. However, with only a few exceptions, drugs from each of these classes have been shown to be significantly effective in treating depressive states when used in adequate dosages. Their major differences from one another are in pharmacokinetics, side effect profiles, toxicity in overdose, potency, drug-drug interactions, and putative mechanisms of action. A thorough knowledge of the pharmacological differences among the various medications is essential to rational prescribing. The characteristics of each major antidepressant are discussed in a later section.

More important to successful treatment than familiarity with the individual drugs, however, is a grasp of the general principles of antidepressant use. Although there is no "right way" to treat depression with medication, clinical experience has defined general guidelines. One of several possible approaches incorporating these guidelines is described below.

Initiating Treatment

After a thorough evaluation has identified a patient in need of treatment and likely to respond, eliminated medical or other psychiatric causes for the depression, and found no clear indication to use (e.g., a family history of response) or avoid (e.g., a side effect sensitivity) a particular medication, the patient should begin a course of an antidepressant, preferably a TCA. This should be done in the hospital if the patient is medically unstable or seriously suicidal.

Imipramine is often a good first choice, particularly with retarded depression, although alternatives include amitriptyline or doxepin (particularly in the agitated, anxious, or sleepless patient who may benefit from

Table 1
Pharmacological Features of Available Antidepressants

Drug	Principal Neurotransmitter Uptake Blockade	Anticholinergic	Sedation	Dose (mg/day)
TCAs				
Imipramine	NE, 5-HT	4+	3+	75–300
Amitriptyline	NE, 5-HT	5+	5+	75–300
Doxepin	NE, 5-HT	4+	5+	75–300
Desipramine	NE	1+	1+	75–300
Nortriptyline	NE	3+	2+	40–150
Protriptyline	NE	3+	1+	20–60
Trimipramine	NE, 5-HT	3+	4+	75–200
Newer antidepressants				
Alprazolam	—	1+	5+	4–8
Amoxapine	NE, [DA]*	2+	3+	200–300
Bupropion	DA	1+	1+	200–600
Maprotiline	NE	2+	2+	50–225
Mianserin	Alpha-2 presynaptic blocker	1+	4+	60–150
Trazadone	5-HT	1+	3+	100–600
Fluoxetine	5-HT	0-1+	0	20–80
Fluvoxamine	5-HT	0-1+	1+	100–300
MAOIs				
Phenelzine	MAO changes	1+	1+	45–90
Isocarboxazid	influence	1+	1+	30–60
Tranylcypromine	NE, 5-HT	1+	0	20–60

*Postsynaptic DA receptor blocker.

sedative side effects) or the less sedating, less anticholinergic desipramine (particularly in the elderly patient sensitive to side effects). The physician should be familiar with the use of several of these standard medications, ideally those that present different spectrums of side effects, and should make initial, and subsequent, drug selections based in part on the side effect pattern. Although the literature is inconclusive, many therapists recommend starting with a tertiary TCA (e.g., imipramine or amitriptyline), partly because secondary tricyclic antidepressants (e.g., desipramine and nortriptyline) are generated as metabolic products and partly because the tertiary drugs are felt by some to be slightly more effective.

An often neglected principle when beginning drug treatment for depression is to provide a complete trial of each medication introduced, when possible. Although side effect problems or patient resistance frequently interrupt a drug trial prematurely, every effort should be made to continue a medication until its clinical limit has been reached—until it has been shown to be clearly effective or ineffective. Insufficient dosage is the most common reason for an antidepressant failure (39, 47).

A clinical antidepressant trial typically depends on an empirical, dose-response approach: one introduces a single medication, raises it in steps to a clinically determined upper limit, and, after a suitable time, concludes the trial to be a success if the patient is sufficiently improved and a failure if he is not. Recovery generally takes several weeks (the patient should be informed of this). If imipramine is the initial drug, it should be begun slowly (perhaps with a 50-mg test dose—25 mg or lower in the elderly—using divided doses), raised to 150 mg over the following 7 to 10 days, maintained at 150 mg for two weeks (dose may then be given all at nighttime), raised to 200 mg for another 1 to 2 weeks, and then raised to 300 mg for a final one to two weeks (77). If side effects interfere at any point, it may be possible merely to slow the rate of dosage increase and continue, rather than to abandon the trial altogether. It occasionally is advisable for the patient to be in the hospital as the trial continues into the higher dosages, particularly if he is experiencing significant side effects. Only after one to two weeks at 300 mg is it safe to conclude that the patient is unresponsive to imipramine (see below), and then only if it is certain that he has been taking the medication as prescribed. Similar stepwise trials can be pursued for other antidepressants, at equivalent dosages.

Use of Antidepressant Blood Levels

The time-honored clinical trial described above, however useful, is flawed. It leaves too indirect the connection between oral dose and clinical change. We know, for instance, that there can be more than a 30-fold interindividual variability in steady-state TCA plasma concentration with an identical oral dose (29), much of this variability due to genetically controlled differences in elimination rates (5). Thus, a failure to improve may be due to a resistant depression, to poor drug absorption or rapid metabolization resulting in low drug plasma levels, or to drug noncompliance by the patient. Likewise, serious side effects at normal drug doses may reflect an unusual patient sensitivity or an elevated plasma level. Antidepressant plasma (35) levels, which appear to be directly related to brain tissue concentrations (25), can help answer these questions and can provide a degree of sophistication and accuracy to drug trials that was previously unavailable.

Unfortunately, well-studied and reasonably well-understood plasma level/clinical response relationships are available for only four antidepressants (71): imipramine, nortriptyline, desipramine, and amitriptyline. Each has a defined therapeutic drug plasma range (if samples are collected 10 to 14 hours after the last dose [29] and carefully analyzed [62]), although improvement can occur outside these ranges and failure within: imipramine (plus desipramine), 150–300 ng/ml; desipramine, 125–300 ng/ml; amitriptyline (plus nortriptyline), 150–300 ng/ml; nortriptyline, 50–160 ng/ml. Imipramine (82) has no therapeutic upper limit (use at higher doses is limited primarily by the development of side effects), while nortriptyline (88) and possibly desipramine (12) have a therapeutic window and become ineffective at higher plasma levels. Amitriptyline functions as though it has a window (8, 84) because severe side effects routinely occur at plasma levels not far above a clearly therapeutic range.

Plasma drug level measurements (97) are useful for and can identify (1) the poorly responsive patient who is a rapid metabolizer maintaining a low plasma level on normal oral drug doses, (2) the lowest effective drug dosage for those who are elderly or medically unstable, (3) drug noncompliance, (4) dangerously high plasma levels that are either unsuspected or symptomatic, (5) asymptomatic but unnecessarily high plasma levels, (6) a subtherapeutic trial, and (7) a therapeutic dose by rapid means, particularly in patients needing urgent treatment. On the other hand, minor side effects are poorly correlated with such measures (72). In general, plasma drug levels can reduce the time needed to produce a response, reducing suffering and cost. However, debate continues about whether plasma levels should be routine. Because many tricyclic drug trials are successful and uncomplicated, plasma levels may be best reserved for the unresponsive or problem patient. However, as the need for rapid dose adjustment and scrupulous minimization of the oral dose increases, the indications for plasma levels may broaden.

For most TCAs, a steady-state plasma level is reached within a week at a constant drug dose. Thus, a plasma level measured in a patient who has failed to respond after two to three weeks of 150 mg of imipramine will accurately help define whether the trial should continue at a higher dosage or needs to be discontinued. If the plasma level of imipramine (plus its metabolite desipramine) is 150–300 ng/ml or above, there is little reason to increase the oral dose or continue the trial, while if the level is low, the patient is either a rapid metabolizer or noncompliant. In this way TCA plasma levels have modified and improved the older dose-response method of selecting an antidepressant. However, in spite of this advancement, the "gold standard" for dose adjustment remains the presence of side effects and clinical response, not the plasma level.

The usual way of using plasma levels to adjust drug dosage is to use a level drawn after five days of a constant oral drug dose. However, rapid oral dose adjustment on the basis of a plasma drug level obtained 24 hours after a test dose of antidepressant appears promising (58) yet demands further validation. Most patients seem to tolerate well a rapid increase to therapeutic levels. If routinely useful, it could reduce hospital stays by a week or more. Finally, it should be borne in mind that almost all TCA plasma level studies have been done on inpatients with major depression. How useful plasma levels are with outpatients or individuals with mild depression remains to be seen—preliminary evidence suggests the plasma concentration : clinical response relationship is less strong than in endogenously depressed patients (8).

The Treatment-Resistant Patient

If a patient doesn't respond to a thorough trial with a TCA, and the pressure of time does not dictate ECT, other antidepressants are worth trying. As many as 60 to 70% of patients will respond to the first drug, but over 80% will have responded after trials of several medications. Although the choice is ultimately empirical, several general principles help in the selection of a second antidepressant.

Choose a nontricyclic; select an MAOI or one of the newer antidepressants. This principle, however, is suspect because many patients who fail on one TCA have responded to a second. The more important variable may be the mechanism of action of the second drug: e.g., if the first drug was primarily noradrenergic, choose one that is primarily serotonergic, etc. Of course, our lack of fundamental knowledge about the mechanism of action of the antidepressants as well as the role neurotransmitters play in depression limits the accuracy of this approach. For example, a hint of the psychobiological complexity involved is seen in our growing suspicion that the NE and 5-HT receptor systems are inextricably linked in depression. It is postulated that the essential element of antidepressant action is the ability of a drug to decrease the number and/or sensitivity of the beta-adrenergic (and possibly the 5-HT) receptors ("down-regulation"—a process that takes several weeks and thus correlates with the time of onset of action of most antidepressants) (93). Thus, it possibly matters less what neurotransmitter the drug affects if the secondary effect of down-regulation is accomplished.

Search for a satisfactory side effect pattern. Avoid drugs that produce side effects similar to those which troubled the patient during the first antidepressant trial. Evaluate the drug's toxicity in light of the patient's suicide potential.

Provide a complete trial: at least four to six weeks, with two of those weeks at maximal dosage. Intolerance is not ineffectiveness. Although it may take less time to demonstrate the patient intolerant to the drug, it requires six weeks to prove the drug ineffective. Drug plasma levels will be of no help here because most antidepressants do not have a defined therapeutic range as yet.

Clinical necessity, patience, finances, and common sense all help determine how many different drugs receive trials. Three or four complete trials are not uncommon; more may be made, if trials are interrupted by drug intolerance. However, after two or three satisfactory but unsuccessful trials, it is advisable to carefully reevaluate the patient in search of unrecognized underlying medical conditions, contributory psychodynamic or environmental factors, or an inaccurate diagnostic formulation. ECT, focused psychotherapy, and/or a structured, long-term hospital setting may be required in the subset of patients in whom drugs have failed.

Ongoing Treatment

Response to antidepressants of any type typically occurs after two to six weeks: sleep and appetite usually return first, then an improved mood. The patient may return to baseline but frequently retains residual symptoms and social impairment; particularly those patients with long-standing depression ("double depression"). Moreover, one-quarter of the improved patients relapse during the first four months (40). Ongoing psychotherapy should complement medication in many of those patients who experience incomplete recovery, although some patients require only medication management.

Drug treatment of uncomplicated depression should last six to nine months after a first episode and one to two years if the depression is recurrent. The dose should be about the same as or modestly lower than acute treatment doses; however, this point has not been well studied. The medication should then be tapered and discontinued over a period of several weeks, since anxiety, headache, myalgia, and nausea can occur with abrupt withdrawal. The patient always should be reviewed for signs of relapse several weeks after the medication has been stopped, and then on a regular basis for the next 6 to 12 months.

If a depression has recurred two or more times, prophylactic treatment should be instituted. Lithium is recommended for bipolar prophylaxis (75) (0.45–0.8 meq/L [11]), while lithium, or amitriptyline or imipramine (at one half or more the dose required for acute illness) seem to be equally effective in preventing episodes of unipolar depression (24, 74). Prophylaxis is most likely to be successful in patients who have had infrequent, acute, and retarded or psychotic episodes of depression and who have cleared completely between episodes and is least likely to be successful in unipolar patients who are chronically dysphoric or bipolar patients who are rapid cyclers (1, 2).

Because recovery is often incomplete or doesn't occur, and because relapse is so common (40), care of a significant percentage of seriously depressed patients becomes a long-term, ongoing concern of the physician which requires attention over years. These are the patients who demand the highest level of psychopharmacological and psychotherapeutic skills.

CHARACTERISTICS OF AVAILABLE ANTIDEPRESSANTS

This section discusses the traditional tricyclic antidepressants, the newer antidepressants, the MAOIs, and drugs occasionally used for depression. Not all of these medications are available everywhere: e.g., some drugs have been used for years in Europe and Canada and are just becoming available in the United States. Although most of these drugs are clearly effective in treating classic depression, the range of depressive spectrum conditions improved by them is not known. Moreover, the effects of some of these medications on CNS neurotransmitters are not well understood either. Thus, clinical use of all but the "classic" TCAs and MAOIs is empirical.

Tricyclic Antidepressants

Imipramine
Amitriptyline
Doxepin
Desipramine
Nortriptyline
Protriptyline
Trimipramine
Clomipramine
Dothiepin

The tricyclics (TCAs) are the first choice in treating most serious depressions. Their mechanisms of action are unknown but are thought to be related to their effects, each to its own degree, as norepinephrine and serotonin reuptake blockers. Much has been made of the fact that some TCAs, the 2° amines (desipramine, nortriptyline, and protriptyline), are metabolites of other TCAs, the 3° amines (amitriptyline, imipramine, trimipramine, and doxepin). This now seems to have limited clinical relevance, although the 2° TCAs display fewer side effects of all types.

TCAs are absorbed rapidly and completely from the small bowel, experience an enterohepatic cycle, but eventually reach the blood stream, developing peak plasma levels in two to eight hours. They are fat-soluble and bind strongly to tissue and plasma proteins. Metabolism is by the liver and excretion by the kidney, with a half-life of approximately one day.

Side effects can be severe and may control pharmacotherapy. They vary with both the patient and the drug used (Table 1), but frequently can be relieved by time or medication (68). Most common among the side effects are the anticholinergic problems due to muscarinic cholinergic receptor blockade: dry mouth (associated with stomatitis and tooth cavities), blurred vision (near vision 2° to mydriasis and cycloplegia; avoid TCAs in narrow-angle glaucoma), constipation (dangerous in the elderly), urinary retention, and central anticholinergic syndrome (anxiety, agitation, confusion and delirium, warm and dry skin, absent bowel sounds; treat carefully with physostigmine 1–2 mg slowly i.v., repeated in 30 to 60 minutes). If severe, these side effects can often be treated with bethanechol, 10–30 mg p.o., q.d. to t.i.d.; begin low and raise dosage slowly, watching for cholinergic symptoms.

Other side effects include orthostatic hypotension (probably secondary to alpha-adrenergic receptor blockade; can be severe; treat with patient education, exercise, support stockings, salt tablets, 600–1800 mg p.o. q.d.

to b.i.d., possibly thyroxine, 0.1–0.2 μg q.d., or methylphenidate, 5 mg p.o. q.d.; lowest incidence is with nortriptyline), weight gain (a common source of patient noncompliance), anorexia, and rashes and allergic reactions. Autonomic effects are common (sweating; impaired sexual arousal, erection, ejaculation, and orgasm), as are central nervous system (CNS) effects: tremor (fine, rapid; treat with diazepam, 5–10 mg p.o. b.i.d., or propranolol, 10–20 mg p.o. q.i.d.), sedation (in many), restlessness and insomnia (in a few), confusion (in some elderly), and tardive dyskinesia (20, 109).

Cardiovascular side effects are often of great concern to the therapist, yet serious problems are infrequent at therapeutic doses. In overdose, however, cardiac problems are the rule and are related to the severity of the overdose (22). Atrioventricular block, ventricular conduction defects, and QT prolongation occur in moderate cases, and ventricular arrhythmias can develop when the overdose is severe. The QRS duration appears to be a helpful measure of the dangerousness of the clinical condition (seizures with a QRS greater than 0.10 seconds; ventricular arrhythmias with a QRS greater than 0.16 seconds), as is the drug plasma level (7). At therapeutic doses, TCAs increase cardiac rate, reduce ventricular arrhythmias (21) (they are used as antiarrhythmic agents in cardiac patients), and produce modest intraventricular conduction delays (23). Thus, they are safe in patients with arrhythmias but should be used cautiously in patients with a severe, preexisting heart block (86).

Individual TCAs are often recommended for certain types of patients because of the side effect spectrum: e.g., amitriptyline or doxepin in the agitated depressive, desipramine in the elderly patient with anticholinergic intolerance, protriptyline if sedation is a problem, nortriptyline if orthostatic hypotension is excessive, and clomipramine if the depression is complicated by obsessive-compulsive features.

Drug interactions are common and can be severe: TCA blood levels are increased by stimulants, antipsychotics, Antabuse, thyroid, and guanethidine and decreased by alcohol, barbiturates, and smoking. TCAs are synergistic with other drugs having anticholinergic effects and can increase the half-life of anticoagulants, impair the effectiveness of antihypertensives, and produce CNS depression when combined with hypnotic-sedatives, antipsychotics, alcohol, and anticonvulsants.

Newer Antidepressants

Although little is known about the mechanisms of action of the newer antidepressants, they seem to offer no improvement in efficacy, speed of onset, or range of disorders treated. However, several are structurally and pharmacologically different from the tricyclics (81), which may explain why the side effect spectrum and toxicity are significantly different in some cases and why these drugs may be useful for patients unable to tolerate or respond to the TCAs.

An exception to this diverse group of agents with diverse neurotransmitter effects are the "pure" serotonin uptake inhibitors, which seem as effective as TCAs with major depression and which also may address a group of depressed patients previously poorly responsive to medication (52). Furthermore, because of their limited side effect pattern, these drugs are better tolerated (and actually preferred) by most patients.

Trazadone. A mild serotonin uptake blocker without cholinergic muscarinic binding (and therefore free of anticholinergic activity); generally free of cardiac side effects except in overdose, although a few patients predisposed to conduction defects have developed ventricular arrhythmias; can produce orthostatic hypotension, sedation, gastrointestinal (GI) distress, peripheral edema, headaches, mixed cognitive and memory impairment, and irreversible priapism (90) (rarely).

Amoxapine. A metabolite of the neuroleptic loxapine; can occasionally produce tardive dyskinesia and other EPS side effects as well as hyperprolactinemia. Of possible use in psychotic depressions; has fewer cardiac problems in overdose, but does produce seizures and renal failure; it is reputed to have a more rapid onset of action than TCAs.

Maprotiline. A tetracyclic that is pharmacologically similar to the TCAs; there is increased risk of seizures at higher therapeutic doses; less cardiotoxicity in overdose than with the TCAs.

Bupropion. Unique pharmacology; a DA uptake blocker which resembles the amphetamines structurally; free of the usual side effects (sedation, postural hypotension, weight gain, cardiac problems, anticholinergic effects) and safe in overdose but can produce insomnia and sweating; withdrawn (temporarily?) due to a high incidence of seizures.

Mianserin. Unique pharmacology: an alpha-2 presynaptic and H-1 receptor blocker; very sedative and may display a peculiar symptom of small-joint swelling; safer than TCAs in overdose.

Alprazolam. A benzodiazepine that may be antidepressant in higher doses; it seems to down-regulate beta-adrenergic receptors; it has few side effects except for significant sedation and a risk of addiction. Safe in overdose.

Serotonin reuptake blockers. Low sedation and anticholinergic side effects but can produce nausea and GI upset, insomnia, restlessness and agitation, sweating, and weight loss.

Fluoxetine
Fluvoxamine
Sertraline

Monoamine Oxidase Inhibitors

Phenelzine
Isocarboxazid
Tranylcypromine
Clorgyline
Pargyline
Deprenyl

MAO is an intraneuronal (also present extraneuronally), mitochondria-bound enzyme which inactivates the catecholamines dopamine, norepinephrine, and serotonin as well as several other amines such as tyramine and tryptamine. It occurs in two uniquely localized, substrate-specific forms: MAO-A (37) (in brain, liver, sympathetic nerves, and intestine), which deaminates NE and 5-HT, and MAO-B (108) (in brain, liver, and platelets), which deaminates benzylamine and phenylethylamine. Both forms deaminate dopamine and tyramine. By inhibiting MAO, MAO inhibitors (MAOIs) raise CNS monoamine concentrations acutely, although those levels fall toward normal with time. This elevation of NE and 5-HT levels is thought to be related to the antidepressant effect of MAOIs.

Three MAOIs are currently in general use as antidepressants: phenelzine and isocarboxazid (both hydrazine drugs) and tranylcypromine (a nonhydrazine compound). All three inhibit both MAO-A and MAO-B. In addition, several specific MAO subtype inhibitors exist which may have clinical utility in the future: clorgyline, an inhibitor of MAO-A, and pargyline and deprenyl, specific inhibitors of MAO-B. Clorgyline, because of its presumed effects on NE and 5-HT, is postulated to have the greater antidepressant potential, and an early comparison study with pargyline supported this notion (57). Likewise, the MAO-B inhibitors, because they are not involved in intestinal wall deamination, are expected to have fewer GI-related side effects, and early studies supported this as well (54).

MAOIs are rapidly absorbed from the intestine, distributed widely, and inactivated in part by acetylation. Speed of acetylation is apparently genetically controlled and ranges from slow to rapid: slow acetylators develop high drug levels more quickly and may display a more rapid therapeutic response (66), although this advantage is lost with time. Like TCAs, the MAOIs usually require two to six weeks for a response.

MAOIs, the oldest of the antidepressants, have been accused of being both ineffective and dangerous, and some experts argue that their use should be abandoned (104). Their reputation for ineffectiveness seems to have arisen from the inadequate doses recommended during the early years of their use. Recent work finds them to be as effective or nearly as effective as the TCAs in treating classic depression when administered in sufficient dosage (64). Moreover, a number of studies have suggested that MAOIs are especially useful in treating patients with atypical depression, particularly patients with significant anxiety (44, 65, 83), panic reactions, phobias, somatization and chronic pain (80), mood lability, or rejection sensitivity (38). Thus, MAOIs are perhaps more "broad spectrum" antidepressants than are TCAs. A trial at a higher dose is advised unless contraindicated by side effect problems (110): phenelzine, 75–90 mg/day, isocarboxazid, 50–60 mg/day, tranylcypromine, 40–60 mg/day. A decrease in platelet MAO-B activity of at least 80% has been used in research settings as the cutoff point for adequate dosage of phenelzine (85), yet the clinical utility of this guide is uncertain.

MAOIs are safe for most patients but can present problems for the poorly compliant patient. They have a full range of side effects (78, 79): particularly orthostatic hypotension, insomnia (and the elimination of REM sleep [107]), impotence and/or anorgasmia, and nervousness and/or hypomania, but also dry mouth, ankle edema, constipation, weight gain, dizziness, drowsiness in a few patients, and the possibility for abuse (30). On the other hand, they have few of the cardiovascular side effects of many of the other antidepressants and thus are safer for patients with arrhythmias (27, 102). In overdose, MAOIs can be fatal, with muscular weakness and agitation, hypertension, hyperthermia, confusion, seizures, and circulatory collapse—often developing many hours after ingestion. Treatment can include support, gastric lavage (there is decreased GI motility), urine acidification (99), and hemodialysis.

More important, however, MAOIs can produce (rarely) an acute, potentially life-threatening hypertensive crisis and hyperpyrexia following ingestion of tyramine or other pressor amines. They prevent the MAO in the gut wall from deaminating the tyramine in ingested food. The result can be a generalized sympathetic effect beginning with a sudden occipital or temporal headache and accompanied by sweating, fever, neck stiffness, and photophobia, which can progress to coma, intracranial hemorrhage, and death. Furthermore, this reaction can occur up to several weeks after the MAOI has been discontinued (17).

The foods most likely to produce this reaction and which the patient must avoid include primarily strong cheeses, but also pickled or kippered herring, dried and salted fish, chicken livers or liver paté, any slightly spoiled meat, nondistilled alcohol, and broad beans. Certain drugs also can precipitate a hypertensive crisis: cocaine, amphetamines, anorectics (they stimulate NE release from adrenergic neurons), sympathomimetic precursors (dopamine, methyldopa, levodopa), catecholamines (epinephrine, NE), and sympathomimetic amines (ephedrine, phenylephrine, phenylpropanolamine, pseudoephedrine, over-the-counter cold and hay fever medication). The "cheese reaction" is unusual and unpredictable and its risk has been exaggerated (19, 92), yet when it occurs, it can be fatal: the patient must be carefully instructed about dietary restrictions. A reaction can be treated with slow i.v. administration of phentolamine. Resolution usually occurs in a matter of hours. A patient may be encouraged to carry a single dose of Thorazine or other potent alpha-adrenergic phenothiazine with him to take orally if signs of a crisis appear.

Phenelzine is the most commonly used of the MAOIs and may be the most effective, but it is also the most likely to be hepatotoxic. Tranylcypromine is pharmacologically unique (it metabolizes to amphetamine) and may be worth trying for that reason, yet a few patients find it too stimulating and it may be the most likely to produce a hypertensive crisis. Pargyline, an MAO-B inhibitor available as an antihypertensive, currently is felt to have modest antidepressant features.

Occasional Antidepressants

Lithium. Lithium is an effective antidepressant with both bipolar and unipolar patients (18) although its efficacy is less than that of the TCAs in patients with unipolar depression (53) (but see Worrall et al. [106] for a contrasting view). However, it may be the drug of choice in those bipolar depressed patients in whom TCAs precipitate rapid cycling. Moreover, lithium becomes a natural maintenance medication in these patients. Finally, lithium is the preferred drug to prevent depressive recurrence in bipolar patients (76) as well as one of several useful drugs for prophylaxis in unipolar depression (55).

Carbamazepine. Carbamazepine, an anticonvulsant used primarily for epilepsy and pain syndromes, has been shown useful as an alternative to lithium in acute mania (67) and in prophylaxis of mania and depression (15, 69). However, it may also have broader utility in depression; case reports suggest effectiveness with depression in bipolar illness (61) and psychotic depression (89) while a recent double-blind study has demonstrated a moderate impact on major depression (57% of patients were improved on an average daily dosage of 971 mg/day) (70). Thus, carbamazepine should be considered as an alternative antidepressant, particularly in depressed bipolar patients who have a tendency to cycle on TCAs (101) or in those patients with atypical or seizure-related phenomena. However, although dose-related side effects like sedation and dizziness are common, the therapist should be on the watch for more serious problems: e.g., aplastic anemia, hepatitis (56).

Stimulants. Stimulants such as amphetamine, dextroamphetamine, and methylphenidate, although they have a long tradition of occasional use in depression, are not good antidepressants (51). Their only use may be in the short-term treatment of the exhausted, nonfunctional patient with mild depression or in the depressed, medically ill patient (105).

COMBINATION PHARMACOTHERAPY

Combined drug therapy for treatment-resistant patients is occasionally effective but totally empirical. Uniformly increased efficacy for combinations has not been demonstrated. In most of the combinations discussed, however, the second medication can be added safely and without a significant increase in side effects and thus may be worth a try if the patient is unimproved or only partly improved after one or more trials with a single medication. Combinations displaying some success are listed below.

TCA and an MAOI

Although long considered dangerous, a TCA/MAOI combination is now felt to be relatively safe (64) and useful (103). However, clinical experience suggests that imipramine probably should be avoided, as should non-TCA serotonin reuptake–inhibiting antidepressants (49, 50). On the other hand, nortriptyline or amitriptyline combined with an MAOI repeatedly has been found useful, while amitriptyline also may provide partial protection from a tyramine-induced hypertensive crisis (63). Begin the two drugs simultaneously (do not add a TCA to an MAOI [4]), start slowly, and keep doses lower than if you were using each drug alone.

Antidepressant and Lithium

Adding lithium to an antidepressant occasionally can induce a marked improvement within the first several days of the change (14). Most experience is with augmentation of TCAs (32), but improvement has occurred in patients taking MAOIs as well (73, 95). This combination seems applicable to both unipolar and bipolar depression (36), as well as to some patients with a psychotic depression (46, 60).

Antidepressants and Antipsychotics

This combination is specifically useful for psychotic depression (91). In fact, antidepressants alone are generally ineffective with this population, while the response rate of the combination is above 80%. (However, amoxapine *may* be an exception since it seems to have both antidepressant and antipsychotic properties.) Be aware, however, that antipsychotics significantly raise the steady-state plasma level of TCAs (33, 59).

Antidepressants and Thyroid

A few patients (apparently primarily females) seem to improve if their antidepressant regimen is augmented with thyroid (28). It is not known whether a subtle thyroid dysfunction is a precondition for this (somewhat modest) response (94).

Other Combinations

Possible combinations seem almost endless and they certainly present many possibilities that have not yet been studied by controlled trials. Examples (to be considered, but used with caution) include: a TCA, MAOI, and stimulant (16); a TCA or an MAOI, lithium, and L-tryptophan (10, 31); a TCA and tryptophan (98); lithium and tryptophan (9); an MAOI and benzodiazepine (13); TCA and reserpine (3, 34).

REFERENCES

1. Abou-Saleh, M. T., & Coppen, A. (1987). Acute treatment, long-term management, and prophylaxis of affective disorders. *Psychiatr. Ann.*, *17*, 301–308.
2. Abou-Saleh, M. T., & Coppen, A. (1986). Who responds to prophylactic lithium? *J. Affect. Disord.*, *10*, 115–125.
3. Amsterdam, J. D., & Berwisk, N. (1987). Treatment of refractory depression with combination reserpine and tricyclic antidepressant therapy. *J. Clin. Psychopharmacol.*, 7, 238–242.
4. Ananth, J., & Luchins, D. (1977). A review of combined tricylic and MAOI therapy. *Compr. Psychiatry*, *18*, 221–230.
5. Asberg, M., Price-Evans, D. A., & Sjoqvist, F. (1971). Genetic control of nortriptyline kinetics in man: A study of relatives of propositi with high plasma concentrations. *J. Med. Genet.*, *8*, 128–135.
6. Beck, A. T. (1976). *Cognitive therapy and the emotional disorders*. New York: International Universities Press.
7. Boehnert, M. T., & Lovejoy, F. H. (1985). Value of the QRS duration versus the serum drug level in predicting seizures and ventricular arrhythmias after an acute overdose of tricyclic antidepressants. *N. Engl. J. Med.*, *313*, 474–478.
8. Boyer, W. F., & Lake, C. R. (1987). Initial severity and diagnosis influence the relationship of tricyclic plasma levels to response: A statistical review. *J. Clin. Psychopharmacol.*, 7, 138–142.
9. Brewerton, T. D., & Reus, V. I. (1983). Lithium carbonate and L-tryptophan in the treatment of bipolar and schizoaffective disorders. *Am. J. Psychiatry*, *140*, 757–760.
10. Bridges, P. K. (1983). " . . . and a small dose of an antidepressant might help." *Br. J. Psychiatry*, *42*, 626–629.
11. Coppen, A., Abou-Saleh, M. T., & Milln, P. (1983). Reducing lithium dose reduces morbidity and side effects in affective disorders. *J. Affect. Disord.*, *6*, 53–66.
12. Coryell, W., Turner, R. O., & Sherman, A. (1987). Desipramine plasma levels and clinical response: Evidence for a curvilinear relationship. *J. Clin. Psychopharmacol.*, 7, 138–142.
13. Deicken, R. F. (1987). Combined alprazolam and phenelzine treatment of refractory depression with panic attacks. *Biol. Psychiatry*, *22*, 762–766.
14. DeMontigyn, C., Elie, R., & Caille, G. (1985). Rapid response to the addition of lithium in iprindole-resistant unipolar depression: A pilot study. *Am. J. Psychiatry*, *142*, 220–223.
15. Fawcett, J., & Kravitz, H. M. (1985). The long-term management of bipolar disorders and lithium, carbamazepine, and antidepressants. *J. Clin. Psychiatry*, *46*, 58–60.
16. Feighner, J. P., Herbstein, J., & Damlouji, N. (1985). Combined MAOI, TCA, and direct stimulant therapy of treatment-resistant depression. *J. Clin. Psychiatry*, *46*, 206–209.
17. Feinberg, M., deVigne, J. P., & Kronfol, Z. (1981). Duration of action of phenelzine in two patients. *Am. J. Psychiatry*, *138*, 379–380.
18. Fieve, R. R., & Peselow, E. D. (1983). Lithium: Clinical applications. In G. D. Burrows, T. R. Norman, & B. Davies (Eds.), *Antidepressants* (pp. 277–321). Amsterdam: Elsevier.
19. Folks, D. G. (1983). Monoamine oxidase inhibitors: Reappraisal of dietary considerations. *J. Clin. Psychopharmacol.*, *3*, 249–252.
20. Gardos, G., & Casey, D. E. (1984). *Tardive dyskinesia and affective disorders*. Washington, DC: American Psychiatric Press.
21. Giardina, E. G. V., & Bigger, J. T. (1982). Antiarrhythmic effect of imipramine hydrochloride in patients with ventricular premature complexes without psychological depression. *Am. J. Cardiol.*, *50*, 172–179.

22. GLASSMAN, A. H., & DAVIS, J. M. (1987). Overdose and tricyclic drugs. *Psychiatr. Ann., 17*, 410–411.
23. GLASSMAR, A. H., & ROOSE, S. P. (1987). Cardiovascular effects of tricyclic antidepressants. *Psychiatr. Ann., 17*, 340–342.
24. GLEN, A. M. I., JOHNSON, A. C., & SHEPHERD, M. (1981). Continuation therapy with lithium and amitriptyline in unipolar depressive illness: A controlled clinical trial. *Psychol. Med., 11*, 409–416.
25. GLOTZBACH, R. K., & PRESKORN, S. H. (1982). Brain concentrations of tricyclic antidepressants: Single-dose kinetics and relationship to plasma concentrations in chronically dosed rats. *Psychopharmacology, 78*, 25–27.
26. GOFF, O. C. (1986). The stimulant challenge test in depression. *J. Clin. Psychiatry, 47*, 538–543.
27. GOLDMAN, L. S., ALEXANDER, R. C., & LUCHINS, D. J. (1986). Monoamine oxidase inhibitors and tricyclic antidepressants: Comparison of their cardiovascular effects. *J. Clin. Psychiatry, 47*, 225–229.
28. GOODWIN, F. K., PRANGE, A. J., POST, R. M., et al. (1982). Potentiation of antidepressant effects by L-triiodothyronine in tricyclic nonresponders. *Am. J. Psychiatry, 139*, 34–38.
29. GRAM, L. F., SONDERGAARD, I., CHRISTIANSEN, J., et al. (1977). Steady-state kinetics of imipramine in patients. *Psychopharmacology, 54*, 255–261.
30. GRIFFIN, N., DRAPER, R. J., & WEBB, M. G. T. (1981). Addiction to tranylcypromine. *Br. Med. J., 283*, 346.
31. HALE, A. S., PROCTER, A. W., & BRIDGES, P. K. (1987). Clomipramine, tryptophan and lithium in combination for resistant endogenous depression. *Br. J. Psychiatry, 151*, 213–217.
32. HENINGER, G. R., CHARNEY, D. S., & STERNBERG, D. E. (1983). Lithium carbonate augmentation of antidepressant treatment—An effective prescription for treatment of refractory depression. *Arch. Gen. Psychiatry, 40*, 1335–1342.
33. HIRSCHOWITZ, J., BENNETT, J. A., ZEMLAN, F. P., & GARVER, D. L. (1983). Thioridazine effect on desipramine plasma levels. *J. Clin. Psychopharmacology, 3*, 376–378.
34. HOPKINSON, G., & KENNY, F. (1975). Treatment with reserpine of patients resistant to tricyclic antidepressants. *Psychiatr. Clin., 8*, 109–114.
35. HULLETT, F. J., LEVY, A. B., & TACHIKI, K. H. (1984). Serum imipramine concentrations lower than plasma values. *J. Clin. Psychiatry, 45*, 516–518.
36. JEFFERSON, J. W., & AYD, F. J. (1983). Combining lithium and antidepressants. *Clin. Psychopharmacol., 3*, 303–307.
37. JOHNSTON, J. P. (1968). Some observations on a new inhibitor of monoamine oxidase in brain tissue. *Biochem. Pharm., 17*, 1285–1297.
38. KAYSER, A., ROBINSON, D. S., NIES, A., et al. (1985). Response to phenelzine among depressed patients with features of hysteroid dysphoria. *Am. J. Psychiatry, 142*, 486–488.
39. KELLER, M. B., LAVORI, P. W., KLERMAN, G. L., et al. (1986). Low levels and lack of predictors of somatotherapy and psychotherapy received by depressed patients. *Arch. Gen. Psychiatry, 43*, 458–466.
40. KELLER, M. B., SHAPIRO, R. W., LAVORI, P. W., et al. (1982). Relapse in major depressive disorder. *Arch. Gen. Psychiatry, 39*, 911–915.
41. KLERMAN, G. L., WEISSMAN, M. M., ROUNSAVILLE, B. J., & CHEVRON, E. S. (1984). *Interpersonal psychotherapy of depression*. New York: Basic Books.
42. KUHN, R. (1957). Uber die behandlung depressiver zustande mit einem iminodibenzylderivat. *Schweiz. Med. Wochenschr., 87*, 1135.
43. LANGER, G., KOINIG, G., HATZINGER, R., et al. (1986). Response of thyrotropin to thyrotropin-releasing hormone as predictor of treatment outcome. *Arch. Gen. Psychiatry, 43*, 861–868.

44. Liebowitz, M. R., Quitkin, F. M., Stewart, J. W., et al. (1984). Phenelzine v. imipramine in atypical depression. *Arch. Gen. Psychiatry, 41* 669–677.
45. Loomer, H. P., Saunders, J. C., & Kline, N. S. (1957). A clinical and pharmacodynamic evaluation of iproniazid as a psychic energizer. *Psychiatr. Res., 8*, 129–134.
46. Louie, A. K., & Meltzer, H. Y. (1984). Lithium potentiation of antidepressant treatment. *J. Clin. Psychopharmacol., 4*, 316–321.
47. Lydiard, R. B. (1985). Tricyclic-resistant depression: Treatment resistance or inadequate treatment. *J. Clin. Psychiatry, 46*, 412–417.
48. Maas, J. W., Kowlow, S. H., Katz, M. M., et al. (1984). Pretreatment neurotransmitter metabolite levels and response to tricyclic antidepressant drugs. *Am. J. Psychiatry, 141*, 1159–1171.
49. Marley, E., & Wozniak, K. M. (1983). Clinical and experimental aspects of interaction between amine oxidase inhibitors and amine re-uptake inhibitors. *Psychol. Med., 13*, 735–749.
50. Marley, E., & Wozniak, K. M. (1984). Interaction of a non-selective monoamine oxidase inhibitor, phenelzine, with inhibitors of 5-hydroxytryptamine, dopamine or nor-adrenaline re-uptake. *J. Psychiatr. Res., 18*, 173–189.
51. Mattes, J. A. (1985). Methylphenidate in mild depression: A double-blind controlled trial. *J. Clin. Psychiatry, 46*, 525–527.
52. Mendels, J. (1987). Clinical experience with serotonin reuptake inhibiting antidepressants. *J. Clin. Psychiatry, 48* (Suppl.), 26–30.
53. Mendels, J. (1976). Lithium in the treatment of depression. *Am. J. Psychiatry, 133*, 373–378.
54. Mendis, N., Pare, C. M. B., Sandler, M., et al. (1981). Is the failure of (−) deprenyl, a selective monoamine oxidase B inhibitor, to alleviate depression related to freedom from the cheese effect? *Psychopharmacology, 73*, 87–90.
55. Mood disorders (1985). Pharmacologic prevention of recurrences [NIMH/NIH Consensus Development Conference Statement]. *Am. J. Psychiatry, 142*, 469–476.
56. Moore, N. C., Lerer, B., Meyendorff, E., & Gershon, S. (1985). Three cases of carbamazepine toxicity. *Am. J Psychiatry, 142*, 974–975.
57. Murphy, D. L., Cohen, R. M., Siever, L. J., et al. (1983). Clinical and laboratory studies with selective monoamine-oxidase inhibiting drugs. *Mod. Prob. Pharmacopsychiatry, 19*, 287–303.
58. Nelson, J. C., Jatlow, P. I., & Mazure, C. (1987). Rapid desipramine dose adjustment using 24-hour levels. *J. Clin. Psychopharmacol., 7*, 72–77.
59. Nelson, J. C., & Jatlow, P. I. (1980). Neuroleptic effect on desipramine steady-state plasma concentrations. *Am. J. Psychiatry, 137*, 1232–1234.
60. Nelson, J. C., & Mazure, C. M. (1986). Lithium augmentation in psychotic depression refractory to combined drug treatment. *Am. J. Psychiatry, 143*, 363–366.
61. Nurnberg, H. G., & Finkel, J. A (1985). Carbamazepine in bipolar-depressed disorder complicated by tricyclic antidepressant switching: Case report. *J. Clin. Psychiatry, 46*, 485–487.
62. Oraulak, P. J. (1986). Therapeutic monitoring of antidepressant drugs: Current methodology and applications. *J. Clin. Psychiatry, 47* (Suppl.), 39–52.
63. Pare, C. M. B., Al Mousawi, M. Sandler, M., et al. (1985). Attempts to attenuate the "cheese effect." Combined drug therapy in depressive illness. *J. Affect. Disord., 9*, 137–141.
64. Pare, C. M. B. (1987). Monoamine oxidase inhibitors in treatment of affective disorders. *Psychiatr. Ann., 17*, 309–315.
65. Paykel, E. S., Rowan, P. R., Parker, R. R., et al. (1982). Response to phenelzine and amitriptyline in subtypes of outpatient depression. *Arch. Gen. Psychiatry, 39*, 1041–1048.

66. Paykel, E. S., West, P. S., & Rowan, P. R. (1982). Influence of acelylator phenotype on antidepressant effects of phenelzine. *Br. J. Psychiatry, 141*, 242–248.
67. Placidi, G. F., Lenzi, A., Lazzarini, F., et al. (1986). The comparative efficiency and safety of carbamazepine versus lithium: A randomized, double-blind 3-year trial in 83 patients. *J. Clin. Psychiatry, 47*, 480–494.
68. Pollack, M. H., & Rosenbaum, J. F. (1987). Management of antidepressant-induced side effects: A practical guide for the clinician. *J. Clin. Psychiatry, 48*, 3–8.
69. Post, R. M., Uhde, T. W., Ballenger, J. C., et al. (1983). Prophylactic efficacy of carbamazepine in manic-depressive illness. *Am. J. Psychiatry, 140*, 1602–1604.
70. Post, R. M., Uhde, T. W., Roy-Byrne, P. P., & Joffe, R. T. (1986). Antidepressant effects of carbamazepine. *Am. J. Psychiatry, 143*, 29–34.
71. Preskorn, S. H. (1986). Tricyclic antidepressant plasma level monitoring: An improvement over the dose-response approach. *J. Clin. Psychiatry, 47* (Suppl.), 24–30.
72. Preskorn, S. H., Weller, E., Weller, R., et al. (1983). Plasma levels of imipramine and adverse effects in children. *Am. J. Psychiatry, 140*, 1332–1335.
73. Price, L. H., Charney, D. S., & Heninger, G. R. (1985). Efficacy of lithium-tranylcypromine treatment in refractory depression. *Am. J. Psychiatry, 142*, 619–623.
74. Prien, R. F., Klett, C. J., & Caffey, E. M. (1974). Lithium prophylaxis in recurrent affective illness. *Am. J. Psychiatry, 131*, 198–203.
75. Prien, R. F., Kupfer, D. J., & Mansky, P. A. (1984). Drug therapy in the prevention of recurrences in unipolar and bipolar affective disorders. *Arch. Gen. Psychiatry, 41*, 1096–1104.
76. Quitkin, F. M., Kane, J., Rifkin, A., et al. (1981). Prophylactic lithium carbonate with and without imipramine for bipolar I patients. *Arch. Gen. Psychiatry, 38*, 902–907.
77. Quitkin, F. M. (1985). The importance of dosage in prescribing antidepressants. *Br. J. Psychiatry, 147*, 593–597.
78. Rabkin, J., Quitkin, F., Harrison, W., et al. (1984). Adverse reactions to monoamine oxidase inhibitors. Part I. A comparative study. *J. Clin. Psychopharmacol., 4*, 270–278.
79. Rabkin, J., Quitkin, F., & McGrath, P. (1985). Adverse reactions to monoamine oxidase inhibitors. Part II. Treatment correlates and clinical management. *J. Clin. Psychopharmacol., 5*, 2–4.
80. Raft, D., Davidson, J. R. T., Wasik, J., et al. (1981). Relationship between response to phenelzine and MAO inhibition in a clinical trial of phenelzine, amitriptyline, and placebo. *Neuropsychobiology*, 7, 122–126.
81. Richelson, E. (1984). The newer antidepressants. *Psychopharmacol. Bull., 20*, 213–223.
82. Rigal, J. G., Albin, H. C. H., Duchier, A. R., et al. (1987). Imipramine blood levels and clinical outcome. *J. Clin. Psychopharmacol.*, 7, 222–229.
83. Rivaris, C. L., Robinson, D. S., Ives, J. O., et al. (1980). Phenelzine and amitriptyline in the treatment of depression. *Arch. Gen. Psychiatry, 37*, 1057–1080.
84. Robinson, D. S., Cooper, T. B., Howard, D., et al. (1985). Amitriptyline and hydroxylated metabolite plasma levels in depressed outpatients. *J. Clin. Psychopharmacol., 5*, 83–88.
85. Robinson, D. S., Nies, A., Ravaris, C. L., et al. (1978). Clinical pharmacology of phenelzine. *Arch. Gen. Psychiatry, 35*, 629–635.
86. Roose, S. P., Glassman, A. H., Giardina, E. G. V., et al. (1987). Tricylic antidepressants in depressed patients with cardiac conduction disease. *Arch. Gen. Psychiatry, 44*, 273–277.
87. Ross, C. A. (1986). Biological tests for mental illness: Their use and misuse. *Biol. Psychiatry, 21*, 431–435.
88. Rubin, E. H., Biggs, J. T., & Preskorn, S. H. (1985). Nortriptyline pharmacokinetics and plasma levels: Implications for clinical practice. *J. Clin. Psychiatry, 46*, 418.

89. Scheffer, C. B., Mungas, D., & Rockwell, E. (1985). Successful treatment of psychotic depression with carbamazepine. *J. Clin. Psychopharmacol.*, *5*, 233–235.
90. Scher, M., Krieger, J. N., & Juergens, S. (1983). Trazodone and priapism. *Am. J. Psychiatry*, *140*, 1362–1363.
91. Spiker, D. G., Weiss, J. C., Dealy, R. S., et al. (1985). The pharmacological treatment of delusional depression. *Am. J. Psychiatry*, *142*, 430–436.
92. Sulliven, E. A., & Shulman, K. I. (1980). Diet and monoamine oxidase inhibitors: A reexamination. *Can. J. Psychiatry*, *29*, 707–711.
93. Sulser, F. (1987). Serotonin-norepinephrine receptor interactions in the brain: Implications for pharmacology and pathophysiology of affective disorders. *J. Clin. Psychiatry*, *448* (Suppl.), 13–18.
94. Targum, S. D., Greenberg, R. D., Harmon, R. L., et al. (1984). The TRH test and thyroid hormone in refractory depression. *Am. J. Psychiatry*, *141*, 463–466.
95. Tariot, P. N., Murphy, D. L., Sunderland, T., et al. (1986). Rapid antidepressant effect of addition of lithium to tranylcypromine. *J. Clin. Psychopharmacol.*, *6*, 165–167.
96. Task Force on Laboratory Tests in Psychiatry (1987). The dexamethasone suppression test: An overview of its current status in psychiatry. An APA Task Force Report. *Am. J. Psychiatry*, *144*, 1253–1263.
97. Task Force on the Use of Laboratory Tests in Psychiatry (1985). Tricyclic antidepressants—Blood level measurements and clinical outcome. An APA Task Force Report. *Am. J. Psychiatry*, *142*, 155–162.
98. Thompson, J., Rankin, H., Ashcroft, G. W., et al. (1982). The treatment of depression in general practice: A comparison of L-tryptophan, amitriptyline and a combination of L-tryptophan and placebo. *Psychol. Med.*, *12*, 741–751.
99. Turner, P., Young, J. R., & Peterson, J. (1967). Influence of urinary pH on the excretion of tranylcypromine sulfate. *Nature*, *215*, 881–882.
100. Veith, R. C., Bielski, R. J., Bloom, V., et al. (1983). Urinary MHPG excretion and treatment with desipramine or amitriptyline: Prediction of response, effect of treatment, and methodological hazards. *J. Clin. Psychopharmacol.*, *3*, 18–27.
101. Wehr, T. A., & Goodwin, F. K. (1979). Rapid cycling in manic-depressives induced by tricyclic antidepressants. *Arch. Gen. Psychiatry*, *36*, 555–559.
102. White, K., O'Leary, J., Razani, J., et al. (1971). Electrocardiographic effects of tranylcypromine vs. amitriptyline. *Arch. Gen. Psychiatry*, *24*, 145–155.
103. White, K., & Simpson, G. (1981). Combined MAOI-tricyclic antidepressant treatment: Reevaluations. *J. Clin. Psychopharmacol.*, *1*, 264–282.
104. White, K., & Simpson, G. (1985). Should the use of MAO inhibitors be abandoned? *Integr. Psychiatry*, *3*, 34–45.
105. Woods, S. W., Tesar, G. E., Murray, G. B., & Cassem, N. H. (1986). Psychostimulant treatment of depressive disorders secondary to mental illness. *J. Clin. Psychiatry*, *47*, 124–125.
106. Worrall, E. P., Moody, J. P., Peet, M., et al. (1979). Controlled studies of the acute antidepressant effects of lithium. *Br. J. Psychiatry*, *135*, 255–262.
107. Wyatt, R. J., Fram, D. H., Kupfer, D. J., & Synder, F. (1981). Total prolonged drug-induced REM sleep suppression in anxious-depressed patients. *Am. J. Psychiatry*, *138*, 379–380.
108. Yang, H., & Neff, N. H. (1974). The monoamine oxidase of brain. Selective inhibition with drugs and the consequences for the metabolism of biogenic amines. *J. Pharm. Exp. Ther.*, *189*, 733–740.
109. Yassa, R., Camille, Y., & Belzile, L. (1987). Tardive dyskinesia in the course of antidepressant therapy: A prevalence study and review of the literature. *J. Clin. Psychopharmacol.*, *7*, 343–346.
110. Zisook, S. (1985). A clinical overview of monoamine oxidase inhibitors. *Psychosomatics*, *26*, 240–251.

20

DRUG THERAPY AND DEPRESSION IN CHILDREN

PAUL J. AMBROSINI, M.D.

Associate Professor of Psychiatry,
Director, Child Psychiatry Outpatient Services
Medical College of Pennsylvania
Eastern Pennsylvania Psychiatric Institute
Philadelphia, Pennsylvania

and

CLAUDIA METZ, M.D.

Assistant Clinical Professor of Psychiatry,
Assistant Director, Child Depression Clinic,
Case Western Reserve University
Cleveland, Ohio

INTRODUCTION

Within the last two decades our understanding of the phenomenology of child and adolescent affective disorder has advanced substantially. The development of standardized assessment techniques and a strong commitment to diagnostic reliability and research design among investigators have helped to delineate the natural history, prevalence, genetic, biological, and psychosocial correlates of affective disorder in the young. However the breadth of our knowledge of child and adolescent affective disorders lags behind the progress achieved in adults because of an initial debate about the validity of the disorder in this age group and because of the lack of suitable diagnostic instruments for identifying child and adolescent psychopathology.

This work was supported in part by NIMH grant MH 41684.

Nowhere is this lack of progress more evident than in the domain of treatment. Numerous double-blind, placebo-controlled studies of adult depressives have conclusively shown that pharmacotherapy is effective both in alleviating the acute morbidity of this disorder and in maintaining recovery (46). Furthermore, the synergistic benefits of pharmacotherapy and psychotherapy are also well documented (6, 62). There are, however, few well-designed studies of pharmacotherapy in depressed youngsters, and there are no investigations of the concurrent use of pharmacotherapy and psychotherapy. Ethical constraints have also limited the use of organic therapies in depressed youngsters before they are proven safe and effective in the adult population. Pharmacotherapy nonetheless is the one treatment modality systematically studied in child and adolescent affective disorder, no doubt because of the major technical difficulties in implementing a psychotherapy protocol (103).

This chapter reviews our current understanding of the efficacy of pharmacotherapy and discusses the clinical implementation of such treatment. Because no double-blind, placebo-controlled study has shown tricyclics to be superior to placebo in the treatment of depressed children and adolescents but clinical experience has clearly identified responders, a thorough understanding of the appropriate use of antidepressants is essential for the practicing clinician. Since proper diagnosis is mandatory prior to initiating pharmacotherapy, the validating characteristics and diagnosis of child and adolescent major depressive disorder (MDD) are briefly reviewed before the discussion of pharmacotherapy.

CLINICAL CHARACTERISTICS OF DEPRESSION IN THE YOUNG

While depression in adults has been recognized for thousands of years, the existence of childhood depression still remains in some circles relatively controversial. In the 1950s and 1960s people questioned whether depression was psychodynamically possible in childhood since the superego was not considered to be fully developed and internalized before adolescence (93, 94). More recently it was hypothesized that while affective disorder may indeed exist in childhood, children are unable to express feelings of sadness and depressed mood directly; thus a diagnosis of depression must be deduced from a variety of symptoms or behaviors which "mask" the underlying dysphoria (22). Behavior problems, school difficulties, and somatic or psychosomatic complaints were considered to be "depressive equivalents," i.e., symptoms that even in the absence of a depressed mood could be considered evidence of depression. It was, however, never shown how to reliably differentiate when these symptoms existed in their own right versus when they should be considered symptoms of depression. Today there is a growing consensus that child, adolescent, and adult depression exist on a single continuum with common clinical symptoms, although the clinical presentation may vary somewhat given the child's level of cognitive and emotional development (16). In this light, depressive equivalents are best understood as common presenting complaints in a depressed child rather than in and of themselves as evidence of the depressive syndrome (48).

Symptom-Syndrome Differentiation

In any discussion of childhood depression, it is important to differentiate between depression as a symptom (the sad mood that may occur in response to a variety of stressors) and depression as a syndrome, that is, a unique constellation of affective, cognitive, motivational, psychomotor, and vegetative symptoms which temporally cluster together. Thus, for example, in the Isle of Wight study (96), parents reported that 10% of their children aged 10 and 11 were depressed or unhappy but only 1.4% of these were actually found to have the depressive syndrome. Similarly Carlson and Cantwell (14), studying children in an inpatient and outpatient psychiatric setting, found that while about 60% of children may describe depressive symptoms on a screening self-report questionnaire, only about 1/3 of these actually have a depressive syndrome. The point prevalence of the depressive syndrome among nine-year-old children is estimated to be about 1 to 2%, and it is equally common among boys and girls (41). Among adolescents, lifetime prevalence increases to 5 to 13% and the sex ratio approaches the two female : one male ratio found in adults (19).

Diagnostic Criteria and Depressive Subtypes

In order to make a diagnosis of major depression, DSM-III-R requires the presence of a dysphoric mood and/or pervasive anhedonia plus at least four of the following symptoms: 1) appetite disturbance, 2) sleep disturbance, 3) psychomotor agitation or retardation, 4) loss of interest or pleasure in usual activities, 5) fatigue or loss of energy, 6) excessive guilt or feelings of worthlessness, 7) decreased concentration, and 8) recurrent thoughts of death or suicide. These symptoms must be present for at least two weeks and must not be superimposed on schizophrenia, organic mental disorder, or uncomplicated bereavement. The major subtypes of depression identified in adults have also been found in children and adolescents.

Endogenous MDD occurs in a proportion of depressed youngsters who exhibit a specific clustering of symptoms such as a qualitatively distinct depressed mood that is not relieved by pleasant environmental events, anhedonia, diurnal variation in depressed mood with dysphoria worse in the morning hours, psychomotor agitation or retardation, early-morning awakening, and appetite or weight loss. These symptoms are similar to those characterizing melancholic depression, but there is not a total overlap. Although it is suggested that the endogenous-melancholic subtype is the more "biologically" based disorder, and there is some supportive evidence for this in depressed youngsters (71, 80), it has not been shown that these children respond preferentially to pharmacotherapy or that they exhibit a similar symptom pattern if their depression recurs.

Psychotic depression, characterized by mood-congruent delusions or hallucinations, is found in about one-third of prepubertal children with major depression (17). Psychotic symptoms are more common with endogenous than with nonendogenous depression. Hallucinations are most commonly auditory, especially command hallucinations, but religious, persecutory, or conversing voices may also be reported. Hallucinations are much less commonly visual or tactile. Mood congruence implies that the hallucinating themes are usually morbid and/or dysphoric—e.g. denigrating voices, suicidal commands, or visions of death or of a dead relative. Furthermore, they are temporally related to the depressed state and resolve with resolution of the depressive syndrome. About 7% of prepubertal depressions are accompanied by delusions. These too are usually mood congruent and involve delusions of persecution, guilt, or sin. When hallucinations or delusions are bizarre or mood incongruent, depression is less likely and a diagnosis of schizophrenia or schizoaffective disorder should be considered. On the other hand, auditory hallucinations of noises or of one's name being called or other hallucinatory phenomena (illusions, imaginary companions, hypnagogic or hypnopompic hallucinations) are relatively common phenomena in childhood and should not be considered diagnostic of psychopathology (28).

Additional subtypes of affective disorder include dysthymic disorder (49, 50) and cyclothymic disorder (1). These are chronic disturbances of affect present for at least one year in which the severity, number and duration of affective symptoms do not meet criteria for a major depression or bipolar disorder and in which the affective symptoms may be interspersed with periods of normal mood lasting from several days up to two months. Little is known about the pharmacotherapy of these syndromes in children.

Bipolar disorder, characterized by alternating periods of mania and depression, commonly has its onset in adolescence or young adulthood (40, 58). Mania is quite rare in prepuberty. In one study by Strober and Carlson (107), approximately 1/5 of an inpatient adolescent sample who presented with major depression progressed to a bipolar outcome within three to four years. Particularly at risk are those with a positive family history of affective disorder, prominent psychomotor retardation, rapid symptom onset, mood-congruent psychotic features, or a hypomanic response to tricyclic antidepressants. Although several authors (63, 116) contend that early onset of bipolar disorder is associated with a relatively poor prognosis with more rapid switches between mania and depression, increased number of episodes, and increased risk of suicide later in life, Zis and colleagues (117) noted that early age of onset is associated with a lower probability of relapse.

Atypical affective disorders are characterized by all the symptoms of MDD but particularly increased appetite and weight, and hypersomnia during depressive episodes. Persons with these disorders are very reactive to their environment, are particularly sensitive to rejection, and have marked difficulties in interpersonal relationships (56). While rare in childhood, such depressions may first make their appearance in adolescence. It is important to distinguish them from nonatypical major depression because of their tendency to respond preferentially to monoamine oxidase inhibitors (MAOI) rather than to tricyclic antidepressants (89).

Despite the widening use of adult symptom criteria and subtyping to define MDD in the young, skepticism still remains regarding the appropriateness of this trend without incorporating a developmental perspective on the expression of psychopathology. The issue of age-related changes in the phenomenology of childhood depression has been discussed and empirically analyzed by several investigators (16, 18, 51). These authors contend that the relationship between development, maturation, and the expression of specific depressive symptoms is more complex than simply accepting behavioral isomorphism in the observed signs and symptoms of depression across different aged children. Clearly, more rigorous work is needed before the clinical spectrum of the depressive syndrome is fully elucidated in the young.

Syndrome and Symptom Comorbidity in Child and Adolescent Depression

While associated symptomatology in depressed children may differ from that typical in the depressed adult because of the child's maturational level, the clinical picture is often complicated by the coexistence of other psychiatric disorders. These syndromes may appear after the onset of the depressed mood, or their symptoms may represent the presenting complaints diverting attention from the underlying depression. In a prospective longitudinal study of school-aged children, Kovacs et al. (49) found that 79% of children with major depressive disorder had a concurrent psychiatric diagnosis. The most common was dysthymic disorder (38%). One-third had a coexisting anxiety disorder and 7% a conduct disorder that clearly antedated the major depression. While these diagnoses do not influence the rate of recovery, a concurrent dysthymic disorder ("double depression") does increase the risk of recurrence of the major depression. Obsessive-compulsive–disordered adolescents frequently have a history of MDD (91), while about one-third of prepubertal depressed boys had a concurrent conduct disorder (76). Anxiety symptoms also frequently co-occur with major depression in children (38). In fact, the rate of anxiety symptoms in subjects with MDD was similar to the rate in subjects with a nondepressed, emotional disorder (87). Separation anxiety disorder is significantly more common in prepubertal than postpubertal depressives (30).

There appears to be a complex relationship between depression and anorexia/bulimia nervosa as well (109). Many eating-disordered children have a positive family history of depression, and one follow-up study (12) of anorexia nervosa in adolescence found that after the anorectic symptoms subsided, 1/3 of the group met criteria for an affective disorder. It may be that anorectics with MDD have a higher family loading for depression compared to anorectics without depression (7).

While hyperactivity used to be considered a "depressive equivalent," there is minimal evidence that depression is associated with attention deficit disorder (ADD). In a family study of ADD, Biederman et al. (8) did, however, find a higher risk for MDD among relatives of these probands compared to nonpsychiatric control families. At the same time, since the psychomotor agitation and poor concentration associated with depression may be misdiagnosed as hyperactivity, all hyperactive children should be carefully assessed for possible depressive symptoms. Similarly, while enuresis used to be considered a symptom of depression since it frequently responded to tricyclic antidepressants, more recent studies suggest that the antienuretic and antidepressant effects of these medications represent different pharmacological mechanisms (4).

Suicide

Suicide is very rare among children under 12, and the rates have remained fairly stable over the past few decades. Among teenagers, the suicide rate has increased significantly over the past years, doubling between 1961 and 1975. Suicide now represents the number 3 cause of death in 15-to-19-year age range in the United States, following accidents and homicide (102). However, the rates of symptomatic versus syndromatic depression in those with suicidal ideation, suicidal attempts, or completed suicide and the rates of suicidal behaviors in those symptomatically or syndromatically depressed are only recently being rigorously investigated. Several groups report higher rates of syndromatic depression with increasing severity of suicidal ideation (15); also, from one-quarter to two-thirds of suicidal attempters have a depressive disorder (15, 16, 112). Conversely, while 90% of symptomatic depressives have suicidal ideation (47), only 38% of syndromatically depressed youngsters attempt suicide (20). Suicidal ideation, attempts, and completed suicides all increase in frequency with increasing age (60, 102), as does the rate of depressive disorder in children and adolescents. Although an affective disorder diagnosis is correlated with the lethality of suicidal behavior (11), the rates of MDD in completed suicide in the young remain to be clarified.

CLINICAL ASSESSMENT METHODOLOGY

Understanding of the phenomenology and the effects of pharmacotherapy of the depressed child was greatly advanced by promulgation of specific diagnostic criteria and by development of reliable assessment interviews. Weinberg et al. (113) were the first to develop operationally defined diagnostic criteria for childhood depression. They modified the Feighner criteria (27) for diagnosing adult major depressive disorder for use in childhood. Puig-Antich et al. (75) used unmodified Research Diagnostic Criteria (RDC) to diagnose and treat prepubertal children with major depressive disorder.

A variety of assessment tools are available to diagnose childhood depression and quantify its severity. These include both interviews and self-rating scales. The childhood version of the Schedule for Affective Disorders and Schizophrenia (K-SADS), developed by Puig-Antich and Chambers (78), is a semistructured interview based on the adult SADS. It allows for the systematic assessment of specific symptoms required to make DSM-III and RDC diagnoses of illness and elicits information from parents and child about the duration and timing of various symptoms. The Diagnostic Interview Schedule for Children (DISC) (21), developed by Costello and colleagues, and the Diagnostic Interview for Children and Adolescents (DICA), developed by Herjanic and Welner (37), are primarily used in epidemiological surveys and clinical studies by nonprofessional interviewers. They too provide diagnoses based on DSM-III and RDC criteria.

To supplement information derived from these clinical interviews, Poznanski et al. (72) adapted the Hamilton Depression Scale for adults as the Children's Depression Rating Scale (CDRS). Several self-rating scales have also been developed. The Beck Depression Inventory (BDI) can be used in adolescents (106) and was modified by Kovacs for use in the 7-to-17-year age range as the Child Depression Inventory (CDI) (52). These scales do not diagnose depression, but rather provide useful information for assessing the *severity* of illness and thus for monitoring the response to treatment. Kazdin and Petti (43) have systematically reviewed most of the scales and interviews used in child and adolescent depression.

VALIDATION OF THE DEPRESSIVE SYNDROME IN THE YOUNG

Evaluating the validity of a psychiatric disorder is a multistage process. It involves assessing internal validators such as the consistency of symptoms that differentiate the syndrome from other disorders and evaluating external validators such as biological correlates, family aggregation, psychosocial characteristics, natural outcome, and response to treatment (13). If the disorder has true validity, it is assumed that these parameters will define a unique cluster of patients when compared to normals or psychiatric controls.

The external validators investigated in child and adolescent MDD have been those parameters characteristically altered in adult depressives. The biological tests studied include cortisol hypersecretion, the dexamethasone suppression test, growth hormone response to insulin-induced hypoglycemia, growth hormone secretion during sleep, thyroid-stimulating hormone (TSH) response to thyrotropin-releasing hormone (TRH), and polysomnographic variables. Family aggregation studies have investigated the prevalence of depressive disorder in both the children of depressed adults and the parents of depressed children. Psychosocial variables measured in this group include relationships with parents, peers, siblings, and school functioning. Finally, the outcome of MDD has been compared with that of dysthymic disorder and adjustment disorder with depressed mood in a naturalistic (untreated) cohort.

Biological Validators

Neuroendocrine investigations in child and adolescent MDD are an attempt to test the catecholamine hypothesis of depression, which suggests that serotonin and norepinephrine are deficient in this syndrome. Since neuroendocrine systems are intimately affected by these catecholamines, an abnormality of these systems would be indirect proof of this hypothesis. A second goal of this work in depressed youngsters is to evaluate the continuity of the depressive syndrome from childhood to adulthood since it is already known that several neuroendocrine abnormalities occur in depressed adults. Studying prepubertal and adolescent depression offers a unique opportunity for assessing the influence of age and therefore maturational development on the depressive syndrome. Numerous methodological constraints, however, remain to be overcome in this neuroendocrine paradigm (95).

Cortisol. Twenty-four-hour cortisol is not significantly elevated in prepubertal depressives since only about 10% of an endogenous sample hyposecretes cortisol (86). Conservative estimates of dexamethasone nonsuppression (DST) in hospitalized prepubertal depressives is approximately 80% with a similar specificity (57, 68, 110, 115), although the sensitivity is considerably lower in outpatient samples (29, 72). Puig-Antich, however, did not corroborate these findings in prepubertal depressives (86). In inpatient adolescent depressives, DST nonsuppression has an approximate sensitivity of 40%, with a specificity of 75% (2, 26, 36, 39, 45, 111). Since weight loss and dexamethasone nonabsorption may cause DST nonsuppression, these confounding variables must be controlled for proper interpretation of these tests (59, 69).

Growth hormone. Growth hormone response to insulin-induced hypoglycemia is blunted in prepubertal endogenous depressives compared to nondepressed psychiatric controls (80). Over 60% of these children and approximately 50% of all major depressive prepubertal youngsters hyposecrete growth hormone in the insulin tolerance test (ITT). Specificity of the ITT ranges from 87% to 94%. It is also reported that about one-half of prepubertal depressives hypersecrete growth hormone during sleep (81). This was significantly different than a psychiatric and normal control group. Both the growth hormone ITT and growth hormone sleep abnormalities remain significantly abnormal when studied in the drug-free, fully recovered state (82, 83).

Thyroid hormone. Blunted TSH response to intravenous TRH does not differentiate prepubertal depressives from a control group (86). Similar negative results are reported in adolescence (35).

Polysomnography. Classical polysomnographic abnormalities found in adult MDD, such as shortened REM latency, increased REM density, decreased delta sleep, decreased sleep efficiency, and an abnormal temporal distribution of REM sleep, were not identified in prepubertal MDD during active illness (77); however, shortened REM period latency emerged in this group on recovery (79). Classical REM sleep findings were also not present in actively depressed adolescents (34).

Family studies. Family aggregation studies suggest that children of depressed adults are at significantly increased risk for major depression compared to nondepressed controlled families (114). The rate of MDD in children of depressed probands ranges from 15% to 41%, and the chronicity of depression in parents increases the overall psychiatric morbidity in their children (44). Similarly, first- and second-degree relatives of depressed children are at high risk for affective disorder (range 20% to 50%) (86, 108).

Psychosocial characteristics. The psychosocial impairment seen in prepubertal depressives suggests a deficit in verbal and affective communication with parents and siblings (84). Even after recovery from the depressive syndrome, those youngsters with initial severe deficits have only moderate improvement in their psychosocial skills (85).

Outcome. Kovacs et al. (49, 50), studying the naturalistic outcome of prepubertal major depression, found that the median time to recovery from onset of MDD was 7.2 months, with a maximal recovery rate of 92% attained by 1½ years. Approximately 9% relapse within the first year after recovery and 32% have relapsed after two years. However, in those youngsters with double depression (dysthymia and major depression), the comparable figures are 43 and 54%, respectively, suggesting that double depression has a higher morbidity rate. The mean duration of adolescent depression is also approximately seven months (108).

Although the validating correlates just reviewed do not all directly coincide with the findings in adult MDD, these findings clearly establish the validity of MDD in children and adolescents. Those areas which differ from adult findings probably reflect the influence of age and maturation on the phenotypic expression of this syndrome across the ages. Studies of pharmacotherapeutic response also are an external validating paradigm.

PHARMACOTHERAPY

Overview

Over the last 20 years tricyclic antidepressants (TCA) have been used in children and adolescents to treat a variety of disorders, including enuresis (104), school phobia (33), and attention deficit disorder (24). This experience has shown that with proper administration TCAs can be safely administered to the pediatric age group.

The use of TCAs in depressed children began in the 1960s, yet the majority of this work is hampered by poor methodological design. Heterogeneous samples of children with anxious, behavioral, or psychotic features were treated; few reports delineated the diagnostic or recovery characteristics; dose and duration of medication treatment were inadequate or not specified. This body of work therefore describes the treatment of the symptom of depression and not necessarily the depressive syndrome (5, 67).

By the mid-1970s more rigorously designed investigations were undertaken from which we have gained the most knowledge of TCA efficacy in child and adolescent depression. Parameters of such studies include the following characteristics: double-blind, placebo-controlled design with random assignment to each treatment cell; placebo washout; sufficient sample size; adequate dosing and duration of pharmacotherapy; and plasma tricylic monitoring. Only eight studies (32, 42, 53, 66, 73, 75, 88, 98) are available that have incorporated most of these design characteristics; no study to date has included all of these parameters. These studies have tested the efficacy of imipramine, nortriptyline, and amytriptyline. Clinical reports are also avialable for the use of maprotiline (61), mianserin (25), and fluoxetine (105); however, the two former works are methodologically weak and the latter work presents preliminary data from an ongoing project.

Of the eight well-designed studies, four are open medication trials (32, 73, 75, 98) with a total sample size of 84, while four studies are double-blind designs (42, 53, 66, 88) with a total sample size of 73. Only two studies (53, 98) investigated the efficacy of TCAs in adolescence; the remainder studied prepubertal MDD. None of the double-blind studies found TCAs superior to placebo although they were considered beneficial in most open trials. It should also be noted that Puig-Antich's group studied approximately half of all these patients (75, 88, 98). A detailed critique of these studies is available (5).

A summary of the pharmacotherapy response is most illuminating. Using conservative estimates of recovery, approximately 62% and 55% of prepubertal children with MDD responded to either TCA or placebo, respectively. The comparable figures in adolescent MDD are 52% and 60%. These figures do not as yet support the clinical efficacy of TCAs in depression in the young; furthermore, the high placebo rate will make it difficult to prove TCA efficacy in properly designed studies without a very large sample size. However, several facts can be gleaned from a more detailed reading of these investigations.

1. Prepubertal depressives may exhibit a different pharmacological response since their improvement was correlated with plasma TCA levels, in contrast with adolescent depressives who did not show this pattern (73, 88).
2. Pharmacotherapy response is similar in the endogenous and non-endogenous subtypes but less likely in the psychotic prepubertal depressives (88, 98).
3. A minimum plasma imipramine plus desipramine level of 150 ng/ml appears to maximize response in prepubertal depressives (73, 88).
4. Nortriptyline may exhibit a "therapeutic window" in prepubertal depressives, with maximal response in the 60 to 100 ng/ml range (36).

Indications for Pharmacotherapy

Since the efficacy of pharmacotherapy in child and adolescent MDD remains marginal in placebo-controlled studies, the question remains as to when TCAs should be used. Before this is discussed several facts must be emphasized. The depressive syndrome in youngsters is not a transient phenomenon since the mean duration is approximately seven months (49, 108) and a diagnosis of MDD implies functional impairment. Efficacy of non-pharmacological interventions also remains unproven although cognitive behavioral and relaxation training may benefit those youngsters with depressive symptoms (92). Therefore, after a proper diagnostic assessment and lack of response to more traditional interventions, a six-week trial of TCAs is indicated. Clearly, if there is prior history of medication responsiveness, pharmacotherapy could be introduced sooner.

Administering Tricyclics in Depressed Children

Knowledge of dosing and titration schedules (90), physiological side-effects (31, 54, 97, 99, 101), and overdose characteristics and management

(3, 9, 10, 100) are necessary for safe pharmacotherapeutic treatment of the depressed child. Furthermore, an initial medical clearance is preferable prior to administering antidepressants. The tricyclics imipramine and desipramine are generally prescribed on a mg/kg basis, while nortriptyline is titrated to achieve a specific plasma drug level (90). Specific plasma tricyclic levels or ranges, particularly in prepubertal MDD, are correlated with maximal response (32, 73, 88). In responders, medication should be continued for at least three months in youngsters and up to six months in adolescents following full remission of the depressive syndrome. Tapering of medication should be gradual over one to two weeks to minimize withdrawal-emergent symptoms (55). Nonresponsiveness may be a particular problem in adolescence. A combination of TCAs and monoamine oxidase inhibitors (MAOI) may augment response in those refractory to imipramine (99). Such a drug combination may also offer protection against the hypertensive response noted in those taking MAOIs and ingesting tyramine-containing foods (64, 65). Lithium carbonate may be beneficial in adolescents with symptoms of significant irritability, hypomanic or maniclike features, or a family history of bipolar disorder (23). Carbamezepine, which has been reported beneficial in adult affective illness (70), could also be tried in nonresponding adolescents. However, its efficacy in this population has not been systematically studied. A more detailed discussion of drug treatment is available (3).

CONCLUSIONS

The validity of child and adolescent MDD is being more clearly demonstrated through systematic research involving epidemiological, biological, treatment, outcome, and family study strategies. Although there is not a complete concordance between characteristics of adult depression and depression in the young, findings to date clearly support the fact that the depressive syndrome is a disorder affecting all ages. Some of the differences may reflect influences of maturation and aging, yet it may also be valid to view major depression as exhibiting age-specific characteristics. This pattern would not be unique to depressive disorder, but rather is commonplace in other pathological states such as juvenile diabetes and rheumatoid arthritis.

The failure to demonstrate the superiority of pharmacotherapy over placebo in child and adolescent MDD is still based on a limited number of studies. A great deal of work remains to be done to more clearly understand the limits of pharmacotherapy in depressed youngsters. Combining pharmacotherapy trials with assessment of other biological parameters (e.g., DST) may help identify specific subsets of drug-responsive patients. Continuation and prophylactic studies are necessary to understand more precisely how long treatment should continue, but such projects are not yet available because the superiority of pharmacotherapy over placebo is still in doubt. Nonpharmacological treatment studies are similarly required. Nonetheless, great strides have been made in our knowledge of the depressive syndrome in the young. Today it appears that we are on the forefront of a major movement that will expand our understanding of the depressive syndrome and its treatment in children and adolescents.

REFERENCES

1. Akiskal, H. S., Downs, J., et al. (1985). Affective disorders in referred children and younger siblings of manic-depressives. *Arch. Gen. Psychiatry*, *42*, 996.
2. Alessi, N. E., & Robbins, D. R. (1984). Symptoms and subtypes of depression among adolescents distinguished by the dexamethasone suppression test: A preliminary report. *Psychiatr. Res.*, *11*, 177.
3. Ambrosini, P. J., Rabinovich, H., et al. (1984). Biological factors and pharmacological treatment in major depressive disorder in children and adolescents. In H. Sudak et al. (Eds.), *Suicide in the young*. Boston: John Wright.
4. Ambrosini, P. J. (1984). A pharmacological paradigm for urinary incontinence and enuresis. *J. Clin. Psychopharmacol.*, *4*, 247.
5. Ambrosini, P. J. (1987). Pharmacotherapy in child and adolescent major depressive disorder. In H. Y. Meltzer (Ed.), *Psychopharmacology: The third generation of progress*. New York: Raven Press.
6. Beck, A. T., Hollon, S. D., et al. (1985). Treatment of depression with cognitive therapy and amitriptyline. *Arch. Gen. Psychiatry*, *42*, 142.
7. Biederman, J., Rivinus, T., et al. (1985). Depressive disorders in relatives of anorexia nervosa patients with and without a current episode of nonbipolar major depression. *Am. J. Psychiatry*, *142*, 1495.
8. Biederman, J., Munir, K., et al. (1987). High rate of affective disorders in probands with attention deficit disorder and in their relatives: A controlled family study. *Am. J. Psychiatry*, *144*, 330.
9. *Biol. Ther. Psychiatry* [newsletter] (1984), *7*, 26.
10. Boehnert, M. T., & Lovejoy, F. H. (1985). Value of the QRS duration versus the serum drug level in predicting seizures and ventricular arrhythmias after an acute overdose of tricyclic antidepressants. *N. Engl. J. Med.*, *313*, 474.
11. Brent, D. A. (1987). Correlates of the medical lethality of suicide attempts in children and adolescents. *J. Am. Acad. Child Adol. Psychiatry*, *26*, 87.
12. Cantwell, D. P., Sturzenberger, S., et al. (1977). Anorexia nervosa: An affective disorder? *Arch. Gen. Psychiatry*, *34*, 1087.
13. Cantwell, D. P. (1985). Depressive disorders in children. Validation of clinical syndromes. *Psychiatr. Clin. N. Amer.*, *8*, 779.
14. Carlson, G. A., & Cantwell, D. P. (1980). A survey of depressive symptoms, syndrome and disorder in a child psychiatric population. *J. Child Psychol. Psychiatry*, *21*, 19.

15. Carlson, G. A., & Cantwell, D. P. (1982). Suicidal behavior and depression in children and adolescents. *J. Am. Acad. Child Psychiatry, 21*, 361.
16. Carlson, G. A., & Garber, J. (1986). Developmental issues in the classification of depression in children. In M. Rutter, C. E. Izard, et al. (Eds.), *Depression in young people*. New York: Guilford Press.
17. Chambers, W. J., Puig-Antich, J., et al. (1982). Psychotic symptoms in prepubertal major depressive disorder. *Arch. Gen. Psychiatry, 39*, 921.
18. Cicchetti, D., & Schneider-Rosen, K. (1986). An organizational approach to childhood depression. In M. Rutter, C. E. Izard, et al. (Eds.), *Depression in young people*. New York: Guilford Press.
19. Cohen, P., Velez, C. N., & Garcia, M. (1985). The epidemiology of childhood depression. Presented at the American Academy of Child Psychiatry, San Antonio.
20. Cohen-Sandler, R., Berman, A. L., et al. (1982). Life stress and symptomatology: Determinants of suicidal behavior in children. *J. Am. Acad. Child Psychiatry, 21*, 178.
21. Costello, A. J., Edelbrock, C., et al. (1984). *Diagnostic Interview Schedule for Children* (DISC). Pittsburgh: Western Psychiatric Institute & Clinic.
22. Cytryn, L., & McKnew, D. H. (1972). Proposed classification of childhood depression. *Am. J. Psychiatry, 129*, 149.
23. DeLong, G. R., & Neiman, G. W. (1983). Lithium-induced behavior changes in children with symptoms suggesting manic-depressive illness. *Psychopharmacol. Bull., 19*, 258.
24. Donnelly, M., Zametkin, A. J., et al. (1986). Treatment of childhood hyperactivity with desipramine: Plasma drug concentration, cardiovascular effects, plasma and urinary catecholamine levels, and clinical response. *Clin. Pharmacol. Ther., 39*, 72.
25. Dugas, M., Mouren, M. C., et al. (1985). Treatment of childhood and adolescent depression with mianserin. *Acta Psychiatr. Scand., 72* (Suppl. 320), 48.
26. Extein, I., Rosenberg, G., et al. (1982). The dexamethasone suppression test in depressed adolescents. *Am. J. Psychiatry, 139*, 1617.
27. Feighner, J. P., Robins, E., et al. (1972). Diagnostic criteria for use in psychiatric research. *Arch. Gen. Psychiatry, 26*, 57.
28. Garralda, M. E. (1984). Hallucinations in children with conduct and emotional disorders. I. The clinical phenomena. *Psychol. Med., 14*, 589.
29. Geller, B., Rogol, A. D., et al. (1983). Preliminary data on the dexamethasone suppression test in children with major depressive disorder. *Am. J. Psychiatry, 140*, 620.
30. Geller, B., Chestnut, E. C., et al. (1985). Preliminary data on DSM-III associated features of major depressive disorder in children and adolescents. *Am. J. Psychiatry, 142*, 643.
31. Geller, B., Farooki, Z. Q., et al. (1985). Serial ECG measurements at controlled plasma levels of nortriptyline in depressed children. *Am. J. Psychiatry, 142*, 1095.
32. Geller, B., Cooper, T. B., et al. (1986). Preliminary data on the relationship between nortriptyline plasma level and response in depressed children. *Am. J. Psychiatry, 143*, 1283.
33. Gittelman-Klein, R., Klein, D. F., et al. (1971). Controlled imipramine treatment of school phobia. *Arch. Gen. Psychiatry, 25*, 204.
34. Goetz, R. R., Puig-Antich, J., et al. (1987). Electroencephalographic sleep of adolescents with major depression and normal controls. *Arch. Gen. Psychiatry, 44*, 61.
35. Greenberg, R., Rosenberg, G., et al. (1985). The dexamethasone suppression test and the thyrotropin-releasing hormone test in adolescent major depressive disorder. *Proc. Am. Acad. Child Psychiatry, 1*, 42.
36. Ha, H., Kaplan, S., et al. (1984). The dexamethasone suppression test in adolescent psychiatric patients. *Am. J. Psychiatry, 141*, 421.
37. Herjanic, B., & Welner, Z. (1983). *The Diagnostic Interview for Children and Adolescents* (DICA). St. Louis: Washington University School of Medicine.

38. Hershberg, S. G., Carlson, G. A., et al. (1982). Anxiety and depressive disorders in psychiatrically disturbed children. *J. Clin. Psychiatry, 43*, 358.
39. Hsu, L. K. G., Molcan, K., et al. (1983). The dexamethasone suppression test in adolescent depression. *J. Am. Acad. Child Psychiatry*, 5, 470.
40. Joyce, P. R. (1984). Age of onset in bipolar affective disorder and misdiagnosis as schizophrenia. *Psychol. Med., 14*, 145.
41. Kashani, J. H., McGee, R. O., et al. (1983). Depression in a sample of 9-year-old children. *Arch. Gen. Psychiatry, 40*, 1217.
42. Kashani, J. H., Shekim, W. O., et al. (1984). Amitriptyline in children with major depressive disorder: A double-blind crossover pilot study. *J. Am. Acad. Child Psychiatry*, 3, 348.
43. Kazdin, A. E., & Petti, T. A. (1982). Self-report and interview measures of childhood and adolescent depression. *J. Child Psychol. Psychiatry, 23*, 437.
44. Keller, M. B., Beardslee, W. R., et al. (1986). Impact of severity and chronicity of parental affective illness on adaptive functioning and psychopathology in children. *Arch. Gen. Psychiatry, 43*, 930.
45. Klee, S. H., & Garfinkel, B. D. (1984). Identification of depression in children and adolescents: The role of the dexamethasone suppression test. *J. Am. Acad. Child Psychiatry*, 4, 410.
46. Klein, D. F., Gittelman, R., et al. (1980). *Diagnosis and drug treatment of psychiatric disorders: Adults and children*. Baltimore: Williams & Wilkins.
47. Kosky, R., Silburn, S., et al. (1986). Symptomatic depression and suicidal ideation. A comparative study with 628 children. *J. Nerv. Ment. Dis., 174*, 523.
48. Kovacs, M., & Beck, A. T. (1977). An empirical-clinical approach toward a definition of childhood depression. In J. G. Schulterbrandt & A. Raskin (Eds.), *Depression in childhood: Diagnosis, treatment, and conceptual models*. New York: Raven Press.
49. Kovacs, M., Feinberg, T. L., et al. (1984). Depressive disorders in childhood. I. A longitudinal prospective study of characteristics and recovery. *Arch. Gen. Psychiatry, 41*, 229.
50. Kovacs, M., Feinberg, T. L., et al. (1984). Depressive disorders in childhood. II. A longitudinal study of the risk for a subsequent major depression. *Arch. Gen. Psychiatry, 41*, 643.
51. Kovacs, M., & Paulauskas, S. L. (1984). Developmental stage and the expression of depressive disorders in children: An empirical analysis. In D. Cicchetti & K. Schneider-Rosen (Eds.), *Childhood depression*. San Francisco: Jossey-Bass.
52. Kovacs, M. (1985). The Children's Depression Inventory (CDI). *Psychopharmacol. Bull., 21*, 995.
53. Kramer, A. D., & Feiguine, R. J. (1981). Clinical effects of amitriptyline in adolescent depression. *J. Am. Acad. Child Psychiatry, 20*, 636.
54. Lake, C. R., Mikkelsen, E. J., et al. (1979). Effect of imipramine on norepinephrine and blood pressure in enuretic boys. *Clin. Pharmacol., 26*, 647.
55. Law. W., Petti, T. A., et al. (1981). Withdrawal symptoms after graduated cessation of imipramine in children. *Am. J. Psychiatry, 138*, 647.
56. Liebowitz, M. R., & Klein, D. F. (1979). Hysteroid dysphoria. *Psychiatr. Clin. North Am., 2*, 555.
57. Livingston, R., Reis, C. J., et al. (1984). Abnormal dexamethasone suppression test results in depressed and nondepressed children. *Am. J. Psychiatry, 141*, 106.
58. Loranger, A. W., & Levine, P. M. (1978). Age at onset of bipolar affective illness. *Arch. Gen. Psychiatry, 35*, 1345.
59. Lowy, M. T., & Meltzer, H. Y. (1987). Dexamethasone bioavailability: Implications for DST research. *Biol. Psychiatry, 22*, 373.
60. McClure, G. M. G. (1984). Recent trends in suicide amongst the young. *Br. J. Psychiatry, 144*, 134.

61. Minuti, E., & Gallo, V. (1982). Use of antidepressants in childhood: Results of maprotiline (Ludiomil) treatment in 20 cases. *Adv. Biochem. Psychopharmacol., 32*, 223.

62. Murphy, G. E., Simons, A. D., et al. (1984). Cognitive therapy and pharmacotherapy. *Arch. Gen. Psychiatry, 41*, 33.

63. Olsen, T. (1961). Follow-up study of manic-depressive patients whose first attack occurred before the age of 19. *Acta Psychiatr. Scand., 37* (Suppl. 162), 45.

64. Pare, C. M. B., & Kline, N. (1982). Will amitriptyline prevent the "cheese" reaction of monoamine-oxidase inhibitors? *Lancet, 2*, 183.

65. Pare, C. M. B., Al Mousawi, M., et al. (1985). Attempts to attenuate the "cheese effect." *J. Affect. Disord., 9*, 137.

66. Petti, T. A., & Law, W. (1982). Imipramine treatment of depressed children: A double-blind pilot study. *J. Clin. Psychopharmacol., 2*, 107.

67. Petti, T. (1983). Imipramine in the treatment of depressed children. In D. P. Cantwell & G. A. Carlson (Eds.), *Affective disorders in childhood and adolescence. An update.* New York: SP Medical & Scientific Books.

68. Petty, L. K., Asarnow, J. R., et al. (1985). The dexamethasone suppression test in depressed, dysthymic, and nondepressed children. *Am. J. Psychiatry, 142*, 631.

69. Pfohl, B., Coryell, W., et al. (1986). Body weight and reported versus measured weight loss as confounders of the dexamethasone suppression test. *Biol. Psychiatry, 21*, 931.

70. Post, R. M., Uhde, T. W., et al. (1984). The efficacy of carbamazepine in affective illness. In E. Usdin, et al. (Eds.), *Frontiers in biochemical and pharmacological research in depression*. New York: Raven Press.

71. Poznanski, E. O., Carrol, B. J., et al. (1982). The dexamethasone suppression test in prepubertal depressed children. *Am. J. Psychiatry, 139*, 321.

72. Poznanski, E. O., Grossman, J. A., et al. (1984). Preliminary studies of the reliability and validity of the Children's Depression Rating Scale. *J. Am. Acad. Child Psychiatry, 2*, 191.

73. Preskorn, S. H., Weller, E. B., et al. (1982). Depression in children: Relationship between plasma imipramine levels and response. *J. Clin. Psychiatry, 43*, 450.

74. Preskorn, S. H., Weller, E. B., et al. (1983). Plasma levels of imipramine and adverse effects in children. *Am. J. Psychiatry, 140*, 1332.

75. Puig-Antich, J., Blau, S., et al. (1978). Prepubertal major depressive disorder. A pilot study. *J. Am. Acad. Child Psychiatry, 17*, 695.

76. Puig-Antich, J. (1982). Major depression and conduct disorder in prepuberty. *J. Am. Acad. Child Psychiatry, 21*, 118.

77. Puig-Antich, J. Goetz, R., et al. (1982). Sleep architecture and REM sleep measures in prepubertal children with major depression. A controlled study. *Arch. Gen. Psychiatry, 39*, 932.

78. Puig-Antich, J., Chambers, W. J., et al. (1983). The clinical assessment of current depressive episodes in children and adolescents: Interviews with parents and children. In D. P. Cantwell & G. A. Carlson (Eds.), *Affective disorders in childhood and adolescence. An update.* New York: SP Medical & Scientific Books.

79. Puig-Antich, J., Goetz, R., et al. (1983). Sleep architecture and REM sleep measures in prepubertal major depressives. Studies during recovery from the depressive episode in a drug free state. *Arch. Gen. Psychiatry, 40*, 187.

80. Puig-Antich, J., Novacenko, H., et al. (1984). Growth hormone secretion in prepubertal children with major depression. I. Final report on repsonse to insulin-induced hypoglycemia during a depressive episode. *Arch. Gen. Psychiatry, 41*, 455.

81. Puig-Antich, J., Goetz, R., et al. (1984). Growth hormone secretion in prepubertal children with major depression. II. Sleep-related plasma concentrations during a depressive episode. *Arch. Gen. Psychiatry, 41*, 463.

82. Puig-Antich, J., Novacenko, H., et al. (1984). Growth hormone secretion in prepubertal children with major depression. III. Response to insulin-induced hypoglycemia after recovery from a depressive episode and in a drug-free state. *Arch. Gen. Psychiatry, 41*, 471.

83. Puig-Antich, J., Goetz, R., et al. (1984). Growth hormone secretion in prepubertal children with major depression. IV. Sleep-related plasma concentrations in a drug-free, fully recovered clinical state. *Arch. Gen. Psychiatry, 41*, 479.

84. Puig-Antich, J., Lukens, E., et al. (1985). Psychosocial functioning in prepubertal major depressive disorders. I. Interpersonal relationships during the depressive episode. *Arch. Gen. Psychiatry, 42*, 500.

85. Puig-Antich, J., Lukens, E., et al. (1985). Psychosocial functioning in prepubertal major depressive disorders. II. Interpersonal relationships after sustained recovery from affective episode. *Arch. Gen. Psychiatry, 42*, 511.

86. Puig-Antich, J. (1987). Affective disorders in children and adolescents: Diagnostic validity and psychobiology. In H. Y. Meltzer (Ed.), *Psychopharmacology: The third generation of progress*. New York: Raven Press.

87. Puig-Antich, J., & Rabinovich, H. (1986). Relationship between affective and anxiety disorders in childhood. In R. Gittelman (Ed.), *Anxiety disorders of childhood*. New York: Guilford Press.

88. Puig-Antich, J., Perel, J. M., et al. (1987). Imipramine in prepubertal major depressive disorders. *Arch. Gen. Psychiatry, 44*, 81.

89. Quitkin, F. M., Harrison, W., et al. (1984). Defining the boundaries of atypical depression. *J. Clin. Psychiatry, 45*, 19.

90. Rancurello, M. D. (1985). Clinical application of antidepressant drugs in childhood behavioral and emotional disorders. *Psychiatr. Ann., 15*, 88.

91. Rapoport, J., Elkins, R., et al. (1981). Childhood obsessive-compulsive disorder. *Am. J. Psychiatry, 138*, 1545.

92. Reynolds, W. M., & Coats, K. I. (1986). A comparison of cognitive-behavioral therapy and relaxation training for the treatment of depression in adolescents. *J. Consult. Clin. Psychol., 54*, 653.

93. Rie, H. E. (1966). Depression in childhood: A survey of some pertinent contributions. *J. Am. Acad. Child Psychiatry, 5*, 653.

94. Rochlin, G. (1959). The loss complex: A contribution to the etiology of depression. *J. Amer. Psychoanal. Assoc., 7*, 299.

95. Rubin, R. T. (1985). The prospects for clinical psychoneuroendocrinology: Has the curtain been drawn across the neuroendocrine window? *Psychol. Med., 15*, 451.

96. Rutter, M., Tizard, J., et al. (1970). *Education, health and behavior*. London: Longmans.

97. Ryan, N. D., Puig-Antich, J., et al. (1987). The relative safety of single vs. divided dose imipramine in adolescent major depression. *J. Am. Acad. Child Psychiatry, 26*, 400.

98. Ryan, N. D., Puig-Antich, J., et al. (1986). Imipramine in adolescent major depression: Plasma level and clinical response. *Acta Psychiatr. Scand., 73*, 275.

99. Ryan, N. D., & Puig-Antich, J., et al. (1988). MAOI's in adolescent major depression unresponsive to tricyclic treatment. *J. Am. Acad. Child. Adol. Psych., 27*, 755.

100. Salzman, C. (1985). Clinical use of antidepressant blood levels and the electrocardiogram. *N. Eng. J. Med., 313*, 512.

101. Saraf, K. R., Klein, D. F., et al. (1978). EKG effects of imipramine treatment in children. *J. Am. Acad. Child Psychiatry, 17*, 60.

102. Shaffer, D., & Fisher, P. (1981). The epidemiology of suicide in children and young adolescents. *J. Am. Acad. Child Psychiatry, 20*, 545.

103. Shaffer, D. (1984). Notes on psychotherapy research among children and adolescents. *J. Am. Acad. Child Psychiatry, 23*, 552.

104. Shaffer, D., & Ambrosini, P. J. (1985). Enuresis and sleep disorders. In J. M. Weiner (Ed.), *Diagnosis and psychopharmacology of childhood and adolescent disorders.* New York: Wiley.

105. Simeon, J. G., & Ferguson, H. B. (1986). Efficacy and safety of fluoxetine in the treatment of depressive disorders in children. *Proc. Am. Acad. Child Adol. Psychiatry, 2*, 27.

106. Strober, M., Green, J., et al. (1981). Utility of the Beck Depression Inventory with psychiatrically hospitalized adolescents. *J. Consult. Clin. Psychol., 49*, 482.

107. Strober, M., & Carlson, G. (1982). Bipolar illness in adolescents with major depression. *Arch. Gen. Psychiatry, 39*, 549.

108. Strober, M. (1985). Depressive illness in adolescence. *Psychiatr. Ann., 15*, 375.

109. Swift, W. J., Andrews, D., et al. (1986). The relationship between affective disorder and eating disorders: A review of the literature. *Am. J. Psychiatry, 143*, 290.

110. Targum, S. D., Chastek, C. T., et al. (1981). Dexamethasone suppression test in prepubertal conduct disorder. *Psychiatr. Res., 5*, 107.

111. Targum, S. D., & Capodanno, A. E. (1983). The dexamethasone suppression test in adolescent psychiatric inpatients. *Am. J. Psychiatry, 140*, 589.

112. Taylor, E. A., & Stansfeld, S. A. (1984). Children who poison themselves. I. A clinical comparison with psychiatric controls. *Br. J. Psychiatry, 145*, 127.

113. Weinberg, W. A., Rutman, J., et al. (1973). Depression in children referred to an educational diagnostic center: Diagnosis and treatment. *J. Pediatr., 83*, 1065.

114. Weissman, M. M. (1987). Psychopathology in the children of depressed parents: Direct interview studies. Presented at the American Psychopathological Association, New York.

115. Weller, R., Weller, E. B., et al. (1985). A comparison of the cortisol suppression index and the dexamethasone suppression test in prepubertal children. *Am. J. Psychiatry, 142*, 1370.

116. Welner, A., Welner, Z., et al. (1979). Psychiatric adolescent inpatients. Eight to ten year follow-up. *Arch. Gen. Psychiatry, 36*, 698.

117. Zis, A. P., Grof, P., et al. (1979). The natural course of affective disorders: Indications for lithium prophylaxis. In T. B. Cooper et al. (Eds.), *Lithium: Controversies and unresolved issues.* Amsterdam: Excerpta Medica.

21

THE RELATIONSHIP BETWEEN TARDIVE DYSKINESIA AND AFFECTIVE DISORDERS

JAMES T. WEGNER, PH.D.

Associate in Research,
Department of Psychiatry,
Yale University School of Medicine
New Haven, Connecticut

and

WILLIAM M. GLAZER, M.D.

Associate Professor of Psychiatry;
Director, Tardive Dyskinesia Clinic,
Department of Psychiatry,
Yale University School of Medicine
New Haven, Connecticut

INTRODUCTION

Tardive dyskinesia (TD) remains a major concern in the long-term use of neuroleptic medications. This problem is particularly compelling since it has been demonstrated that maintenance medication plays an important role in the prevention of relapse in schizophrenia (25), including first-episode schizophrenics (58, 89). The lack of a proven, effective treatment for TD (55) and its irreversibility in a proportion of patients (19) emphasize the importance of identifying subgroups of psychiatric patients who may be at higher risk for developing this movement disorder. The purpose of this chapter is to examine in some detail the role affective disorders may play as a risk factor in the development of TD, and to present data from the TD Clinic at Yale University (41) relevant to this body of literature. Moreover, we review what TD is and explore briefly other risk factors that have emerged in the literature which may render an individual more vulnerable to TD development.

Background and Description

This iatrogenic syndrome was originally described in the late 1950s (97, 98) and was initially considered rare. Tardive dyskinesia is now a well-recognized side effect of prolonged neuroleptic treatment (4), and its status as a public health concern has been commented on (38). While differences in syndrome definition, patient populations, and examining techniques preclude accurate prevalence determination, Kane and Smith (59) reviewed 56 studies in which TD prevalence ranged from 0.5% to 56% (mean, 20.1%), and preliminary findings from a prospective study of TD development suggest a TD incidence of 24% after seven years of neuroleptic exposure (62). While TD may occur at any point in the course of neuroleptic treatment, its emergence usually is delayed by many months or years. It may also appear suddenly following withdrawal of neuroleptic medication after a period of prolonged use.

The most typical symptom cluster consists of the buccolingual-masticatory (BLM) syndrome, which involves lip smacking, puckering of the lips, chewing and sucking movements, jaw movements, and tonic, clonic, and choreoathetoid movements of the tongue (56). Although, typically, the upper regions of the face are spared, spasmodic blinking, blepharospasm, and involuntary movements of the frontalis muscle may occur in a small percentage of patients (21, 107). However, Stevens (105) has reported that schizophrenics display spontaneous abnormal eye blink rate, which suggests that in schizophrenics, the presence of blinking may represent schizophrenic pathology and not a manifestation of TD. Occasionally, facial tics, grunting vocalizations, and grimacing may also accompany the clinical picture.

In patients over the age of 50, BLM symptomatology is the rule. Less frequently, choreoathetoid movements of the limbs and trunk may occur as well (56). Choreoathetoid movements of the fingers and wrists, ballistic movements, abnormal movements of the toes, rotation and flexion of the ankles, axial hyperkinesia, as well as other disturbances of the neck and trunk can all occur in TD. Abnormal trunk movements, however, usually accompany the more severe forms of the disorder. Pediatric and adolescent cases of TD are typically characterized by the presence of choreoathetoid movements of the distal extremities, ataxia, and ballistic movements (30), and by the absence of BLM symptomatology, although some case reports have described the coexistence of both BLM and extremity involvement in pediatric samples (87). The relationship between younger patients having TD symptoms in the extremities and older patients having TD predominantly in the orofacial region is analogous to the effect of age on the topographic distribution of movements in torsion dystonia (29, 107).

The majority of patients seen show mild cases of TD. Although many patients are unaware of their dyskinetic movements (2, 93, 101), there are some who are and who find their movements distressing, which may lead to social withdrawal (38). However, a number of reports and case studies raise concern over more serious sequelae arising from TD. Dyspnea and chest pain (115), increased respiratory rate (53), and life-threatening respiratory, gastrointestinal and renal complications have been reported (14, 71). Moreover, Mehta et al. (78) found a higher mortality rate in their TD patients than in their control sample. Jackson et al. (53) speculated that the increased respiratory rate may compromise the functioning of other systems, and that this component is associated with TD and increased mortality.

RISK FACTORS IN THE DEVELOPMENT OF TARDIVE DYSKINESIA

While dyskinetic movements, particularly choreic movements, were noted in psychiatric patients in the preneuroleptic era (90), the epidemiological evidence implicating neuroleptic treatment as the most significant etiological factor for TD is extremely strong. Kane and Smith (59), in their review of 56 studies involving 35,000 neuroleptic-treated patients, found a mean prevalence rate of 20%, while the average prevalence among 19 untreated samples involving 11,000 patients was 5%. The statistical difference between these two findings was $p<10^{-5}$. Moreover, because of the difficulties TD imposes on the clinical management of psychiatric patients, extensive work has been done in attempting to identify factors that may predispose an individual to the development of TD.

Age

It is generally agreed that TD is more common among the elderly than among younger patients. Smith and Baldessarini (100), in reviewing the literature, showed that a linear correlation exists between age and both the prevalence and severity of TD irrespective of duration of neuroleptic exposure. They also found that remission of TD symptomatology varied inversely with age. Retrospective data or point-prevalence studies that examine age as a possible risk factor are difficult to interpret, however, since it is frequently impossible to ascertain when the dyskinetic movements first appeared. Moreover, age may be correlated with the presence of mild organic brain syndromes and the development of spontaneous dyskinesia, thus rendering age as epiphenomenal to perhaps more critical variables.

Gender Differences

While most investigators report that increasing age is an important predisposing factor in the development of TD, the results concerning the importance of sex in this regard have been contradictory. Some studies (10, 65) have reported that female samples have twice the prevalence of this disorder as male samples. Other studies (54) have found no difference in the prevalence of TD in women versus men, and two studies (17, 84) noted a slightly higher prevalence in men. Jeste and Wyatt (56), in reviewing 20 studies that examined gender as a predisposing factor, found that the prevalence of TD was about 41% higher in women than in men. Smith et al. (102) found that while women had a linear increase with age in the prevalence of TD, males displayed a significant curvilinear relationship, with the prevalence in men decreasing after age 70. However, it is conceivable that differences in endocrine status affecting neuroleptic metabolism (45), sex-related differences in enzyme levels (81), differential drug responsiveness (52), and differences in treatment patterns with female patients (26, 70, 99) could contribute to differing prevalences of TD between sexes. Glazer et al. (46) found that estrogen replacement therapy improved involuntary movements in postmenopausal women with TD significantly more than placebo. Thus, the finding of sex differences in TD is somewhat complex, and treatment- and patient-related variables are probably interacting with this effect in some as of yet undetermined way.

Neuroleptic Treatment Variables

Numerous studies have examined the relationship between TD and neuroleptic variables, including the length of neuroleptic exposure (22, 99), maximum daily dose (20, 39, 57, 102), cumulative drug exposure (22, 65), the use of polypharmacy (57, 102), type of neuroleptic (40, 65, 85, 102), and drug holidays (9, 47, 54). Thus far, there is no compelling evidence that any of these neuroleptic variables contribute to the development of TD in any significant way. However, the examination of these neuroleptic treatment effects are methodologically complex since the investigator typically has to rely on retrospective chart review for gathering information on treatment history. Moreover, some variables, such as type of neuroleptic and its effect on the development of TD, are almost impossible to adequately assess, since it is extremely rare for a patient to have been exposed to one type of neuroleptic over the entire course of treatment.

Other risk factors have been examined, including history of extrapyramidal side effects (18), history of antiparkinsonian medication (67), organic impairment (112, 113, 122), history of ECT (32), premorbid asociality (112), and so forth, and the results have generally been equivocal. The relationship between TD and psychiatric diagnosis has also been explored, and while there are no clear-cut findings regarding this, a body of literature is emerging that suggests a relationship between affective disorders and TD. This interesting finding may be of etiopathological significance and will be explored in more detail below.

AFFECTIVE ILLNESS AND TARDIVE DYSKINESIA

Tardive dyskinesia has frequently been described in schizophrenics probably because they are the group of patients most likely to receive neuroleptic treatment, and thus they are more at risk for developing the disorder. The early literature stressed that TD occurred almost exclusively in chronically impaired schizophrenics or patients suffering from organic brain syndromes, but later studies reported TD in outpatient schizophrenics (8) and in neuroleptic-treated nonpsychotic patients (66). To date, however, there does not appear to be any direct relationship between schizophrenia and TD.

Affective Diagnosis and Tardive Dyskinesia

In 1976, two extended case reports appeared in the literature that suggested that patients with affective disorders may be at higher risk for developing TD. Davis et al. (24) reported that of their 14 patients evaluated for TD, nine met Feighner criteria (33) for depression. In another study, Alpert et al. (3) noted that over the course of their patients' psychiatric illness, depressive trends were evident.

Rosenbaum et al. (94) retrospectively examined all cases of TD at the Mayo Clinic, and of their 12 patients, nine had a diagnosis of depression. In addition, these investigators also interviewed a cohort of TD patients and found that 15 of their 18 patients met Feighner criteria (33) for depression.

Rush et al. (95) retrospectively examined the presenting signs and symptoms of 11 patients with and eight patients without TD during their first hospitalization. The results of this case-control study showed that while the no-TD patients had higher overall ratings of symptom severity during their first admission, the TD patients had significantly higher ratings on mood and affective disorder, but not psychomotor retardation. Moreover, when these patients were rediagnosed using RDS (103) criteria, it was found that 7 of the 11 TD patients had affective disorders and the other four were nonschizophrenic. In the control group, six were RDC schizophrenics and two schizoaffective, mainly schizophrenic. These findings suggested that patients who go on to develop TD are more likely to exhibit depressive symptomatology early in the course of their illness.

In an attempt to replicate the findings of Rush et al. (95) and using a case-control design, Yassa and Schwartz (125) retrospectively examined the charts of 26 patients with and 26 patients without TD for the presence of depressive symptomatology in their first admission, and in subsequent admissions. The results showed that 18 (68.4%) of the 26 TD patients had depressive episodes during their first hospitalization, as compared to five no-TD patients (19.2%), and that over the course of their illness, the TD patients had a total of 85 depressive episodes while the no-TD patients had 43 depressive episodes. Both these findings were significantly different. However, there was no difference between the two groups in the number of manic episodes, and there was no relationship between the severity of TD and the number of depressive episodes.

Hamra et al. (49), also using a case-control design, retrospectively reviewed the charts of 17 outpatients with TD and 17 randomly selected patients without TD. Their findings regarding psychiatric diagnosis showed that patients with affective disorders and paranoid schizophrenia had significantly more TD. However, their criteria for TD was any case with an Abnormal Involuntary Movement Scale (AIMS) score of >1, a score that could potentially result in a high number of false positive cases of TD.

Yassa et al. (123), in a prevalence study of TD, examined 83 neuroleptic users attending an affective disorders clinic and all patients admitted to their hospital with a diagnosis of affective disorder. Of the 83 patients, 35 (41%) were found to have TD. Considering that the mean prevalence for TD is about 20% for all psychiatric patients (59), a rate of 41% is rather high.

In a prevalence study of 328 patients, Yassa, Nair, and Schwartz (124) identified 101 cases of TD. They found that the diagnosis of organic mental syndrome (41%) and bipolar disorder (42%) was significantly more frequent than the diagnosis of schizophrenia (24.5%) in the patients with TD.

Kane et al. (61), in analyzing the results of their incidence study, examined the relationship between affective illness and the development of TD. The results of a life-table analysis revealed that at the end of six years of cumulative neuroleptic exposure, the incidence for TD in the schizoaffective/affective group was 26%, while for the schizophrenic group, it was 18% ($p < .05$; Lee Desu test). However, the diagnosis used in the analysis was based on the hospital chart (usually DSM-II criteria). Moreover, potentially confounding variables were not controlled for in the life-table analysis. To that end, using a case-control design, they matched 54 TD patients with 54 prospectively followed no-TD patients, and using RDC criteria, they found that the rate of affective disorders was not significantly different across the two groups They concluded that their results provided at least some support for the role of affective disorders as a risk factor for TD development.

Wolf et al. (121), in a prevalence study, examined the relationship between TD and primary psychiatric diagnosis and found that patients with affective disorders with alcoholism were at highest risk for developing the disorder while young schizophrenics with a short hospitalization were at the lowest risk. Moreover, parkinsonism and low scores on the Mini-Mental-State (36) were associated with TD in affective disorder but not schizophrenic patients.

Mukherjee et al. (79) examined the prevalence of TD in their sample of DSM-III–diagnosed bipolar disorder outpatients. Of the 96 patients who received neuroleptic treatment of at least three months' duration, 34 (35.4%) were diagnosed as having persistent TD based on RD-TD criteria. In their multivariate analysis of relevant variables, longer cumulative duration of neuroleptic treatment and shorter exposure to lithium carbonate treatment accounted for 36% of the variance of the prevalence of TD.

Symptoms and/or Mood-State Effects on Dyskinetic Symptomatology

While these studies have investigated the relationship between TD and primary psychiatric diagnosis of affective illness, a number of other studies have examined either the effect of affective symptoms or the effect the mood state itself has on the symptomatology of TD.

Karson et al. (63) examined the relationship between psychopathology and TD in chronic schizophrenics by retrospectively evaluating the Brief Psychiatric Rating Scale (BPRS) (83) scores of 17 TD patients and 30 no-TD patients who were undergoing a medication withdrawal period. In this case-control design, a number of trends emerged from the data, including the finding that patients with TD tended to have higher depressive symptomatology scores than did the no-TD cohort.

In a discontinuation study of outpatients suffering from TD, Glazer et al. (42) examined the relationship between psychological symptoms and dyskinetic movements. They found that in the nonschizophrenic TD group, the BPRS "depressed mood" item correlated negatively with the total AIMS score ($r = -.40$, $p < .052$). Thus, more depression was associated with less TD.

Price and Levin (88) presented a case report in which the patient's TD and depressive symptomatology improved after a course of ECT. Interestingly, ECT has also been reported to alleviate both depression and extrapyramidal symptoms in some depressed Parkinson's disease patients (7, 72). Similar to the findings of Glazer et al. (42), Himmelhoch and Neil (51) reported on a bipolar patient whose symptoms of TD regularly lessened during depressive states. However, a number of other case reports have noted an exacerbation of TD during depressive episodes and its disappearance during normal mood states (5, 23), and similar improvement during manic periods (23, 27, 74, 116, 120). Finally, Goswami et al. (48) reported that their bipolar disorder patient's TD lessened during his depressive and manic states but was exacerbated during periods of euthymia. These findings of mood state and its effect on TD symptomatology are difficult to interpret since they are all based on case reports. Moreover, the normal fluctuation of TD symptoms over time as well as possible treatment effects may be influencing the outcome of these mood-dependent findings in TD. For instance, previous case studies in the literature have reported that tricyclic antidepressants can cause choreoathetosis (31) and other dyskinetic movements, particularly amoxapine (69, 73), and that lithium carbonate has been reported to be beneficial in treating TD symptomatology in some patients (16), as well as causing choreoathetoid movements (126).

The Relationship Between Affective Illness and the Course of Tardive Dyskinesia

Only a handful of studies have examined the association of affective illness and the course of the movement disorder itself. Kane et al. (60) reported on a cohort of psychiatric patients who were considered as being at high risk for TD, which they defined as anyone developing the disorder after less than one year of cumulative exposure to neuroleptics. Five of their seven patients were diagnosed as having affective disorders using RDC criteria (103), which suggests that affectively ill patients may be more sensitive to TD development early in their treatment. This finding was replicated in a larger sample (61), in which they also found that the affectively ill patients frequently had more severe TD than that found in schizophrenics.

Glazer et al. (43), in factor-analyzing the seven anatomical scores of the AIMS, found three statistically independent factors of abnormal movements: jaw/tongue, face/lips, and extremities/trunk. Using logistic regression to predict severity of these factors, one of the findings showed that the severity of the orofacial scores was positively correlated with a diagnosis of schizoaffective or affective disorder.

In an extension of the study mentioned above (42), Glazer et al. (44) followed 49 TD patients off neuroleptic medication on a monthly basis for as long as five years. Thirty-eight of these patients did not have SADS-L-RDC diagnoses of schizophrenia. The majority of these 38 patients had affective diagnoses, including two with schizoaffective disorder. Multivariate analyses revealed that a nonschizophrenic diagnosis signficantly predicted a shorter time to reaching an observable improvement in TD, i.e., a decrease in the total AIMS score by 50% or more from the baseline value. Furthermore, nonschizophrenic patients exhibited a greater decrease in the average of all AIMS scores measured over time. Thus, this study found that nonschizophrenic patients (mainly affective) with TD improved faster and to a greater degree than patients with a schizophrenic diagnosis. This study, together with Kane et al.'s (60, 61), suggests that affective patients develop TD faster when exposed to neuroleptic medication and recover more quickly and more considerably than patients with schizophrenic diagnoses.

Putative pharmacological mechanisms. There are interesting pharmacological data that may provide a framework for understanding the link between affective disorders and TD. The monoamine hypothesis of depression (11, 96) suggests that depression results from a deficiency in norepinephrine and/or serotonin. It has been known for quite some time that there are direct and indirect connections between these neurotransmitters and central dopamine systems. Several investigators have generated animal models for noradrenergic-dopaminergic interactions (28, 108). In addition, serotonin-dopamine interactions in the nigrostriatal system have been demonstrated via behavioral (68, 75), biochemical (110), and electrical (1) techniques. Recently, McMillen (77) demonstrated that buspirone, a predominantly serotonergic receptor agonist, reversed striatal postsynaptic dopamine supersensitivity resulting from chronic neuroleptic exposure in rats. Assuming that postsynaptic supersensitivity in the rat represents the pathomechanism underlying TD, and assuming that the effect from buspirone is via serotonin, one can see a possible explanation for the relationship between depression and TD. It is possible that serotonin depletion in certain patients with depression renders the nigrostriatal dopamine system more vulnerable to the dyskinetogenic effects of neuroleptics. Further studies of the treatment of TD with serotonergic agonists are indicated.

Familial Occurrence of Affective Illness in the First-Degree Relatives of Patients with Tardive Dyskinesia

One study has appeared in the literature that examined familial aggregation of psychiatric disorders in the first-degree relatives of schizophrenics with TD. Wegner et al. (112), using the family history method for ascertaining psychiatric diagnosis in a case-control design, found that schizophrenics with TD had a higher familial loading for affective disorders in their first-degree relatives than no-TD schizophrenic controls. A morbidity risk of 21.7% in the TD group was over twice that found in the control group (9.6%). Previous studies have revealed that the morbidity risk for affective illness in the first-degree family members of schizophrenic probands is between 7.0% (109) and 11.4% (64), and these rates are similar to the control group finding of Wegner et al. (112). Interestingly, Galdi et al. (37), in their psychopharmacogenetic study, found that schizophrenics who had depressed relatives tended to exhibit more severe drug-induced parkinsonism regardless of the type of neuroleptic used in their treatment. These studies suggest that schizophrenics with a positive family history of affective illness may be more susceptible to the development of both TD and parkinsonian side effects.

Affective Disorders, Organic Impairment, and Tardive Dyskinesia

A number of reports in the literature have suggested that organically impaired patients with a primary psychiatric diagnosis of affective illness may be particularly at risk for developing TD. Wolf et al. (122) found affective disorder patients with TD showed more impairment on the Wechsler Memory Scale (111) and the Rey Auditory-Verbal Learning Test (91) than affective disorder patients without TD. This was not found in their comparison between schizophrenics with and without TD. Moreover, Mukherjee et al. (80) found that neurological soft signs were associated with bipolar disorder patients with TD. Furthermore, Wegner et al. (113) psychometrically evaluated a large cohort of psychiatric patients prior to the development of TD using the Conceptual Level Analogy Test (CLAT) (118) and the Trailmaking Test (6). While the results showed that patients who subsequently develop TD have a significantly worse baseline CLAT score, there was an interesting trend noted which showed that affective disorder patients who develop TD had worse CLAT scores than schizophrenics who develop TD. These results were surprising since schizophrenics as a group traditionally perform more poorly than affective disorder patients on tests of cognitive functioning. Of related interest is the electroencephalographic (EEG) finding of Wegner et al. (114) which showed that one EEG abnormality, the B-Mitten pattern, was associated with TD. Past research has suggested a primary relationship between mittens and affective dysregulation (106). These neuropsychological findings, while not definitive, do suggest that organically impaired affective disorder patients may be at higher risk for TD development than affective disorder patients who are organically intact.

Affective Disorders and Other Movement Disorders

Closely related to these findings of a possible relationship between affective disorders in patients with TD is a body of literature that has emerged in examining the association of affective illness and idiopathic movement disorders. In Parkinson's disease, there is a high prevalence of depression in the early stages of the illness, which is not just reactive to the illness but appears to accompany it (7, 15, 92). In fact, Harvey (50) reported that depression is the most common psychiatric complication in Parkinson's disease, with an incidence higher than that found in the general population. Moreover, in studies examining the psychiatric status of patients with Huntington's disease, it has been reported that about one-half are also diagnosed as psychotic. While the proportion of patients diagnosed as schizophrenic or major affective disorder varies across studies, Folstein and Folstein (35) found that 41% of Huntington's disease patients suffered from a major depressive disorder at some time in their lives.

Studies examining the prevalence of psychiatric disorders in first-degree family members of probands with Parkinson's disease or Huntington's disease have suggested a familial relationship between affective disorders and these movement disorders. Stein et al. (104), in a pilot study, found a 24%

frequency of primary affective disorder in the first-degree relatives of Parkinson's disease patients. However, in examining a larger group of parkinsonian patients, this same group of investigators were unable to replicate their earlier findings (119). Folstein et al. (34), in examining family members with Huntington's disease, dichotomized their Huntington's disease probands into those with and without a major affective disorder. They found that when the Huntington's disease proband had a history of affective illness, 87% of the family members also had both Huntington's disease and an affective disorder, while in probands without an affective disorder, only 22% of the family members had a history of affective illness. Their data suggest that in families where affective disorder is a prominent symptom, the illness seems to segregate with the Huntington's disease gene (117).

Thus, these data suggest a possible association between affective disorders and both Parkinson's and Huntington's disease. Accompanying these disease states are profound changes in various neurotransmitter systems, including deficiencies of dopamine (82), serotonin, and norepinephrine (12) in Parkinson's disease, and gamma-aminobutyric acid (GABA) (76, 86) and acetylcholine (76) in Huntington's disease. Several of these neurotransmitters have also been implicated in the etiology of depression, and thus, it is conceivable that the structural brain changes inherent to these disorders impinge on neurotransmitter systems and the development of affective symptomatology as a result of this interaction.

SUMMARY

Tardive dyskinesia remains a troublesome side effect of neuroleptic treatment. Moreover, while these medications have been proven to be effective in the treatment of psychoses, particularly schizophrenia, the risk of tardive dyskinesia development has become a prominent aspect of the psychiatrist's decision-making process in examining the risks versus benefits of neuroleptic therapy in a given patient. However, in order to assist the clinician and to identify causes of psychiatric disorders, it is important for researchers to continue to identify subgroups of patients who may be more susceptible to TD development.

This chapter reviews a number of risk factors in TD, with a predominant focus on the recently emerging issue of whether affective illness patients are at higher risk for TD. The data suggest a trend that a diagnosis of affective illness confers greater risk for the development of TD. In addition, the literature suggests that affectively ill as well as schizophrenic patients (112) who also have some form of neuropsychological impairment are at even greater risk for TD development. These results suggest a complex interaction among the variables of TD, affective disorders, and cognitive impairment.

Pharmacological studies provide possible mechanisms to explain the apparent relationship between affective illness and TD. Specifically, further understanding of interactions between serotonin and the nigrostriatal dopamine system may eventually explain the observations delineated in this chapter.

We are conducting a prospective study that will allow us to delineate the extent to which affective disorder predicts TD incidence. Furthermore, we are planning to use a familial aggregation design to see whether genetic factors explain why patients with affective disorders are more vulnerable to TD development.

The emerging evidence implicating affective illness as a risk factor for the development of TD should temper an already conservative approach for the use of neuroleptics in nonschizophrenic patients. Future studies should clarify the role neuroleptic medications play in treating the course of chronic affective disorder. Judicious short-term use of neuroleptics in affectively ill patients is the goal for the clinician in the responsible utilization of these medications (13).

REFERENCES

1. Aghajanian, G. K. (1981). The modulatory role of serotonin at multiple receptors in brain. In B. L. Jacobs & A. Gelperin (Eds.), *Serotonin neurotransmission and behavior*. Cambridge, MA: MIT Press.
2. Alexopoulos, G. S. (1979). Lack of complaints in schizophrenics with tardive dyskinesia. *J. Nerv. Ment. Dis.*, *167*, 125.
3. Alpert, M., Diamond, F., & Friedhoff, A. J. (1976). Tremorgraphic studies in tardive dyskinesia. *Psychopharmacol. Bull.*, *12*, 5.
4. American College of Neuropsychopharmacology–FDA Task Force (1973). Neurological syndromes associated with antipsychotic drug use. *Arch. Gen. Psychiatry*, *28*, 463.
5. Appelbaum, P. S. (1982). Dyskinesia and unipolar depression. *Am. J. Psychiatry*, *139*, 140.
6. Armitage, S. G. (1946). An analysis of certain psychological tests used for the evaluation of brain injury. *Psychol. Monogr.*, *60* (whole no. 277).
7. Asnis, G. (1977). Parkinson's disease, depression and ECT: A review and case study. *Am. J. Psychiatry*, *134*, 191.
8. Asnis, G. E., Leopold, M. A., Duvoisen, R. C., & Schwartz, A. H. (1977). A survey of tardive dyskinesia in psychiatric outpatients. *Am. J. Psychiatry*, *134*, 1367.
9. Branchy, M., & Branchy, L. (1984). Patterns of psychotropic drug use and tardive dyskinesia. *J. Clin. Psychopharmacol.*, *4*, 41.

10. Brandon, S., McClelland, H. A., & Protheroe, C. (1971). A study of facial dyskinesia in a mental hospital population. *Br. J. Psychiatry, 118*, 171.
11. Bunney, W. E., & Davis, J. M. (1965). Norepinephrine in depressive reactions: A review. *Arch. Gen. Psychiatry, 32*, 1357.
12. Carlsson, A. (1973). Brain monoamines in basal ganglia disease. In M. D. Yahr (Ed.), *Current concepts in the treatment of parkinsonism*. New York: Raven Press.
13. Casey, D. E. (1984). Tardive dyskinesia and affective disorders. In G. Gardos & D. E. Casey (Eds.), *Tardive dyskinesia and affective disorders*. Washington, DC: American Psychiatric Press.
14. Casey, D. E., & Rabins, P. (1978). Tardive dyskinesia as a life-threatening illness. *Am. J. Psychiatry, 135*, 486.
15. Celesia, G. G., & Wanamaker, W. M. (1972). Psychiatric disturbances in Parkinson's disease. *Dis. Nerv. Syst., 33*, 577.
16. Cole, J. O., Gardos, G., Raphen, R. M., Gelernter, J., Haskell, D., Moore, P., Schniebolk, S., & Bird, M. (1984). Lithium carbonate in tardive dyskinesia and schizophrenia. In G. Gardos & D. E. Casey (Eds.) *Tardive dyskinesia and affective disorders*. Washington, DC: American Psychiatric Press.
17. Crane, G. E. (1968). Dyskinesia and neuroleptics. *Arch. Gen. Psychiatry, 19*, 700.
18. Crane, G. E. (1972). Pseudoparkinsonism and tardive dyskinesia. *Arch. Neurol., 27*, 426.
19. Crane, G. E. (1973). Persistent tardive dyskinesia. *Br. J. Psychiatry, 122*, 395.
20. Crane, G. E. (1974). Factors predisposing to drug-induced neurologic effects. In I. S. Forrest, C. J. Carr, & E. Usdin (Eds.), *The phenothiazines and structurally related drugs*. New York: Raven Press.
21. Crane, G. E., & Naranjo, E. R. (1971). Motor disorders induced by neuroleptics: A proposed new classification. *Arch. Gen. Psychiatry, 24*, 179.
22. Crane, G. E., & Smeets, R. A. (1974). Tardive dyskinesia and drug therapy in geriatric patients. *Arch. Gen. Psychiatry, 30*, 341.
23. Cutler, N. R., Post, R. M., Rey, A. C., & Bunney, W. E. (1981). Depression-dependent dyskinesias in two cases of manic-depressive illness. *N. Engl. J. Med., 304*, 1088.
24. Davis, K. L., Berger, P. A., & Hollister, L. E. (1976). Tardive dyskinesia and depressive illness. *Psychopharmacol. Commun., 2*, 125.
25. Davis, J. M. (1975). Overview, maintenance therapy in psychiatry, I: Schizophrenia. *Am. J. Psychiatry, 132*, 1237.
26. Degwitz, R., & Wenzel, W. (1967). Persistent extrapyramidal side effects after long-term application of neuroleptics. In H. Brill (Ed.), *Neuro-psycho-pharmacology*. New York: Excerpta Medica.
27. DePotter, R. W., Linkowski, P., & Mendlewicz, J. (1983). State-dependent tardive dyskinesia in manic-depressive illness. *J. Neurol. Neurosurg. Psychiatry, 46*, 666.
28. Deutch, A. Y., Tam, S-Y., & Roth, R. H. (1985). Footshock and conditional stress increase DOPAC in the ventral tegmental area but not substantia nigra. *Brain Res., 333*, 143.
29. Eldridge, R. (1970). The torsion dystonias: Literature review and genetic and clinical studies. *Neurology, 20*, 57.
30. Englehardt, D. M., Polizos, P., & Waizer, J. (1975). CNS consequences of psychotropic drug withdrawal in autistic children: A follow-up report. *Psychopharmacol. Bull., 1*, 6.
31. Fann, W. E., Sullivan, J. L., & Richman, B. W. (1976). Dyskinesia associated with tricyclic antidepressants. *Br. J. Psychiatry, 128*, 490.
32. Faurbye, A., Rasch, P. J., Petersen, P. B., Brandborg, G., & Pakkenberg, H. (1964). Neurological symptoms in pharmacotherapy of psychoses. *Acta Psychiatr. Scand., 40*, 10.

33. Feighner, J. P., Robins, E., Guze S. B., Woodruff, R. A., Winokur, G., & Munoz, R. (1972). Diagnostic criteria for use in psychiatric research. *Arch. Gen. Psychiatry, 26*, 57.
34. Folstein, S. E., Abbott, M. H., Chase, G. A., Jensen, B. A., & Folstein, M. F. (1983). The association of affective disorder with Huntington's disease in a case series and in families. *Psychol. Med. 13*, 537.
35. Folstein, S. E., & Folstein, M. F. (1983). Psychiatric features of Huntington's disease. *Psychol. Dev., 2*, 193.
36. Folstein, M., Folstein, S., & McHugh, R. (1975). Mini-mental state: A practical method for grading the cognitive state of patients for the clinician. *Psychiatry Res., 12*, 189.
37. Galdi, J., Rieder, R. O., Silbur D., & Bonato, R. B. (1981). Genetic factors in the response to neuroleptics in schizophrenia: A psychopharmacogenetic study. *Psychol. Med., 11*, 713.
38. Gardos, G., & Cole, J. O. (1980). Overview: Public health issues in tardive dyskinesia. *Am. J. Psychiatry, 137*, 776.
39. Gardos, G., Cole, J. O., & LaBrie, R. (1977). Drug variables in the etiology of tardive dyskinesia—Application of discriminant function analysis. *Prog. Neuropsychopharmacol., 1*, 147.
40. Glazer, W. M., Hafez, H. M., & Benarroche, C. L. (1985). Molindone and haloperidol in tardive dyskinesia. *J. Clin. Psychiatry, 46*, 4.
41. Glazer, W. M., & Moore, D. C. (1981). A tardive dyskinesia clinic in a mental health center. *Hosp. Community Psychiatry, 32*, 574.
42. Glazer, W. M., Moore, D. C., Schooler, N. R., Brenner, L. M., & Morgenstern, H. (1984). Tardive dyskinesia. A discontinuation study. *Arch. Gen. Psychiatry, 41*, 623.
43. Glazer, W. M., Morgenstern, H., Niedzwieki, D., & Hughes, J. (In press). Heterogeneity of tardive dyskinesia: A multivariate analysis. *Br. J. Psychiatry.*
44. Glazer, W. M., Morgenstern, H., Schooler, N., Berkman, C., & Moore, D. C. (In preparation). Predictors of improvement in tardive dyskinesia following discontinuation of neuroleptic medication.
45. Glazer, W. M., Naftolin, F., Moore, D. C., Bowers, M. B., & MacLusky, N. J. (1983). The relationship of circulating estradiol to tardive dyskinesia in men and postmenopausal women. *Psychoneuroendocrinology, 8*, 429.
46. Glazer, W. M., Naftolin, F., Morgenstern, H., Barnea, E. R., MacLusky, N. J., & Brenner, L. B. (1985). Estrogen replacement and tardive dyskinesia. *Psychoneuroendocrinology, 10*, 345.
47. Goldberg, S. C., Shensy, R. S., Sadler, A., Hamer, R., & Ross, B. (1981). The effects of a drug holiday on relapse and tardive dyskinesia in chronic schizophrenics. *Psychopharmacol. Bull., 17*, 116.
48. Goswami, U., Narayanan, H. S., & Channabassavanna, S. M. (1985). A study of state-dependent reversal of tardive dyskinesia: Phenomenological probe in humans. *J. Clin. Psychopharmacol., 5*, 48.
49. Hamra, B. J., Nasrallah, H. A., Clancy, J., & Finn, R. (1983). Psychiatric diagnosis and risk for tardive dyskinesia. *Arch. Gen. Psychiatry, 40*, 346.
50. Harvey, N. S. (1986). Psychiatric disorders in parkinsonism: 1. Functional illnesses and personality. *Psychosomatics, 27*, 91.
51. Himmelhoch, J., & Neil, J. (1980). Neuroleptics—Mood state and lithium-provoked tardive extrapyramidal syndromes. In E. Usdin (Ed.), *Phenothiazines and structurally related drugs*. Amsterdam: Elsevier.
52. Hogarty, G. E., Goldberg, S. C., Schooler, J., & Uhlrich, R. F. (1974). Drug and sociotherapy in the aftercare of schizophrenics II. Two year relapse rates. *Arch. Gen. Psychiatry, 31*, 603.

53. JACKSON, I. V., VOLAVKA, J., JAMES, B., & REKER, D. (1980). The respiratory components of tardive dyskinesia. *Biol. Psychiatry, 15*, 485.
54. JESTE, D. V., POTKIN, S. G., SINHA, S., FEDER, S., & WYATT, R. J. (1979). Tardive dyskinesia—Reversible and persistent. *Arch. Gen. Psychiatry, 36*, 585.
55. JESTE, D. V., & WYATT, R. J. (1982). Therapeutic strategies against tardive dyskinesia: Two decades of experience. *Arch. Gen. Psychiatry, 39*, 803.
56. JESTE, D. V., & WYATT, R. J. (1982). *Understanding and treating tardive dyskinesia.* New York: Guilford Press.
57. JUS, A., PINEAU, R., LACHANCE, R., PELCHAT, G., JUS, K., PIRES, P., & VILLENEUVE, R. (1976). Epidemiology of tardive dyskinesia. Part II. *Dis. Nerv. Syst., 37*, 257.
58. KANE, J. M., RIFKIN, A., QUITKIN. F., NAYAK, D., & RAMOS-LORENZI, J. (1982). Fluphenazine vs. placebo in patients with remitted, acute first-episode schizophrenia. *Arch. Gen. Psychiatry, 39*, 70.
59. KANE, J. M., & SMITH, J. M. (1982). Tardive dyskinesia: Prevalence and risk factors. *Arch. Gen. Psychiatry, 39*, 473.
60. KANE, J. M., STRUVE, F. A., WEINHOLD, P., & WOERNER, M. (1980). Strategy for the study of patients at high risk for tardive dyskinesia. *Am. J. Psychiatry, 137*, 1265.
61. KANE, J. M., WOERNER, M., WEINHOLD, P., LIEBERMAN, J., & BORENSTEIN, M. (1984). Incidence and severity of tardive dyskinesia in affective illness. In G. Gardos & D. E. Casey (Eds.), *Tardive dyskinesia and affective disorders.* Washington, DC: American Psychiatric Press.
62. KANE, J. M., WOERNER, M., WEINHOLD, P., WEGNER, J. T., & KINON, B. (1984). Incidence of tardive dyskinesia: Five year data from a prospective study. *Psychopharmacol. Bull., 20*, 39.
63. KARSON, C. N., JESTE, D. V., & BIGELOW, L. B. (1985). Tardive dyskinesia and psychopathology in chronic schizophrenia: A cross-sectional study. *Compr. Psychiatry, 26*, 388.
64. KENDLER, K. S., MASTERSON, C. C., UNGARO, R., & DAVIS, K. L. (1984). A family history study of schizophrenia-related personality disorders. *Am. J. Psychiatry, 141*, 424.
65. KENNEDY, P. F., HERSHON, H. I., & MCGUIRE, R. J. (1971). Extrapyramidal disorders after prolonged phenothiazine therapy. *Br. J. Psychiatry, 118*, 509.
66. KLAWANS, H. L., BERGEN, D., BRUYN, G. W., & PAULSON, G. W. (1974). Neuroleptic-induced tardive dyskinesia in nonpsychotic patients. *Arch. Neurol., 30*, 338.
67. KLAWANS, H. L., & RUBOVITS, R. (1974). Effect of cholinergic and anticholinergic agents on tardive dyskinesia. *J. Neurol. Neurosurg. Psychiatry, 27*, 941.
68. KUCZENSKI, R. (1979). Effects of parachlorophenylalanine on amphetamine and haloperidol-induced changes in striatal dopamine turnover. *Brain Res., 164*, 217.
69. LAPIERRE, Y. D., & ANDERSON, K. (1983). Dyskinesia associated with amoxapine and antidepressant therapy: A case report. *Am. J. Psychiatry, 140*, 493.
70. LASKA, E., VARGA, E., & WANDERLING, J. (1973). Patterns of psychotropic drug use for schizophrenia. *Dis. Nerv. Syst., 34*, 294.
71. LAZARUS, A. L., & TOGLIA, J. U. (1985). Fatal myoglobinuric renal failure in a patient with tardive dyskinesia. *Neurology, 35*, 1055.
72. LEBENSOHN, Z. M., & JENKINS, R. B. (1975). Improvement of parkinsonism in depressed patients treated with ECT. *Am. J. Psychiatry, 132*, 283.
73. LESSER, I. (1983). Case report of withdrawal dyskinesia associated with amoxapine. *Am. J. Psychiatry, 140*, 1358.
74. LINNOILA, M., KAROUM, F., CUTLER, N. R., & POTTER, W. Z. (1983). Temporal association between depression-dependent dyskinesia and high urinary phenylethylamine output. *Biol. Psychiatry, 18*, 513.
75. LUCKI, I, & HARVEY, J. A. (1979). Increased sensitivity to *d*- and *l*-amphetamine action

after midbrain raphe lesions as measured by locomotor activity. *Neuropharmacology, 18*, 243.

76. Martin, J. B., & Gusella, J. F. (1986). Huntington's disease: Pathogenesis and management. *N. Engl. J. Med., 315*, 1267.
77. McMillen, B. A. (1985). Comparative chronic effects of buspirone or neuroleptics on rat brain dopaminergic neurotransmission. *J. Neural Transm., 64*, 1.
78. Mehta, D., Mallya, A., & Volavka, J. (1978). Mortality of patients with tardive dyskinesia. *Am. J. Psychiatry, 135*, 371.
79. Mukherjee, S., Rosen, A. M., Caracci, G., & Shukla, S. (1986). Persistent tardive dyskinesia in bipolar patients. *Arch. Gen. Psychiatry, 43*, 342.
80. Mukherjee, S., Shukla, S., & Rosen, A. (1984). Neurological abnormalities in patients with bipolar disorder. *Biol. Psychiatry, 19*, 337.
81. Nies, A., Robinson, D. S., Freedman, M. J., & Green, R. (1977). Relationship between age and tricyclic antidepressant plasma levels. *Am. J. Psychiatry, 134*, 790.
82. Olsson, R., & Roos, B. E. (1968). Concentration of 5-hydroxyindoleacetic acid and homovanillic acid in the cerebrospinal fluid after treatment with probenecid in patients with Parkinson's disease. *Nature, 219*, 502.
83. Overall, J. E., & Gorham, D. R (1962). Brief psychiatric rating scale. *Psychol. Rep., 10*, 789.
84. Perényi, A., & Arató, M. (1980). Tardive dyskinesia on Hungarian psychiatric wards. *Psychosomatics, 21*, 904.
85. Perris, C., Dimitrijevic, P., & Jacobson, L. (1979). Tardive dyskinesia in psychiatric patients treated with neuroleptics. *Br. J. Psychiatry, 135*, 509.
86. Perry, T., Hanson, S., & Koster M. (1973). Huntington's chorea: Deficiency of gamma-aminobutyric acid in brain. *N. Engl. J. Med., 22*, 107.
87. Petty, L. K., & Spar, C. J. (1980). Haloperidol-induced tardive dyskinesia in a 10-year-old girl. *Am. J. Psychiatry, 137*, 745.
88. Price, T. R. P., & Levin, R. (1978). The effects of electroconvulsive therapy on tardive dyskinesia. *Am. J. Psychiatry, 135*, 991.
89. Rabiner, C. J., Wegner, J. T., & Kane, J. M. (1986). Outcome study of first-break psychosis, I. Relapse rates after 1 year. *Am. J. Psychiatry, 143*, 1155.
90. Reiter, P. J. (1926). Extrapyramidal motor disturbances in dementia praecox. *Acta Psychiatr. Scand., 1*, 287.
91. Rey, A. (1964). *L'Examen Clinique en Psychologie*. Paris: Presses Universitaires de France.
92. Robins, A. H. (1976). Depression in patients with parkinsonism. *Br. J. Psychiatry, 128*, 141.
93. Rosen, A. M., Mukherjee, S., Olarte, S., Varia, V., & Cardenas, C. (1982). Perception of tardive dyskinesia in outpatients receiving maintenance neuroleptics. *Am. J. Psychiatry, 139*, 372.
94. Rosenbaum, K. H., Niven, R. G., Hanson, N. P., & Swanson, E. W. (1977). Tardive dyskinesia. Relationship with a primary affective disorder. *Dis. Nerv. Syst., 38*, 423.
95. Rush, M., Diamond, F., & Alpert, M. (1982). Depression as a risk factor in tardive dyskinesia. *Biol. Psychiatry, 17*, 387.
96. Schildkraut, J. J. (1965). The catecholamine hypothesis of affective disorders: A review of supporting evidence. *Am. J Psychiatry, 122*, 509.
97. Schönecker, M. (1957). Ein eigentrumliches Syndrom im oralen Bereich bei Megaphen Applikation. *Nervenartzt, 28*, 35.
98. Sigwald, J., Bouttier, D., Raymond, C., & Piot, C. (1959). Quatre cas de dyskinesie facio-buccio-linguo-masticatrice a evolution prolongie secondaire a un traitment par les neuroleptiques. *Rev. Neurol., 100*, 751.
99. Simpson, G. M., Varga, E., & Lee, J. H. (1978). Tardive dyskinesia and psychotropic drug history. *Psychopharmacology, 58*, 117.

100. Smith, J. M., & Baldessarini, R. J. (1980). Changes in prevalence, severity and recovery in tardive dyskinesia with age. *Arch. Gen. Psychiatry, 37*, 1368.
101. Smith, J. M., Kucharski, L. T., Oswald, W. T., & Waterman, L. J. (1979). A systematic investigation of tardive dyskinesia in inpatients. *Am. J. Psychiatry, 136*, 918.
102. Smith, J. M., Oswald, W. T., Kucharski, L. T., & Waterman, L. J. (1978). Tardive dyskinesia: Age and sex differences in hospitalized schizophrenics. *Psychopharmacology, 58*, 207.
103. Spitzer, R. L., Endicott, J., & Robins, E. (1978). Research diagnostic criteria: Rationale and reliability. *Arch. Gen. Psychiatry, 35*, 773.
104. Stein, S. L., Hurtig, H. I., & Mendels, J. (1977). Psychiatric illness in relatives of patients with Parkinson's disease: A preliminary report. *Am. J. Psychiatry, 134*, 443.
105. Stevens, J. R. (1978). Eye blink and schizophrenia: Psychosis or tardive dyskinesia. *Am. J. Psychiatry, 135*, 223.
106. Struve, F. A., & Klein, D. F. (1976). Diagnostic implications of the B-Mitten EEG pattern: Relationship to primary and secondary affective dysregulation. *Biol. Psychiatry, 11*, 599.
107. Tarsy, D., & Baldessarini, R. J. (1976). The tardive dyskinesia syndrome. In H. L. Klawans (Ed.), *Clinical neuropharmacology*. New York: Raven Press.
108. Tassin, J. P., Reibaud, M., Blanc, G., Studler, J. M., & Glowinski, J. (1984). Regulation of the sensitivity of D_1 receptors in the prefrontal cortex and the nucleus accumbens by nondopaminergic pathways. In (Eds.), *Catecholamines: Neuropharmacology and central nervous system – Theoretical aspects*. New York: Alan R. Liss.
109. Tsuang, M. T., Winokur, G., & Crowe, R. R. (1980). Morbidity risks of schizophrenia and affective disorders among the relatives of patients with schizophrenia, mania, depression, and surgical controls. *Br. J. Psychiatry, 137*, 147.
110. Waldmeier, P. C., & Delini-Stula, A. A. (1979). Serotonin-dopamine interaction in the nigrostriatal system. *Eur. J. Pharmacol., 55*, 363.
111. Wechsler, D. (1946). A standardized memory scale for clinical use. *J. Psychol., 19*, 87.
112. Wegner, J. T., Catalano, F., Gibralter, J., & Kane, J. M. (1985). Schizophrenics with tardive dyskinesia: Neuropsychological deficit and family psychopathology. *Arch. Gen. Psychiatry, 42*, 860.
113. Wegner, J. T., Kane, J. M., Weinhold, P., Woerner, M., Kinon, B., & Lieberman, J. (1985). Cognitive impairment in tardive dyskinesia. *Psychiatry Res., 16*, 331.
114. Wegner, J. T., Struve, F. A., Kantor, J. S., & Kane, J. M. (1979). Relationship between the B-Mitten EEG pattern and tardive dyskinesia. *Arch. Gen. Psychiatry, 36*, 599.
115. Weiner, W. J., Goetz, C. G., Nausieda, P. A., & Klawans, H. L. (1978). Respiratory dyskinesia: Extrapyramidal dysfunction and dyspnea. *Ann. Intern. Med., 88*, 327.
116. Weiner, W. J., & Werner, T. R. (1982). Mania-induced remission of tardive dyskinesia in manic-depressive illness. *Ann. Neurol., 12*, 229.
117. Wexler, N. (1984). Huntington's disease. In D. V. Jeste & R. J. Wyatt (Eds.), *Neuropsychiatric movement disorders*. Washington, DC: American Psychiatric Press.
118. Willner, A. E. (1971). *Conceptual Level Analogy Test*. New York: Cognitive Testing Service.
119. Winokur, A., Dugan, J., Mendels, J., & Hurtig, H. I. (1978). Psychiatric illness in relatives of patients with Parkinson's disease: An expanded survey. *Am. J. Psychiatry, 135*, 854.
120. Wolf, M. E., Almy, G., Toll, M., & Mosnaim, A. D. (1982). Mania associated with the use of baclofen. *Biol. Psychiatry, 17*, 757.
121. Wolf, M. E., DeWolfe, A. S., Ryan, J. J., Lips, O. & Mosnaim, A. D. (1985). Vulnerability to tardive dyskinesia. *J. Clin. Psychiatry, 46*, 367.
122. Wolf, M. E., Ryan, J., & Mosnaim, A. D. (1983). Cognitive functions in tardive dyskinesia. *Psychol. Med., 13*, 671.

123. Yassa, R., Ghadirian, A. M., & Schwartz, G. (1983). Prevalence of tardive dyskinesia in affective disorder patients. *J. Clin. Psychiatry, 44*, 410.
124. Yassa, R., Nair, V., & Schwartz, G. (1984). Tardive dyskinesia and the primary psychiatric diagnosis. *Psychosomatics, 25*, 135.
125. Yassa, R., & Schwartz, G. (1984). Depression as a predictor in the development of tardive dyskinesia. *Biol. Psychiatry, 19*, 441.
126. Zorumski, C. F., & Bakris, G. L. (1983). Choreoathetosis associated with lithium: Case report and literature review. *Am. J. Psychiatry, 140*, 1621.

22

CONVULSIVE THERAPY: A REAPPRAISAL

MAX FINK, M.D.

Professor of Psychiatry,
School of Medicine, SUNY at Stony Brook,
Long Island, New York

INTRODUCTION

Repeated failure of modern drug therapies to relieve patients with major depressive disorders has renewed interest in convulsive therapy—a treatment first introduced into psychiatry in 1934 by the Hungarian neuropsychiatrist Ladislas Meduna for the treatment of dementia praecox (58). The treatment's early success led to its widespread use, but the introduction of modern psychotropic drugs in the 1960s promised to replace it, as well as insulin coma and leukotomy, the other major somatic treatments of the time.

But the pharmacotherapies are neither as safe nor as effective as first heralded. Increasing numbers of "therapy-resistant" patients lead clinicians to seek other effective interventions, including convulsive therapy. Our better understanding of the predictors of a good therapeutic response, improved techniques and instruments, and answers to the vexing question "Is a seizure really necessary for therapeutic efficacy?" encourage a reassessment of convulsive therapy and its increasing use. This chapter describes the present practice of convulsive therapy in the treatment of the severely mentally ill.

Aided, in part, by grants from the International Association for Psychiatric Research, Inc., St. James, New York 11780.

INDICATIONS FOR USE

Convulsive therapy is ordinarily reserved for patients so ill as to warrant hospitalization. Although patients may be treated as outpatients, the need for anesthesia makes it akin to surgery and reserves it for those who require a major intervention. Also, present philosophy gives priority to trials with medications, despite clear indications of a greater efficacy and safety of convulsive therapy for many conditions. Prior treatment failure is a precondition of the use of convulsive therapy in many venues (6, 25, 52, 66).

Depressive Disorders

Convulsive therapy relieves the mood disorder of affectively ill patients, regardless of subtype. It is equally effective in those with unipolar and bipolar histories, especially when accompanied by psychosis. It is particularly effective in patients with melancholia. Recently, we have recognized another group of depressed patients, those who exhibit a dementia often labeled "dementia of the Alzheimer type." The depression of such patients may also be helped by convulsive therapy, including a remarkable resolution of their dementia. When this occurs, the dementia is relabeled "reversible dementia" or "pseudodementia" (12, 56).

Depression accompanied by psychosis, especially delusions of guilt, somatic concern, or infidelity, responds well to convulsive therapy. These signs are considered a poor prognostic sign for treatment with antidepressant drugs; in such patients, convulsive therapy may be considered a primary treatment (25).

Elderly patients who are affectively ill often do not respond to conventional antidepressant treatments, and others are intolerant of the side effects of these agents. Convulsive therapy is often successful among the elderly, and when such patients recover from their depressed mood, they show an astonishing enthusiasm for their renewed life.

Not all depressed patients are good candidates. Those with dysthymia (previously called neurotic depression) do not respond well; neither their depressive symptoms nor the accompanying symptoms of anxiety, hypochondriasis, or hysteria improve. Patients with character disorders, or with drug dependence, in whom depressive symptoms may be situational and secondary to their social difficulties, are also miserable candidates for convulsive therapy, often complaining more bitterly of their symptoms than before treatment.

Schizophrenia

Convulsive therapy is effective in patients with schizoaffective psychoses and syndromes of catatonia, where the results may be lifesaving, particularly in those whose feeding is interrupted and inanition and electrolyte imbalance are prominent features of their condition. The results with convulsive therapy in acutely ill schizophrenic patients are generally equivalent to the results with neuroleptic drugs (74). Since drug therapies are easier and less costly to administer, these are generally favored. In schizophrenic patients who fail to respond to drug therapy, and who exhibit symptoms of delusions, hallucinations, and periods of overactivity and excitement, however, the addition of convulsive therapy to their ongoing neuroleptic drug treatment program is often salutary (36, 41).

Other Conditions

Other applications for convulsive therapy are among patients who are suicidal or suffering from delirium, and among medically ill patients, especially those with severe cardiovascular disorders. The cardiovascular effects of the tricyclic antidepressant drugs and the monoamine oxidase inhibitors may be disabling, warranting referral for convulsive therapy. In patients with cardiac dysrhythmia or hypertension, monitoring of the treatment is easier during convulsive treatments than in drug therapies. In convulsive therapy, the patient is monitored during the whole intervention, so that the effects on cardiovascular performance may be treated immediately. In treatment with antidepressant drugs, monitoring is infrequent and the risks of cardiovascular complications greater.

A special indication for convulsive therapy is among pregnant women with severe psychiatric illnesses, such as melancholia or mania, where the risks of teratogenicity in the fetus preclude the general use of psychoactive drugs. The anesthesia of the treatment is short and seems not to affect the developing fetus (20).

CONTRAINDICATIONS

There are no physical or medical contraindications to the use of convulsive therapy in patients with conditions where there is a likelihood for benefit. Yet, "absolute" and "relative" contraindications are described. When treatment of a psychiatric condition is sufficiently compelling, as when patients are suicidal, debilitated, or starving, the absolute contraindications are set aside and convulsive therapy is considered a prudent intervention. Such conditions include patients with recent myocardial infarction, cerebrovascular accident, intracranial mass lesion, or cerebral vascular malformation, whose psychosis is so severe as to interfere with recovery from their medical illness. Patients with serious medical conditions are considered *high-risk* cases, requiring special expertise on the part of therapists. The prudent physician will not treat patients with these conditions with a therapy of any risk, unless the need is compelling. But when compelled, as when convulsive therapy is a less riskful alternative, treatments have been given. At such times, the skill of the psychiatrist and that of the anesthesiologist determine the outcome.

RISKS

Fracture, death, fear, tardive seizures, and impairment of memory and cognition were prominent risks of convulsive therapy in the first decades. The use of barbiturate anesthesia and succinylcholine by well-trained physicians has dissipated these concerns, except for the effects on cognition. Impairment is usually described for the time of the illness and the events associated with the treatments, but there are some patients who describe a loss of memory to events earlier than the time of the illness (55).

Cognitive impairment results, in part, from the type and amount of electrical energy and the path of the electric currents used. The selection of electrode placement and current type and dose for the induction of the seizure can do much to limit the degree and duration of the cognitive effects. There is a lag in education, however, so that these techniques are not well known, and the risk of cognitive impairment remains high.

CONSENT

The stigma of "shock therapy" is another risk of the treatment for the patient and the family, and, unfortunately, for the therapist. Convulsive therapy is seen as a controversial treatment, and both patients and their families are confused as to why it is recommended (14). Indeed, concerns about its application may come as strenuously from the therapist's peers and co-workers as from lay persons. The information about the risks and reasons for recommending the treatment that is shared with the patient and the family is central to a good outcome and good management. It is no longer acceptable to depend on a patient's signature on a single-sentence consent to treatment as valid and informed.

Our practice is to provide each patient and close members of the family with a detailed explanation of the treatment—what it entails, its risks and benefits, and our understanding of its mechanism of action. This information is provided in a detailed consent form, which is discussed by a knowledgeable member of the treatment team (25). This discussion is accompanied by viewing a videotape describing the benefits and risks of the treatment and demonstrations of actual treatments (75). The viewing of a videotape, produced in our own facility, has been very useful not only in assuring "informed" consent, but in meeting our institutional legal and ethical concerns.

MEDICAL EXAMINATIONS

When the decision to treat is made and consent is obtained, the medical history and physical examination are reviewed. Many patients referred for convulsive therapy need continuing treatment for medical conditions that increase the risks of anesthesia, such as hypertension, arrhythmia, diabetes, pulmonary disease, and arthritis. Therapies should be optimized and consultation with the patient's physician may be useful. Some recent reviews describe the management of patients with medical conditions (2, 48, 68, 79) or neurological conditions (21, 46).

There are no laboratory tests required before treatment. Spine x-rays are no longer routinely obtained. In patients who have had prior courses of convulsive therapy, or in whom a disorder of the spine is suggested by the medical history, dorsal spine x-rays are done. (If done prior to treatment, x-rays are usually repeated after the course of therapy.) A pretreatment electrocardiogram is requested in patients with a history of cardiovascular disease or in those over the age of 40 years. Electroencephalogram, CT scan, and neuropsychological assessment are not routine examinations and serve no useful purpose in planning a course of convulsive therapy; these should be requested when the patient's history or examination raises questions for which the procedure may be helpful.

A dental examination is useful, particularly in older patients, to determine the presence of loose teeth or dentures. If the patient's condition permits, these should be secured by proper treatment before convulsive therapy is given. The anesthesiologist should also meet with the patient, review the medical record, and reassure the patient.

For a few years, there was a wave of enthusiasm that the dexamethasone suppression test would be a useful guide to treatment, but recent findings have not been reassuring (30). Interest in the test as applied to convulsive therapy has waned.

"Clearance"

In some institutions, medical "clearance" for treatment is requested of consultants. It is unclear what is expected. The decision to administer convulsive therapy is the responsibility of the attending psychiatrist, who must make the decision based on the severity of the patient's illness, treatment history, and a risk-benefit analysis of the available psychiatric therapies. The most one can expect of consultants is a better understanding and an optimization of the patient's medical condition, especially treatment for associated medical conditions. To ask for "clearance for treatment," as if medical consultants have a divine guidance to judge the safety of a procedure as complex as convulsive therapy, is to ask more than most consultants can answer. Such practice should not be condoned.

DRUG INTERACTIONS

Since patients receive various medications for anesthesia, drug-drug interactions must be considered. Benzodiazepine or barbiturate use for nighttime sedation raises seizure thresholds, making induction more difficult. The quality of the treatment may also be reduced, needlessly extending the course of therapy. Benzodiazepines should be discontinued before treatment.

Some antiarrhythmics, notably lidocaine, raise seizure thresholds (44) and substitutes such as propranolol should be considered. Theophylline may increase the duration of seizures, including the development of prolonged seizures, especially when administered at high levels (65). Patients with glaucoma may continue their medications, unless they are receiving echothiopate, which should be discontinued (73). Diabetic patients should continue their medications, although dosages may be modified on treatment days. In patients with epilepsy, some authors decrease antiepileptic medications, especially phenytoin and phenobarbital. This is not necessary, although the electrotherapist should be aware that seizure thresholds may be elevated and special maneuvers may be necessary to assure an adequate seizure.

Whether or not to continue psychotropic drugs during convulsive therapy is a complex issue. For tricyclic antidepressant drugs and monoamine oxidase inhibitors, we find no evidence of a synergistic therapeutic action. As cardiovascular risks are enhanced with the use of tricyclic antidepressant drugs, especially in elderly patients, and therapeutic efficacy may be reduced, combined use is not recommended and dosages of tricyclic drugs are tapered during treatment. Concerns have been expressed that a recent intake of monoamine oxidase inhibitors (MAOI) may increase the risks of hypertension during convulsive therapy, and some authors recommend that treatment be deferred until MAOI use has been suspended for two weeks. Neither Freese (35) nor Remick et al. (69) found evidence to support this practice, and such delay is not necessary.

Lithium administration may increase the risks of an organic mental syndrome and prolonged apnea, and most therapists reduce dosages rapidly when convulsive therapy is being considered. But the justification for such advice has been questioned, and combined therapy need not be proscribed (71).

For neuroleptic drugs, on the other hand, there may be a synergism in the combination with convulsive therapy, particularly in the treatment of manic and schizophrenic patients (36, 41). These medications are usually continued during the course of convulsive therapy. Some reports of cardiovascular complications and death when reserpine was used with convulsive therapy suggest that such combined use is hazardous, but this injunction is limited to reserpine and is not generalized to other neuroleptic drugs. There is little information as to the safety of the concurrent use of anticholinergic drugs, so that most therapists use these substances only when clearly necessary.

TREATMENT PROCEDURES

The present practice of convulsive therapy has undergone much change and the image of unmodified convulsive therapy so frequently pictured in the cinema is no longer realistic. As convulsive therapy is usually given with barbiturate-succinylcholine anesthesia, an intravenous infusion line is established with dextrose in water or normal saline. Physiological monitors are put in place: blood pressure by cuff; ECG by three leads; and frontal EEG (32, 51). For electric stimulation, the skin over the two stimulation sites is cleansed by a fat solvent (ethyl acetate, alcohol, or acetone). Electrodes are applied using electrode-conducting jelly. The impedance of the circuit is checked, and the contact of the electrodes adjusted to an impedance within the specification of the instrument manufacturer.

For bilateral electrode placement, the electrodes are placed on both temples. For unilateral electrode placement, one electrode is placed on a temple, about midway between the outer canthus of the eye and the meatus of the ear. Many locations for the second electrode over the homolateral scalp have been proposed. As there is little therapeutic advantage for one locus over another, the second electrode is usually placed as far back on the scalp as is possible, near the midline (d'Elia location) as it induces a seizure with lower electrical dosage (19, 24).

Some authors recommend the administration of intravenous atropine (0.6–1.2 mg) or glycopyrrolate (0.2–0.4 mg) to reduce the vagal effects of a seizure, especially in patients with cardiovascular disorders. Results in studies of such practice are ambiguous and their use is considered optional (59).

When an airway is assured, intravenous methohexital (0.5–1.0 mg/kg) is given as a bolus. A blood pressure cuff is inflated on an extremity and intravenous succinylcholine (0.5–1.5 mg/kg) given. The degree of motor paralysis is tested by the knee jerk, foot withdrawal to stroking the sole of the foot, or response to a nerve stimulator. Oxygenation is maintained throughout. When motor reactions are obtunded, a bite block or mouthguard is inserted, and the treatment given.

A concern in the treatment is the immediate effect of the seizure on blood pressure and heart rate. Both hypertension and hypotension occur, as does transient heart block and irregular heart rhythms (18, 37). These effects ordinarily require no intervention, as they spontaneously normalize by the end of the seizure.

For patients with established hypertension, intervention may be warranted. The first maneuver is to dissolve one or two nitroglycerine tablets (0.3–0.6 mg) under the tongue, two to four minutes prior to treatment. If hypertension is severe, or blood pressure control critical, the rapid-acting ganglionic blocking agent, trimethaphan camsylate (Arfonad) drip is used.

For patients with a history of malignant hyperthermia, or those who develop fever with treatment, succinylcholine may be replaced by curare (3–6 mg/kg) or atracurium (0.5 mg/kg) (22, 43).

Seizure Induction

The appearance of a bilateral grand-mal seizure is the hallmark of an effective induction. Subconvulsive or sham treatments are less effective (50, 63). The most recent reports of the Northwick Park, Leicestershire, and Nottingham studies in Great Britain conclude that there is a distinct therapeutic advantage for treatments with induced grand-mal seizures compared to sham treatments, both in patients with depression and those with schizophrenia (10, 11, 40, 47).

Current type. Two current types are in use—sinusoidal and brief pulse. Seizures induced with sinusoidal currents use higher amounts of total energy and elicit greater cognitive and EEG effects than those induced with brief pulse currents. While the efficacy of seizures induced by the two currents may be unequal, and clinical trials are in progress, there is an acceptance of the use of brief pulse current instruments for routine use (55).

The lesser cognitive effect of brief pulse currents was thought to result from the lower total energy used. As a consequence, the use of low total energy has been a recent aim of therapists. Treatments using threshold energies were tested and were found less effective than treatments given with suprathreshold stimulation (55). Lowered efficacy was particularly apparent with unilateral electrode placements. But, if high induction energies are used, patients exhibit greater cognitive deficits.

What is the prudent therapist to do? Present practice aims to use induction energies that are substantially above threshold, but not so high as to be associated with excess cognitive deficits or prolonged seizures. We use the cuff-monitored seizure duration as a guide. When seizure durations are between 25 and 30 seconds, we generally increase the dosage of the stimulation for the next treatment by 10%; when seizure duration is longer than 90 seconds, we reduce the dosage by about 10% for the next treatment.

Electrode placement. Cognitive impairment is less with unilateral electrode placement than with bilateral (45), and in the belief that the efficacy of unilateral and bilateral treatments was equal, unilateral placement was generally recommended (6). However, recent studies demonstrate greater efficacy for seizures using bilateral placements than those using unilateral, and the earlier recommendations have been modified (1, 4). Many observers, however, contend that treatments through unilateral electrode placements, when properly done, are equally effective to those in which bilateral electrode placements have been used (45, 77).

Seizure inductions with unilateral electrode placement over the nondominant hemisphere and brief pulse currents at higher than threshold intensity are generally recommended for all affectively ill patients, except the most suicidal or most severely ill and those with mania, in whom bilateral treatments are preferred (4, 60). Bilateral treatments are also recommended in the most severely ill, and in those who have not responded within five to six unilateral treatments (4, 5, 57, 67).

"Adequate seizure." An "adequate seizure" is conventionally defined as one with a duration greater than 25 seconds with cuff monitoring, with bilateral cerebral generalization as evinced by bilateral tonic and clonic components, and perhaps with a postseizure period of electrical silence, usually defined by an abrupt EEG seizure termination. An adequate seizure results from the interaction of patient's age, degree of anesthesia, type and dosage of electrical current, and electrode placement.

The amount of energy necessary to induce a seizure increases with age, and is generally higher in men than in women. Thresholds are higher for bilateral electrode placements than unilateral. Thresholds rise during the course of therapy. It is necessary, therefore, for the therapist to monitor seizures for adequacy. From time to time, seizure durations remain short and seizures are considered inadequate despite changes in electrical dosage, electrode placement, and even electrical current form. In such instances, therapists first check the fit of the electrodes, assuring an adequate contact (low impedance) between electrodes and the patient. Dosages of barbiturate anesthetic may be reduced, or etomidate may be used instead of methohexital (13). If seizure durations remain short, augmentation by an analeptic agent may be tried. Pentetrazol augmentation using an intravenous bolus of 500–800 mg pentetrazol, 60 to 90 seconds before the electrical induction, is useful. Or an intravenous bolus of caffeine sodium benzoate (500–750 mg), 5 to 10 minutes before seizure induction, may be successful (72). If seizures are unusually prolonged, e.g., persisting for longer than 180 seconds, the seizure may be interrupted by intravenous methohexital (30–50 mg) or diazepam (2.5–5.0 mg) (39).

Postseizure monitoring. The recovery period is a time of continued risk for the patient, and observation should be continued by trained personnel, able to manage an impaired airway or changes in cardiovascular status. Monitoring continues through the postseizure recovery period, until the patient is returned to his room. It is useful to develop a simple scale of orientation and tests of aphasia during recovery, to determine whether the organic features are prolonged or aphasia is prominent. In such instances, a change in electrode placement may be considered.

Number and Frequency of Seizures

Both the frequency and number of treatments are defined by clinical progress. It is conventional in the United States to treat patients three times a week, while in Great Britain and Ireland, the pattern is twice weekly. Affectively ill patients show improvement, usually in the relief of vegetative symptoms and mood, within four to five treatments. When such changes are not observed, electrode placement or current type should be changed. In severely ill patients, particularly those in manic delirium, daily treatments are useful. Some authors describe multiple treatments in one session—up to six seizures with one anesthesia—as being more effective and reducing the period of incapacity (54). The evidence that such modifications are more effective and as safe as conventional ECT is not compelling.

The number of treatments averages seven to nine for patients with severe affective disorders, and from 12 to 20 for patients with mania and therapy-resistant psychosis. The end-point of a course is defined by the patients' relief of symptoms.

Continuation Therapy

Convulsive therapy is an effective therapy, but the duration of the effects is often short, and continuation therapy is essential. In psychoactive drug treatments, therapy is generally continued for months. Indeed, despite such continuation, many affectively ill patients relapse. In convulsive therapy, continuation with antidepressant drugs or lithium reduces relapse rates when compared with no continuation or with sedative drugs (16, 25). Treatment is usually maintained at half the clinical therapeutic dose, usually 150 mg/day for the tricyclic antidepressants.

Continuation therapy with weekly or biweekly convulsive therapy was a regular feature of practice in the 1950s (49). It is reasonable to assume that the same factors that require continuation in drug therapies will also require continuation after convulsive therapy. Unfortunately, the data are not available to provide an adequate guideline. In patients who rapidly relapse after a course of therapy, some practitioners induce seizures at weekly and biweekly intervals, proceeding to monthly intervals (34, 78). Such continuation is usually prescribed for six months after recovery.

FACILITIES

Psychiatrists administering convulsive therapy should be qualified, by preceptorship and experience, to assume responsibility for this complex treatment. The complexities of the treatment no longer allow a cavalier attitude, an attitude that accepts the least-qualified intern or junior as competent to manage these procedures. It is a reflection of the inherent safety of convulsive therapy and the tolerance of our patients for seizures that more reports of adverse effects do not fill the medical and legal literature. There is no accreditation procedure for practice, so it is the responsibility of each medical center to establish guidelines for the proficiency of physicians responsible for these treatments (29, 62). In addition to the psychiatrist, a trained nurse and nursing assistant with experience in intensive care and resuscitation are usually required. The role of the nurse has been defined by the Royal College of Nursing (70).

The administration of anesthesia, even for a procedure as short as convulsive therapy, requires skill in airway management and, occasionally, in resuscitation after cardiac or respiratory failure. Anesthesiologists and nurse-anesthetists are usually qualified in these practices, and in major institutions, especially in those equipped to treat high-risk cases, their skills should be part of the treatment team (28).

Convulsive therapy is best given in a suite consisting of a treatment room and a recovery area on the psychiatric treatment unit. The use of operating rooms invariably inhibits its proper use. It is neither required by the procedure nor does it facilitate the proper treatment of patients. Such a requirement usually reflects the dogmatism of the anesthesiologist or the hostility of an administration to proper psychiatric practice.

Equipment to induce seizures has undergone many modifications and there is little justification for the use of equipment designed or built prior to 1980. Convulsive therapy is a repeated treatment, so that records are helpful in optimizing the treatment of individual patients. Records should include anesthetic doses and adjuvant drugs; seizure induction parameters (instrument, dose, time, electrode placement); seizure duration measurements; blood pressures; and notes as to any untoward events. In addition to the records maintained in patient charts, a duplicate record kept in the treatment room is helpful, to assist in treating patients readmitted after relapse.

Some educational materials are useful: the Consensus Development Conference Statement (15); the experiences of a patient described in the autobiography titled *Holiday of Darkness*, by Norman Endler (23); and the reports by the APA Task Force (6) and Pippard and Ellam (66) for the Royal College. The textbooks by Fink (25), Fraser (34), Abrams and Essman (3), Glenn and Weiner (38), Taylor, Sierles, and Abrams (78), and Abrams (2) should be part of the library. Instruction manuals and videotapes describing treatment practice accompany many new instruments. An educational videotape for health professionals and students is available (76). A videotape made especially for patients and their families provides a useful resource for consent (75). The quarterly journal *Convulsive Therapy*

(Raven Press, New York), now in its fifth year of publication, is a source of case and research material, especially about high-risk cases. Subscribers and authors may also avail themselves of a citation service and "hotline" for consultation.

MECHANISM OF ANTIDEPRESSANT ACTION

The essential ingredient for the effect of convulsive therapy on mood disorders remains the repeated induction of bilateral grand-mal seizures, two to five times weekly, for 7 to 12 seizures. To explain the therapeutic effect, we search for biochemical changes in the brain that may follow repeated seizures. But seizures involve massive electrical and biochemical changes in brain tissues, stimulation of the autonomic nervous system, release of substances from endocrine glands, and, unless there is neuromuscular blockade, severe tonic and clonic movements of body muscles. These activities elicit so many changes in biochemistry and physiology of the body that there is no dearth of demonstrable effects. Our difficulty lies not in demonstrating changes, but in differentiating those which may be central to a therapeutic effect and those which may be clearly secondary (25, 31).

The same difficulties that beset psychiatric research also affect convulsive therapy research: diagnostic and symptomatic variability among patients, limitations on experimentation in humans, inaccessibility of brain tissues for direct study, anxieties raised by such simple procedures as cerebrospinal fluid examinations, and the cost of any procedure that delays treatment. These limitations compel studies in animals, but these have been of little help in our understanding of the convulsive therapy process. What progress has been made has come from human research, precisely because the conditions under study, the affective and psychotic disorders, have no duplicate in animal species or animal tissues.

Indeed, where suggestions from animal studies have been examined in patients, they usually do not replicate. Cerebrospinal fluid (CSF) studies do not find relations between catecholamine metabolites and seizures, and studies of naloxone fail to find connections between opioid receptors and convulsive therapy (26, 27, 42, 64). Perhaps the single compelling observation from animal studies that has been replicated in humans is the increase in dopaminergic activity in centrencephalic regions following electroconvulsive shock (ECS). The suggestion that patients with parkinsonism may be helped by repeated seizures has been verified, clarifying the role of this neurohumor in parkinsonism (7–9, 61).

Two theories have recently been proposed to explain the clinical efficacy of convulsive therapy. One focuses on the same neurohumoral mechanisms as have been used to explain the action of antidepressant drugs. In this formulation, the acute release of norepinephrine and dopamine and the increase in the turnover of norepinephrine in the brain that occur during ECS are emphasized. Receptor sensitivity is also increased during ECS. Sensitivity to agents mimicking the actions of brain monoamines is increased, such that postsynaptic responses mediated by serotonin, dopamine, and norepinephrine are enhanced. These biochemical changes are seen as reversing the pathophysiology of the depressive disorder (17, 53).

The other view focuses on the signs of neuroendocrine dysregulation which are so prominent in patients with affective disorders, and which normalize during the recovery process. In this view, hypothalamic dysfunction (probably hypofunction) is postulated as central to endogenous depressive disorders. The antidepressant activity of convulsive therapy is seen to result from the stimulation of hypothalamic-pituitary centers, releasing natural substances, probably peptides, that modify mood, vegetative symptoms, and behavior associated with mood disturbances (25, 33).

The theory takes into account observations that the grand-mal seizure, with its centrencephalic features and release of brain substances, is essential to the treatment response. It claims nothing from the induction process or the peripheral manifestations. It recognizes that convulsive therapy is particularly effective in relieving melancholic features in patients with a prominence of vegetative symptoms. And it takes advantage of the observations that seizures release peptides from the central nervous system; that some peptides are behaviorally active; and that increased permeability of the blood-brain barrier is a regular feature of the convulsive therapy process.

CONCLUSION

Convulsive therapy has undergone many assessments in the past decade, and each has found the treatment useful. The indications for treatment have been clarified and the practice has become more secure, more humane, and safer. New instruments with safer designs and more efficient currents have been developed. But the complexity of the treatment has increased, and there is a need for the training of a cadre of personnel to safely administer the treatment. Much of the research energy has been directed to clarifying the indications and the technical aspects of treatment; little has been directed to an understanding of its mode of action.

The challenge of the next decade is to define its mechanism of action, and to increase our understanding of the pathophysiology of affective illnesses. The progress of the past decade encourages our belief that progress will be made, and that this complex, labor-intensive, and expensive treatment will be replaced by one that has more direct effects on pathology and is more efficient in delivery.

REFERENCES

1. Abrams, R. (1986). Is unilateral electroconvulsive therapy really the treatment of choice in endogenous depression? *Ann. NY Acad. Sci.*, *462*, 50–55.
2. Abrams, R. (1988). *Electroconvulsive therapy* (231 pp.). New York: Oxford University Press.
3. Abrams, R., & Essman, W. B. (Eds.) (1982). *Electroconvulsive therapy. Biological foundations and clinical applications*. (270 pp.). New York: Spectrum.
4. Abrams, R., & Fink, M. (1984). The present status of unilateral ECT. Some recommendations. *J. Affect. Dis.*, 7, 245–247.
5. Abrams, R., Taylor, M. A., Faber, R., Ts'o, T. O., Williams, R. A., & Almy, G. (1983). Bilateral vs. unilateral electroconvulsive therapy: Efficacy in melancholia. *Am. J. Psychiatry*, *140*, 463–465.
6. American Psychiatric Association (1978). *Electroconvulsive therapy*. Task Force Report #14. (200 pp.). Washington, DC: American Psychiatric Association.
7. Balldin, J., Granerus, A. K., Linstedt, G., Modigh, K., & Walinder, J. (1981). Predictors for improvement after electroconvulsive therapy in parkinsonian patients with on-off symptoms. *J. Neural. Transm.*, *52*, 199–211.
8. Balldin, J., Granerus, A. K., Lindstedt, G., Modigh, K., & Walinder, J. (1982). Neuroendocrine evidence for increased responsiveness of dopamine receptors in humans following electroconvulsive therapy. *Psychopharmacology*, *76*, 371–376.
9. Baruch, P., Jouvent, R., Vindreau, C., Drouillon, C., Widlocher, D., & Agid, Y. (1985). Improvement of parkinsonism in ECT-treated depressed patients: Parkinson's disease or depression-related extrapyramidal disorder. *World Cong. Biol. Psychiatry Abstr.*, p. 425.2.
10. Brandon, S., Cowley, P., McDonald, C., Neville, P., Palmer, R., & Wellstood-Eason, S. (1984). Electroconvulsive therapy: Results in depressive illness from the Leicestershire trial. *Br. Med. J.*, *288*, 22–25.
11. Brandon, S., Cowley, P., McDonald, C., Neville, P., Palmer, R., & Wellstood-Eason, S. (1985). Leicester ECT trial: Results in schizophrenia. *Br. J. Psychiatry*, *146*, 177–183.
12. Bulbena, A., & Berrios, G. E. (1986). Pseudodementia: Facts and figures. *Br. J. Psychiatry*, *148*, 87–94.
13. Christensen, P., Kragh-Sorenson, P., Sorenson, C., Thomsen, H. Y., Iversen, A. D., Christensen, K. S., Hüttel, M., & Tønnesen, E. (1986). EEG-monitored ECT: A comparison of seizure duration under anesthesia with etomidate and thiopentone. *Convuls. Ther.*, *2*, 145–150.
14. Consensus Conference (1985). Electroconvulsive therapy. *JAMA*, *254*, 103–108.
15. Consensus Development Conference Statement (1985). *Electroconvulsive therapy*. 5(#1). Washington, D.C.: US DHEW.
16. Coppen, A., Abou-Saleh, M. T., Milln, P., Bailey, J., Metcalfe, M., Burns, B. H., & Armond, A. (1981). Lithium continuation therapy following electroconvulsive therapy. *Br. J. Psychiatry*, *139*, 284–287.

17. Costain, D. W., Cowen, P. J., Gelder, M. G., & Grahame-Smith, D. G. (1982). Electroconvulsive therapy and the brain: Evidence for increased dopamine-mediated responses. *Lancet, 1*, 400–404.
18. Dec, G. W., Jr., Stern, T. A., & Welch, C. (1985). The effects of electroconvulsive therapy on serial electrocardiograms and serum cardiac enzyme values. A prospective study of depressed hospitalized inpatients. *JAMA, 253*, 2525–2529.
19. d'Elia, G. (1970). Unilateral electroconvulsive therapy. *Acta Psychiatr. Scand., 215* (Suppl.) 5–98.
20. Dorn, J. B. (1985). Electoconvulsive therapy with fetal monitoring in a bipolar pregnant patient. *Convuls. Ther., 1*, 217–221.
21. Dubovsky, S. L. (1986). Using electroconvulsive therapy for patients with neurological disease. *Hosp. Community Psychiatry, 37*, 819–824.
22. Dwersteg, J. F., & Avery, D. H. (1987). Atracurium as a muscle relaxant for electroconvulsive therapy in a burned patient. Case report. *Convuls. Ther., 3*, 49–53.
23. Endler, N. S. (1982). *Holiday of darkness* (169 pp.). New York: Wiley.
24. Erman, M. K., Welch, C. A., & Mandel, M. R. (1979). A comparison of two unilateral ECT electrode placements; efficacy and electrical energy considerations. *Am. J. Psychiatry, 136*, 1317–1319.
25. Fink, M. (1979). *Convulsive therapy: Theory and practice* (306 pp.). New York: Raven Press.
26. Fink, M. (1984a). Theories of the antidepressant efficacy of convulsive therapy (ECT). In R. M. Post & J. C. Ballenger (Eds.), *Neurobiology of manic depressive illness* (pp. 721–730). Baltimore: Williams & Wilkins.
27. Fink, M. (1984b). Neuroendocrine aspects of the relief of melancholia by induced seizures (ECT). In E. Usdin, M. Asberg, L. Bertilsson, & F. Sjoqvist (Eds.), *Frontiers in biochemical and pharmacological research in depression. Adv. Biochem. Psychopharmacol., 39*, 345–357.
28. Fink, M. (1985). Anesthesia in electroconvulsive therapy (Editorial). *Convuls. Ther., 1*, 155–157.
29. Fink, M. (1986). Training in convulsive therapy (Editorial). *Convuls. Ther., 2*, 227–230.
30. Fink, M., Gujavarty, K., & Greenberg, L. B. (1987). Serial dexamethasone suppression tests and clinical outcome in ECT. *Convuls. Ther., 3*, 111–120.
31. Fink, M., Key, S., McGaugh, J., & Williams, T. (Eds.) (1974). *Psychobiology of convulsive therapy*. Washington, DC: V. H. Winston.
32. Fink, M., & Johnson, L. (1982). Monitoring duration of ECT seizures: "Cuff" and EEG methods compared. *Arch. Gen. Psychiatry, 39*, 1189–1191.
33. Fink, M., & Ottosson, J-O. (1980). A theory of convulsive therapy in endogenous depression: Significance of hypothalamic functions. *Psychiatry Res., 2*, 49–61.
34. Fraser, M. (1982). *ECT: A clinical guide* (134 pp.). Chichester: Wiley.
35. Freese, K. J. (1985). Can patients safely undergo electroconvulsive therapy while receiving monoamine oxidase inhibitors? *Convuls. Ther., 1*, 190–194.
36. Friedel, R. O. (1986). The combined use of neuroleptics and ECT in drug resistant schizophrenic patients. *Psychopharmacol. Bull., 22*, 928–931.
37. Gerring, J. P., & Shields, H. M. (1982). The identification and management of patients with a high risk for cardiac arrhythmias during modified ECT. *J. Clin. Psychiatry, 43*, 140–143.
38. Glenn, M. D., & Weiner, R. D. (1985). *Electroconvulsive therapy: A programmed text* (147 pp.). Washington, DC: APA Press.
39. Greenberg, L. B. (1985). Detection of prolonged seizures during electroconvulsive therapy: A comparison of electroencephalogram and cuff monitoring. *Convuls. Ther., 1*, 32–37.
40. Gregory, S., Shawcross, C. R., & Gill, D. (1985). The Nottingham ECT study. A double-blind comparison of bilateral, unilateral and simulated ECT in depressive illness. *Br. J. Psychiatry, 146*, 520–524.

41. Gujavarty, K., Greenberg, L., & Fink, M. (1987). Electroconvulsive therapy and neuroleptic medication in therapy-resistant postive-symptom psychosis. *Convuls. Ther.*, *3*, 185–195.
42. Haskett, R. F., Zis, A. P., & Albala, A. A. (1985). Hormone response to repeated electroconvulsive therapy: Effects of naloxone. *Biol. Psychiatry*, *20*, 623–633.
43. Hicks, F. G. (1987). ECT modified by atracurium. Case report. *Convuls. Ther.*, *3*, 54–59.
44. Hood, D. D., & Mecca, R. S. (1983). Failure to initiate electroconvulsive seizures in a patient pretreated with lidocaine. *Anesthesiology*, *58*, 379–381.
45. Horne, R. L., Pettinati, H. M., Sugerman, A. A., & Varga, E. (1985). Comparing bilateral to unilateral electroconvulsive therapy in a randomized study with EEG monitoring. *Arch. Gen. Psychiatry*, *42*, 1087–1092.
46. Hsiao, J. K., Messenheimer, J. A., & Evans, D. L. (1987). ECT and neurological disorders: A review. *Convuls. Ther.*, *3*, 121–136.
47. Johnstone, E. C., Deakin, J. F. W., Lawler, P., Frith, C. D., Stevens, M., McPherson, K., & Crow, T. J. (1980). The Northwick Park electroconvulsive therapy trial. *Lancet*, *2*, 1317–1320.
48. Kalinowsky, L. B., Hippius, H., & Klein, H. E. (1982). *Biological treatments in psychiatry* (424 pp.). New York: Grune & Stratton.
49. Karliner, W., & Wehrheim, H. K. (1965). Maintenance convulsive treatments. *Am. J. Psychiatry*, *121*, 113–115.
50. Kiloh, L. G. (1985). The trials of ECT. *Psychiatr. Dev.*, *3*, 205–218.
51. Larson, G., Swartz, C., & Abrams, R. (1984). Duration of ECT-induced tachycardia as a measure of seizure length. *Am. J. Psychiatry*, *141*, 1269–1271.
52. Latey, R. H., & Fahy, T. J. (1985). Electroconvulsive therapy in the Republic of Ireland 1982: A summary of findings. *Br. J. Psychiatry*, *147*, 438–439.
53. Lerer, B. (1984). Electroconvulsive shock and neurotransmitter receptors: Implications for the mechanism of action of electroconvulsive therapy. *Biol. Psychiatry*, *19*, 361–383.
54. Maletzky, B. M. (1986). Conventional and multiple-monitored electroconvulsive therapy: A comparison in major depressive episodes. *J. Nerv. Ment. Dis.*, *174*, 257–264.
55. Malitz, S., & Sackeim, H. (Eds.) (1986). *Electroconvulsive therapy: Clinical and basic research issues. Ann. NY Acad. Sci.*, *462*, 1–424.
56. McAllister, T. W., & Price, T. R. P. (1982). Severe depression pseudodementia with and without dementia. *Am. J. Psychiatry*, *139*, 626–629.
57. McAllister, T. W., Price, T. R. P., & Ferrell, R. B. (1985). Bilateral sinusoidal ECT following poor response to five unilateral brief-pulse ECTs. *J. Clin. Psychiatry*, *46*, 430–431.
58. Meduna, L. (1985). Autobiography. *Convuls. Ther.*, *1*, 43–57, 121–136.
59. Miller, M. E., Gabriel, A., Herman, G., Stern, A., Shagong, U., & Kupersmith, J. (1987). Atropine sulphate premedication and cardiac arrhythmia in electroconvulsive therapy (ECT). *Convuls. Ther.*, *3*, 10–17.
60. Milstein, V., Small, J. G., Klapper, M. H., Small, I. F., & Kellams, J. J. (1987). Uni- versus bilateral ECT in the treatment of mania. *Convuls. Ther.*, *3*, 1-9.
61. Modigh, K., Balldin, J., Eden, S., Granerus, A. K., & Walinder, J. (1981). Electroconvulsive therapy and receptor sensitivity. *Acta Psychiatr. Scand.*, *290* (Suppl.) 91–99.
62. Moscarillo, F. M. (1986). Electrotherapy certification. *Convuls. Ther.*, *2*, 129–131.
63. Palmer, R. L. (1981). *Electroconvulsive therapy: An appraisal* (316 pp.). New York: Oxford University Press.
64. Papakostas, Y. G., Stefanis, C. S., Markianos, M., & Papadimitriou, G. N. (1985). Naloxone fails to block ECT-induced prolactin increase. *Biol. Pscyhiatry*, *20*, 1326–1327.

65. PETERS, S. G., WOCHOS, D. N., & PETERSON, G. C. (1984). Status epilepticus complicating electroconvulsive therapy in the presence of theophylline. *Mayo Clin. Proc.*, *59*, 568–570.
66. PIPPARD, J., & ELLAM, L. (1981). *Electroconvulsive treatment in Great Britain, 1980* (162 pp.). London: Gaskell.
67. PRICE, T. R. P. (1981). Unilateral electroconvulsive therapy for depression. *N. Engl. J. Med.*, *304*, 53.
68. REGESTEIN, Q. R., & REICH, P. (1985). Electroconvulsive therapy in patients at high risk for physical complications. *Convuls. Ther.*, *1*, 101–114.
69. REMICK, R. A., JEWESSON, P., & FORD, R. W. J. (1987). MAO inhibitors in general anesthesia: A re-evaluation. *Convuls. Ther.*, 196–203.
70. ROYAL COLLEGE OF NURSING (1987). RCN nursing guidelines for ECT. *Convuls. Ther.*, *3*, 158–160.
71. RUDORFER, M. V., LINNOILA, M., & POTTER, W. Z. (1987). Combined lithium and electroconvulsive therapy: Pharmacokinetic and pharmacodynamic interactions. *Convuls. Ther.*, *3*, 40–45.
72. SHAPIRA, B., ZOHAR, J., NEWMAN, M., DREXLER, H., & BELMAKER, R. H. (1985). Potentiation of seizure length and clinical response to electroconvulsive therapy by caffeine pretreatment: A case report. *Convuls. Ther.*, *1*, 58–60.
73. SIBONY, P. A. (1985). ECT risks in glaucoma. *Convuls. Ther.*, *1*, 283–284.
74. SMALL, J. G. (1985). Efficacy of ECT in schizophrenia, mania and other disorders. I: Schizophrenia. *Convuls. Ther.*, *1*, 263–270.
75. SOMATICS, INC. (1986a). Informed ECT for patients and families. Videotape. 22 min. (910 Sherwood Drive, Lake Bluff, IL 60044.)
76. SOMATICS, INC. (1986b). Informed ECT for health professionals. Videotape. 24 min. (910 Sherwood Drive, Lake Bluff, IL 60044.)
77. STRÖMGREN, L. S. (1984). Is bilateral ECT ever indicated? *Acta Psychiatr. Scand.*, *69*, 484–490.
78. TAYLOR, M., SIERLES, F. S., & ABRAMS, R. (1985). *General hospital psychiatry* (463 pp.). New York: Free Press.
79. WEINER, R. D., & COFFEY, C. E. (1987). Use of electroconvulsive therapy in patients with severe medical illness. In A. Stoudemire and B. Fogel (Eds.), *Treatment of psychiatric disorders in medical-surgical patients* (pp. 113–133). New York: Grune & Stratton.

23

ADVANCES IN LITHIUM THERAPY

ALAN H. ROSENBAUM, M.D.

Comprehensive Psychiatric Services, P.C., Southfield, Michigan

INTRODUCTION

The most exciting area of lithium use has been in the augmentation of antidepressants (tricyclics and MAOIs) in resistant depressions (5). Preliminary data in uncontrolled studies showed the combination to be promising (2, 7, 11, 14, 16, 19, 22). Himmelhoch et al. contended that MAOIs and lithium worked better than the tricyclic/lithium combination (4). DeMontigny et al., demonstrated a rapid effect within 48 hours of adding lithium to tricyclic treatment (2). In 74% of their patients, there was a 50% improvement in HDRS scores (13). Others have questioned it (9, 24).

Besides deMontigny, the Yale group of Charney, Price, and Heninger have repeatedly shown a synergistic effect for tricyclics (13, 21, 23), MAOIs (12), and even the addition of lithium to a combination of an antipsychotic and antidepressant for treatment of psychotic depressions (25). Lingjaerde et al. (24), in an early multinational study, found one group showing a significant synergistic effect, while the others did not, leading to a lack of conclusive evidence. Nelson and Mazure (26) found a good response to the combination in bipolar patients (eight of nine) but not in unipolar (3 of 12) psychotic depressions. Louie and Meltzer (9) also had a poor overall response.

TRICYCLIC COMBINATION

In a recent study, the Yale group attempted to see whether downgrading of the β-adrenergic receptor which appears to correlate with clinical improvement could be enhanced with a yohimbine-desmethylimipramine combination. Theoretically the increased NE flow would desensitize the β receptor more rapidly. In their group of resistant depression, which had a relatively high 24-hour urine MHPG level, they had none respond to the combination but had a significant response to the lithium/tricyclic or MAOI combination (21).

IN UNIPOLAR ACUTE DEPRESSION – DEPRESSIVE SUBTYPES

Attempts have been made to subtype unipolar depressive disorders. Recent studies have shown that out of 50 (34) patients who met criteria for severe depression (Hamilton Depression Rating Scale [HDRS] scores – 21 items were greater than 28) who had low MHPG (3 methoxy-4 hydroxyphenyl glycol), less than 1900 μgm/24h, responded well to tricyclic antidepressants (>70% of patients improved 60% on HDRS) at four weeks. The middle group responded poorly, as did the high group, which also appeared to cycle in mood (6, 18). A pilot study of six patients with high MHPG and high 24-hour urine free cortisol who failed to respond to 150 mg or greater antidepressant dose for four weeks had more than 60% reduction in HDRS within two weeks of the addition of lithium (27).

DeMontigny and the Yale group have hypothesized that lithium augmented the serotonin effect (13). In addition, our group hypothesized that middle and high MHPG groups which were poor clinical responders to tricyclics might be a serotonin-deficient group or a group with high cholinergic response and/or decreased sensitivity of the adrenergic receptor (17, 28). The response to lithium would be consistent with their hypothesis.

However, Linnoila et al. found rapid-cycling bipolars responding to lithium had a decreased amount of dopamine metabolite in their urine (8). These findings would be consistent with the findings of Bennett et al. (29) of a rapid clinical response with desipramine-thioridazine (a dopamine blocker).

The side effects of this combination are not without significance. Prien et al. concluded an increase in side effects occur which is more than the effect of either drug alone (30). Others have stated that there is an increase in cycling and mania (31).

CRITICAL REVIEW

This author has treated over 2,000 patients with an antidepressant/lithium combination. The rapid 48-hour response is rare unless one uses large loading doses of lithium. Most responses are in five to nine days, with some responses occurring two to three months later.

Tremors are not uncommon, but dose adjustment can be made by lowering either the lithium or the tricyclic. Rarely does one need a tricyclic dose >125 mg, and usually the 75–125 mg range suffices. Tremors can be so severe that some patients can't raise a cup to their mouth.

Postural hypotension can become more severe, and one should be cautious not to add lithium to a high-dose antidepressant, as the standing blood pressure will drop. Interestingly, this combination will lower the blood pressure lying and standing, especially when there is a response (even in hypertensives). Further, as one takes away the antidepressant, the blood pressure will rise (32).

A strange pseudopregnant state will occur with lower-abdominal protrusion and sometimes breast enlargement with weight gain and craving of sweets in good responders. Marked edema can occur.

Nelson and Mazure (26) made a critical error in their retrospective study of lithium augmentation to a tricyclic-phenothiazine. Many patients need a two-to-three-week withdrawal of the phenothiazine before lithium can be added. Adding lithium too early, especially to substantial doses of antipsychotic drugs, causes severe tremor and worsening of the depression, as they describe (15). This does not mean, as they show, that phenothiazines can't be used, but only that they must be used judiciously and usually in very small doses (i.e., 0.25–3 mg haldol or 1–6 mg of perphenazine or trifluoperazine).

Louie and Meltzer (9) did the above and had a good response in a psychotic unipolar patient who initially responded to a phenothiazine tricyclic combination and then cycled down into a depression. After a four-week trial off the phenothiazine, lithium stabilized the mood swing in combination with doxepin and elevated the mood of the delusional depression. In another case, they added lithium to amoxapine, which has a potent antipsychotic metabolite, and the patient gradually deteriorated.

Caution must be used in patients on phenothiazines in the depressed state. These patients can become organic, very Parkinsonian, and develop markedly abnormal EEGs. Those with tardive dyskinesia can become worse. If one waits three weeks at a maximum, this potentially dangerous condition can be avoided. Keeping in mind that lithium works only 50% of the time, the addition of a small dose of phenothiazine is sometimes needed in highly anxious, delusional, and hostile depressions, when initially adding lithium or if there is a partial response and more antipsychotic effect is needed.

Ataxia is not uncommon and problems with proprioception—especially difficulty with stairs—are common. Seizures have been reported (31).

The overall response rate by this author has not been as high as the 74% rate reported by deMontigny et al. (22). However, it has not been as low as the 16% reported by Louie and Meltzer (9).

Lithium is certainly worth a try in patients with resistant depressions who have no response or become more anxious, somatic, hostile, irritable, and have palpitations and urinary retention with tricyclics or MAOIs.

When patients become manic or cycle more rapidly, carbamazepine can be added and/or the antidepressant discontinued, as lithium won't stop the cycling in those cases.

A large number of patients develop decreased urine-concentrating ability on lithium (1). Recent work indicates that amiloride and other K^+-sparing diuretics may be useful. This technique, initially reported by Himmelhoch, was reviewed by Kasten and Forrest (33).

Further, Miller et al. (10) found a trend toward higher urine osmolality in patients on slow-release lithium than in those on regular lithium.

Relationships between high lithium levels and decreased concentrating ability have not been found because of increased thirst and increased fluid intake with resultant lower lithium levels.

Kidney damage, initially reported by Hestbech et al. (3), has not proven to be common. Five to ten percent develop irreversibly reduced tubular function due to tubulointerstitial nephropathy, and glomerular changes are less prevalent and less severe than tubular changes (1). Renal damage may be partly related to age (20).

While adverse effects can be greater than with either drug alone, once the depression resolves one can usually slowly decrease the antidepressant and maintain the patients on very low doses or lithium alone before attempting to discontinue it.

REFERENCES

1. BENDZ, H. (1983). Kidney function in lithium treated patients: A literature survey. *Acta Psychiatr. Scand.*, *68*, 303–324.
2. DEMONTIGNY, C., GRUNBERG, F., MAYTER, A., et al. (1981). Lithium induces rapid relief of depression in tricyclic antidepressant drug non-responders. *Br. J. Psychiatry*, *138*, 252–256.
3. HESTBECH, J., HANSEN, H. E., ANDISEN, A., et al. (1977). Chronic renal lesions following long term treatment with lithium. *Kidney Int.*, *12*, 210–213.
4. HIMMELHOCH, J. M., DETRE, T., KUPFER, D. J., et al. (1972). Treatment of previously intractable depressions with tranylcypromine and lithium. *J. Nerv. Ment. Dis.*, *155*, 216–220.
5. JEFFERSON, J. W., & AYD, F. J. (1983). Combining lithium and antidepressants. *J. Clin. Psychopharmacol.*, *3*, 303–307.
6. JIMERSON, D. C., INSEL, T. R., REUS, V. I., et al. (1983). Increased plasma MHPG in dexamethasone-resistant patients. *Arch. Gen. Psychiatry*, *40*, 173–176.

7. Joyce, P. R., Hewland, H. R., & Jones, A. V. (1983). Rapid response to lithium in treatment-resistant depression. *Br. J. Psychiatry, 142*, 204–205.
8. Linnoila, M., Karoum, F., & Potter, W. Z. (1983). Effects of antidepressant treatments on dopamine turnover in depressed patients. *Arch. Gen. Psychiatry, 40*, 1015–1017.
9. Louie, A. K., & Meltzer, H. Y. (1984). Lithium potentiation of antidepressant treatment. *J. Clin. Psychopharmacol., 4*, 316–321.
10. Miller, A. L., Bowden, C. L., & Plewes, J. (1985). Lithium and impairment of renal concentrating abilities. *J. Affect. Dis.*, 9, 115–119.
11. Nelson, J. C., & Byck, R. (1982). Rapid response to lithium in phenelzine non-responders. *Br. J. Psychiatry, 141*, 85–86.
12. Price, L. H., Charney, D. S., & Heninger, G. R. (1985). Efficacy of lithium-tranylcypromine treatment in refractory depression. *Am. J. Psychiatry, 142*, 619–623.
13. Price, L. H., Charney, D. S., & Heninger, G. R. (1986). Variability of response to lithium augmentation in refractory depression. *Am. J. Psychiatry, 143*, 1387–1392.
14. Rosenbaum, A. H., Niven, R. G., Hansen, N. P., et al. (1977). Tardive dyskinesia: Relationship with a primary affective disorder. *Dis. Nerv. Syst., 38*, 423–427.
15. Rosenbaum, A. H. (1978). Tardive dyskinesia and pharmacotherapy (letter to editor). *Am. J. Psychiatry, 135*, 506.
16. Rosenbaum, A. H., Maruta, T., Duane, D. D., et al. (1980). Tardive dyskinesia in depressed patients: Successful therapy with antidepressants and lithium. *Psychosomatics, 21*, 715–719.
17. Rosenbaum, A. H., Maruta, T., Schatzberg, A. F., et al. (1983). Toward a biochemical classification of depressive disorders. VII: Urinary free cortisol and urinary MHPG in depressions. *Am. J. Psychiatry, 140*, 314–318.
18. Schatzberg, A. F., Rosenbaum, A. H., Orsulak, P. J., et al. (1981). Toward a biochemical classification of depressive disorders. III: Pre-treatment urinary MHPG levels as predictors of response of treatment with maprotiline. *Psychopharmacology (Berlin)*, 75, 34–38.
19. Tariot, P. N., Murphy, D. L., Sunderland, T., et al. (1986). Rapid antidepressant effect of addition of lithium to tranylcypromine. *J. Clin. Psychopharmacol.*, 6, 165–167.
20. Walker, R. G., Davies, B. M., Holwill, B. J., et al. (1982). A clinicopathological study of lithium nephrotoxicity. *J. Chronic Dis., 35*, 685–695.
21. Charney, D. S., Price, L. H., & Heninger, G. R. (1986). Desipramine-yohimbine combination treatment of refractory depression. *Arch. Gen. Psychiatry, 43*, 1155–1161.
22. deMontigny, C., Cournoyer, G., Morissette, R., et al. (1983). Lithium carbonate addition in tricyclic antidepressant resistant unipolar depression. *Arch. Gen. Psychiatry, 40*, 1327–1334.
23. Heninger, G. R., Charney, D. S., & Sternberg, D. E. (1983). Lithium carbonate augmentation of antidepressant treatment: An effective prescription for treatment-refractory depression. *Arch. Gen. Psychiatry, 40*, 1335–1342.
24. Lingjaerde, O., Edlund, A. H., Gormsen, C. A., et al. (1974). The effect of lithium carbonate in combination with tricyclic antidepressants in endogenous depression. *Acta Psychiatr. Scand., 50*, 233–242.
25. Price, L. H., Conwell, Y., & Nelson, J. C. (1983). Lithium augmentation of combined neuroleptic-tricyclic treatment in delusional depression. *Am. J. Psychiatry, 140*, 318–322.
26. Nelson, J. C., & Mazure, C. M. (1986). Lithium augmentation in psychotic depression refractory to combined drug treatment. *Am. J. Psychiatry, 143*, 363–366.
27. Rosenbaum, A. H., & Schatzberg, A. F. (1981). (Unpublished observations.)
28. Schildkraut, J. J., Orsulak, P. J., Schatzberg, A. F., Cole, J. O., & Rosenbaum, A. H. (1981). Biochemical discrimination of subgroups of depressive disorders based on differences in catecholamine metabolism. In E. Usdin & I. Hanin (Eds.), *Biological*

markers in psychiatry and neurology, Proceedings of a Conference at Ochsner Clinic, New Orleans (pp. 23–33). Elmsford, NY: Pergamon Press.

29. Bennett, J. A., Hirschowitz, J., Zemlan, F., et al. (1984). Combined thioridazine and desipramine: Early antidepressant response. *Psychopharmacology, 82*, 263–265.
30. Prien, R. F., Kupfer, D. J., Mansky, P. A., et al. (1984). Drug therapy in the prevention of recurrences in unipolar and bipolar disorders. *Arch. Gen. Psychiatry, 41*, 1096–1104
31. Jefferson, J. W., Greist, J. H., Ackerman, D. T., et al. (1987). *Lithium encyclopedia for clinical practice* (2nd ed.) (p. 664). Washington, DC: APA Press.
32. Zachariah, P. K., & Rosenbaum, A. H. (1982). Stabilization of high blood pressure with tricyclic antidepressants and lithium combinations in hypertensive patients. *Mayo Clin. Proc., 57*, 625–628.
33. Kasten, T. R., & Forrest, J. N. (1986). Treatment of severe lithium-induced polyuria with amiloride. *Am. J. Psychiatry, 143*, 1563–1568.
34. Schildkraut, J. J., Orsulak, P. J., Schatzberg, A. F., et al. (1981). Possible pathophysiological mechanisms in subtypes of unipolar depressive disorders based on differences in urinary MHPG levels. *Psychopharmacology Bulletin, 17*, 90–91.

NAME INDEX

SUBJECT INDEX